Lecture Notes in Computer Science

Commenced Publication in 1973
Founding and Former Series Editors:
Gerhard Goos, Juris Hartmanis, and Jan van Leeuwen

Felix F. Ramos   Victor Larios Rosillo
Herwig Unger (Eds.)

Advanced Distributed Systems

5th International School and Symposium, ISSADS 2005
Guadalajara, Mexico, January 24-28, 2005
Revised Selected Papers

Springer

Volume Editors

Felix F. Ramos
CINVESTAV Div. Guadalajara
Prol. Lopez Mateos Sur 590, Guadalajara, Jal. 45000, Mexico
E-mail: framos@gdl.cinvestav.mx

Victor Larios Rosillo
Universidad de Guadalajara, CUCEA
Department "Sistemas de Informacion"
799, Periferico Norte, Ed. L308, Zapopan, Jal. 45100, Mexico
E-mail: vlarios@acm.org

Herwig Unger
Universität Rostock, Institut für Informatik
Albert-Einstein-Str. 23, 18051 Rostock, Germany
E-mail: hunger@informatik.uni-rostock.de

Library of Congress Control Number: 2005932536

CR Subject Classification (1998): C.2.4, I.2.11, D.2.12, D.1.3, D.4, H.3, H.4

ISSN   0302-9743
ISBN-10   3-540-28063-4 Springer Berlin Heidelberg New York
ISBN-13   978-3-540-28063-7 Springer Berlin Heidelberg New York

Springer is a part of Springer Science+Business Media

springeronline.com

© Springer-Verlag Berlin Heidelberg 2005
Printed in Germany

Typesetting: Camera-ready by author, data conversion by Olgun Computergrafik
Printed on acid-free paper   SPIN: 11533962   06/3142   5 4 3 2 1 0

Preface

It is our pleasure to present the papers accepted and presented at the 5th International School and Symposium on Advanced Distributed Systems (ISSADS) in this LNCS volume. The symposium was held in the city of Guadalajara, Mexico from January 24 to 28, 2005. The organization team was composed of members of CINVESTAV Guadalajara, Rostock University in Germany, the CUCEI and CUCEA campuses of Guadalajara University, and Instituto Tecnológico y de Estudios Superiores de Occidente, ITESO. The symposium is already a well-established annual meeting, at which scientists and people from the industrial field meet and discuss the progress of applications and the theory of distributed systems in a forum during the last week of January. This year, more than 250 people from 3 continents attended the conference. Most of them are scientists, teachers, students and engineers from the local industry.

The papers presented in the sessions of the symposium cover not only the subjects of distributed systems from the system level and applications, but also contributions from the area of theory and artificial intelligence concepts. These papers were selected out of more than 100 submissions. There was a selection filter in which each paper was evaluated by at least three members of the international Program Committee, who came from research institutions of good reputation all over the world.

We were pleased to listen to an invited talk given by Ali Hurson, a distinguished lecturer of ACM, on distributed data bases, and another one presented by Carlos Coello who become famous by its works in evolutive computation.

Besides the scientific sessions, ISSADS 2005 followed a tradition by offering six high-level tutorials covering the important topics of security, emerging technologies, knowledge management, multi-agent systems, design of complex systems, and modern Internet technologies. Furthermore, the conference was also a forum for presentations by the main industrial companies in the area of distributed systems – this year INTEL, HP, Texas Instruments and IBM took part in our event. All events enabled the participants to extend their knowledge in certain areas, to have a lot of worthwhile discussions, and to establish new, interesting and useful contacts.

We would like to extend our gratitude to all the members of the Program and Organizing Committees as well as their teams. We would like to note our special appreciation of Dr. Francisco Medina, Director of the Council of Science and Research of Jalisco, Mexico, for his financial support. We also thank J. Luis Leyva, Director of CINVESTAV, for all his help, and we thank Dionisio de Niz from ITESO, and Patricia Mendoza, Luis Gutierrez and Carlos Franco from Guadalajara University for their logistic support during all the events. Last but not least, we are grateful to the Chambers of Electronic and Information Technologies of Jalisco, Mexico. Gabriela Tagliaprieta put a lot of effort into supporting all participants. Finally, a special recognition is given to all the researchers who submitted their papers to ISSADS 2005. They led to the success of ISSADS. We would be happy to see all of you and hopefully some new participants at ISSADS 2006, which will be held again in our nice city, Guadalajara, Mexico.

February, 2005   Félix F. Ramos C.
                                                               Victor Larios Rosillo
                                                                      Herwig Unger

Program Committee

Chair Félix Francisco Ramos Corchado, Cinvestav Guadalajara
Co-chair Victor Manuel Larios Rosillo, CUCEA, Universidad de Guadalajara
Editor Herwig Unger, Rostock University, Germany

Scientific Committee

Anastase Adonis
Alain Bui
Anbulagan
Arbad Farhad
Gilbert Babin
Barradas Hector Ruiz
Jean Paul Barthès
Nadia Bennani
Thomas Böhme
Pierre Boulanger
Marc Bui
Humberto Cervantes
Hugo Coyote
Diaz Michel
Didier Donsez
Drira Khalil
Estivill Castro Vladimir
Eduardo Fernandez

Alexander Gelbukh
Emmanuelle Grislin
Guzmán Arenas Adolfo
Guilherme Bittencourt
Hervé Luga
Hubert Kihl
Kim Kane
Jean-Luc Koning
Peter Kropf
Sylvain Lecomte
Linpeng Huang
Guerrero Miguel López
Aurelio López
M.L. Ernesto López
Maralin Jimenez Ricardo
M. Nakano Miyatake
René Mandiau
Andrei N. Tchernykh

Elizabeth Pérez Cortéz
Meana Hector Pérez
Pires Ramos Milton
Ren Fuji
Román Graciela
Scalabrin Edson Emilio
Sybertin Blanc
Tazi Said
Thierry Delot
Torres Deni
Helena Unger
Joaquin Vila
Ricardo Vilalta
Thierry Villemur
Young-Hwan Park
Yves Duthen
Andreas Zekl

Organization

Public Relations and Logistics-Chair Ana Gabriela Tagliapietra,
     CINVESTAV Guadalajara
Logistics and Webmasters Joel Espinosa and Jorge Hernández,
     CINVESTAV Guadalajara

Table of Contents

Database Systems

Distributed and Parallel Algorithms

Real-Time Distributed Systems

Cooperative Information Systems

Fault Tolerance

Information Retrieval

Modeling and Simulation

Wireless Networks and Mobile Computing

Artificial Life and Multi-agent Systems

ISSADS 2004

Database System Architecture – A Walk Through Time: From Centralized Platform to Mobile Computing Keynote Address

Ali R. Hurson and Yu Jiao

Department of Computer Science and Engineering
The Pennsylvania State University, University Park, PA 16802, USA
{hurson,yjiao}@cse.psu.edu

Abstract. Classical distributed database systems monolithically offer distribution transparency and higher performance. This is made possible by making data available and closer to the application domain(s) that uses it by means such as the data distribution, duplication, and fragmentation. However, with the advances in technologies this monolithic and top down approach becomes insufficient. In the new networked computational environment, the data distribution issue has evolved into data integration from several heterogeneous and autonomous data sources. Heterogeneous distributed databases are designed to deal with issue of data integration and interoperability. They are developed to allow timely and reliable access to heterogeneous and autonomous data sources in an environment that is characterized as "sometime, somewhere."

The concept of mobility, where users access information through a remote connection with portable devices, has introduced additional complexities and restrictions to the heterogeneous distributed database system. This keynote address first introduces a three dimensional space to classify and identify the evolution of different classes of database systems. It also extensively discusses Heterogeneous Distributed Database Systems (HDDBS) and Mobile Data Access Systems (MDAS). Finally, it will address several research issues and their potential solutions.

1 Information Everywhere, Computers Everywhere

Advances in computation and communication technologies have enabled users to access information at anytime, from anywhere. However, this flexibility comes at the expenses of new challenges. These challenges stem from the diversity in the range and the exponential growth of information that is available to a user at any given time. The spread of computer networks, the wide breadth of access devices with different physical characteristics, and the extensive need for information sharing have created a demand for cooperation among pre-existing, distributed, heterogeneous, and autonomous information sources in an infrastructure that is characterized by:

- Low bandwidth,
- Frequent disconnection,
- High error rates,
- Limited processing resources, and
- Limited power sources.

Binary data was the main data format in 1970s and it has evolved into text, images, multi media, and sensor data during the past decades. In mid 1980s, it was estimated

F.F. Ramos et al. (Eds.): ISSADS 2005, LNCS 3563, pp. 1–9, 2005.

that the U.S. Patent Office and Trademark has a database of size 25 terabytes (1 tera-bytes = 10^{12} bytes) subject to search and update. In 1990s, it was estimated that the NASA's Earth Observing Project would generate more than 11,000 terabytes of data during the 15-year time-period. Recently, it was estimated that the amount of new information generated in 2002 was about 5 exabytes (1 exabyte = 10^{18} bytes).

The diversity in representation, the growth in size, and the increased availability of information also introduced new challenges in areas such as security and resource management (e.g., power and network bandwidth). The cost associated with viruses, unsolicited emails, and other attacks has grown exponentially. For example, it is esti-mated that 7000 new computer viruses were discovered in 2003 and the FBI approxi-mated that computer viruses cost businesses $27 million during that time. As another example, in 2003, unsolicited email cost businesses $20 billion worldwide due to lost productivity, system overhead, user support, and anti-spam software.

The availability of heterogeneous, autonomous, and partially unreliable informa-tion in various forms and shapes brings out the following challenges:
- How to locate information intelligently, efficiently, and transparently?
- How to extract, process, and integrate relevant information efficiently?
- How to interpret information intelligently?
- How to provide uniform global access methods?
- How to support user and data source mobility?

2 Database Systems Taxonomy

Different parameters can be used to classify the architecture of data base systems. We classify data base systems along the following three parameters:
- **Physical infrastructure:** This dimension refers to the underlying platform com-posed of homogeneous/heterogeneous processing devices interconnected through different communication medium. The processing devices ranging from powerful parallel machines to portable units communicating with each other via a wide va-riety of communication medium ranging from land-based connection to wireless medium.
- **Services:** Along this dimension one can distinguish two classes in which either there is no distinction between services, or there is a distinction between user processes and data processes.
- **Distribution:** This dimension distinguishes distribution of processing, data, and control (also known as autonomy). Note that data distribution also includes data fragmentation and data replication.

2.1 Centralized Databases

A centralized database system is the one that runs on a single computer platform and does not interact with other computer systems. Based on our taxonomy, a centralized database is characterized by: its single processing unit, without distinction between its services, and without any notion of distribution. The centralized database systems can be further classified as, single-user configuration and multi-user configuration. Natu-rally, database systems designed for single-user configuration do not provide many facilities needed for a multi-user system e.g., concurrency control, and security.

2.2 Parallel Databases

Let us inject processing distribution into the scope of the centralized database system. This brings out the so called parallel database systems, in which several processing resources in cooperation with each other are intended to resolve users' requests. Note that in this environment there exist no notion of data and control distribution. In addition, there is no distinction between services that are provided by the database management system. Parallel configurations are aimed at improving the performance and throughput by distribution of a task at different granularity (fine, medium, or coarse) granularity among several processing units. The literature has introduced four classes of parallel systems:

- Shared Memory (tightly coupled) – All processors share a common global memory.
- Shared Disk (loosely coupled) – All processors share a common set of disks.
- Share Nothing – The processors share neither a common memory nor common disks.
- Hierarchical – A hybrid of the other models.

As noted in the literature; the shared memory configuration is not scalable and the communication network is the system bottleneck. Raid technology can be used to improve performance and reliability of the disk subsystem. The shared nothing configuration offers scalability at the expenses of high inter-processor communication cost. Finally, in the hierarchical topology, at the higher level, system acts as a shared nothing organization and at the lower level, each node could be a shared memory and/or a shared disk system.

2.3 Client/Server Topology

In sections 2.1 and 2.2 we looked at two configurations that did not make any distinction between the services provided by the database management system. Along the *services*, we distinguish two classes of functions:

- The data functions (the back end processes) – query processing, query optimization, concurrency control, and recovery.
- The user functions (the front end processes) – report writer and Graphical User Interface facilities.

This brings out the so called client/server topology that has functionality split between a server and multiple clients. The client/server topology can be grouped into multiple client/single server and multiple client/multiple server configurations. Functionality and processing capability of the client processors and communication speed between the client and server also distinguishes two classes of the client/server topology, namely, transaction server (thin client) and data server (fat client). The client/server topology is one step towards distributed processing. It offers a user-friendly environment, simplicity of implementation, and high degree of hardware utilization at the server side.

2.4 Peer-to-Peer Topology

This topology is a direct evolution of the client/server topology. Note that in the client/server topology functionality is split into user processes and data processes, in

which user processes handle interaction with the user and data processes handle interaction with data. In a Peer-to-Peer topology, one should expect to find both classes of
processes placed on every machine. From a data logical perspective, client/server
topology and Peer-to-Peer topology provide the same view of data - data distribution
transparency. The distinction lies in the architectural paradigm that is used to realize
this level of transparency.

2.5   Distributed Databases

Distributed databases are based on data distribution. It brings the advantages of distributed computing to the database management domain. A distributed system is a
collection of processors, not necessarily homogeneous, interconnected by a computer
network. Data distribution is an effort to improve performance by reducing communication costs and to improve quality of service in case of network failure. Based on our
taxonomy, a distributed database system has the following characteristics: data is
distributed (possibly replicated and/or fragmented) stored in locations close to the
application domain(s) that uses it (e.g. increased availability), processors do not share
resources (i.e., disks and memory) and processes are more distinct, and the underlying
platform is possibly parallel. In comparison to parallel systems in which processors
are tightly coupled and constitute a single database system, a distributed data base
system is a collection of loosely coupled systems that share no physical components.

How to distribute data in order to improve performance, reliability, and accessibil-
ity, and how to provide transparency are the key issues in the design of distributed
databases. Table 1 enumerates some important issues that one needs to consider in the
design of distributed database systems.

Table 1. Issues in distributed database systems

ISSUES	REMARKS
Data Distribution	How data should be distributed/replicated/fragmented in order to improve performance/reliability/accessibility
Distribution Transparency	Distribution transparency includes network (location), replication, and fragmentation transparency
Keeping Track of Data	Keeping track of the data distribution, fragmentation, and Replication
Replicated Data Management	Which replica to access, how to maintain consistency, and how to control number of replica
Database Recovery	Recover from individual site crashes and system failures
Query Processing and Query Optimization	Query resolution, generation of sub-queries, and aggregation of partial results
Transaction Management	Concurrency control protocols
Security	Authenticate users, enforce authorization and access control, and auditing

2.6   Multidatabases

Adding control distribution to the definition of distributed databases as discussed in
section 2.5 results in an environment with the following characteristics:

- Data is distributed and stored in several locations,
- Processes are more distinguished,
- Underlying platforms could be parallel, and
- Processing nodes are autonomous.

This brings out a new computational paradigm that is referred to as multidatabase or heterogeneous distributed database. Due to the autonomy, local databases can join or leave the global information infrastructure at will. As noted in the literature, the autonomy comes in the form of design autonomy, communication autonomy, execution autonomy, and association autonomy. Reading between the lines, autonomy implies heterogeneity. Therefore, autonomy and heterogeneity are the major features that distinguish a multidatabase system from a traditional distributed database system.

To conclude, multidatabases are more dynamic and robust than distributed databases – i.e., system expands and shrinks more rapidly. The design of multidatabase is a bottom up approach – i.e., integration and interoperability of pre-existing data bases. Consequently, while data distribution is a major concern in the design of distributed databases, data integration is the major concern in the design of multidatabases. Research issues in multidatabases (see table 2) are similar to the ones in distributed databases, however, their implementations are becoming more complicated because of the autonomy and heterogeneity of local databases.

Table 2. Issues in multidatabases

ISSUES	REMARKS
Site Autonomy	Local databases have complete control over local data and local processing
Heterogeneity	Support of providing local translation capability from the local model to the common global model
Differences in Data Representation	This includes issues such as name differences, formal differences, structural differences, abstraction differences, and missing or conflicting data
Global Constraints	Need for some method for specifying and enforcing integrity constraints on inter-database dependencies and relationships
Query processing and Query Optimization	Query decomposition and optimization in face of the component databases which could be unavailable, unwilling, and uncooperative
Transaction Management	Concurrency control protocols in the face of global/global and global/local conflicts among transactions
Security	Potential conflicts between global security protocols and local security protocols
Local Node Requirements	Computational and storage capabilities of local nodes to fulfill some global functions

2.7 Mobile Computing

Remote access to various types of data is not a new concept. Traditional distributed databases and multidatabases relying on fixed network connectivity have addressed many of the issues involved in accessing remote data. However, the concept of mobility, where a user accesses data through a remote connection with a portable device, has introduced several disadvantages for traditional database management systems. These include:

- Reduced network connectivity,
- Processing and resource restrictions, and
- Effectively locating and accessing information from a multitude of sources.

The mobile computing environment is based on wireless communication that allows the user to access information anywhere at anytime without direct physical link to the network. The wireless network (Figure 1) is mainly composed of the following:

- A number of network servers enhanced by wireless transceivers, called mobile support stations (MSS), scattered along a geographical area and
- A varying number of mobile hosts (MHs) free to move at will.

The MSS provides a link between the wireless network and the wired network. The link between a MSS and the wired network could be either wireless (shown as dashed line) or wire based. The area covered by the individual transceiver is referred to as a cell. The size of the area covered by each cell varies widely, depending on the technology being used. The MH is relatively small, light weight, and portable. It is designed to preserve space and energy, and it usually has limited amount of resources (memory, processing power, etc.). Most of the time, the MH relies on temporary power sources such as batteries as its main power source. To save energy, the MH is design to operate in different operational modes (i.e. active doze, sleep, nap) that consume different amount of power.

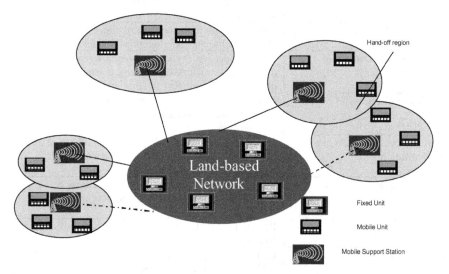

Fig. 1. Architecture of the mobile computing environment

Within the scope of this infrastructure, two types of services are available to the users:

- On-demand-based services, and
- Broadcast-based services.

On-Demand-Based Services. In this configuration, users obtain answers to requests through a two-way communication with the database server (s) – the user request is pushed, data sources are accessed, query operations are performed, partial results are collected and integrated, and generated information is communicated back to the user. In order to overcome the shortcomings of a mobile computing environment effectively, a suitable solution must address issues such as; Security and access control, isolation and autonomy, data heterogeneity, data integration, distribution transparency, location transparency, browsing, query processing and query optimization, transaction processing and concurrency control, limited resources, and limited power sources. Table 3 enumerates issues of importance in this environment.

Table 3. Issues in on-demand-based environment

ISSUES	REMARKS
Site Autonomy	Local control over resources and data. The degree of autonomy required depends upon the degree of mobile support offered by the system
Heterogeneous Interoperability	Hardware and software heterogeneity
Disconnect and Weak Connection Support	A mobile system should provide a means to provide access to data while faced with a disconnection or weak connection
Support for Resource Scarce Systems	A mobile system should address the inherent limitations of various resource scarce access devices. These include processing, storage, power, and display limitations.
Transaction Management and Concurrency Control	Correct transaction management should satisfy the ACID properties (Atomicity, Consistency, Isolation, and Durability)
Distribution Transparency	Distribution of data is transparent to the user
Location Transparency	The location of the data is transparent to the user
Location Dependency	The content of the data is physically dependent upon the location of the user
System Transparency	The user should be able to access the desired data irrespective of the system
Representation Transparency	Representation transparency includes naming differences, format differences, structural differences, and missing or conflicting data
Intelligent Search and Browsing of Data	The system should provide a means for the user to efficiently search and browse the data
Intelligent Query Resolution	The system should be able to efficiently process and optimize a query submitted by the user

Broadcast-Based Services. Many applications are directed towards public information that are characterized by i) the massive number of users and ii) the similarity and simplicity in the requests solicited by the users. The reduced bandwidth attributed to the wireless environment places limitations on the rate and amount of communication. Broadcasting is a potential solution to this limitation. In broadcasting, information is generated and broadcast to all users of the air channels. Mobile users are capable of searching the air channels and pulling their required data. The main advantage of broadcasting is the fact that it scales up as the number of users increases, eliminating the need to multiplex the bandwidth among users accessing the air channel. Furthermore, broadcasting can be considered as an additional storage available over the air for the mobile clients. This is an attractive solution because of the limited storage capability of the mobile unit. Within the scope of broadcasting one needs to address three issues:

- Data selection,
- Effective data organization on the broadcast channel, and
- Efficient data retrieval from the broadcast channel.

3 Our Research

Our research is intended to develop an information infrastructure that allows anytime, anywhere, transparent, intelligent, secure, timely, reliable, and cost effective access to global information regardless of:

- Heterogeneity of access devices,
- Heterogeneity of communication medium, and
- Heterogeneity and autonomy of data sources.

As part of our research we developed an Intelligent Search Engine – Summary Schemas Model, which can automatically identify the semantic similarity among different access terms. It uses linguistic relationships between schema terms to build a hierarchical global metadata, which describes the information available in all local databases in an increasingly abstract form. The hierarchical metadata is a collection of summary schemas. A summary schema is a concise, abstract description of the semantic contents of a group of input schemas. Through extensive simulation study it has been shown:

- The hierarchical metadata of the summary schemas model is by orders of magnitude smaller than the metadata generated by the global-schema approach.
- The summary schemas model preserves local autonomy.
- The summary schemas model provides good system scalability.
- The summary schemas model reduces average search time.
- The summary schemas model resolves imprecise queries.

The SSM has also been prototyped based on the client/server and mobile agent paradigms. In addition, the scope of the SSM was extended by allowing mobility both at the client side and the database side. Within the scope of this mobile computing environment several issues as numerated in table 4 have been researched.

4 Conclusion

The following is a partial list of challenges that deserve attention of researchers:

- Intelligent energy management,
- Interoperability across platforms,
- Portability,
- Security,
- Location dependent services, and
- Pervasiveness

Table 4. Our research efforts

UNDERLYING ENVIRONMENT	RESERARCH ISSUES
On-Demand-Based Services	Transaction processing Query processing Data caching and data duplication Power management Security
Broadcast-Based Services	Access latency and power management Application of index and organization of objects on single broadcast channel Application of index and organization of objects on parallel broadcast channels Conflict resolution and scheduling of data retrieval from parallel broadcast channels

References

1. Bright, M.W., Hurson, A.R. and Pakzad, S.H., "Issues in Multidatabase Systems," IEEE Computers, 25(3):50-60, 1992.
2. Bright, M.W., Hurson, A.R. and Pakzad, S. "Automated Resolution of Semantic Heterogeneity in Multidatabases," ACM Transactions on Database Systems, 19(2):212-253, 1994.
3. Haridas, H., Hurson, A.R., and Jiao, Y., "Security Aspects of Wireless Heterogeneous Databases – Protocol, Performance, and Energy analysis", IEEE WiSPr 2003, pp. 417 -424.
4. Hurson, A.R., Ploskonka, J., Jiao, Y., and Haridas, H., "Security issues and Solutions in Distributed heterogeneous Mobile Database Systems," Vol., 61, Advances in Computers, 2004, pp. 107-198.
5. Hurson, A.R. and Jiao, Y., "Data Broadcasting in a Mobile Environment", Wireless Information Highway, 2004.
6. Jiao, Y. and Hurson, A.R., "Application of Mobile Agents in Mobile Data Access Systems - A prototype", Journal of Database Management, 15(4):1-24, 2004.
7. Lim, J.B., Hurson, A.R., "Heterogeneous Data Access in a Mobile Environment - Issues and Solutions," Advances in Computers, Vol. 48, 1999, pp. 119-178.
8. Lim J.B., and Hurson A.R., "Transaction Processing in Mobile, Heterogeneous Database Systems," IEEE Transactions on Knowledge and Data Engineering, 14(6):1330-1346, 2002.
9. Ngamsuriyaroj, S., Hurson, A.R., and Keefe, T.F., "Authorization Model for Summary Schemes Model", *Proceedings of the International Database Engineering and Applications Symposium,* IDEAS 2002, pp. 182-191.
10. Orchowski, N. and Hurson, A.R., "Energy-Aware Object Retrieval from Parallel Broadcast Channels", *Proceedings of the International Database Engineering and Applications Symposium,* IDEAS 2004, pp. 37-46.
11. Segun, K., Hurson, A.R., Desai, V., Spink, A., and Miller, L.L., "Transaction Management in a Mobile Data Access System," Annual Review of Scalable Computing, Vol. 3, 2001, pp.85-147.
12. Sun, B., Hurson, A.R., and Hannan J., "Energy-Efficient Scheduling Algorithms of Object Retrieval on Indexed Parallel Broadcast Channels", International Conference on Parallel Processing, 2004, pp. 440-447.

Extending Wide-Area Replication Support with Mobility and Improved Recovery*

Hendrik Decker, Luis Irún-Briz, Francisco Castro-Company,
Félix García-Neiva, and Francesc D. Muñoz-Escoí

Instituto Tecnológico de Informática
Universidad Politécnica de Valencia
Ciudad Politécnica de la Innovación, Campo de Vera, s/n
46022 Valencia, Spain
{hendrik,lirun,fcastro,fgarcia,fmunyoz}@iti.es

Abstract. We survey the MADIS architecture. It supports high availability, fault tolerance and seamless error recovery in computer networks for distributed web services. MADIS is open for plugging in different protocols for replication, failure resilience and recuperation. We outline ongoing research which aims at improving fault tolerance and error recovery by a dynamic adaptation of protocols plugged into MADIS. Future development of MADIS envisages an extension with functionality supporting web-based services also for mobile users, possibly including an integration of voice and data traffic over a single internet link.

1 Introduction

Web services usually rely on one or several underlying databases. Such databases either serve to manage application-specific information, e.g., stored or screened versions of ongoing and previous session data, or more general knowledge provided by third parties, e.g., geographical information systems. Typical examples of such web services are web-based communication and collaboration, digital libraries, web-based information systems, etc.

Failure resilience, fault tolerance and seamless error recovery of the databases underlying such web services are key factors for their performance as well as their user acceptance. A tried and tested principle for supporting availability, fault tolerance and transparent error recovery is *distributed replication* [9] [25]. This principle has been adopted by the middleware MADIS [18].

Traditionally, fault tolerance and transparent error recovery is provided by redundant hardware and a software layer which manages a seamless failover from a failing hardware component to a pre-positioned substitute which then is able to continue to function and perform in place of the defunct component. Hardware redundancy works well in local-area networks, such as ethernets or wireless local-area networks.

With MADIS, high availability, fault tolerance and error recovery have been scaled up for communication and computing networks distributed over wider areas, based on the TCP/IP or UDP/IP protocol suites. Stored data items of a given web service are consistently replicated over all network nodes, so that the data and services it provides

---

* This work has been supported by the Spanish MCyT grant TIC2003-09420-C02-01

F.F. Ramos et al. (Eds.): ISSADS 2005, LNCS 3563, pp. 10–20, 2005.

become more available, more fault tolerant and more efficient with recovering from failures.

In section 2, we outline the MADIS architecture. In section 3, we recapitulate several different protocols and outline how a seamless error recovery in data communication networks can be further optimized by a dynamic adaptation of replication strategies. Section 4 addresses future extensions of MADIS with mobility features. In section 5, we conclude.

2   The Main Ideas

MADIS [18] is a more efficient, JDBC-based follow-up of the middleware COPLA [16] [7], developed in the GlobData project [8] [24]. A key feature inherited from its antecedent is that MADIS is not only a system for supporting replication and failure resilience of data communication networks, but also a platform for developing such support systems for specific applications.

Adaptivity of MADIS is achieved via pluggable protocols. They can be chosen and plugged into the middleware according to service-specific requirements, different network properties and various attributes of terminal devices and user profiles. The use of pluggable protocols in MADIS for web-based information systems and voice/data-integated collaboration has been described in [2] [1] [6].

Already the predecessor COPLA of MADIS offered a considerable flexibility of adapting its replication management to different degrees of availability [22]. MADIS can be tuned so as to satisfy lower or higher degrees of availability and fault tolerance, which typically is traded off against increasing or relaxing the requirements on the consistency of replicas, and vice-versa. The essential advances of MADIS over COPLA are the following.

Firstly, the latter provided mappings to fully object-oriented user interfaces, which resulted in "fat" code and large performance overheads for underlying databases of relational kind. As opposed to that, MADIS is much thinner. It complies with the standard relational database paradigm, using just JDBC, instead of cumbersome combinations of JDBC and CORBA.

Secondly, the adaptation of protocols was focused on the tradeoff between consistency and availability. Additionally, MADIS allows to trade off replication consistency also against fault tolerance.

Thirdly, MADIS provides much more flexibility for choosing and swapping suitable protocols than COPLA. MADIS offers a range of different pluggable protocols (synchronous, asynchronous, hybrid, with eager or lazy replication, different relaxations of the ACID properties, etc), so as to satisfy lower or higher degrees of availability and fault tolerance, which is traded off against increased or relaxed requirements of replica consistency. By storing complete sets of metadata for different protocols, it is possible to swap them not only at well-defined break-points (e.g., at the end of sessions), but even while the system is running.

Future development of MADIS envisages an extension of supporting the high availability of web services also for mobile users. An extension for wireless communication services, involving an integration of voice and data traffic over a single internet link, is addressed in section 4.

2.1 The MADIS Architecture

MADIS is structured by three main layers, as shown in fig. 1. On top, the users layer is the interface for developing and using web services, while the core management layer supports their distributed operation. This middle layer includes the transparent management of replica, precautionary measures to prevent any non-availability of data and services, and the seamless recovery of broken nodes. On the bottom, the storage layer provides access to the underlying database, using triggers via JDBC. Also the interaction between users and core management layer goes through JDBC, using the Java Remote Method Invocation mechanism. Both interfaces are described in [17]. The MADIS core management is described in the following subsections.

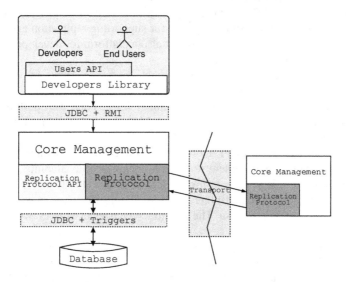

Fig. 1. MADIS Layered Architecture

2.2 The Core Management Layer

The core management of MADIS has a fixed and an exchangeable part. The fixed part manages transactions, including the delegation of requests to the protocols module, which constitutes the exchangeable part. It is exchangeable in the sense that protocols for communication, replication and recovery can be plugged in and out, so as to adapt the system's behaviour to the needs of given applications, network loads and user requirements. Thus, a network administrator can always choose and plug in suitable protocols, in order to adapt the system conveniently.

Maintaining consistency of replicated data and restoring it upon recovery, the protocols module communicate with the core management modules at the other network nodes, by means of message passing. Essentially, the duties of these modules are, to

– cater for requests by users and application programs,
– update local data,

– disseminate a session's updates to other managers,
– monitor group membership,
– keep track of consistency of stored data,
– support recovery of broken nodes,
– decide when to commit or abort transactions.

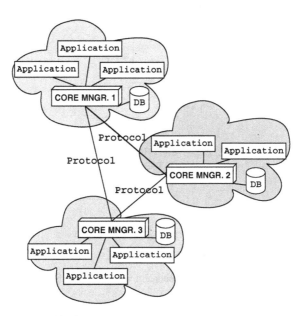

Fig. 2. Networked MADIS Core Managers

In MADIS, protocols specifically tailored to the needs of particular applications can be selected at convenience. For instance, eager or lazy protocols, attuned to eager or lazy update policies (cf. [27] [3]) can be used. Examples of protocols have been discussed, e.g., in [23] [26] [15]. The appropriate choice of suitable protocols depends on the applications, their use cases (e.g., casual or business), network properties (e.g., mobile or fixed nets, the current load, peculiarities of providers, bearers, backbones etc) and user profiles.

2.3   Peer-to-Peer and Client-Server Configurations

MADIS can be used either in *peer-to-peer* or *client/server* scenarios. "Peer-to-peer" here means that data are replicated transparently at the site of each node. Note that each node can be either client or server to each other node, in dynamically interchangeable roles.

Typically, using MADIS in a client/server scenario means that some or all users have access to a virtual database server which does not necessarily belong to the site of any node. Rather, it would be a (public or commercial) third party's repository. Thus, such users behave as clients of a virtual server which actually is a network of replicas.

As shown in fig. 3, client/server and P2P scenarios can be combined orthogonally. Users of one or several external MADIS-supported database servers may at the same

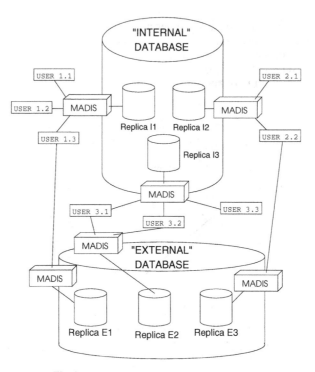

Fig. 3. Users as clients and peers of MADIS

time use replicas of one or several internal peer databases that are also made highly available and failure resilient by MADIS. Then, each installation of MADIS can (and should) be independently tuned according to their own particular requirements. That is, different protocols can be plugged into different installations of MADIS that are running simultaneously.

For example, in a web-based collaboration service, session participants may consult an external distributed database containing time tables or routes of public transport for arranging a meeting, and they may also seek agreement on which documents to bring to the meeting, by retrieving related data in an internal database.

Now, suppose that both the external and the internal database are replicated using MADIS, as illustrated in fig. 3 (the large cylinders suggests that users perceive distributed replicas, represented by small cylinders, as a single system). Then, the external database is probably best served by plugging in a protocol that guarantees a very high degree of consistency, since the provided data are supposed to be accurate at all times. And since it will rarely be written while being read frequently, it will not be a high performance burden to memorize at each node an incremental history of all updates, such that recovery will be very fast after a node's failure, because hardly any additional net communication will be needed for quickly re-installing the current state. Recovery protocols which pursue such a recovery-preventive strategy are described in section 3.

On the other hand, consistency requirements for the internal database can be more relaxed. This is because it neither really matters nor is it possible at all that the latest version of shared collaboration data are always immediately replicated and displayed on each screen at the very same time. Rather, delays of up to a some seconds are usually tolerable in web-based data communication for collaborative dialogues. Hence, protocols used in the internal database may take advantage of such delays by allowing to slightly defer activities for achieving consistency of all replica.

Relaxation of consistency can then be conveniently traded off in favour of other virtues of the protocols. For instance, a higher precaution can be taken in terms of failure prevention and seamless error recovery, which improves the availability of shared data as well as their recovery in case of a network breakdown or a node's failure. Again, we refer to section 3 for details on how protocols may invest in such preventive measures.

3 Speeding up Recovery by Swapping Protocols

For web services the replicas of which are distributed over wide areas, error recovery is more complicated than in local-area clusters, due to the geographical distance and the instability of links between nodes. Clearly, instability further increases in mobile networks. Hence, particular care has to be taken for providing a seamless recovery from failures in a wide-area mobile network.

In general, the idea of replication is that, in case of a node's failure or breakdown, some other replica can be charged with the load of the broken node while the latter is recovering. In wide-area networks, however, recovery entails not just local, but additional system-wide costs of data processing and re-transmission of transactions that have been missed by the broken nodes. This is further aggravated in failure-prone mobile networks.

For minimising the amount of additional communication which is necessary for recovery, we have developed a uniform total order communication protocol which uses a reliable multicast algorithm. Uniform means that the protocol ensures that all network nodes (not just one) are always up-to-date with regard to committed transactions. Moreover, it ensures that each node not only receives, but also maintains locally a record of all delivered messages on hard disc. That way, even after a total breakdown, broken nodes can recover themselves from their own memory, such that only the recent incremental changes that have been missed during its downtime need to be re-transmitted for recovery, instead of possibly huge amounts of transactions or even entire database states.

Conformant with the general philosophy of protocol adaptiveness in MADIS, this uniform total-order communication protocol can be parametrised with different kinds of recovery protocols. For instance, CLOB (*Configurable LOgging for Broadcast protocols*)[4] is a suite of broadcast protocols, used as a basis for database replication. CLOB allows for an easy combination of automatic log-based and protocol-specific version-based recovery techniques. Such a combination provides recovery solutions with optimal performance, but requires some additional storage for maintaining both the log of missed messages and the version-based information needed for recovery. However, version-based information is only a little percentage of the usual log-based one, as has been shown in several examples [11, 23], and the additional storage is easily compensated by the obtained performance gains.

In [4], we describe in more detail how CLOB manages the logging of missed messages in the broadcast protocol core. It provides automatic recovery in short-term failures, but discards the log and accordingly notifies the database replication protocol modules in case of long-term outages. This kind of support can be easily combined with version-based recovery protocols, as follows. Once a failure is detected, the replication protocol uses a traditional version-based management strategy for recovery, which however will be discarded if the replica is able to rejoin the system soon. Then, CLOB automatically propagates the missed update messages to the recovering replica, thus avoiding any delays both in the source and destination replicas. If, on the other hand, the outage period exceeds a given threshold, the reliable broadcast service will notify the replication protocol about that, discard the message logs maintained by CLOB and delegate the recovery management to the upper-layer components.

For dealing with longer-term outages, MADIS offers a recovery protocol called FOBr [5], which uses node identifiers for deploying a concept of object ownership. The key of load balancing then is that each node contributes with a subset of the whole set of objects to be recovered, so that it is free to attend other user requests. The use of node identifiers for identifying object versions imposes very low requirements of additional storage space for keeping track of objects missed during outages. Thus, only the last version of an object needss to be migrated, as oppossed to techniques where complete transaction logs are maintained and each object is transferred as many times as updates had been applied to it. This obviously is very advantageous for wide area networks, since network traffic is significantly reduced.

Current research is concerned with finding optimal trade-off points for CLOB and FOBr on an axis which quantifies outage intervals. By a complementary combination of runtime experiments and analytical methods [10], we are trying to find out for which intervals the outage time is short enough so that a CLOB protocol should be used, and from which interval length onwards it turns out that using FOBr is more advantageous, for speeding up recovery.

4   Enhancing MADIS with Mobility (an Outlook)

We are targeting an extension of MADIS for supporting mobility. New protocols will have to be designed and implemented for taking into account an increased volatility of mobile data, a higher risk of network failures, and limited capacities of communication channels and devices. Additionally, we envisage the incorporation of multimedia communication, at a later stage.

In the following subsection, we revisit a web-based collaboration project called MOVE, which supports both mobility and multimedia collaboration. Since the architectures of MOVE and MADIS are fairly distinct and orthogonal, an integration of both is conceivable.

4.1   MOVE

The main objective of the project MOVE (Mobile Middleware with Voice-Enabled Services) [12] [13] was the integration of voice (real-time data) and multimedia services (real-time and non-real-time data) for mobile GSM-, UMTS- and Web-based collaboration [14]. MOVE is a middleware platform which supports the initiation, maintenance and termination of mobile voice-enabled collaborative multimedia sessions, connecting to each session participant via a single, possibly wireless web link, while simultane-ously, a dynamic quality adjustment of integrated voice/data streams is provided. Sim-ilar to MADIS, the MOVE middleware also provides location transparency of network nodes.

As a demonstration scenario, a collaborative call center application involving web-based VoIP phone conferencing and a hotel-booking service for mobile users, has been developed. It was shown to wide acclaim at the 1999 edition of ITU Telecom in Geneva. That exhibit marked the first time in the history of IP-based telecommunication that a seamless handoff between HSCSD-, GSM- and DECT-based mobile network base sta-tions could be demonstrated in the kbit/s range; handoffs between Wave-LAN base sta-tions even performed in the Mbit/s range.

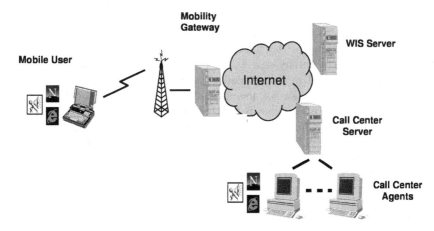

Fig. 4. MOVE collaboration scenario

Figure 4 shows that, along with the mobile user and the call centre, third parties such as a web-based information system or any security service may be involved. The icons besides the screens of user and call center agents indicate that MOVE is not only independent of different browser technologies, but that it also adapts to the peculiarities of some of the more prominent web browsers on the market.

In MOVE, the streaming of voice, video and webcam data meet established trans-mission quality standards. Voice and other real-time data streams are transmitted with higher priority, relative to non-real-time data. If, in spite of clever coding and sophisti-cated compression, the available bandwidth or other resources would otherwise not al-low a timely transmission, then visual data are downsized suitably. Typically, attributes of secondary importance are then scaled down. For instance, fine-grained colour palettes may be coarsened, or mapped to gray tone scales, or to black-and-white binaries. Spe-cial attention is paid to the monitoring and adaptation of heterogeneous media streams, concerning their adjustment to a wide range of quality-of-service parameters.

4.2   Adaptivity in MOVE and MADIS

Adaptivity in web-based collaboration systems usually refers to one of two distin-guished sets of issues. First, adaptivity caters for bridging differences caused by the geographic distance between network nodes and session participants, such as time zone, language, currency, cultural issues, etc. Second, adaptivity refers to a middleware-supported adjustment to (or overruling of) technical idiosyncrasies such as bandwidth limitations, device properties, mobility, user profiles and locations, transmission delays and jitters, vendor-specific hardware and software properties, as well as different types, capacities, carriers, bearers and backbones of various network services. Neither MOVE nor MADIS is concerned with the first kind of adaptivity, which consequently will not be further addressed.

The MOVE adaptivity is of the second kind, as documented in [14] and the project's final report [19]. In addition to its seamless adaptivity as characterized above, MOVE also offers a patented, dynamically adaptive quality-of-service support [21] [20] for the integration of real-time voice and non-real-time data communication over a single internet link, which responds to essentially the same parameters as those determined by the aforementioned network-, location-, vendor- and user-related technicalities.

The MADIS adaptivity does not fall into any of the two categories mentioned above. Although it does offer adaptivity to network load, bandwidth limitations and other static and dynamic properties of web-based collaboration sessions, it does not do so by by means of any web service. Rather, the adaptation of MADIS functionality to the requirements of collaborative sessions is realized, first by choosing, then by monitoring and then suitably exchanging pluggable networking protocols, if the monitoring results advise such an exchange. This is an administrator's job, which so far has not been automated, nor built into the middleware as an autonomous functionality. In some more detail, the MIDAS adaptivity is recapitulated in the conclusion.

5   Conclusion

We have surveyed the middleware MADIS, for supporting an adaptive wide-area replication of distributed data, and thereby the fault tolerance and seamless error recovery of web-based communication networks and services. Moreover, we have outlined an extension of MADIS with functionality as provided by the the middleware MOVE, which supports adaptive voice/data-integrated mobile web-based collaboration services. We have emphasised the adaptivity of both, and contemplated an integration of their respective functionalities into a single web-based collaboration platform which supports mobility.

Adaptivity in communication networks usually refers to one of two distinguished sets of issues. First, adaptivity caters for bridging differences caused by the geographic distance between network nodes and session participants, such as time zone, language, currency, cultural issues, etc. Second, adaptivity refers to a middleware-supported adjustment to (or overruling of) technical idiosyncrasies such as bandwidth limitations, device properties, mobility, user profiles and locations, transmission delays and jitters, vendor-specific hardware and software properties, as well as different types, capacities, carriers, bearers and backbones of various network services.

However, the MADIS adaptivity does not fall into any of the two categories mentioned above. Although it does offer adaptivity to network load, bandwidth limitations and other static and dynamic properties of web-based collaboration sessions, it does not do so by by means of any web service. Rather, adaptivity here consists in the possibility to choose among several protocols, which may favour either lazy or eager update propagation, optimistic or pessimistic concurrency control, and may opt for either a primary-copy or an update-everywhere policy. According to the fine-tuning of such parameters, more or less strong requirements of consistency, availability and responsiveness can be guaranteed. Adaptation to the requirements of network communication is realized, first by choosing, then by monitoring and then suitably swapping pluggable networking protocols, if monitoring results advise such a swap. This is an administrator's job. Its partial automation and integration into the middleware as an autonomous functionality is envisaged in the further development of MADIS.

Currently, we are developing new protocols for supporting an even higher availability and failure resilience than what can so far be guaranteed already by MADIS. The price to pay for that are further relaxations of consistency guarantees, which however are feasible, due to the interactive nature of most web services. A higher performance penalty also has to be paid for additional precautionary measures of memorizing transaction data, in order to enable a seamless recovery from network failures. However, these additional costs are justified by the fact that network failures are much more likely to happen in wide-area mobile networks than in hardwired local-area clusters. Thus, the investment made at times when network nodes operate without faults pays off whenever those nodes are recovering from brakdowns without the need of re-transmissions of huge amounts of data.

An intended future enhancement of MADIS with mobile integrated voice/data features is expected to be particularly beneficial with respect to the demands of web-based communication with small devices via mobile links, as well as for potentially huge volumes of streaming data. In general, different kinds of multimedia data and devices have quite different requirements with regard to timeliness, bandwidth demand and suitability for replication. For instance, voice tends to be elusive and ephemeral, and since it is rather "for the moment" than for the record, it is likely not to be stored, let alone replicated. Hence, the flexibility of MADIS to choose well-suited protocols for satisfying particular requirements will be especially welcome.

References

1. J. Bataller, H. Decker, L. Irún, F. Muñoz: Replication for Web-Based Collaboration. *Proc. 4th Int'l Workshop on Web Based Collaboration*, 15th DEXA, IEEE Computer Society, 2004.
2. J. Bataller, H. Decker, L. Irún, F. Muñoz: A Distributed Web Information Systems Platform Supporting High Responsiveness and Fault Tolerance. *Proc. CAiSE Workshops*, Vol. 1, 79-91, Riga Tech. Univ., 2004.
3. Y. Breitbart, R. Komondoor, R. Rastogi, S. Seshadri, A. Silberschatz: Update propagation protocols for replicated databases. *SIGMOD Record* 28(2):97-108, 1999.
4. F. Castro, J. Esparza, M. Ruiz, L. Irún, H. Decker, F. Muñoz: CLOB: Communication Support for Efficient Replicated Database Recovery. To appear in *Proc. 13th Euromicro Conference on Parallel, Distributed and Network-based Processing*, 2005.
5. F. Castro, L. Irún, F. García, F. Muñoz: FOBr: a version-based recovery protocol for replicated databases. To appear in *Proc. 13th Euromicro Conference on Parallel, Distributed and Network-based Processing*, 2005.
6. H. Decker, F. Muñoz, L. Irún, J. Bataller, P. Galdámez, R. García: Augmenting Web-based Collaboration with Adaptive Replication and Mobility. In M. Matera, S. Comai (eds): *Engineering Advanced Web Applications*, Rinton Press, 2004.

7. H. Decker, F. Muñoz, L. Irún, P. Castro, A. Calero, J. Esparza, J. Bataller, P. Galdámez, J. Bernabéu: Enhancing the Availability of Networked Database Services by Replication and Consistency Maintenance. *Proc. Parallel and Distributed Databases*, 14th DEXA, 531-535. IEEE Computer Society, 2003.
8. http://globdata.iti.es
9. R. Guerraoui, A. Schiper: Fault-Tolerance by Replication in Distributed Systems. *Proc. Int'l Conf. Reliable Software Technologies*, 38-57. Springer LNCS 1088, 1996.
10. L. Irún, F. Castro, H. Decker, F. Muñoz: An Analytical Design of a Practical Replication Protocol for Distribute d Systems. *Applying Formal Methods: Testing, Performance and M/ECommerce (Pro c. FORTE Workshops)*, 248-261. Springer LNCS 3236, 2004.
11. L. Irún, F. Castro, F. García, A. Calero, F. Muñoz: Lazy recovery in a hybrid database replication protocol. *Proc. XII Jornadas de Concurrencia y Sistemas Distribuidos*, 2004.
12. http://www.cordis.lu/infowin/acts/rus/projects/ac343.htm
13. M. Wallbaum, D. Carrega, M. Krautgärtner, H. Decker: A Mobile Middleware Component Providing Voice over IP Services to Mobile Users. *Proc. ECMAST '99*, 552-563. Springer LNCS Vol. 1629, 1999.
14. D. Carrega, H. Muyal, H. Decker, M. Wallbaum: Integrating voice and data services for mobile internet collaboration with the MOVE middleware architecture. *Proc. 1st Int'l Workshop on Web Based Collaboration*, 12th DEXA, 532-536. IEEE Computer Society, 2001.
15. L. Irún, F. Muñoz, J. Bernabéu: An Improved Optimistic and Fault-Tolerant Replication Protocol. *Proc. 3rd Int'l Workshop on Databases in Networked Information Systems*, 188-200. Springer LNCS 2822, 2003.
16. L. Irún, F. Muñoz, H. Decker, J. Bernabéu: COPLA: A Platform for Eager and Lazy Replication in Networked Databases. *Proc. 5th ICEIS*, Vol. 1, 273-278, 2003.
17. L. Irún, R. de Juan-Marín, F. Castro, H. Decker, F. Muñoz: Dealing with Readsets and Writesets in the MADIS Architecture. *submitted*, 2004.
18. http://www.iti.upv.es/madis
19. ftp://ftp.cordis.lu/pub/infowin/docs/fr-343.pdf
20. M. Wallbaum, H. Decker: Enabling Quality-of-Service Management for Voice/Data-Integrated Mobile Communication. *Proc. ICDCS 2000 Workshops, section D: Wireless Networks and Mobile Computing*, 87-93. IEEE Computer Society, 2000.
21. H. Decker, M. Krautgärtner: Flexible Quality-of-Service Technology for Supporting Voice/Data-Integrated Nomadic Networking. *Flexible Working – New Network Technologies*, 215-224. IOS Press, 1999.
22. F. Muñoz, L. Irún, J. Bataller, P. Galdámez, J. Bernabéu, J. Bataller, C. Bañuls, H. Decker: Flexible Management of Consistency and Availability of Networked Data Replications. *Proc. FQAS'02*, 289-300, Springer LNCS 2522, 2002.
23. F. Muñoz, L. Irún, P. Galdámez, J. Bernabéu, J. Bataller, M.C. Bañuls: GlobData: Consistency Protocols for Replicated Databases. *Proc. YUFORIC'01*, 97-104. IEEE Computer Society, 2001.
24. F. Muñoz, L. Irún, P. Galdámez, H. Decker, J. Bernabéu, J. Bataller, C. Bañuls: GlobData: A Platform for Supporting Multiple Consistency Modes. *Proc. Information Systems and Databases*, 104-109, Acta Press, 2002.
25. T. Özsu, P. Valduriez: *Principles of Distributed Database Systems*, 2nd Edition. Prentice Hall, 1999.
26. L. Rodrigues, H. Miranda, R. Almeida, J. Martins, P. Vicente: The GlobData Fault-Tolerant Replicated Distributed Object Database. *Proc. EurAsia-ICT*, 426-433. Springer LNCS 2510, 2002.
27. M. Wiesmann, A. Schiper, F. Pedone, B. Kemme, G. Alonso: Database replication techniques: A three parameter classification. *Proc. 19th Sympos. Reliable Distributed Systems*, 206-217. IEEE Computer Society, 2000.

Extending Databases to Precision-Controlled Retrieval of Qualitative Information

Victor Polo de Gyves[1], Adolfo Guzman-Arenas[1,2], and Serguei Levachkine[2]

[1] SoftwarePro International
degyves@gmail.com, a.guzman@acm.org
[2] Centro de Investigación en Computación, Instituto Politécnico Nacional
07738 Mexico City, Mexico
sergei@cic.ipn.mx

Abstract. A hierarchy is an arrangement of qualitative values in a tree with certain properties. Hierarchies allow to define the confusion *conf(r, s)* in using qualitative value r instead of the intended or correct value *s*. From here, "predicate P holds for object *o*", written P(*o*), is generalized to "P holds for *o* within confusion ε", written $P_\varepsilon(o)$. These *precision-controlled predicates* are useful to retrieve approximate answers, where the error (confusion) is known.
The predicates are implemented through an extended SQL that uses *confusion* to retrieve information from a database. We show how to extend *any* database for precision-controlled retrieval. Limiting the total error is also useful, and this is achieved by predicate P^ε. Examples are given.

1 Introduction and Related Work

A datum makes sense only within a context. Intuitively, we know that "computer" is closer to "office" than to "ocean" or to "dog." A "cat" is closer to "dog" than to "bus station." "Burning" is closer to "hot" than to "icy." How can we measure these similarities?

A hierarchy describes the structure of qualitative values in a set S. A **(simple, normal) hierarchy** is a tree with root S and if a node has children, these form a partition of the father [1]. A simple hierarchy describes a hierarchy where S is a set (thus its elements are not repeated not ordered). For example: live being{animal{mammal, fish, reptile, other animal}, plant{tree, other plant}}. In a **percentage hierarchy** [3], the size of each set is known[1], for instance: AmericanContinent(640M){North America(430M) {USA(300M), Canada(30M), Mexico(100M)} Central America (10M), South America(200M)}. The nodes of a percentage hierarchy are bags (sets where repetition is allowed). In an **ordered hierarchy** [2], the nodes of some partitions obey an ordering relation (they are ordered sets): object{tiny, small, medium, large}*[2]. Finally, a **mixed hierarchy** combines the three former types. Other works on retrieval of approximate answers are referenced in [4].

For these four types of hierarchies we define *conf(r, s)* as the confusion or error in using value r instead of s, the intended or correct value. These definitions agree with the human sense of estimation in closeness for several wrong but approximate answers to a given question; each is applicable to particular endeavors.

---

[1] Notation: after each set we write its size in parenthesis. Here we write number of inhabitants
[2] Notation: an * is placed at the end of the partition, to signify that it is an *ordered* partition

F.F. Ramos et al. (Eds.): ISSADS 2005, LNCS 3563, pp. 21–32, 2005.

The main trust of the paper is in implementation. We define an extended SQL syntax (XSQL) that deals with approximate queries on elements in a database holding qualitative values hierarchically structured. XSQL expresses precision-controlled predicates (§3). The user writes his queries in XSQL. A program (§4.1) converts an XSQL expression back to (pure) SQL. Another program (§4.2) converts hierarchies into tables (storing confusion values) that are added to the (normal) database. Thus, the extension (to precision-controlled retrieval) of *any* database is possible. Some examples are given, mainly for simple and percentage hierarchies, due to page limit.

2   Confusion in Hierarchies

Who wrote *Leaves of Grass?* Walt Whitman is the right answer; Edgar Allan Poe a close miss, Michael Jordan a fair error, and Mexico City or cellphone a gross error. What is closer to a *violin*, a *harp*, a *flute* or a *camel*? Can we measure these errors? Yes, with hierarchies of symbolic values. Some definitions from [1-4] are:

Let H be a simple hierarchy. If r, s $\in$ H, then the confusion in using r instead of s, written conf(r, s), is:

- conf (r, r) = conf (r, s) = 0, where s is any ascendant of r;   (1)
- conf (r, s) = 1 + conf (r, father_of(s)) $\blacklozenge$ (2)

To measure *conf*, count the descending links from r to s, the intended or correct value. Function *conf* is not a distance, nor an ultradistance. To differentiate from other linguistic terms like relatedness or closeness, we prefer to use 'confusion.' *Example:* in table 8, conf(Florida, USA)=1, conf(USA, Florida)=0, conf(USA, Mexico City)=2.

Let H be an ordered hierarchy. The confusion in using r instead of s, conf'' (r, s), is defined as follows:

- conf'' (r, r) = conf (r, any ascendant of r) = 0;
- If r and s are distinct brothers, conf''(r, s) = 1 if the father is not an ordered set; else, conf''(r, s) = the relative distance from r to s = the number of steps needed to go from r to s in the ordering, divided by the cardinality-1 of the father;   (3)
- conf'' (r, s) = 1 + conf''(r, father_of(s)). $\blacklozenge$

This is like conf for *simple hierarchies* (formed by sets), except that in them the error between two brothers is 1, and here it is a number in (0, 1]. *Example*: Let Temp = {icy, cold, normal, warm, hot, burning}*. Then, conf''(icy, cold)= 1/5, while conf'' (icy, burning)=1.

Let H be a percentage hierarchy. Let S be the set at the root of H. The **similarity** in using r instead of s, sim^b (r, s), is:

- sim^b (r, r) = sim^b(r, any ascendant_of (r)) = 1;
- if r is ascendant of s, sim^b(r, s)= number of elements of S$\cap$r$\cap$s / number of elements of S$\cap$r = relative popularity of s in r. $\blacklozenge$ [3]

The confusion in using r instead of s, conf'(r, s), is 1 – sim^b (r, s). $\blacklozenge$ (4)

---

[3] Relative popularity or percentage of s in r = number of elements of S that are in r and that also occur in s / number of elements of S that are also in r

Example: If baseball player(9) = {pitcher(1), catcher(1), base player(3){first base (1), second base(1), third base(1)}, field player(3){left fielder(1), center fielder(1), right fielder(1)}, shortstop(1)}, then *(a)* conf'(field player, baseball player)= 1 − sim^b(fielder, baseball player)= 0; *(b)* conf'(baseball player, field player)= 1 − 1/3 = 2/3; *(c)* conf' (baseball player, left fielder)= 8/9; *(d)* conf' (base player, left fielder) = 2/3. This ends the definitions taken from [1-4].

Let H be a mixed hierarchy. To compute *sim(r, s)* in a mixed hierarchy:

- apply rule (1) to the *ascending* path from *r* to *s*;
- in the descending path, use rule (3) instead of rule (2), if p is an ordered set[4]; or use rule (4) instead of (2), when sizes of p and q are known. ♦ That is, use (4) instead of (2) for percentage hierarchies.

This definition is consistent with and reduces to previous definitions for simple, ordered, and percentage hierarchies.

3 Querying a Database with Predicates that Are Imperfectly Fulfilled

Precision-controlled predicates. A powerful use of *confusion* is to define predicates over objects having attributes with domains on hierarchies, and to define some "looseness of fit" for these predicates. That is, a predicate P shall be satisfied within a given confusion [1]. Let *Hv* stand for a hierarchical variable, and *v* its value for object *o*. We define predicate P_ε thus [1]:

P holds for object o with *confusion* ε (written P_ε holds for o, or $P_\varepsilon(o)$) if:

- When *P* is of the form: *(Hv = s)*, iff conf(v, s) ≤ ε. (footnote[5])
- When *P* is of the form *P1* ∨ *P2*, iff *P1* holds for *o* or *P2* holds for *o*.
- When *P* is of the form *P1* ∧ *P2*, iff *P1* holds for *o* and *P2* holds for *o*.
- When *P* is of the form ¬*P1*, iff *P1* does not hold for *o*. ♦

Examples (Figs. 2, 4 and 5): the predicate *(address = North_America)$_0$* will match any person living in North America or any of its regions (subsets). The predicate *(address = Mexico City)$_1$* will match any person living in Mexico City, Jalisco, Guadalajara or Mexico. The predicate *(address = Mexico City ∨ industrial_branch = Mexican food)$_1$* is equal to *(address = Mexico City)$_1$* ∨ *(industrial_branch = Mexican food)$_1$* = {Garcia Productores, Mole Doña Rosa} ∪ {Luigi's Italian Food, Mole Doña Rosa}. The predicate *(address = Mexico City ∧ industrial_branch = Mexican food)$_1$* is equal to *(address = Mexico City)$_1$* ∧ *(industrial_branch = Mexican food)$_1$* = {Mole Doña Rosa}.

From the definition of P_ε holds for o, it is true that $(P \lor Q)_\varepsilon = (P_\varepsilon \lor Q_\varepsilon)$. This means that for $(P \lor Q)_a = (P_b \lor Q_c)$, a = min(b, c). Similarly, for $(P \land Q)_a = (P_b \land Q_c)$, we have a = max(b, c).

---

[4] Here, p and q are two consecutive elements in the path from r to s, where q immediately follows p. That is, r → ...p→q... →s

[5] That is, the value *v* of property *Hv* for the object *o* can be used instead of *s* with confusion ε

In addition, we define a predicate with "delimited" confusion ε if the sum of the partial confusions is $\leq \varepsilon$, thus:

P holds for object *o*, but **delimited by** ε [read P^ε *delimited by* ε, *holds for o;* written $P^\varepsilon(o)$], when *P* is of the form $P1 \wedge P2 \wedge ...Pk$ and $\exists \varepsilon 1, \varepsilon 2,... \varepsilon k \geq 0$ such that $P1_{\varepsilon 1}(o)$ and $P2_{\varepsilon 2}(o)...$ and $Pk_{\varepsilon k}(o)$ and $\varepsilon 1 + \varepsilon 2 + ... + \varepsilon k \leq \varepsilon$. ◆ P "delimited by ε" means that the accumulated confusions should not exceed ε. Note that the "delimited" confusion does not apply to disjunctive predicates (of type $P1 \vee P2 \vee ...$), because these hold even when only one Pi holds, and therefore it does not make sense to add the confusion of the Pi's not holding. Example (Figs. 2, 4 and 5): *(address = Mexico City $\wedge$ industrial branch = computer)[1]* = {Garcia Productores} because, for each of the customers of Fig. 2, the accumulated confusion is, respectively, 2+0, 0+0.7, 2+0.7, 2+0, 2+0.7, 2+0.7, 1+0.7, 2+0.7, 2+0.7, 2+0.7.

3.1 Extended SQL (XSQL)

To query with controlled precision a table T of a database, SQL is extended by these constructs:

- `conf(R,s)`$\leq \varepsilon$, an XSQL representation for $(R=s)_\varepsilon$, is a condition procedure used in a WHERE or HAVING clause, which is true iff conf(r, s)$\leq \varepsilon$. R is the name of a column of T that is a hierarchical variable (a variable or column having hierarchical values), *r* is each of these values, and *s* is the intended or expected qualitative value. ◆ *Example*: `conf(address,mexico)`≤ 0 represents in XSQL the predicate *(address = mexico)$_0$* and will select all rows from figure 2 whose address is Mexico with confusion 0; that is, all rows where *(address = r)* and conf(r, mexico)≤ 0. It will return rows 2 and 7.
- `conf(R)` is an XSQL expression [a shorthand for `conf(R,s)`], used in 'SELECT `conf(R)`', or 'GROUP BY `conf(R)`' or 'ORDER BY `conf(R)`', which returns for each row of table T, the value conf(R,s). ◆ That is, `conf(R)` returns for table T a list of numbers corresponding to the confusion of the value of property R for each row of T. *Example*: see figure 3.

3.2 The User Writes a Query EXPR in XSQL When He Has P_ε or P^ε in Mind

The algorithm EXPR= replace(P) to substitute (the user thinks about precision-controlled predicate P and writes EXPR instead) predicate P by its equivalent XSQL expression EXPR is:

- *(R = s)$_\varepsilon$* should be replaced by 'conf (' *R* ',' *s* ')$\leq$' ε, when R is the name of a column of a table, and s a symbolic value.
- *(P1 $\vee$ P2)$_\varepsilon$* should be replaced by ' (' replace(*P1$_\varepsilon$*) ' OR ' replace (*P2$_\varepsilon$*) ') '.
- *(P1 $\wedge$ P2)$_\varepsilon$* should be replaced by ' ('replace(*P1$_\varepsilon$*) ' AND ' replace (*P2$_\varepsilon$*)') '.
- ¬*P* should be replaced by 'NOT (' replace (*P*) ') '.
- *(P1 $\vee$ P2)$^\varepsilon$* should be replaced by ' ('replace(*P1*) ' AND ' replace(*P2*) ' AND (conf (' *P1* ') +conf (' *P2* ')) $\leq$' ε')'. ◆

Example: (industrial branch = food)$_0$ $\wedge$ [(address = pasadena) $\vee$ (address = mexico city)]$_1$ is replaced by conf (industrial_branch, food)$\leq$ 0 AND (conf(address, pasadena)$\leq$ 1 OR conf (address, mexico city)$\leq$ 1). *Example*: *(address = Mexico City $\wedge$ industrial branch = computer)^1* is replaced by (conf(address, Mexico City)$\leq$1 AND conf (industrial_branch, computer) $\leq$1 AND (conf(address)+conf (industrial_branch))$\leq$1).

3.3   Queries: Retrieving Objects That Match P$_\varepsilon$

Example: (address = usa)$_1$ becomes the XSQL query conf(address, usa)$\leq$1, which returns any object whose value of property address can be used instead of usa with confusion 1. *Example*: Figure 1 shows customers (of figure 2) for which *(address = california)$_1$*. This returns every record, except for Mole Doña Rosa [its address is somewhere in Mexico and conf(mexico, california)=2, by figure 4]; except for Garcia Productores [its address is in Mexico City and conf (mexico city, california)=2]; except for Luigi's Italian food [its address is somewhere in North America and conf(north america, california)=2]; except for Canada seeds [because conf(canada, california)=2]. Figure 3 sorts the result set based on the confusion.

```
select customer.name, customer.address
from customer
where conf(customer.address,'california')<=1

NAME                ADDRESS
East coast meat     florida
Media Tools         new york
Tom's Hamburgers    pasadena
Microsol            silicon valley
Tampa tobacco       tampa
Texas fruits        texas
```

Fig. 1. Querying conf(address, california)$_1$: any customer in California with confusion 1

name	industrial_branch	address	discount
Media Tools	computers	new york	0
Garcia Productores	tequila	mexico city	0
Tom's Hamburgers	food	pasadena	0
Microsol	software	silicon valley	0
East coast meat	meat	florida	0
Luigi's italian food	italian food	north america	0
Mole Doña Rosa	mexican food	mexico	0
Texas fruits	fruits	texas	0
Tampa tobacco	cigars	tampa	0
Canada seeds	food	canada	0

Fig. 2. Table of customers

```
select customer.name, customer.address,
conf(customer.address) from customer where
conf(customer.address,'california')<=1
order by conf(customer.address)

NAME              ADDRESS         CALIFORNIA
Tom's Hamburgers  pasadena        0
Microsol          silicon valley  0
Media Tools       new york        1
Tampa tobacco     tampa           1
Texas fruits      texas           1
East coast meat   florida         1
```

Fig. 3. Querying, sorting and showing values for conf(address, california)[1]

```
Property: address;
hierarchy: world{
                    north_america{
                      usa{
                        california{
                            silicon valley,
                            pasadena, },
                        new york{
                            new york city
                        },
                        florida{
                            miami,
                            tampa
                        },
                        texas
                      }
                      canada,
                      mexico{
                        mexico city,
                        jalisco{
                            guadalajara } } } }
```

Fig. 4. The addresses of customers form a simple hierarchy. Hierarchies are used in §4.2 to generate confusion tables such as that of figure 7

```
Property: industrial branch;
hierarchy:
industrial branch(1){
    computer(.3){
        software(.12),
        hardware(.18)
    },
    human consumption(.7){
        food(.56){
            prepared food(.112){
                mexican food(.0448),
                italian food(.0672)
            },
            meat(.168),
            fruits(.28)
        }
        drinks and cigars(.14){
            drinks(.056){
                whiskey(.0112),
                beer(.028),
                tequila(.0168)
            },
            cigars(.084) } } }
```

Fig. 5. Mixed hierarchy of industrial branch for customers, using percentage values. The percentage values represent the products consumed in a business organization

Precision-controlled retrieval in percentage hierarchies can also be done. *Example:* Give me the customers whose industrial branch (figure 5) is food (with confusion of 1), sort and show the confusion values. Results are in figure 6.

```
select customer.name, customer.industrial_branch,
conf(customer.industrial_branch) from customer
where conf(customer.industrial_branch,'food')<=1 order by
conf(customer.industrial_branch)

NAME                      INDUSTRIAL_BRANCH FOOD
Luigi's italian food italian food       0
Tom's Hamburgers         food            0
Canada seeds             food            0
Texas fruits             fruits          0
East coast meat          meat            0
Mole Doña Rosa           mexican food    0
Garcia Productores       tequila         0.44
Tampa tobacco            cigars          0.44
Microsol                 software        0.44
```

Fig. 6. Querying, sorting and showing values for *(industrial_branch = food)$_1$* for customers of figure 2

4   Implementation of Confusion-Controlled Queries

An *extension kit* permits *any database* to handle imprecise retrieval: First, a parser is used to translate (§4.1) XSQL predicates to a (pure) SQL query able to use pre-calculated *confusion* tables (called SCTs). Then, execution of the new SQL predicate is carried out. §4.2 explains how these tables are created.

4.1   Translating (by the Parser) XSQL Queries to Valid SQL Queries

Since we extended SQL by adding only conf(R, s) and conf(R), we need to deal only with these two. If S is a valid XSQL SELECT query containing conf (R, s) ≤ε or conf(R):

1. Let t(R) = R's table name and r(R) = R's column name.
2. Add t(R) to the list of tables (FROM clause).
3. Translate any conf (R, s) ≤ε as '(confusion.' t(R) '_' r(R) 'norm.name=' t(R) '.' r(R) ' AND confusion.' t(R) '_' r(R) '_norm.' s '≤' ε ')'.
4. Translate any conf (R) as 'confusion.' t(R) '_' r(R) '_norm.' s.

Example: select customer.name from customer where conf (customer.industrial_branch, 'food') <=1 translates to select customer.name from customer, confusion.customer_industrial_branch_norm where (confusion.customer_industrial_branch_norm.name = customer.industrial_branch AND confusion.customer_industrial_branch_norm.food <=1).

If S is a valid XSQL `UPDATE/DELETE` arising from a predicate using P^ε or P_ε and containing `conf(R,s)` $\leq\varepsilon$ only in the `WHERE` section:

1. Let $t(R) = R$'s table name and $r(R) = R$'s column name.
2. Create a valid SQL `SELECT`, named S2= '(`SELECT` ' R ' `FROM` ' t(R) ' `WHERE` conf (' R '.' r(R) ')` $\leq$ ' ε ')'.
3. Translate S2 [to get rid of the conf(R.r(R))<ε], generating a new expression S2'.
4. Replace every appearance of `conf(R,s)` $\leq\varepsilon$ in S by S2'.

For `INSERT` sentences, no confusion is valid, except for `INSERT...SELECT`. In that case, translate the `SELECT` part as described.

4.2 Implementing the Calculation of Confusion Values in Databases

Applying *conf (R, s)*$\leq\varepsilon$ in a database table *T* involves the use of a function *f* that, for every record $x \in T$, takes the *r* value stored in the *R* property of *x* and calculates *conf (r, s)*. If less or equal to ε, the record is returned. Doing this calculation for every query is slow. Instead, sets of pre-calculated database tables of confusion (SCT's) are used to speed up the query process. This process is shown (displayed) in figure 7.

4.3 Two Examples Using Confusion with Mixed Hierarchies
for Retrieval of Information in Databases

In example 4.3.1 we need to hire one computer specialist (from candidates of figure 10) with some special characteristics. The problem is to select the best candidate fulfilling the desired requirements. It would be good to use confusion, specially if there are few or no candidates covering all of the requirements. Figures 9, 11, 12 and 13 define the hierarchies. In example 4.3.2 we update groups of objects that depend on hierarchical structures.

4.3.1 Limiting the Errors

Sort candidates to hire. Here we analyze the use of P^ε. It is a way to limit the total error in predicates: A list of candidates is given to cover available jobs on a new enterprise. The requirements for the job is given in a predicate P. While P_ε can select and sort this list for a given value of ε, it is better to limit the sum of confusions produced by each candidate (due to imperfect match of his qualifications). This is accomplished by P^ε, where ε is such limit. We will use figures 9-13. We begin by using P = (degree = 'high school computer')$_2$ $\wedge$ (programming language = 'java')$_2$ $\wedge$ (previous work = 'system analyst')$_2$ $\wedge$ (experience = 'solaris')$_3$.

We may reduce the *confusion* in P by querying with small ε's, such as in P2= (degree = 'high school computer')$_1$ $\wedge$ (programming_language = 'java')$_2$ $\wedge$ (previous_work = 'system analyst')$_1$ $\wedge$ (experience = 'solaris')$_2$, so that now only *Alfred* fulfills P. But, what if we need more employees to hire? This is where P^ε goes. It allows to use the sum of confusion values to delimit the objects that P holds for. So, we can delimit P of figure 15 as follows: $P^5 =$ ((degree = 'high school computer')$_2 \wedge$ (programming_language = 'java')$_2 \wedge$ (previous_work = 'system analyst')$_2 \wedge$ (experience = 'solaris')$_3$)^5. Having done this, now we are controlling the list of resulting objects using the *sum of confusions* (figure 14):

Step	Example
Let *T* be a database table. $Tp=\{a_1...a_n\}$ are properties of *T*; $Th=\{a_m...a_n\}$ are hierarchical properties of *T* and $Th \subseteq Tp$.	T = customer (see table customer in Fig. 2) Tp = {name, industrial_branch, address, discount} Th = {industrial_branch, address}
Consider each $a_x \in Th$, and form $H=\{ h_x \mid h_x$ is the hierarchy corresponding to $a_x\}$	H = {h$_\text{industrial\_branch}$, h$_\text{address}$} = the set of hierarchies of T.
Let $CT =$ $\{confusion.T\_a_m\_norm, ...,$ $confusion.T\_a_n\_norm \}$ where $a_x \in Th$. For each element $e_x \in CT$, a pre-calculated confusion table will be created, as described later.	CT = {confusion.customer_industrial_branch_norm, confusion.customer_address_norm}
Given an element $e_x \in CT$, the set of properties *sp* for e_x is a function defined as: $sp(e_x) = \{$ *'name'*, $h_{x1}...h_{xn}\}$ where h_{xy} is an element in the hierarchy h_x and $h_x \in H$.	sp(confusion.customer_industrial_branch_norm)={name, industrial_branch, computer, human consumption, software, hardware, food, drinks and cigars, prepared food, meat, fruits, drinks, cigars, mexican food, italian food, whiskey, beer, tequila } sp(confusion.customer_address_norm)={name, world, north america, canada, usa, mexico, california, new york, florida, texas, mexico city, jalisco, silicon valley, pasadena, new york city, miami, tampa, guadalajara}
Given an element $e_x \in CT$, the set of objects *so* for e_x is a function defined as: $so(e_x)= \{ \{h_{x1}, conf(h_{x1}, h_{x1})... conf(h_{x1},h_{xn}) \},... \{h_{xn}, conf(h_{xn},h_{x1})... conf(h_{xn}, h_{xn}) \} \}$, where h_{xy} is an element in the hierarchy h_x and $h_x \in H$.	so(confusion.customer_industrial_branch_norm)={ {industrial_branch,0.0,0.6,0.4,0.8,0.7,0.5,0.8,0.9,0.8,0.7,0.9,0.9,0.9, 0.9,0.9,0.9,0.9}, {computer,0.0,0.0,0.4,0.8,0.7,0.5,0.8,0.9,0.8,0.7, 0.9, 0.9,0.9,0.9,0.9,0.9,0.9}, ... {tequila,0.0,0.6,0.0,0.8,0.7,0.5,0.0,0.9,0.8,0.7,0.0,0.0,0.8,0.9,0.9,0.9,0.8,0.0} } *(the complete set of objects is not shown)* so(confusion.customer_addres_norm)={ {world, 0 ,1 ,2 ,2 ,2 ,3 ,3 ,3 ,3 ,3 ,3 ,4 ,4 ,4 ,4 ,4 ,4}, {north america,0 ,0 ,1 ,1 ,1 ,2 ,2 ,2 ,2 ,2 ,2 ,3 ,3 ,3 ,3 ,3 ,3}, ... {guadalajara, 0 ,0 ,1 ,1 ,0 ,2 ,2 ,2 ,2 ,1 ,0 ,3 ,3 ,3 ,3 ,3 ,0} } *(the complete set of objects is not shown)*
Finally, given an element $e_x \in CT$, the SQL confusion table for e_x is an SQL table defined as $sp(e_x)$ and filled with elements in $so(e_x)$; the name of the table will be e_x. $SCT=\{e_m,...,e_n\}$ is the set of confusion tables for *T*.	

Fig. 7. Steps to compute a confusion table (CT) for a table T. The example uses for T the table of Fig. 2, and the hierarchies in figs. 4 and 5. Two CT's are produced, one is shown in Fig. 8

name	world	north america	canada	usa	mexico	california	new york	florida	texas	mexico city	jalisco	silicon valley	pasadena	new york city	miami	tampa	guadalajara
world	0	1	2	2	2	3	3	3	3	3	3	4	4	4	4	4	4
north ame	0	0	1	1	1	2	2	2	2	2	2	3	3	3	3	3	3
canada	0	0	0	1	1	2	2	2	2	2	2	3	3	3	3	3	3
usa	0	0	1	0	1	1	1	1	1	2	2	2	2	2	2	2	3
mexico	0	0	1	1	0	2	2	2	2	1	1	3	3	3	3	3	2
california	0	0	1	0	1	0	1	1	1	2	2	1	1	2	2	2	3
new york	0	0	1	0	1	1	0	1	1	2	2	2	2	1	2	2	3
florida	0	0	1	0	1	1	1	0	1	2	2	2	2	2	1	1	3
texas	0	0	1	0	1	1	1	1	0	2	2	2	2	2	2	2	3
mexico c	0	0	1	1	0	2	2	2	2	0	1	3	3	3	3	3	2
jalisco	0	0	1	1	0	2	2	2	2	1	0	3	3	3	3	3	1
silicon va	0	0	1	0	1	0	1	1	1	2	2	0	1	2	2	2	3
pasadena	0	0	1	0	1	0	1	1	1	2	2	1	0	2	2	2	3
new york	0	0	1	0	1	1	0	1	1	2	2	2	2	0	2	2	3
miami	0	0	1	0	1	1	1	0	1	2	2	2	2	2	0	1	3
tampa	0	0	1	0	1	1	1	0	1	2	2	2	2	2	1	0	3
guadalaja	0	0	1	1	0	2	2	2	2	1	0	3	3	3	3	3	0

Fig. 8. SQL confusion table for confusion.customer_address_norm, as generated by the algorithm of figure 7. Each row is r while each column is s. Another confusion table (for confusion.customer_industrial_branch_norm, not shown) is generated, too. Thus, the set SCT generated in figure 7 contains these two confusion tables (CT)

```
degree{
    mathematics{
        computer{high school computer, college computer},
        physics college,
        electric{electric college, electronics college, electric high
                school},
    }
    biology{medical, biologist},
    humanities{history college, languages college}
}
```

Fig. 9. Hierarchy for degree. It is a simple hierarchy, as defined in §1

NAME	DEGREE	LANG	PREVIOUSWORK	OPERATINGSYSTEM
Alfred	college_computer	java	system_analyst	unix
Brenda	high_school_computer	basic	hackman	windows_xp
John	high_school_computer	prolog	secretary	none
Thomas	electronics_college	python	programmer	linux
Susan	electronics_college	basic	programmer	windows_2000
Abraham	electric_college	cpp	operator	bsd
Natalie	electric_high_school	pascal	secretary	none
Martin	physics_college	lisp	manager	solaris
Alex	physics_college	lisp	programmer_leader	windows_2000
Ernest	college_computer	shell	operator	linux
Ann	history_college	none	other	none
Sam	biologist	none	other	linux
Fred	languages_college	prolog	manager	macos9
Robert	electric_college	java	database_administrator	linux
Bill	high_school_computer	cpp	other	solaris

Fig. 10. Candidates and their qualifications. The ideal candidate should have a college degree related to computers; should know Java; should have worked previously as system analyst, and should have experience in Solaris

```
work{
    computers related{programmer, programmer leader, system
        analyst, database administrator},
    administration related{chief executive, manager},
    operations related{operator, secretary, hackman}
    other
}
```

Fig. 11. Hierarchy for work, pertinent to column PREVIOUSWORK of figure 10

```
languages{
    programming languages{
        artificial intelligence{prolog, lisp},
        object oriented{cpp, java, python},
        other{pascal, basic, shell}
    },
    none
}
```

Fig. 12. Hierarchy for programming language

```
systems{
    operating systems{
        unix{   linux, solaris, bsd}
        microsoft{windows 2000, windows nt 4, windows xp}
        apple{macos9, macosx}
    }
    none
}
```

Fig. 13. Hierarchy for operating systems.

```
select candidates.name from candidates where
conf(candidates.degree,'high_school_computer')<=2 AND
conf(candidates.programminglanguage,'java')<=2 AND
conf(candidates.previouswork,'system_analyst')<=2 AND
conf(candidates.operatingsystem,'solaris')<=3 AND
conf(candidates.degree)+conf(candidates.programminglanguage)+conf
(candidates.operatingsystem)+conf(candidates.previouswork) <= 5"
NAME      CONF_SUM
Alfred    2
Robert    4
Thomas    5
Bill      3
```

Fig. 14. Querying with P^ε to use the *sum of confusions* as a way to have a control of the returning objects. The column showing the sum of confusion values for each object was added by hand: it is not part of the query

4.3.2 Update

Give a discount to customers having food as industrial branch. *(Update)*. Hierarchies in figures 4 and 5 are used, where customers (figure 2) buy from a supermarket. The supermarket wishes to give a discount of 7% to customers related to food, because another supermarket is trying to have these customers. It is possible to do this update using pure SQL, but it involves the execution of several SQL sentences. Using XSQL to update objects delimited by hierarchical qualitative values provides a simpler and faster way to execute to the database server. Use

```
update customer set discount=0.07 where customer.name in
conf (customer.industrial_branch,'food')<=0
```

The 'confusion way' is efficient because the update is solved by filtering the customer's table using joins with SCT's tables. The update result appears in figure 15.

```
NAME                       INDUSTRIAL_BRANCH DISCOUNT
Media Tools                computers         0.0
Garcia Productores         tequila           0.0
East coast meat            meat              0.07
Luigi's Italian food       italian food      0.07
Mole Doña Rosa             mexican food      0.07
Texas fruits               fruits            0.07
Tampa tobacco              cigars            0.0
Canada seeds               food              0.07
Tom's Hamburgers           food              0.07
Microsol                   software          0.0
```

Fig. 15. Update results to customers related to food in the `INDUSTRIAL_BRANCH` property; the sentence was `update customer set discount=0.07 where cus-tomer.name in conf(customer.industrial_branch,'food')<=0`

5   Conclusions

The similarity among symbolic values that form hierarchies is exploited through use of confusion. Predicates with controlled precision $P_\varepsilon(o)$ (called "P holds for o with precision ε") and $P^\varepsilon(o)$ (called "P delimited by ε, holds for o") allow us to define precision-controlled retrieval of hierarchical values. These predicates permit "loose retrieval" (retrieval with defined confusion bounds) of objects that sit in a relational database. Moreover, such database could be an existing "normal" database (where no precision-controlled retrieval was possible), to which one or more definitions of hierarchies are attached. This in fact provides a procedure (a "kit") to extend *any* (existing) database to another in which imprecise retrievals are possible. Furthermore, this extension can be done without recompiling application programs. Old programs (with no precision retrieval) still work as before, whereas new application programs can exploit the database with precision-controlled queries. Thus, a "normal" database now becomes a "precision-controlled" database when the kit is applied to it.

Acknowledgments

Work was partially supported by CONACYT Grant 43377. First and second authors have a SNI National Scientist Award.

References

1. Guzman-Arenas and S. Levachkine. Hierarchies Measuring Qualitative Variables. *Lecture Notes in Computer Science* LNCS **2945** (Computational Linguistics and Intelligent Text Processing), (Springer-Verlag 2004). 262-274.
2. Guzman-Arenas and S. Levachkine. Graduated errors in approximate queries using hierarchies and ordered sets. *Lecture Notes in Artificial Intelligence* LNAI **2972**, (Springer-Verlag 2004). 139-148. ISSN 0302-9743
3. S. Levachkine and A. Guzman-Arenas. Confusion between hierarchies partitioned by a percentage rule. Unpublished manuscript.
4. S. Levachkine and A. Guzman-Arenas. Hierarchy as a new data type for qualitative variables. Submitted to *Data and Knowledge Engineering*.

An Approach for Solving Very Large Scale Instances of the Design Distribution Problem for Distributed Database Systems*

Joaquín Pérez O.[1], Rodolfo A. Pazos R.[1], Juan Frausto-Solís[2], Gerardo Reyes S.[1],
Rene Santaolaya S.[1], Héctor J. Fraire H.[3], and Laura Cruz R.[3]

[1] Centro Nacional de Investigación y Desarrollo Tecnológico (CENIDET)
AP 5-164, Cuernavaca, Mor., 62490, México
{jperez,pazos,greyes,rene}@cenidet.edu.mx
[2] ITESM, Campus Cuernavaca
Reforma 182-A, Temixco, Mor., 62589, México
juan.frausto@itesm.mx
[3] Instituto Tecnológico de Ciudad Madero, México
{lcruzr,hfraire}@prodigy.net.mx

Abstract. In this paper we deal with the solution of very large instances of the design distribution problem for distributed databases. Traditionally the capacity for solving large scale instances of NP-hard problems has been limited by the available computing resources and the efficiency of the solution algorithms. In contrast, in this paper we present a new solution approach that permits to solve larger instances using the same resources. This approach consists of the application of a systematic method for transforming an instance A into a smaller instance A' that has a large representativeness of instance A. For validating our approach we used a mathematical model developed by us, whose solution yields the design of a distributed database that minimizes its communication costs. The tests showed that the solution quality of the transformed instances was on the average 10.51% worse than the optimal solution; however, the size reduction was 97.81% on the average. We consider that the principles used in the proposed approach can be applied to the solution of very large instances of NP-hard problems of other problem types.

1 Introduction

The increasing popularity of the Internet and e-business has generated a great demand of applications of distributed databases (DDB's). These applications are developed using Distributed Database Management Systems (DDBMS's). Despite the advanced technology of DDBMS's, the design methodologies and tools have many limitations. Consequently, database administrators carry out the distribution design using empirical and informal approaches due to the problem complexity. In this paper a formal and systematic methodology is proposed aimed at overcoming the limitations.

The distribution design problem consists of determining data fragmentation and allocation so that the communication costs are minimized. Like many other real problems, this is a combinatorial NP-hard problem. The solution of large scale instances is

---

* This research was supported in part by CONACYT and COSNET

F.F. Ramos et al. (Eds.): ISSADS 2005, LNCS 3563, pp. 33–42, 2005.

usually carried out solving a simplified version of the problem or using approximate methods [1, 2]. General purpose nondeterministic heuristic methods are at present the best tools for the approximate solution of this class of problems [3, 4]. In the balance these methods will be referred to as heuristic methods.

For several years we have worked on the distribution design problem and its solution with heuristic methods. In [5] we proposed an on-line method to set the control parameters of the Threshold Accepting algorithm. In [6] a mechanism for automatically obtaining some control parameter values for genetic algorithms is presented.

2   Related Work

The distribution design problem has been dealt with by many researchers [7–11]. The approach for solving large scale instances, used in those works, consists of modeling the problem and using an exact or heuristic algorithm for solving the instances. The largest instance size that can be solved is limited by the available computing resources and the efficiency of the algorithm used. In [12] the location problem with limited replication (four replicas) is solved. A relevant aspect is that the paper reports instances with up to 50,000 queries. However, it utilizes the same approach used in previous works for solving large scale instances.

Random sampling is a technique that is used to obtain information from very large volumes of data examining only a small part of them. In computational applications, the use of sampling allows minimizing the large consumption of computing resources when processing large volumes of data. In spite of this advantage, its application has been scarce since it is necessary to previously estimate the most suitable sample size to assure the process efficiency. An alternative for tackling this problem is the use of progressive sampling [13–16]. This technique has been used, with good results, in the solution of problems of digital image transmission, statistical studies on agriculture, and data mining.

In this article we present a new approach for solving large scale instances, which permits to increase the size of instances that can be solved using a given set of computing resources. This approach consists of the application of methods for transforming an instance A into a smaller instance A', which has a high representativeness of instance A.

3   Distribution Design Problem

This section describes the distribution design problem and the mathematical model used for validating the proposed approach.

3.1   Formal Description

The DDB distribution design problem consists of allocating DB-objects, such that the total cost of data transmission for processing all the applications is minimized. A DB-object is an entity of a database that requires to be allocated, which can be an attribute, a tuples set, a relation or a file. DB-objects are independent units that must be allocated in the sites of a network. A formal definition of the problem is the following:

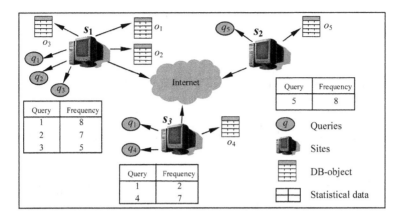

Fig. 1. Distribution design problem

Let us consider a set of DB-objects $O = \{o_1, o_2, \ldots, o_{no}\}$, a computer communication network that consists of a set of sites $S = \{s_1, s_2, \ldots, s_{ns}\}$, where a set of queries $Q = \{q_1, q_2, \ldots, q_{nq}\}$ are executed, the DB-objects required by each query, an initial DB-object allocation schema, and the access frequencies of each query from each site in a time period. The problem consists of obtaining a new replicated allocation schema that adapts to a new database usage pattern and minimizes transmission costs. Figure 1 shows the main elements related with this problem.

3.2 Mathematical Model

Traditionally it has been considered that the distributed database distribution design consists of two sequential phases, fragmentation and allocation. Contrary to this widespread belief, it has been shown that it is simpler to solve the problem using our approach which combines both phases. A key element of this approach is the formulation of a mathematical model that integrates both phases.

The mathematical model objective function (1) includes four terms: the first models the cost of processing read-only queries, the second models the cost of read-write queries, the third models the migration cost of the DB-objects, and the last one models the storage cost of DB-objects in the sites. Table 1 shows the main elements used in the model formulation.

$$\min z = \sum_k \sum_j f_{kj} \sum_m \sum_i q_{km} l_k c_{ji} w_{jmi} + \sum_k \sum_j f'_{kj} \sum_m \sum_i q'_{km} l'_k c_{ji} x_{mi} + \sum_j \sum_m \sum_i w'_{jmi} c'_{ji} d_{mi} + \sum_m \sum_i C A_i b_m x_{mi} \tag{1}$$

4 Proposed Methodology

This section describes the methodology proposed for the solution of large scale instances of the distribution design problem. Three strategies that can be used for the

Table 1. Model elements

no	Number of DB-objects to distribute.
ns	Number of sites in the network.
nq	Number of user queries.
f_{ki}	Frequency matrix of integer values that describes the emission frequency of read-only query k from site i, in a given time interval.
q_{km}	Usage matrix that indicates the DB-objects that are used by the different read-only queries; $q_{km} = 1$ if query k uses DB-object m; $q_{km} = 0$ otherwise.
l_{km}	Communication packets required to transmit a DB-object m to satisfy a read-only query k, $l_{km} = (b_m \cdot s_k)/PA$ where b_m is the size in bytes of the DB-object m, s_k is the selectivity of the query k and PA is the size in bytes of the communication packet.
f'_{ki}	Frequency matrix of integer values that describes the emission frequency of read-write query k from site i, in a given time interval.
q'_{km}	Usage matrix that indicates the DB-objects that are used by the different read-write queries; $q'_{km} = 1$ if query k uses DB-object m; $q'_{km} = 0$ otherwise.
l'_k	Communication packets required to transmit a write instruction $l'_k = P_k/PA$ where P_k is the size in bytes of the write instruction required by query k.
d_{mi}	Communication packets required to create a DB-object m replica in site i.
CA_i	Storage cost for byte in site i.
c_{ji}	Matrix that contains the transmission costs between sites.
x_{mj}	Binary variable that indicates if DB-object m is located in site j. $x_{mj} = 1$ if DB-object m is in site j, otherwise $x_{mj} = 0$.
w_{jmi}	Binary variable that indicates if DB-object m located in site i is required by a read-only query located in site j. $w_{jmi} = 1$ if DB-object m located in site i is required by a read-only query in site j, otherwise $w_{jmi} = 0$.
w'_{jmi}	Binary variable that indicates if DB-object m that must be located in site i is currently located in site j. $w'_{jmi} = 1$ if DB-object m that must be located in site i, is currently located in site $j \neq i$, otherwise $w'_{jmi} = 0$.

approximate solution of a large scale instance are: transforming the instance into another instance whose solution requires fewer resources, choosing the algorithm that has had the best performance on instances of the same type, or using a model that requires less computing cost. For solving a large scale instance, the main strategy of the methodology consists of applying approximation techniques of this type. The following definition formally describes this approach.

Definition: Solution Strategy

Given:
  π: NP-hard problem,
  I: instance set of π,
  R: finite set of transformations of instances of π,
  M: finite set of models of π,
  A: finite set of solution algorithms for the models,

if $s \in R \times A \times M$ then s is a solution strategy of a given instance of π (Figure 2).

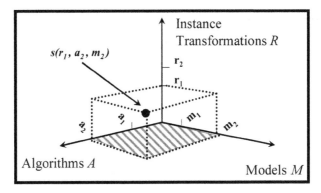

Fig. 2. Taxonomy of solution strategies

For a given instance $i \in I$, the purpose of the methodology is finding a strategy $s = (r, a, m)$ that permits solving instance i using transformation r, algorithm a and model m. A major difference from other approaches is that, when these choose a model and an algorithm, the strategy lies at a point on the dark plane of Figure 2. In our approach, the addition of a transformation dimension extends the possibilities beyond the dark plane. The transformation mechanisms must be devised so as to permit solving larger instances with a given set of computing resources. The following section describes an instance transformation method that attains this design objective and shows the feasibility of this approach.

4.1   Instance Transformation Using Progressive Sampling

This section presents an instance transformation method that uses progressive sampling techniques. The basic idea is generating a representative sample (subset) of the instance queries and solving the problem instance that involves only the queries in the sample; thus the new problem is a reduced version of the original one. Notice that any feasible solution to the transformed instance A' is also a feasible solution to the original instance A, but the optimal solution to A' is generally a suboptimal solution to A, whose quality (closeness to the optimum) depends on the representativeness of A'.

For very large problem instances, if the number of sites is much smaller than the number of queries, the access pattern of queries to data will appear repeatedly in the frequency matrix. Since the access pattern of a query is a binary vector of ns size, the maximum number of different access patterns is 2^{ns}. Because of the exponential growth of this number, only instances with a maximum of 15 sites will be considered. In these circumstances it is reasonable to suppose that a progressive sampling process can identify the access pattern of queries using relatively small samples. The process has as input the original instance and yields the transformed instance. A sample with the optimal size is called a minimal representative sample (MRS). The concepts introduced below constitute the basis for the instance transformation process that is proposed.

Tuple cluster. Let $C = \{c_1, c_2, \ldots, c_n\}$ denote a partition of relation R tuples. Each element of C is a tuple cluster, which for simplicity will be called cluster.

Cluster access probability. Ratio of the cluster size to the relation size.

$$p_{c_i} = \frac{Size(c_i)}{\sum\limits_{j=1}^{n} Size(c_j)} \qquad \begin{array}{l} Size(c_i)\text{: size of cluster } c_i \\ n\text{: number of clusters} \end{array} \qquad (2)$$

Query access probability. Ratio of the number of query accesses to the number of accesses to the relation.

$$p_{q_i} = \frac{Acc(q_i)}{\sum\limits_{j=1}^{nq} Acc(q_j)} \qquad \begin{array}{l} Acc(q_i)\text{: number of accesses of query } q_i \\ nq\text{: number of queries} \end{array} \qquad (3)$$

Joint query probability. Query access probability multiplied by the sum of the probabilities of access to the clusters used by the query.

$$P_{q_i} = p_{q_i} \cdot \sum_j P_{c_j} \qquad \forall c_j \in q_i \qquad (4)$$

Relevant queries of a sample. Sample queries such that their joint query probabilities is larger or equal to $\lambda = P_{min} + \alpha(P_{max} - P_{min})$; where P_{min} and P_{max} are the minimum and maximum joint probabilities of the sample queries and $\alpha \in (0, 1)$ is a factor used for setting the relevance boundary. The set of all relevant queries of a sample is denoted by RS.

Sample representativeness. Average joint probability of the relevant queries.

$$r_{m_i} = \bar{P}(RS) \qquad \text{where} \qquad \bar{P}(RS) = \frac{\sum\limits_{q_i \in RS} P_{q_i}}{\|RS\|} \qquad (5)$$

Similarity between two samples m_a and m_b. It is defined as 1 minus the absolute value of the difference of their representativenesses.

$$sim(m_a, m_b) = 1 - |r_{m_a} - r_{m_b}| \qquad (6)$$

An important property of sample similarity is that it converges to 1 if and only if the representativeness of the samples converges to a fixed value. Therefore, the convergence of the sample representativeness can be determined through the similarity convergence.

A sampling program specifies the sample sizes to be considered $S = \{n_0, n_1, n_2, \ldots, n_k\}$. A geometric program is defined as $S = \{n_0 k^n\}$ where n_0 and k are fixed values and $n = 0, 1, 2, 3, \ldots\}$. In order to evaluate the sampling program $S = \{n_0, n_1, n_2, \ldots, n_k\}$, the algorithm in the Figure 3 is applied [15].

The algorithm progressively determines the representativeness of the programmed samples and stops when this indicator stays consistently in the interval from $R - \delta$ to $R + \delta$, for a fixed value R that must be determined in the process and a given tolerance δ. Since the similarity converges to 1 if and only if the samples representativeness converges to some fixed value, then we can stop the process when the similarity of

```
i ← 0
n ← n_i
Generate a random sample M of size n
r ← Determine the representativeness of M
while r does not converge do
        i ← i + 1
        n ← n_i
        Generate a random sample M of size n
        r ← Determine the representativeness of M
end while
```

Fig. 3. Progressive sampling algorithm

the consecutive program samples stabilizes in the interval from $1 - \varepsilon$ to 1, for a given tolerance ε.

Once the size of the optimal sample is determined, a random sample of this size is extracted from the original instance. Finally, the parameters of the original instance are modified so as to include only the sample queries. The resulting instance is the transformed instance.

5 Experimental Results

In order to evaluate the merit of the proposed approach, a set of experiments were conducted using instances of different sizes and characteristics. For each experiment 30 random instances were used with the same number of clusters, sites and queries. Disperse and dense instances were used. For the first ones, queries access at most 20% of the sites; while for the second ones, queries access up to 80% of the sites.

For each instance of a particular experiment, the size of the minimal representative sample is determined. In the progressive sampling process the query relevance factor was set to $\alpha = 0.5$. The geometric program was $S = \{10, 20, 40, 80, \ldots\}$ corresponding to the values $n_0 = 10$ and $k = 2$. Afterwards the transformed instance is generated, and the original and the transformed instances are solved. Using the model generated for the original instance, the optimal distribution cost of the transformed instance is determined and is compared with the optimal distribution cost of the original instance. This process is repeated for the rest of the experiment instances.

Table 2 shows a fragment of the data obtained for each of the experiments. The table includes a consecutive number (CN), the number of clusters (C), sites (S) and queries (Q), the instance size in bytes (Size) and the optimal solution (Z_o) of the experiment instances. Since each transformed instance A' has the same clusters and sites as the original instance A, the table only includes the number of queries (Q') of the transformed instance, which equals the size of the optimal sample (MRS). Finally, the table includes the size (Size') and optimal solution (Z'_o) of the transformed instance. For each experiment the instance sizes and the optimal solution values were accumulated, and the global reduction and the error generated by the transformation were calculated. All the instances generated for a particular experiment have the same size, since the instances

Table 2. Fragment of the data obtained for an experiment

CN	C	S	Q	Size	Z_o	Q'	Size'	Z'_o
				Instance A			Instance A'	
1	40	6	2,000	201,410	93	80	4,408	75
2	40	6	2,000	201,410	92	80	4,408	81
3	40	6	2,000	201,410	87	80	4,408	86
4	40	6	2,000	201,410	91	80	4,408	81
⋮	⋮	⋮	⋮	⋮	⋮	⋮	⋮	⋮
30	40	6	2,000	201,410	90	80	4,408	82

have the same number of clusters, sites and queries; a similar situation occurs with all the transformed instances of a particular experiment.

Table 3 is a representative sample of the experiments results. The table includes the experiment code (EC), which includes the number of clusters, sites and queries of each experiment instances. The second column shows the ratio of the number of queries to the number of sites, and the experiments are ordered according to this ratio. The table includes the accumulated size of all the generated instances (ASize) and transformed instances (ASize'), and the accumulated optimal values of the generated instances (AZ_o) and transformed instances (AZ'_o). Finally, the table shows the global error percentage (%E) and size reduction (%R) of the experiment.

Table 3. Reduction value and effect on quality

EC	Q/S	ASize	ASize'	AZ_o	AZ'_o	%E	%R
T20.3.100	33	186,660	32,700	2,801	1,342	52.08	82.48
T20.5.200	40	436,860	43,080	1,689	822	51.33	90.13
T30.7.300	42	771,990	48,720	1,423	913	35.83	93.68
T50.10.1000	100	3,908,460	102,840	2,844	1,830	35.65	97.36
T20.3.1000	333	1,644,450	69,750	3,059	2,562	16.24	95.75
T40.6.2000	333	6,042,300	132,240	2,692	2,409	10.51	97.81

Table 3 shows that the method efficiency increases as the queries-to-sites ratio grows. In the solution of the largest instances a global size reduction of 97.81% is attained at the expense of a quality reduction of 10.51%. Therefore, under the established conditions and assumptions, this shows the feasibility of reducing the resources required for solving large scale instances with a reasonable reduction in solution quality.

6   Conclusions and Future Work

This paper shows the feasibility of the proposed solution approach for large scale instances. The general strategy includes, unlike other approaches, an additional dimension for transforming the instance to be solved. The transformation method introduced converts an instance A into a smaller instance A'. The transformation mechanism was devised in such a way that A' has a high representativeness of A.

A set of experiments were conducted for evaluating quantitatively the size reduction that can be achieved and its effect on the solution quality. Table 3 shows that the efficiency of the method increases as the queries-to-sites ratio of the original instance grows. In the experiments involving the largest instances, a global size reduction of 97.81% was obtained at the expense of a solution quality reduction of 10.51%. This shows that, given a set of computing resources, it is now possible to solve instances much larger than those previously solvable.

Given the encouraging results, at the moment we are working on the implementation of a transformation method based on clustering techniques, the implementation of the module for solving instances, and the use of this approach to the solution of large scale instances of other problem types.

References

1. Garey, M. R. and Johnson, D. S.: Computers and Intractability: A Guide to the Theory of NP-completeness: Freeman (1979).
2. Papadimitriou, C., Steiglitz, K.: Combinatorial Optimization: Algorithms and Complexity: Dover Publications (1998).
3. Barr, R.S., Golden, B.L., Kelly, J., Steward, W.R., Resende, M.G.C.: Guidelines for Designing and Reporting on Computational Experiments with Heuristic Methods: Proceedings of International Conference on Metaheuristics for Optimization. Kluwer Publishing. Norwell, MA (2001) 1–17.
4. Michalewicz, Z., Fogel, D.B.: How to Solve It: Modern Heuristics: Springer Verlag (1999).
5. Pérez, J., Pazos, R.A., Frausto, J., Romero, D., Cruz, L.: Vertical Fragmentation and Allocation in Distributed Databases with Site Capacity Restrictions Using the Threshold Accepting Algorithm. Lectures Notes in Computer Science, Vol. 1793. Springer-Verlag, (2000) 75–81.
6. Pérez, J., Pazos, R.A., Frausto, J., Rodríguez,G., Cruz, L., Fraire, H., Mora, G.: Self-Tuning Mechanism for Genetic Algorithms Parameters, an Application to Data-Object Allocation in the Web. Lectures Notes in Computer Science, Vol. 3046. Springer-Verlag (2004) 77–86.
7. Ceri, S., Navathe, S., Wiederhold, G.: Distribution Design of Logical Database Schemes. Proc. IEEE Transactions on Software Engineering, Vol. SE-9, No. 4. (1983) 487–503.
8. S. Navathe, Ceri, S., Wiederhold, G., Dou, L.: Vertical Partitioning Algorithms for Database Design, ACM Trans. On Database Systems, vol. 9, no. 4, Dic. 1984, pp.680–710.
9. Apers, M.G.: Data Allocation in Distributed Database Systems. ACM Transactions on Database Systems, Vol. 13, No. 3. (1988) 263–304.
10. Lin, X., Orlowska, M.: An integer Linear Programming Approach to Data Allocation with the Minimum Total Communication Cost in Distributed Database Systems. Information Sciences 85. (1995) 1–10.
11. March, S., Rho, S.: Allocating Data and Operations to Nodes in Distributed Database Design. Transactions on Knowledge and Data Engineering. Vol. 7, No. 2. (1995) 305–317.
12. Visinescu, C.: Incremental Data Distribution on Internet-Based Distributed Systems: A Spring System Approach: Master of Mathematics in Computer Science thesis, supervised by Tamer Ozsu; University of Waterloo (2003).
13. Eldar, Y., Lindenbaum, M., Porat, M., Zeevi, Y.: The Farthest Point Strategy for Progressive Image Sampling: IEEE Trans. On Image Processing, Vol. 6, No. 9. (1997) 1305–1315.

14. Stamatopoulos, C.: Observations on the Geometrical Propeties of Accuracy Growth in Sampling with Finite Populations. FAO Fisheries Technical Paper 388 (ISSN 0249-9345). Food and Agricultura Organization of the United Nations, Rome (1999).
15. Provost F., Jensen, D., Oates, T.: Efficient Progressive Sampling. Proceedings of the Fifth ACM SIGKDD International Conference on Knowledge Discovery and Data Mining. ACM (1999) 23–32.
16. Parthasarathy, S.: Efficient Progressive Sampling for Association Rules. Proceedings of the 2002 IEEE International Conference on Data Mining (ICDM 2002). IEEE Computer Society 2002. ISBN 0-7695-1754-4 (2002) 354–361.

On the Abstraction of Message-Passing Communications Using Algorithmic Skeletons
A Case Study*

Horacio González-Vélez

University of Edinburgh, School of Informatics,
King's Buildings, Edinburgh EH9 3JZ, UK
h.gv@ed.ac.uk
http://homepages.inf.ed.ac.uk/s0340602/

Abstract. This is an initial case on exploring the application of algorithmic skeletons to abstract low-level interprocess communication in MPI. The main purpose is intended to illustrate the competitive performance demonstrated by the skeletal approach when compared to utilization of the pure MPI, whilst providing an abstraction with reusability advantages. This initial work involves the implementation of the Wagar's hyperquicksort algorithm in conjunction with the MPI-based *eSkel* skeleton library. The reported results compare three MPI-based implementations of hyperquicksort. Firstly a canonic MPI one; secondly, two implementations using the MPI-based skeletal library *eSkel*. Lastly, the S3L_sort routine, part of its optimized numerical libraries from Sun, is employed as baseline. This overall comparison demonstrates that the use of algorithmic skeletons caused a slight performance degradation, while providing some promising guidance on the use of abstraction for low-level communication operations using the *eSkel* model.

1 Introduction

Portability, control, and scalability have always been adumbrated among the main strengths of message-passing, and in particular, of the Message Passing Interface standard (MPI) [1]. On the other hand, its enhanced low-level approach can be error-prone when developing complicated codes.

Having been conceived as higher order functions corresponding to good parallel algorithmic techniques [2], the algorithmic skeletons have proved to be a reliable method for the design of high-level, structured parallel programming solutions. The term structured parallelism is often assigned to skeletal programming owing to an implicit association with principles of the structured sequential programming model where the programmer must adhere to top-down design and construction, limited control structures, and limited scope of data structures [3].

---

* This work has been partly supported by the EC-funded project HPC-Europa, contract number 506079. The author would like to thank Murray Cole for useful discussions and advice.

F.F. Ramos et al. (Eds.): ISSADS 2005, LNCS 3563, pp. 43–50, 2005.

Fig. 1. Skeletons within the context of hardware and software

Since skeletons possess intrinsic parallelism, the actual expression of algorithms using skeletal programming is not necessarily more complicated than a sequential one. The skeletal paradigm describes the purpose of the algorithm rather than its implementation. It may, therefore, be argued that the corresponding algorithm formulation is simpler owing to the fact that the skeleton transformational programming approach and its inherent reusability are not tied to any particular implementation or architecture. An overall layered schema is presented in Figure 1.

Skeletons do not rely on specific hardware or software for their portability and it benefits entirely from any performance improvements in the systems infrastructure. It is important to mention that the skeletal paradigm has been successfully implemented through assorted imperative and functional programming environments [4]. It compares favorably to other related approaches to reusable distributed and parallel programming such as templates, patterns, and archetypes [5].

In exploring these assumptions, light can be shed by analyzing problems associated with parallel sorting. That is to say, how structural parallel programming can help to express the sorting problem class.

This is an initial study with a reduced test set using hyperquicksort and *eSkel* (an MPI-based skeleton library). The main objectives of this work is to demonstrate that skeletons can simplify programming whilst not degrading performance through their utilization. If the case pertaining to the fact that employing skeletons does not cause degradation of system response time, it may lead to a wider utilization of skeletons amongst research and commercial communities.

The remainder of this work describes the *eSkel* library and places it within context. It is followed by a description of the hyperquicksort algorithm and how the *eSkel* functions and skeletons fit into place. Next, there is a report on the results of several MPI executions of three hyperquicksort implementations: One without skeletons and two with skeletons. The Sun S3L_sort routine acts as the baseline. Finally, future directions and extensions to this work are mentioned.

2   *eSkel*

eSkel is a skeletal library built using on C and MPI. It was developed by the Structured Parallelism Group at the University of Edinburgh. The source code for the current version of the library as well as its manuals and related publications, are publicly accessible online [6].

The *eSkel* implementation model is based on the single-program multiple-data (SPMD) programming paradigm. It is currently employed within a C program, (or one capable of performing C function calls) within a pre-initialized MPI environment. Indeed, it is a upper-layer MPI component that extends the functionality of MPI and benefits from its features, such as thread-safe routines or optimized collective operations. It has been proven under test conditions to work with open-source and vendor-specific implementations of MPI.

The *eSkel* approach allows for decomposition to be applied whilst easing the mapping, communication and synchronization of threads by decoupling the design of the algorithm from its actual implementation. Moreover, the developer does not require a full command of the message-passing techniques. That is to say, when programming a parallel algorithm one starts to design it by mapping the algorithm into its corresponding skeleton, without any attention being paid to the implementing architecture, the communication structure, or the inter-process synchronization.

The design of *eSkel* is flexible enough to ease the communication and control tasks while allowing the programmer to retain control over the program behavior. This is achieved by the *eSkel* access model which extends the scope of communication objects in MPI by introducing the concepts of the *eSkel* Data Model (eDM). Since new communicators are declared in the library, access may be required by the programmer. Then, the eDM permits the use of intrinsic data and structures with the use of eDM atoms and eDM collections [7].

In a nutshell, eDM provides a high-level abstraction of MPI communications. In addition to general routines aimed at initializing the environment and managing the internal communication structures, this version of *eSkel* library includes the following interaction functions on eDM atoms:

- *Give* Send-like function includes spread and inheritance
- *Take* Receive-like function includes spread and inheritance
- *Exchange* Used to interchange information with the notions of process partner locality. Employed in the Butterfly skeleton
- *eSkel_atom_t* Wrapper to encapsulate an array of data and its length. Useful in conjunction with *Give/Take/Exchange* functions

The spread and inheritance of the *give-take* duad allows the seamless distribution of data (*spread*) whilst simultaneously providing a mechanism to keep track of multiple levels of control on MPI data structures.

The above functions constitute the foundation for activity code interaction, since they include implicit invocations to interaction functions in its implementation and provide an abstraction of the low-level communication operations *send* and *receive*.

Traditionally, the abstraction of low-level operations has been the subject of study in skeletons. As a matter of fact, it has been suggested that low-level *send-receive* operations can be considered harmful and ought to be replaced by collective operations in the parallel setting, due to its simplicity, expressiveness, programmability, performance and predictability [8].

The current version of *eSkel* also includes:

– *Farm* Skeleton with variations for load-balancing, 1for1, simple and simple1for1 interaction
– *Pipeline* Skeleton with variations for standard and 1for1 interaction
– *Butterfly* This a tree-based divide-and-conquer skeleton which includes the notion of neighbor locality

In this work the *Butterfly* skeleton and the interaction functions *Give* and *Take* are bestowed. The complete documentation of the *eSkel* library and APIs is included in the downloadable tarball [6].

On the portability side, *eSkel* has been tested in shared and distributed memory architectures using open and vendor versions of MPI. The use of portable high-level multi-platform libraries has previously proved to be effective and without a performance trade-off.

3   Implementation

Hyperquicksort is a multi-step parallel sorting algorithm based on the Hoare's quicksort, originally developed for hypercubic computer system topologies [9]. A quick description of the hyperquicksort algorithm is presented in Figure 2.

The hyperquicksort is of particular interest because it can be implemented using a divide-and-conquer approach, uses several rounds of communication with

IN: S Sequence of n elements; p Processors OUT: S' where $S'[n-1] \geq S'[n-2] \geq \ldots \geq S'[1] \geq S'[0]$

Base   Each hypercube node sorts n/p elements locally

Pivot   The "host" hypercube node broadcasts its median key m.
          Each node divides elements as:
          $elements < m$ and $elements > m$

Comm. Nodes exchange elements within *dimension*.
          Node with $0 \cdots$ address transmits its $elements > m$
          to neighbor with $1 \cdots$ address.
          Conversely, neighbor returns $elements < m$.
          Incoming elements are merged into sorted sequence

Recur   Call recursively using the $p/2$-node subcubes

Fig. 2. Hyperquicksort algorithm

good load balancing (provided there exists a random distribution of elements), and its MPI implementation is widely used as an illustrative approach to message passing programming.

The choice of pivot elements in hyperquicksort has major effects on the workload distribution [10] and its analysis and implications to the execution time are beyond the scope of this assay. Randomization is employed to ensure, to some extent, an average case distribution. The first hyperquicksort implementation employed is a public version [11]. The second and third versions are its skeletal counterparts using *eSkel* linked with the thread safe Sun mpi_mt library (ver. 2) and the standard Sun mpi library (ver. 3). The source code for the skeletal version deployed is bundled with the standard *eSkel* distribution under the name butterflyhqs.c [6].

As the evaluation baseline, we have used the Sun S3L_sort sorting routine, part of the Sun numerical library. The S3L_sort routine implements an optimized version of the sample sort [12]. The binary code of the MPI and numerical libraries is bundled with the Sun HPC ClusterTools distribution.

The deployed skeletal implementation of hyperquicksort employs the *Butterfly* skeletons in conjunction with the *Give* and *Take* functions to structure the control and communications within the hypercubic topology.

These three constructions aimed at abstracting the internodal communication mapping, important to the hyperquicksort algorithm implementation. The resulting code was extremely fast to generate. Therefore, it is arguable that their use plays a role in the simplification of the coding of this algorithm by providing a higher-level of abstraction. A C code extract to give the substance of the inclusion is outlined in figure 3.

```
/* Exchange information with partner within hyperquicksort function */
if (myrank() >= mycommsize() / 2) { /*       Send        lower
half        to        partner       */
    Give(lower, lowerlen);
    halflen = MAX_ARRAY;
    half = Take(&halflen);
} else { /*        Receive lower half from partner */
    halflen = MAX_ARRAY;
    half = Take(&halflen);
/*        Send        upper        half        to        partner       */
    Give(upper, upperlen);
}

/*                              ... main() */
    Butterfly(dimension,level, MPI_INT, mycomm());
```

Fig. 3. Extract from the butterflyhqs.c file

4   Results

In order to have a representative execution time, a 64-million integer number set was selected whilst varying the dimension of the hypercube from 0 (1 process)

Table 1. Hyperquicksort on 64-million integer numbers generated randomly. All figures are expressed in seconds. Key: 1.- Non-skeletal MPI; 2.- *eSkel* linked with thread-safe mpi_mt library; 3.- *eSkel* linked with standard mpi library; Baseline.- Sun S3L_sort

Ver. #Proc	1	2	3	Baseline
1	74.18	70.68	70.05	54.09
2	45.74	44.25	44.74	59.46
4	29.44	28.41	28.31	25.20
8	18.60	20.57	19.48	14.49
16	15.48	16.20	15.07	10.89
32	12.67	14.28	13.03	n/a

to 5 (32 processes). We have mapped every mpirun process to a single machine processor. All program executions were carried out in a dedicated Sun Fire 15K server with 48 UltraSPARC-III processors at 900MHz/8MB-cache running Solaris 9, located at the Edinburgh Parallel Computing Centre in the UK. The executables were produced using the Sun Forte Developer 7 C compiler version 5.4 and the Sun HPC ClusterTools 5 suite, using Sun Grid Engine as queue manager.

The actual results from the execution of the 64-million key sort on the three hyperquicksort implementations plus the baseline are presented in Table 1 and depicted in Figure 4. The table entries report the real time in seconds and include all the sorting execution time. To the best of our knowledge, we have

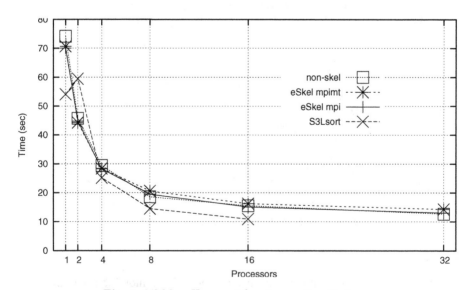

Fig. 4. 64M-key Hyperquicksort execution timings

tried to adhere to algorithm engineering practices in order to accurately report the results from the experiments [13].

Although the scalability on more than 8 processors of the implementations examined is far from linear, it is interesting to note that the overhead incurred by the use of *eSkel* versions is hardly noticeable. The scalability issue can be track down to the low computing to communications ratio for the the hyperquicksort.

It can be argued that there is almost no trade-off for the augmented flexibility and simplicity provided. The latter, is difficult to quantify and, therefore, to justify. This is to minimize the argument that an increase in abstraction always comes with a corresponding performance degradation.

A notable resulting side-effect of the experimentation is that the baseline case exploiting the Sun S3L_sort routine shows a performance degradation for the 2-processor case. It is believed to be attributable to a cache peculiarity. However, the source code for the routine is not available for a full profiling analysis. Once this particular problem size and configuration are varied the oddity disappears.

In addition to this, it did not execute the 32-processor run for the problem size specified, nor for anything above 24 processors. No further account can be provided. The difference between the non-skeletal and the skeletal versions is in the order of 5% in most cases. The one and two processor skeletal versions are faster than their non-skeletal counterpart.

In summary, the additional changes in the program, incurred by the use of skeletons are minimum, non-disruptive, and aimed at easing the coding while providing acceptable performance. These results help us to claim that the skeletal model performs well. Indeed, the ease of implementation is difficult to evaluate and verification would necessitate a separate study purely devoted to this.

5   Future Directions

We believe that these initial experimentations have shown some promising performance figures, while providing an important source of information. Although the results are by no means conclusive, the fact that *eSkel* does not pose a burden to MPI in this particular case is *per se* auspicious.

Indeed, this performance evaluations is by no means comprehensive. Thus, development of a set of testing codes is being planned in order to further test the communication primitives of *eSkel*. Planned extensions include the use of a broader spectrum of test cases and algorithms to form a more comprehensive evaluation and the benchmark execution on distributed environments. This may lead to the definition of a basic MPI benchmark suite for *eSkel*.

We would like this to include not only "just-performance" tests but also usability and performance estimation methods.

References

1. Message Passing Interface Forum: MPI standard and documentation. www.mpi-forum.org/docs/docs.html (2003)

2. Cole, M.: Algorithmic Skeletons: Structured management of parallel computation. MIT Press (1989)
3. Cole, M.: Algorithmic skeletons. In Hammond, K., Michaelson, G., eds.: Research Directions in Parallel Functional Programming. Springer-Verlag, London, UK (1999) 289–304
4. Rabhi, F.A., Gorlatch, S., eds.: Patterns and skeletons for parallel and distributed computing. Springer-Verlag, London, UK (2003)
5. González-Vélez, H., de Luca, A., González-Vélez, V.: A comparative study of intrinsic parallel programming methodologies. In: Int Conf on Electrical and Electronics Engineering, Acapulco, Mexico, IEEE CS (2004)
6. Structured Parallelism Group, University of Edinburgh: eSkel. homepages.inf.ed.ac.uk/mic/eSkel/ (2003)
7. Cole, M.: Bringing skeletons out of the closet: a pragmatic manifesto for skeletal parallel programming. Parallel Computing 30 (2004) 389–406
8. Gorlatch, S.: Message passing without send-receive. Future Generation Computer Systems 18 (2002) 797–805
9. Wagar, B.: Hyperquicksort: A fast sorting algorithm for hypercubes. In Heath, M., ed.: Hypercube Multiprocessors, SIAM (1987) 292–299
10. Blelloch, G.E., Leiserson, C.E., Maggs, B.M., Plaxton, C.G., Smith, S.J., Zagha, M.: An experimental analysis of parallel sorting algorithms. Theoretical Computer Science 31 (1998) 135–167
11. Rochester Institute of Technology: MPI implementation of hyperquicksort. (2003) www.cs.rit.edu/usr/local/pub/ncs/parallel/mpi/hqs.c.
12. Sun Microsystems: Sun HPC ClusterTools 5 software user's guide. (2003) docs.sun.com/source/817-0084-10.
13. Bader, D.A., Moret, B.M.E., Sanders, P.: Algorithm engineering for parallel computation. In Fleischer, R., Moret, B.M.E., Schmidt, E.M., eds.: Experimental Algorithmics. Volume 2547 of LNCS., Springer-Verlag (2002) 1–23

Implementing Distributed Mutual Exclusion on Multithreaded Environments: The Alien-Threads Approach

Federico Meza[1,*], Jorge Pérez R.[1], and Yadran Eterovic[2]

[1] Depto. de Ingeniería de Sistemas, Universidad de Talca
Camino Los Niches Km. 1, Curicó, Chile
`{fmeza,jperez}@utalca.cl`
[2] Depto. de Ciencia de la Computación, Pontificia Universidad Católica de Chile
Casilla 306, Santiago 22, Santiago, Chile
`yadran@ing.puc.cl`

Abstract. We present a simple implementation of a token-based distributed mutual exclusion algorithm for multithreaded systems. Several per-node requests could be issued by threads running at each node. Our algorithm relies on special-purpose *alien threads* running at host processors on behalf of threads running at other processors. The algorithm uses a tree to route requests for the token. We present a performance simulation study comparing two versions of our algorithm with a known algorithm based on path reversal on trees. Results show that our algorithm performs very well under a high load of requests while obtaining acceptable performance under a light load.

Keywords: Distributed mutual exclusion, multithreading, parallel programming, concurrent programming, distributed shared memory.

1 Introduction

Mutual exclusion aims to provide synchronized access to shared resources ensuring that, at any time, at most one process can be executing in its critical section. Distributed mutual exclusion algorithms focus on mutual exclusion on distributed environments lacking shared memory. Several algorithms address the distributed mutual exclusion problem for systems where only one process is running at each processor. Multithreaded distributed systems allow the existence of several threads of execution within each distributed process. Thus, there is a need to provide mutual exclusion to a large number of distributed threads. We are particularly interested in Distributed Shared Memory systems [1] with support for multithreading and thread migration.

In this work, we present an algorithm for distributed mutual exclusion in a multithreaded system. The algorithm is token-based, and it uses a tree to route requests issued to acquire the token. We rely on special-purpose *alien threads* running at host processors on behalf of threads running at other processors.

* Federico Meza was supported by Fondecyt under grant 2990074.

F.F. Ramos et al. (Eds.): ISSADS 2005, LNCS 3563, pp. 51–62, 2005.

When a thread asks for permission to enter its critical section, if the token is not present at the processor it is running at, a remote alien thread is activated in order to obtain the token and send it to the requesting processor. Alien threads behave just like ordinary threads, and must compete for the token with other user threads. Thus, our algorithm is simple but correct.

We performed a simulation study comparing two versions of our algorithm with a previously proposed algorithm based on path reversal on trees. This algorithm is, to the best of our knowledge, the only documented implementation addressing the same problem. Results obtained from the simulation are encouraging. Our algorithm performs very well under high load conditions, outperforming the other proposal as the number of threads per node increases.

Our algorithm was successfully implemented on *DSM-PEPE*, a multithreaded distributed system with support for thread migration [2].

2   The Algorithm

2.1   System Model

The system is a loosely-coupled network of computers, consisting of n processors: $p_1, p_2, ..., p_n$. At any time, at each processor p_i, there are m_i threads running. Threads are allowed to migrate according to some system policy, for instance, pursuing load balancing or minimal message exchange.

Processors communicate through message passing. We assume that message delivery is guaranteed by the network. We also assume that two messages issued at one processor and addressed to the same node are received in the same order at the destination. This is the usual behavior of switched local area networks, where there is only one possible route between each pair of computers.

A thread wishing to enter its critical section must obtain permission by calling `Acquire()`. The thread could be delayed until mutual exclusion can be guaranteed. Once the thread leaves the critical section, it must notify the system by calling `Release()`. Mutual exclusion must be ensured between the call to `Acquire()` and the call to `Release()`.

2.2   Brief Description

Our algorithm is token-based. A thread wishing to enter its critical section must obtain a single system-wide token. Uniqueness of the token guarantees the mutual exclusion [3]. At the higher level, ownership of the token is not granted directly to threads but to processors. Once a processor owns the token, threads running at that processor can compete for it. Requests issued at each processor are stored in a local queue owned by the processor. Ownership of the token is granted to one of the processors during initialization. For the remaining processors a unique path must exist to allow them to reach the actual owner of the token. This is accomplished through a chain of *probable owners*, building up a tree rooted at the first owner.

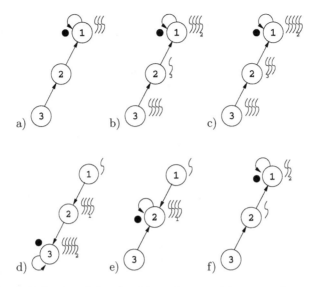

Fig. 1. Behavior of the algorithm when servicing several requests

Requests made by threads running at the processor currently owning the token are serialized and served according to their arrival time. A request issued by a thread running at a processor not owning the token involves sending a request to the probable owner. Our algorithm accomplished this task, by signaling a special-purpose thread running at the probable owner of the token.

At any processor, there are $n - 1$ *alien threads*, each acting on behalf of one of the remaining $n - 1$ processors in the system. Alien threads behave just like ordinary threads, but they are blocked most of the time. An alien thread at processor p_i is signaled when some thread at the home processor – that is, the processor for which the alien thread is working on behalf of – is requiring the token, and it is presumed that the token is held by processor p_i, that is, the probable owner at the home processor is set to p_i. The woken alien thread asks for the token at its host processor. Then, once the token is granted, the alien thread sends the token to the processor it is representing.

Note that it is possible for a woken alien thread to find out that the token is no longer on its host processor. When this situation occurs, the alien thread acts like an ordinary thread requesting the token. The alien thread signals the alien thread on the processor where the token apparently went to, that is, the probable owner on its host processor. This scenario could appear several times, until the processor currently holding the token is reached. This kind of forwarding resembles the algorithm described by Raymond for distributed mutual exclusion of single-threaded processors [4].

Figure 1 shows the behavior of our algorithm in a system with 3 nodes. Initially, node 1 owns the token – represented as a filled circle – and several threads are blocked at that node, each waiting to enter its critical section (Figure 1a). Note that node 1, the owner of the token, is at the root of the tree used to route the requests. At this moment, several requests are issued from threads running at node 3. The first of these requests produces a signal to an alien thread on node 2, to wake up and act on behalf of node 3 (Figure 1b). However, since the token is not present at 2, the recently woken alien thread blocks, producing a signal to an alien thread on node 1, to wake up and act on behalf of node 2. This alien thread waits at the end of the local queue of node 1. Note that the request made by a thread running at node 3 produced two requests at remote nodes, issued by alien threads. After that, some threads issued new requests at nodes 1 and 2, producing their local enqueueing (Figure 1c). At this point it is important to note the behavior of the alien threads currently active in the system. An alien thread is waiting for the token at node 1, the current owner of the token, on behalf of 2, and another alien thread is waiting for the token at node 2, on behalf of 3. The thread that issued the original request is waiting for the token at node 3. A node only sees a queue of requests, some issued by local threads and some issued by alien threads. Eventually, the alien thread running at node 1 on behalf of 2 obtains the token, and sends it to node 2. Since the queue was not empty at this time, that is, there are pending requests at node 1, an alien thread on node 2 is signaled to bring the token back to node 1. At the head of the queue at node 2 was the alien thread that acts on behalf of node 3, so it sends the token to node 3, and an alien thread on node 3 is signaled to bring the token back to node 2. Note that, at node 2 there are several pending requests, including one that will bring the token back to node 1 (Figure 1d). Eventually, the token returns to node 2 (Figure 1e) and to node 1 (Figure 1f).

2.3   Detailed Description

Each processor must hold the following information:

- **probOwner**: process identifier – pid – of the processor last known as the token owner. Initially set in such a way that there is a single path, following the probOwners chain, from each node to the initial owner of the token. The first owner sets probOwner to its pid.
- **tokenRequested: true** if there are pending requests for the token issued from this processor, *i.e.*, a request for the token has been already sent. Initially **false** at every processor.
- **numLocal**: number of requests for the token that have been issued locally; initially 0 at every processor. Recall that only the first request actually makes an alien thread to be signaled.

Local mutual exclusion for the operations showed below is mandatory. However it has been omitted intentionally to illustrate the solution more clearly. Semantics of the *wait* and *signal* operations are consistent with those on conditions variables. A signal across processors involve sending a message to the target processor.

A thread acquiring the token must execute:

```
Acquire() {
   numLocal++;
   if (probOwner != pid) && (! tokenRequested) {
      // Not owner and not previously requested => Request token
      signal(alien thread on probOwner);
      tokenRequested = true;   // to avoid multiple requests
      wait(for signal from the alien thread);
      probOwner = pid;         // processor becomes owner
      tokenRequested = false;
   }
   else {
      // Processor owns token, or token has been requested already
      if (numLocal > 1) {
         wait(for signal from another local thread);
      }
   }
}
```

If the token is not currently held by the processor it must be requested, by
signaling the alien thread on the probable owner. The thread blocks waiting for
the token to arrive. If some other thread has previously called Acquire, we must
prevent multiple requests. If the token is held by the processor, or it has been
requested already, there is no need for remote requests. If the token is held but
free the thread is allowed to enter its critical section.

A thread releasing the token must execute:

```
Release() {
   numLocal--;
   signal(local thread waiting for the token);
}
```

Note that the thread being signaled could be a user thread or an alien thread.

The alien thread executing on processor *host* on behalf of processor *home*
must execute the following code:

```
alienThread(host_pid, home_pid) {
   while(true) {
      wait(for signal from home processor);        // stay idle
      Acquire();                  // acquire token on host processor
      signal(thread waiting for the token on the home processor);
      probOwner = home_pid;  // update host-processor's probOwner
      numLocal--;
      if (numLocal > 0) {
         // Request the token on behalf of host processor
         tokenRequested = true;   // to avoid multiple requests
         signal(alien thread on home processor on behalf of host);
      }
   }
}
```

An alien thread waits until signaled from its home processor. Then, it acquires the token, competing with local threads on the host processor, as well as with other alien threads trying to get the token on behalf of their homes. Once an alien thread succeeded on acquiring the token, it signals its home processor, allowing a remote waiting thread to resume under mutual exclusion. It is possible to have additional threads left on the local queue when an alien thread acquires the token delivering it to its home processor. If this happens, the alien thread requests the token before turning idle. This is accomplished by signaling the alien thread that represents its host on its home processor. A simple improvement to the algorithm presented involves *piggybacking* this request on the same signaling message that delivers the token.

The behavior of an alien thread holding the token is slightly different from the behavior of a user thread. A user thread is expected to release the token once it leaves the critical section. However, an alien thread does not release the token, but delivers it directly to another thread at his home processor instead.

2.4   A Variant on the Proposed Algorithm

An alien thread forwards requests when the token is not present at its host processor. This is done by signaling the alien thread on the probable owner, on behalf of its host processor. Thus, the token is forced to follow exactly the same path followed by the requests. This behavior is desirable under high requests load, because there will be always pending requests on the returning path of the token, avoiding the exchange of extra messages. However, under a light load, the token could be sent directly to the processor that issued the first request, avoiding the extra steps produced by the forwarding. Only the code executed by the alien threads must be modified in order to implement this variant:

```
alienThread(host_pid, home_pid) {
  while(true) {
    wait(for signal from home processor);       // stay idle
    if ((probOwner != host_pid) && (numLocal == 0)) {
      signal(alien thread on behalf of home, on host's probOwner);
    }
    else {
      // Behaves like the original alien thread
      Acquire();              // acquire token on host processor
      signal(thread waiting for the token on the home processor);
      probOwner = home_pid;  // update host-processor's probOwner
      numLocal--;
      if (numLocal > 0) {
        // Request the token on behalf of host processor
        tokenRequested = true;   // to avoid multiple requests
        signal(alien thread on home processor on behalf of host);
      }
    }
  }
}
```

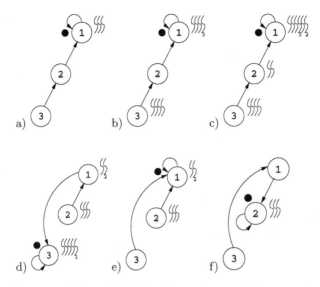

Fig. 2. Behavior of the modified algorithm when servicing several requests

Instead of simply forwarding requests, the improved alien thread checks first if there are local requests at its host processor that justify acquiring the token. Otherwise, it signals an alien thread on behalf of its home processor, avoiding the passing of the token across its host processor.

Figure 2 shows the behavior of the modified algorithm for the same requests sequence used in the example of the original algorithm in Section 2.2. Note that, when the first request by a thread running at node 3 is issued, the alien thread at node 2 does not remain active because the queue at node 2 is empty. It just forwards the signal to an alien thread at node 1, to wake up and act on behalf of node 3 instead (Figure 2b). Eventually, this alien thread obtains the token, and sends it directly to node 3 (Figure 2d).

The path followed by the token back to the requester node is not necessarily the same path previously followed by the request on its way to the owner of the token. Note that several alien threads in the request path just forwarded the request, changing the topology of the tree.

3   Proof Outline

A mutual exclusion algorithm must satisfy several conditions. The following is an outline of the proof of correctness for three of these conditions, considering the original algorithm.

Mutual exclusion: It must be assured that, at any time, at most one thread can be executing in its critical section. Our algorithm is token-based: there is a single system-wide token, owned by the node having `probOwner == pid`. This condition is enforced during initialization. A thread asks for the token by executing `Acquire` and could be delayed on two conditions: (1) when the token is currently held by its host node but it is assigned to another thread, or (2) when the token is not locally present at the time. Either way, the thread is allowed to continue executing in its critical section only when the thread currently holding the token relinquished it by executing `Release`, or when an alien thread signals the blocked thread remotely. In the former, it is straightforward to verify that mutual exclusion is assured. In the latter, the signaling alien thread previously obtained the mutual exclusion by executing `Acquire` on its host processor. Since an alien thread does not have a critical section, it relinquishes the mutual exclusion on behalf of the thread that made the request on its home processor. This way, mutual exclusion among threads is assured.

Deadlock freedom: It is easy to verify that a deadlock can not occur under some reasonable restrictions. For a deadlock to occur there must be a circular-wait condition involving two or more threads in the system. Assuming that a thread executing in its critical section is not allowed to execute `Acquire` again, this condition will never occur.

Starvation freedom: If we assume the use of a fair policy for serving local requests at each node starvation will not occur. Recall that we have a single path from each node to the node currently holding the token. Note that a request issued at a node not owning the token results in an alien thread being queued at the node currently owning the token. If the local service policy is fair, the alien thread eventually obtains the token and allows the thread it is acting on behalf of, to enter its critical section.

4   Performance

Analytic studies of distributed mutual exclusion algorithms are hard to perform, due to the rapid growth of the cardinality of the state space as the number of nodes increases [5]. In multithreaded systems, the size of the state space grows even faster. For this reason, we choose a simulation approach to study the performance of our proposal.

4.1   Simulation Model

We use a simulation model based on similar studies [5], [6]. We assume that requests to enter the critical section arrive at each node according to a Poisson process with parameter λ. Thus, the time elapsed between critical section requests behaves according to an exponential distribution. We assume that, at every node, requests are made by randomly-chosen user threads. It is important to note that the simulation process remains under Poisson behavior as long as any running – not waiting – local thread exists in a node. When all the threads running at a node are waiting to enter to its critical section, the process stops until the first local thread completes its critical section.

The λ parameter will give us a notion of the load of the entire system. The time taken by a thread to execute its critical section is modeled as a constant C. The message propagation delay is a constant M multiplied by a random number having a uniform distribution between 0 and 1.

We are interested in two main measures: the average number of messages exchanged per critical section entry, and the average waiting time for the permission to enter the critical section.

To obtain statistically reliable results we made long-time simulations executing 100,000 critical section entries. On each experiment we use $N = 31$ nodes, because we have a binary complete tree for the initial state. We simulate a variable number of threads per node. The parameter λ takes values in the $[0, 1]$ interval. The parameter M was taken as 0.1 and the parameter C as 0.01. These values are consistent with those used in similar studies [5],[6].

4.2   Results

Figures 3 through 5 show the results of the simulations for the two versions of our algorithm – using piggybacking – as well as the algorithm proposed by Mueller [7], using 1, 5 and 10 threads per node. In Figure 3 there is a single thread per node. In this case, the first implementation of our algorithm resembles the algorithm by Raymond [4]. Obtained results are consistent with that fact [6].

Under a light load, the second version of our algorithm requires fewer messages than the first one, because the token is sent from the releaser node to the requester directly. The alien thread that was waiting for the token at the releaser node, acts on behalf of the requester node. The first implementation enforces the token to travel along the tree structure to reach the requester node. This is so because several alien threads need to be signaled in the path previously followed by the requests. The algorithm proposed by Mueller has the best comparative performance under a light load, considering the number of messages exchanged. This is due to the *aggressive path compression* technique, characteristic of the path reversal approach [8].

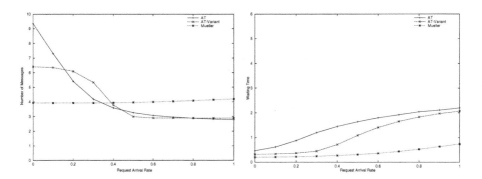

Fig. 3. Performance comparison of the 3 algorithms with a single thread per node

Considering the waiting time, the second version of our algorithm behaves better than the first one under all loads. The algorithm proposed by Mueller outperforms the other two.

Under a high load, both versions of our algorithm need almost the same number of messages per critical section. When the first alien thread associated to a request is signaled, it is most likely that the token was already requested on the host node. This will make both versions of the algorithm behave the same way. This situation can be easily observed in the code of the alien thread: both versions will execute the same code under high load conditions. This is also the cause of the very small number of messages exchanged per critical section under high loads. Both implementations of the alien thread algorithm outperform Mueller's algorithm.

When we turn to multithreaded scenarios (Figures 4 and 5) the relative behavior among the two versions of our algorithm remains unchanged. Moreover, the waiting time is almost identical, for every number of threads per node. Besides, an important decrease in the number of messages exchanged per critical section entry is achieved under high loads as the number of per-node threads increases. Once a request has been sent from a node – that is, an alien thread

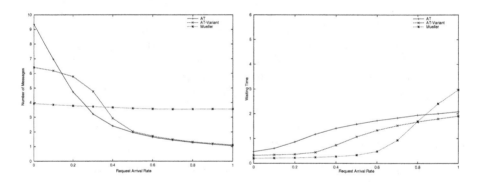

Fig. 4. Performance comparison of the 3 algorithms with 5 threads per node

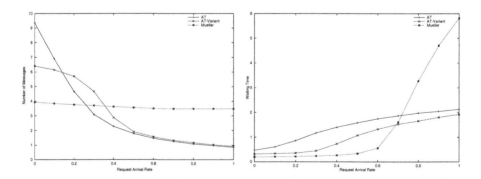

Fig. 5. Performance comparison of the 3 algorithms with 10 threads per node

has been signaled –, subsequent requests issued by threads on the home node do not involve the sending of additional messages. Thus, most of the requests issued by threads wishing to enter the critical section will be served without message exchange. The algorithm proposed by Mueller does not show any of these behaviors. The number of messages exchanged does not change significantly as the number of threads per node increases. Waiting time increases abruptly as the system load increases. The growing rate of the waiting time in the Mueller's algorithm, also increases as the number of threads per node increases. His algorithm is very sensitive to load growth on multithreaded scenarios.

The second version of the alien thread algorithm outperforms the initial version in all aspects. The algorithm proposed by Mueller showed better performance under a light load. Under high loads, the alien thread algorithm showed better results.

5   Related Work

Several distributed mutual exclusion algorithms have been proposed in the literature. They can be classified as *permission-based* or *token-based* [9]. We focus our study on token-based distributed algorithms, excluding those algorithms that use a central coordinator.

Token-based algorithms rely on a unique token which must be acquired by a process wishing to enter its critical section. The token could be traveling from one process to another continuously or could be obtained by sending a request. The algorithms proposed by Raymond [4], by Neilsen and Mizuno [10], by Banerjee and Chrysanthis [11], and by Naimi, *et al.* [8] fall into this category.

Distributed mutual exclusion for multithreaded environments has not been studied extensively. The design and implementation of distributed synchronization primitives are presented by Mueller, focusing on the impact of multithreading on synchronization [7]. Distributed mutual exclusion is based on a token-passing mechanism based on the algorithm described by Naimi, *et al.* [8].

6   Conclusions

We presented a simple implementation of a token-based algorithm providing mutual exclusion to distributed threads running on a loosely-coupled system. This mechanism has been successfully implemented on a Distributed Shared Memory system supporting thread migration.

We developed two versions of the algorithm and compare them to a known implementation of another algorithm, targeting to the same problem. A simulation of performance shows that both of our algorithms outperforms the other implementation under high load conditions. The difference increases as the number of threads per node increases. Under a light load, our algorithms still perform within reasonable limits.

The first version of our algorithm, limited to a single user thread per node, behaves just like a well-known single-threaded distributed mutual exclusion algorithm [4]. The third algorithm considered in our study [7], was originally conceived as an extension of another single-threaded algorithm based on path reversal on trees [8]. Our intention is to extend the study to several single-threaded algorithms for distributed mutual exclusion, exploring the feasibility of extend them using the same ideas used to develop the alien-threads algorithm.

References

1. Li, K., Hudak, P.: Memory Coherence in Shared Virtual Memory Systems. ACM Transactions on Computer Systems **7** (1989) 321–359
2. Meza, F., Campos, A.E., Ruz, C.: On the Design and Implementation of a Portable DSM System for Low-Cost Multicomputers. In: Proc. of the Intl. Conference on Computational Science and its Applications (ICCSA '2003). Volume 2667 of Lecture Notes in Computer Science., Springer (2003)
3. Hélary, J.M., Mostefaoui, A., Raynal, M.: A General Scheme for Token- and Tree-Based Distributed Mutual Exclusion Algorithms. IEEE Transactions on Parallel and Distributed Systems **5** (1994) 1185–1196
4. Raymond, K.: A Tree-Based Algorithm for Distributed Mutual Exclusion. ACM Transactions on Computer Systems **7** (1989) 61–77
5. Chang, Y.: A Simulation Study on Distributed Mutual Exclusion. Journal of Parallel and Distributed Computing **33** (1996) 107–121
6. Johnson, T.: A Performance Comparison of Fast Distributed Mutual Exclusion Algorithms. In: Proceedings of the 9th International Symposium on Parallel Processing (IPPS'95), Los Alamitos, CA, USA, IEEE Computer Society Press (1995) 258–264
7. Mueller, F.: Decentralized Sinchronization for Multithreaded DSM. In: Proc. of the 2nd. Workshop on Software Distributed Shared Memory (WSDSM '2000). (2000)
8. Naimi, M., Trehel, M., Arnold, A.: A $log(N)$ Distributed Mutual Exclusion Algorithm based on Path Reversal. Journal of Parallel and Distributed Computing **34** (1996) 1–13
9. Raynal, M.: A Simple Taxonomy for Distributed Mutual Exclusion Algorithms. ACM SIGOPS Operating Systems Review **25** (1991) 47–50
10. Neilsen, M., Mizuno, M.: A DAG-Based Algorithm for Distributed Mutual Exclusion. In: Proc. of the 11th. International Conference on Distributed Computing Systems (ICDCS '96). (1991) 354–360
11. Banerjee, S., Chrysanthis, P.: A New Token Passing Distributed Mutual Exclusion Algorithm. In: Proc. of the 16th. International Conference on Distributed Computing Systems (ICDCS '96). (1996) 717–725

On Time Analysis of Random Walk Based Token Circulation Algorithms

Alain Bui[1,*] and Devan Sohier[1,2]

[1] CReSTIC-LICA, Université de Reims Champagne Ardenne, BP1039 F-51687
Reims cedex, France
{alain.bui,devan.sohier}@univ-reims.fr
[2] LRIA – EPHE rue G. Lussac, F-75005 Paris, France

Abstract. The problem of evaluating time complexity of random distributed algorithms is considered. A common and natural way to randomize a distributed algorithm is to use random walks *i.e.* memoryless stochastic processes: a "token" message circulates in the system and, at each step, the node that owns it sends it to one of its neighbors chosen at random. The token usually contains some pieces of information or part of the result of some distributed computing for instance. In this paper we focus on the cover time, defined by the expected time to visit all nodes in the system. This quantity often appears in the complexity of random walk based distributed algorithms. We provide a general method to compute the cover time on any arbitrary graph modeling a distributed system.

1 Introduction

Let $G = (V, E, \omega)$ an undirected connected graph representing a distributed system. V is the set of nodes E a set of edges, and ω the weight function ($\omega(i, j)$ is the weight of edge (i, j)). We define $|V| = n$ and $|E| = m$. A random walk is a sequence of nodes of G visited by a token that starts at a node i and visits other vertices according to the following transition rule: if the token is at i at time t then, at time $t+1$, it will be at one of the neighbors of i chosen at random among all of them proportionaly to the weight of the links starting from i). An algorithm using this mechanism is called a random walk based token circulation algorithm.

Original solutions using random walks have been designed for various problems related to distributed computing *e.g* [6] for self-stabilizing mutual exclusion, [3] for mobile agent in wireless networks, [2] for token circulation in dynamic network in faulty environment or as an alternative way to flooding in decentralized and unstructured peer-to-peer networks (especially to achieve low bandwidth consumption) [10].

Similarly to deterministic distributed algorithms, the time complexity of random walk based token circulation algorithms can be viewed as the number of "steps" it takes for the algorithm to achieve the network traversal. With only

---

* Corresponding author

F.F. Ramos et al. (Eds.): ISSADS 2005, LNCS 3563, pp. 63–71, 2005.

one walk at a time (which is the case we deal), it is also equal to the message complexity.

Random walks-based distributed algorithms must be analyzed through probabilistic tools. It can be shown that a random walk will visit all the sites in a graph in a finite time, but there is no hope to give hard bounds to the time it will take: the classical worst-case analysis cannot be applied in this case, and we are led to use an average-case analysis.

The cover time C – the average time to visit all nodes in the system – and the hitting time denoted by h_{ij} – the average time to reach a node j for the first time starting form a given node i – are two important values that appear in the analysis of random walk-based distributed algorithms. For instance, the cover time will be the average time needed to build a spanning tree thanks to a random walk token circulation algorithm.

In this paper, we propose a method to exactly compute the cover time. To our knowledge, this is the first solution ever designed to solve this problem.

2   Related Work

Random walks and resistive networks A tight link exists between random walks and resistive networks (*cf.* [5]). We build an electrical network from a graph G by replacing each of its edges by a resistor such that the conductance value (*i.e.* the inverse of the resistance) is equal to the weight of the edge in the graph (see fig. 1).

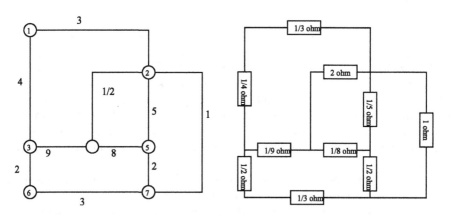

Fig. 1. the electrical circuit built from a weighted graph

The effective resistance R_{ij} between nodes i and j is defined as the resistance of the resistor to be placed between i an j to ensure the same electrical properties in the whole network. In other words, R_{ij} is the potential difference (in volts) between i and j when a $1A$ current flows from j to i. R denotes the maximal effective resistance between two nodes of the network *i.e.* $R = \max_{(i,j) \in V^2} R_{ij}$.

[4] shows that:

$$mR < C < O(mR \log n)$$

and [9] that:

$$h_{ij} = \frac{1}{2} \sum_k \deg(k)(R_{ij} - R_{ik} + R_{jk})$$

In [8], we generalized the above results to weighted graphs:

$$h_{ij} = \frac{1}{2} \sum_k \omega(k)(R_{ij} - R_{ik} + R_{jk})$$

Efficient computation of the hitting times and potentials We propose in [1] to compute automatically the hitting times by computing equivalent resistances in the associated resistive network. In [8], we improve this to allow an application to large network. We use the Millman's theorem, which is based on the application of the Kirchhoff's laws to all the vertices and leads to the square linear system:

$$V_i = \frac{\sum_{j=0,}^k \frac{V_j}{r(i,j)}}{\sum_{j=1}^k \frac{1}{r(i,j)}}$$

that is

$$\frac{V_i - V_0}{r(i,0)} + \frac{V_i - V_1}{r(i,1)} + \frac{V_i - V_2}{r(i,2)} + \cdots + \frac{V_i - V_k}{r(i,k)} = 0$$

where $1, \cdots, k$ are the neighbors of i, $V_1, \cdots, V_k$ are the voltages on each of these nodes.

This system is not invertible. This corresponds to its physical interpretation: to compute the voltages one needs also to know at least the potential on one node. Thus, we suppress one equation (the first one, for example), and add an equation setting the potential on a node (say $V_0 = 0$). The matrix is then invertible, and we can obtain all the potentials by inverting it, and setting two of them (the ones *"wired to the generator"*). Then the equivalent resistances are:

$$R_{ij} = \Delta_2^{-1}(i,j) - \Delta_2^{-1}(j,j) - \Delta_2^{-1}(i,i) + \Delta_2^{-1}(j,i)$$

with Δ_2 the square matrix associated to the modified equation system. The overall complexity required to compute all the hitting times is thus $O(n^3)$ [8].

Many papers deal with bounds on cover time *e.g.* [7] (see references section of [1] for more complete bibliography). But none of them – to our knowledge – has established an *effective way* to compute the cover time for arbitrary graphs.

In [1], we have studied an alternative approach through the cyclic cover time notion, which is close to the cover time notion and much easier to compute. The cyclic cover time is defined by the average time to visit all the vertices in the best deterministic arrangement ($CCT = \min\{\sum_{k=1}^{n-1} h_{\sigma(k)\sigma(k+1)}/\sigma \in \mathcal{S}_n\}$, where $\mathcal{S}_n$ is the set of permutations over $\{1, \ldots, n\}$). The cyclic cover time can be easily deduced thanks to the previous method: "computing the hitting time through their expression in terms of resistances". This method has been generalized to weighted networks and improved to allow application to large networks [8].

In the following, we focus on the cover time, and we provide a general method to compute the cover time on any arbitrary graph.

3   Cover Time

The cover time is the expected time for a random walk – called here the token
– starting from a given node to visit all the nodes in the distributed system. To
compute the cover time, we need a criterion to determine whether every vertex
has been visited by the token.

Consider $G = (V, E)$ the undirected connected graph modeling a distributed
system. We build from G an associated graph $\mathcal{G}$ such that the cover time of
G can be expressed in terms of hitting times in $\mathcal{G}$. To express results on cover
time using hitting times, we have to take into account the token trajectory. So
$\mathcal{G}$ should reflect some history-dependant data.

3.1   Construction of the Associated Graph $\mathcal{G}$

First let define $\mathcal{G} = (\mathcal{V}, \mathcal{E})$ where $\mathcal{V}$ is a set of nodes and $\mathcal{E}$ a set of directed edges.

- $x \in \mathcal{V}$ is defined by $x = (P, i)$ with $P \in \mathcal{P}(V)$ where $\mathcal{P}(V)$ is the power set
  of V – set of nodes of G – and $i \in V$. P represents the set of nodes in G
  already visited by the token, and $i \in V$ the vertex on which the token is
  currently on.
- any edge $(x, y) \in \mathcal{E}$ is of the form $(x, y) = ((P, i), (Q, j))$ with $(x, y) \in \mathcal{V} \times \mathcal{V}$
  and $(i, j) \in E$ (is an edge).

Suppose that, initially, the token is at node i in G, and next the token moves
to j neighbor of i, and next moves back to i. In the associated graph $\mathcal{G}$, we have
the following path $((\{i\}, i); (\{i, j\}, j); (\{i, j\}, i))$.

Note that $\mathcal{E}$ is a set of *directed* edges $((P, i), (Q, j))$. Edges in $\mathcal{E}$ are defined
by:

- $((P, i), (P, j))$, where i and j are neighbors; this case corresponds to a token
  transmission to the node j and j has already been visited by the token.
- $((P, i), (P \bigcup \{j\}, j))$ where i and j are neighbors; this case corresponds to a
  token transmission to the node j and j is holding the token for the first time.

The probability to obtain a given path in G is equal to the probability to
obtain the associated path in $\mathcal{G}$. Indeed, for $i \in P \subset V$ and $j \in V$, there exists
some $Q \subset V$ such that the transition probability from (P, i) to (Q, j) and the
transition probability from i to j are the same: $Q = P$ if $j \in P$, else, $Q = P \bigcup \{j\}$.

A token in G has visited every node *iff* the associated token in $\mathcal{G}$ has reached
a node (P, i) such that $P = V$. Then, we deduce that the cover time in G is the
average time it takes to a token in $\mathcal{G}$ starting from a node i to reach any arbitrary
node k for the first time while having visited all nodes, that is

$$C_i(G) = h_{(\{i\}, i), \{(V, k)/k \in V\}}(\mathcal{G})$$

The token has covered G when the associated token in $\mathcal{G}$ has hit any vertex
in $F = \{(V, k)/k \in V\}$. We do not care at which node (V, k) the token reaches
in $\mathcal{G}$, then we lump all nodes in F into a single one called f (in fact we obtain an
absorbing Markov Chain). Now, the cover time in G is obtained by the average
number of steps needed before entering f starting in node $(\{i\}, i)$.

3.2 Cover Time Computation

$\mathcal{G}$ being directed, we cannot apply the procedure of section 2 to compute $h_{(\{i\},i),\{(V,k)/k\in V\}}(\mathcal{G})$.

Let $\mathcal{N}_o(x)$ be the set of vertices that have an incoming edge from x: $\{y \in V/(x,y) \in \mathcal{E}\}$.

Since f can be reached from any vertex (if not, some of the h_{xf} would be undefined) we have,

$$\begin{cases} \forall x \in V, h_{xf} = 1 + \sum_{y\in\mathcal{N}_o(x)} p_{xy}h_{yf} \\ h_{ff} = 0 \end{cases} \quad (1)$$

The square linear system (1) has a single solution (vector $h_{\cdot f}$) then the hitting time between all nodes and a given node can be computed by inverting one matrix.

Thus, the cover time of any graph G is computed by building $\mathcal{G}$ and by computing $h_{(i,\{i\}),f}(\mathcal{G})$, which requires the inversion of an approximatively $n2^n \times n2^n$ matrix.

Let G be the graph on figure 2. Then $\mathcal{G}$ is partially represented by the graph on figure 3.

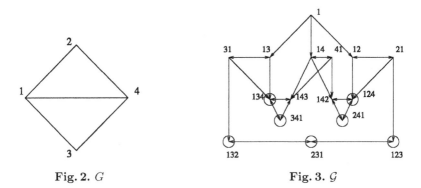

Fig. 2. G Fig. 3. $\mathcal{G}$

In figure 3, we use the following notation: $ij\mathbf{k}$ corresponds to node $(\{i,j,\mathbf{k}\},\mathbf{k})$ (e.g. 31 corresponds to $(\{1,3\},1)$ and 13 corresponds to $(\{1,3\},3)$). We only built the part of $\mathcal{G}$ that corresponds to situations where the token started in node 1. We did no write the states in which all vertices are visited: for the sake of legibility, we circled the sites that lead to such a state. Thus, in state 134, the token will reach 2 and finish to cover the graph with probability $\frac{1}{3}$, reach 3 (the state being 143) or 1 (341) also with probability $\frac{1}{3}$.

Since we merge all the states in which the token has covered the graph, every circled state leads to the new site f with a directed vertex.

The matrix of $\mathcal{G}$ is then:

	1	12	14	13	21	124	41	142	143	31	134	123	132	241	341	231	f
1	0	1	1	1	0	0	0	0	0	0	0	0	0	0	0	0	0
12	0	0	0	0	1	1	0	0	0	0	0	0	0	0	0	0	0
14	0	0	0	0	0	0	1	1	1	0	0	0	0	0	0	0	0
13	0	0	0	0	0	0	0	0	0	1	1	0	0	0	0	0	0
21	0	1	0	0	0	1	0	0	0	0	0	1	0	0	0	0	0
124	0	0	0	0	0	0	0	1	0	0	0	0	0	1	0	0	1
41	0	0	1	0	0	0	0	1	1	0	0	0	0	0	0	0	0
142	0	0	0	0	0	1	0	0	0	0	0	0	0	1	0	0	0
143	0	0	0	0	0	0	0	0	0	0	1	0	0	0	1	0	0
31	0	0	0	1	0	0	0	0	0	0	1	0	1	0	0	0	0
134	0	0	0	0	0	0	0	0	1	0	0	0	0	0	1	0	1
123	0	0	0	0	0	0	0	0	0	0	0	0	0	0	0	1	1
132	0	0	0	0	0	0	0	0	0	0	0	0	0	0	0	1	1
241	0	0	0	0	0	1	0	1	0	0	0	0	0	0	0	0	1
341	0	0	0	0	0	0	0	0	1	0	1	0	0	0	0	0	1
231	0	0	0	0	0	0	0	0	0	0	0	1	1	0	0	0	1
f	0	0	0	0	0	0	0	0	0	0	0	0	0	0	0	0	0

The system we have to solve to obtain the cover time is:

$$
\begin{pmatrix}
1 & -\frac{1}{3} & -\frac{1}{3} & -\frac{1}{3} & 0 & 0 & 0 & 0 & 0 & 0 & 0 & 0 & 0 & 0 & 0 & 0 & 0 \\
0 & 1 & 0 & 0 & -\frac{1}{2} & -\frac{1}{2} & 0 & 0 & 0 & 0 & 0 & 0 & 0 & 0 & 0 & 0 & 0 \\
0 & 0 & 1 & 0 & 0 & 0 & -\frac{1}{3} & -\frac{1}{3} & -\frac{1}{3} & 0 & 0 & 0 & 0 & 0 & 0 & 0 & 0 \\
0 & 0 & 0 & 1 & 0 & 0 & 0 & 0 & 0 & -\frac{1}{2} & -\frac{1}{2} & 0 & 0 & 0 & 0 & 0 & 0 \\
0 & -\frac{1}{3} & 0 & 0 & 1 & -\frac{1}{3} & 0 & 0 & 0 & 0 & 0 & -\frac{1}{3} & 0 & 0 & 0 & 0 & 0 \\
0 & 0 & 0 & 0 & 0 & 1 & 0 & -\frac{1}{3} & 0 & 0 & 0 & 0 & 0 & -\frac{1}{3} & 0 & 0 & -\frac{1}{3} \\
0 & 0 & -\frac{1}{3} & 0 & 0 & 0 & 1 & -\frac{1}{3} & -\frac{1}{3} & 0 & 0 & 0 & 0 & 0 & 0 & 0 & 0 \\
0 & 0 & 0 & 0 & 0 & -\frac{1}{2} & 0 & 1 & 0 & 0 & 0 & 0 & 0 & -\frac{1}{2} & 0 & 0 & 0 \\
0 & 0 & 0 & 0 & 0 & 0 & 0 & 0 & 1 & 0 & -\frac{1}{2} & 0 & 0 & 0 & -\frac{1}{2} & 0 & 0 \\
0 & 0 & 0 & -\frac{1}{3} & 0 & 0 & 0 & 0 & 0 & 1 & -\frac{1}{3} & 0 & -\frac{1}{3} & 0 & 0 & 0 & 0 \\
0 & 0 & 0 & 0 & 0 & 0 & 0 & 0 & -\frac{1}{3} & 0 & 1 & 0 & 0 & 0 & -\frac{1}{3} & 0 & -\frac{1}{3} \\
0 & 0 & 0 & 0 & 0 & 0 & 0 & 0 & 0 & 0 & 0 & 1 & 0 & 0 & 0 & -\frac{1}{2} & -\frac{1}{2} \\
0 & 0 & 0 & 0 & 0 & 0 & 0 & 0 & 0 & 0 & 0 & 0 & 1 & 0 & 0 & -\frac{1}{2} & -\frac{1}{2} \\
0 & 0 & 0 & 0 & 0 & -\frac{1}{3} & 0 & -\frac{1}{3} & 0 & 0 & 0 & 0 & 0 & 1 & 0 & 0 & -\frac{1}{3} \\
0 & 0 & 0 & 0 & 0 & 0 & 0 & 0 & -\frac{1}{3} & 0 & -\frac{1}{3} & 0 & 0 & 0 & 1 & 0 & -\frac{1}{3} \\
0 & 0 & 0 & 0 & 0 & 0 & 0 & 0 & 0 & 0 & 0 & -\frac{1}{3} & -\frac{1}{3} & 0 & 0 & 1 & -\frac{1}{3} \\
0 & 0 & 0 & 0 & 0 & 0 & 0 & 0 & 0 & 0 & 0 & 0 & 0 & 0 & 0 & 0 & 1
\end{pmatrix}
h_{.f}(\mathcal{G}) =
\begin{pmatrix}
1 \\ 1 \\ 1 \\ 1 \\ 1 \\ 1 \\ 1 \\ 1 \\ 1 \\ 1 \\ 1 \\ 1 \\ 1 \\ 1 \\ 1 \\ 1 \\ 0
\end{pmatrix}
$$

When solving this system, we obtain that

$$
h_{.f}(\mathcal{G}) = \left(\frac{34}{5};\frac{109}{20};\frac{13}{2};\frac{109}{20};\frac{49}{10};4;\frac{13}{2};5;5;\frac{49}{10};4;\frac{9}{4};\frac{9}{4};4;4;\frac{5}{2};0\right) \text{ Thus, } C_1 = \frac{34}{5}
$$

3.3 Efficient Cover Time Computation

The matrix to be inverted in the previous method is large (about $n2^n \times n2^n$: we give no exact value since the graph size can be reduced by suppressing the unreachable states), leading to a complexity approaching $n^3 8^n$.

However, this graph has some particularities we want to exploit to improve the efficiency of the computation. The subgraphs constituted by all the vertices (P, i) with the same P are undirected. The cover time can be computed thanks to:

$$h_{(P,i),f} = 1 + s(P,i) + \sum_j p(P,i,j) h_{(P \cup \{j\}, j), f}$$

where

- $p(P, i, j)$ is the probability that the first vertex outside P hitten by a random walk starting at i is j;
- $s(P, i)$ the average time the walk starting at i stays in P

We can express both of those quantities in terms of equivalent resistances and potentials, making it possible to use results of part 2:

- $p(P, i, j)$ is the potential in i when $V_j = 1$ and all other sites in $V \backslash P$ have potential 0
- $s(P, i) = h_{i(V \backslash P)}(G(P \cup \{j\}))$

Those quantities can be computed thanks to a $|P| \times |P|$ matrix inversion.

In fig. 4, we represented $\mathcal{G}$ and circled subgraphs that are not directed. Each of them is also a subgraph (connected and containing 1) of G. We have to compute the time the random walk spends in each of the subgraph, considering its arrival point. In fig 5, we highlighted the directed edges joining the various subgraphs: each of them represent the discovery of a new vertex. We have to compute the probability that the walk crosses each of these edges, depending on the vertex of the subgraph it arrives on. Then, using those information, we can compute the cover time with the above formula.

The complexity of this procedure is one $k \times k$ matrix inversion for each subgraph of size k appearing. The complexity is then at most $O(n^3 2^n)$. However,

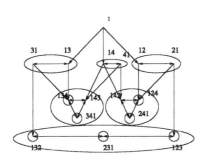

Fig. 4. G

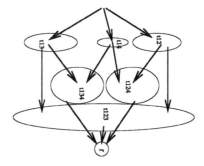

Fig. 5. $\mathcal{G}$

it highly depends on the topology of G. If G is a chain, only n subgraphs appear (a subgraph occurs in the computation *iff* it contains the state 1 and is connected), and the complexity is $O(n^4)$.

4 Conclusion

We provide in this paper a new method to compute cover times on a graph modeling a distributed system. Since a long time, cover time is used as a bound on the complexity of numerous random walk-based algorithms. But only bounds on the cover time were known. Knowing exact cover times may help to test the efficiency of random walk-based algorithms compared to deterministic algorithms, both in terms of execution time and in terms of used bandwidth.

Many works are currently led on dynamic networks (P2P, *ad-hoc*, ...): the topology of those networks evolves too fast to consider a loss of connection or a new connection as a failure. In this kind of networks, the bandwidth is often limited, and solutions are often based on broadcasting a message by flooding the network. Random walk-based distributed algorithm may provide a less expensive scheme to structure networks (see [10] for example), even if it will be less efficient (in terms of execution time).

This loss of efficiency has to be counter-parted by a gain in bandwidth, and we need a theoretical tool to test this and the validity of the trade-off. We think that an efficient computation of the cover time is part of such a tool along with an efficient computation of the hitting time and a study on the use of several random walks.

This theoretical study may also lead to the determination of a *"good"* size and topology of networks (in terms of the use of random walks), which could not be achieved by simulations. Topology on which the cover time is weak (with respect to the size of the graph) are highly desirable to achieve a low complexity of most of random walk based distributed algorithms. And to improve their efficiency, we are willing to cluster sites in subnetworks on which random walks are efficient, *i.e.* the cover time is low.

References

1. T. Bernard, A. Bui, M. Bui, and D. Sohier. A new method to automatically compute processing times for random walks based distributed algorithms. In *International Symposium on Parallel and Distributed Computing*, pages 31–37. IEEE Comp. Soc. Press, 2003.
2. Thibault Bernard, Alain Bui, and Olivier Flauzac. Topological adaptability for the distributed token circulation paradigm in faulty environment. In *ISPA 2004*, pages 146–155. LNCS 3358, Springer, 2004.
3. Marc Bui, Sajal K. Das, Ajoy Kumar Datta, and Dai Tho Nguyen. Randomized mobile agent based routing in wireless networks. *International Journal of Foundations of Computer Science*, 12(3):365–384, 2001.
4. A. K. Chandra, P. Raghavan, W. L. Ruzzo, and R. Smolensky. The electrical resistance of a graph captures its commute and cover times. pages 574–586, 1989.

5. Peter G. Doyle and J. Laurie Snell. *Random Walks and Electric Networks*. 2000 (first edition 1984 Mathematical Association of America).
6. Amos Israeli and Marc Jalfon. Token management schemes and random walks yield self-stabilizing mutual exclusion. In *9th ACM symposium on Principles of distributed computing*, pages 119–131, 1990.
7. László Lovász. Random walks on graphs: A survey. In T. Szõnyi ed. D. Miklós, V. T. Sós, editor, *Combinatorics: Paul Erdos is Eighty (vol. 2)*, pages 353–398. János Bolyai Mathematical Society, 1993.
8. D. Sohier and A. Bui. Hitting times computation for theoretically studying peer-to-peer distributed system. In *IPDPS'04 - Sixth Workshop on Advances in Parallel and Distributed Computational Models - APDCM*. IEEE CS Press, 2004.
9. P. Tetali. Random walks and effective resistance of networks. *J. Theoretical Probability*, 1991.
10. D. Tsoumakos and N. Roussopoulos. A comparison of peer-to-peer search methods. In *Sixth International Workshop WebDB'03*, 2003.

Architecture for Media Streaming Delivery over P2P Networks

Francisco de Asís López-Fuentes and Eckehard Steinbach

Institute of Communication Networks, Media Technology Group
Technische Universität München, 80333 München, Germany
{fcoasis,Eckehard.Steinbach}@tum.de

Abstract. Peer-to-Peer networks (P2P) exhibit specific characteristics that can be exploited for media streaming delivery. In this paper we propose a P2P-based architecture for video streaming delivery incorporating reputation, cooperation, and semantic clustering strategies. We believe that the integration of those strategies will lead to significant improvements of P2P-based media streaming delivery. In our approach all peers cooperate and share resources. They inform each other about these resources using a resource ticket. Only the best peers are selected and shown in an access ticket. Reputation is proposed as a way for supervising and keeping the media stream of acceptable quality for end-peers.

1 Introduction

In recent years considerable research effort has been conducted in the areas of Peer-to-Peer (P2P) technologies. Also, media streaming over the Internet has gained significant popularity due to the continuous increase in network access rate of the end-users. In today's Internet, media streaming applications based on Content Delivery Networks (CDN) have several limitations. We believe that P2P networks provide characteristics and possibilities that can deal with these limitations. However, P2P networks still pose many challenges such as dynamically changing transmission capacity and availability. Query processing in P2P networks is inefficient and does not scale well. Quality of Service (QoS) support for media distribution is very limited or nonexistent. Due to the limited serving capacity of peers the media files typically have to be streamed from multiple peers simultaneously [1]. The requesting peer therefore has to manage several connections concurrently. For instance, if the outbound transmission rate offered by a supplying peer is less than the original playback rate of the media data, it is necessary to involve multiple supplying peers in one real-time streaming session. A scheduler has the responsibility to download the packets from a set of possible nodes before their scheduled display time to guarantee non-disruptive playback. Timing constraints are crucial, since a packet arriving after its scheduled playback time is useless and considered lost. In a P2P media streaming system only a subset of peers own a certain media file. They stream the media file to requesting peers, which may opt to store segments of the media file for a specific period of time, or forward these segments to other requesting peers in the system. Currently, many researchers are investigating how to implement media streaming in P2P networks in order to provide an efficient and scalable multimedia distribution service.

F.F. Ramos et al. (Eds.): ISSADS 2005, LNCS 3563, pp. 72–82, 2005.

We propose in this paper a novel distributed P2P-based media streaming approach based on cooperation, semantic clustering and reputation among peers. With this model we try to achieve good connectivity among peers and best proximity of resources. A successful streaming media solution requires a framework that is adaptive to content, packet loss, variable transmission capacities, delay, and client capabilities. In our approach we improve self-organisation based on semantics and support QoS by using information from peers with high reputation.

The rest of this paper is organized as follows. Section 2 discusses related work. In Section 3, we introduce our architecture for P2P-based media streaming. Based on the proposed architecture, we develop our operations algorithms in Section 4. We conclude with directions for future work in Section 5.

2   Related Work

Semantic structure, cooperation and reputation strategies have been used in several approaches but in separate ways. Clustering peers with similar documents has been proposed in [2, 3, 4, 5]. The approach in [2] is based on a centralized server to cluster documents and nodes. Clustering nodes with similar interest is proposed in [3], but it is not discussed how to define the interest similarity amongst the peers. One semantic approach using content hierarchies for music files is pursued in [5]. It consists of explicitly identifying distinct semantic groups of documents and building possibly overlapping overlay networks for each group. The concept of reputation is used in several systems such as the online auction system eBay. In eBay's reputation system, buyers and sellers can rate each other after a transaction, and the overall reputation of a participant is the sum of these ratings over the past 6 months. The authors in [6, 7, 8, 9] are proposing reputation systems with the purpose to ensure that peers obtain reliable information about the quality of the resources they are receiving. All these techniques are proposed to support data transfer but not for video transmission. Streaming of video puts more constraints on the network than simple file downloading. Once a video stream has started, data has to arrive at a continuous rate in order to guarantee proper display of the video. Recently, some approaches for media streaming over peer to peer have been presented. In [10, 11, 12] frameworks for simultaneously streaming video from multiple senders to a single receiver are proposed. In [13] several replication techniques for multimedia distribution are revised. Cooperation strategies for media streaming are developed in [14, 15, 16]. CoopNet [16] proposes to build multiple description trees spanning the source and all the receivers, each tree transmitting a separate description of the media signal. CoopNet puts a heavy control overhead on the source. In CoopNet the source must maintain full knowledge of all distribution trees.

3   Architecture for P2P-Based Media Streaming

3.1   General Approach

In our approach all peers cooperate and share resources such as available storage, CPU and available transmission capacity. They inform other peers about these resources using a *resource ticket*. Only the best peers are selected and shown in an *access ticket*. Our approach is illustrated in Fig. 1.

The *access ticket* is used by peers for self-organization based on semantics. A new peer uses the *access ticket* to select the best serving peer or the best serving peer set of a semantic group owning a specific video. A *distributed cashier* that manages the tickets is implemented over a small group of reliable peers named *manager peers*. Several video descriptions are obtained using Multiple Description Coding (MDC). MDC is a source coding technique which encodes a signal into a number of separate bitstreams [17]. Each individual bitstream is called a description. The descriptions are sent through different network paths to a destination. These descriptions are distributed among peers in a semantic group. A reputation mechanism is considered in order to guarantee that the receiving peer obtains a video of high quality from a peer with high reputation.

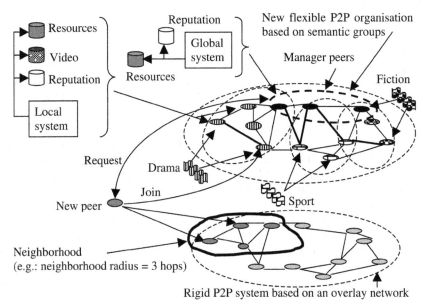

Fig. 1. Overview of the model

With the *access ticket*, a peer can determine "good" peers based on semantics/resources interests and join them. Thus, peers with a high degree of similar interests are connected closely. We call this cluster a semantic group. Initially, when the number of peers is small, the organization has only one cluster. As clients join or leave, this organization will grow or shrink. A reputation mechanism must be implemented in order to guarantee the quality of content delivered by the peers in a group. Our model has a distributed approach that global video (global media) is partitioned into subsets using Multiple Description Coding. The video descriptors are distributed and allocated among best peers. The video descriptors can be replicated in several peers. Thus, *multiple* supplying peers serve one receiving peer in one real-time streaming session. An index server (indicating resources and video available in every peer) is distributed among peers of a semantic group. Every peer builds a local database with information from its neighboring peers, e.g., peers within a neighborhood of three hops. If the neighboring peers do not belong to the same semantic group, a co-operation strategy can be implemented in order to allow temporary replication or caching. Tickets are placed in a set of reliable manager peers with transparency of replication and access. Our model consists of a local scheme within every peer and a global scheme for all peers.

3.2 Local Scheme

Every peer has three local databases: *A metrics database, a video database* and *a reputation database*. The metrics database is built by a peer from the information about the best supplying peers provided by the *access ticket*, from information about other peers that belong to the same semantic group (drama, cartoons or adventures) and from information about its neighbors. The metric database has the following fields: *ID_Peer, CPU, Available Bandwidth (AvB), Storage (AvS), Semantic and Reputation.*

The video database is built with an index of all videos recorded under the same semantics and links. The video database index is replicated in every peer of the semantic group. The video database shows which description of the video is available. This database can be accessed by any peer. The complete database or only some specific fields (e.g. file name and links) can be copied by any peer. The video database is developed with information from the video but also contains additional fields named *link_1* and *link_2*, which points to other peers where the video is also available. An example of a video database for the semantic group "Drama" is shown in Table 1.

Table 1. Video database for the semantic group "Drama"

File Index	File Name	Stored Description	Bit rate (kbit/s)	File size (Mbytes)	Duration (hh:mm:ss)	Link_1	Link_2
1371	Titanic	D1	50	45.90	02:50:30	ID_Peer	ID_Peer
…………						…………	…………
299	Casablanca	D2	60	19.45	02:55:26	ID_Peer	ID_Peer

In the reputation database a peer *p* can file a complaint about peer *q* at any time. A *complaint message* is evaluated in every peer and in the *manager peer* by mechanisms of reputation evaluation. Every peer manages its own local database and decides based on the local database if it has enough information about the involved peers.

3.3 Global Scheme

The global system has three main components: a global resources database and selection mechanism, the cashier system and the global reputation system. It is shown in Fig. 2. The global resources database has information about the resources and reputation from all peers in the system. Here the information that does not appear in the *access ticket* is stored. The global resources database is built in a manager peer or distributed among several manager peers. A *selection mechanism* exchanges a peer in the access ticket when a better peer is identified in the database.

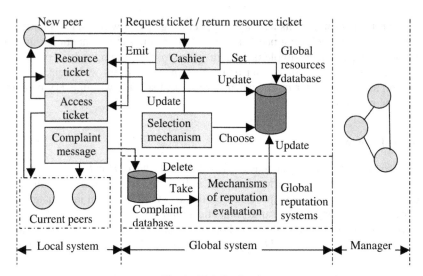

Fig. 2. Global scheme

Our reputation system is inspired by [9]. A transaction made by any peer can be either performed correctly or not. A *complaint message* is evaluated in the *manager peer* (P_m) and the decision is based on the experience about the behavior of the sender peer (reputation of sender peer). We consider the dishonest interactions as relevant. An overview about the operation of our reputation system is shown in Fig. 3. Peers perform transactions and each transaction $t(p_1, p_2)$ can be either performed correctly or not. In our model we considered that a peer is cheating when it supplies the wrong data or serves with lower resources than promised. When a peer p_1 interacts with another peer p_2 in a set of all peers P, we make observations about malicious behavior in each peer. This means, that in a global perspective we take into account all reports about transactions that are made about p_1, but as well as all reports about transactions that are made by p_1. Thus, when peer p_2 is cheating in a transaction with peer p_1, a complaint is sent by p_1 to the global reputation database in the manager peer. Another complaint is recorded in its local reputation database. Let us assume that p_2 also files a complaint about p_1 in order to hide its misbehavior. The manager peer can not distinguish whether p_1 or p_2 is the dishonest peer. It is solved when p_2 cheats in another interaction with p_3. Thus, P_m has two complains for p_2 from p_1 and p_3, and it can conclude that it is very probable that p_2 is the cheater. Then, the reputation for p_2 is decreased in the manager peer and peer p_1. If peer p_2 is in access ticket, it is updated and sent to all peers. The reputation of a peer p can be derived from the manager peer. If a current peer p_5 or a new peer p_4 want to determine the reputation of p_1, they can request it from the manager peer. In addition a global behavior system can be used in order to normalize results obtained about a specific peer.

3.4 Media Streaming Distribution

In our approach we propose to use Multiple Description Coding (MDC) as a method of encoding the video signal into a number of separate streams. In MDC each indi-

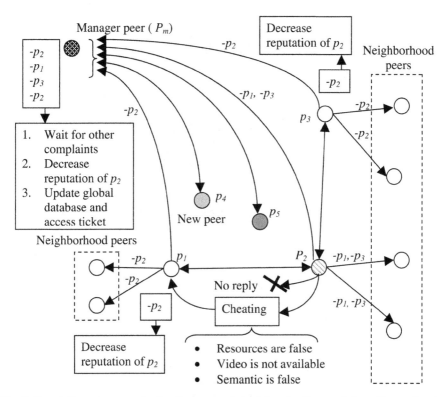

Fig. 3. Reputation scheme. p_2 is cheating, p_5 wants to determine the reputation of p_1 and p_2, but it has no relation with them. (P_m: manager peer, p: peers, p_4: is a new peer)

vidual stream is called a description, such that any subset of these descriptions can be received and decoded into a signal with distortion (with respect to the original signal). The level of distortion depends on the number of descriptions received. That is, the more descriptions are received, the lower the distortion of the reconstructed signal (i.e., the higher the quality). The descriptions are sent through different network paths to a destination. The receiver can make a useful reproduction of the signal when at least one of the descriptions is received. In [18] it is demonstrated that using MDC in combination with packet path diversity improves the robustness of real-time video applications significantly. In a scenario using MDC over P2P a MDC encoded video is streamed simultaneously from multiple geographically distributed peers. Fig. 4 illustrates that peer p_5 wants to receive video file C which is available in the MDC format on p_7, p_2 and p_6. We consider in this example that the video is encoded using two descriptions, D_1 and D_2. Peers p_7 and p_2 are chosen based on a performance metric (eg.: response time, number of hops). Thus they can simultaneously serve the video file C, each one providing a complementary description. As is demonstrated in [12], if any of the descriptions is affected by packet loss or excessive delay, the receiver can still decode and display video C but at the expense of degradation of the quality, as the descriptions are independently decodable.

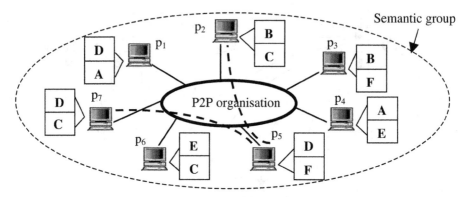

Fig. 4. Video streaming over a P2P network. The supplying peers belong to the same semantic group and serve complementary descriptions of the video

4   Algorithms for Operation

When a new peer p_n requests content for the first time, it must advertise its resources and must acquire the *access ticket* from a cashier installed in the *manager peers*. A manager peer could be the first peer that started the group or a set of reliable peers (e.g. a manager peer for each semantic group).

The manager peer can emit in addition an empty *resource ticket* and an empty *complaint message*. Initially these three tickets are acquired by a new peer. In the empty *resource ticket*, a new peer must put information of its own resources that it is able to share. A peer fills the *complaint message* and sends it to other peers only when it has a complaint about a specific peer. The access ticket has information about the best peers for each semantic group. Algorithm 1 in Fig. 5 manages the tickets. Here, the *manager peer* (P_m) defines an initial database with N semantic styles, which is named *global metrics database* (DB_{gm}). The DB_{gm} records donated resources from other peers. Two best peers in each semantic group are selected and put in the access ticket. When P_m receives a request for an access ticket from any peer P_n, P_m searches in DB_{mg} if P_n is recorded, then P_m sends an update access ticket to P_n. If P_n is not recorded in DB_{mg}, then P_m sends a resource ticket and semantic style classification to P_n, in order to receive donated resources from it. When P_n returns information about its donated resources to P_m, it will send an access ticket to P_n and update the global metric database. Also, a peer can update its donated resources in P_m without requesting an access ticket. In our approach only the manager peers can change the information recorded in the *access ticket* in order to guarantee the credibility of the *access ticket*. This information is based on a combination of resource metrics and reputation for each peer.

When the requesting peer P_n receives the access ticket, it chooses the best peer P_b of a specific semantic group. This is considered by algorithm 2 in Fig. 6. When P_n has video files to share, it sends a semantic classification P_m and P_b in order to update the system. If the requested content is available from the selected peer P_b, the content is delivered to the requestor directly. If the content is not available, then links to other origin peers P_o recorded in the local database are searched. The local database has an

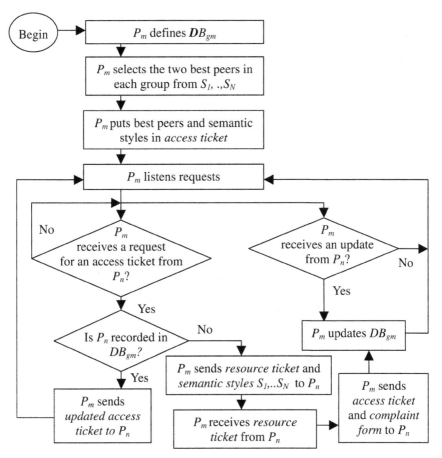

Fig. 5. Algorithm for management of tickets. (P_m: manager peer, P_n: new peer, P_b: best peer, DB_{gm}: global metrics database)

index with information about other peers within the same semantic group and in the local neighborhood. In this way, a query for "Drama" video will go directly to the nodes that have "Drama" content, reducing the time that it takes to answer the query. If the content is not in the same semantic group, then it is searched in other semantic groups.

When the control system decides to download a particular video stream from a specific origin peer P_o, the requesting peer sends a request message (REQ) to the intended sending peer. The name of the file and description number is in the REQ message. Then the receiver sets a time to wait for media (T_{wfm}). A process for the monitoring of link candidates is initiated. If the packet arrives before T_{wfm} expires, the time is reset and the whole process is repeated. T_{wfm} is recomputed every n received packets in order to obtain the best average time. If a new packet does not arrive within T_{wfm}, the receiver assumes that peer P_o is not available and switches to other available peers. The receiver computes the next frame and asks the new supplying peer about

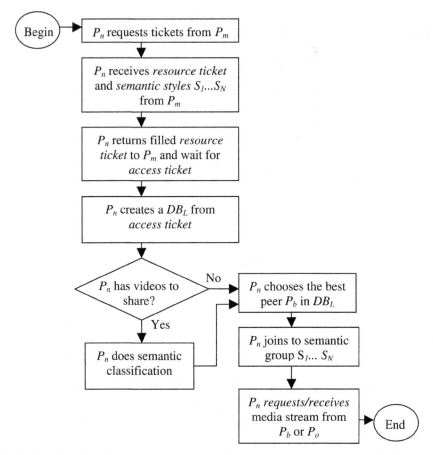

Fig. 6. Algorithm for joining a semantic group. (P_m: manager peer, P_n: new peer, P_b: best peer, P_o: origin peer, DB_L: local metrics database)

the corresponding description. The REQ message specifies the starting frame number to be transmitted.

A STOP message is send to P_o with the purpose of avoiding duplicated packets when it is restored. When peer P_o receives a REQ message from any peer, it reads the received FILE_ID, searches the video and immediately starts sending the file from the frame number requested. The server sends the packets according to the rate of the video signal.

5   Conclusions

In this paper, we presented an architecture for media streaming over P2P networks. We have examined the issues of semantic clustering, cooperation and reputation. We considered source peer selection, which depends on its semantic organization and performance metrics. The use of MDC in combination with packet path diversity is proposed in order to improve the robustness of the video delivery. Algorithms for the management of tickets and the participation in the video systems are proposed. The ticket concept is introduced as a way to make a best selection of peers.

In our proposed architecture only a shared resources approach is presented for cooperation amongst peers. In the future other cooperation strategies or incentives could be integrated to improve the system. An incentive mechanism is for instance useful for concurrency control in the best peer. In addition, some replication strategies will be studied in order to make a localization of video in the proximity of the requesting peer to improve performance and quality in the group.

Currently, we are in the process of implementing our architecture. We are implementing these strategies and algorithms in our P2P network simulation environment and will present the results in the near future.

References

1. Hefeeda, M. M. and Bhargava, B. K.: On-Demand Media Streaming Over the Internet. Proceedings of the 9th IEEE Workshop on Future Trends of Distributed Computing Systems. San Juan, Puerto Rico (2003)
2. Bawa, M., Manku, G. S., Raghavan, P.: SETS: Search enhanced by topic segmentation. Proceedings of ACM SIGIR (2003) 306–313
3. Iamnitchi, A., Ripeanu, M., Foster, I. T.: Locating Data in (small-world?) Peer- to-Peer Scientific Collaborations. Proceedings of the 2nd International Workshop on Peer-to-Peer Systems, Berkeley, CA, USA (2002) 232–241
4. Li, M., Lee W. C., Sivasubramanian, A., Lee D. L.: A Small World Overlay Network for Semantic Based Search in P2P. Proceedings of the 2nd Workshop on Semantics in Peer-to-Peer and Grid Computing (SemPGrid), in conjunction with the 13th World Wide Web Conference, New York, NY, USA (2004)
5. Crespo, A., García-Molina, H.: Semantic Overlay Networks for P2P Systems; Technical Report, http://www-db.stanford.edu/crespo/publications/op2p.pdf (2002)
6. Cornelli, F., Damiani, E., Vimercati, S.D.C.D., Paraboschi, S., Samarat, S.: Choosing Reputable Servents in a P2P Network. Proceedings of the 11th World Wide Web Conference, Hawaii, USA (2002)
7. Kamvar, S.D., Schlosser, M.T., Garcia-Molina, H.: The EigenTrust Algorithm for Reputation Management in P2P Networks. Proceedings of the 12th World Wide Web Conference WWW, Budapest, Hungary (2003)
8. Gupta, M., Judge, P., Ammar, M.: A Reputation System for Peer-to-Peer Systems. Proceedings of ACM NOSSDAV 2003, Monterey, CA (2003)
9. Aberer, K., Despotovic, Z.: Managing Trust in a Peer-2-Peer Information System. Proceedings of the ACM 10th International Conference on Information and Knowledge Management, New York, USA (2001)
10. Hefeeda, M., Bhargava, B.: On-Demand Media Streaming Over the Internet. CERIAS TR 2002-20, Purdue University, USA (2002)
11. Hefeeda, M., Habib, A., Botev B., Xu D., Bhargava, B.: PROMISE: Peer-to-Peer Media Streaming Using Collect-Cast. Technical report, CS-TR 03-016, Purdue University, USA. (2003)
12. Khan, S., Schollmeier R., Steinbach E.: A Performance Comparison of Multiple Description Video Streaming in Peer-to-Peer and Content Delivery Networks. Proceedings of the IEEE International Conference on Multimedia & Expo, ICME'04, Taipei, Taiwan, (2004)
13. Xiang, Z., Zhang, Q., Zhu, W., Zhang Z., and Zhang Y.: Peer-to-Peer Based Multimedia Distribution Service, IEEE Transactions on Multimedia, Vol. 6. No.2, (2004)
14. Habib A., Chuang, J.: Incentive Mechanism for Peer-to-Peer Media Streaming. Proceedings of the 12th IEEE International Workshop on Quality of Service, Montreal, Canada (2004)

15. Lai K., Feldman M., Stoica I., Chuang J.: Incentives for Cooperation in Peer-to-Peer Networks. Proceedings of the Workshop on Economics of Peer-to-Peer Systems, Berkeley, CA, USA (2003)
16. Padmanabhan, V. N., Wang, H. J, Chou, P. H., Sripanidkulchai K.: Distributing Streaming Media Content Using Cooperative Networking. Proceedings of the NOSSDAV 2002, Miami Beach, FL, USA, (2002)
17. Goyal, V., K.: Multiple Description Coding: Compression Meets the Network. IEEE Signal Processing Magazine, vol. 18, no. 5, pp. 74 – 94, (2001)
18. Apostolopoulos, J., Wong, T., Tan, W., Wee, S.: On Multiple Description Streaming with Content Delivery Networks. Proceedings of the 21st IEEE INFOCOM, New York, NY, USA (2002)

On the Role of Information Compaction to Intrusion Detection[*]

Fernando Godínez[1], Dieter Hutter[2], and Raúl Monroy[3]

[1] Centre for Intelligent Systems, ITESM-Monterrey
Eugenio Garza Sada 2501, Monterrey, 64849, Mexico
fgodinez@itesm.mx
[2] DFKI, Saarbrücken University
Stuhlsatzenhausweg 3, D-66123 Saarbrücken, Germany
hutter@dfki.de
[3] Department of Computer Science, ITESM–Estado de México
Carr. Lago de Guadalupe, Km. 3.5, Estado de México, 52926, Mexico
raulm@itesm.mx

Abstract. An intrusion detection system (IDS) usually has to analyse Giga-bytes of audit information. In the case of anomaly IDS, the information is used to build a user profile characterising normal behaviour. Whereas for misuse IDSs, it is used to test against known attacks. Probabilistic methods, e.g. hidden Markov models, have proved to be suitable to profile formation but are prohibitively expensive. To bring these methods into practise, this paper aims to reduce the audit information by folding up subsequences that commonly occur within it. Using n-grams language models, we have been able to successfully identify the n-grams that appear most frequently. The main contribution of this paper is a n-gram extraction and identification process that significantly reduces an input log file keeping key information for intrusion detection. We reduced log files by a factor of 3.6 in the worst case and 4.8 in the best case. We also tested reduced data using hidden Markov models (HMMs) for intrusion detection. The time needed to train the HMMs is greatly reduced by using our reduced log files, but most importantly, the impact on both the detection and false positive ratios are negligible.

1   Introduction

Probabilistic methods for intrusion detection, e.g. hidden Markov models (HMMs), have proved to be suitable to user profile formation. This profiling can be used both for misuse and anomaly detection. However, profile formation is prohibitively expensive, since these methods consume many computational resources [1, 2] with respect to the amount of information to be analysed. To complement an earlier work [3], in this paper we propose a session folding method that significantly reduces the amount of information a probabilistic method ought to analyse, without missing key details, thus making the use of probabilistic methods feasible.

---

[*] This research is supported by three research grants CONACyT 33337-A, CONACyT-DLR J200.324/2003 and ITESM CCEM-0302-05

At system call level, a session is composed of a finite sequence of system calls. The length of the sequence can vary depending on the activity of the user, it can be as short as a few hundred system calls, or as large as tens of thousand system calls. We have used HMMs both to, classify the service a session belongs to [4], and to detect intrusions. Time complexity for training and parsing of an HMM is directly related to the length of the sequence they ought to analyse.

To shrink a log file, we suggest to fold up the subsequences of system calls that most frequently occur within the sessions in a log file. Our method substitutes each such a repetitive session subsequence with a fresh tag, which can be regarded as a meta-level system call. To identify the most repetitive session subsequences, we use n-gram theory. N-gram theory has been largely used in the context of natural language processing; it has also been used in anomaly detection [5–9].

Let an *n-gram* be a sequence of n symbols, system calls in our case. Then, an *n-gram language model* is used to calculate the probability that a system call s will appear at position n, given the occurrence of an $(n-1)$-gram; that is, a sequence of *n-1* system calls. So the n-gram language model enables us to estimate the likelihood of appearance of a given n-gram along a larger sequence. By using n-gram theory, we have identified the n-grams with the highest rate of occurrence among the log files regardless the service, and within three different services, namely: i) ftp, ii) `telnet` and iii) `smtp`. This paper's key contribution is a collection of n-grams that are very likely to be repetitively found in many computer sessions of the analysed services.

Folding repetitive n-grams significantly reduces the length of a given session. Along our analysis we used n-grams of different length, ranging from bigrams to 100-grams. Our experiments show that we can effectively reduce an input session by an average factor of 4 (3.6, worst case scenario, and 4.8, best case one.)

The reduced log files were tested using an HMM IDS. The time needed to train the HMMs is greatly reduced by using a folded session. The order of HMMs parsing is $O(n^2 l)$ where n is the number of states in the HMM, and l is the length of the parsed sequence. Therefore parsing time is reduced by the same factor by which we reduce the input sequences. More importantly, detection ratio is better than the one obtained with non reduced log files. The false positive ratio is only 1% higher. It is worth mentioning that data used to extract the n-grams do not contain any attacks or anomalies.

The remainder of this paper is organised as follows: Section 2 is an overview of other attempts at log file reduction; Section 3 presents the reason to chose n-grams over other feature extraction methods like HMMs; Section 4 gives a brief overview of how and why we chose data for identifying repetitive n-grams; Section 5 shows the use of the n-gram models to identify the n-grams with higher occurrence frequency; Section 6 summarises the reduct obtained throughout our investigations; Section 7 is a description of our validation experiments and the selected data for such experiments; Section 8 shows the results obtained from applying the validation experiments to a collection of BSM log files and to the service selection module [4]; Section 9 shows the impact of our methodology on intrusion detection; finally, conclusions drawn up from our investigations appear in Section 10.

2   Session Length Reduction Methods

N-gram theory has been largely used in the context of natural language analysis, it also has been used in anomaly detection by Maxion and Tan [6, 7], Marceau [8], Wespi [9], and Forrest et al. [5]. All these papers present ways of using n-grams for anomaly detection and not for log file reduction. Therefore comparing our method with these methods is out of the question. Log file reduction methods are presented below.

Marin et. al. [10] have suggested to use an expert system to approach log file reduction. The expert system first discriminates objects that most frequently occur, using a series of fuzzy rules. Then it clusters the discriminate objects, to form a small number of object classes. Even though its reduction factor is very high, this method is prone to a large false-negative intrusion detection rate. This is because it prunes out key information and is restricted to a 1-gram only. By contrast, we do not get rid of non-commonly used system calls and the scope of our reduction analysis is considerably larger. As we showed, this contributes to keep false-negative intrusion detection rate low.

Lane and Brodley have also addressed the problem of log file reduction [11, 12]. They have proposed two main clustering methods, one based on K-centres and the other on greedy clustering. By applying both methods, each cluster contains a collection of objects sequences, which is then collapsed into only two objects: the cluster centre and the associated mean. The other object sequences are simply disregarded. Lane and Brodley's methods may yield a huge reduction ratio (e.g. 500 different sequences might be shrunk to only 30 ones or even fewer); however, eager sequence elimination inevitably leads to poor or incomplete profiles and therefore to an increase in the false-alarm detection rate. By comparison, even though our technique yields a lower reduction ratio, it does not have a negative impact on the false positive ratio.

Besides from the two methods above mentioned, Lane and Brodley have also explored two heuristic pruning techniques: least recently used (LRU) and least frequently used (LFU). In both techniques the reduction ratio is defined *a priori* and hence a predetermined number of sequences ought to be eliminated from the input session. Both techniques will of course produce a reduction ratio as high as indicated, but at the expense of losing of chief information. Lane and Brodley report on an increment in the false-positive and false-negative ratio (20% and 16% respectively). By comparison, even though our technique yields a lower reduction ratio, it does not have a negative impact on the false positive ratio. But most importantly false positives are reduced.

Knop et. al. [13] have addressed a similar problem, which also aims to make intrusion detection feasible, but does not consider log file reduction. Rather than shrinking an input session, Knop et. al.'s method simplifies its content by calling similar objects with the same name. Let $\Sigma(seq)$ denote the alphabet of symbol sequence seq, then given a sequence s, the method will return a new sequence, s' such that length$(s') =$ length(s) but that $|\Sigma(s')| \ll |\Sigma(s)|$. The method works as follows: it first correlates objects using a method similar to principal component analysis [14]. This way, two objects will be assigned a coefficient equal to

1 if they are completely correlated, and equal to 0 otherwise. Then using this correlation coefficient information, a K-Nearest Neighbours algorithm is applied for achieving object clustering. Object reduction amounts to selecting one object from a cluster discarding the rest of them. Once again, the alphabet simplification factor is very impressive but so is the loss of information. One important limitation of Knop et al.'s approach is that it is in general difficult to apply in the intrusion detection context. This is because the method requires some kind of numerical value to express correlation between objects to be applicable. This is unnatural, since almost every piece of data in sessions are strings. This completes our revision of related work regarding session length reduction. In the next section we will analyse the reasons that to choose n-grams as our reduction methods.

3   The Use of N-Grams as a Reduction Method

N-grams models are generally used to predict the next element in a sequence. To make this prediction an n-gram model has to have a frequency analysis from which a probability of occurrence is extracted. This probability is then used to estimate the probability of occurrence of the next element in the sequence. Other methods can be used to predict the next element in a given sequence, e.g. HMMs.

N-grams can be used to identify the most repetitive subsequences in any sequence of elements. HMMs can also do this job. But the HMMs do not find an specific sequence, they find a family of subsequences, i.e. [15, 16]. If we were to use a method such as HMMs then we can substitute any subsequence described by the family for the same tag. This substitution allows for an attack subsequence to be substituted and regarded as a normal subsequence. By using n-gram models we guarantee a 1-to-1 substitution relation. That way, variations of an attack that pose as a normal sequence (mimicry attacks) are not substituted.

Another thing we want from an IDS is not to lose the capability to return to the original sequence. One reason for wanting the reduction process to be reversible is for forensic analysis. We must assume that after an intrusion is detected, the attacker already has done some harm to the system. Therefore, we will perform a forensic analysis on the data to follow all of the attacker steps. To follow the events we need the track of activity that lead to an insecure state of the system. When designing a security device it is necessary to assume that this device will interact with other devices. And the design of our methods is done so it can provide the most information to other devices in the security chain. In the next section we will describe the data we selected to generate our n-gram models and to extract the most frequent n-grams.

4   Data Selection for N-Gram Extraction

For the process of n-gram selection, we chose to use the 1998 DARPA repository as our data source. We used 5 log files out of 35 log files for the n-gram selection process. This number of log files form a representative sample:

$$n = \frac{N}{1 + Ne^2} \qquad (1)$$

Where, n is the number of samples we need to take to represent a population of size N with a confidence $1 - e$ (or with an error tolerance of e). In our case we chose a confidence of 97.5% ($e = 2.5\%$). We have an average of 250 sessions in each log file. For a population of 8750 sessions we need around 1300 sessions as our sample. So we used 5 log files (close to 1250 sessions) as our representative sample. In order to take a representative sample for a year of log files (52 weeks, equivalent to 65000 sessions), considering the same 97.5% confidence, we would need 1500 sessions. Using 1250 sessions we have a confidence of 97.2% that this sample represents a year of data.

We only used sessions without attacks or anomalies. The rationale behind this is to select only n-grams that identify normal traffic and do not add noise to the intrusion detection process. The selected log files are the ones with less attack sessions, so after discarding attack or anomaly sessions we ended up with the highest possible number of sessions.

A BSM log file is composed of a set of sessions, each of which belongs to a given service. Moreover each session is formed by one or more processes. During our methodology we separated each of these sessions and concatenated all of its processes. Both the number of sessions and processes in each session are variable. By separating log files and ordering them by sessions, we extracted high occurrence frequency n-grams that are part only of a single session without overlapping contiguous sessions. From now on, we will refer to these ordered sessions as the training sessions.

We selected n-grams in two ways: i) extracting them from every available session; ii) extracting them from service specific sessions. Each log file contains a finite number of sessions, each of which belongs to a given service. Some services have a more representative body among the log files. Services with lower number of sessions have n-grams that reduce that service greatly. Since these n-grams have lower frequency than the n-grams of most common services they might get lost in the process. That is why we assigned a priority that uses the number of sessions a service belongs to instead of the total number sessions. In the following section, we will describe the entire selection and reduction process. In these processes we will describe the use of the above mentioned priority.

5   Session Folding Using N-Gram Models

This section aims to describe how we used the n-gram theory to achieve log file reduction through session folding. The reduction is two step procedure, the first step aims at selecting the n-grams with the highest repetition frequency and to attach their corresponding priority, we will call this process n-gram detection and tagging. The second step, is the actual reduction process which makes use of the tagged n-grams extracted in the first step for session folding. N-gram detection and tagging only needs to be performed once and can be done offline. Whereas the reduction is done in real time and for every session.

Following is a description of each step in the n-gram identification process: i) n-gram extraction; ii) n-gram frequency analysis and n-gram priority assignment. Later on we shall describe each step in the reduction process: i) n-gram comparison, aimed at avoiding overlapping; ii) subsequence substitution using a fresh tag.

Step 1 in the identification process is the language model creation process. Step 2 uses the frequency analysis from the language model for a priority assignment (both will be described below).

5.1   N-Gram Identification and Tagging

The first step toward session folding is to extract the n-grams with a higher occurrence frequency and occurrence probability, and then tag them with a priority. The priority is calculated using both a combination of services, and a service exclusive analysis.

N-Gram Extraction. N-Gram extraction consists of the application of a blind, exhaustive procedure. As a result, we obtained the n-grams that occur most frequently in the training sessions. Although in theory n-gram model creation should consider all possible n-grams, in practise only n-grams that exist within the training data are used. For example for a 10-gram with a vocabulary of 200 tokens, the possible number of sequences should be $200^{10} \times 199$. However, in our experiments, we found only 2291. N-Gram extraction prunes all sequences with 0 occurrences. For the final language model a low probability is assigned to pruned sequences. In our calculations, we considered the n-grams that were pruned from the entire log file as well as those pruned from different services within that file.

N-Gram Priority Assignment. Using the n-gram count and the language model, we identified the n-grams with a higher frequency or probability of occurrence. We considered n-grams of different sizes to find n-grams that provide a high reduction rate. If an n-gram is present in the training log files an occurrence frequency is assigned to it. If it is not present then an occurrence probability is assigned.

Using either the n-gram occurrence frequency or probability, we estimated a reduction ratio later used as a priority Pr for every n-gram that was found. The priority is used to select which n-gram to use first in the reduction process. Not only does this ratio consider large n-grams with a high frequency, but it also considers the total number of system calls N on the training sequence sessions from which the n-grams were extracted. We calculated a reduction percentage for every selected n-gram, i.e. how much will a given n-gram reduce a log file.

If we use n-gram occurrence frequency f the n-gram priority Pr is calculated by:

$$Pr = \frac{n \times (f+1)}{N} \qquad (2)$$

By contrast if we use n-gram occurrence probability P the n-gram priority Pr is calculated by:

$$Pr = P \times n \qquad (3)$$

In both cases n is the size of the n-gram. Both equations provide a reduction ratio for the input n-gram. Using Pr we choose the sequences that provide a high reduction rate. Our n-gram selection criterion is divided in two: selection of n-grams with high Pr at log file level, and n-grams with high Pr at service level.

Service Exclusive N-Gram Selection and Priority Assignment. It is possible that a certain n-gram has a high ratio, i.e. in an `smtp` session; but `smtp` sessions are a small segment of an entire log file. This is because some services in the training log files have a less representative body than other services. This situation might exclude n-grams with low reduction ratio at log file level from the reduction set, even though the reduction ratio within a given service is high. The same analysis presented for n-gram priority assignment is done at service level and it is our second criterion for n-gram selection. Assigning a priority to an n-gram is not sufficient to avoid overlapping. Below we will show how we solved this problem.

5.2   Session Folding Using Tagged N-Grams

N-grams tend to overlap with each other, they might intersect at some point. To avoid overlapping when making an n-gram substitution we used a priority queue approach to select the n-gram to substitute. The queue was used to substitute high ratio n-grams. We created a window of size equal to the largest n-gram in the queue. Once the window is full, we tested its content against all n-grams in the queue. The order of the priority queue is given by the ratio defined in equations (2) and (3). By substituting n-grams with higher ratio we warranty that, even if there is an overlapping, only the n-grams that provide maximum reduction are used. Notice that by substituting an n-gram with a new symbol we are avoiding further substitution on that segment resulting in overlapping elimination. We avoid substitution because the newly added symbol is not present in any n-gram used in the substitution.

Log file reduction using n-grams is accomplished by n-gram substitution at session level. In n-gram model creation, overlapping is not considered, but only conditional probability. We need to take the concept even further and include Pr as a reduction measure. Whenever a high priority n-gram is found, it is replaced by a fresh symbol that substitutes the entire n-gram. The first time we use an n-gram, a new symbol is created and added to the symbol dictionary. In the next section we will show how this methodology is applied to session folding and the subsequent reduction.

6   The Methodology in Action

We will provide evidence that as a result of applying our methodology, we obtained a large reduction ratio using a small number of n-grams. For the experiments reported in this paper we used the CMU-Cambridge Statistical Language

Modelling Toolkit [17]. The toolkit provides a series of UNIX tools that facilitate language modelling. Each of the steps required for n-gram substitution and log file reduction is described below.

6.1 N-Gram Extraction

By using the CMU toolkit we extracted the n-grams and the associated frequency. The analysis was made for each log file and also for each service. The results of such an analysis are presented in histograms shown in figure 1 where the first figure corresponds to an all services histogram and the second to a `telnet` histogram. Here, histogram's axises are shown as a right hand coordinate system. The x axis represents the n-grams size. The z axis represents the frequency f for that given n-gram. The y axis is the number of different n-grams of size n with frequency f.

The histograms are used to analyse the amount of n-grams that have a number of repetitions similar to a multiple of the number of different sessions included in the training data. If there are m sessions and the frequency of an n-gram is a multiple of m, then that n-gram is more likely to be common among every session. That is, we prefer n-grams that are repeated in a large number of sessions over n-grams that repeated many times in a couple of sessions. The former are more general n-grams and therefore provide a better reduction ratio for unseen sessions. The same histograms can be used to know in advance, how many n-grams to look for when making the frequency based selection. In what follows we will see such frequency analysis and priority assignment.

6.2 N-Gram Tagging

Based on the occurrence frequency analysis we identified the n-grams with a desired number of repetitions. This analysis makes the extraction of such n-grams much easier and faster. From the extraction we chose 100 n-grams for the reduction. These n-grams are mostly the ones whose occurrence frequency is close to a multiple of the number of sessions. Also, based on the language model probabilities we selected about 50 n-grams with a probability of occurrence above 98%.

We also extracted 50 different n-grams using the analysis over separate services. Selected n-grams have an occurrence frequency similar to a multiple of the number of sessions for that service. This means that such n-grams are common to many sessions of that service. All these n-grams have an associated occurrence count, and the total number of system calls present in the original log file. The n-gram set used in the folding process and the dictionary are available at our web site[1]. Along with the size of the n-grams, the number of system calls will define the reduction ratio. After extracting n-grams for every log file (both all sessions and service separated) a language model is generated. We need to

---

[1] http://webdia.cem.itesm.mx/ac/raulm/ids

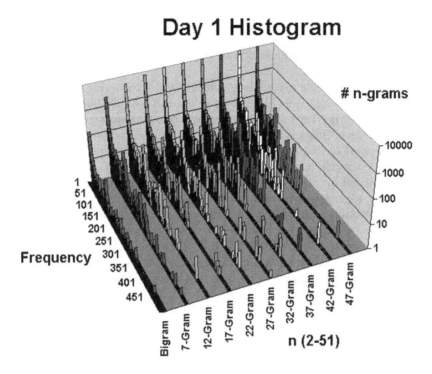

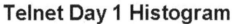

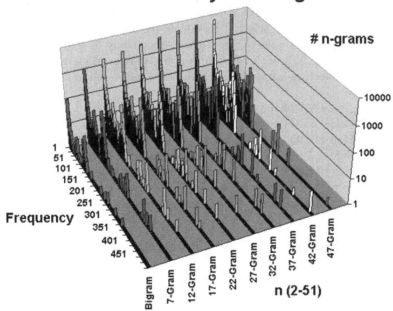

Fig. 1. Mixed Services and Telnet Histograms

explain the selection of the *discounting strategy*. The one provided with the software we used is the good-Turing estimator. N-gram theory is a great method to avoid elimination of unseen n-grams without imposing considerable probability reduction of existing n-grams.

The main overhead of using n-gram language models for reduction is the space required to hold a language model file. For a log file with $800,000$ objects of size 17Mb, a file of 5Mb is needed to hold n-gram occurrence frequency and about 1Gb to hold the language model. The language model and an n-gram occurrence frequency file are used to extract key n-grams. Fortunately, the language model and the frequency file are temporal, as they are eliminated after key n-gram extraction. The format for the language model is described in [17].

After selecting n-grams with high occurrence frequency or probability we calculated the reduction ratio. The reduction ratio will sort selected n-grams in a priority queue for subsequent replacement of such n-grams in the log files. Using the priority queue we substitute, or fold, a given session. Prior to the substitution we load any abbreviation dictionary that we have previously used in order to avoid repetitive abbreviations in sub-sequent reductions. The priority queue is then used to avoid overlapping.

6.3   Session Folding

With the use of the dictionary we selected the next abbreviation that will be used in the folding process. An abbreviation is only generated when an n-gram is used in a substitution, not all n-grams will be assigned an abbreviation. For example from the 100 n-grams selected based on occurrence frequency, only 11 were really used. From the 50 selected based on occurrence probability, only 5 were used and from the 50 selected from each service only 3 were used. This means that about 89% to 93% of the selected n-grams were overlapping. Selected n-grams do not intersect, so after the analysis, subsequent reductions did not consider a priority.

Even by using only 9% of the selected n-grams, we obtained a reduction of 65% in the worst case and a reduction of 82% in the best case. We obtained an average reduction of 74%. This reduction was tested using the n-gram set generated from the first 5 BSM log files to reduce another set of 5 BSM log files. The result is a set of 19 n-grams that provide an average reduction rate of 74%. In the next section we will provide an insight of the experiments we conducted to test our reduction method and the data involved in our experiments.

7   Validation Experiments and Data Selection

To test the reduction capabilities of our method we chose to reduce log files from the 1998 and 1999 DARPA repositories using extracted n-grams from the 1998 repository. By using to different years of log files we aim at showing the generality of our reduction method. As we will see, the results are pretty similar between reductions for each year. This is proof that changes in user activity is not a critical factor for our reduction method. We specifically used the 5 log files used for n-gram selection plus another 5 logs from 1998 and 5 more from 1999. This is a total of 15 log files out of 40. As described in Section 4, this gives us a confidence of 98.8%. The data used in the validation process includes attack and anomaly sessions. The validation procedure is straight-forward, we use the extracted and tagged n-grams, and then apply the reduction methodology to avoid overlapping.

Nonetheless, we still need to prove that our reduction method keeps the information necessary to discern between two events regardless the reduction. To prove this, we compared the service selection results described in [4] using folded sessions against the results of unfolded sessions. We also used this comparison to show the HMM training time difference between folded and unfolded sessions. Another test is to compare the results of using our IDS with mimicry attacks over folded and unfolded sessions. In the next section we present the results of applying the above mentioned experiments.

8   Validation Results

In this section we will explain how the resulting set of n-grams was validated. The validation is performed by means of a reduction of unseen sessions.

Extracted n-grams provide an average reduction of 74% within the training sessions. We also used the n-grams to reduce unseen sessions from 5 different log files from the 1998 repository, and 5 from 1999. As input we have an unseen log file and as output we provide the reduced log file. In tables 1, and 2, we show the reduction ratio over the validation data of 1998 and 1999 respectively (we will

Table 1. Validation Results, 1998 Log Files

Log File ID	Original Object #	Compressed Object #	Reduction %	Used N-grams
1	776,000	270,000	65.3%	7
2	1,800,000	486,000	73%	12
3	1,150,000	344,000	70.1%	5
4	801,000	175,000	78.2%	9
5	1,158,000	392,000	66.2%	5
telnet	209,000	48,000	77.1%	5

Table 2. Validation Results, 1999 Log Files

Log File	Original Object #	Compressed Object #	Reduction %	Used N-grams
1	820,855	248,719	69.7%	9
2	490,896	142,360	71%	8
3	630,457	198,594	68.5%	7
4	520,358	139,456	73.2%	11
5	220,658	52,296	76.3%	13

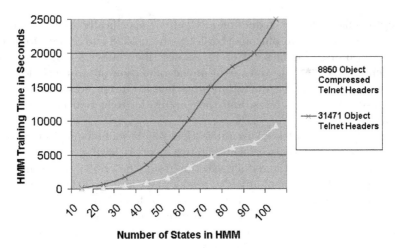

Fig. 2. Telnet Service HMM Training Times, Unfolded Sessions vs. Folded Sessions

only show results for unseen data). The table columns are: log file ID, original number of system calls, compressed number of system calls, and number of n-grams used in the reduction. Last row of the table shows the results of applying the reduction to a file with only `telnet` sessions. By training the HMMs we can validate the impact of our methodology in training times. As we expected training time is significantly reduced by using folded sessions. The reason for time reduction is that the order of the HMMs training algorithm is $O(n^2 l)$, where n is the number of states in the HMM, and l is length of the training sequence. In figure 2 we show training times for the HMMs presented in [4]. In each figure, training times for unfolded sessions and its folded counterpart are contrasted. Also in table 3 we show the comparative results for service selection using folded and unfolded sessions. The first column in the table indicates the service discriminator used. The first row indicates to which service a session belongs to. The table should be read as: the percentage of sessions of service n (first row) classified as service m (first column). The first percentage of each cell corresponds to unfolded sessions and the second result corresponds to folded sessions. The service selection process is explained in [4]. We can see from this table that not only does session folding keeps discernibility information, but it also reduces the number of false positives. The false positive reduction for intrusion detection will be explored in the next section.

Table 3. % of Correct Service Discrimination, Folded vs. Unfolded Sessions

HMMs	`telnet` headers	`smtp` headers	`ftp` headers	`finger` headers
`telnet`	100% vs. 100%	2% vs. 1.8%	1% vs. 1%	0% vs. 0%
`smtp`	1% vs. 0.8%	100% vs. 100%	2% vs. 1.6%	0% vs. 0%
`ftp`	0% vs. 0%	1% vs. 0.7%	100% vs. 100%	0% vs. 0%
`finger`	0% vs. 0%	0% vs. 0%	0% vs. 0%	100% vs. 100%

9   Reduction Impact on Intrusion Detection

One of the major hypothesis to be tested in this thesis states that shrinking the information to be analysed does not get in the way to intrusion detection. This section aims to show that using n-gram reduction allows us to use HMMs with larger sequences than the ones proposed in previous works, such as [1, 2, 18]. HMMs take a large amount of time for training. Wagner, in [19], also describes the disadvantages of using only short sequences as the detection base using HMMs. We used entire sessions containing the attacks for both, our training and testing data. We used a single word network for each attack.

We used 20 instances of each attack to train the HMMs. The tests were conducted against entire sessions of different services, in this case we used folded sessions. Again, we tested against 800 `telnet`, 1000 `smtp`, 50 `ftp` and 150 `finger` sessions.

9.1   Detection Results

By using reduced session we obtained a 98% detection ratio and the false positives were 23 out of 200 detected attacks. With a higher similarity measure, 95%, false positives lowered from 23 to 14 and the detection ratio also lowered but only to 94%. We tested the same attacks for both scenarios. The difference in false positives was found in short attacks as `eject`. Most of the false positives were normal sessions labelled as one of these short attacks. Nevertheless, higher detection ratio is present in variations of these same short attacks. We have successfully detected a significant subclass of general case mimicry attacks which is a great breakthrough since no other research has done anything similar.

For all our experiments we used the "Hidden Markov Model Toolkit (HTK)". The software allows for large HMMs to be used and it also has the ability to use word networks. The software and its documentation can be found at `http://htk.eng.cam.ac.uk/`. We now present the conclusions that we have drawn from our experiments.

10   Conclusions

Based on our results we conclude that we successfully reduced the number of objects in a log file with nearly no impact for intrusion detection. By identifying a small number of key n-grams we reduced BSM log files by a factor of 4. The number of key n-grams is small enough not to increase considerably the vocabulary of system calls. An increase in the vocabulary would impact on the training time of a method such as HMM. Our method allowed us to find a small number of n-grams that provide a large reduction. This reduction ratio is comparable to the ones proposed by rival techniques and even better in most cases. Moreover, our reduction method is capable of returning to the original set of system calls. By contrast, rival techniques are incapable of reverting the reduction process as discussed in section 2.

We also trained some HMMs with unfolded sessions and with folded session, and the difference in training times between them is a considerable improvement. That way we proved that using longer sequences to train HMMs is convenient. In section 9 we showed how folded sessions are equally useful, in some cases better, than unfolded sessions for intrusion detection.

References

1. Warrender, C., Forrest, S., Pearlmutter, B.: Detecting Intrusions Using System Calls: Alternative Data Models. In: Proceedings of the 1999 IEEE Symposium on Security and Privacy, IEEE Computer Society Press (1999) 133–145
2. Yeung, D., Ding, Y.: Host-Based Intrusion Detection Using Dynamic and Static Behavioral Models. Pattern Recognition **Vol. 36** (2003) pp. 229–243
3. Godínez, F., Hutter, D., Monroy, R.: Attribute Reduction for Effective Intrusion Detection. In Favela, J., Menasalvas, E., Chávez, E., eds.: Proceedings of the 2004 Atlantic Web Intelligence Conference, AWIC'04. Number 3034 in Lecture Notes in Artificial Intelligence, Springer-Verlag (2004) 74–83
4. Godínez, F., Hutter, D., Monroy, R.: Service Discrimination and Audit File Reduction for Effective Intrusion Detection. In: Proceedings of the 2004 Workshop on Information Security Applications, WISA'04. Number 3325 in Lecture Notes in Computer Science, Springer-Verlag (2004) 101–115
5. Forrest, S., Hofmeyr, S., Somayaji, A., Longstaff, T.: A Sense of Self for Unix Processes. In: Proceedings of the 1996 IEEE Symposium on Security and Privacy, Los Alamitos, CA, IEEE Computer Society Press (1996) 120–128
6. Maxion, R.A., Tan, K.M.C.: Anomaly Detection in Embedded Systems. IEEE Transactions on Computers **51** (2002) 108–120
7. Maxion, R.A., Tan, K.M.C.: Benchmarking Anomaly-Based Detection Systems. In: Proceedings of the 1st International Conference on Dependable Systems and Networks, New York, New York, USA, IEEE Computer Society Press (2000) 623–630
8. Marceau, C.: Characterizing the Behavior of a Program Using Multiple-Length N-grams. In: Proceedings of the 2000 Workshop on New Security Paradigms, ACM Press (2000) 101–110
9. Wespi, A., Dacier, M., Debar, H.: An Intrusion-Detection System Based on the Teiresias Pattern-Discovery Algorithm. In Gattiker, U.E., Pedersen, P., Petersen, K., eds.: Proceedings of EICAR '99. (1999)
10. Marin, J.A., Ragsdale, D., Surdu, J.: A Hybrid Approach to Profile Creation and Intrusion Detection. In: Proc. of DARPA Information Survivability Conference and Exposition, IEEE Computer Society (2001)
11. Lane, T., Brodley, C.E.: Temporal Sequence Learning and Data Reduction for Anomaly Detection. ACM Transactions on Information and System Security **2** (1999) 295–331
12. Lane, T., Brodley, C.E.: Data Reduction Techniques for Instance-Based Learning from Human/Computer Interface Data. In: Proceedings of the 17th International Conference on Machine Learning, Morgan Kaufmann (2000) 519–526
13. Knop, M.W., Schopf, J.M., Dinda, P.A.: Windows Performance Monitoring and Data Reduction Using WatchTower and Argus. Technical Report Technical Report NWU-CS-01-6, Department of Computer Science, Northwestern University (2001)
14. Rencher, A.: Methods in Multivariate Analysis. Wiley & Sons, New York (1995)

15. Krogh, A., Brown, M., Mian, I.S., Sjölander, K., Haussler, D.: Hidden Markov Models in Computational Biology: Applications to Protein Modeling. Journal Molecular Biology **235** (1994) 1501–1531
16. Hughey, R., Krogh, A.: Hidden Markov Models for Sequence Analysis: Extension and Analysis of Basic Method. Comp. Appl. BioSci **12** (1996) 95–108
17. Young, S., Evermann, G., Kershaw, D., Moore, G., Odell, J., Ollason, D., Povey, D., Valtchev, V., Woodland, P.: The HTK Book for HTK Version 3.2. Cambridge University Engineering Department (2002)
18. Qiao, Y., Xin, X., Bin, Y., Ge, S.: Anomaly Intrusion Detection Method Based on HMM. Electronic Letters **38** (2002) 663–664
19. Wagner, D., Soto, P.: Mimicry Attacks on Host Based Intrusion Detection Systems. In: Proceedings of the Ninth ACM Conference on Computer and Communications Security, Washington, DC, USA, ACM (2002) 255–265

A Hybrid Framework of RR Scheduler
to Ensure Priority, Low Complexity and Delay
with Relative Fairness

John Tsiligaridis[1] and Raj Acharya[2]

[1] Math and Computer Science, Heritage University,
3240 Fort Road Toppenish, WA, 98948, USA
`tsiligaridis_j@heritage.edu`
[2] Computer Science and Engineering, Penn. State University, 220 Pond Lab.,
University Park, PA 16802-6106, USA
`acharya@cse.psu.edu`

Abstract. In order to manage fairly the service of the queueing elements, the support of QoS with a sophisticated packet scheduling algorithms that is a part of the Fair Queuing family can be considered as essential. Two are the main parts that this work focuses; First, the Palindromic Motion (PM) algorithm that works as a timestamp (or sorted priority) scheduler keeping the flow service priority and second, the two backup flexible credit methods for adjustment of the weight which are used instead of the fixed credit method with a lower maximum weight. A feedback mechanism is used for adjusting the weight size considering the current packet size. The provisional increase of the weight is proposed by the two backup methods; the Direct Increase Weight (DIW) algorithm and the Compound Round Robin (CRR) algorithm. Advantages over recent schemes like Group Round Robin (GRR) etc are presented. Simulation experiments are provided.

1 Introduction

High speed networking offers opportunities for new applications that have stringent performance requirements in terms of throughput, delay, delay jitter and loss rate[1]. The conventional packet switching data networks with window based flow control and FCFS discipline cannot provide services with strict performance guarantee. Hence new rate based flow control and rate based service disciplines have been proposed for a connection oriented network architecture with resource allocation and admission control policies[2]. A rate based service is one that usually provides with a minimum service rate independent of the traffic characteristics of other clients.

There are two methods for packet scheduling: the sorted-priority (or timestamp-based) and frame-based [14]. According to the first method each packet is assigned a priority value and is transmitted at an increasing order of their priority. Examples of sorted-priority schemes are Waited Fair Queueing (WFQ), WF2Q (closely to the FFQ)[3], Virtual Clock (VC) [4], Self-Clock Fair Queuing (SCFQ) [5], Leap Forward Virtual Clock (LFVC) [6] and Start Fair Queueing [7]. In general the timestamp schedulers have good delay properties, but they suffer from a sorting bottleneck that results in a time complexity of O(log(N)) per packet. Many of them use virtual times for finding the next servicing packet (WFQ, WF2Q etc) which costs end to end delay and time complexity. Particularly the Leap Forward Virtual Clock attempts to address the sorting problem by the use of a complicated data structure (tree) which is not

F.F. Ramos et al. (Eds.): ISSADS 2005, LNCS 3563, pp. 98–117, 2005.
© Springer-Verlag Berlin Heidelberg 2005

appropriate for hardware implementation. The timestamp schedulers, although they have good fairness and delay properties they have high computational cost and high (time) complexity, that prevents them from being used in practice. The computational complexity, associated with the evaluation of virtual times, is not feasible in a broad-band high speed network.

In the frame–based (or round-robin) approach, time is divided into frames and packets are entered into a frame. Example of this method is the Deficit Round Robin (DRR)[8]. This method is very scalable because the time complexity is only $O(1)$ in contrast to the sorted-priority schemes that require a sorting operation in order a new packet to be inserted.

Our approach works on both kinds of schedulers. The first part provides a kind of timestamp scheduler (the PM) that ensures the priority of the flows while the second one, which belongs to the round robin scheduler, provides a feedback mechanism (DIW, CRR) that guarantees the service of large packets with less service delay.

As far as the first part is concerned, two are the components that costs for the implementation of the Packet Fair Queueing (PFQ) algorithms that have been proposed to approximate the GPS. First is the computation time of the system using virtual time and second is to maintain the relative ordering of the packets using their timestamps in a priority queue mechanism [10].

Many proposed algorithms reduce the complexity of the computation of the system virtual times but the complexity of maintaining the priority queue and therefore the total implementation complexity of PFQ *still remains depending on the number of active sessions.* A number of algorithms have been developed giving virtual time function with complexity $O(1)$ or $O(logN)$. The work of many sorted-priority servers is based on finding the virtual finishing times from the arrival packet (WFQ, WF$_2$Q). The phase of *updating the sorted list* remains and the service of the packets is held according to the increasing order of their virtual finishing times. As to today, no great attention is paid by the current literature to the significance of the sorting operation.

Regarding the rate servers, keeping the fairness in the allocation of resources among the users, is essential. A systematic approach of the *weight sufficiency problem* is much more preferable than the continuous and endless change of the credits' amount in every round as it happens in the Deficit Round Robin (DRR). It is interesting to develop an *adaptively adjustment credit scheme* instead of a fixed weight scheme.

Quite often a fixed-credit scheme using a lower maximum (for some flows), does not perform as well as the flexible variable credit scheme. Many algorithms have been developed *making assumptions on the packet's size* before beginning the transmission. In [8], the DRR clearly states that for having O[1] complexity, the quantum of each flow must be greater than the largest possible packet size. In some cases (1-packets arrival) the fixed value of the DRR weight is not sufficient to provide $O(1)$ complexity. Some of the probable reasons that make *the instantaneous increase of the weight* of a flow a necessity are:

*The short size of the Maximum Transfer Unit (MTU),*an algorithms is used in routers when an increase of weight is needed, to avoid the fragmentation of the segments given the short size of MTU [15]. *The violation of the Service level Agreement (SLA),* is usually the result of the internal conditions of the network, and not because of the particular bad source's behavior. *The Latency,* the service delay of some flows can cause further delay to all the other flows as well. For *the new services (or applications)* (like video on demand) an increase of the weight of the flow is probably needed so that the "empty rounds" are avoided. All the routers along a delivery chain must be able to support the desired type of QoS.

No references have been made in literature in respect of *the automatic variable adjustment of the weight* (if needed), while the scheduler is "on the fly". As to that, our variable and flexible proposed credit schemes succeed in eliminating the "empty rounds" (with instant increase of the bad flow's weight) and guarantee $O(1)$ complexity. When the DRR server remains *uninformed* (delay or lack of information) about the upcoming l-packets, then the service is not *effective, economical or functional* because the fixed value of quantum is too low to service them. Thus, a *re-adjustment* of the weight's size is needed for faster flow service.

Some *assumptions* on the *system design* and fairness are presented below so that the operation of the proposed algorithm cannot be blocked. A *predefined maximum weight* (p_weight) for each flow (not necessarily all equal) is considered but going beyond this limit is not allowed. The scheduler can cope *with all the flows asking simultaneously* to use the p_weight of each flow. The sum of credits assigned to all of the queues by adaptive schemes, should be fixed at a sum of T. *The necessary condition for servicing the l-packets is p_weight $\geq$ MSLP.* Short interval bad behaved flows are examined. Their time period is considered *abnormal*. A *new policy* for the *short interval bad behaved* flows is introduced here. Instead of punishing the flow in the next rounds (penalty solutions, as DRR,SRR provide), it is preferable *to increase the weight provisionally and diminish the service delay by speeding up the service.* The bad behavior of a flow in the *core routers* is frequent because of the internal conditions in the network. The *previously taken increased weight*, during the abnormal period of a flow, is finally shared proportionally with all the other well behaved flows. This can *guarantee the fairness* with all flows. A similar policy was proposed in wireless networks [9].

Based on the way the scheduler takes the additional (until p_weight) weight, the algorithms are; the Direct Increase Weight (DIW), and the Compound Round Robin (CRR). They are similar to the Elastic Round Robin (ERR) scheduler [14], because they can operate *without any assumption* on the maximum size of the packet. The DIW is *oriented to the MSLP*, while the CRR works *no matter* what the MSLP is. Because of this, the second scheme is more *flexible and scalable* to the size of the serviced packets. The scheduler works as a *controller (sensory);* after the l-packets' service is over (abnormal period), and the sequence of the l-packets' size follows the normal row, the flow takes the previous lower quantum size value again.

We present a novel system that reduces the overall complexity of implementing a class of PFQ algorithms. We use only a real clock. The PM using a numbering of the queues and the arrival time of any packet can find when the service will take place after its arrival. It consists of two parts. Firstly, the *scheduler table* where information for arrival packets is registered and secondly based on this information it finds when to begin the service of the next flow. Other data structures, like the calendar queue [11] do not provide the simplicity and the effectiveness of our solution since the initialization step and the dequeue operation are performed without overhands.

A framework is created by the PM and a DIW or CRR so that both kinds of schedulers can cooperate providing the Round Robin with service priority.

The rest of the paper is organized as follows: In Section 2 general issues, associated with special kind of recently proposed schedulers and their properties. In Section 3, and 4 the PM and the DIW with CRR are developed respectively. Simulation experiments are provided in Section 5.

2 Background

There are many scheduling algorithms related to various issues: fairness, intensive throughput, low delay, low complexity. The objective of the fairness of two flows is to ensure that $W_1(t_1,t_2)/r_1 - W_2(t_1,t_2)/r_2$ is as close to 0 as possible, where r_1 and r_2 are the service rates of the two flows. Many algorithms have been proposed in order to reduce the computational complexity of fair scheduling algorithm. According to the WF$_2$Q and SCFQ, packets are scheduled at an increasing order of the finish tags of the packets. The aim of fair is, if N channels share an output trunk they should get 1/N of the bandwidth. This work can be accomplished by doing a bit by bit round robin (BR) but this is not practical to be done. By servicing packets in the order of the finish numbers, it can be shown that Fair Queuing emulates BR [8].

Intuitive descriptions of some very known fair service disciplines which are packet approximation algorithms to the Generalized Processor Sharing (GPS) are presented at the following. The GPS is a general form of head of line processor sharing service discipline(PS). The Virtual Clock (VC) [4], the Weighted Fair Queueing (WFQ) [3], the WF$_2$Q (the continuity of the WFQ) [3], the SCFQ [5], the Start time Fair Queueing (SFQ) [7] are some of the approximations to the fluid GPS system.

More recently proposed schemes Stratified Round Robin (SRR) [17], Group Round Robin (GRR) [18], focus on the attempt to combine the two kinds of schedulers so that fairness and delay properties of timestamp schedulers along with the low complexity of round robin scheduler to be assured. This can be achieved by evolving a round robin scheme (like DRR) and incorporating some essential abilities of the timestamp scheduler.

Our proposed work follows this approach by the Palindromic Motion (PM) Algorithm. Additionally, two new round robin adaptively adjustment credit schemes, for servicing large size packets are provided.

In the Stratified Round Robin [17] the allocation of the slots is beyond the circular basis. The flows are stratified into classes according to their approximately equal weights. The first step (inter-class) scheduling chooses the next servicing class while the second step (intra-class) choose the flow of the selected class. The classification of the flows wastes time that might be critical for the service of some flows. On the other hand the idea of using approximately equal weight speeds up the service negatively affecting fairness especially when one flow approximates the weight value from a lower or upper value. Using more queues for the flows helps the discrimination of the service of any kind of service. The same comments make arise for the Group Round Robin (GRR) [18].

The Smoothed Round Robin (SRR) [19] with the Weight Matrix addresses the output burstiness problem of the DRR. Although the delay bounds of SRR are better than those of DRR, the worst case delay for a packet still remains log(N), N is the number of activated flows.

In Aliquem [20] an Active List queue holds the packets of flows that will be serviced next by finding the round at which a packet of a flow can be transferred. So Aliquem is suitable even for large size of packets' servicing avoiding the additional round time. For large size packets and when the quantum is insufficient to service a packet in a current round the queueing delay exists in their proposed circular array until the time the packet becomes feasible (to be serviced).

The proposed hybrid scheme consisting of a simple timestamp scheduler (Palindromic Motion -PM-) with the two flexible credit schemes the Direct Increasing Weight (DIW) and the Compound Round Robin (CRR) can guarantee both priority and low complexity with low queueing delay. First the PM defines the flow that will be serviced using the *jump* mechanism and then the DIW or CRR can be used for the large packets service.

3   Working with PM Algorithm

3.1   Implementation Complexity

For high speed networks the scheduling algorithms must be implemented in hardware.

In addition the time complexity is desirable to not depend on the number of the active connections in the scheduler. The are the main steps of the implementation of the sorted – priority category scheduler given that V is the maximum number of connections that may share the output link.

- calculation of the timestamps. The WFQ (or PGPS) has the greater complexity since GPS scheduler must be simulated in parallel in order to update the virtual time. This simulation may take $O(V)$ per packet transmissions in the worst case. In a worst case the Virtual Clock and Self-Clocked fair Queuing has $O(1)$ complexity since the time stamp calculation contains only a constant number of computations.
- insertion in a sorted priority list. The first packet of flow's queue must be stored in in a sorted priority list. This it takes $O(\log V)$ steps when a packet arrives into an empty queue.
- selection of a packet with the minimum timestamp in order to be transmitted.

The packet of a sorted priority list with the highest priority may be selected in $O(\log V)$ time.

The last two operations are the same for any sorted priority scheduler. Using our algorithm the work of this kind of scheduler is permitted only to the first operation.

On the other hand for the frame-priority schedulers the implementation time is only $O(1)$. Only the delay bounds may be increased linearly with the number of the connections.

3.2   The Description of the PM Algorithm

It is assumed that the arrival flows are accommodated in queues. The terms "queue", "line", "flow" are used with the same meaning in the text. We can discriminate two time cases for the arrival packets. One is the *ahead arrival* packets, when the value of the real time clock is less than the arrival time of the packets. The other case is the *previous arrival* packets, when the packets arrive during the service of the current packet. The proposed algorithm is activated for both cases. But for the second case in order to avoid the complication of finding when the scheduler will begin the service of other queue it can work only by using the *scheduler table*. The scheduler table is an array where the scheduler register the necessary information (# of queue, arrival time) of the next packet arrival if it belongs to defferent queue. This can be done by registering the information from the packets that are in HOL in each queue when they arrive in the system.

The time is considered in slots, and it works perfectly in ATM networks, where in each slot a packet (cell) is sent. The main point of the algorithm is to find, when it begin servicing the packet of other queue given its arrival time.

The lines with their sessions can be categorized in a similar way to [13] as follows: leading or header line, secondary, waiting, and satisfied. *Leading or header* line, is the h_i line at which a session arrives at time t and start being serviced. *Secondary* line is the s_i line that is activated later than time t starting its service even if the leading line's service has not completed yet and as a result, for some time then they are serviced simultaneously. *Waiting,* line is called the line at which a session arrives later than time t (in time t+), and keeps waiting for service. A line can be characterized as *satisfied,* when its session's service has been completed by time t.

At every session arrival, a new secondary line is established and starts being serviced.

All these secondary lines are projected to the heading one. When header line's service is completed the first secondary line takes its place and now it is named h_{i+1} while the next secondary line becomes first and all the others advance one step forward taking the place of the their preceding line.

The one change service sequence of the header lines in a sequence of secondary lines can be represented before the change as: $h_1 \mid s_1, s_2, s_3, \ldots, s_n$ and after the change, $s_1 ->h_2, s_2->s_1, \ldots s_n->s_{n-1}$ and finally $h_2 \mid s_1, s_2, s_3\ldots s_{n-1}$.

This process continues over and over until the end of all the lines' service.

Two moves of the scheduler, the *horizontal* and the *vertical* regulate the service of a packet. The horizontal move takes place when the service continues to the next packet of the same queue while the vertical move starts when the scheduler changes the serviced queue in order to serve another queue's packet or it jumps to an other queue. The *criterion* by which the scheduler determines the "time and place" that is, at what time and to which queue it is going to jump to, depends on the type of the scheduler algorithm requested. For the case of the Virtual Clock(VC) algorithm, that allows the scheduler skip to the next queue for service only if the header line's service is complete. The next queue for service is regulated by the arrival and finish time of the other sessions, which is the case, of the most of the known scheduling algorithms.

An array (ARR) is responsible to handle all the elements of the arrival of the packets at every queue. These elements are: the number of the queue, the time of the packet's, and the number of the packets. It is taken as an assumption that every flow corresponds to a queue. The algorithm focuses on the concepts of making the scheduler develop decisions, when gradually packets arrives in different queues, such as to start servicing the new coming packets of each queue by processing one by one the lines of the array moving along horizontal or vertical axis. When a session arrives or ends the service, a new line is added to or removed from the ARR respectively. Each time there are *active* and *non active* queues. The main body of PM has been distinguished from further changes that are considered for each type of known schedulers.

The pseudocode of the main algorithm is as follows:

```
The main algorithm steps:
    if (an arrival of a session of i flow exists)    {
            the elements of the session are entered in the array(ARR)
        the scheduler reads the first line of the ARR
            and services the arrival packet (i queue) }
    if (a packet of i flow has been serviced and
            the i session is not serviced)
        the scheduler is searching the ARR to discover
            probable arrivals in j <> i queue
    if (an arrival in j queue is located)
        then it changes the service queue,
                and j queue is now serviced (vertical move)
    else
            it continues servicing the i flow (horizontal move)
```

The scheduler makes horizontal (while servicing packets of the same line) and vertical (servicing packets of different lines) moves according to the especially requested algorithm that we want to produce without using the methodology of the virtual times for each case. It is not necessary the packets have the normal size but it is possible to have large size (l-packets). In each slot a packet is serviced independent of its size.

In order to determine the point at which the scheduler has to make the vertical moves, the point of line for change of service (PLCS) the following steps are followed:

```
The steps for taking vertical move:
  1.  the first arrival defines the header line (h) (from the scheduler table)
  2.  the second arrival defines the first secondary line (j)
  3.  take the difference of two successive arrival times: D_hj=AT(j)-AT(h)
  4.  if (D_hj >0) { //arrivals in various time
  4.     create the variable DF, where DF= D_hj + (#of active queues – 1)
  5.     NST(h)=AT(h)  // initial value
  6.     while (not end of service of all sessions) {
  7.        while (not end of header session)  {
  8.            NST(h)=NST(h) + ST(h)   // ST(h)= the service time of the header
  9.            if (AT(j) + DF = NST(h) + ST)  //the condition for vertical move
 10.                { we reached the point of change service line–PLCS-
 11.                service the new line
 12.                scheduler makes decision for the weight
 13.                    if (large size packet)
 14.                        select the proper algorithm (DIW, CRR)
 15             }
 16.        else
 17.           {continue working with the header line
 18.               until the condition 8 becomes valid} }
 19. header session = the first secondary session //the new header session } }
```

Some explanations of the PM are the following:

- We count the active flows beginning from the first service line (line 1)
- The variable DF represent the number of packets that are interjected between the first arrival packet of the header line and the first packet of the secondary one.
- The lines 12-14 include the case of *scheduler making decision*. The DIW or CRR are activated for the large size packets.

An illustrative example:

We consider the following schema:

#queue	arrival time	#packets
a	3	6
b	5	8
c	6	4

In the array we will have the lines:
Line (1): a, 3, 6
Line (2): b, 5, 8
Line (3): c, 6, 4

I

Analytically the schema for the three lines is:

```
0  1  2  3  4  5  6  7  8
.  .  .  x1 x2 x3 x4 x5 x6            (line 1)
.  .  .  .  .  y1 y2 y3 y4 y5 y6 y7 y8   (line 2)
.  .  .  .  .  .  v1 v2 v3 v4         (line 3)
```

The line 1 is the header line since the session $x1,...,x6$ came up first. At time 3,4,5: the scheduler service $x1,x2,x3$ packets respectively. At time 6, the scheduler *jumps* from the line 1 to line 2 in order to service the $y1$ packet. Then the line 2 becomes the first secondary queue while the header line is still the line 1. At time 6 we have vertical move, after servicing $x4$, $y2$. At time 7, the scheduler finds the second secondary queue (the line 3) and services the $v1$ packet. The other two lines continue to being serviced since they still have packets for service.

For finding the first point of line change service (PLCS) at the end of time 6, the algorithm works as follows:

- $D_{jh}=AT(j) - AT(h) = 5-3=2$
- Header line is the line 1
- $DF= 2 + (1-1)= 2$
- $NST(h)=AT(h)=3$, $ST(h)=1$
- while (not end of header session) {
    - $NST=NST + 1$; // $3+1=4$ ($x1$ service), $4+1=5$ ($x2$ service), $5+1=6$ ($x3$ service)
    - if ($5 + 2 = 6 + 1$)
        {change the service to line 2 for the $y1$, -1st vertical move-
        scheduler decision making for the weight
        probable use of DIW or CRR}

Here DF is for the line 2, equal to 2, because 2 packets the $x2,x3$ are interfered between $x1$, and $y1$ ($x1,x2,x3,y1$). For line 3, DF=4, because, 4 packets are interfered between $x1$, $v1$ ($x1,x2,x3,x4,y2,v1$).

We can take the same results if the header of the line is not in the first order queue. Due to limited space this case is not developed. Fig. 1 shows the proposed scheduler structure with the part of the decision making.

The STAB is updated either by the HOL packets from any queue when there is an arrival (2) or when a packet enters in any queue (1). After finishing the service of a

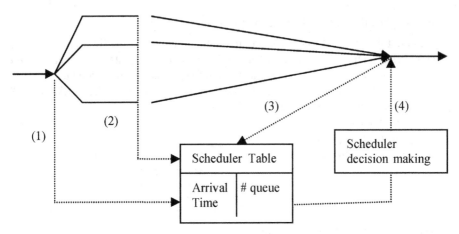

Fig. 1. The scheduler structure using the decision making operation

packet (or cell) the scheduler just goes through the table seeking for a new arrival (3). In order to diminish the number of accesses to the STAB, a variable can be updated so that it indicates whether a non activated queue's packet has arrived. The scheduler makes the decision for increase of weight and services the packet by line (4). In *STAB accepts registrations of new arrivals that do not belong to any currently activated line. The already activated lines are serviced in a RR manner.*

The PM helps the scheduler decide to which slot should make the next move (when to move), in order to service a new secondary line.

The scheduler table (STAB) is updated each time there is an arrival at any queue. Otherwise when a packet is entered in any queue it updates the scheduler table.

After finishing the service of a packet (or cell) the scheduler just checks the table for any arrival. The service is done line by line (FIFO).

It is apparent that in STAB only the new arrival is registered that belongs to a new no activated before line or to an old activated one. In addition, the up to date activated lines are serviced in a RR manner.

It is necessary to compare the *queueing delay* of packets of different queues in order to regulate their service. When there is a difference in the packet size of two queues a delay for the lower size packets can be noticed, due to the service of large packets. The service of the large sessions *burdens* the queuing delay of the normal size packets and this is not fair. Even though fair service of packets can be held in SFQ [7], where the service order of the packets is determined by the use of a sorting mechanism, a queueing delay for the small packets may still appear. The phenomenon of the *aggressive queueing delay* is developed by Lemmas. The Lemmas, and their proves are not included in the present work due to limited space. The service rates of the queues is supposed unchanged. Another method to avoid the queueing delay of the small packets is to *provisionally increase the weight*. The second part of this work is based on this work. Additionally, due to the limited space we can't eleborate with the PM support to the sorted-priority servers and especially to the SFQ [7], where the PM provides the same service order with SFQ, having O(1) complexity, instead of the O(logV).

3.3 Working like Frame-Based Server

The time is split into frames of maximum size F, a flow i is not allowed to send more than s_i packets during a frame period. This structure is like bin type storage [2]. The packets stored in the same bin are queued in a FIFO order and sent to the outgoing link by the scheduler

The difference from the RR service policy is that the service priority in PM is given *according to the header line*. The sooner the service begins for the burden (increasing delay) flow, the lower the queueing delay will be. The PM, using the scheduler table, can provide service priority by changing the *classical* service order of the RR server. Consequently, there is a difference in service order between PM and WRR, where the service order is stable. Thus, *the service order depends on time*. If the weight is insufficient then the DIW or CRR will be used.

Additionally, PM, can avoid the *"empty times"*, the time that the scheduler spends around the queues until finding a non empty one, by using the STAB information.

The delay analysis and the fairness of the PM can be distinguished into two service cases: the normal (no changes of the weight is needed) and abnormal (when an increase of the weight is needed). The abnormal case is developed in the 2nd part of the framework (the adaptive credit schemes). Here PM is restricted to the finding of the next service flow. Due to limited space we present only the PM delay analysis (normal case).

3.4 Delay Analysis (Normal Case)

Let us consider f_1, f_2, f_3 ... f_n the set of flows that are serviced by PM server, and where flow f i has a guaranteed rate of service r i bits/sec. It is evident that the sum of the rate of all flows sharing a link does not exceed the link capacity: $\sum_{i=1}^{n} r_i \leq B$, where B is the link capacity or the outgoing service rate. The sequence of c packets in a particular flow f is denoted by $p_{f,1}$, $p_{f,2}$, ..., $p_{f,c}$, and the size of them as $L_{f,1}$, $L_{f,2}$, ..., $L_{f,c}$.

For each flow a number of slots is devoted s_i. We split the time in frames and assume that F bits are transmitted during a frame period.

Let us consider that at all the n queues are backlogged and an arrival of the kth cell of the last order queue happens at time t. A frame period is T= F/B. During this period F bits will be transferred with the outgoing link.

The number of rounds that takes place until the service of the kth cell lets us be m.

For each round the number of slots that are occupied for cells of flow 1 are s_1, for the cells of flow 2 are s_2 and finally for the cell of flow n are s_n.

For the 1st round the slots that are used: $s_1 + s_2 +...+ s_n = \sum_{i=1}^{n} s_i$

This is repeated for at most m rounds (if in each round one packet is serviced).

So the delay for the kth cell $d(k) = m \sum_{i=1}^{n} s_i \leq m (F / r)$.

4 Working with Adaptive Credit Schemes

4.1 The Direct Increasing Weight (DIW) Algorithm

In order to keep the DRR service discipline [8] and to minimize the overhead of taking and returning the additional bandwidth, we have to retain the following *basic service* statement, for every round: $rem_{r,i}$ + weight $\geq$ l-packet-size   (1)

The remainder of the previous round plus the weight must exceed the size of the l_packet. For the $rem_{r,i}$, the subscripts r and i stands for the remainder at the end of the r round, and the number of the flow respectively. If (1) is not valid the weight should be increased so that the l-packet will be serviced in the *current* round.

Two subcases for the direct increase of the weight (DIW) are presented; the DIW1 where the increased weight take the *complete value* (weight + MSLP) and the DIW2 where the increased value is *the remainder, (rem_p_weight) until p_weight*, (p_weight = MSLP).

There are two states depending on the weight in use for each flow; the *enlarged* and the *diminished* one. Two bounds of the receiving weight are defined: d_{min} (minimum) and d_{max} (maximum), according to the size of the serviced packets. For the diminished (normal) state, we have the same value for both weight bounds, low and high ($d_{max}=d_{min}$). On the other hand, for the enlarged (abnormal) state, we have the maximum value of the weight d_{max}. We define *shell* or $dif = d_{max} - d_{min}$. The DIW2 works like the DIW1. For the DIW1 and the DIW2 when the l-packets are found, the scheduler takes the shell or rem_p_weight respectively, For the normal size packets the scheduler just returns to the initial state *(controller or sensory behavior)*.

4.2 The Compound Round Robin Algorithm (CRR)

The Compound Round Robin (CRR) algorithm has taken its name from the compound of the two kinds of operating phases. In the *recognition* phase, the scheduler gradually increases the weight (DW) and tries to reach its final size, in order to secure the service of the next round no matter what the size of the next packet will be. We can say that it tries to take the MSLP value. The WFA is used to increase the weight. In the *working* phase, the scheduler works without any change of the weight. It is absolutely certain that the length of the weight is greater than any packet size, and there is always a remainder of weight for the next round. It is possible to define the CRR upper bound, setting its value to the same as the DIW bound.

```
The CRR psedocode:
DW=0; NW=weight //initial value
do {
    if ( weight< packets´ size)
        {
        DW=packets´ size – weight  //increase weight' size
        NW=NW + DW
        }
    }
while (NW≤dmax)
```

The maximum value of NW can be less or equal to the maximum value of the weight of the DIW (p_weight).

4.3 Some Analytical Results

A scheduler is considered as *efficient*, only if the whole work complexity for enqueue-ing and dequeing is $O(1)$ for each packet. The work complexity of a packet is $O(1)$ only if it is certain that *at least* one packet for each flow is served within a round. In order the work complexity per packet of the DRR to be $O(1)$, we have to be sure that the quantum value is larger or equal to the size of the maximum size packet [3]. In case that, *no* packet of n flows, located at the head of each queue, can be serviced, because the quantum value with the previous round's remainder are less than the packet size, then the complexity is $O(n)$. Therefore, the scheduler must be *aware* of the maximum size of the servicing packet, in order to obtain $O(1)$ complexity. The Surplus RR (SRR) works like the DRR and penalizes the flow that overdraws its account, in the next round.

Definition: We call *round coefficient (rc)*, the ratio of the number of served flows over the total number of flows.

The limits of the rc are: $0 \leq rc \leq 1$. When rc=1, the complexity of the scheduler is $O(1)$. If rc=0, which means that no packet can be served in a round, the complexity is $O(n)$. On the other hand, if $0 < rc < 1$, some flows may be serviced in the round, but not all of them. As mentioned before, for each algorithm, *the increase of the weight is only held in the current round*, where the remainder of the previous round plus the weight is less than the packets' size at the head of the queue (like ERR). Conse-quently, when rc=1 for *all* the proposed algorithms. ased on this fact it is guaranteed that the HOL packet is going to be serviced during the current round independently of its size.

Two are the *main operations* of our scheduler. The *enqueue* and the *dequeue*. In the first operation the packets are put in a flow, while in the second one packets at the head of each flow are serviced according to the proposed algorithms. In addition an *ActiveList* holds the flows that are active.

Theorem 1. All the proposed algorithms are $O(1)$ complexity.

Proof. We have to confirm that the enqueuing and dequeuing operations are held within a constant period of time for each flow. For the enqueuing process it takes $O(1)$. First, the new packet is inserted in the appropriate flow and if the flow id is not in the ActiveList, the flow is added to it. The addition of a packet to the end of a linked list takes $O(1)$ operation. For the dequeuing process the scheduler determines which flow is going to be serviced next, removes this flow from the head of the Ac-tiveList and adds it back at the tail, and finally updates the remainder and the ask variables with the unused and the additional amount of bandwidth in the current round ,respectively. The above described procedures are held at a constant period of time ($O(1)$ complexity), because all of them represent a constant number of operations. The case that the scheduler does not service packets from all flows in a round *be-comes impossible*. This is due to the fact that the DIW and the CRR increase the weight either directly or gradually (in definite steps), up to the maximum permitted value(p_weight).   ∎

Lemma 1. When the length of the l-packets increases, the corresponding remainder decreases (assuming the weight unchanged).

Proof. In order for all the algorithms to work without any weight increase; the following *basic condition* must be satisfied:

rem $_{r,I}$ + new weight (or weight) $\geq$ length of a l-packet
   or   the equation

rem $_{r,I}$ + new weight (or weight) = length of a l-packet

$$+ \text{ rem }_{r+1,i} \qquad (2)$$

Let's assume an increasing sequence of l-packets ($lp_1 < lp_2 < ... < lp_n$) and $lp_1 >$ weight. We have the following, according to (2):

rem $_{1,i}$ + weight = lp_1 + rem $_{2,i}$

   since: $lp_1 >$ weight => rem $_{1,I} <$ rem $_{2,i}$

......

rem $_{n,i}$ + weight = lp_n + rem $_{n+1,i}$

   and finally rem $_{n,I} <$ rem $_{n+1,i}$

As a result, if the sequence of l-packets is increasing, we receive decreasing sequence of remainders up to zero. Thus, the scheduler has to increase the weight.   ∎

Lemma 2. Let us consider the special case of an increasing sequence of l-packets, (interrupted or not by either another small packet - s-packet - or a sequence of them) and finally followed by the longer l-packet (with the size of MSLP). The service of the MSLP will be realized in the next round, *without any increase of the weight value* (assuming that the weight increases like in CRR).

Proof. We suppose that we have a sequence of increasing l-packets (s1) and a sequence (s2) of small packets followed by the l-packet (MSLP size). In s1, the scheduler increases the weight by the additional bandwidth needed for the l-packets' service. In s2, the scheduler creates remainders of weight while it gets occupied with servicing s-packets followed by an l-packet that is not serviced in the current round. However, there is a possibility that only a part of the weight will be needed for the service the longer l-packet (MSLP size), while the rest will be covered by the remainder. We symbolize: by ask_i the scheduler's request for additional bytes to service the l-packet at the i round, by lp_i the i l-packet, by $weight_i$ the weight of a flow after the i round.

For s1: $weight_0 + ask_0 = lp_1$ $weight_1 = weight_0 + ask_0$ (the new weight)

       .....

       $weight_{n-1} + ask_{n-1} = lp_n$ $weight_n = weight_{n-1} + ask_{n-1}$ (the last weight)

For s2: Final created weight: $weight_n =$ s-packet (s) + rem$_{n,i}$ (3)

This means that the $weight_n$ covers the s-packet(s) and has a remainder: rem$_{n,i}$ resulting from the *unserviced* MSLP in the n round. For the next round (n+1), if $weight_n +$ rem$_{n,i} \geq$ MSLP, the MSLP can be serviced, without any increase of the weight.

Under these conditions, *it is not necessary* for the weight to increase further, when the scheduler meets the MSLP. From this Lemma *first we have to examine if the new created weight (by the CRR) is sufficient to service the MSLP packet* in the next round without any further increase. The new weight has the *autocovering* attribute.   ∎

Example: We consider the simple case of 2 packets in a queue with sizes: spacket=10 and a l-packet with MSLP=40, $weight_n$ = 29. From (3) we find: rem $_{1,i}$ = $weight_n$ (29) - s-packet (10) = 19 (29-10). For the next round we have: rem $_{1,i}$ + $weight_n$ = 19 + 29 = 48 > 40. Consequently, in the next round the MSLP will be serviced without any increase of the weight.

4.4 Fairness

For the fairness measure (FM), we follow the idea of Golestani [10].The worst case difference for the normalized service received by two different backlogged flows at any time interval, is examined. The fairness of the i and j flows, in an interval (t_1, t_2) is defined as the difference between the number of sent packets: $sent_i(t_1, t_2) / f_i - sent_j(t_1, t_2) / f_j$, where f_i, f_j are the share of the i and j flow respectively. For the service discipline of the ideal fluid-flow model, offering small increments of service, the FM becomes zero. We found that DIW2 and CRR have the same relative fairness with DRR. Examining the fairness, we can distinguish *three cases* based on whether a flow is backlogged with one of our algorithms or remains with unchanged weight (DRR):

– Both flows with unchanged quanta, both DRR service discipline *(Case 1)*.
– Both flows with changed quanta (proposed service discipline is used) *(Case 2)*.
– A flow with increasing quantum and the other unchanged quantum (DRR) *(Case 3)*.

Case 1: It is evident that for the first case, the size of the packets is uniformly distributed in the queues and the FM has been found for the DRR in [3] as follows:

$$sent_i(t_1, t_2) / f_i - sent_j(t_1, t_2) / f_j \leq weight_i + MSLP_i / f_i + MSLP_j / f_j \leq 3M.$$

Here, M is the maximum size of all the packets that are being served in any flow.

Case 2: An increasing policy with DIW2.(The DIW1 can be developed similarly by using $p\_weight_i = weight_i + MSLP_i$) and $rem_{k,i} \leq weight_i + MSLP_i$)

Lemma 6. Let us consider an interval (t_1, t_2) during which flows i and j are backlogged. For the i flow, after k rounds, for the DIW2 policy we have:

$$(k-1)*MSLP_i / f_i \leq sent_i(t_1, t_2) \leq (k+1)*MSLP_i / f_i$$

Proof. We consider two queues with the DIW2 service discipline.
For k rounds, the flow i during this interval, the number of bytes that will be served is $k*$ weight. $Serv_{k,i}$ is the number of serviced packet during the defined interval. Until the k round, we can take:

$$serv_{1,i} = weight_{1,i} + rem_{0,i} - rem_{1,i}$$
$$serv_{2,i} = weight_{2,i} + rem_{1,i} - rem_{2,i}$$
$$.....$$
$$serv_{k,i} = weight_{k,i} + rem_{k,i} - rem_{k,i}$$

Adding all the equations and considering that $all\_serv_{k,I} = \sum_{j=1}^{k} serv_{j,i}$ we can take:

$$all\_serv_{k,i} = \sum_{j=1}^{k} weight_{j,I} + rem_{0,i} - rem_{k,i} \qquad (4)$$

We consider that $\forall\ k \in S$, where S is the set of the rounds, $weight_{k,i} \leq p\_weight_i$ (5) the maximum permitted value of the weight for i flow).

For the DIW2, it is apparent that: $p\_weight_i = MSLP_i$ ($p\_weight_i = weight_i + MSLP_i$. can be used for DIW1). We also consider that: $minwei = min\ (weight_i)$ and f_i stands for the share for the i flow. Consequently, $f_i = weight_i / minwei$.

Using (4) and (5): $all\_serv_{k,i} = k* p\_weight_i + rem_{0,i} - rem_{k,i}$

$$\leq k*(MSLP_i) + rem_{0,i} - rem_{k,i}$$

$$\leq k*(MSLP_i) + rem_{0,i}. \qquad (6)$$

Since $rem_{k,i}$ is not negative for all the k values, and $\leq MSLP_i$ we get:

$$all\_serv_{k,i} \leq k* (\ MSLP_i) + (\ MSLP_i\ ).$$

We consider: $sent_i(t_1, t_2) = all\_serv_{k,i}$

Divided by f_i ,we have:

$$sent_i(t_1, t_2) / f_i \leq k* MSLP_i / f_i + MSLP_i / f_i$$

$$= k*MSLP_i / f_i + MSLP_i / f_i$$

$$= (k+1)*MSLP_i / f_i \qquad (7)$$

From (6): $all\_serv_{k,i} = k* p\_weight_i + rem_{0,i} - rem_{k,i}$

$$\geq k* p\_weight_i - rem_{k,i}$$

$$\geq k*(weight_i + MSLP_i) - (weight_i + MSLP_i\ )$$

In the same way we take:

$$sent_i(t_1, t_2) / f_i \geq k* MSLP_i / f_i - MSLP_i / f_i)$$

$$= (k-1)*MSLP_i / f_i \qquad (8)$$

From all the above the Lemma has been proved.   ∎

Theorem 2. The Relative Fairness Measure (RFM) for the DIW is: $3M$

Proof. From (7) we have:

$$sent_i(t_1, t_2) / f_i \leq (k+1)*MSLP_i / f_i$$

For a second flow j according to (8) we take similarly:

$$sent_j(t_1, t_2) / f_j \geq (k'-1)*MSLP_j / f_j \quad (where\ k' \geq k-1,\ or\ k- k' \leq 1\ )$$

After multiplying by (-1): $-sent_i(t_1, t_2) / f_j \leq (1- k')*MSLP_j / f_j$

We consider that: $MSLP_k / f_k \leq M$ $(k=1,..,n,\ n=total\ number\ of\ active\ flows)$

Adding these two inequalities we take:

$$sent_i(t_1, t_2) / f_i - sent_j(t_1, t_2) / f_j = (k+1)*MSLP_i / f_i + (1- k')* MSLP_j / f_j$$

$$\leq (k+1)*M + (1- k')*M$$

$$\leq 2*M + (k- k')*M$$

$$\leq 3*M \ (like\ DRR) \qquad ∎$$

Lemma 7. Let us consider an interval (t_1, t_2) during which flows i and j are back-logged. For the flow i, after k rounds *of the stabilization of the weight*, for the CRR policy, we have:

$$k* minw - MSLP_i / f_i \leq sent_i(t_1, t_2) \leq k*minw + MSLP_i / f_i$$

Proof. We consider two queues with CRR. It is obvious that for the CRR the condition is satisfied: $p\_weight_i = MSLP_i$. In the start period (t_1, t_2) the scheduler increases the weight step by step until its final $(fweight_i)$ value, and serves the i packets. It is obvious that the $fweight_i$ of the CRR is greater than the $fweight_i$ of the CRR.

For both cases, there is an upper bound so that $fweight_i \leq p\_weight_i = MSLP_i$. This happens because according to Lemma 3, *it is possible the l-packets to be serviced at a lower bandwidth value* than $MSLP_i$. On the other hand, for the increased service policy case we have:

f_i = fweight$_i$ / minw (fweight$_i$ ≤ APB$_i$). Working as above, we get:

all_serv$_{k,i}$ ≤ k* fweight$_i$ + rem$_{0,i}$ - rem$_{k,i}$

$$\leq k* \text{fweight}_i + MSLP_i \qquad (9)$$

We consider that: minw= fweight$_i$ / f_i .

Finally: sent$_i$(t$_1$, t$_2$) / f_i ≤ k*fweight$_i$ / f_i + MSLP$_i$ / f_i

$$= k*\text{minw} + MSLP_i / f_i \qquad (10)$$

On the other hand from (9):

all_serv$_{k,i}$ ≤ k* fweight$_i$ + rem$_{0,i}$ - rem$_{k,i}$ ≥ k* fweight$_i$ - rem$_{k,i}$

$$\geq k* \text{fweight}_i - MSLP_i.$$

And finally: sent$_i$(t$_1$, t$_2$)/f_i ≥ k*fweight$_i$/f_i - MSLP$_i$/f_i

$$= k*\text{minw} - MSLP_i/f_i \qquad (11)$$

It is obvious that minw ≤ minwei because fweight$_i$ ≤ p_weight$_i$ ∎

Theorem 3. The Relative Fairness Measure (RFM) for the CRR is: *3M*

Proof. From (10), we take: sent$_i$(t$_1$, t$_2$) / f_i ≤ k*minw + MSLP$_i$ / f_i (12)

From (11), we take: sent$_j$(t$_1$, t$_2$) / f_j ≥   k*minw - MSLP$_j$ / f_j or

sent$_j$(t$_1$, t$_2$) / f_j ≥ k'* weight - MSLP$_j$ / f_j = k'*minw - MSLP$_j$ / f_j or

$$-\text{sent}_j(t_1, t_2) / f_j \leq - k'*\text{minw} + MSLP_j / f_j \qquad (13)$$

After adding (12), (13) for the normalized service for flows i and j (k'≥k-1, k- k'≤1), we get:

sent$_i$(t$_1$, t$_2$) / f_i – sent$_j$(t$_1$, t$_2$) / f_j ≤ (k- k')minw + MSLP$_j$/ f_i + MSLP$_j$/ f_j

$$\leq \text{minw} + MSLP_i / f_i + MSLP_j / f_j .$$

Simplifying, we take: M+M+M = 3M(like DRR)   ∎

Due to limited space Case 3 is not developed.

4.5 Latency

Some applications are quite sensitive to the latency of transmitting data across a network. The end to end latency is due to the latency of physical transmission media and delays introduced by intermediate routers and switches. From [1] we have that a small packet can be delayed only by an amount proportional to its own size by every other flow. Both algorithms belong as DRR to the Latency Rate (LR) class schedulers. The DRR latency depends on the number of sessions sharing the outgoing link, the granularity of bandwidth allocation and the maximum packet size [5].

The amount of total used service rate must be lower than the predefined bound in order to exist a margin so that it will be able to reach the maximum transmission efficiency of the output link. This condition makes the scheduler operate and get through the overload service with the help of the weight increase with no significant latency increase. Moreover, we do not have any more overhead of taking and returning the additional quantum. The effectiveness of our schemes, requires the system's ability to keep a portion of the bandwidth for the real time traffic beyond the amount of bandwidth needed for the best effort traffic (DRR). The system proposed in our analysis is considered rich in resources, so that in a worst case condition (when l-packets sequences appears to all of the queues simultaneously) it can work. This design seems quite attainable.

The delay bounds can be diminished by allocating more bandwidth to the servicing session (l-packets sequence) [5]. As far as the compensation is concerned, the additional amount of bandwidth used for increase the weight, can be proportionally shared with the other flows. No further details are provided for Latency, for the Relative Fairness (RF), short and long term compensation due to the limited space.

5 Simulation

Our present work deals with the experiments of the DIW and CRR which are cooperating with the PM. The PM provides the service priority while the DIW or CRR services the l-packets.

In our simulation experiments, we assume that we have isolated flows and each flow has its own queue. The space of buffers is non-restricted. A system with three levels is developed; the Application, the Queue and the List level. In the *Queue level,* we use the enqueue and dequeue functions according to each queue's service policy. These two essential functions are finally performed in the last internal *list level* with the corresponding functions of *insertAtBack* and *remove FromFront* of the linked lists. *The PM is developed in the Application level (before the DIW,CRR) in order to find, according to the STAB, the next flow for service.* We used Poisson arrivals, random size packets, queues with the same size (l-packets and normal size) and five scenaria.

Scenario 1: Comparison between WRR and PM for the waste time of "empty times" that WRR is making in order to find the next serviced packet (Fig. 2).

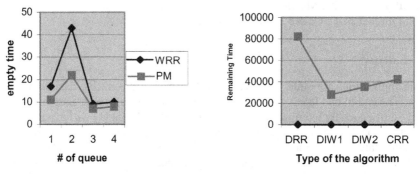

Fig. 2. WRR vs PM for the number of empty times

Fig. 3. The remaining time for: DRR, DIW1, DIW2, CRR

Scenario2: We compare the performance of the algorithms (DRR, DIW1, DIW2, CRR) by using four queues (Fig. 3). *Remaining time or the throughput (in time units) is the amount of time that the packets of a queue are in the system, from the moment of their arrival until they are all serviced.* The DIW2 has greater remaining time than the DIW1 and the CRR, because the weight's increase is less than the DIW1 and the CRR weight. The sooner the DIW1 and the DIW2 meet an "empty round", and the scheduler gets the new weight (shell), the better the packets' service will be. The CRR is the second after the DRR because takes the additional weight little by little. In Fig. 4, the CRR services the packets after the DIW1 and about the same as DIW2.

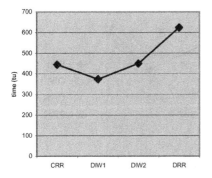 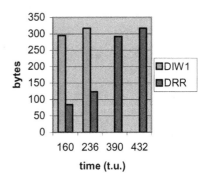

Fig. 4. Comparison of the service time for: DRR, DIW1, DIW2, CRR

Fig. 5. Comparison of DRR and DIW1 with the return phase

Scenario 3: We compare the performance of the DRR and the DIW1 by using two queues including the *return* phase. In Fig. 5, the DIW1 server, taking the shell (after the first empty round), finishes servicing the l-packets sequence, at 160 tu (while the DRR services just a portion) and it *returns* to the previous normal state. Then, it meets the sequence of normal size packets and services them at 236 tu. The DRR finishes servicing the l-packets at 390 tu and the normal size packets at 432 tu.

Scenario 4: We examine (Fig. 6) the total amount of serviced packets in the other streams when queue 2 finishes servicing the 185 mb (the first end serviced queue). At this time (133 t.u.) we see that the DIW is finished and is followed by the CRR. The DRR seems to have the fewer served packets. From all the above, the performance of the algorithms depends on the: number and size of packets, the position of the l-packet sequence in the stream, the value of the upper bound for each flow that can be predefined. If the MSLP is in front of the sequence, it is quite probable to provoke the "empty rounds" and activate the DIW earlier. The position of the MSLP would not play a significant role for the CRR if the already taken weight served the packet without "empty rounds". If the sequence is increasing, it greatly affects the CRR.

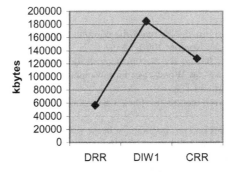

Fig. 6. Comparison of the serviced packets for DRR, DIW1, CRR

Scenario 5: It is clear from Fig. 7, that the DIW1 can compete with the ERR. DIW1 may have better performance than the ERR since it can get a large amount of weight, in a short period of time.

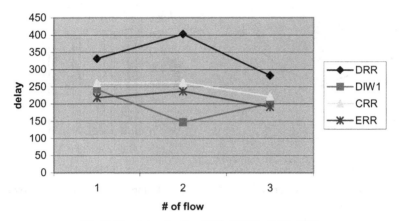

Fig. 7. The delay for the: DRR, DIW1, CRR, ERR

6 Conclusion

The importance of the proposed framework is that two kind of schedulers the PM (sorted-priority) and the DIW or CRR (Round-Robin) with O(1) complexity perfectly cooperate and provide service priority, flexibility on service l-packets, low queueing and service delay and relative fairness (the same with DRR). The key concept of PM is that is able to jump to the next service flow. This combination of operations of the schedulers (jump and provisional weight increase) provide less delay and can be competent with other recently developed schedulers (like: Aliquem, Smoothed Round Robin (SRR), Elastic Round Robin (ERR)). Additionally instead of using a group of flows (like in Group Round Robin (GRR), and Stratified Round Robin (SRR), here we have the ability to work with a large range of queues and maintain the service characteristics of each flow. The usefulness, the efficient and easy implementation makes this proposed framework amenable to several parts of the network (routers).

References

1. D.Ferrari, "Client requirements for real time communication services", *IEEE Communication Magazine,* 28(11), November 1990.
2. S. Cheung, C. Pencea, *"BSFQ: Bin Sort Fair Queuing"*, *Infocom 2002,* June 2002, NY
3. J.Bennett, H.Zhang,"WF2Q: Worst-case Fair Weighted Fair Queueing", *Proc.IEEE Infocom '96,* Mar. 1996, pp.120-128.
4. L. Zhang, " A new Architecture for Packet Switched Network Protocols, PhD Dissertation", *MIT,* July 1989.
5. S.Golestani, "A self-clocked fair queueing scheme for broadband applications", *IEEE Infocom'94,* Toronto, CA, June 1994, pp. 636-646.
6. S.Suri, G.Vargese, G.Chandranmenon, "Leap Forward Virtual Clock: A new fair Queuing Scheme with Guaranteed Delays and Throughput Fairness", *IEEE Infocom 1997,* pp. 557-565, 1997
7. P.Goyal, H.Vin, "Start time Fair Queueing: A scheduling Algorithm for Integrated Services Packet Switching Networks", *IEEE/ACM Trans. On Networking,* Vol. 5, No. 4, Aug. 1997, pp. 561-571.

8. M.Shreedhar, G. Vargese," Efficient Fair Queuing using deficit Round Robin", *ACM/IEEE Trans. on Networking*, Vol. 4, No3, June 1996, pp. 375-385

9. T.Eug.Ng, I.Stoica, H.Zhang, "Packet Fair Queueing Algorithms for Wireless Networks with Location-Dependent Errors",*IEEEInfocom'98*,March98,pp.1103-1111.

10. J. Bennett, D. Stephens, H. Zhang, "High Speed, Scalable, and Accurate Implementation of Packet Fair Queuing Algorithms in ATM Networks", *ICNP'97*, Oct. 97,Atlanta,GA, pp. 7-14.

11. R. Brown, "Calendar Queues: A Fast Priority Queue Implementation for the Simulation Event Set Problem",*Comm. of theACM*,Oct 1988,V. 31,N.10,pp1220-1227

12. K. Wrikson, R. Ladner, A. LaMarca," Optimizing Static Calendar Queues", *Proceedings of IEEE Symp. on Foundation of Computer Science*, Nov. 20-22, 1994

13. J. Rexford, A. Greengerg, F. Bonomi, "Hardware-Efficient Fair Queueing Architectures for High-Speed Networks*", IEEE Infocom '96*, pp. 638-646.

14. S. Kanhere, H. Setha, A. Parekh, *"Fair and Efficient Packet Scheduling using Elastic Round Robin", IEEE Trans. On Parallel and Distributed Systems*, vol.13, No3, March 2000, pp. 324-336.

15. A. Tanenbaum, "Computer Networks", Prentice-Hall, 1996.

16. D.Stiliadis, A. Varma, "Latency-Rate Servers: A general Model for Analysis of Traffic Scheduling Algorithms", *IEEE/ACM Trans. on Networking*, Vol.6, No.5,Oct.98.

17. S. Ramabhadram, J. Pasquale, "Stratified Round Robin: A low Complexity Packet Scheduler with Bandwidth Fairness and Bounded Delay", *Sigcomm '03*, August 2003, Germany

18. B. Carpita, W. Chan, J. Nieh, "Group Round Robin: Improving the Fairness and complexity of Packet Scheduling" ,*Dept of Computer Science, Columbia Univesrity, Technical Report CUCS-018-03*, June 2003

19. G. Chuanxiong, "SRR: An O(1) Time Complexity Packet Scheduler for Flows in Multi-Service Packet Networks", *Sigcomm '01*, August 2001, San Diego, USA

20. L.Lenzini, E. Mingozzi, G. Stea, "Tradeoffs Between Low Complexity, Low Latency, and Fairness with Deficit Round-Robin Schedulers", *IEEE/ACM Transactions on Networking,* Vol. 12, No.4, August 2004, pp.681-693

Data Hiding in Identification and Offset IP Fields*

Enrique Cauich[1], Roberto Gómez Cárdenas[2], and Ryouske Watanabe[2]

[1] Computer Science and Engineering 204B
University of California, Irvine, CA 92717 USA
ecauichz@ics.uci.edu
[2] ITESM-CEM, Depto. Ciencias Computacionales, Km 3.5 Lago Guadalupe,
51296, Atizapan Zaragoza, Edo México, Mexico
{rogomez,A00445577}@itesm.mx

Abstract. Steganography is defined as the art and science of hiding information, it takes one piece of information and hides it within another. The piece more used to hide information are the digital images. In this paper we present a way to use unused fields in the IP header of TCP/IP packets in order to send information between to nodes over Internet.

1 Introduction

Steganography literally means "covered languages" [1,2]. In today's computer world, it has come to mean hiding secret messages in any digital multimedia signals. Steganography works by replacing bits of useless or unused data in regular computer files (such as graphics, sound, text, HTML, or even floppy disks) with bits of different, invisible information. This hidden information can be plain text, cipher text, or even images. Must of the scientific word is focus in hiding information into images. The techniques used have the intention to make impossible to detect that there is anything inside the innocent file, but the recipient must obtain the hidden data without any problem. The most important feature of a steganographic system is the fact that it allows communication between two authorized parties without an observer is aware that the communication is actually taking place.

TCP/IP is the protocol used in Internet. TCP /IP were developed by a Department of Defense (DOD) research project to connect a number different networks designed by different vendors into a network of networks (the "Internet"). IP (Internet Protocol, [3]) is responsible for moving packet of data from node to node, and TCP (Transmission Control Protocol, [4]) is responsible for verifying the correct delivery of data from client to server. The IP protocol defines the basic unit of data transfer through the Internet as a packet. All the data is partitioned into IP packets on the sending computer and reassembled on the receiving computer. Each packet begins with a header containing addressing and system control information. The header packet is divided into The IP packet header consists of 20 bytes of data divided in several fields. Each field has a special purpose, depending on the type of data contained in the packet payload.

Many scientific work has been made in order to create software and methods to hide information into digital images. Our approach take advantage of the unused

---

* The work described here was supported by the Computer Security Research Group at TESM-CEM.

F.F. Ramos et al. (Eds.): ISSADS 2005, LNCS 3563, pp. 118–125, 2005.

fields of the IP header packet. As mentioned earlier we not all the fields of an IP packet are always used. These fields are used to hide the information we want to send without raising any suspicion.

This paper is organized as follows: In section two we present an analysis of steganographic methods. This is followed by an overview of the Internet Protocol in section three. Previous work, that uses a similar approach than us, is analyzed in section four. Our proposal is explained in section five and the implementation and experiments are showed is section six. The last section presents our conclusions, limitations and advantages of our work.

2 Steganography Overview

Communication confidentiality can be accomplish using cryptography, which involves key administration, algorithm implementation and other management issues. Nevertheless, if an eavesdropper is listening he will realize that exists a secret communication between two entities. Steganography will hide the presence of a message in such a way that an eavesdropper (who listen to all the communications) cannot tell that a secret message is being sent. As the goal of steganography is to hide the presence of a message, it has been as the complement of cryptography, whose goal is to hide the content of a message.

The first scientific study of steganography was presented by Simmons in 1983 [5] who formulate it as the "Prisoners problem". The problem is the following one: Two prisoners need to communicate, but all the messages pass through the warden who can detect any encrypted messages. They must find some technique of hiding their message in an innocent looking communication.

The generic embedding and decoding process in steganography is presented in [6,7,8] The first step in embedding and hiding information is to pass both, the secret message and the cover message, into the encoder. Inside the encoder, one or several protocols will be implemented to embed the secret information into the cover message. A key is often needed in the embedding process. This can be in the form of a public or private key. Having passed through the encoder, a stego object will be produced. A stego object is the original cover object with the secret information embedded inside. it will then be sent off via some communications channel, such as email, to the intended recipient for decoding. The recipient must decode the stego object in order for them to view the secret information. The decoding process is simply the reverse of the encoding process. After the decoding process is completed, the secret information embedded in the stego object can then be extracted and viewed.

The most used cover messages are digital images. In [9] Nelson and Jajodia gives an introduction to steganography in digital images. According to them must of the techniques use common approaches that includes least significant bit insertion, masking and filtering and transformations. The LSB method works by using the least significant bits of each pixel in one image to hide the most significant bits of another. Masking and filtering techniques hide information by marking an image, in a manner similar to paper watermarks. Transformation take advantages of algorithms and coefficients form processing the image or its components to hide information. One example of this technique is the discrete cosine transformation. In [10] the authors uses digital imagery as a cover signal to hide information. In [11] the authors propose to use random bit-sequences generated by linear shift registers (LFSRs) within the pixel-byte instead of just the LSB. They established that such changes within any given pixel of the image will result in better hiding of the data and hence secure data transmission.

Other covert messages include audio signals or slack space in disks. In [12] propose a technique that uses autocorrelation modulation, with several variations, to hide information within audio-signals. A MP3 resistant oblivious data hiding technique is presented in [13].

Like many security tools, steganography can be used for a variety of reasons, some good, some not so good. Legitimate purposes can include things like watermarking images for reasons such as copyright protection. Digital watermarks (also known as fingerprinting, significant especially in copyrighting material) are similar to steganography in that they are overlaid in files, which appear to be part of the original file and are thus not easily detectable by the average person.

Attacks on steganographic systems exists and are named steganalysis. Their goal is to determine whether or not they have a payload encoded into them, and, if possible, recover that payload. More information can be found in [14,15,16]. An interesting analysis of limits of steganography is presented in [17]; the authors presents a discussion of the obstacles that lie in the way of a general theory of information hiding systems.

3   The Internet Protocol

Internet use the Internet Protocol (IP) as a standard way to transmit information and actually almost al the network is based in the IP version 4. The header of this protocol usually uses some fields that have some redundancy or normally are not used during the transmissions. We can use this fields that are not used for our purposes, but first we will analyze how the IP header works. For the aim of our investigation we will focus in just the second and third 32-bit worlds of the header; it mean's; the identification, flags, fragment offset, Time to Live, protocol and Checksum fields of the header.

Vers	HLen	TOS	Total Length	
Identification			Flags	Fragment Offset
Time to Live		Protocol	Header Checksum	
Source Address				
Destination Address				
Options				Padding

Fig. 1. Fields of an IP header

When the transmission over the internet occurs; the information is wrapped by different protocols at different layers of the TCP/IP network model. Two of these layers are the Physical layer and the Transport layer. The communication over the transport layer is standardized by the IP protocol, but over the network layer exists some different technologies and implementations, which implies that each technology has a maximum size of data it can carry per transmission or Maximum Transfer Unit(MTU).

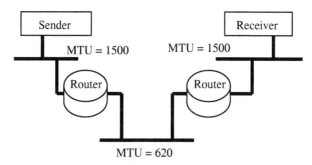

Fig. 2. MTU example

The Transport layer solve this problem with the fields located at the second and third 32-bit words. During the transmission of an IP packet, if the MTU of the source network is smaller there is not problem; but if not, the router needs to fragment the IP packet.

When fragmentation occurs; the router splits the IP datagram with a maximum size of the new MTU. The new headers has the same information, but now the bit of More Fragments is turned on and the Fragment Offset indicates the offset of the data. Otherwise, if fragmentation does not occur; both fields, the Flags Field and the Fragment Offset, are set in zero.

Finally when the packet arrive to its destination, this device must be able to join the packet again; therefore, IP needs to assure when the device joins the pieces again; that each one corresponds to the original packet. To assure it, IP uses the Identification field.

There are other modification that occurs over the IP header every time that a packet pass trough a router. When a packet reach to a router, the field of Time to Live in the header decreases its value, originally set in 30, by one. If a packet reaches the router with a value of zero in the Time to Live field, the packet is dropped; this is because IP need to assure that a packet will no be forever traveling over the network without reaching its destiny. At least, because of all the modifications that occur in the IP header while traveling, the Checksum field is modified every time the packet reaches a router.

4   Previous Work of Steganography in IP

Our proposal is to use some of the fields described in the previous section. Similar approaches have been published in [15] and [16].

In [15] the authors idea resides in the manipulation of the IP Identification Field. The Identification Field of the IP Packet is assigned by the original sender. This number consist basically in a random number generated while the packet was being constructed. The Identification Field is only used when fragmentation occurs. Therefore; if we assure that no fragmentation will occur because of the size of the packet; it is possible to hide data in this field without any consequence in the transmission.

The advantages in this work is that it is used to send information from point to point, but the limitations are the quantity of information that you send. Furthermore if by any circumstances the datagram is fragmented, the receiver will listen noise in the transmission because it will receive the same information more than one time with every new fragment of the datagram.

In [16] the work is focused in the manipulation of the Do Not Fragment Bit. There is possible to indicate if we do not want that our packet be fragment by the routers in the way. In consequence; again, if we assure that our packet will be not fragmented because of the size of it; we can hide information in the Do not fragment Bit at the flags field.

In this work the problem of the size of data is worst than the Identification Field, because here we can only transmit one bit for each datagram. Imagining that the datagram does not carry any data but the header, then the ratio useful information to total data is 1:160, it means that if you want to transmit the phrase "hello world" you will need to transmit 88 datagrams producing and overhead of almost 2 Kb for just 11 bytes.

5 Our Proposal

Our idea is not really to hide information, but to use the non-used bits to send messages and information, node to node, related with the router performance, best routes or even to update the new routes between the gateways without generating more traffic. For this purpose we will analyze two fields that are not quite often used in a IP datagram transmission.

As it was mentioned, the Fragmentation Offset Field always is set to zero if fragmentation does not occur at all and the Identification Field also becomes useless if there it occurs. Unfortunately, we cannot be sure of it because we are not sure that the source MTU is the smaller in the travel that the packet will take; furthermore, we are not sure of which path the packet will take during the travel. In consequence we can not use the Fragmentation Offset Field or the Identification Field if we want to transmit point to point information, but in node to node.

5.1 Packet Fragmentation

There are two scenarios when a IP packet cross from one network to other. The first one is that it is fragmented because the MTU of the second one is smaller the former, in which case the More Fragments bit of the Flags Field is set to 1 and the Fragment Offset became used. The second scenario is when fragmentation is not necessary; therefore, the Fragment Offset will be zero, and the only two modifications that the datagram will receive is the decrement of the TTL field and a recalculation of the Header Checksum.

It is in the second scenario when it is possible to substitute the fragment offset by some data without any consequence.

5.2 Datagram Selection to Carry Information

Now the problem is how we can identify when a datagram is loading information of fragmentation in the Offset field or when the datagram is loading our information. It's not possible to know only with the More Fragment bit, because it is set to one in every fragment except the last one. Therefore, in the last fragment we will have a

More Fragment bit in zero and nonzero Fragment Offset. Furthermore we cannot track if the datagram is part of a fragmented one or not because maybe every fragment can take a different path. Moreover, if this could be possible we will require storing the ID of the fragment with the destination IP address.

The solution to this problem is to use a non used bit, than can be every reserved bit of the header that actually is not used. It can be the two less significant bits of the TOS field or the most significant bit of the Flags field. For convenience we will use the bit of the Flags field, because its only necessary to do an "AND" in a 32 bit length word to extract if the datagram is carrying any data in the unused fields. Another advantage of this approach is that in case the datagram is carrying any data we had already been extracted the data with the same "AND" operation. We also need to discern when a router can use a datagram; it can be used only under two circumstances. The first one is when the datagram has the chosen reversed bit on, meaning that the datagram carries data of the previous gateway, so we need to extract the data, but also we can reuse this datagram for sending data to the next router in the path. The second case occurs when the More Fragments Bit is off and also the Fragment Offset is set to zero that indicates that the datagram has not been fragmented and has not been used by the previous router, so it can be used for sending data to the next router in the path.

After the gateway extracts the information we embedded in the datagram, these fields are replaced with a random value in the Identification Field and set to zero in the Offset Field if there is no information we need to transmit to the next router, or with the new information in the other case.

6   Implementation and Tests

The code that implements our proposal uses the LibNet library for the construction of the packets two computer Pentium running Open BSD 2.x.

Our environment test was constituted by two computers Pentium running OpenBSD 2.x that work as the gateways. One of them (R1) was running the program that injects the information within the datagram. The principal roll of this program was to read from the internal interface the datagram, check if it has fragmentation. If not if there was some information to send to R2, it sets the reserved bit from the flags field to one and write down the information in the ID and Offset Field. After the decrement of the TTL and the recalculation of the checksum the datagram is sent through the external interface to the next network.

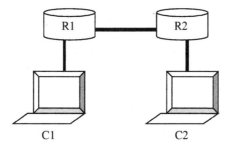

Fig. 3. Implementation architecture

The information that R1 sent was write down in a text file in R1. And it was sent while there exists traffic in the network from C1 to C2 and the EOF of the text file was no reached.

The second gateway (R2) was running the program that take out the information and reestablish the packet. This program read the flags field of the datagram, if it has the reserved bit on and the fragmentation bit of then it takes out the information of the ID and fragment Offset field and reestablishes the value of the Offset field to zero, copies the Checksum to the ID field (this because we need any number in this field), decreases the TTL and recalculates the Checksum. The information that R2 received was displayed to the screen of R2.

C1 and C2 was to laptops running Windows 2000 that was doing ping and telnet. Also both of them was running ethereal to check the structure and the data that the datagrams were carrying. Additionally we connected and sniffer between R1 and R2 in order to maintain a tracking of the packets and the information that they were carrying.

7 Conclusions

We have presented a new another technique to hide information over a valid communication channel. The covert messages were the Identification and Offset IP fields of the TCP/IP packets used in a communication between two valid entities. The experiments shown some limitations but they also presented some advantages over similar steganographic techniques.

As we mention above; it is not possible to send information point to point because we cannot assure that the IP datagram will be not fragmented. Furthermore we do not know exactly which way the packet will take, so is not possible to be sure in our information will arrive to destiny or the datagram will take another way that never pass thought our destination. That is caused because the owner of the datagram is not ours. Actually there are two ways to assure the packet will cross thought a gateway.

The first way when we route the datagram thought a known interface with a known MAC address of a known gateway at the same network segment.

The second way is to put a static rout in the Options field of the datagram, but with this we are doing and extra work that causes overloading at the gateway and also and overheading at the network that is what we try to avoid.

Another limitation is that in presence of an Intrusion Detection System (IDS), and depending the configuration of, it is possible that the datagram can be identified as a malicious one.

By the other hand, our work presents several advantages. The first advantage is that we have an effective 12-bit word to be used in every datagram that is not fragmented, and the only extra work that the gateway need to do is to replace the data carried at the Offset Field with zeros. There is no more work for the gateway because finally every time a datagram cross thought a gateway the TTL field is decreased and the checksum must be recalculated.

Furthermore, with the use of this methodology to send information between to gateways that are back to back, they can share routes, the load of each route or the quality of service, throughput of each route without generating overloading in the network.

References

1. D Kanh, The History of Steganography, Proceedings: Information Hiding. First International Workshop, Cambridge UK pp1-5 1996
2. W Bender et al. Techniques for Data Hiding IBM Systems Journal Vol 35 Nos. 3&4, pp 313-336, 1996 15. Craig H. Rowland, Covert Channels in the TCP/IP protocol suite. First Monday, 2003.
3. RFC 793, Transmission Control Protocol, Darpa Internet Program, Protocol Specification, September 1981
4. RFC 791 Internet Protocol, Darpa Internet Program, Protocol Specification, September 1981
5. Simmons, G. J. Prisoners' problem and the subliminal channel., Advances in Cryptology: Proceedings of CRYPTO 83. D. Chaum, ed. Plenum, New York, 1983, pp. 51-67.
6. Neil F. Johnson and Sushil Jajodia, Steganalysis of Images Created Using Current Steganography Software, Proceedings Second Information Hiding Workshop held in Portland, Oregon, USA, April 15-17, 1998, Lecture Notes in Computer Science, Vol. 1525, pp 273-289
7. L.M. Marvel, C.T. Retter, C.G. Boncelet, Jr, Hiding information in images, 1998 International Conference on Image Processing (ICIP '98) 3-Volume Set-Volume 2 October 04 - 07, 1998 Chicago, Illinois
8. Neil F. Johnson and Sushil Jajodia, Steganalysis: The Investigation of Hidden Information,. IEEE Information Technology Conference, Syracuse, New York, USA, September 1st - 3rd, 1998: 113-116.
9. Neil F. Johnson, Sushil Jajodia, Exploring Steganography: Seeing the Unseen, IEEE Computer, February 1998 (Vol. 31, No. 2) pp 26-34
10. L. M. Marvel, C. G. Jr. Boncelet and C. T. Retter, "Spread spectrum image steganography", IEEE Transactions on Image Processing, Volume: 8, August 1999
11. Jamil, T.; Ahmad, A.; An Investigation into the application of Linear Feedback Shift Registers for Steganography SoutheastCon, 2002. Proceedings IEEE, 5-7 April 2002 pp 239 - 244
12. Petrovic, R.; Winograd, J.M.; Jemili, K.; Metois, E.; Data hiding within audio signals Telecommunications in Modern Satellite, Cable and Broadcasting Services, 1999. 4th International Conference on ,Volume: 1, 13-15 Oct. 1999
13. Litao Gang; Akansu, A.N.; Ramkumar, M.; MP3 resistant oblivious steganography Acoustics, Speech, and Signal Processing, 2001. Proceedings. (ICASSP '01). 2001 IEEE International Conference on, Volume: 3, 7-11 May 2001, pp:1365 - 1368 vol.3
14. Huaiqing Wang, Shuozhong Wang; Cyber warfare: steganography vs. steganalysis, Communications of the ACM archive, Volume 47, Issue 10 (October 2004) pp. 76 - 82
15. Jessica Fridrich and Miroslav Goljan, Practical steganalysis of digital images: state of the art, Proceedings of SPIE -- Volume 4675 Security and Watermarking of Multimedia Contents IV, April 2002, pp. 1-13
16. Chandramouli,R.; Subbalakshmi, K.P., Active steganalysis of spread spectrum image steganography Circuits and Systems, 2003. ISCAS '03. Proceedings of the 2003 International Symposium on, Volume: 3, May 25-28, 2003
17. Anderson, R.J. Petitcolas, F.A.P., On the limits of steganography Comput. Lab., IEEE Journal on Communications, May 1998, Volume: 16, Issue: 4 pp. 474-481
18. Rowland, Craig H, Covert channels in the TCP/IP protocol suite, DoIS Documents in Information Science, May 1997
19. K. Ahsan and D. Kundur, Practical data hiding in TCP/IP, Proc. ACM Workshop on Multimedia Security, 2002.

Interpretation of UML Sequence Diagrams as Causality Flows

Christophe Sibertin-Blanc, Omar Tahir, and Janette Cardoso

Université Toulouse 1 / IRIT
21 allée de Brienne F-31042 Toulouse cedex
{sibertin,otahir,jcardoso}@univ-tlse1.fr

Abstract. UML Interaction diagrams (Sequence diagrams (SD), Collaboration diagrams or Communication diagrams) lack a formal semantics; they include some amount of ambiguity so that formal techniques cannot be applied e.g. for automatically deriving the behavior of the objects (as Statecharts or State-Transition diagrams) from the SD where they appear. To overcome this situation, this paper first analyses and simplifies the semantic relationships among the concepts that intervene in the definition of SDs: *synchronous / asynchronous, activator* and *return* messages. Then it proposes an interpretation of the *precedence association* among messages that yields to an operational semantics of SDs that orders the actions of emitting and receiving messages according to a causality relationship.

1 Introduction

UML is a semi-formal language widely used in software development processes for the specification, design and documentation of systems. It proposes a tool-kit of diagrams to describe the structure and behavior of a system according to different aspects and views.

A UML-based modeling process begins with the identification of use cases with their scenarios describing the executions of interest. Each use case corresponds to a system function and it is accompanied with one or several scenarios. Scenarios are used in system requirement phase to illustrate how the use case is performed. Each one describes a sequence of interaction between the system's components and its external actors, and it may be graphically represented by a sequence diagram (SD) which shows message exchanges arranged along a time sequence.

From this functional specification, it would be very interesting to assist a part of the design activities by automatically deriving the statechart diagrams of the objects within the system, that is an abstract executable specification of their observable behavior. Computer support for this translation from specification to design is important for successful application developments.

Unfortunately, UML lacks a formal semantics and does not offer semantic relationships between the diagrams of dynamics. In particular, SDs do not have an operational semantics describing formally how to carry out such diagrams. The definition of SD in UML deals only with the scheduling of messages and does not say anything about the scheduling of the actions of sending ($!m$) and receiving ($?m$) a message m. In the case of SDs having a single thread of control, the message ordering directly defines the scheduling of the message sending and receiving actions; only one object

F.F. Ramos et al. (Eds.): ISSADS 2005, LNCS 3563, pp. 126–140, 2005.

being active at any moment, no concurrency is possible and there is no scheduling issue. This does not hold in the case of distributed systems where several objects can be active simultaneously. For instance, the SD depicted in Fig. 1 says that message m has to precede message m', but it does not specify e.g. whether the receiving action $?m$ must precede the send action $!m'$.

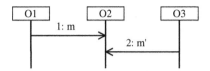

Fig. 1. A simple UML Sequence Diagram

To provide SDs with an operational semantics consists in defining a partial order relation among the actions of sending and receiving messages. Any such scheduling of actions has to account for the fact that a message can not be received before it has been sent, thus we always have for any message m: $!m$ before $?m$.

Then, there are several ways to schedule the sending and receiving actions of a SD. The first one is to read a SD as a Message Sequence Chart (MSC) [3], that is to ignore the UML global ordering of messages and to just consider the local ordering of actions performed by each object along its life-line. According to this definition, we just have for the SD of Fig. 1: $!m$ before $?m$, $!m'$ before $?m'$ and $?m$ before $?m'$.

A second way to schedule the actions is defined and studied in [1]. This semantics just considers the ordering of messages: if a message m precedes a message m', m exists before m' and thus we must have $!m$ before $!m'$. As a consequence, this semantics imposes a total serialization on the set of emission actions, even for those sent by different objects. According to this definition, we have for the SD of Fig. 1: $!m$ before $?m$, $!m'$ before $?m'$ and $!m$ before $!m'$.

In this paper, we introduce a third way to schedule the actions of a SD; it accounts for the UML global ordering of messages while also dealing with the causality relationship among the actions, that means that two actions $a1$ and $a2$ are serialized only if $a1$ causes $a2$ in some way. According to this latter conception, we just have for the SD of Fig. 1: $!m$ before $?m$ and $!m'$ before $?m'$.

Indeed, there is nothing that enables to relate $!m$ performed by $o1$ and $!m'$ performed by $o3$, and as a result there is no way to causally relate the receptions $?m$ and $?m'$ performed by $o2$. The main property of this new scheduling of actions is that it orders two actions only if there is a necessity reason for that. Any requirement on actions ordering is a constraint put on the executions of the system. Thus, the main quality of this new operational semantics for SDs is to alleviate the behavior of a system from the execution constraints that are not rigorously justified.

Provided with such a well-defined scheduling of the message sending and receiving actions, the functional requirements expressed by a set of SDs may be used to design the system's components. Indeed, SD become provided with an operational semantics as Message Sequence Charts do. This allow to apply the results concerning the "realization" of a set of MSCs [6, 7, 9], that consists in synthesizing from a set of MSC an automaton for each of the objects involved in these MSCs. This automaton includes all the sequences of message sending and receiving that the object must be able to perform in order to fulfill the requirement expressed by the MSCs. In [8], an informal way is given to derive the statecharts of the objects appearing in a set of SDs.

The remainder of this paper is organized as follow: section 2 introduces the basic concepts of UML SDs. Section 3 discusses the interpretation of these concepts in order to start from a well-founded definition of UML Sequence diagrams. In section 4, we define the causality semantics of SD in terms of partial order between actions. Section 5 applies this definition on a traditional alarm clock example and, before to conclude, section 6 presents some related works.

2   The UML Definition of SD

Any formal semantics has to be based on the abstract syntax of the interaction diagrams, i.e. on their definition in term of the metamodel of UML [2]. Fig. 2 shows how interactions are defined in the UML 1.5 metamodel.

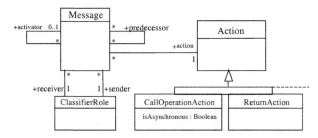

Fig. 2. Extract of the UML metamodel

An interaction is a unit of behavior that focuses on the observable exchange of information between a set of participating objects. More precisely, it contains a set of partially ordered messages, each specifying one communication.

Graphically, an interaction is represented either as a SD to emphasize the chronology of the exchanges of messages, or as a Collaboration Diagrams (CD) to stress the organization of the system. A SD shows a temporal view of the interactions by putting the accent on the scheduling of the messages between objects, while a CD shows a structural view of the interactions by stressing links between the participating objects. These two diagrams are semantically equivalent since they are described by the same concept – *collaboration* – in the metamodel. Many UML tools automatically translate one diagram type to the other.

2.1   Message

A message is the specification of a communication between two objects, or an object of the system and its environment. It unifies invocation of operation, send of signal, return of a result after an operation call, creation and destruction of an object.

Each message has a sender and a receiver, which is an instance of a class of objects, or more precisely the role that plays this instance in the interaction. Each message is sent by an action, which specifies the statement that causes the communication specified by the message.

The attribute *isAsynchronous* associated with an action indicates whether the message sending is asynchronous or synchronous. In the case of an asynchronous invocation, the sender continues its execution immediately without concern for the behavior launched by the message at the receiver object side; in the case of a synchronous invocation, the sender is blocked as long as the receiver does not send a ReturnMessage that is a result or an acknowledgement of delivery. A signal is always asynchronous, whereas an operation call can be either synchronous or asynchronous [2]. Graphically, an asynchronous message is represented with a stick arrowhead while a synchronous message is represented with a filled solid arrowhead. Finally, each message has a set of predecessor messages and, optionally, an activator message. The following sections explain the meaning of the predecessor and activator associations.

2.2 The Predecessor Association

The messages of a SD are partially ordered by the predecessor association. The scheduling of those messages is based on the execution thread they belong to. Within each thread, messages are sent in sequential order whereas messages belonging to different threads are sent in parallel or in arbitrary order. This partial order among messages is defined by the association predecessor. For each message, its predecessors are "The set of Messages whose completion enables the execution of the current message. All of them must be completed before execution begins." [2]. In the concrete notation [4], this predecessor association is expressed by the sequential numbering of messages: message *2.4:m1* precedes message *2.5:m2*, whereas messages *2.A:m1* and *2.B:m2* belong to different threads: they are independent and thus concurrent.

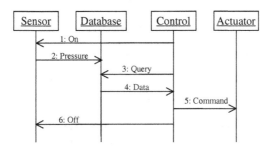

Fig. 3. Scenario for a Boiler Control system

2.3 The Activator Association

An interaction also specifies the activator of each message. The activator of a message is the message that invoked the procedure that in turn invokes the current message.

In fact, the set of messages activated by a message constitutes a transaction, or a procedure. The execution of this procedure is triggered by the reception of the activator message, and it ends at the sending of the last of these messages; it must be sent by *ReturnAction*, i.e. an action that returns a result or a control flow to the sender of the activator message.

In the concrete notation, the activation association is expressed by the hierarchization of the sequence number associated with messages: a message of form *2.4.1:m2* is activated by a message *2.4:m1*.

2.4 Definition of an Interaction

As a conclusion, a UML SD may be defined as a sextuple *(O, M, to, from, $\mathfrak{R}_{Pre}$, $\mathfrak{R}_{Act}$)*, where:

– is a finite set of instances or objects;
– *M* is a finite set of messages, each message being either isSynchronous or isAsynchronous, and some of them being additionally tagged as ReturnMessage;
– *From* and *To* are two functions from *M* to *O*. *From(m)* denotes the instance which sends message *m*, while *To(m)* denotes the instance which receives message *m*;
– $\mathfrak{R}_{Pre}$ is *an* order relation defined on *M*, it corresponds with the predecessor association defined in the UML metamodel;
– $\mathfrak{R}_{Act}$ is a function from *M* to $\mathcal{P}(M)$, the powerset of M. For each message *m*, $\mathfrak{R}_{Act}(m)$ denotes the set (possibly empty) of messages activated by *m*. It corresponds to the activation association defined in the UML metamodel.

Beyond this formal definition, there are several constraints on these predecessor and activator relations; with *M* the set of messages of an interaction. The following constraints have to be satisfied [2, 10].

a) The graph *(M, $\mathfrak{R}_{Pre}$)* with $\mathfrak{R}_{Pre}$ the predecessor relation is acyclic,
b) For *m'*, *m''* $\in$ *M*, if *m'* transitively precedes *m''* then either both have the same activator *m* $\in$ *M* or both have no activator,
c) For *m* $\in$ *M*, if the action of *m* is synchronous call then there is an *r* $\in$ *M* such that (1) the action of *r* is *ReturnAction*, (2) *m* activates *r* and (3) *m'* transitively precedes *r* for all *m'* $\in$ *M* such that *m* activates *m*; thus each synchronous message is activator such as the last activated message is sent by a ReturnAction.

Moreover, we say that a SD is *locally controllable* iff for all messages *m*, *m'* $\in$ *M*, *m* $\mathfrak{R}_{Pre}$ *m'* => *From(m)* = *From(m')* or *To(m)* = *From(m')*, i.e., for two directly consecutive messages, either they are sent by the same object or the second message is sent by the recipient of the first. In a locally controllable SD, each object has enough information to know when a send action must be performed, so that the global ordering of actions is ensured by the local controls in each object.

The SD depicted in Fig. 3 extracted from [9] describes a scenario for a Boiler Control System. The *Control* unit operates a *Sensor* and an *Actuator* to control the *pressure* of a steam boiler. A *Database* is used as a repository to buffer *Sensor* information while the *Control* unit performs calculations and sends *commands* to the *Actuator*. This SD states that there must be some pressure registered into the Database before any queries is treated.

This SD is not locally controllable. The *Control* object cannot know whether the sensor has registered pressure in the *Database*, it does not have enough local information to know at which time it must emit the request *Query*. Thus, in order to ensure that any request is treated after pressure has been registered, there is a need either for a centralized controller that activates each object when it has a send action to perform or for the addition of a synchronization message from the *Sensor* to the *Control* as described in [1].

Another solution is to consider a new operational semantics that does not impose a total serialization on the emission and reception actions of successive messages sent by different objects. Since the *Pressure* and *Query* messages are not causally related, it imposes no constraint on the ordering of their reception; instead, it considers that the sending of a message is caused by the reception of the precedent messages and thus imposes that the sending of a message is postponed after the reception of all these precedent messages.

According to this causally based semantics, we have for the Boiler Control system: the send and receive actions of the two messages *Pressure* and *Query* are not ordered, that is the Control object can send the *Query* message without regard for the sending of the *Pressure* message by the Sensor, and the Database can receive these two messages in any order. On the other hand the emission of the *Data* message is conditioned by the reception of both the *Pressure* and the *Query* messages. As a matter of fact, this SD has exactly the same semantics than the SD where the *Pressure* and *Query* messages are in the inverse order, *Query* being numbered 2 and *Pressure* 3.

This semantics will be formally described in section 4.

3   Interpretation of the UML Associations in Terms of Actions

In order to give a formal semantics to SD, we need a more simple definition of UML SD that especially clarifies the relationships between the *predecessor* association, the *activator* association and the *isAsynchronous* property. To this end, we will integrate the three in a *precede* relation among all the messages.

The main difficulty results from the ambiguity in the definition of the predecessor relationship given in the manual reference [2], since the meaning of *"message completion"* is not specified.

Among all reasonable and tractable interpretations we can quote that given by [5]: the completion of a message means the termination of the action related to the sending of the message and performed by the sender. In case of asynchronous communication, the termination of the message is simply sending the message, while in case of synchronous communication it includes the resumption of the sender execution that was blocked after the sending of the message.

Nevertheless, we adopt a finer interpretation that takes into account both the sending and the receiving actions of the message. Indeed, each emission of message goes with a send action realized by the sender object and a reception action realized by the receiver object, which corresponds to the activity carried out after the reception of the message. Thus the message completion concerns the two objects, the completion relating to sender object means the end of the execution of the send action and in the case of a synchronous message the reception of the expected result, whereas the completion related to the receiver object means the end of the activity carried out by the receiver object.

For each message m we will consider its sending action $!m$ and also its receiving action $?m$. Thus, we complete the UML definition of SD that only identifies the send action and does not say anything on the reception of the message.

The *predecessor* association in the UML metamodel only relates messages which belong to a same activation. Indeed, UML contains the following constraint [2] :*"the predecessors of a message have the same activator as it"*, therefore the activator of a message does not precede it. It is however necessary to schedule the set of all the messages, including those which are in different hierarchical levels. Thus, we translate the activator association into the predecessor association by defining a new *extended predecessor association* $\mathfrak{R}^e{}_{Pre}$ between the messages which extends the $\mathfrak{R}_{Pre}$ predecessor relation. This translation accounts for the synchronous or asynchronous character of the message activator.

3.1 The Synchronous Case

Let m be a synchronous message (then m is an activator message according to the assumption (c) stated in section 2.4 and m' be any message activated by m, that is $m' \in \mathfrak{R}_{Act}(m)$. Then:

(a) If m' is without predecessor, then $m \; \mathfrak{R}^e{}_{Pre} \; m'$; that means that a activator message precedes necessarily the first message of an activation. In other words, the actions of an activation are carried out after the beginning of this activation.

(b) if $m1$ is a successor of m and m' is without successors, then $m' \; \mathfrak{R}^e{}_{Pre} \; m1$; that means that if a message activator m is synchronous then all the actions of this activation must be carried out before a message $m1$ which succeeds m can be sent.

3.2 The Asynchronous Case

Let m be an asynchronous message and m' be a message activated by m, that is $m' \in \mathfrak{R}_{Act}(m)$. Then

(a) If m' is without predecessors, then $m \; \mathfrak{R}^e{}_{Pre} \; m'$, as in the previous synchronous case (a).

(b) if $m1$ is a successor of m, m' is without successor and $From(m1) \neq From(m)$, then $m' \; \mathfrak{R}^e{}_{Pre} \; m1$.

The synchronous character of a message sending characterizes the behavior of the sender object and not the activity carried out by the reception of the message. In the case of an asynchronous activator, the activity carried out at the receiver side is concurrent with that at the sender object side.

These rules express that (a) the actions of an activation must be carried out after the beginning of the activation. But (b) the end of the activation of an asynchronous message must be carried out before the messages which succeed the message activator is sent, except for the messages transmitted by the same object as the message activator.

Once the activator relation is transcribed in a predecessor relation, and taking into account the constraints stated in section 2.4, in particular (c), the synchronous messages are considered and treated exactly as the asynchronous messages, since we considerer that each synchronous message is also an activator for which the last activated message is sent by a *ReturnAction* that is explicitly shown. So we can consider a SD as defined by a 5-uple $(O, M, to, from, \mathfrak{R}^e{}_{Pre})$ where no additional property is associated to the messages of M.

4   A Causality Based Semantics for SD

We are now provided with a single acyclic precede relation $\mathfrak{R}^e_{Pre}$ among the set of messages that catches the meaning of the UML predecessor and activator associations together with the isAsynchronous property. In this section we define an order relation on the set of the actions that send and receive these messages.

This order is a balance between on the one hand the MSC-order that ignores the UML global ordering of messages and only considers the local ordering of actions along the life-line of each object; and on the other hand the predecessor-order that funds the scheduling of local actions only on the global ordering of messages. This latter ordering considers that "message m precedes message m'" always implies "action $!m$ precedes action $!m'$" and it is counter intuitive in the case of SDs that are not locally controllable since the correct execution of these SD requires either the use of a centralized controller or the addition of hidden messages.

Thus the causality-based order relation defined in this section accounts for the precede relation among messages as far as all the synchronization between objects are realized by the exchanged messages, without the use of a global controller or the addition of other messages. It is founded on the synchronizations between objects operated by the messages – the sending precedes necessarily the reception – and on the local scheduling of actions in each object.

4.1   Local Scheduling of Messages

We start by defining a local ordering of the messages sent or received by each object o. This relation, denoted $<_{DS,\,o}$, is the order relation induced by the predecessor association $\mathfrak{R}^e_{Pre}$ on the object o. It is the order according to which, while following the life line of an object o from top to down, we encounter the send or receive action of messages. It is defined in the following way:

$<_{DS,\,o} = \{(m, m')$ such as:

1. $m, m' \in M$ are sent or received by the object o,
2. $m\,\mathfrak{R}^e_{Pre}{}^*\,m'$, that is m precedes m'
3. $\forall\, m'' \in M$ sent or received by the object o, $\Rightarrow (m''\,\mathfrak{R}^e_{Pre}{}^*\,m)$ or $(m'\,\mathfrak{R}^e_{Pre}{}^*\,m'')\}$[1]

The third clause allows to consider in $<_{DS,\,o}$ only the pairs of messages that are directly consecutive with regard to the object o. $<_{DS,\,o}$ is a minimal acyclic relation that contains no transitive implicates.

4.2   Causality Rules Between Actions

One retains four rules to determine whether an action may be considered as the cause of another action and thus must precede this latter. The two firsts rest on a very natural concept of causality, the two others on an interpretation of the predecessor association between the messages.

Beyond the obvious clause: "a message can be received only if it were sent previously", we briefly describe the key concepts of the causality notion. First, we consider

---

[1] Let R be an acyclic relation, R* denotes the transitive closure of R.

that the sending of a message is caused by the reception of the precedent messages and thus imposes that the sending of a message is postponed after the reception of all these precedent messages. Second, We consider that if two directly successive messages are sent by the same object, then the respective emission actions must be ordered; on the other hand, if they are emitted by two different objects, the emission actions are completely independent and thus are not ordered. This new operational semantics thus does not impose a total serialization on the emission and reception actions of successive messages sent by different objects. Third clause complements the preceding one, in the particular case where two messages sent by the same object o are addressed to the same object o': if they are emitted in this order by o, it is to that they are treated in the same order by o', then their respective reception actions must be ordered.

Synchronization Relationship $<_{SYNC}$. This rule says that the $?m$ action of receiving a message m is caused by the $!m$ action of sending that message. It does not require a long justification, a message can be received only if it were sent previously. Formally: $<_{SYNC} = \{(!m, ?m) ; m \in M\}$

Reception-Emission Relationship $<_{RE}$. A reception of message is the cause of the actions of emission that are directly consecutive to it: these emissions constitute the reaction of the object to that it has just received. In terms of causality, a send action is caused by any receive action that has been specified to occur earlier. Fig. 4.a illustrates this rule: the send action of message $m3$ is caused by the reception actions of $m1$ and $m2$, that means the message $m3$ can be sent only after having received the two messages $m1$ and $m2$. Formally: $<_{RE} = \{(?m, !m') ; m, m' \in M, \exists o \in O$ such as :

1. $to(m) = from(m') = o, m <_{DS, o}* m'$ and
2. $\forall m'' \in M, m <_{DS,o}* m'' <_{DS,o}* m' \Rightarrow to(m'') = o\}$.

Again, the second clause allows to consider in $<_{RE}$ only pairs of actions that are directly consecutive with regard to this relation: $(?m, !m') \in <_{RE}$ implies that there is no send action between $?m$ and $!m'$.

Emission-Emission Relationship $<_{EE}$. This rule keeps as far as possible the idea that, if a message m precedes another message m', then m must be created and sent before m'. There is no difficulty to observe this principle in the case where m and m' are sent by the same object. In the other hand, if the two messages are sent by two different objects then the respective emissions are not ordered by this $<_{EE}$ relation since the interpretation of the precedence relation is local in each object, consequently the emission of the second message does not await the termination of the first. This rule is illustrated in Fig. 4, the object o sends the message $m4$ after having sent the message $m3$. Formally: $<_{EE} = \{(!m, !m') ; m, m' \in M, \exists o \in O$ such as $o = From(m) = From(m')$ and $m <_{DS, o} m'\}$.

Reception-Reception $<_{RR}$. This rule complements the preceding one, in the particular case where two messages sent by the object o are addressed to the same object o': if they are emitted in this order by o, it is to that they are treated in the same order by o'. As shown in Fig. 4.b, if the object o sends to o' two messages $m3$ and $m4$ in this order, then they must be treated in this order by o'; consequently between two objects message lines do not cross. Formally: $<_{RR} = \{(?m, ?m') ; m, m' \in M$ such that $!m <_{EE}* !m'$ and $to(m) = to(m')\}$.

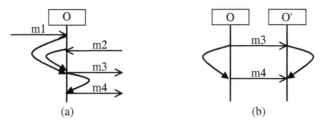

Fig. 4. Causality Rules

4.3 Global Order Relation

There are two types of order relations between the actions of sending and receiving messages: the *inter*-object order relation $<_{SYNC}$, allowing the objects to synchronize their respective behaviors, and the *intra*-objects order relations $<_{RE}$, $<_{EE}$ and $<_{RR}$ deduced from the $<_{DS, O}$ local order relations between messages within each object.

The global causal-order relation among the actions is defined as the transitive closure of the above relations, that is $<_G = <_{SYNC} \cup <_{EE} \cup <_{RR} \cup <_{RE}$.

This relation represents the global behavior of the modeled system. By considering the transitive closure of the global order $<_G^*$, we obtain all the causal dependencies between actions. The local order inside an object o, that we note $<_o$, is obtained by the projection of the global order $<_G^*$ on the object o: $<_o = \{(a, b);$ a, b actions performed by object o and a $<_G^*$ b$\}$ is the set of all the causal dependencies among the actions inside the object o. We can notice that this order can comprise pairs of actions which do not appear in $<_{EE} \cup <_{RR} \cup <_{RE}$ but are deduced by transitivity with $<_{SYNC}$. It is for example the case of the *!on* and *?data* actions performed by the *Control* object in the Boiler Control system, Fig. 3. The same holds for the actions *!Register* and *?AlarmTimeReached* in the object *Manager* of the example presented in the following section, Fig. 8. In these two cases, a receipt action is caused by a send action in the same object. But the causality is indirect and goes through another object. Indeed, a basic idea of the causal-order is that an object cannot be the cause of a message that it receives, except if the received message is sent as a result to one of its own sending. That is, *!m* $<_o$ *?m'* always is deduced by transitivity from a sequence *!m* $<_{SYNC}$ *?m* $<_{RE}$ *!m'* $<_{SYNC}$ *?m'*.

5 Application Examples

In order to illustrate the meaning of the different order relations above defined, we first consider the SDs pictured in Fig. 5.

For these two SDs, the message ordering *precede* association is: *m1* $\mathcal{R}_{Pre}$ *m2* $\mathcal{R}_{Pre}$ *m3*. There is no Activator message. These SDs have the same local scheduling of the messages: $<_{DS, o1} = (m1, m3)$, $<_{DS, o2} = (m2, m3)$ and $<_{DS, o3} = (m1, m2)$. The global order $<_G$ for SD1 and SD2 are represented in Fig. 6.a and 6.b. respectively.

In SD1, each object locally controls its activity, and the relation *!m1* $<_G$ *?m3* is gained by transitivity. All the actions of sending and receiving are purely sequential. This serialization results from the send-receive constraints of the messages and from the *reception-emission* relation $<_{RE}$, where each reception of message causes the emis-

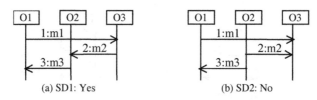

Fig. 5. Locally controllable SDs

Fig. 6. Global Order for SDs on Fig. 5

Fig. 7. Causal-order equivalent SDs

sion of the following message. For this SD, the three semantics coincide – the MSC-order, the UML predecessor-order and the causal-order. As a matter of fact, the UML predecessor-order and the causal-order semantics are equivalent on the sub-class of Locally controllable SDs.

In SD2, three sequences of actions can be carried out in parallel: *!m1;?m1* in parallel with *!m2;?m2*, in parallel with *!m2;!m3;?m3*. This results from the fact that the actions *!m1* and *!m2* are carried out by two distinct objects while there is no way to relate them by transitivity. As a consequence, SD2 is causal-order equivalent to the SD SD3 shown in Fig. 7.a, where the order of *m2* and *m3* is preserved while *m1* is postponed after *m2*. However, SD2 is not causally equivalent to SD4 shown in Fig. 7.b where *?m3* causes *!m1*.

Let us now consider a more complex example: The use of an alarm clock. The Fig. 8 presents a SD comprising the objects User, Controller, Alarm and Timer, describing a scenario of one alarm clock use. The messages are ordered according to their sequence number in the SD.

This SD do not contain messages activators (then $\mathcal{R}^e{}_{Pre} = \mathcal{R}_{Pre}$). From the UML precede association $\mathcal{R}_{Pre}$, we compute the message local orders $<_{DS, o}$ for each object. Then, to obtain the global order relation $<_G$, it is necessary to make the union of the order relations ($<_{SYNC}$, $<_{EE}$, $<_{RR}$, $<_{RE}$) defined in the previous section. Finally, the local order $<_O$ of the actions carried out by each object is obtained by projection of the global order relation $<_G$* on each object.

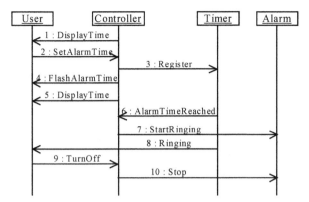

Fig. 8. Scenario of using an alarm clock

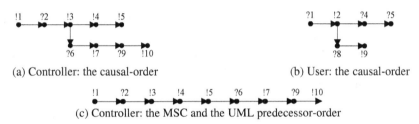

(a) Controller: the causal-order   (b) User: the causal-order

(c) Controller: the MSC and the UML predecessor-order

Fig. 9. The Order Relations $<_O$

The careful examination of this realistic SD is interesting because it features properties that are very common in the practice of UML modeling but seldom fully accounted for. First, the *AlarmTimeReached* message makes this SD not locally controllable, and this is an intrinsic property that cannot be avoided, since reaching the alarm time may happen at any moment after the registration of this time. In fact, this message is caused by the *Register* message and this fact cannot be expressed with the UML predecessor-order relating !*DisplayTime* and !*AlarmTimeReached* is not erroneous and no other similar solution effectively describe the behavior of an alarm clock; as for the MSC-order, a correct modeling requires two other SDs with the reception of *AlarmTimeReached* before the sending of *DisplayTime* or *FlashAlarmTime*.

On the other hand, our causal order, that serializes actions only when necessary, reveals that the activity of the *Controller* and *User* object is better described if it is split in two threads of control. Concerning the *Controller*, see Fig. 9.a, the sequence of actions !*FlashAlarmTime* ; !*DisplayTime* deals with the User while the sequence ?*AlarmTimeReached* ; !*StartRinging* ; ?*TurnOff* ; !*Stop* deals with the Alarm. This distinction is fully relevant and was not apparent at the visual examination of the SD shown Fig. 8. In a similar way concerning the User, only the application of the causal-order, Fig. 9.b, reveals that the sequence ?*FlashAlarmTime* ; ?*DisplayTime* concerns looking at the screen while the sequence ?*Ringing* ; !*TurnOff* concerns hearing the ringing. This splitting of the object activities in distinct threads does not entail that the objects are able to support an internal concurrency among actions. It just means that any sequence interleaving the actions belonging to the threads – more formally: any extension of the $<_o$ relation in a total order relation – is a correct realization of the SD.

6 Related Work

There are mainly two types of papers related to semantics of UML SD. The first kind is called transformational approach in which SDs are translated to existing formalism, such as PVS, Z, Petri-Nets, etc. [11] suppose that the semantics of a SD is given in the form of traces of events associated with each object of the interaction. The common factor of these approaches is the fact that they regard a SD as a MSC. The definition of the SD is thus not in conformity with its definition in the metamodel, since we schedule the actions but not the messages. The advantage of this approach is that tools exist for well established reasoning after the translation. The second approach attempts to interpret or to give a semantics to the SD, then to represent this semantics by a formal language. Our work belongs to the second approach. [12] initially enumerated a number of anomalies from which DS suffer, then proposed a solution which consists in removing the relation of problematic activation. On the other hand, it did not define mathematical process allowing to deduce from the actions of emission and reception starting from scheduling from the messages. [13] is particularly interested by locally controllable SDs, where scheduling of the actions is relatively very simple.

The various semantics can be compared according to whether there are applied on a locally controllable SD or not. In the case of a SD not locally controllable, according with semantics described in [3], there is a need either for a centralized controller that activates each object when it has a send action to perform or for the addition of a synchronization messages. However, the new semantics which we proposed based on the causality of the actions relax this constraint. This semantics is cleaned up by removing all sequencing that has no causal basis by scheduling the least possible the actions. In addition, The precedence over the messages does not necessarily involve that their emissions are ordered.

7 Conclusion

This paper proposes a new operational semantics for UML SD in the form of a scheduling of the actions of sending and receiving messages. This semantics serializes as least as possible these actions, and a precedence between two messages in the SD does not necessarily entail that their emissions are ordered. This semantics is based on the causality relationship among actions, which means that we serialize two actions $a1$ and $a2$ only if $a1$ causes $a2$ either directly or by transitivity.

The semantics proposed in [1] is based on the scheduling of the messages, in which a precedence between two messages implies a precedence between the corresponding sending actions. In this case, an additional synchronization message is needed to ensure that *!FlashAlarmTime* is performed before *!AlarmTimeReached*. As a consequence, the local order of the actions performed by the Controller object, shown in Fig. 9.c, is a total ordering.

Providing SDs with a semantics that imposes slighter scheduling constraints on the behavior of objects results in more expressive SDs, since each SD describes a larger number of acceptable behaviors. As an example, the DataBase object in the SD shown in Fig. 3 may receive the *2:Pressure* and *3:Query* messages in any order, the *4:Data* message will be sent only once both of them have been received. This is clearly the intended meaning of the designer of this SD, which is relieved to draw the SD in which the *2:Pressure* and *3:Query* messages are in the reverse order. When a great number of cases have to be considered, due to the interleaving of actions performed by independent objects, this larger expressive power eases the task of the designer. Notice that this larger expressive power does not mean any ambiguity in the behavior specified by a SD: When editing a SD, the user can ask the generation of all the SDs having the same causal semantics but a different graphical representation.

Another serious benefit of this semantics is that, at the early steps of a development process, it is more convenient than semantics that totally order the actions in each object, as the MSC-order does and partly the UML predecessor-order too. At the early steps, as long as the design of the system is not yet investigated, a SD involves subsystems and large parts of the whole system; it does not involve fine grained components because they are not yet identified, the detailed architecture is still to be drawn. These subsystems will be later breakdown into basic components featuring sequential behaviors. But as long as they are considered as global components, the specification of their interaction with others subsystems by message sending and receiving needs some amount of internal concurrency is not allowed to avoid over-specification that biases following steps of the process by implicit design constraints. Using a semantics that totally orders the actions performed by each component leads to over-specify the behavior of the system: the designer is enforced to detail how the fine grain components interleave their message sending and receiving actions while these components are not even identified.

References

1. J. Cardoso, C. Sibertin Blanc. An operational semantics for UML interaction: sequencing of actions and local control. European Journal of Automatised Systems, APII-JESA 36, p 1015-1028, ISBN 2-7462-0573-4, Hermès-Lavoisier, 2002.
2. OMG Unified Modeling Language Specification : version 1.5 Mars 2003. http://www.omg.org/.
3. « ITU-T recommendation Z.120. Message Sequence Charts (MSC'96), » May 1996, ITU Telecommunication Standardization Sector.
4. G. Booch, I. Jacobson, J. Rumbaugh. "The Unified Modeling Language User Guide". Addison-Wesley Object Technology Series, Addison-Wesley 98, ISBN 0201571684.
5. S. Bernadi, S. Donatelli, J. Merseguer. "From UML Sequence Diagrams and Statecharts to analysable Petri Models". Proceedings of the third international workshop on Software and performance Rome, Italy, 2002. p. 35 – 45 ISBN:1-58113-563-7
6. R. Alur, K. Etessami, M. Yannakakis. "Inference of Message Sequence Charts". Proceedings of the 22nd international conference on Software engineering. Limerick, Ireland 2000. p. 304 – 313 ISBN:1-58113-206-9
7. M. Mukund, K.N. Kumar, and M. Sohoni, "Synthesizing distributed Finite-state systems from MSCs," in CONCUR 2000 :Concurrency Theory, 11th International Conference, LNCS 1877, pp. 521-535. Springer, 2000.
8. Jon Whittle, Johann Schumann. "Generating Statechart Designs From Scenarios". Proceedings of the 22nd international conference on Software engineering, Limerik, Ireland, 2000 Pages: 314 – 323 ISBN:1-58113-206-9

9. S. Uchitel, J. Kramer and J. Magee. "Detecting Implied Scenarios in Message Sequence Chart Specifications". In Proc. Of the European Software Engineering Conference (ESEC/FSE'01), Vienna 2001.

10. Alexander Knapp. "A Formal Semantics for UML Interactions". In Proc. of the 2nd International Conference on the Unified Modeling Language UML'99. October 28-30, 1999 Fort Collins, Colorado, USA. LNCS 1723, pp. 116-130, Springer 1999.

11. Demissie B. Aredo. A Framework for Semantics of UML Sequence Diagrams in PVS Journal of Universal Computer Science (JUCS), 8(7), pp. 674-697, July 2002.

12. Simon Pikin. PhD thesis. Test des composants logiciels pour les télécommunications. Université de Rennes, France, 2003.

13. Xiaosha n Li, Zhiming Liu, Jifeng He: A Formal Semantics of UML Sequence Diagram. In Proc. Australian Software Engineering Conference 2004, April 2004, Australia.

A Proposal for On-Line Reconfiguration Based upon a Modification of Planning Scheduler and Fuzzy Logic Control Law Response

Héctor Benítez-Pérez*, A. García-Zavala, and Fabian García-Nocetti

Departamento de Ingeniería de Sistemas Computacionales y Automatización, IIMAS, UNAM, Apdo. Postal 20-726. Del. A.Obregón, México D.F., 01000, México
Tel: ++52 5622 36 39, ++52 5622 35 69, Fax: ++52 5616 01 76
hector@uxdea4.iimas.unam.mx, agarciaz@yahoo.com
fabian@uxdea4.iimas.unam.mx

Abstract. Nowadays on-line reconfiguration for computer networks is pursued as an alternative approach to keep performance levels when a mal function is presented in the system. In this case, reconfiguration is proposed in three stages. Firstly, computer network presents a degradation in time communication due to the appearance of certain local faults. Secondly, based upon this scenario a strategy for on-line reconfiguration is pursued in order to cover faults where new time delays appear between elements. These delays modify the behaviour of the dynamical response of the system. During third stage, the control law needs to be modified in terms of current time delays. Therefore, in this paper, on-line system reconfiguration as multivariable and multi-stage problem is pursued based upon a quasi-dynamic scheduler that takes into account those predetermined time delays and the related control law. Control law reconfiguration is pursued as soon as structural computer network reconfiguration is taken place by using current system performance.

1 Introduction

Nowadays, on-line reconfiguration is an open field for several applications such as computer network based systems and safety critical systems. The complexity of on-line reconfiguration modifies several conditions within the application like communication performance and system behaviour [1]. Moreover, on-line reconfiguration can be reached by the use of several strategies like research operations [2] or scheduling algorithms [3]. In this work, the authors follow second strategy because it presents a feasible technique in order to keep real-time requirements which are necessary for safety critical systems. As mention before, different variables need to be measured in order to perform on-line reconfiguration for a safety critical system, then, a scheduling algorithm cannot reach this goal by its own because it does not consider system performance. It is necessary to take into account several measures such as, the planning analysis, the square error of the application response and the degradation of the system behaviour

The scope of this work is related to safety critical systems response during on-line reconfiguration, where an ad-hoc procedure is presented in order to get on-line recon-

---

* Contact author.

F.F. Ramos et al. (Eds.): ISSADS 2005, LNCS 3563, pp. 141–152, 2005.
© Springer-Verlag Berlin Heidelberg 2005

figuration. This paper is focused into the definition of a method based upon two algorithms. First algorithm is the planning scheduler that is used to define which plans are valid during an off-line stage. This algorithm takes into account the performance from the related control law (second algorithm) of each plan under the related structural conditions. The problem is to overcome performance degradation from the control law when local time delays appear due to structural reconfiguration. The solution stated above is the goal of this work (the proposal of two algorithms). The goal of this paper is to present an approach for on-line reconfiguration for a safety critical computer network system based upon two algorithms, one for structural reconfiguration (scheduler) and another for system dynamics reconfiguration (reconfigurable control law).

A similar strategy is presented by [4] where an interesting analysis is proposed based upon a trade-off between schedulability and real-time control performance. Alternative strategies have been pursued such as that presented by [5] where a complete framework is reviewed for the design and analysis of distributed real-time control systems. Moreover, [6] have proposed an interesting overview of how time delays related to communication systems are integrated to the control law. An alternative strategy has been presented by [7] where a foundation for optimal controller design is defined for multiple time delays. These delays are caused by a distributed communication system. The result defines a very interesting structure for the same scope addressed in this paper, nevertheless, it presents the constraint of a complete observable system where not always is possible. Moreover, time delays are considered constant where as in here, these are considered time variable based upon scheduling algorithm. This method is focused in a combination of two issues. On one hand, the reconfiguration of a computer network due to certain exogenous demands named as structural reconfiguration. On the other hand, control law reconfiguration as a result of the same exogenous demands named as a dynamic reconfiguration.

This procedure, as first step, proposes a reconfiguration plan. If this is validated (second step) from a comparison procedure explained in a latter section, bus controller takes the correspondent actions to further develop structural reconfiguration over the computer network. At the same time, if the selected plan allows reconfiguration, the bus controller node sends a message to control law node in order to select the related control law (third step). When this last action takes place, control law node gets synchronized to bus controller node to perform both reconfigurations. It is important to define that both databases are determined during offline process. Therefore, two stages are needed, off-line and on-line. During off-line performance a scheduling algorithm tests a group of plans in order to validate some of them. Afterwards (but still in off-line stage), these plans are tested as separate scenarios into the computer network dynamical system with a predefined control law who takes into account the related time delays inherent to current plan. If the response is satisfactory both, the tested plan and the control law are saved into the respective databases. The scheduling algorithm used is the planning scheduler [8] for planning analysis during off-line performance and for scheduling construction during on-line stage. For online stage, the request for reconfiguration from an exogenous agent is carried out. As soon as this requisition is dispatched, this plan is verified within the bus controller node and the control law node where both (the selected plan and the related control law) are delivered to the system. The verification procedure is based upon a simple comparison of the proposed plan and the valid plan database. This database is to be referred as table subsequently. For on-line stage, planning scheduler is used just to build tasks distribution.

In this paper, a case study has been used; this is based upon a ball and beam example [9]. Third section gives a review of this case study.

This computer network system has been implemented on RTLinux [10] and case study has been simulated in MATLAB 5.3 [11]. This paper has been divided in six sections. First section is current introduction. Second section is planning scheduler revision. Third section is the modification proposal of this last scheduling algorithm. Fourth section presents case study and dynamic reconfiguration. Fifth section presents some preliminary results. Finally, concluding remarks are presented in section sixth.

2   Planning Scheduling Review

This scheduler has been proposed by [8]. It is composed of several components such as tasks, main plan consumption time and elementary cycles. Each task is defined by a local consumed time (c) and local period (T). The main plan consumption time (W) is divided into several elementary cycles (EC) where each EC is divided into local time windows named as esp_i. These last divisions result into a more efficient time managing based upon a preemptive strategy. This proposal (planning scheduler) divides a time window into a more complex time division to that presented by rate monotonic [12].

This planning scheduler is based upon eqns 1, 2 and 3 where U is the total consumption time with respect to related periods. N is the total number of tasks, X is the maximum wasted time between time windows EC's.

$$U = \sum_{i=1}^{N} \frac{c_i}{T_i} \tag{1}$$

$$U = \sum_{i=1}^{N} \frac{c_i}{T_i} \langle N\left(2^{1/N} - 1\right) * \frac{E - X}{E} \tag{2}$$

$$X = \max_{i=1...N}(X_i) \leq \max_{i=1...N}(C_i) \tag{3}$$

In this case, time performance is increased in comparison to Rate Monotonic due to re-order of useless time spaces. It presents the advantage of a possible dynamical modification every time window W who is defined as the time window where a very task is executed at least one time. This characteristic makes the system pseudo dynamic in terms of reconfiguration. This algorithm (planning scheduler) is enhanced in order to incorporate new measures such as system performance. As explained in first section, these measurements are taking into account during off-line performance in order to define a suitable control law for those valid plans. This implementation is further reviewed in next section.

3   The Proposed Method

Having reviewed the planning scheduler, this paper proposes a modification based upon the increment of case study efficiency taking into account dynamic system performance.

This procedure is divided in two main stages (Fig. 3.1). Firstly, the off-line stage (First Step) is performed by the use of several combinations of c's (consumed time by local task) and T's (Periodicity related to local task) from the total number of tasks. The list of combinations is conformed in a classification who is named table and it is conformed of a fixed number of lists that are tested by the planning scheduler in order to select those who are valid (Second Step). This new group is tested in case study simulation considering a suitable control law (Third Step). This step generates a smaller group of valid lists with suitable control laws. In this step, two groups are formed, the valid plans and the valid control laws. Both have a one to one relation. Both groups integrate the valid response of case study for different dynamical configuration scenarios. This is named as final table.

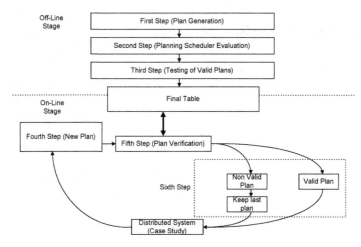

Fig. 3.1. Modified Planning Scheduler

Second stage represents the on-line performance. Firstly, an external element proposes a plan candidate (Fourth Step). This is verified by a simple comparison against those plans presented in final table (Fifth Step).

This comparison is based on an inner product between current proposed plan and those valid plans. If the maximum resultant value from all products is bigger than a determined threshold, current plan is declared as valid. The related control is selected as well.

If plan candidate is valid, this is distributed to every task during a particular time window (Sixth Step). If this plan is not valid, then, current plan is kept for next time window W (Sixth Step).

During second stage if one of the valid plans is selected, then, the related control law is performed as well.

It is essential to remember that reconfiguration and plan distribution takes place between time windows W. In this case, reconfiguration is allowed just during a fixed period of time.

Initially, the modification of scheduler strategy is based upon local faults of peripheral elements.

4 Case Study

Having explained current approach, a case study is reviewed in order to perform case based evaluation. This case study represents a ball and beam with different optical sensors and two actuators [13]. The linearised mathematical model of the ball and beam is next:

$$A(z^{-1})y(t) = z^{-d}B(z^{-1})u(t-1) + c(z^{-1})e(t)$$
$$B = 0 + 0.0013z^{-1} + 0.0016z^{-2}$$
$$C = 1 + 1.5977z^{-1} + 0.8258z^{-2} \tag{4}$$
$$A = 1 + 2.018z^{-1} + 1.032z^{-2}$$

This model is separated in different modules such as peripheral elements and the control law strategy. Sensor and actuator dynamics are neglected for clarity purposes.

This implementation is based upon RT-Linux module. This approach has been followed due to synchronization requirements.

Having shown the main structure of this case study, modelling dynamics are taking into account based upon eqn. 4 where sensors and actuators are considered to be linear. In Fig 4.1 it is shown the actual strategy for reconfigurable control.

In this case, the proposed method is performing *on-line stage*, meaning that on-line reconfiguration takes place based upon previous *off-line stage* depuration and current plan comparison. During this *on-line stage* Modified Planning Scheduler module takes into account an external act in order to perform reconfiguration. This external act is based upon local actuators and sensors behaviour in terms of local faults who are not studied in this work.

This Modified Planning Scheduler module is based upon an inner product between current proposed plan and already defined plans (Defined within Final Table). From the result of this operation if one of the plans produces a result bigger than a defined threshold reconfiguration takes place based upon proposed plan (from external act) and the related control law.

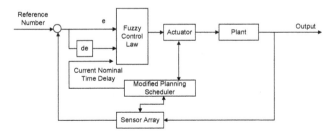

Fig. 4.1. Fuzzy Control Law

Fuzzy control has been chosen rather than gain-scheduler controller and smith's predictor because it has a smooth transition between scenarios. Furthermore, the chosen operating points are the reference elements of proposed fuzzy control. Thus, any degradation from time delays would degrade control law but the plant keeps a stable response. Time delay degradation is bounded from communication protocol as explained by [14].

Current approach follows Mamdani strategy rather than Takagi Sugeno (TKS) proposal. Further on TKS is focused into future work pursued as the integration of time delays into subsequent part of fuzzy rules.

The actual structure of this controller for fault free scenario is proposed in Fig. 4.2. This is based upon [15]. Membership functions are gaussian bells, where *e* variable has six membership functions (PB, PM, PS, NS, NM, NB), *de* has 6 membership functions (PB, PM, PS, NS, NM, NB). The output variable has eight membership functions (PB, PM, PS, PZ, NZ, NS, NM, NB). Additional variable named Current Nominal Time Delay (CNTD) has three membership functions (N, Z, P). Stability issue is not pursued in this paper. The interested reader may consult [16].

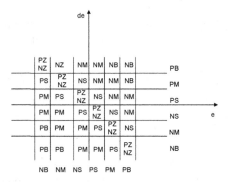

Fig. 4.2. Classical Structure for Fuzzy Control Law

This implementation is a common approach for fuzzy control. For the case of second and third scenarios, Fig. 4.3 shows actual implementation.

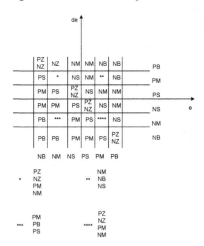

Fig. 4.3. Modification for Fuzzy Control Law

Fig. 4.3 (Fault Scenario II) shows different possibilities at the same condition. This case is proposed due to the possible situation that may be presented at next stage. This is at 100 percent time delay. For instance, condition *de* is NM and *e* is PM has a result

NZ, PZ for fault free scenario (Fig. 4.2). However, Fig. 4.3 presents same scenario with four possible solutions NM, PM, NZ and PZ. This is the result of considering where e and de suppose to be with 100 percent delayed. In this case every new state in terms of fuzzy control is considered equally possible.

Both control laws have been established firstly from try and error approach, afterwards, the use of a classical cluster technique such as fuzzy C-Means is used in order to validate both control laws [17]. The results are similar to those presented in Figs. 4.2 and 4.3.

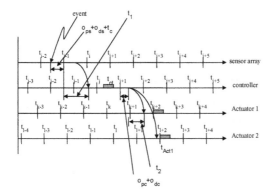

Fig. 4.4. Scheduler for Fault Free Scenario

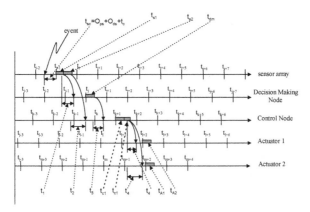

Fig. 4.5. Scheduler for Fault Scenario

Having defined the structure of control reconfiguration, it is necessary to determine those time delays who are the result of system reconfiguration and inter-node communication. These results from each node are transmitted as part of the information flow of control system (sensor-control-actuator). Related to time delays, control node may produces either t_{ff} (time spent for fault free scenario) or t_{fsI} (time spent for fault scenario I) based upon the stage of peripheral elements, furthermore, it gets an estimation of time spent by actuator node and its communication (t_{A1}). Having obtained these sources of time delay, control node produces a global time delay Δt_* This value is composed of time spent by sensor, communication time spent between sensor and control, time spent by control node. Δt_* has three different values as shown in eqns. 6, 8 and 10. These values depend on the current scenario. This Δt_* value is considered as an extra input for controller [9]. First scenario is named as fault free scenario. Fig. 4.4 presents a result of time performance. Total time spent during this scenario is 11.5 milliseconds according to table 1.a and eqn. 5.

$$t_{ff} = t_1 + o_{ps} + o_{ds} + t_{ct} + o_{pc} + o_{dc} + t_2 + t_{A1} \tag{5}$$

Where t_{ff} is the total time spent during fault free scenario. This time is a measure related to scheduling scheme shown in Fig. 4.5.

Table 1a. Time variable from Fault Free Scenario

Var	Name	Time Consume (micro seconds)
c	Communication	450
b	Blocking	50
i	Interference	0
t_c	Capture sensor information	100
O_{ps}	Overhead time from pre-processing sensor information	3000
O_{ds}	Overhead time from post-processing sensor information	3000
t_1	Communication time from sensor node to control node	575
O_{pc}	Overhead of Pre-processing Information from control node	1000
O_{dc}	Overhead of Process Information from control node	1000
t_{ct}	Control Process Time	250
t_2	Communication time from control node to actuator node	575
t_{A1}	Processing time from actuator 1 and 2	2000

Table 1b. Time variables from Fault Scenario

Var	Name	Time Consume
O_{ps}	Overhead time from pre-processing sensor information	1000
O_{ds}	Overhead time from post-processing sensor information	1000
t_c	Capture sensor information	1000
c	Communication	450
b	Blocking	50
i	Interference	0
t_1	Communication time from sensor node to decision making module	575
t_2	Communication time from sensor node to control node	575
t_{s1}	Processing time before sending information	2000
t_{s2}	Processing time before sending information	2000
O_{dm}	Overhead of Pre-processing Information	3000
O_{pm}	Overhead of Process Information	3000
t_{dm}	Sending information from Decision Making to Controller	1000
$t_{c1} = t_{c2}$	Processing time from control node	1000
t_3	Communication time from Decision making node to control node	575
t_4	Communication time from control node to actuator node	575
t_{A1}	Processing time from actuator 1 and 2	2000

Global time delay (Δt_*) is defined from the occurrence of an event until the information reaches control node. Following eqn. 5 actuator its time consumption and time communication are estimated from previous event. Eqn 6 shows this result.

$$t_{ff} - t_{A1} = \Delta t_{ff} \tag{6}$$

Where t_{ff} represents global time spent, t_{A1} represents time delay spent by actuator at fault free scenario and Δt_{ff} represents time delay at fault free scenario. In nominal conditions Δt_{ff} value is zero. For fault scenario I, see Fig. 4.10 (Table 1.b), the summation of this graph is as follows

$$t_{fsI}=t_{dm}+t_{s2}+t_{s1}+ t_2+t_3+t_{c2}+t_4+ t_{c1}+{}^{t_{A1}}+t_1+ t_{sc} \tag{7}$$

This case presents another time delay result due to the appearance of an extra element identified as decision maker module. New communication transactions between sensor and control nodes appear due to this extra element. As a result of this interaction an extra time delay is sum as shown in eqn. 7. As soon as last time delay from actuator node $\hat{t}_{A1}$ is estimated from previous scenario. Final result is equal to equation 8.

$$t_{fsI} - t_{A1} = \Delta t_{fsI} \tag{8}$$

This time delay represents how long control action is taken to be ready before actuator node acts upon the plant. In nominal conditions this value represents 20–40% from worst case scenario.

For second fault scenario shown in Fig, 4.10. A similar situation of former case is exposed due to appearance of extra elements. Eqn. 9 shows total time consumed in this scenario.

$$t_{fsII}=t_{dm}+t_{s2}+t_{s1}+ t_2+t_3+t_{c2}+t_4+ t_{c1}+{}^{t_{A1}}+t_1+ t_{sc} \tag{9}$$

This third scenario is shown as

$$t_{fsII} - t_{A1} = \Delta t_{fsII} \tag{10}$$

Although t_{fsII} and t_{fsI} are similar in nominal terms, it is expected to be modified due to fault conditions. Nevertheless, the differences between scenarios are not explored in this paper. As result of these three scenarios three time delays are obtained. For the case of this simulation, CANbus standard is used to establish the communication between elements and clock synchronisation is time stamping over each communication process. The implementation of this scheduler as well as the case study is based upon State-Flow toolbox from [11].

5 Preliminary Results

The evaluation of the system consists of three scenarios during on-line stage. First scenario is a fault free scenario where the response of the plant is ideal. Second scenario is a fault scenario based upon the loss of "smart" sensor output. Finally a catastrophic condition is presented, then the control law no longer uses the current sensor output.

For these three scenarios the current input of the plant is a pulse train whose indicates the current position of the ball. The output of the plant represents the force applied to the beam. In order to switch to last two scenarios a fault is applied to one of the sensors. The fault is noise that modifies the output of the sensor that measures current position of the ball.

Fig. 5.1 shows the response of the sensor, the plant and the controller during a fault free scenario. Fig. 5.2 shows the response of the system when a fault is presented at 2000 seconds. In here, the control law is second fuzzy logic control (Fig. 4.6) where the input of the faulty sensor is still considered. This fault is active during 500 seconds.

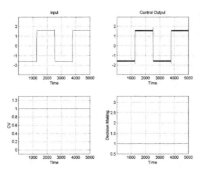

Fig. 5.1. Fault Free Scenario

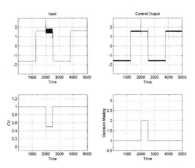

Fig. 5.2. Fault Scenario Starting at 2000 Seconds

As mention in third section the comparison between proposed plan and Final Table is performed by an inner product between them. From the result of this operation a vector is obtained, the maximum element from this vector is considered the winner. If this value is bigger than a defined threshold the proposed plan is taken into account for reconfiguration. The related to control law is switched as well. As depicted in Fig. 5.3 the number of accepted plans is presented taking into those selected with no adequate response from structural reconfiguration. For instance, some tasks would not have enough time to be sampled and executed. This result is presented as the percentage of the adequate use of structural reconfiguration during on-line stage. In this case, current control law is modified according to time delays status. Case study produces an error due to structural and control reconfiguration. This is evaluated in order to declare a valid plan or not.

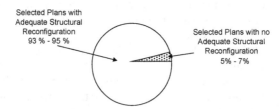

Fig. 5.3. Percentage of Selected Valid Plans for Structural Reconfiguration

Having defined the percentage related to those adequate plans during structural reconfiguration, this is taking as 100 % and is evaluated in terms of control law performance. The results are presented in Fig. 5.4. In here, 97% of the valid plans have a valid response in terms of the mean square error response from the dynamic response of case study.

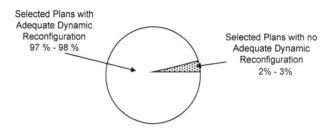

Selected Plans with
Adequate Dynamic
Reconfiguration
97 % - 98 %

Selected Plans with no
Adequate Dynamic
Reconfiguration
2% - 3%

Fig. 5.4. Percentage of Selected Valid Plans for Control Law Reconfiguration

As preliminary conclusion it can stated that on-line reconfiguration will not always be successful by just taking into account the isolate response of control law. It is necessary to take into account the transitions from one configuration to another.

On-line reconfiguration is pursued during a fixed time window named W equal to 200 ms. This is presented as a drawback, however, it does keep a safety standard in terms on time dependability.

6 Conclusions

Present approach has shown how on-line reconfiguration can be pursued based upon dynamic system performance defined from time delays appearance. In order to define these time delays, it is necessary to determine those scenarios where reconfiguration would take place. This selection of suitable scenarios is an *off-line stage* where planning scheduler selects those suitable scenarios and the related control laws. During *on-line* procedure, a simple comparison between a proposed plan and the already selected plan allows on-line reconfiguration. The related control is dispatched at the same time when the selected plan is send to the rest of the elements in the computer network.

Although, this approach is based upon two separate problems, it presents an ad hoc view of how control performance needs to be taken into account in order to develop on-line system reconfiguration based upon a quasi-dynamic scheduler algorithm. Further work is required in terms of a more precise comparison between current proposed plan and Final Table. In this case, two different approaches may be pursued, the use of Neural Networks for pattern classification and genetic algorithms for table optimisation.

Acknowledgements

The authors would like to thank the financial support of UNAM-PAPIIT (IN106100 and IN105303) Mexico in connection with this work.

References

1. Cervin A., Eker J., Bernhardsson B., Arzen, K.; "Feedback-Feedforward Scheduling of Control Tasks"; Real-Time Systems, Kluwer Academic Publishers, Vol. 23, No. 25-53, 2002.
2. Cheng A.; "Real-Time Systems"; Wiley Interscience, USA, 2003.
3. Liu J.; "Real-Time Systems"; Ed. Prentice Hall, 2000.
4. Seto D., Lehoczky J., Sha, L., and Shin, K.; "Trade-Off Analysis of Real-Time Control Performance and Schedulability"; Real-Time Systems, Vol. 21, pp. 199-217, 2001.
5. Törngren, M., and Redell, O.; "A Modelling Framework to support the Design and Analysis of Distributed Real-Time Control Systems"; Microprocessors and Microsystems, vol. 24, pp. 81-93, 2000.
6. Cervin A., Henriksson, D., Lincoln B., Eker, J., and Arzen K.; "How Does Control Timming Affect Performance"; IEEE Control Systems Magazine, Vol. 23, No. 3, pp. 16-30, 2003.
7. Lian F. Moyne J. and Tilbury D. ; "Optimal Controller Design and Evaluation for a Class of Networked Control Systems with Distributed Constant Delays"; American Control Conference, pp. 3009-3014, May 2002a.
8. Almeida L., Pasadas R. and Fonseca J. A.; "Using a Planning Scheduler to Improve the Flexibility of Real-Time Fieldbus Networks"; *Control Engineering Practice*, vol 7, pp. 101-108, Pergamon,1999.
9. Benítez-Pérez H. and García-Nocetti F.; "Switching Fuzzy Logic Control for a Reconfigurable System considering Communication Time Delays"; Proceedings, CD-ROM, European Control Conference; ECC03, UK, September 2003b.
10. Ripoll, J.; "Tutorial of Real-Time Linux"; http://bernia.upv.es/~iripoll/rt-linux/rtlinux-tutorial/index.html, 2001.
11. Mathworks (1998). *MATLAB User's Guide*, MATLAB.
12. Liu L., and Layland L.; "Scheduling Algorithms for Multiprogramming in a Hard Real-Time Environment" Journal of ACM., Vol. 20, pp. 46-61, 1973.
13. Benítez-Pérez, H., and García Nocetti, F.; "Reconfigurable Distributed Control using Smart Peripheral Elements ", Control Engineering Practice, vol. 11, No. 9, pp. 975-988, 2003a.
14. Lian F. Moyne J. and Tilbury D. ; "Network Design Consideration for Distributed Control Systems"; IEEE Transactions on Control Systems Technology, Vol. 10, No. 2, pp. 297-307, March 2002b.
15. Driankov, D., Hellendoorn, H., Reinfrank, M.; " An Introduction to Fuzzy Logic Control"; Springer-Verlag, 1994.
16. Nguyen H., Prasad N., Walker C., and Walker E.; "Fuzzy and Neural Control"; Ed. CRC, 2003.
17. Höppnner F., Klawonn F., Kruse R., and Runkler T.; "Fuzzy Cluster Analysis"; Ed. John Wiley, 2000.

Integrated Tool for Testing Timed Systems

Hacène Fouchal[1], Sébastien Gruson[2], Ludovic Pierre[2],
Cyril Rabat[2], and Antoine Rollet[2]

[1] GRIMAAG, Université des Antilles et de Guyane,
F-97157 Pointe-à-Pitre, Guadeloupe, France
Hacene.Fouchal@univ-ag.fr
[2] CReSTIC/LICA, Université de Reims Champagne-Ardenne,
BP 1039 F-51687 Reims Cedex, France
{Cyril.Rabat,Antoine.Rollet}@univ-reims.fr

Abstract. Some new protocols handle time constraints to model important aspects (delays, timeouts, ..). This issue has to be taken into account in every step during its development life cycle, in particular in the testing step. This paper presents an integrated tool which permits to specify a timed system in various models (RT-LOTOS, IF, Timed automata) and then generates test sequences using a new efficient algorithm. Illustrated examples show the differents steps of this new test generation method.

Keywords: Protocol Engineering, Validation, Conformance Testing, Timed Automata, Automata Theory.

1 Introduction

In software development, conformance testing is highly needed in order to avoid catastrophic errors and to tackle the industrial development of the product with confidence. Since a couple of years, time is considered as a crucial feature of many sensitive systems as multimedia protocols, embedded systems, air traffic systems. Then it should be seriously considered by designers and developers.

In this paper, we present a tool which is able to accept three different (RT-LOTOS, IF, Timed automata) models to describe any system to test. RT-LOTOS [1] is an extension to the ISO language LOTOS [2]. In this part we use the RTL tool to derive Input Output Timed Automata. IF [3] is an intermediate form which may come from SDL or any other formal technique. We developed a translater able to derive Input Output Timed Automata from IF specifications. We have also taken into account the possibility to handle Timed automata used in the Uppaal [4] tool. Then we apply a technique of test sequence generation on the derived Timed Input Output Automaton (TIOA). A Timed Input Output Automaton (defined as an automaton where each transition can bear either an input action or output action and sometimes timing constraints), widely used for the description of timed systems.

Our work is deeply inspired by the protocol engineering area where researchers usually deal with two main validation techniques:

- the *verification approach*, which handles the system specification and tries to prove its correctness (in this case the system is a white box). Usually, the user properties are expressed by another formalism as temporal logics and must be verified on the specification by using a model-checker for example,

F.F. Ramos et al. (Eds.): ISSADS 2005, LNCS 3563, pp. 153–166, 2005.

– the *testing approach*, which uses the implementation of the system and tries to find any faulty behavior on it without having a priori any information about the structure of the system (in this case the system is a black box). The test generation produces sequences of inputs (actions) from the specification, and the implementation must be able to execute these sequences (called *'test sequences'*) and to answer with the expected outputs.

In this paper, we will deal with the second technique where the aim is to derive for each controllable state of the system a specific test sequence. The purpose is to check if every controllable state is correctly implemented on the Implementation Under Test (IUT). This technique is integrated in the whole tool in order to permit to specify and then to derive test sequences for any system. This tool will use the output files produced by other tools (most of them are dedicated to the verification issue).

This paper is structured as follows: Section 2 contains related works to the timed testing field. Section 3 describes the timed automata model and its main features. In section 4, we present all specification tools that we used in order to generate timed automata.

Then, in Section 5.3, we present an algorithm which produces, for each controllable state, a sequence of actions able to identify it. Section 6 gives the conclusion and some ideas about future works.

2   Related Work

There are many works dedicated to the verification of timed automata [5–7]. Some tools [4, 8] have been developed for this purpose. But some other studies proposed various testing techniques for timed systems.

[9] deals with an adaptation of the canonical tester for timed testing and it has been extended in [10]. In [11], the authors derive test cases from specifications described in the form of a constraint graph. They only consider the minimum and the maximum allowable delays between input/output events. [12] presents a specific testing technique which suggests a practical algorithm for test generation. They have used a timed transition system model. The test selection is performed without considering time constraints. [13] gives a particular method for the derivation of the more relevant inputs of the systems. [14] suggests a technique for translating a region graph into a graph where timing constraints are expressed by specific labels using clock zones. [15] suggests a selection technique of timed tests from a restricted class of dense timed automata specifications. It is based on the well known testing theory proposed by Hennessy in [16]. [17] derives test cases from Timed Input Output Automata extended with data. Automata are transformed into a kind of Input Output Finite State Machine in order to apply classical test generation technique.

[18] gives a general outline and a theoretical framework for timed testing. They proved that exhaustive testing of deterministic timed automata with a dense interpretation is theoretically possible but is still difficult in practice. They suggested to perform a kind of discretization of the region graph model (which is an equivalent representation of the timed automata model). Clock regions are only equivalence classes of clock valuations. Their discretization step size takes into account the number of clocks as well as

the timing constraints. Then they derive test cases from the generated model. The second study [19] differs from the previous one by using discretization step size depending only on the number of clocks which reduces the timing precision of the action execution. The resulting model has to be translated into a kind of Input/Output Finite State Machine which could be done only under strong and unrealistic assumptions. Finally they extract test cases by using the Wp-method [20].

As we can notice, there are different ways to tackle the problem of timed testing. All of these studies focus on reducing the specification formalism in order to be able to derive test cases feasible in practice. In contrast to these studies, we use the timed automata model without neither translation nor transformation of labels on transitions.

3   Timed Automata Model

In this section, we will recall the definitions of *timed input output automata* model.

3.1   Definitions

Timed input output automata have been proposed to model finite-state real-time systems. Each automaton has a finite set of *states* and a finite set of *clocks* which are real-valued variables. All clocks proceed at the same rate and measure the amount of time that has elapsed since they were started or reset. Each transition of the system might reset some of the clocks, and has an associated enabling condition which is a constraint on the values of the clocks. A transition can be taken only if the current clock values satisfy its enabling condition.

The following definitions are mainly identical to those given in [21], but some of them have been modified in order to widen the field of application of the method, and also to eliminate some repeated and useless information.

Definition 1. *(Clock constraints and clock guard) A* clock constraint *over a set C of clocks is a boolean expression of the form x* **oprel** z *where $x \in C$,* **oprel** *is a classical relational operator $(<, \leq, =, \geq, >)$, and z is either an integer constant n, or a clock y, or their sum $y + n$.*

A clock guard *over C is a conjunction of clock constraints over C.*

It is important to notice at once that all these constraints can be expressed by a relation such as: $\Theta(x_1, \ldots, x_{|C|})$ **oprel** 0 where θ is linear.

Definition 2. *(Timed Input Output Automata) A timed input output automaton [21] A is defined as a tuple $(\Sigma_A, L_A, l_A^0, C_A, E_A)$, where:*

- *Σ_A is a finite alphabet, split in two sets: $\Im$ (input actions) beginning with a "?", and $\mathcal{O}$ (output actions) beginning with a "!".*
- *L_A is a finite set of states,*
- *$l_A^0 \in S$ is the initial state,*
- *C_A is a finite set of clocks,*
- *$E_A \subseteq L_A \times L_A \times \Sigma_A \times 2^{C_A} \times \Phi(C_A)$ is the set of transitions.*

An edge (l, l', a, λ, G) represents a transition from state l to state l' on input or output symbol a. The subset $\lambda \subseteq C_A$ allows the clocks to be reset with this transition, and G is a clock guard over C_A. $\Phi(C_A)$ is the set clock guards over C_A.

4 Tools

In this section we develop briefly the external tools used in our toolbox in particular to model timed systems.

4.1 The KRONOS Tool

In fact KRONOS [22] is a set of tools which deal with timed automata. It provides a verification engine in order to be integrated in a real-time environment. It has been developped by VERIMAG Laboratory at the University of Grenoble. It does not deal with Input Output Automata. In this tool, we only use its timed automata internal form as basic form for our tool box.

The KRONOS Description Form is as follows (the KRONOS file extension is **tg**):

- The file heading contains the automaton state number, the transition number and the clock number (with their labels).
- The automaton is completely defined in the file body, with a set of expressions corresponding to each state and which contains: the outgoing number of the state, its label, its invariant conditions on clocks and its set of transitions (going from the state). Each transition is described with a guard (timing constraint on the transition), a label, a set of clocks to be reset, and finally the destination state.

The form used in our tool box is the KRONOS one. But other tools often use different forms of timed automata. For our case, it is necessary to translate these forms into the KRONOS one in order to handle them.

4.2 The UPPAAL Tool and Its XML Form

UPPAAL [4] is a tool for modeling and validation of real-time systems, modeled as timed automata networks. The UPPAAL file form is XML (the older versions of UPPAAL accept TA and XTA forms, but it tends to disappear).

Each automaton of the system represents a process and communicates with other processes via channels. Each automaton has clocks that can be local (i.e. just for this automaton) or global (i.e. for the whole system). All automata have to be deterministic.

4.3 The IF Environment

IF [3] is a free environment for the validation of distributed systems. It is based on the SDL (Specification and Description Language) language.

The IF files contain the description of a system composed of different processes communicating via communication buffers, probably with exchanges of signals or with shared variables. Processes may be non-deterministic and more than one transition may be fired from any state. The language provides also the dynamic creation and destruction of processes.

From IF or UPPAAL Form to KRONOS Form. This part is an analyser called if2tg that translates IF files into KRONOS files based on [3]. The principle of translation from XML to KRONOS is quite similar.

Each IF file describes a whole system, composed by different processes. Each process is considered as a timed automaton. Since the IF language is more powerful than the KRONOS, some options are ignored during the translation, such that priorities, atomicity of actions or informations about the routes of signals.

Notice that several input (the field `input`) and output actions (`output` actions) may be on one transition. So, we need to create a new state for each input/output action so that one action corresponds to one transition. The new states have no guard.

An other problem on the transitions is that the language allows `while` loops and `if/then/else` conditions.

4.4 The RTL Tool

RTL is a tool for modeling timed automata using the RT-LOTOS language.

The RT-LOTOS language (Real Time LOTOS), used in the tool RTL, is an extension of the LOTOS language (Language Of Temporal Ordering Specification). RT-LOTOS is dedicated especially for the specification of real-time systems, with temporal operators added to LOTOS (delay, latency, temporal violation).

The tool RTL provides a lot of functionalities. We particularly use one of them: the possiblity to compile an RT-LOTOS specification (.lot extension) into a kind of timed automaton: a Dynamic Timed Atomaton (DTA) (.dta extension). Actually, a DTA is a tuple (S, N_{Clocks}, E, s_0) obtained as:

- **S** a finite set of controllable states
- N_{Clocks} a function associating an index to the clocks constraints
- **E** a finite set of transitions where each transition is a tuple (s, a, K, C, θ, s') with:
  - s is the source state of the transition
  - s' is the destination of the transition
  - K is the timing condition
  - a is the label of an associated action
  - $C \subseteq \{1 \ldots N_{Clocks}(s')\}$ defines the indexes of clocks that have to be reset
  - $\theta \in N^+_{Clocks}$ represents the functions(s) associated to the transition
- s_0 is the initial state

From DTA Form to KRONOS Form. This part of translation from DTA filesin to KRONOS files is called dta2kronos. It is the result of some modifications on the initial tool (with the same name) given in RTL (http://www.laas.fr/RT-LOTOS /distrib/dta2kronos.0.7.tar.gz). We made these modifications for technical reasons. One of these modifications is the possibility to count the state number in the automaton.

4.5 The Polylib Library

The Polylib [23] library provides a software package to handle polyhedrons. It provides a set of operations on sets obtained by union of polyhedrons, or for example on matrix or vectors.

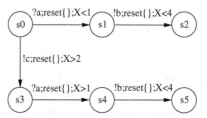

Fig. 1. Example of Timed automaton

In our tool, the Polylib is used to calculate the intersection of two inequality sets. Indeed, two transitions with the same label may be different if their timing condition (the guard) are different. Thus the guards have to be compared.

On Figure 1, state s_0 accepts the sequence $(?a, X < 1), (!b, X < 4)$. Similarly, state s_3 accepts the sequence $(?a, X > 2), (!b, X < 4)$. However, these two sequences are considered as different since the intersection between $(X < 1)$ and $(X > 2)$ is empty. If we had have $(X < 1)$ et $(X < 2)$, the two sequences would have been considered as accepted by the two states.

5 Test Sequence Generation

Our main contribution is described in this section. We detail our test generation algorithm. We ullistrate each part of the algorithm by an example.

5.1 Assumptions

The following assuptions are required for our systems.

Assumption 1: the tester will handle its own set of clocks which run in the same rate than the IUT one. There may be some resets which are not correctly implemented on the IUT. We will show later how our method is able to detect that IUT is faulty without a precise diagnostic about this fault.

In order to increase our ability to control and observe as best as possible the IUT, we should be able at each moment to know what we have to do. Then, a system cannot have a choice of an input action or an output one.

Assumption 2: we consider that each state in $\mathcal{TA}$ has either only outgoing transitions labeled with input actions or only outgoing transitions labeled with output actions.

We handle only deterministic systems, ie, from each state we cannot have two outgoing transitions with the same label. In fact, we have no idea about how timing constraints are implemented, then we cannot observe the implementation if the two target states by both transitions are correctly implemented.

Assumption 3: we assume also that we cannot have two outgoing transitions labeled by the same output action even if their timing constraints are different.

Assumption 4: we assume also that we cannot have two outgoing transitions labeled by two distinct output actions where the intersection of their timing constraints is not empty.

Assumption 5: all the systems that we are able to deal with should be described by minimal automata. If there are some redundant states in any automaton, there is no way to distinguish them. That means our algorithm will fail.

5.2 Definitions

We consider the following notations. Let's have a Timed automaton $\mathcal{T}\!A = (\Sigma, \mathcal{S}, s_0, \mathcal{C}, \mathcal{T})$. $\mathcal{S}$ is the set of states. $\mathcal{C}$ is the set of clocks. $\mathcal{G}$ is the set of guards over $\mathcal{C}$. Σ is the set of actions, $\Sigma = \mathcal{I} \cup \mathcal{O}$ where $\mathcal{I}$ set of input actions and $\mathcal{O}$ set of output actions $\mathcal{T} = \{t_1, ..., t_M\}$ where $t_i = \langle a_i, g_i, Rset_i \rangle$ $(1 \le i \le N)$ and $a_i \in$, $g_i \in \mathcal{G}$ and $Rset_i \in \mathcal{C}$.

The basis of our test sequence generation algorithm is to identify states of the specification on the implementation. The specification timed automaton is denoted $\mathcal{T}\!A_\mathcal{S}$ and the implementation timed automaton is denoted $\mathcal{T}\!A_\mathcal{I}$. But the only states that we are able to identify are those having outgoing transitions with input actions. These states are called controllable states. We denote $\mathcal{OS}$ this set, $\mathcal{OS} = \{os_1, ..., os_{OSN}\}$ (OSN length of this set). The set denoted $\mathcal{NOS}$ contains not controllable states (they have outgoing transitions labeled by output actions).

Definition 3 (Controllable state). os is a controllable state if $os \in \mathcal{S}$ and $Out(os) = \{t_1, ..., t_n\}$ $\forall t_j$, $t_j \in (T)$ and $t_j = \langle a_j, G_j, Rset_j \rangle$ and $a_j \in \mathcal{I}$

Definition 4 (Possible identification sequence). seq_i is a Possible identification sequence if seq_i is defined as $\{t_{i_1}, ..., t_{i_n}\}$ where $\forall j, 1 \le j \le n$ $t_{i_j} \in \mathcal{I}$ and $t_{i_1} = \langle a_{i_1}, G_{i_1}, Rset_{i_1} \rangle$ and $a_{i_1} \in \mathcal{I}$ and $t_{i_n} = \langle a_{i_n}, G_{i_n}, Rset_{i_n} \rangle$ and $a_{i_n} \in \mathcal{O}$.

Example: On Figure 2, s_1 has a possible identification sequence: $(?a;X{<}7),(!b,X{<}4)$

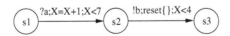

Fig. 2. Example of a specification

Definition 5 (Recognized sequence). *se is a recognized sequence (with depth d) from a controllable state os_i and denoted $sequence_i^d$ if seq_i appears in $\mathcal{T}\!A$ from os_i and if seq_i contains d input actions.*

Definition 6 (Recognized sequence set). *Let os_i an controllable state, let D the maximum number of input actions required in an identification sequence. RSS_i (Recognized Sequence Set) is the set of all recognized sequences of os_i having at maximum D input actions. $RSS_i = RSS_{i_1} \cup ... \cup RSS_{i_D}$ where $RSS_{i_j} = \{sequence / sequence = sequence_i^j\}$*

Definition 7 (Identification sequence). *Id_i is the identification sequence for the controllable state os_i if Id_i is a Possible Identification Sequence of os_i and $\forall os_j \in \mathcal{OS}$, $Id_i \notin RSS_j$*

Definition 8 (Identified state). *os_i is an identified state if $\exists seq_i$ and seq_i is an identification sequence for os_i.*

Example: On Figure 3, state s_0 is controllable. We consider then the following test sequences:

1. $(?a, X < 4), (!b, X > 2),$
2. $(?d, X < 1), (!d, X > 2), (!e, X < 4),$
3. $not[(?b, X > 1), (!c, X > 6)].$

This set of sequences is recognized by state s_0. Indeed:

- $(?a, X < 4), (!b, X > 2)$ is recognized by s_0,
- $(?d, X < 1), (!d, X > 2), (!e, X < 4)$ is recognized by s_0,
- $(?b, X > 1), (!c, X > 6)$ is not recognized by s_0.

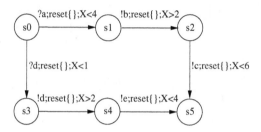

Fig. 3. Set of sequences example

5.3   Test Sequence Generation Algorithm

The algorithm for the generation of test sequences is presented in [24]. The idea is to find for any controllable state a set of sequences in order to identify the state (see 5.2 p. 159). This algorithm is divided into three steps, described below.

First Step. The first part consists of generating for each controllable state all the possible sequences accepted by itself, with a given maximum depth. Then we check for each sequence if an other state accepts it. There are two possibilities:

- If no other state recognizes this sequence, then the current state is considered as identified by this sequence. We store the sequence, mark the state and we continue with next states
- Else we try all the possible sequences until one of them identifies the state or until there is no more sequence to try. If none of them can identify the state, we store the sequence which has been accepted by the lower number of states. It will be used during the second step of the algorithm.

If all the states have been identified at the end of this step, then the algorithm stops.

Example

On the automaton of Figure 4, four states are controllable: all the transitions going from these states are input transitions. These states are: s_1, s_3, s_5 and s_7.

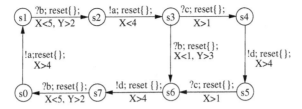

Fig. 4. Automaton on which only the first step is necessary

For a depth equal to 1, we find all these possible sequences:

- s_1 : one sequence : $(?b, !a)$,
- s_3 : two sequences : $(?c, !d)$ et $(?b, !d)$,
- s_5 : one sequence : $(?c, !d)$,
- s_7 : one sequence : $(?b, !a)$.

For the states s_1 and s_7, the resulting sequences have the same labels. However, the guards of the second transition of these sequences are distinct. Thus these sequences are considered as different, and then the states s_1 and s_7 are identified.

For s_3, the only sequence that identifies it is $(?b, !d)$. On the other hand, there is no sequence in this set that may identify s_5 since its single sequence is accepted by s_3 too. So we need to reach the depth 4 in order to find a identifying sequence for s_5: $(?c, !d, ?e, !a)$. Indeed, the depth 3 gives no valid sequence since a sequence has to end with an output.   Let us summarize the results:

- s_0 : not controllable,
- s_1 : controllable, identified with sequence $(?b, !a)$,
- s_2 : not controllable,
- s_3 : controllable identified with sequence $(?b, !d)$,
- s_4 : not controllable,
- s_5 : controllable identified with sequence $(?c, !d, ?e, !a)$,
- s_6 : not controllable,
- s_7 : controllable identified with sequence $(?b, !a)$.

Second Step. This step uses as inputs the results of the previous step. Here, we built a tree where the root contains all the states to be identified. We try then to split this set as follows:

- We choose a sequence recognized by one of the remaining states (one of those found by the first step but which has been also recognized by other states)
- We apply this sequence on every state of the set
- All states which recognize this sequence will be gathered on the right child node
- All other states will be gathered on the left child node

We proceed recursively on all child nodes until the situation where we cannot split any set. The set may contain only one state or no sequence can distinguish between states. At the end of the step, we will consider two kinds of leafs of the resulting tree:

- leafs with only one state, that means this state is identified by the set of all sequences of the path going from the root to this state. Of course some sequences of the path (those of the left nodes) should not be recognized by the state.
- leafs with more than one state, that means these states cannot be distinguish with this step. But we keep the set of the sequences of the path going from the root to this node: this sequence set will distinguish the state set from all others.

If at the end of this step, all controllable states have been identified, the algorithm will end.

Notice: When a set of sequences distinguishes a set of states from others, it is true for the step two, but we should also check if this sequence set is not recognized by states identified in the first step.

If we find such states, then we add the unique sequence of states (first step) to the set of sequences and we precise that this unique sequence should not be recognized by the set of states of the second step.

Example

We consider the automaton of Figure 5. Let us choose 1 as the maximum depth in this case. Then, the states $\{0, 4$ and $7\}$ will not be identified in the step one. As best sequence for each state, we will have respectively $(?b, !c)$, $(?c, !d)$ et $(?a, !c)$. All of these sequences are recognized by two states at least.

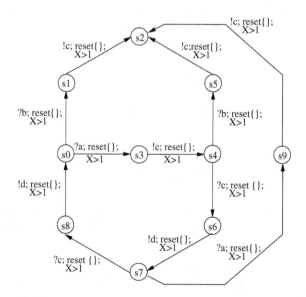

Fig. 5. Automaton which needs step two without step three

We start with a tree having at its root all of these states. Then we choose the first of these (here 0) and we check if the sequence $(?b, !c)$ is recognized. 0 and 4 recognize it but not 7. We gather the first two states on the right node and the other in the left node.

The right node should be split.

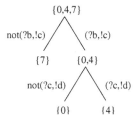

Fig. 6. Obtained tree after the second step on the automaton of Figure 5

We select the state 4 and its sequence $(?c, !d)$. 0 does not recognize it, we put it in the left node and 4 in the right one. As we said, the resulting tree is interesting since all the leafs contain single states. The obtained tree is in the Figure 6. The test sequences obtained after this step are:

- s_0 : controllable with the sequences $(?b, !c)$ et not$(?c, !d)$,
- s_1 : not controllable,
- s_2 : not controllable,
- s_3 : not controllable,
- s_4 : controllable by $(?b, !c)$ and $(?c, !d)$,
- s_5 : not controllable,
- s_6 : not controllable,
- s_7 : controllable by$(?a, !c)$ and not$(?b, !c)$
- s_8 : not controllable,
- s_9 : not controllable.

Step Three. In this last step, we only consider each state set not split in the step two. Then, we apply for each of them the same process of the step two: we build a tree begining at the root with the whole set and we choose a sequence able to divide the state set on two parts: a part of states which recognizes the sequence and another part which will not recognize it. But here, we consider all possible sequences going from each state. The final result is to have leafs with only one state.

Example

We consider the example of Figure 7. The controllable states are $\{0, 2, 7$ et $9\}$.

If we choose as depth value 1, no state could be identified after step 1. After step 2 only two sets are gathered $\{0, 9\}$ and $\{2, 7\}$ (the first set recognizes the sequence $(?a, !b)$ but not the second one).

We deal with the first set with depth value 1, then we have the following results: state 1, one sequence $(?a, !b)$; state 3, no sequence and state 4, 1 sequence $(?a, !b, ?b, !c)$, both states react in a similar way. Thus, in order to distinguish them, we should find a sequence having a depth value equal to 5 which is $(?a, !b, ?b, !c, !b)$ (another may be possible $(?a, !b, ?b, !c, !d)$). The state 0 accepts also this sequence but not the state 9. We add this sequence to the one found in step 2.

We proceed in a similar way for 2 and 7. At the depth value 1, the only possible sequence $(?b, !c)$ is not able to distinguish the sets. But with depth value equal to 3, $(?b,$

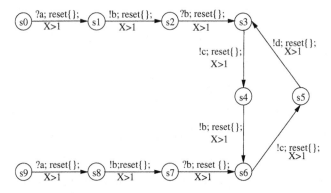

Fig. 7. Automaton which needs the step three

!c, !b) will distinguish the two states (2 will recognize but not 7). We add then this one to not(?a, !b).

We also add to the states 2 and 7 their best sequences found in step one (?b, !c).

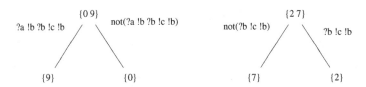

Fig. 8. Resulting tree after step 3 on the automaton of Figure 7

Finally, here are the results of the whole algorithm:

- s_0 : controllable and identified by (?a, !b) and (?a, !b, ?b, !c, !b),
- $s_1, s_3, s_4, s_5, s_6, s_8$: not controllable,
- s_2 : controllable and identified by (?b, !c), not(?a, !b) and (?b, !c, !b),
- s_7 : controllable and identified by (?b, !c), not(?a, !b) and not(?b, !c, !b),
- s_9 : controllable and identified by (?a, !b) and not(?a, !b, ?b, !c, !b).

6   Conclusion

In this paper, we have presented a toolbox able to handle timed systems from the specification step to the test sequence generation step. We have used external tools well known in the area of timed systems modeling and verification (RTL, UPPAAL, KRONOS, IF). We have adapted their description formats and used them in order to apply our test sequence generation algorithm. Our toolbox is shown in Figure 9

Our main contribution is the implementation of a test generation algorithm for timed systems using only timed automata. We have illustrated the three parts of this algorithm on simple examples.

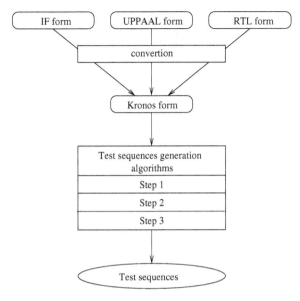

Fig. 9. The scheme of the integrated tool

We are currently working on the specification and the test sequence generation for a real protocole (t PGM protocole) dedicated to a real-time video transfer. We need to improve the adaptation of external formats since there are some specific situations where we cannot deal with specifications written in UPPAAL and RTL.

References

1. Courtiat, J.P., Santos, C., Lohr, C., Outtaj, B.: Experience with RT-LOTOS, a Temporal Extension of the LOTOS Formal Description Technique. Computer Communications **23** (2000) 1104–1123
2. Bolognesi, T., Brinksma, E.: Introduction to the ISO specification language LOTOS. In Eijk, P.v., Vissers, C., Diaz, M., eds.: The formal description technique LOTOS, Elsevier Science Publishers (1989) 23–73
3. Bozga, M., Fernandez, J.C., Ghirvu, L., Graf, S., Krimm, J.P., Mounier, L.: IF: A validation environment for timed asynchronous systems. In: Computer Aided Verification. (2000) 543–547
4. Bengtsson, J., Larsen, K., Larsen, F., Petterson, P., Yi, W., Weise, C.: New Generation of UPPAAL. In: Proceedings of the International Workshop on SOftware Tools and Technology Transfer (Aalborg, Denmark, July 12-13). (1998)
5. Alur, R., Courcoubetis, C., Henzinger, T.: The observational power of clocks. In Jonsson, B., Parrow, J., eds.: Proceedings CONCUR 94, Uppsala, Sweden. Volume 836 of Lecture Notes in Computer Science. Springer-Verlag (1994) 162–177
6. Daws, C., Olivero, A., Yovine, S.: Verifying ET-LOTOS programs with KRONOS. In Hogrefe, D., Leue, S., eds.: Proceedings of the 7th International Conference on Formal Description Techniques, FORTE'94, North-Holland (1994) 207–222

7. Daws, C., Yovine, S.: Two examples of verification of multirate timed automata with KRO-NOS. In: Proceedings of the 1995 IEEE Real-Time Systems Symposium, RTSS'95, Pisa, Italy, IEEE Computer Society Press (1995)

8. Daws, C., Olivero, A., Tripakis, S., Yovine, S.: The tool Kronos. In Alur, R., Henzinger, T., Sontag, E., eds.: Hybrid Systems III. Volume 1066 of Lecture Notes in Computer Science, Springer-Verlag (1995)

9. Koné, O.: Designing test for time dependant systems. In: Proceedings of the 13th IFIP International Conference on Computer Communication *Séoul, South Korea.* (1995)

10. Laurencot, P., Castanet, R.: Integration of Time in Canonical Testers for Real-Time Systems. In: International Workshop on Object-Oriented Real-Time Dependable Systems, California, IEEE Computer Society Press (1997)

11. Clarke, D., Lee, I.: Automatic generation of tests for timing constraints from requirements. In: Proceedings of the Third International Workshop on Object-Oriented Real-Time Dependable Systems, Newport Beach, California. (1997)

12. Cardel-Oliver, R., Glover, T.: A practical and complete algorithm for testing real-time systems. In: Proc. of the 5th. Formal Techniques in Real-Time and Fault-Tolerant Systems. Volume 1486 of Lecture Notes in Computer Science., SpringerVerlag (1998) 251–261

13. Raymond, P., Nicollin, X., Halbwatchs, N., Waber, D.: Automatic testing of reactive systems, madrid, spain. In: Proceedings of the 1998 IEEE Real-Time Systems Symposium, RTSS'98, IEEE Computer Society Press (1998) 200–209

14. Petitjean, E., Fouchal, H.: From Timed Automata to Testable Untimeed Automata. In: 24th IFAC/IFIP International Workshop on Real-Time Programming, Schloss Dagstuhl, Germany. (1999)

15. Nielsen, B., Skou, A.: Automated Test Generation from Timed Automata. In Margaria, T., Yi, W., eds.: Proceedings of the Workshop on Tools and Algorithms for the Construction and Analysis of Systems, Genova, Italy. Volume 2031 of Lecture Notes in Computer Science., Springer-Verlag (2001) 343–357

16. De Nicola, R., Hennessy, M.: Testing equivalences for processes. Theoretical Computer Science **34** (1984) 83–133

17. Hogashino, T., Nakata, A., Taniguchi, K., Cavalli, A.R.: Generating Test Cases for a Timed I/O Automaton Model. (2001)

18. Springintveld, J., Vaandrager, F., D'Argenio, P.R.: Timed Testing Automata. Theoretical Computer Science **254** (2001) 225–257

19. En-Nouaary, A., Dssouli, R., Khendek, F., Elqortobi, A.: Timed test cases generation based on state characterization technique. In: 19th IEEE Real Time Systems Symposium (RTSS'98) Madrid, Spain. (1998)

20. Fujiwara, S., Bochmann, G., Khendek, F., Amalou, M., Ghedamsi, A.: Test selection based on finite-state models. IEEE Transactions on Software Engineering **17** (1991) 591–603

21. Alur, R., Dill, D.: A theory of timed automata. Theoretical Computer Science **126** (1994) 183–235

22. Yovine, S.: Kronos: A verification tool for real-time systems. International Journal on Software Tools for Technology Transfer (STTT) **1** (1997) 123–133

23. at IRISA, D.W.: (Site officiel de polylib)
    http://icps.u-strasbg.fr/~loechner/polylib/.

24. Fouchal, H., Higashino, T.: An efficient test generation algorithm for timed automata (2002)

Conformance Testing of Real-Time Component Based Systems

Abbas Tarhini[1,*] and Hacène Fouchal[2]

[1] CReSTIC/LICA, Université de Reims Champagne-Ardenne,
BP 1039 F-51687 Reims Cedex, France
Abbas.Tarhini@univ-reims.fr
[2] GRIMAAG,
Université des Antilles et de Guyane,
F-97157 Pointe-à-Pitre, Guadeloupe, France
Hacene.Fouchal@univ-ag.fr

Abstract. In this paper, we suggest a methodology for testing Real Time Component Based Systems (RTCBS). A RTCBS is described as a collection of components where each component is modeled as a Timed Input-Output Automaton (TIOA). The first part of this study is devoted to the generation of timed-test sequences. Our algorithm for test sequence derivation extracts executable timed test sequences from a synchronous product between a timed test purpose (a property required on the system) and the corresponding component(s) specification.

The second part presents an adequate test architecture consisting of the System Under Test (SUT) components, and a distributed tester that consists of a set of co-ordinating testers. Each tester is dedicated to test a single SUT component. A test execution algorithm is presented. Testing the SUT is divided into two phases. In the first phase, each of the testers tests its corresponding component in isolation. In the second phase, each tester executes only its corresponding communication timed test sequences to test the interaction between components integrated in a RTCBS, taking into consideration the synchronization of events between testers themselves.

Keywords: Component based systems, conformance testing, distributed testing, timed automata, validation, formal methods, real-time systems.

1 Introduction

In recent years, software is becoming more complex consisting of many independent distributed components running concurrently on heterogeneous networks; consequently, facilitating the creation of emerging technologies such as commercial Off-The-Shelf (COTS) products which are becoming a market reality [19]. Traditional testing methods that ordinary COTS products undergo are not thorough enough to guarantee reliability; still, many of these products are integrated temporally in critical real time component based systems. Such integration may lead to architectural mismatches when assembling components with incorrect behavior [8], leaving the system in a hostile environment.

---

* Also at Lebanese American University, Beirut, Lebanon

F.F. Ramos et al. (Eds.): ISSADS 2005, LNCS 3563, pp. 167–181, 2005.

Testing such complex distributed real time component based systems requires not only the validation of components' behavior in isolation, but also the validation of components' integration into a component-based system taking into consideration their temporal aspects.

This paper deals with the conformance testing of Real-Time Component-Based Systems (RTCBS). We present (1) a simple test architecture consisting of (a) a set of Timed Input-Output Automata (TIOA) each of which represents the specification of each SUT component, and (b) a distributed tester that consists of a set of coordinating testers. Each tester is dedicated to test a single SUT component (see Figure 1).

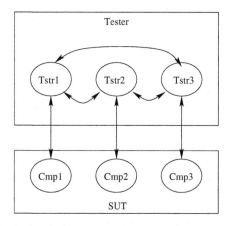

Fig. 1. Distributed architecture for testing a RTCBTS

Moreover, based on the test purpose method [6, 16], for each component we (2) generate *timed-test sequences* from the corresponding component's TIOA specification. Then, (4) we focus on the execution of these timed test sequences. A *timed-test sequence* is defined as a set of test inputs and expected results restricted with execution conditions (timing constraints). Timed-test sequences are extracted from the combination of a *timed-test purpose* and the corresponding transitions in the component's specification by synchronizing their events and execution instants. Such a combination is called a *synchronous product*. Software architects generate a *timed-test purpose* by defining relevant sequence of events and associated timing constraints. The extracted timed-test sequences are divided into two sets. The first set is used to validate each component in isolation, and the second set is used to test the communication between the components integrated in a RTCBS.

The execution of timed test sequences on the SUT is divided into two phases. In the first phase, the tester tests each component in isolation by executing the generated timed-test sequences, and produces a verdict success, failure or inconclusive. The verdict is success, if the component's implementation conforms to both its specification and test purpose; thus it is a valid stand-alone object; otherwise, component's implementation is faulty. The verdict is inconclusive, if the components' implementation conforms only to its specification but not to its test purpose. In the second phase, the tester executes only the second set of timed test sequences to test the interaction between components integrated in a RTCBS.

In both phases, our main concern is to cover the entire timing interval where an action has to be submitted to the implementation. For this reason, the action of a transition will be submitted by the tester as soon as we enter the timing interval of that action and at the ending instant of that timing interval.

The contribution of this method is (a) avoiding exhaustive testing by generating restrictive test sequences for each component rather than generating extensive test sequences from the specification of the whole CBS; still, we are (b) performing automatic testing for the RTCBS that is able to generate from the first phase valid-reusable components. Along with each component (c) we attach a set of communication timed-test sequences that are used whenever the components are integrated in any RTCBS. (d) A test execution algorithm adapted to our method is presented. It tests the (i) components in isolation, (ii) validates the timing constraints, and tests the time synchronization between components. Moreover, it is able to test almost all the RTCBS behavior by testing all communications related to the most wanted test purposes.

In what follows we present our proposed approach in details. Section 2 provides a review on related works done on the development and testing of distributed and component based systems. Section 3 provides a background of different modeling techniques used to represent RTCBS. In Section 4 we focus on our method for testing Real Time Component Based Systems, first we describe the TIOA definitions and formalization; next, the timed test sequence generation method is presented. In Section 5, we detail the testing architecture as well as the test execution process. Finally, we conclude in Section 6.

2   Related Work

In this section we present some works done on the construction of component based systems [17],[22],[20]. We also address selected research in the area of testing component based [3], [23] and distributed real-time systems [10], [11].

Components in distributed or component based systems (CBS) may communicate with every other component, and must interact with different external elements by sending and/or receiving messages through one or more communication channel. Those components may be reused in different CBSs and may run on single, distributed or network systems in a sequential or individual concurrent manner. Such systems require a tight/loose coupling of components of diverse granularity [17], taking into consideration some requirements such as, flexibility, time-to-market, quality, and cross-department standardization.

Different models have been suggested to design CBS. We highlight some of these models to show the complexity of building such systems and the need for testing them thoroughly. [20] presents a novel concept of acpectual component-based real-time system development (ACCORD), where (1) systems are decomposed into components and aspects, next, (2) it provides a real-time component model (RTCOM) that supports the notation of time and temporal constraints, space and resource management constraints, and composability. [22] presented a model based on the feedback control paradigm of control engineering that takes into consideration the interaction of components with external elements. It is a non-trivial task to build and test such fault tolerant systems, which meets specific safety requirements [14]. Therefore, such systems need to be thoroughly tested for some aspects of real-time systems such as behavior, synchronization, scheduling events and temporal attributes.

Distributed testing was studied with different test architectures. [11] proposed a distributed tester, and a method that projects a global test sequence (GTS) generated from the specification of the whole system (ignoring the distribution of the IUT) into local test sequences to be executed over local testers. The advantage of this work is discussing the inaccurate clock synchronization and the fault detectability problems. Moreover, based on the (GTS) method, [10] also proposed a centralized test architecture for distributed real-time systems where conditions that guarantee controllabilty (controlling instant of inputs) and observability (observing instant of outputs) are determined. In spite of the advantages of such methods, they may not be suitable to be applied on vast CBS. A GTS generated from the specification of the whole system would be exhaustive, and projecting such a sequence into local test sequences would need restrictive synchronization and timing conditions so that these sequences would be executable. Moreover, such sequences would test the component in a specific environment and thus it would not be possible to tell about the correctness of each component as as stand-alone object.

Generally, conformance testing consists of generating test sequences and applying them to the system under test (SUT) aiming at checking whether the SUT conforms to its specification. In this work we perform conformance testing, noting that testing component-based systems needs to validate not only the components themselves, but also the interaction and order of messages among components aiming at validating the whole system, taking into consideration their temporal aspects.

Formal testing CBS was tackled in only few studies. In [3], testing a CBS is based on modeling the Software architecture (SA) dynamics using a Labeled Transition System (LTS) model, which is tremendous amount of information flattened into a graph. In order to make such information usable by a designer, a suitable abstraction of the LTS (abstract views of LTS), called the abstract LTS (ALTS) is used. ALTS specify precise views of the SA dynamics by concentrating on features seen relevant by the software architect. Test sequences are derived by traversing paths covering the ALTS. This method did not consider timing constraints; moreover, it generates test sequences from extensive graph of information which would be quite hard for the software designer to single out from such a graph relevant observations of the system behavior.

In the protocol engineering area, testing systems modeled as LTS has been investigated in many studies. [21] and [1] present a part of these studies; they mainly studied a conformance testing theory based on conformance equivalences and preorders (check if the specification is included in the implementation) between the specification and the implementation. In order to ensure this conformance, they have developed efficient technique to extract pertinent traces from the specification respecting a given coverage criteria.

3   Modeling Component Based Systems

Modeling component-based systems requires us to recall the definition of components that are the building blocks of such system. Szyperski [19] defined components as:

> *a component is a unit of composition with contractually specified interfaces and fully explicit context dependencies that can be deployed independently and is subject to third-party composition.*

Software architecture (SA) dynamics that represent the individual components and their interactions are used in building component-based systems. [4] distinguished between the following perspectives of CBS: (1) the individual component *implementation*: the executable realization of a component, (2) the component *interface (interaction)*: summarizes the properties of the component that are externally visible to the other parts of the system, and (3) real-time component: component technology for real-time systems should support specification and prediction of timing.

In fact, the time factor problem in reactive real-time component based systems (RTCBS) is not enough investigated [4]. The time issue should be included in the model of such systems, where an action from the environment is modeled as an input event, while the reaction from the system is an output event. A Timed Input Output Automata (TIOA) is able to specify a sequence of inputs and their corresponding outputs; moreover, it shows timing constraints on events occurring in the system. Consequently, a TIOA best represents the (SA) dynamics of a RTCBS.

In our model, we use continuous time. This is due to the fact that is more realistic. A solid theoretical foundation of a timed automata (TA) is defined by Alur-Dill [2] as a finite set of states and a finite set of clocks which are real-valued variables. All clocks proceed at the same rate and measure the amount of time that has elapsed since they were started or reset. Each transition of the system might reset some of the clocks, and has an associated enabling condition (EC) which is a constraint on the values of the clocks. A transition is enabled only if its corresponding state is reached and the current clock values satisfy its enabling condition.

In this study, we choose to model the individual components of the RTCBS as TIOA. In the next section, we, first, present a formal definition of the TIOA, then a representation of a single component; next, we describe the test sequence generation method.

4   A Methodology for Testing Component Based Systems

4.1   Preliminaries

Definition 1 (Timed Input Output Automaton (TIOA)). *A* **TIOA** *is defined by* $M = (S, A, C, T, s_0)$ *where S is a finite set of states, s_0 is the initial state, and A is a set of actions. A is partitioned into 2 sets: A_I is the set of input actions (written ?i), A_O is the set of output actions (written !o). C is a set of clocks.*

T *is a transition set having the form* $\{Tr_1.Tr_2...Tr_n\}$. Tr_i = <s; a; d; EC; C_s>, *where* **s** *and* **d** *are starting and destination states.* '**a**' *is the action of the transition.* **EC** *is an enabling condition that evaluates to the result of the formula* $a \sim b$ *where* $\sim \in$

{ <, >, ≤, ≥, = } or to a constant valued either true or false. C_s is a set of clocks to be reset at the execution of a transition. A transition Tr_i is enabled if the current state of TIOA is s_i and the current instant satisfies the guard EC. Whenever enabled, if Tr_i is an output transition, it should be immediately executed reaching state 'd' without staying indefinitely in state **s**. The initial state of TIOA is s_0. s_0 can execute only input actions. After the execution of Tr_i all clocks in C_s are reset.

A TIOA M is said to be *input-complete* if for each state of M it has at least one transition for each input symbol. A TIOA M becomes *minimal* if every pair of states s_i, s_j that belongs to M, there is no sequence of events Σ when applied to both states, M reaches the same state s_r. A TIOA M is *strongly connected* if for every pair of states s_i, s_j belong to M there exists a sequence of events Σ such that state s_j is reachable from s_i if Σ is applied. A TIOA M is *completely specified* if all states of M accept any action $\sigma \in A$.

4.2   Single Component Representation

In this paper, both the specification and implementation of each component are represented by input-complete, minimal, strongly connected, and completely specified TIOA. A component may send output to other components or to the environment. The component's specification contains information about the destination of the output sent from its component.

Figure 2 shows an example of an TIOA M with initial state s_0. A transition is represented by an arrow between two states and labeled by the action, its enabling condition, and the clock to be reset. For example, from state s_0, M reaches state s_1 on the reception of '?a' or it reaches s_2 on the reception of "?c". From s_1, it proceeds to s_2 on the sending of "!b". From s_2 M reaches s_0 on the sending of "!c".

The set of actions A ={?a, !b, ?c, !c}; and the set of states $S = \{s_0, s_1, s_2\}$.

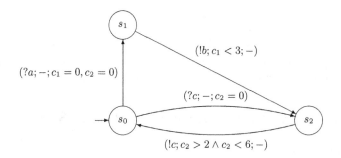

Fig. 2. An Example of TIOA

4.3   Test Sequence Generation for a Single Component

Background: The next issue to study is the test sequence generation for our proposed model. A lot of contributions are done in this matter, most of which are done in the framework of protocol engineering. Below we briefly summarize some of these techniques. In the next section we discuss our method of test generation.

[15] gives a particular method for the derivation of the more relevant inputs of the systems. In [12] we suggest a technique for translating a region graph into a graph where timing constraints are expressed by specific labels using clock zones.

[9] derives test sequences from Timed Input Output Automata extended with data. Automata are transformed in a kind of Input Output Finite State Machine in order to apply classical test generation technique.

[18] gives a general outline and a theoretical framework for timed testing. They proved that exhaustive testing of deterministic timed automata with a dense interpretation is theoretically possible but is still difficult in practice. They suggested performing a kind of discretization of the region graph model (which is an equivalent representation of the timed automata model). Clock regions are only equivalence classes of clock valuations. Their discretization step size takes into account the number of clocks as well as the timing constraints. Then they derive test cases from the generated model. The second study [5] differs from the previous one by using discretization step size depending only on the number of clocks which reduces the timing precision of the action execution. The resulting model has to be translated into a kind of Input/Output Finite State Machine which could be done only under strong and unrealistic assumptions. Finally they extract test cases by using the Wp-method [7].

Test Sequence Generation Method: Our test sequence generation method, proposed for a component-based real-time system, consists of four main steps. In step 1, we generate test purposes which are timed traces of events with constraints seen relevant by the software architect. In step 2, respecting the same order of actions in the test purpose, extract their corresponding transition sequences (TSq) from the specification. Step 3 generates a synchronous product from the TSq and the generated timed test purposes. Finally, step 4 generates the timed test sequences by traversing all possible paths in the synchronous product. In what follows we detail each of these steps preceded by the needed notations.

Notation 41 P_m, Ts_m, LTs_m, CTs_m:
P_m is a component indexed 'm'. $Ts_m = \{Ts_m^1, Ts_m^2, ..., Ts_m^n\}$ is a set of test sequences for component P_m. Each Ts_m^i, having the form $<Tr_1.Tr_2....Tr_n>$, maybe either a local test sequence (LTs_m^i) if every transition Tr_i tests only the local behavior of the component, or a communication test sequence (CTs_m^i) if at least one transition Tr_i requiring a component "P_m" to get input from (resp. send output to) another component "P_k".

Notation 42 $T_m, O_m^{T_i}$:
T_m is a tester for component "P_m". $O_m^{T_i}$ is an output from a component 'P_m' sent to tester T_i (tester for component 'P_i') through tester T_m.

Step 1: Timed Test Purpose
In classical (untimed) test purpose based methodologies, a test purpose is an expected abstract description of part of the specification. It helps the designer to choose behaviors to test particular functionality and to reduce the specification exploration.

A test purpose is represented by a path where final states may be either 'accept' states (the purpose is reached) or 'refuse' states (behavior parts which would be rejected). That is, all events in the test purpose path ending with an 'accept' state conforms to the specification, and at least one event in the test purpose path ending with a 'refuse' state does not conform to the specification. Events in the test purpose should also be found in the specification.

For timed systems, test purposes must also contain timing properties. We define such a purpose as a Timed Test Purpose (TTP).

Definition 2 (Timed Test Purpose (TTP)). *A timed test purpose is defined as a path with edges labeled by timed events. Each path starts from the root and expresses a partial trace on the specification. The TTP nodes do not need to have the same labels as the ones in the specification.*

Figure 3 gives an example of a timed test purpose required on the system described in Figure 2. It is clear in figure 2 that the event !c is executed on state s_2, and our purpose here is to check whether the execution of !c is enabled when c_2 is greater than 3. We should notice that timed test purposes are not exact parts of the specification, but they are sequences containing behavior and timing properties of the specification. Note that the sequence of events in the test purpose path in figure 3 ends with an accept state that is they conform with the specification.

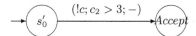

$$(!c; c_2 > 3; -)$$
$$s_0' \longrightarrow Accept$$

Fig. 3. A Timed Test Purpose

Step 2: Extraction of Transition Sequences

In this step we extract transition sequences (TSq) from the specification containing all actions of the test purpose and having the same order of occurrence. Such sequences are named TSq1(Sp), ..., TSqn(Sp). If this set is empty, the process terminates and the following steps cannot be performed. Figure 4 shows an example of extracted transition sequences matching the test purpose in Figure 3. Note that, for each action !c (our test purpose) we have to traverse from s_0 either action ?a followed be action !b, or only action ?c; therefore, we have two transition sequences one for each path.

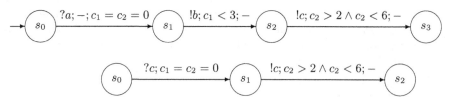

Fig. 4. Extracted Transition Sequences

Step 3: Synchronous Product

Transition sequences extracted from the specification in step 2 still lack the constraints of the test purpose; therefore, in this step we perform a synchronization between the test purpose and the corresponding transition sequences. Such a synchronization is called synchronous product. The transitions of the generated synchronous product are labeled with computed time constraints according to the following definition:

Definition 3 (Synchronous Product). *Let $S = (S^s, A^s, C^s, T^s, s_0^s)$, be a TIOA representing the specification and $Tp = (S^t, A^t, C^t, T^t, s_0^t)$ be a TIOA representing a test purpose. Tp is a particular TIOA composed by only one path.*
Let $T^t = \{tp_1, ..., tp_n\}$ be the successive transitions of the test purpose Tp.
Let $PS = \{ps_1, ..., ps_m\}$ be the set of all possible paths of S starting from the state s_0^s, where $ps_j = \{tps_1.tps_2.....tps_n\}$, and tps_k is a transition in ps_j.
The synchronous product S^p is a set of paths $= \{sp_1, ..., sp_l\}$, where $sp_i = \{tsp_1.tsp_2.....tsp_n\}$, and tsp_k is a transition in sp_i. S^p is defined as:
$S^p \subset PS$ *and*
$\forall\, tp_i \in T^t, \forall\, ps_j \in PS$, *where event$(tp_i)$ = event(tps_k), $\exists\, sp_i \sim ps_j$ such that:*
$$EC_F(tsp_l) = !EC(tps_k),\ and$$
$$EC_I(tsp_l) = EC(tps_k)/EC(tp_i),\ and$$
$$EC_P(tsp_l) = EC(tps_k) \cap EC_P(tp_i).$$

Note that the Enabling Condition in any transition of the synchronous product is composed of three sets:

EC_F: set of events and time that does not match the specification.

EC_I: set of events and time that matches the specification but not the test purpose.

EC_P: set of events and time that matches the specification and test purpose.

The set PS is composed of all possible paths of the specification. In each transition Tr of any path EC_F(Tr) and EC_I are set to ϕ and EC_P contains the set corresponding to the enabling condition in Tr. Event(tr) is the action allowed by the transition.
Figure 5 shows the synchronous product of the test purpose (figure 3) and extracted test sequence (figure 4).

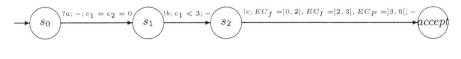

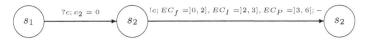

Fig. 5. Synchronous Product of a Test Purpose and an extracted transition sequence

Step 4. Timed Test Sequence Generation
In this section, for each component (P_m), we derive the set of all timed test sequences (Ts_m). Each test sequence in Ts_m corresponds to a path in the synchronous product. For example, the test sequences generated from figure 5 are:

$Ts_1^1 = <?a; -; c_1 = c_2 = 0> . <!b; c_1 < 3; -> . <!c; EC_f =]0, 2], EC_I =]2, 3], EC_P =]3, 6[; ->$
$Ts_1^2 = <?c; c_2 = 0; -> . <!c; EC_f =]0, 2], EC_I =]2, 3], EC_P =]3, 6[; ->$

These test sequences may be of two types (1) local test sequences, LTs_m, that test the internal component's behavior, and (2) communication test sequences, CTs_m, that contains events to test the interaction among other components. The set of generated test sequences is able to tell about the behavior of each component and the behavior of the whole system.

5   Test Architecture and Execution

In this work, we consider a component-based system that consists of several components each of which is able to interact with the environment. Figure 6 illustrates the test architecture. It consists of a set of distributed local testers. For each component "P_m" of the system, a dedicated Tester "T_m" is assigned. This test architecture is inspired from the work done in [13] which is dedicated to timed systems. Below we present the notations needed in this section. In the following subsections, we describe the scheme for component's communication; next, we present the architecture of each local tester, then the tester coordination, and finally we explain the test execution process.

Notation 51 ITs_m, Tr_j^m, ioQ:
ITs_m : is an interoperable test sequence set that contains all CTs_m^i. Tr_j^m : is a transition indexed j and is an input from tester T_m. $ioQ = \{ioQ_1, ioQ_2, ..., ioQ_N\}$ where each ioQ_m is an input/output priority queue dedicated for tester T_m. ioQ_m holds inputs sent from any tester T_i to component P_m.

Notation 52   wait(T_m), signal(T_m):
Wait and signal are two atomic functions. Wait(T_m): will pause the execution of tester T_m. Signal(T_m): will resume the execution of tester T_m.

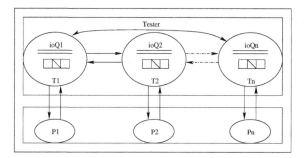

Fig. 6. Test Architecture for the whole system

5.1   Component Communication Scheme

For simplicity, we assume one-port communication components; that is, components communicate with each other and with the environment via the same port through their corresponding testers. Moreover, information about the destination of the output is given in the component's specification. Therefore, an output from component P_i to component P_j is done by sending the output to tester T_i which in turn sends to tester T_j, next, T_j forwards the output to P_j.

5.2   Local Tester Representation

Local testers execute generated test sequences (Ts_m/ITs_m) on their corresponding components (P_m) by sending input actions and receiving output actions in the form

O_m^{Ti} (i = {1,..,m,..N}). Each local tester consists of the following: (1) a test executer unit **(TEU)**, (2) a test monitor unit **(TMU)**, and (3) a local input/output queue (ioQ), and (4) a local clock.

The job of the test executer unit **(TEU)** is to apply test sequences to a component, and the job of the test monitor unit **(TMU)** is to validate the feedback from the components with the corresponding test sequence. ioQ_m is a local input/output priority queue dedicated for tester T_m. ioQ_m holds inputs sent by any tester T_i to component P_m. Embedding the clocks in testers, enables the tester to tell about the time an event occurred instantaneously with no communication delay. All testers' clocks are supposed to be synchronized with a reference clock. Moreover, each tester's clock is assumed synchronized with its corresponding component's clock. The assumption of synchronization between a tester's clock and the corresponding component's clock is essential; otherwise, we will not be able to tell about the clock of the black-box component.

5.3   Tester Coordination

Testers work in parallel with some synchronization. Testers communicate with each other through the input/output queues (ioQ). In their communication, the following testers's communication scheme is respected. The output transition from tester T_i, sent as an input, to tester T_j will wait on queue ioQ_j until this transition is enabled in T_j. On the other hand, the execution of a communication test sequence CTs_j by tester T_j will pause if this test sequence requires P_j to wait for an input from component P_i. The execution in tester T_j will resume after receiving the needed input from tester T_i; and thus, testers give a higher priority to handle inputs received from the components over inputs received from other testers that are stored in local testers' queues. Coordinating testers are able to detect livelocks (at the end of test sequence a component is locked by waiting for an event), and deadlocks (at least two components are locked and some test sequences may not be executed completely).

5.4   Test Execution

A time-test execution scheme is defined as follows: A time-test execution will be declared as success iff **the execution of all events in a** test sequence terminates in a(n) accept (resp. refuse) state and satisfies (resp. at least one event does not satisfy) the timed-enabling conditions of their transitions. Otherwise, it will be declared as failure.

The testing execution process is done in two phases. The first phase tests each component separately, and the second phase tests the communication among components.

In both phases, each tester T_m executes, using **TEU**, the corresponding test sequences and validates, using **TMU**, the feedback from each component with its corresponding test sequence.

In the first phase, we ignore all communication requests from other components; and thus, all inputs to component P_m from corresponding or other testers are sent at the instants those inputs are needed based on the information in the test sequence (i.e, component's specification S^{P_m}) without considering the communication from any other tester T_i, and therefore, here we are checking the validation of the component in isolation, without taking any communication input from other components. An execution of tester T_m to a test sequence Ts_m gives a verdict success, iff the reception of all the outputs from "P_m" are exactly as those in the test sequence Ts_m, and their timing constraints respect the time-test execution scheme defined above.

The identified communication test sequences CTs_m are added to the set ITs_m to be re-executed in the second phase after abstracting their behavior. At any failure, the component and the failed test sequence are identified.

In the second phase, respecting the scheme of testers' coordination mentioned in section 5.3, each tester T_m executes, using **TEU**, its corresponding communication test sequence in ITs_m. An execution of tester T_m to a communication test sequence in ITs_m gives a verdict success, iff the sending of inputs and reception of outputs $O_m^{T_i}$ from P_m or T_i are exactly as those in the synchronous product. Below we present the test execution algorithm, and an example of test coordination is presented in figure 7.

Algorithm 2: Test execution – **This code is executing on component / tester indexed "m".**
Input: S^{Pm} Test sequences: Ts_m, ITs_m ; ITs_m initially is empty
Output: verdict pass, fail: set of failed components.
Phase 1:
1 For all components P_m
2   For all test sequences Ts_m
3   Select a test sequence Ts_j^m
4   At the entering and leaving instants of timing interval EC_P, apply all events of Ts_j^m via tester $T_m toP_m$ while the expected outputs are valid with its $EC_I or EC_P$.
5   If output $O_m^{T_i}$ from P_m is valid
6   If $O_m^{T_i}$ represents a communication event
7   Build interoperable test sequences ITs_m.
8   Identify P_m as a failing component on test sequence Ts_j^m based on the following:
             – The output is not valid and the last state is success.
             – The output is valid but does not respect the $EC_I or EC_P$ and last state is success.
             – The whole execution of the test sequence is success but the last state reached is fail.

Phase 2:**This code is executing on component / tester indexed "m".**
9 For all components:
10   For all test sequences ITs_m
11   Select a test sequence ITs_j^m from ITs_m
12   For all transitions Tr_k of ITs_j^m
13   If (current event of ITs_j^m is a local transition:Tr_k^m)
14   At the entering and leaving instants of EC_P, T_m applies current event of ITs_j^m on component P_m.
15   T_m receives and validates the output $O_m^{T_i}$ from P_m.
16   If valid output $O_m^{T_i}$ and the instant of reception is within $EC_P or EC_I$
17   T_m forwards the *appropriate* output of $O_m^{T_i}$ to io-queue ioQ_i of tester T_i.
18   If (tester T_i is waiting on this input)
19   Tester T_m Signals Tester T_i to resume execution:**Signal**(T_i).
20   else if current event is not local transition: Tr_k^i
21   if transition $Tr_k^i is$ found in (already sent to) current local queue ioQ_m
22   Respecting EC_P of Tr_k^i,T_m applies Tr_k^i to P_m.
23   else if the other tester T_i is not waiting on an input from this tester
24   pause execution of T_m until it gets input from T_i: **wait** (T_m).
25   else if (the other tester T_i is waiting on an input from this tester T_m)
26   Supply T_m with the appropriate input from S^{Pm} to be applied on P_m.
             Identify a deadlocks state on test sequence ITs_j^m.
28   Signal all testers waiting on T_m.
29 Assign the appropriate verdict (Pass | Fail | Inconclusive)
30 Identify all faulty components based of the following:
             – The output is not valid and the last state is success.
             – The output is valid but does not respect the $EC_I or EC_P$ and last state is success.
             – The whole execution of the test sequence is success but the last state reached is fail.

In the above algorithm, phase 1(lines 4- 8) is used to test each component in isolation. Lines 6-7 build the ITs_m to be used in phase 2. In phase 2: Block 1 (lines 13-19) executes transitions that are not input from other testers. Block 2 (lines 20-29) executes transitions that are input from other tester. Lines 21-22: executes a transition if it is already found in the local tester io-queue. Lines 23-27: Checks and handles deadlock between testers. Lines 23-24: pause the execution of T_m by executing a $wait(T_m)$ statement, on a condition that T_i is not waiting for an input from Tm; otherwise, deadlock occurs. Lines 25-26: identify deadlock on the current test sequence, and continue execution by supplying the component P_m needed information from S^{P_m}. Line 28 signals all waiting testers. Line 29 Identify all faulty components that failed to pass a test sequence. Figure 7 illustrates testers'coordination while executing in phase 2.

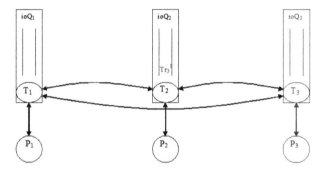

Fig. 7. Example of Testes' Coordination - Phase 2: Test execution

Instant	Tester1	Tester 2
1:	Tr_1^1	Tr_1^2
2:	Tr_2^1	Tr_2^2
3:	Tr_3^1	$wait(T_2)$
4:	Tr_4^1	...
5:	$Tr_5^1 : Signal(T_2)$	Tr_3^1
6:	Tr_6^1	Tr_4^2

Tester T_1 executes test sequence: $CTs_1 = Tr_1^1.Tr_2^1.Tr_3^1.Tr_4^1.Tr_5^1(O_1^{T_2}).Tr_6^1$, and tester T_2 executes test sequence: $CTs_2 = Tr_1^2.Tr_2^2.Tr_3^1.Tr_4^2$
From CTs_1 and CTs_2 it is clear that tester T_1 sends output to tester T_2 at the fifth transition Tr_5^1. and tester T_2 waits for this information at the third transition Tr_3^1. The execution goes as follows: at instances 1 and 2, both testers execute their local transitions. At instance 3, tester T_1 executes its transition Tr_3^1; however tester T_2 cannot execute it because the corresponding input for tester T_2 is not found in its local queue ioQ_2; therefore, tester T_2 will block itself waiting on an input from tester T_1. At instance 4, tester T_1 executes its transition Tr_4^1, but tester T_2 is still waiting. At instance 5, tester T_1 executes transition Tr_5^1 which passes the information to ioQ_2 of tester T_2 and thus we signal T_2 so that it is able to execute its third transition Tr_3^1.

6 Conclusion and Future Work

Formal Testing for real-time component-based systems is discussed in this article. The most interesting studies done in this field are summarized in section 2. In this paper, we present a formal method for testing real-time component-based systems using distributed test architecture. Test sequence generation is done automatically but controlled by the designer since he has to provide a test purpose (a property) to be respected by the system, and the test execution is done in two phases: the first one takes into account the local behavior of each component and the second phase deals with communication aspects between components. Three main contributions are noticeable in this method:

The first is the generation of a reduced test sequence set that is able to detect a faulty component. The designer provides a timed test purpose and we compute a timed synchronous product between the test purpose and the specification.

The second contribution is that by the end of the first phase of the test execution, we are able to tell about all non-faulty stand-alone components. Moreover, along with every component we attach a set of test sequences to test the communication among other components whenever integrated in a real-time component-based system.

A third contribution is the test-execution algorithm that executes and synchronizes test sequence execution on local testers. The synchronization is done via tow atomic statements, Signal() and Wait(), and a set of input-output queues. A queue is attached to each tester. The synchronization respects the timing constraints of both components involved in the communication.

This technique can be applied in a realistic environment since the time taken by testers is much reduced compared to the time needed by the system to work.

As a future work, we intend to take into account the time delay which may be introduced by the components composition. We need also to experiment this methodology in a real case study such as industrial control software. We intend also to handle other formalisms able to consider, in addition to behavior description, the data exchange between components.

References

1. A.V. Aho, A.T. Dahbura, D. Lee, and M.Ü. Uyar. An optimization technique for protocol conformance test generation based on UIO sequences and Rural Chinese Postman Tours. *IEEE Transactions on Communications*, 39(11):1604–1615, 1991.
2. R. Alur and D. Dill. A theory of timed automata. *Theoretical Computer Science*, 126:183–235, 1994.
3. A. Bertolino, F. Corradini, P. Inveradi, and H. Muccini. Deriving test plans from architectural descriptions. In *ACM Proceedings, International Conference on Software Engineering ICSE2000, June 2000*, June 2000.
4. Ed Brinksma, Geoff Coulson, and Ivica Crnkovic. Project ist-2001-34820 - artist- advanced real-time systems. roadmap: Component-based design and integration platforms. http://www.systemes-critiques.org/ARTIST/.
5. A. En-Nouaary, R. Dssouli, F. Khendek, and A. Elqortobi. Timed test cases generation based on state characterization technique. In *19th IEEE Real Time Systems Symposium (RTSS'98)* Madrid, Spain, 1998.

6. Hacène Fouchal, Eric Petitjean, and Sébastien Salva. An User-Oriented Testing of Real Time Systems. In *Proceedings of the International Workshop on Real-Time Embeded Systems RTES'01 (London), IEEE Computer Society*, dec 2001.

7. S. Fujiwara, G. Bochmann, F. Khendek, M. Amalou, and A. Ghedamsi. Test selection based on finite-state models. *IEEE Transactions on Software Engineering*, 17(6):591–603, June 1991.

8. D. Garlan, R. Allen, and J. Ockerbloom. Architectural mismatch: Why reuse is so hard. *IEEE software*, 12(6):17–26, Novr 1995.

9. Teruo Hogashino, Akio Nakata, Kenichi Taniguchi, and Ana R. Cavalli. Generating Test Cases for a Timed I/O Automaton Model. In *Proceedings of the 13th International Workshop on Test of Communicating Systems 2001 (Beinjin, China)*. North-Holland, October 2001.

10. A. Khoumsi. Testing distributed real-time reactive systems using a centralized test architecture. In *North Atlantic Test Workshop (NATW), Gloucester, Massachusetts, USA, May 2001*, May 2001.

11. A. Khoumsi. Testing distributed real-time systems in the presence of inaccurate clock synchronization. *Journal of Information Soft. Technology (IST)*, 45, Dec 2003.

12. E. Petitjean and H. Fouchal. From Timed Automata to Testable Untimeed Automata. In *24th IFAC/IFIP International Workshop on Real-Time Programming, Schloss Dagstuhl, Germany*, 1999.

13. Eric Petitjean and Hacène Fouchal. A Realistic Architecture for Timed Systems. In *5th IEEE International Conference on Engineering of Complex Computer Systems, Las Vegas, USA*, pages 109–118, 1999.

14. S. Philippi. Analysis of fault tolerance and reliability in distributed real-time system architectures. *Reliability Engineering and System Safety*, 82(2), Nov 2003.

15. P. Raymond, X. Nicollin, N. Halbwatchs, and D. Waber. Automatic testing of reactive systems, madrid, spain. In *Proceedings of the 1998 IEEE Real-Time Systems Symposium, RTSS'98*, pages 200–209. IEEE Computer Society Press, December 1998.

16. Sébastien Salva, Eric Petitjean, and Hacène Fouchal. A simple approach to testing timed systems. In *Workshop on Formal Approaches to Testing of Software, FATES'01 (Aalborg, Danmark), August 25, 2001 (Workshop of CONCUR'01)*, pages 93–107, aug 2001.

17. H. Schmidt. Trustworthy components-compositionality and prediction. *The Journal of Systems and Software*, 65:215–225, 2003.

18. J. Springintveld, F.W. Vaandrager, and P. R. D'Argenio. Timed Testing Automata. *Theoretical Computer Science*, 254(254):225–257, 2001.

19. C. Szyperski. *Component Software: Beyond Object Oriented Programming*. Addison Wesley, Harlow, England, 1998.

20. A. Tesanovic, D. Nystrom, J. Hansson, and C. Norstrom. Towards aspectual component-based development of real-time systems. In *Proceeding of the 9th International Conference on Real-Time and Embedded Computing Systems and Applications (RTCSA 2003), February 2003*, February 2003.

21. J. Tretmans. Test generation with inputs, outputs and repetitive quiescence. *Software - Concepts and Tools*, 17:103–120, 1996.

22. J. Zalewski. Developing component-based software for real-time systems. In *27th Euromicro Conference 2001: A Net Odyssey (euromicro'01)*, September 2001.

23. Peter Zimmerer. Test architectures for testing distributed systems. In *12th International software quality week (QW'99)*, May 1999.

Modeling Multiple Interactions
Using Coloured Petri Nets: A Case Study

Francisco Camargo-Santacruz[1], Juan Frausto-Solís[2], and Fernando Ramos-Quintana[2]

[1] Instituto Tecnológico y de Estudios Superiores de Monterrey, Campus Estado de México,
Carretera al Lago de Guadalupe, Km. 3.5, Atizapán, 52926, Estado de México, México
phone ++52-55-5864 5560, fax ++52-55-5864 5557
fcamargo@itesm.mx
http://www.itesm.mx
[2] Instituto Tecnológico y de Estudios Superiores de Monterrey, Campus Cuernavaca,
Carretera al Lago de Guadalupe, Km. 3.5, Atizapán, 52926, Estado de México, México
{juan.frausto,fernando.ramos}@itesm.mx

Abstract. The dynamic nature of cooperative information systems (CIS) makes considerably more difficult the task of modeling interactions among agents. One of the most difficult problems related to the dynamic of a system is how to model and control simultaneously multiple interactions among agents in a friendly way. So far, traditional approaches deal with the problem of modeling interactions in static conditions and commonly with only two agents participating concurrently in cooperative tasks. Consequently, expressiveness becomes a problem related with the representation of multiple interactions in a satisfactory way, particularly in dynamic environments, such as e-business. The paper illustrates the application of a methodology based on Coloured Petri Nets (CP nets) in order to model the interaction mechanism in a CIS in an expressive way. This reduces the associated complexity in the representation of the dynamic of the system in a contact center environment, which is the start point to customer service, where concurrent interactions among users, technical people, process center and the contact center constitute a dynamic process that needs to be permanently monitored and controlled. The methodology provides us important advantages in the representation and reasoning for the interaction mechanism modeled in CIS. The use of CP nets allows analyzing the behavior of the system in the dynamic model using the individual and structural model.

Keywords: Cooperative Information Systems, Coloured Petri Nets, Interaction, Agent-Based Software Engineering, Multi-Agent Systems, E-Business.

1 Interaction, Cooperative Information Systems and Formal Methods

A Cooperative Information System (CIS) supports daily activities in the organization. It is a cooperative multi-agent system [16] integrated by a set of agents, data, and procedures, working in a cooperative way. They have a common goal, exchange information, and work together in order to achieve the objective [14]. The Contact Center systems are considered CIS and they pose a set of particular characteristics, by their dynamic and interactive natures that require to be modeled in an expressive way. We represent the CIS by the expression CIS= {A, Cg, Gk, I}, where A is the agent set, Cg is the common goal, Gk is the global knowledge and I is the interaction set.

F.F. Ramos et al. (Eds.): ISSADS 2005, LNCS 3563, pp. 182–193, 2005.

To model a CIS in dynamic environments is a complex task and the static modeling approaches are insufficient for representing system behavior over time. The reason is that they provide no way to represent how the system's state will change as time passes. Lacking such provisions, static models can not handle the dynamic of the interactions properly [12]; on the contrary, a dynamic modeling is one that can represent both the structure and the behavior of a system at any time of the process.

We consider that the *Cooperation* problem involves several layers [15]: a *Communication* layer, an *Interaction* layer, and the *Coordination* layer. At the lowest level we have a Communication Protocol, which enables the information exchange among the agents of the system and produces a change of the system state [3]. The Interaction mechanism is a set of behavior rules that defines the information exchange among agents [4], [5]. The Coordination mechanism establishes the action sequence and execution according to the agents' individual goals and the common goal of the CIS [5], [13]. Finally, at the higher level we have a Cooperation, which is understood by the agent's behavior to coordinate interaction and information exchange in order to achieve a common goal.

The interaction mechanism is the central theme for the cooperation in CIS, because it is the bridge between the communication protocol and the coordination mechanism for the agents in the system. The interaction problem for CIS is immersed in a natural dynamic world, consequently, the interaction modeling and control are hard to manipulate and normally they have ambiguity and control problems [11]. The use of different formal methods in order to model the interaction mechanism are present in related literature such as: The First Order Logic [10], State Transition Diagrams [3] [8], Condition/Event (C/E) Petri Nets [6]. They are practical to specify the structure of the interaction mechanism when they appear in insolated communication situations, but they are not useful to model complex protocols with several interactions simultaneously in CIS. Other works that model interactions using CPN are El Fallah et al. [5] and Cost et al. [4]. El Fallah et al., focuses on the study of the pragmatic of multiagent systems design, combining two paradigms: 1) Distributed observation to capture the interactions between agents and 2) CPN as a formalism to identify interaction-oriented designs. Cost et al., focuses in the construction of a language for conversation specification, named Protolingua within the framework of the Jackal agent development environment, and they proposed to use CPN as a model underlying a language for conversation specification. In our approach the use of CP nets ease us to reduce ambiguity in the interaction model and allows to simulate the system dynamic which is related to multiple simultaneous interactions [2].

A Petri net is a formal and graphic appealing language, which is appropriate for modeling complex systems with concurrency [12]. The coloured Petri nets are a high level Petri net where each token of a different color represents arbitrary data values. This extension increases the descriptive power for modeling. The firing of transitions is then made dependent on the availability of an appropriately coloured token [12]. A CP net has a graphical structure with associated computer language statements. The coloured Petri nets are a good formalism for describing concurrency, synchronization and causality [1], and are suitable for modeling, analyzing and prototyping dynamic systems with parallel activities [4] as CIS in our approach. In this work, we propose the use of CP nets, because they have relevant characteristics for modeling interaction in CIS, such as: 1) the graphical representation, 2) the well defined semantics, 3) the formal analysis of the models and 4) the capacity for modeling the system hierarchically. The use of CP net computer tools, such as CPN Tools [12], helps us make a dynamic simulation of the system interaction, and to find problems before the system implementation. CPN Tools simulator provides interactive simulation, so we can run the model step by step watching the state changes and token flow for every step. CP nets provide an extremely effective dynamic modeling paradigm. This paper present an upgrade of the methodology introduced in [15] and the details of the proposed interaction reasoning analysis that can be done with the CPN models using CPN Tools. The structure of the paper began with the interaction modeling tool, the Action Basic Loop. In section 3, the architecture for modeling the interactions in CIS are discussed and used for the case study presented in section 4. Finally, the conclusions and further works are presented.

2   Interaction Modeling

The CIS analysis is centered on the interactions among agents, where it is defined who talks to whom and in which way. The interaction mechanism is modeled using the Action Basic Loop [8], [9]. They propose an ontology of communicative acts: *Request*, *Promise*, *Inform* and *Declare*, and an execution process which join together four steps: *Preparation*, *Negotiation*, *Execution* and *Evaluation*. In Fig. 1 we present the loop process and the communicative acts.

Fig. 1. The Action Basic Loop and the Communicative Acts

A brief description of the execution process is: a) Agent 1 *prepares* the *request* for Agent 2 in a conversation. b) Agent 1 and Agent 2 make a *negotiation* about the *request*, and Agent 2 issues a *promise*. c) Agent 2 *executes* the *promise* and when they finish the task, they give an *inform* to Agent 1. d) Agent 1 makes a *declaration* for the *evaluation* of Agent 2 assignment.

The basic action loop helps us to have a coordinate conversation between agents, and to join more than two agents simultaneously in the coordinate conversation, building an interaction. In order to model multiple simultaneously interactions among agents is necessary to relate many conversations in a system interaction. The Interaction Diagram, shown in Fig. 2, is the used tool. The methodology proposes a documentation set and a notation for the interaction model and the details are shown in [15].

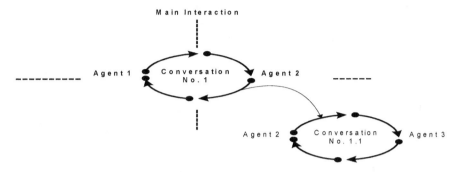

Fig. 2. Interaction Diagram

3   The Architecture for Modeling Interaction in CIS

The CIS frequently perform complex tasks that are distributed over space and time, which involve discrete flows of objects and/or information [14]. Among other things, CIS are complex due to their dynamic nature and the management of many simultaneous interactions and the software specification is hard to be implemented due to the reasons stated above. A proper structured way of building software for the aforementioned needs, is relevant to facilitate the specification of complex systems. We center our research in two areas: analysis and design of interactions in CIS. We actually hold different views about the system: 1) the *explicit specification* for the static view and 2) the *implicit specification* for the dynamic view. These views are part of the architecture.

We propose the use of CP nets in order to represent the agent's behavior and its intentions, and to simulate the resulting model. In Fig. 3 we can see the integration of the models in the architecture. At the lowest layer we have the *individual model*, in which we describe the agents separately. At the medium layer, we have the *structural model*, in which the interactions among agents are described, and finally, at the highest layer we have the *dynamic model*, in which the simulation of the system interaction is observed and controlled. It is important to note that the implicit specification is based on the explicit specification.

The CP net model captures in the specification both, the static of the system in the structural model and the behavior in the dynamic model.

In order to model interactions in CIS, we use the IMCIS methodology proposed previously in [15], which has the following steps:

IMCIS *(Interaction Methodology for CIS)*

Explicit Specification:
1. Individual Model:
   ° Identify agents and their intentions.
2. Structural Model:
   ° Build the agents diagram.
   ° Build the interaction diagrams.
   ° Design the messages and the agent ports.
   ° Specify the interaction mechanism using Coloured Petri Nets.

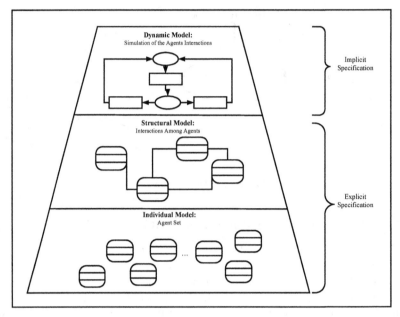

Fig. 3. The Architecture for Modeling Interaction in CIS

Implicit Specification:
3. Dynamic Model:
   ° Simulate the system interactions evolution.

In the early specification stages, the explicit specification is relatively large and the knowledge of its execution behavior may be imprecise. A CP net model helps give the definition and subsequently shows the dynamic behavior of different agent interactions.

The architecture is designed to have a recursive and iterative software engineering life cycle in order to make a model step by step refinement. The CP net is the most important factor in the integration between the structural model and the dynamic model.

4   Modeling Multiple Interactions in a Contact Center Application

The Contact Center, shown in Fig. 4, is the only central point to customer services. Frequently they have an impact in customer satisfaction and loyalty. This kind of system requires hard coordination in order to manage and control multiple simultaneously interactions. Some characteristics of the Contact Center, which are common to other kind of CIS, are:

- Multiple simultaneously interactions among Process Center, Technical People and Customers.
- High cooperation and coordination work environment.
- Intensive use or telecommunication systems and contact media like telephone, internet and fax, among others.

- The need of a common goal and cooperation among agents to reach the solution.
- Working in a distributed, heterogeneous and dynamic environment.

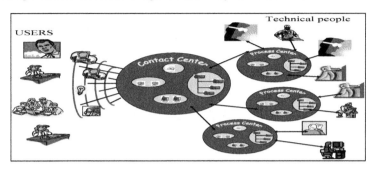

Fig. 4. The Contact Center

The Fig. 5 shows the Agent Diagram, where the conversations between agents like: request service, service evaluation, assign ticket, assign technical people and close request are identified.

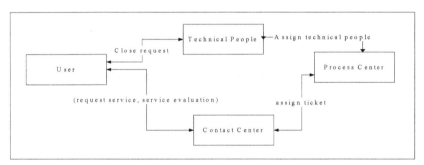

Fig. 5. The Agent Diagram

The main interaction in the Contact Center environment is: *Request Service*, which is integrated by five conversations:

- User *Request Service* Contact Center.
- Contact Center *Assign Ticket* Process Center.
- Process Center *Assign Technical People* Technical People.
- Technical People *Close Request* User.
- User *Service Evaluation* Contact Center.

The result Interaction Diagram, where all conversations are integrated, is shown in Fig. 6.

We represent the CIS by the expression: CIS={A, Cg, Gk, I}, where:

- Agent Set, A = {(User, To request an effective solution for his needs of information or process), (Contact Center, Take care of the relationship with the User and transfer the request to the appropriate Process Center), (Process Center, Do his work with the defined standards in order to satisfy the Users needs), (Technical People, Do the assigned work with impeccability, efficiency and efficacy)}.

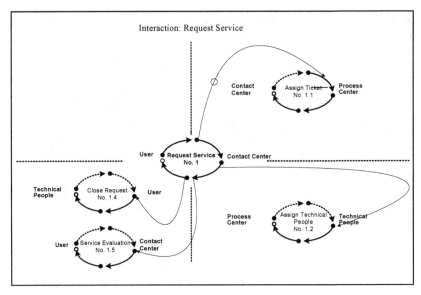

Fig. 6. The Interaction Diagram

- Common Goal, Cg= Resolve the Users requests in a coordinate, efficient and efficacy way using one contact point.
- Global Knowledge, Gk= {Request, Technical People Availability, Technical Documentation}.
- Interaction Set, I= {Service Request}.

The interaction mechanism is modeled with a set of CP nets, where each of them represents the conversations between the Client and the Provider. We remark that the User, Contact Center, Process Center and Technical People play the roles of client or provider in the different steps of the interaction. The tokens in the CP nets represent the interactions among the different agents. The basic elements used of CP nets are: 1) Place to represent states of the conversation; 2) Transitions to represent communicative acts; 3) Arc inscriptions to represent the different system interactions and the function to calculate the next communicative act; and 4) Guards to control the transition fire.

We use a coloured token in order to model and control simultaneously multiple interactions in an expressive way. The use of CP nets in addition to the general interaction model ease the definition of complex data type for each token component in the interaction. The interaction is represented by a color token, which is a record with a user list (user), the contact center (cc), the list of process center (pc), the technical people list (lt), the service request (therequest) and the actual communicative act (nextaction). The token is shown in Table 1. The actual CPN model do not include the agent goals modeling.

The dynamic model in a Contact Center environment is tested in order to analyze and validate the expressivity of the representation and the behavior of the interaction.

1. **Service Request**: One User, one Contact Center, n Process Center, one Technical People and one request without conflict.

Table 1. The Coloured Token Interaction Definition

color Tinteraction = record
user:Tlistuser *
cc: TCCenter *
pc:TlistPCenter *
lt: TlistTech *
therequest: Trequest *
nextaction: TPorts;

2. **Multiple simultaneous interactions**: m Users, one Contact Center, n Process Center, k Technical People and x request without conflict.
3. **Service Request with conflict**: One User, one Contact Center, n Process Center, one Technical People and one request with conflict like the no availability of technical people where this situation force the Negotiation step.
4. **Multiple simultaneous interactions with conflict**: m Users, one Contact Center, n Process Center, k Technical People and x request with conflict like the no availability of technical people where this situation force the Negotiation step.

In order to explain the results observed in the interaction analysis using the CPN Tools, the initial and final states in the conversation are identified: Initial State: *Preparation*. Final States: *Closed Satisfied*, *Closed Canceled*, *Closed Declined*, *Closed Revoked*. It is important to remark that all simulations must be ended with a mark in some of the Final States. In the opposite one we can conclude that the interaction never ends and this suggests a potential problem like a deadlock, the need for some resource or some similar situation.

At Fig. 7 we have a middle step of three simultaneously interactions, where the users identified with the numbers 1 and 2, in the tokens, are in different steps like *Countered* and *Acceptance no agreement*, while the user identified with the number 3 is in some state that is not shown in this particular CP net. The transactions can be fired according with the state of each transaction and the communicative acts like C_CancelNoAgr, C_DeclineToAcceptNoAgr and C_CancelMakeNewRequest, in the place *Acceptance (no agr)*. In the place *Countered*, the communicative acts are: C_Counter, C_DeclineCounteroffer, C_CancelMakeNewRequest, C_CancelNoAgr, C_AgreeToCounteroffer and C_DeclareSatisfactionNoAgr.

Fig. 8 shows the final mark of the interactions. The conversation of users 2 and 3 is ended with a mark in the state *Closed Canceled*, and this is one of the correct final state. The user number 1, at this time, is in some state that is not shown in this particular CP net.

5   Conclusion and Further Works

This paper propose the representation of the interaction among agents in Cooperative Information Systems by means of the use of the Interaction Diagram represented by CPN in the explicit specification, and the formal specification using Coloured Petri Nets at the implicit specification, to deal with the associated complexity for modeling the dynamic of the interactions in CIS. The use of the basic action loop in order to model the organization interaction in the CIS, like the Contact Center, that helps us understand and represent different situations with a common action and coordination language.

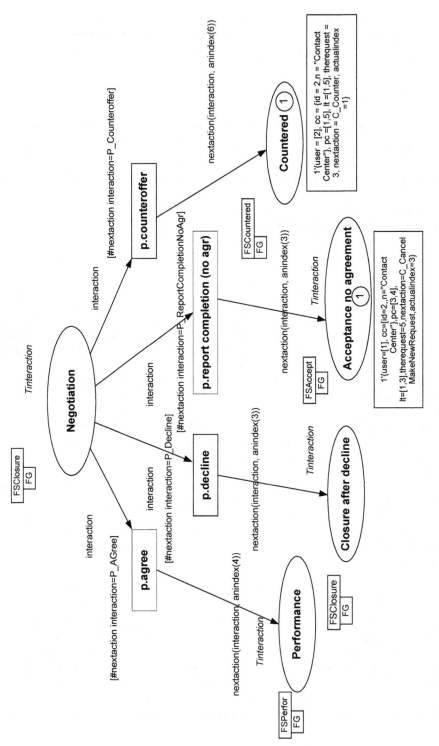

Fig. 7. A Middle Contact Center Simulation Step

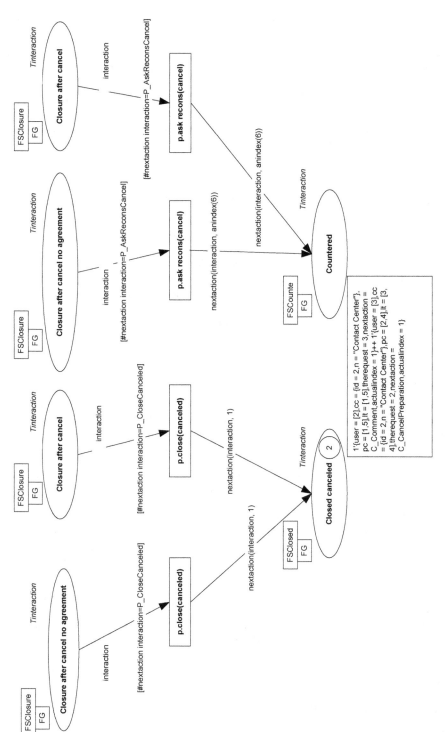

Fig. 8. A Final Contact Center Simulation Step

Relevant characteristics in the proposed architecture and modeling methodology are:

a) It allows the characterization of the cooperation problem in CIS by means of a multilevel model that includes communication, interaction, coordination and co-operation.
b) It allows to easily model the state of simultaneous interaction among more than two agents in an expressive way.
c) It allows to model and control multiple simultaneous interactions using CP Nets.
d) It allows to simulate the system interaction dynamics by the use of CPN Tools.
e) It allows to share models among collaborative software engineering's teams in an easy way.

The following CP nets characteristics allow to manage the complexity in the modeling of multiple interactions:

a) The use of fusion place for modeling the system hierarchically is a viable solution for representing the communication medium.
b) The use of colors helps us model complex data types and allows to model and control multiple simultaneous interactions among agents.
c) The representation of the interaction states like place and the communicative acts like a transition in the CP net.
d) The use of CPN Tools to model and simulate the CP nets, in order to understand the dynamic of the agent's interactions in the CIS.

References

1. Cabac Lawrence, Moldt Daniel und Heiko Rölke. "A Proposal for Structuring Petri Net-Based Agent Interaction Protocols". In: W. v. d. Aalst und E. Best (Herausgeber), Proceedings of the International Conference on Application and Theory of Petri Nets 2003, Band 2679 von Lecture Notes in Computer Science, Seiten 102 {120. Springer-Verlag, Berlin Heidelberg New York, 2003.
2. Camargo-Santacruz F., Ramos-Quintana F., Frausto-Solis J., "Modeling Interaction in Cooperative Information Systems Using Coloured Petri Nets","The 7th World Multi-Conference on Systemics, Cybernetics and Informatics", Orlando, Florida, USA, July 2003.
3. Cohen P.R., and H.J. Levesque, "Communicative actions for artificial agents", Proceedings of the International Conference on Multi-Agent Systems, AAAI Press, San Francisco, June, 1995.
4. Cost R.S., Y. Chen, T. Finin, Y. Labrou and Y. Peng, "Using Coloured Petri Nets for Conversation Modeling", IJCAI '99, 1999.
5. El Fallah A., S. Haddad and H. Mazouzi, "Protocol Engineering for Multi-agent Interaction", 9th European Workshop on Modelling Autonomous Agents in a Multi-Agent World, MAAMAW'99, Springer, 1999.
6. Demazeau Y, J.L. Koning, and G. Françoise, "Formalization and pre- validation for interaction protocols on multi-agent systems", Distributed AI and Multi-agent Systems, p- 298-302, 1998.
7. FIPA, Foundation for Intelligent Physical Agents, "Agent Communication Language Specification", http://www.fipa.org, 2004.
8. Flores F., and T. Winograd, "Understanding computer and cognition, a new foundation for design", Addison Wesley, 1986.

9. Flores F., "Introducción al Ciclo Básico de la Acción ("Loop")", Business Design Associates, Inc., 1996.
10. Haddadi A., "Towards a Pragmatic Theory of Interactions", Morgan Kaufmann Publishers, San Francisco, California, United States of America, 1998.
11. Huhns M., and M.P. Singh, "Readings in Agents", Morgan Kaufmann Publishers, San Francisco, California, United States of America, 1998.
12. Jensen K., "Coloured Petri Nets, Basic Concepts, Analysis Methods and Practical Use", volume 1, 2, 3, second edition, Springer, Germany, 1997, http://www.daimi.au.dk/PetriNets/.
13. Lesser V., "Reflections on the nature of multi-agent coordination and its implications for the agent architecture", Autonomous agents and multi-agent systems, Kluwer academic publishers, 1, 89-111, July 1998.
14. Papazoglou M., and G. Schlageter, "Cooperative Information Systems, Trends and Directions", Academic Press, 1998.
15. Ramos-Quintana F., Frausto-Solis J. and Camargo-Santacruz F., "A Methodology for Modeling Interactions in Cooperative Information Systems Using Coloured Petri Nets", International Journal of Software Engineering and Knowledge Engineering, World Scientific, Vol. 12, No. 6 (2002) 619-635, http://www.worldscinet.com/117/12/1206/S0218194002001104.html, 2002.
16. Wooldidge H.J., and N.R. Jennings, "Intelligent Agents: Theory and Practice", The Knowledge Engineering Review, 10 (2), p. 115-152, 1995.

A Framework for Information Integration with Uncertainty

Ali Kiani and Nematollaah Shiri

Dept. of Computer Science & Software Engineering
Concordia University
Montreal, Quebec, Canada
{ali_kian,shiri}@cse.concordia.ca

Abstract. Uncertainty management and information integration have been challenging issues in AI and database research. The literature is vast and rich on either of these two issues, however, they have not been studied simultaneously in the same setting. In this work, we make a first attempt and propose a framework for information integration with uncertainty, which uses the *information source tracking (IST)* model [9] as the underlying certainty model. The *IST* model is an extension of the relational data model in which every tuple t is annotated with (a set of) fixed length vectors, called *agent vectors*, representing the (human or sensor) agents which confirmed t or contributed to it. Our framework consists of a dynamic collection of autonomous but cooperating *IST* databases, called the information *sources* or *sites*, in which each relation r is annotated with a *site vector*, indicating which sites contributed to the definition of r. We extend the relational algebra from the basic *IST* model accordingly to manipulate agent and site vectors. We also extend the reliability calculation algorithm from the basic model to compute the certainty of each answer tuple as a function of the reliabilities of the contributing agents and sites. We have developed a running prototype of the proposed framework for which we mainly used SQL programming for query rewriting and manipulation of agent and site vectors.

1   Introduction

Many real-life applications require the ability to represent and manipulate deficient data. Examples of deficiency in data include incompleteness, uncertainty, inconsistency, and imprecision. The problem of representing and manipulating uncertain data has been studied extensively in AI and database systems. Parson [6] surveys approaches to handling deficient information in data and knowledge bases. Lakshmanan and Shiri [5] survey uncertainty in logic programming and deductive databases. Silberschatz et. al. identified uncertainty as a challenging issue in database research [11].

Sadri [9] proposed *IST* to model uncertainty in relational databases. Each tuple in an *IST* database is annotated with *agent* vectors, representing the agents which contributed to that tuple. (In [9], agent vectors were called *source vectors*.) Each agent vector is a list of fixed length vector over $\{-1, 0, 1\}$, or a set of such

F.F. Ramos et al. (Eds.): ISSADS 2005, LNCS 3563, pp. 194–206, 2005.

vectors, in general. Standard relational algebra was extended in *IST* which takes into account the presence of agent vectors.

In this paper, we propose a framework which consists of a "dynamic" collection of autonomous but cooperative *IST* databases, each of which is stored as a site/node in the integrated model, in which nodes can be easily added or removed. Each relation r in our framework is denoted by r/p, where r is an extended relation in the *IST* model, and p is a special attribute of r, called the *site vector*, indicating the sites that contributed to the definition of r. In this work, we use sources and sites interchangeably. For ease of presentation, we consider p as a list of sites, sorted on their id's/names. Note the difference between the two kinds of vectors; agent vectors are associated with tuples whereas source vectors are associated with relations, independent of the tuples they may contain.

We extended the relational algebra operations in the basic *IST* model to manipulate both types of agent and site vectors. For this, we have defined and used some auxiliary functions to manipulate site vectors. We have implemented, in Java, a prototype of our integrated framework, in which each source is an *IST* database under the Oracle 9i DBMS. In addition to showing the feasibility and usefulness of the ideas in this work, the prototype developed provides a basis to further study various issues such as query rewriting and optimization involved in our context of information integration with uncertainty. To our knowledge, this is a first attempt of its kind.

The rest of this paper is organized as follows. Section 2 reviews the basic *IST* model. In section 3, we introduce our framework for information integration with uncertainty. Section 4 presents an extend relational algebra for our model which takes into account the presence of agent and site vectors. In section 5, we report details of a prototype of the proposed model and illustrate query rewriting and processing. A reliability calculation algorithm is presented in section 6. Concluding remarks and future directions are provided in section 7.

2   Background and Notation

In this section, we quickly review the *IST* model [9]. This model extends the relational database model, in which each tuple t in an *IST* database is annotated with *agent vectors* indicating which agents contributed to t and the kind of its contribution. The length of the agent vectors in an *IST* database is fixed, and is determined when we design the database.

Each entry in an agent vector is an element in $L = \{-1, 0, 1\}$. Normally, tuples in base relations are entered with agent vectors which have one entry of 1, and the rest being 0. For derived relations, such as answers to queries and views, the tuples may be associated with agent vectors that have multiple entries of 1 and/or -1, in general. Intuitively, if the i-th entry in an agent vector associated with tuple t is 1, it indicates agent i contributed positively to t. If this entry is 0, it indicates agent i did not contribute to t. If this entry is -1, it indicates agent i contributed negatively to t. This last case arises when a query involves the set difference operation. Each tuple inserted in base relations in an

IST database is associated with a single agent vector, however, in query results or views, tuples may be associated with sets of agent vectors, in general, with multiple entries over L. In any case, as in the standard case, users do not consider agent vectors when formulating queries. Compared to the standard case, a user in the *IST* model would see the agent vectors associated with the tuples in the query result. Optionally, the user can get the reliability of each answer tuple, which is a value in $[0, 1]$ calculated based on the reliabilities of the agents.

Formally, an *extended relation schema* R in an *IST* database D is a set of attributes $\{A_1, \ldots, A_n, I\}$, where $A_1, \ldots, A_n$ are regular attributes, and I is the *agent attribute*. Suppose $I = \{a_1, \ldots, a_k\}$ is the set of agents for D. The domain of each regular attribute A_i is denoted as D_i, $i = 1, \ldots, k$. For the agent attribute I, the domain D_I is the set of agent vectors of length k, i.e., $D_I = \{\langle a_1, \ldots, a_k \rangle \mid a_i \in \{-1, 0, 1\}, i = 1, \ldots, k\}$.

Each tuple in an extended relation R is an element of $D_1 \times \ldots \times D_n \times D_I$. That is, each tuple is of the form $t@u$, where t is "regular" part of the tuple corresponding to the regular attributes $A_1, \ldots, A_n$, and $u \in D_I$ is the "agent" part of the tuple corresponding to the agent attribute I. We simply refer to t as the "pure tuple" and to u as its (agent) vector. A relation instance r on R is a set of tuples over R.

2.1   Relational Algebra in *IST*

In the basic *IST* model, the standard relational algebra operations of selection, projection, union, intersection, Cartesian product, and set difference were extended to manipulate agent vectors [9]. Since we use this algebra as a basis and extend it in our work, we recall the definitions of these operations, which use the auxiliary functions: *3Or*, *Union*, and *Negation*, defined as follows. To better understand these definitions, note that $L = \{-1, 0, 1\}$ is a poset with the two orderings: $0 \prec -1$, and $0 \prec 1$, with $\oplus$ as the least upper bound operator.

Given any pair of agent vectors $u = \langle a_1 \ldots, a_m \rangle$ and $v = \langle b_1 \ldots, b_m \rangle$, the *3Or* of u and v, denoted by $u \parallel v$, is an agent vector $w = \langle c_1 \ldots, c_m \rangle$ such that $c_i = \oplus(a_i, b_i)$. As a special case, if $\oplus(a_i, b_i) = \top$, then this means agent i has been contradictory w.r.t. a tuple t, interpreted as "over-specified." In this case, to support manipulation of the agent vectors, we use the agent vector with all entries set to 0. The *3Or* function is extended, in a natural way, to sets of agent vectors, as follows. Given $x = \{u_1, \ldots, u_p\}$ and $y = \{v_1, \ldots, v_q\}$, the *3Or* of x and y is defined pair-wise as: $x \parallel y = \{u_1 \parallel v_1, \ldots, u_1 \parallel v_q, \ldots, u_p \parallel v_1, \ldots u_p \parallel v_q\}$. The function *Negation* is defined as follows. Let $u = \langle a_1, \ldots, a_m \rangle$ be an agent vector and let $a_{d_1}, \ldots, a_{d_n}$ be the non-zero elements of u. The *Negation* of u, denoted by $\#(u)$, is a set of agent vectors $\{v_{d_1}, \ldots, v_{d_n}\}$ of length m such that the entries of v_{d_j} are all zero except for the d_j-th entry, which is 1 if $a_{d_j} = -1$, and is -1 if $a_{d_j} = 1$. The *Negation* of a set of agent vectors $x = \{u_1, \ldots, u_p\}$ is defined as $\#(x) = \#(u_1) \parallel \ldots \parallel \#(u_p)$. The *Union* of two sets of source vectors is defined in the standard way: given source vectors $x = \{u_1, \ldots, u_p\}$ and $y = \{v_1, \ldots, v_q\}$, $x \cup y = \{u_1, \ldots, u_p, v_1, \ldots, v_q\}$.

Using the above three functions, the extended relational algebra operations in *IST* are defined as follows.

$\sigma_C(r) = \{t@u : t \text{ satisfies condition } C \text{ and } t@u \in r\}$

$\pi_X(r) = \{t[X]@u : t@u \in r\}$, where $t[X]$ is the restriction of t to X.

As in the standard case, tuples defined on the same set of regular attributes are assumed to be compatible, which is required for the union, intersection, and set difference operations. We next define the extended binary operations of union, intersection, cartesian product, and natural join, which use the *3Or* function to manipulate agent vectors.

$r \cup s = \{t@x : t@u \in r \lor t@v \in s\}$

$r \cap s = \{t@(u \parallel v) : t@u \in r \land t@v \in s\}$

$r \times s = \{t_1 \cdot t_2@(u \parallel v) : t_1@u \in r \land t_2@v \in s\}$

where $t_1 \cdot t_2$ denotes the concatenation of t_1 and t_2.

Finally, the set difference operations uses *Negation* (#) and *3Or* ($\parallel$) functions:

$r - s = \{t@x : (t@x \in r \land \nexists y \; t@y \in s) \lor (t@u \in r \land t@v \in s \land x = u \parallel \#(v))\}$.

3   The Proposed Framework

We now present our framework for information integration with uncertainty, obtained by extending the basic *IST* model. Our integrated model is a collection of cooperative *IST* databases, to each of which we refer as an information source or a site. The agents in each information source are assumed to be fixed and different from those in other sources. These sources form the local schemas of the integrated framework. We exploit the LAV and GAV mappings [4, 7, 12] in query processing to map the global and local schemas. While our framework uses the *IST* model as the basis, it differs in two ways, as we consider a collection of *IST* sources. The first difference is that no two sites may have the same information agent, while they may have the same number of agents. Secondly, in our integrated framework, evaluating a query in a site may require the contributions of other sites, which is determined at the integration level and is transparent to the users.

In our model, tuples are similar to the basic *IST* model. However, the definition of relations is further extended to take into account the presence of site vectors. That is, an extended relation schema in our model is denoted by R/J, in which R is an *IST* relation and J is a special attribute, which we call the *site attribute* or *site vector*, for short. The semantics of R/J is that at least one relation in each site listed in J has contributed to the definition of R.

Let $N = \{s_1, \ldots, s_n\}$ be the set of id's of the sites in our integrated model. The domain D_J of the site attribute J is the set of all non-empty, sorted lists of sources in N. The reason for using the list as the structure of site vectors is to simplify the definitions of operations on agents. To define D_J, we introduce the function *Sort*, denoted $\mathbb{S}(V)$, such that for $V \subseteq N$, it returns the sorted list of id's in V. That is, $\mathbb{S}(V) = \{\langle s_i, \ldots, s_j \rangle : s_i, \ldots, s_j \in V \text{ and } s_i < \ldots < s_j\}$. Using this function, we have $D_J = \{\mathbb{S}(V) : V \subseteq N, V \neq \emptyset\}$. We will use $\mathbb{S}(V)(i)$ to denote the i-th element in the list $\mathbb{S}(V)$.

Therefore, an *agent vector* associated with a tuple in an extended relation R/J is a non-empty set of vectors of size m defined as: $I = \{\langle a_{i_1}, a_{i_2}, \ldots, a_{i_m}, \ldots, b_{j_1}, b_{j_2}, \ldots, b_{j_n}\rangle\}$, where $J = \langle s_i, \ldots, s_j \rangle$ is the list of sites used in defining R. Note that the number of information agents at different sites s_i and s_j may be different. Also note that while the domain of tuples in any instance r of R is $D_1 \times D_2 \ldots D_n \times D_I$, we represent the relation schema as R/J, even though J is not explicitly mentioned in the tuple expression $t@u$, where $u = \langle a_{i_1}, a_{i_2}, \ldots, a_{i_m}, \ldots, b_{j_1}, b_{j_2}, \ldots, b_{j_n}\rangle$.

Associating a site vector with each relation in our model has an intuitive appealing and is justified as it makes it explicit, an assumption that is implicitly made in standard relational databases. This is explained as follows. First, note that our model reduces to the basic *IST* model when there is only one site, i.e., $|N| = 1$. In this case, the site vector may naturally be ignored. Furthermore, our model reduces to standard relational databases if there is only one information agent. In this case, we can ignore the agent and site vectors, and hence back to the standard case. One may argue that our integrated model may be viewed simply as an *IST* model in which information agents are partitioned into (possibly different) size) groups, where each group denotes the site vector of a virtual source. While this is a correct view in terms of modeling, it is inefficient in space utilization due to the presence of potentially many non-contributing agents. Besides, this view ignores the fact that sources actually exist and operate independently in the integrated model. We also remark that the clear redundancy in this view compared to our proposed model is similar to the redundancy of a universal relation compared to a collection of normalized relations.

We next illustrate our integrated model using the following example. Suppose we have a relation r in the global schema about the teams qualified for the World Cup Soccer. Also suppose there is a base relation r_1 stored at site s_1, which corresponds to r. An instance of r_1 is shown in Fig. 1, which has four contributing agents, as indicated. We can think of these agents, numbered 1 to 4, as different sport magazines.

Example 1. Consider query Q: *"List all the teams qualified in the World Cup 2002 but not in 1998."* Processing this query is restricted to site s_1, the result of which is shown in Fig. 1(b). The site vector $\langle s_1 \rangle$ at the top-right corner of table (b) indicates that this result is obtained from relation(s) in site s_1.

Name	Year	I $\langle s_1 \rangle$
Brazil	1998	1 0 0 1
England	1998	1 0 0 0
France	1998	0 1 0 0
Korea	2002	0 0 1 0
England	2002	0 0 1 0

(a)

Name	I $\langle s_1 \rangle$
England	-1 0 1 0
Korea	0 0 1 0

(b)

Fig. 1. (a) Relation r_1 stored at site s_1. (b) The result of query $Q(r)$

Example 2. In addition to relation r_1 above, suppose an instance of r_2, shown in Fig. 2(a), is stored at site s_2. Also suppose that there is a mapping from relation r in the global schema to r_2 at s_2.

Name	Year	I $\langle s_2 \rangle$
France	2002	1 0 0
Korea	1998	0 0 1

(a)

Name	I	$\langle s_1, s_2 \rangle$
England	**-1 0 1 0 0 0 0**	
Korea	**0 0 1 0 0 0 -1**	
France	**0 0 0 0 1 0 0**	

(b)

Fig. 2. (a) An instance of r_2 stored at site s_2. (b) The result of query $Q(r)$, in which the agent vectors at site s_1 are shown in bold

The answer to query Q from the integrated model is shown in Fig. 2(b). As indicated, s_1 and s_2 are the contributing sites. The first 4 entries in the agent vector in Fig. 2(b) indicate the contribution of the agents of site s_1, and the last 3 entries indicate that of agents of s_2. The emphasis here is that whenever a query refers to relations from different sites, their agent vectors should be expanded "properly" for query processing.

Name	Year	Goals	I $\langle s_1 \rangle$
Brazil	1998	14	1 0 0 0
England	2002	6	1 1 0 0
France	1998	15	1 0 0 1

(a)

Team	WYear	Games	I $\langle s_2 \rangle$
Brazil	1998	7	1 0 0
England	2002	5	1 0 1
France	1998	7	0 1 0

(b)

Fig. 3. (a) Relation instance s at site s_1. (b) Relation instance t at site s_2

For relations r_3 and r_4 in the global schema, consider their instances shown in Fig. 3. Relation r_3 records the number of goals each team scored, and r_4 records the number of games each team played in different world cups. Using a LAV or GAV view, we can obtain the tuples in r_3 from site s_1 and those in r_4 from site s_2. Since these relations are stored in different sites, to perform any operation on both, their agent vectors should be expanded with respect to the contributing sites, $\langle s_1, s_2 \rangle$ in our example. We elaborate on this in section 5.

4   Extended Relational Algebra

In this section, we present an extension of relational algebra operations in our context. For this, in addition to function $\mathbb{S}(V)$ defined earlier, we introduce the following functions to manipulate agent and site vectors.

(a) *Length*: This function, denoted by $\mathbb{L}$, takes a source name/id, s_j, as input and returns the number of entries of the agent attribute I_j, associated with every relation in s_j. That is, $\mathbb{L}(s_j)$ is the length of the agent vectors in s_j.

(b) *Flatten*: This function, denoted by $\mathbb{F}$, changes a list to a set. The input is an agent/site vector p and the output is the set of agents mentioned in p.

(c) *Pattern*: This function, denoted by $\mathbb{P}$, takes two site vectors p and q and returns an "expanded" site vector, called *pattern*, which has an entry 1 for every agent specified in p, and has a 0 for the entry of those agents in q which are not in p. The position of each sequence of 0's or 1's is determined by the sorted order of the id's of the sites specified in sites p and q. For example, suppose $p = \langle s_1, s_3 \rangle$ and $q = \langle s_2 \rangle$. Then the agent vectors associated with any tuple in a relation defined by contributions of sites s_1 and s_3 would be of the form $\langle a_1, \ldots, a_i, c_1, \ldots, c_k \rangle$. Similarly, the agent vectors associated with any tuple in a relation defined by the contribution of s_2 would be of the form $\langle b_1, \ldots, b_j \rangle$. Here, $i = \mathbb{L}(s_1)$, $j = \mathbb{L}(s_2)$, and $k = \mathbb{L}(s_3)$. Therefore, $\mathbb{P}(p, q) = \langle 1, \ldots, 1, 0, \ldots, 0, 1, \ldots, 1 \rangle$, where the lengths of the two sequences of 1's are i and k, and the length of the sequence of 0's in the middle is j. Also note that in this example, $\mathbb{P}(q, p) = \langle 0, \ldots, 0, 1, \ldots, 1, 0, \ldots, 0 \rangle$, with i number of 0's, followed by j number of 1's, followed by k number of 0's. Formally, $\mathbb{P}(p, q)$ is a string over $\{0, 1\}$ of the form $\langle p_1 p_2 \ldots p_n \rangle$, in which each p_i is a sequence of all 0's or all 1's, defined as follows, where $V = \mathbb{F}(p) \cup \mathbb{F}(q)$, $n = |V|$, $i \in [1..n]$, $s_i = \mathbb{S}(V)(i)$, and $k = \mathbb{L}(s_i)$:

$$
p_i = \begin{cases} 1^k & \text{if } s_i \in \mathbb{F}(p) \\ 0^k & \text{otherwise} \end{cases}
$$

(d) *Expand*: This function, denoted by $\mathbb{E}$, takes an agent vector u and a pattern p as the inputs and returns an expanded vector u' with respect to the p generated by $\mathbb{P}$. In the formulation below, λ is the empty string and "." is the concatenation operation on strings. This function produces a 0 if there is a 0 at position j in the pattern; otherwise, it gets the next entry from u if the entry at position j is 1.

$$
E(u, p) = \begin{cases} \lambda & \text{if } p = \lambda \\ b.E(u', p') & \text{if } p = 1.p', \ u = b.u' \\ 0.E(u, p') & \text{if } p = 0.p' \end{cases}
$$

We are now ready to present the extended relational algebra in our framework which takes into account the presence of both agent and site vectors. For any query, if at least two sites contribute, then we need to use the expand function in general. In our algebra operations below on relations r/p and s/q, the result is of the form t/w, in which $w = \mathbb{S}(\mathbb{F}(p) \cup \mathbb{F}(q))$. In other words, the site vector of the result is the non-repeated sequence of all the sites in p and q, sorted on their id's. Note that if $p = q$, then $w = p$.

- Selection: The select operation returns every tuple in r that satisfies condition C. That is, $\sigma_C(r/p) = \{t@u : t@u \in r/p \text{ and } t \text{ satisfies condition } C\}/p$.
- Projection: This projects the tuples in r on the attributes that appear in the argument list. That is, $\pi_X(r/p) = \{t[X]@u : t@u \in r/p\}/p$, where $t[X]$ denotes the restriction of tuple t to the attributes in X.

- Union: This is similar to the standard case, except that we need to expand the agent vectors of the contributing tuples from r and s with respect to the sites mentioned in q or p. We refer to this process as *reconfiguration of agent vectors*, which unifies the agent vectors of the answer tuples in that the ith entry in every agent vector would refer to a fixed agent.

  $r/p \cup s/q = \{t@x : (t@u \in r/p, \ x = \mathbb{E}(u, p_1), \ p_1 = \mathbb{P}(p, q))$ *or*
  $\qquad\qquad\qquad (t@v \in s/q, \ x = \mathbb{E}(v, p_2), \ p_2 = \mathbb{P}(q, p))\}/w.$

- Intersection: As before, we need to reconfigure the agent vectors of the tuples involved in this operation.

  $r/p \cap s/q = \{t@x : t@u \in r/p, \ t@v \in s/q, \ x = \mathbb{E}(u, p_1) \ \| \ \mathbb{E}(v, p_2),$
  $\qquad\qquad \text{where } p_1 = \mathbb{P}(p, q) \text{ and } p_2 = \mathbb{P}(q, p)\}/w.$

- Cartesian Product: Given any pair of tuples $t_1@u \in r/p$ and $t_2@v \in s/q$, their cross product generates the tuple $t@x$, where $t = t_1 \times t_2$. If u' and v' are the reconfigured agent vectors associated with t_1 and t_2, then the vector x associated with t is the *3Or* of u' and v'.

  $r/p \times s/q = \{t_1 \cdot t_2 @x : \ t_1@u \in r/p, \ t_2@v \in s/q, \ x = \mathbb{E}(u, p_1) \ \| \ \mathbb{E}(v, p_2),$
  $\qquad\qquad \text{where } \ p_1 = \mathbb{P}(p, q) \text{ and } p_2 = \mathbb{P}(q, p)\}/w.$

- Difference: To define *difference*, we have the following two cases to consider.
  1. Tuple $t@u$ is in r/p, but t does not appear in s/q. In this case, we just need to reconfigure the agent vector u before producing the result.
  2. For a tuple t, $t@u$ is in r/p and $t@v$ is in s/q. In this case, the agent vector x associated with t in the query result is defined as $x = u' \ \| \ \#(v')$.

  Formally:

  $r/p - s/q = \{t@x : (t@u \in r/p \text{ such that } \forall v : t@v \notin s/q, \ x = \mathbb{E}(u, p_1))$ *or*
  $\qquad\qquad (t@u \in r/p, \ t@v \in s/q, \ u' = \mathbb{E}(u, p_1), \ v' = \mathbb{E}(v, p_2),$
  $\qquad\qquad x = u' \ \| \ \#(v'), \text{ where } p_1 = \mathbb{P}(p, q) \text{ and } p_2 = \mathbb{P}(q, p))\}/w.$

5 System Architecture

Fig. 4 depicts the three-layer architecture of the prototype *IIST* of the integrated model we developed. As can be seen from the figure, standard database sources (DS) are at the lowest layer, the *IST* is in the middle, and the integration layer is at the top. This is further explained as follows. The lowest layer stores standard relations with the agent attribute I. The components representing this layer are $DS_1, \ldots, DS_n$. Each DS_i is an *IST* database, implemented and wrapped with the *IST* layer. That is, given a query in SQL, the wrapper rewrites the query so that the underlying relational database appears as an *IST* database. The top layer in the integration layer provides to the user of integrated model, a transparent access to our collection of data sources.

There are basically three major activities at the top layer: query pre-processing, query shipping, and post-processing, described as follows. As shown in Fig. 4, each *IST* node can initiate and/or participate in these activities.

The pre-processing module rewrites the user query to support *IST* data model to deal with agent vectors. The steps are as follows. First the user query is divided into sub-queries. Each sub-query is then rewritten to be suitable to *IST* model.

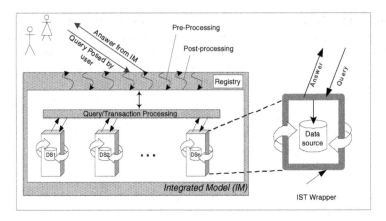

Fig. 4. Architecture of the prototype

The rewritten subqueries are then put back together into a single query. For example, let us consider the following query:

```
select * from r natural join
        (select Name, Year, Goals, Games from s, t
         where s.Name=t.team and s.year=t.WYear);
```

Then the result of rewriting this query is as follows, which uses *or3way* to compute $r.I \parallel u.I$ and also $s.I \parallel t.I$.

```
select r.Name,r.Year,u.Goals, u.Games, or3way(r.I,u.I) as I
from r, (select s.Name,s.Year,Goals,Games,or3way(s.I,t.I) as I
         from s,t where s.Name=t.team and s.year=t.WYear) u
where r.Name=u.Name and r.Year=u.Year;
```

The next step in the pre-processing phase is identify which sites/sources will participate in answering the query. In our prototype, this is done using the information in the system registry. In our prototype, a user may restrict evaluation of a query on a selected set of sources, if desired. This module would also be responsible to identify the "best" plan for data/query shipping over the integrated system. This is an important optimization issue, not discussed in this work. In our example, suppose the *IIST* includes two sites, s_1 and s_2, and suppose there is a set of mappings between relations r, s, and t, and their correspondences at s_1 and s_2, i.e., relation s (Fig. 3(a)) in the query comes from site s_1, relation r (Figures 1(a) and 2(a)) come from sites s_1 and s_2, and relation t (Fig. 3(b)) comes from s_2. Then an execution plan would be to transfer a copy of relations r and t to site s_1, justified if we assume the size of the data at site s_1 to be more than that at s_2.

Our prototype includes a module that performs necessary query and/or data shipping. If required, it also expands agent vectors of the *IST* relations with respect to the contributing sources. Suppose in our example, source s_1 is decided to process the query. As shown in Fig. 5, after query/data shipping, s_1 will have all the required relations to evaluate the query.

Name	Year Goals	I $\langle s_1, s_2 \rangle$
Brazil	1998 14	**1 0 0 0 0 0 0**
England	2002 6	**1 1 0 0 0 0 0**
France	1998 15	**1 0 0 1 0 0 0**

(b)

Name	Year	I	$\langle s_1, s_2 \rangle$
Brazil	1998	**1 0 0 1 0 0 0**	
England	1998	**1 0 0 0 0 0 0**	
France	1998	**0 1 0 0 0 0 0**	
Korea	2002	**0 0 1 0 0 0 0**	
England	2002	**0 0 1 0 0 0 0**	
France	2002	**0 0 0 0 1 0 0**	
Korea	1998	**0 0 0 0 0 0 1**	

(a)

Team	WYear Games	I $\langle s_1, s_2 \rangle$
Brazil	1998 7	**0 0 0 0 1 0 0**
England	2002 5	**0 0 0 0 1 0 1**
France	1998 7	**0 0 0 0 0 1 0**

(c)

Fig. 5. Relations r (a), s (b), and t (c) originally residing at s_1 and s_2 are stored at s_1

Name	Year	Goals	Games	I $\langle s_1, s_2 \rangle$
Brazil	1998	14	7	**1 0 0 1 1 0 0**
England	2002	6	5	**1 1 1 0 1 0 1**
France	1998	15	7	**1 1 0 1 0 1 0**

Fig. 6. Query answer from Integrated IST

During query execution, some revisions in agent/site vectors may be necessary to deal with some run-time issues. For instance, it is possible that a relation mentioned in a query may not contribute to the answer, e.g., due to the selection condition. In a different scenario, a relation used may become unavailable during query processing. In such cases, the agent/site vectors, which are already expanded by query pre-processing module, need to be "shrunk" to exclude vectors related to such relations. Fig. 6 shows the query result in this example.

6 Computing Certainties

We now present an algorithm to convert agent vectors in the answer tuples into certainty/reliability values. This is obtained by extending the method proposed in [9] to take into account the site vectors, in addition to agent vectors. Each agent a at site s has a reliability v_a, which is value in $[0, 1]$. The reliability of a tuple t is then defined as a function of reliabilities of the agents contributed to t. More precisely, the reliability of t is "the probability of correctness of t confirmed by its contributing agent(s)." Thus, if an agent a has contributed to the definition of relation r/p, then v_a is used in computing the reliability of every tuple in r/p. Recall that p is a sorted list of sites. The contribution of agent a is recorded at some fixed position, j, in p, once the agents in p are sorted according to site id and the result is viewed as a single, long agent vector. We use $\mathbb{R}(j, p)$ to denote the reliability of the agent at position j in this long vector, and is defined as follows, where $rel(j, s)$ denotes the reliability of the jth agent at site s.

$$\mathbb{R}(j, p) = \begin{cases} rel(j, s) & \text{if } j \leq \mathbb{L}(s) \quad \text{where } s = \mathbb{S}(p)(1) \\ \mathbb{R}(j', p') & otherwise \quad s = \mathbb{S}(p)(1), \ j' = j - \mathbb{L}(s), \ p' = p - s \end{cases}$$

We remark that this definition of $\mathbb{R}(j,p)$ reduces to the reliability of agent defined in the *IST* model. Intuitively, $j > \mathbb{L}(s)$ means that j is referring to an agent, a_j, in the expanded agent vector in which s is the first element of the site vector P. Therefore, in order to obtain the reliability of an agent a_j in p, we remove this site s from the beginning of p and decrease j by the length of the agent vector in the remaining entries until $j \leq \mathbb{L}(s)$, i.e., until j is referring to the agent in the desired site.

We consider four different cases for computing the reliability of any tuple t in relation r/p. First, when every tuple t is associated with a single agent vector and not a set of such vectors. In this case, we further distinguish two cases (i) and (ii), explained as follows. In case (i), there are no two tuples in r/p with t as the pure part. That is, if $t@u$ is in r/p, then for no v different from u, $t@v \in r/p$. Now suppose $i_1, i_2, \ldots, i_d$ are all the entries in u having value 1 and $j_1, j_2, \ldots, j_m$ are all those having -1. In this case, the reliability of t in r/p is:

$$\mathbb{R}(t,p) = \mathbb{R}(i_1, p) \times \ldots \times \mathbb{R}(i_d, p) \times [1 - \mathbb{R}(j_1, p)] \times \ldots \times [1 - \mathbb{R}(j_m, p)].$$

Note that we used $\mathbb{R}$ to denote the reliability of an agent as well as the reliability of a tuple. This abuse of notation is justified upon noting that the reliability of a tuple is defined as a function of the reliabilities of agents. In case (ii), tuple $t@x$ appears only once in relation r/p, where $x = \{u_1, \ldots, u_j\}$ is a set of agent vectors. If we assume that the agents are pairwise independent, then reliability of t is defined as: $\mathbb{R}(t,p) = 1 - [1 - \mathbb{R}(t@u_1, p)] \times \ldots \times [1 - \mathbb{R}(t@u_j, p)]$.

If the agents are not independent, we may use the following algorithm to compute reliabilities. Suppose $t@u_1, t@u_2, \ldots, t@u_p$ are all the tuples in r/p with the pure part t. Let

$$K_1 = \sum_{i=1}^{d} \mathbb{R}(u_i, p), \quad K_2 = \sum_{i=1}^{d} \sum_{j>i}^{d} \mathbb{R}(u_i||u_j, d), \quad K_3 = \sum_{i=1}^{d} \sum_{j>i}^{p} \sum_{k>j}^{d} \mathbb{R}(u_i||u_j||u_k, p), \ldots$$

Then the reliability of tuple t would be $\mathbb{R}(t,p) = K1 - K2 + K3 - K4 + \cdots$

We next consider the case in which a pure tuple t appears multiple times in r/p, which we further classify into cases (iii) and (iv), described as follows. In case (iii), every occurrence of t in r/p is associated with an agent vector (and not a set of vectors). That is, $t@u_1, t@u_2, \ldots, t@u_k$ are the only tuples in r/p with the pure part t, where u_i is an agent vector. This corersponds to a situation in which each agent confirms t, each with a reliability that is identical to the reliability of the agent itself. In this case, different user-defined algorithms may be employed for computing the reliability of t by combining the multiple reliabilities of t.

Finally, in case (iv), suppose $t@x_1, \cdots, t@x_k$ are all the tuples with the pure part t in r/p, where x_i's are sets of agent vectors, one of which contains at least two agent vectors. That is, we have $x_1 = \{u_{11}, \ldots, u_{m1}\}$, $x_2 = \{u_{12}, \ldots, u_{m2}\}$, ..., and $t@x_k = \{u_{1k}, \ldots, u_{mk}\}$. In this case, we first compute the reliability of t for each $t@x_i$ and then obtain the overall certainty of t by combining these reliabilities, using a user-defined function mentioned in the previous case.

Our framework also models data inconsistency, which may arise when an agent a is contradictory with respect to some tuple t, in the sense that a has contributed positively and negatively to t. In this case, user-defined inconsistency resolution algorithms could be incorporated within our framework [1].

7 Conclusions and Future Work

In this paper, we proposed a framework for information integration with uncertainty, by extending the *IST* model which associates with each tuple a set of agent vectors. Our framework is a collection of cooperative information sources, in which each source is an *IST* database. We introduced the concept of "contributing sites" associated with the relation schemas in the integrated model. We further extended the relational algebra operations accordingly to manipulate agent and site vectors. We developed a prototype of the proposed framework, and used SQL programming to implement schema mapping and query rewriting. We also implemented in Java a reliability calculation module which converts the agent vectors associated with each answer tuple into a value in $[0, 1]$ as the reliability of the tuple. Our experiment with the prototype system indicates that the ideas and techniques employed in this work are useful both in theory and practice. In addition to modeling inconsistency, as discussed, our framework also supports *lineage tracing* in a natural way through the agent and site vectors.

As a future work, more efficient reliability computation algorithms are required, noting that agent vectors could be large when many sources contribute to a query result. Furthermore, various (semi-)automatic resolution techniques may be suitable in this context to deal with inconsistency [1]. We did not consider much the efficiency of query processing in this work. For this we need to improve on selecting candidate sites to perform query rewriting and shipping [10]. Extending this work to a peer-to-peer model is another future direction for this work [3]. In this paper, we did not consider schema matching [8] and schema management [2]. Rather we assumed this information exists and used it through SQL programming for query transformation. Incorporating this capabilities within our framework is under investigation.

Acknowledgements

This work was in part supported by Natural Sciences and Engineering Research Council (NSERC) of Canada and by Concordia ENCS grants. Philippe Legaul implemented the client/server and the communication layer in the prototype. Srividya Kadiyala implemented the GUI to manage information sources.

References

1. P. Anokhin and A. Motro. Data integration: Inconsistency detection and resolution based on source properties. In *Proc. FMII-01, International Workshop on Foundations of Models for Information Integration*, 2001.
2. P. Bernstein. Generic model management: A database infrastructure for schema manipulation. In *Proc. (CoopIS01)*. Springer-Verlag, LNCS-2172, 2001.

3. Neil Daswani, Hector Garcia-Molina, and Beverly Yang. Open problems in data-sharing peer-to-peer systems. In *ICDT '03: Proceedings of the 9th International Conference on Database Theory*, pages 1–15. Springer-Verlag, 2002.

4. Alon Y. Halevy. Answering queries using views: A survey. *The VLDB Journal*, 10(4):270–294, 2001.

5. Lakshmanan, Laks V.S. and Shiri, Nematollaah. Logic programming and deductive databases with uncertainty: A survey. In *Enclyclopedia of Computer Science and Technology*, volume 45, pages 153–176. Marcel Dekker, Inc., New York, 2001.

6. Simon Parsons. Current approaches to handling imperfect information in data and knowledge bases. *Knowledge and Data Engineering*, 8(3):353–372, 1996.

7. Lucian Popa, Yannis Velegrakis, Renee J. Miller, Mauricio A. Hernandez, and Ronald Fagin. Translating web data. In *Proceedings of VLDB 2002, Hong Kong SAR, China*, pages 598–609, 2002.

8. Erhard Rahm and Philip A. Bernstein. A survey of approaches to automatic schema matching. *VLDB Journal:*, 10(4):334–350, 2001.

9. Sadri, Fereidoon. Modeling uncertainty in databases. In *Proc. 7th IEEE Intl. Conf. on Data Eng.*, pages 122–131, April 1991.

10. Subhabrata Sen and Jia Wong. Analyzing peer-to-peer traffic across large networks. In *Second Annual ACM Internet Measurement Workshop*, November 2002.

11. Silberschatz Avi, Stonebraker Michael, and Ullman J.D. Database systems: Achievements and opportunities, 1990. The Lagunita report of the NSF workshop on the future of database systems research held in Palo Alto, California.

12. Jeffrey D. Ullman. Information integration using logical views. *Theoretical Computer Science*, 239(2):189–210, 2000.

Model Fragmentation for Distributed Workflow Execution: A Petri Net Approach

Wei Tan and Yushun Fan

Department of Automation
Tsinghua University, 100084 Beijing, P.R. China
tanwei@mails.tsinghua.edu.cn, fanyus@tsinghua.edu.cn

Abstract. Workflow is the key technology for business process automation, while distributed workflow is the solution to deal with the decentralized nature of workflow applications and the performance requirements of the whole system. In this paper the architecture of distributed workflow execution is given, and the centralized model called CWF-net, which is based on colored Petri net, is presented. Based on the centralized model, a novel model fragmentation algorithm is proposed. This algorithm partitioned the centralized model into fragments by duplicating the places shared by transitions which are executed in different sites. The behavioral equivalence between the CWF-net and resulted fragments are guaranteed by the extended firing rules. Then the correctness of the fragmentation algorithm is discussed, the correctness criteria comprises completeness of the fragmentation, completeness of each fragment, and the behavioral equivalence after fragmentation. Finally the future research work is pointed out.

1 Introduction

Workflow is the key technology for the coordination of various business processes, such as loan approval and customer order processing [1]. By setting up the process model and enacting it in the workflow server, it can help to streamline the business process, deliver tasks and documents among users, and monitor the overall performance of the process.

Traditional workflow systems are often built upon the client/server architecture, in which a single workflow server will be responsible for the operation of the overall process. But this sort of centralized systems may bring about many disadvantages. First of all, in the internet age, the process itself may be distributed among geographically dispersed business partners, therefore the workflow applications are inherently distributed. Secondly, the reliability of the centralized system cannot be guaranteed since there can be a single point of failure. Last but not the least, the performance of the centralized system may be drastically degraded when there are too many process instances to handle.

To solve the problem that centralized workflow systems cannot overcome, many distributed workflow systems are designed from different approaches. The Exotica system [2] developed by IBM Almaden Research center proposes a completely distributed architecture, in which the information among servers is transferred by the persistent message queue. And by this means, the reliability of the system is highly enhanced.

The Mentor Project [3] of the University of Saarland developed a traceable and scalable workflow architecture. A formal model called state chart is used for workflow

F.F. Ramos et al. (Eds.): ISSADS 2005, LNCS 3563, pp. 207–214, 2005.

specification, and a model partitioning method is proposed by mapping a centralized state chart to distributed ones, each comprises a single state. A theorem has showed that this mapping is a homomorphism between state charts, which means that the transformation preserves the behavior of the original specification.

The Dartflow [4] project has shown the use of the mobile agents in distributed workflow execution. In Dartflow, the workflow model is fragmented dynamically, i.e., when one task is completed, the remaining model, which has not been executed, is partitioned, and the partitions are carried by mobile agents and sent to different sites which are responsible for them.

Workflow specification, or process model provides the information of the process, and it's the basis to computationally support business processes automation. In distributed workflow execution paradigm, the whole process must be partitioned into fragments before execution, and each fragment is designated to a workflow server at which it is to be executed. However, the research works in this field mainly focus on the design of the system architecture and the implementation based on specific communication mechanism. As far as we know, little attention has been paid to the formal method of model fragmentation. Mentor project proposes an approach for model partition, but it just separates states from a state chart, and does not consider which ones are to be executed at the same server.

In this paper we propose a Petri net based approach for model fragmentation. First we discuss the distributed workflow execution architecture, through which we explain how a workflow process is handled by multiple servers. Our centralized process model is based on the well known colored Petri net, and we present the algorithm to partition the centralized model into fragments. The partition is done by duplicating the places connecting different transitions which are not to be executed at the same server. An example is also given to illustrate the algorithm. Another contribution of this paper is that the correctness of our fragmentation algorithm is analyzed in three aspects, i.e., completeness of the fragmentation, completeness of each fragment and the behavioral equivalence after fragmentation. Finally the future work is presented and a conclusion is drawn.

2   Distributed Workflow Execution Architecture

In traditional workflow system, there is a single workflow server to take charge of the operation of the overall process, so the workflow engine must communicate with each task agent, deliver necessary information and retrieve the outcome of a task, as it shows in Fig. 1 (a).

While in the distributed paradigm, there are many workflow *servers* (also called *sites*, for the reason that the servers are often geographically dispersed), and each task is designated to be executed in one of them. After each task is labeled with a server identifier, the process model is separated into several fragments, each coordinated by one server. For example, in Fig. 1 (b), first the centralized model is given. Then *task 1* to *task 8* are labeled with the server name of which they are designated to (*task 1* and *task 2* are designated to *server 1*, *task 4* is designated to *server 2*, *task 3* and *task 5* are designated to *server 3*, *task 6, 7* and *8* are designated to *server 4*). After labeling, it's natural to see that the model is divided into four fragments, i.e., f_1, f_2, f_3 and f_4, and each fragment consists of one or more adjacent tasks which are designated to the same

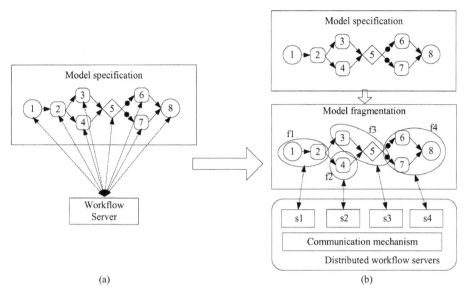

Fig. 1. Architecture for Centralized and Distributed Workflow Execution

server. Note that servers must communicate when the execution is transferred from one sever to others.

3 Centralized Workflow Model

The workflow model used in this paper is an extension of the WF-net [5] proposed by Van der Aalst. WF-net is a special class of Petri net, which prevails in workflow modeling field because of its graphic nature and theoretical foundation. The WF-net has shown its advantages in workflow model verification [5], whereas it's hard to be used to model a real business process because it cannot depict the relevant data and the precondition for tasks. In the meantime, it's well known that colored Petri net [6] can be used in modeling data and condition for tasks, so we combine the WF-net and the colored Petri net for the modeling of workflow in this paper. Below is the definition of CWF-net, which is used for centralized workflow modeling.

Definition 1 (CWF-Net). *A colored Petri net CPN (Σ, P, T, A, N, C, G, E, I) is a colored WF-net (CWF-net) if and only if:*
  (i) (P, T, A, N) forms a WF-net, i.e.,
    a) CPN has two special places: i and o. Place i is a source place: $^{\bullet}i=\Phi$. Place o is a sink place: $o^{\bullet}=\Phi$;
    b) If we add a transition tn to CPN which connects place o with i (i.e., $^{\bullet}tn=\{o\}$ $tn^{\bullet}=\{i\}$), then the resulting Petri net is strongly connected.
  (ii) Σ= {ID×DataList}, ID = {id|id is the identifier of process instances}
       DataList = {$d_1,d_2,...,d_n$|$d_1,d_2,...,d_n$ are workflow relevant data items}
  (iii) $\forall p \in P$, $|C(p)_{MS}| = 1$; $\forall a \in A$, E(a) = I(i), i is the source place.

From the definition above we know that a CWF-net is a kind of colored Petri net with the structure characteristics of a WF-net. The color sets for all places are the same, and the token identifies the process instance as well as the relevant data items. There is at most one token in each place, each arc expression represents the initial token in source place, and the guard functions on transitions are used to model the conditional dependencies between tasks. Fig. 2 is an example of CWF-net, which represents the centralized model in Fig. 1. Note that the guard functions at t_6 and t_7 are mutually exclusive so that only one transition is enabled when p_6 holds one token.

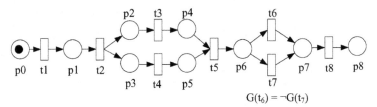

$$G(t_6) = \neg G(t_7)$$

Fig. 2. An Example of a CWF-net

We call a colored WF-net $(\Sigma, P, T, F, C, G, E, I)$ sound if and only if (P, T, A, N) is a sound WF-net, in this paper it's assumed that before fragmentation the centralized model has been verified for its correctness, therefore we assume that the CWF-net is sound.

4   Fragmentation Algorithm

There are two kinds of fragmentation scheme, the static one and the dynamic one. In this paper we only consider the static fragmentation method, that is, the whole model is fragmented when the workflow process is ready to instantiate.

The basic idea about static fragmentation is that when the centralized model is given and each task is labeled with the server (site) id, the model is fragmented. The method for decomposition (or fragmentation) is inspired by the idea that if the adjacent activities are planned to execute on the same site, then they can be put into a single fragment and sent to the site they are designated to. In a CWF-net, activities are represented by transitions and connected by places. When we decompose the whole process model into smaller parts that can be executed at different sites, we must assure that each resulted fragment is started and ended by places, just as the original CWF-net does.

For the sake of simplicity, we define some functions which will be used throughout this paper.

Definition 2 (Some Functions). *In a CWF-net (P, T, A, N)*

$\forall t \in T$, *function site(t) returns the id of the site at which task t is executed.*
$\forall T' \subseteq T$, *site(T') = {s| s = site(t), t\in T' }*
$\forall p \in P$ *function dup(p, k) returns a set of duplicated places of p, i.e., { $p_1, p_2, ..., p_k$ }*
$\forall p_d \in dup(p, k) = \{ p_1, p_2, ..., p_k \}$, *dups($p_d$) = { $p_1, p_2, ..., p_k$ }*
For example, in Fig. 2, *site(t_1) = s_1, site(t_8) = s_4; dup(p_3, 2) = {p_{31}, p_{32}}; dups(p_{31}) = dups(p_{32}) = p_3.*

Fragmentation Algorithm

Algorithm 1 shows our method for model fragmentation. Through Algorithm 1, a CWF-net is divided into a set of colored Petri nets, and each represents a fragment that can be executed in one site. When we impose Algorithm 1 to the CWF-net in Fig. 2, four fragments are obtained, as it shows in Fig. 3. Note that in Fig. 3, the fragments are encircled by dashed rectangles and duplicated places are grouped by ellipses.

Algorithm 1 (Model decomposition)
Given a CWF-net $(\Sigma, P, T, A, N, C, G, E, I)$
For each p_i in P
    If $(k=|site(^\bullet p_i \cup p_i^\bullet)|>1)$
        Let $\{s_1, s_2, ...,s_k\} = site(^\bullet p_i \cup p_i^\bullet)$
        Let $\{ p_{i1}, p_{i2}, ...,p_{ik} \} = dup(p_i, k)$
        For each t_j in $^\bullet p_i$
            $s_m = site(t_j)$
            $t_j^\bullet = \{t_j^\bullet\}\backslash\{p_i\}\cup\{p_{im}\}$
        End For
        For each t_j in $p_i^\bullet$
            $s_n = site(t_j)$
            $^\bullet t_j = \{^\bullet t_j\}\backslash\{p_i\}\cup\{ p_{in} \}$
        End for
    End If
End For

Firing Rules in Fragments

From Fig. 3 we know that in the fragments we obtained, places are classified into two categories, one is the kind of places which exist in the original CWF-net, for example, p_0 and p_1 in fragment f_1, we call this kind of places *common places*; the other is the places generated by the *dup* function, we call them *duplicated places*, for example, p_{21} and p_{31} in fragment f_1. For places of different types, we have different firing rules.

1. Local firing rule: for the common places, the firing rule is the same as ordinary Petri nets.
2. Global firing rule: for the duplicated places, we suppose that if a duplicated place p_d possesses one token, then this token is shared among all duplicated places generated by the same place in original WF-net, i.e., $dups(p_d)$. And once any duplicated place p_d fires a transition then this token is removed and cannot be used by any other duplicated places in $dups(p_d)$.

For example, in Fig. 3 place p_0 and p_1 are common places, so the firing rule is the same as ordinary Petri nets. After the firing of t_1 and t_2, duplicated places p_{21} and p_{31} hold one token respectively. Because p_{21} and p_{31} are duplicated places, according to the global firing rule, the token in p_{21} is shared with p_{23}, so transition t_3 is enabled. With the same reason, p_{31} shares the token it holds with p_{32}, so transition t_4 is enabled. By firing t_3 and t_4, fragment f_2 and f_3 become active and the process is executed continuously.

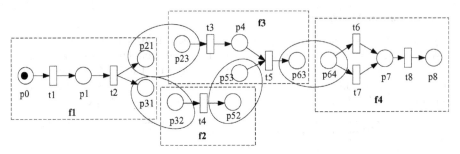

Fig. 3. Results after Fragmentation

5   Correctness of Fragmentation Algorithm

In this section we come to the correctness issue of the fragmentation algorithm. Generally the following three aspects are taken into account, i.e., completeness of the fragmentation, completeness of each fragment and the behavioral equivalence after fragmentation. We are going to discuss the three aspects respectively.

5.1   Completeness of the Fragmentation

The completeness of the fragmentation concerns whether all the fragments can be put together to rebuild the original model.

Through Algorithm 1, a CWF-net is partitioned by duplicating the places which are shared by different fragments. For brevity, we only concern the structure of the fragment, hence we can denote a CWF-net as $PN(P, T, F)$, in which P is the set of places, T is the set of transitions, and F is the set of arcs.

Suppose that by applying Algorithm 1, PN is partitioned into m fragments, i.e., $\{f_1, f_2, \dots, f_m\}$, and $f_i = (P_i, T_i, F_i)$ for $1 \leq i \leq m$. We know that if we define $p = \cup dup(p, k)$ for $p \in P$, then we have

$$T_1, T_2, \dots, T_m \subseteq T, \quad T_1 \cup T_2 \cup \dots \cup T_m = T;$$
$$P_i = {}^\bullet T_i \cup T_i{}^\bullet; \qquad F_i = F \cap ((P_i \times T_i) \cup (T_i \times P_i))$$

This kind of partition of a Petri net is called union decomposition in [7], and from the equation above we know that no information about the CWF-net is lost after fragmentation.

5.2   Completeness of Each Fragment

The completeness of each fragment concerns whether each fragment has sufficient information to execute. From Algorithm 1 we know that each fragment is started by one or more places, which denotes the pre-conditions for tasks; and ended by one or more places, which denotes the post-conditions for tasks. In case of conflict, which task to be executed is determined by the local and global firing rule, together with the guard functions on transitions. So we can conclude that each fragment has sufficient information to execute.

5.3   Behavioral Equivalence Between CWF-Net and Fragments

The behavioral equivalence between the CWF-net and the fragments concerns whether the fragments have the same behavioral characteristics with the original CWF-net. Because the fragmentation algorithm imposes union decomposition on the CWF-net, and with the extended firing rules we proposed (i.e., the local firing rule and the global firing rule), the reachability graphs of the fragments and the CWF-net are the same, which means they are behavioral equivalent.

6   Conclusions

In this paper a formal model fragmentation method for distributed workflow execution is discussed. Given the architecture for distributed workflow execution, we partitioned the centralized CWF-net into fragments by duplicating the places shared by tasks executed at different sites, and the behavioral equivalence between the CWF-net and resulted fragments are guaranteed by the extended firing rules.

The correctness of the fragmentation algorithm is ensured because no information is lost after fragmentation, each fragment has sufficient context to execute, and the fragments are behavioral equivalent to the original CWF-net.

Future research issues include the dynamic fragmentation method and the fragmentation policies. This paper only deals with static fragmentation method, i.e., in the situation that the execution site of each task is designated before the process is going to initiate. But when the process is enacting among different sites, some sites may become very busy, or even unavailable, so it's reasonable to believe that designating execution sites for tasks and do fragmentation dynamically will increase the flexibility and performance of the system.

Another issue is the fragmentation policies, that is, the biases we take when we group adjacent tasks into fragments. There are many factors influencing the fragmentation policy. For example, sometimes the tasks belong to the same organizational unit or located at the same place should be put into one fragment for management convenience. And in the data-intensive processes, tasks which exchange large volume of data should be put into one fragment to reduce the data transfer amount among sites. And sometimes which tasks are to be put into one fragment is decided by the process user. All these policies must be studied in detail to improve the availability and performance of the workflow system.

References

1. Georgakopoulos, D., Hornick, M., Sheth A.: An Overview of Workflow Management: from Process Modeling to Workflow Automation Infrastructure. Distributed and Parallel Databases 3 (1995) 119-153
2. Mohan, C., Alonso, G., Guenthoer, R., Kamath, M., Reinwald, B.: An Overview of the Exotica Research Project on Workflow Management Systems. In: Proc. 6th International Workshop on High Performance Transaction Systems, Asilomar, CA (1995)
3. Muth, P., Wodtke, D., Weissenfels, J., et al.: From centralized workflow specification to distributed workflow execution. Journal of Intelligent Information Systems 10 (1998) 159-184

4. T, Cai, P, Gloor, S, Nog.: DartFlow: A Workflow Management System on the Web using Transportable Agents. Technical Report of Dartmouth College, Hanover, USA (1996)
5. WMP Van der Aalst. The application of Petri nets to workflow management. Journal of Circuits Systems and Computers 8 (1998) 21-66
6. Kurt Jensen.: Coloured Petri nets: basic concepts, analysis methods, and practical use. Springer-Verlag, Berlin Heidelberg New York (1992)
7. Wang, P.L,, Zhao Y.J., Ye Z.B.: Union decomposition of Petri net. Control theory and applications 18 (2001) 116-118 (in Chinese with English abstract)

An Online Component Deployment System for Dynamic Collaborative Sessions

Emir Hammami, Thierry Villemur, and Khalil Drira

LAAS-CNRS, 7 avenue du Colonel Roche,
31077 Toulouse, France
{ehammami,villemur,drira}@laas.fr

Abstract. Component deployment within collaborative sessions is the process through which collaborative tools viewed as monolithic or composite components are made available to session members. Existing approaches dealing with this process adopt an offline exhaustive and static deployment technique. This kind of deployment is not applicable for collaboration where the session structure evolves in time and changes during the collaborative work. In this case, the component distribution is affected by session dynamics. Deploying components can be efficiently and correctly automated by using a formal session model based on collaboration graphs. In this paper, we introduce the problem of dynamic deployment for collaborative sessions, and we describe CDS, a first prototype system we have developed that supports both the initial and the subsequent deployment process according to a formal session model, while satisfying low-level constraints resulting from the heterogeneity of the target environment.

1 Introduction

Computer Supported Collaborative Work (CSCW) and groupware provide a group of collaborating distributed users with the facility to communicate and share data in a coordinated way [1]. Users are involved in collaborative sessions. In particular, synchronous sessions enable people in different geographic locations to bridge time and space by sharing and jointly manipulating different data types in real-time.

In the current approaches, collaborative environments presuppose the availability of collaborative tools used for communications, like videoconferencing tools and shared editors, on each participant site before any coherent starting of the session. In this case, the deployment of these tools adopts an offline exhaustive and static deployment technique according to predefined and unchanged criteria.

On the other hand, with the recent advances in networking in particular available bandwidth increasing and wireless connectivity, and in communication services like true multipoint, new requirements appear:

- **Session evolution:** In a typical collaborative scenario, users join and quit online sessions at any moment whenever they want. Moreover, the role assigned to each participant may change during the working time. Session dynamics lead to modifications of the tool configuration required by each participant.
- **Heterogeneity:** sites used to join to the collaborative session may cover a large panel of capabilities, from tiny devices like PDA to highly powerful portable computers and workstations.

F.F. Ramos et al. (Eds.): ISSADS 2005, LNCS 3563, pp. 215–225, 2005.
© Springer-Verlag Berlin Heidelberg 2005

For these reasons, support for automated deployment when required becomes crucial. Collaborative tools, viewed as monolithic or composite entities, are formed by components which can be instantiated as a producer or a consumer of a special data type. The collaborative deployment aims to provide dynamic distribution of components according to the session structure while satisfying constraints resulting from the heterogeneity of the target environment.

To enable an efficient and correct deployment, a coherent session model based on directed labeled graphs has been proposed [2]. This model describes how a collaborative synchronous session is intended to be structured and has been used as a basis for the deployment system.

This paper focuses on providing a dynamic deployment facility within collaborative sessions. The proposed system, called Collaborative Deployment System (CDS), provides a new approach for deploying components used in a session. Based on session requirements, the system first discovers available components. It selects the most appropriate ones that satisfy constraints then deploys them onto the concerned hosts.

This approach requires additional mechanism like component discovery, included in peer-to-peer (P2P) platforms. It avoids drawbacks of more classic client/server approaches.

The paper is structured as follows. In Section 2, we further motivate the need for online deployment by defining dynamic collaborative sessions and by illustrating how it is important to ensure session coherence in response to session events. In Section 3, based on research and development efforts dealing with the deployment paradigm in the context of component-based applications, we introduce our proposition. Section 4 describes the Collaborative Deployment System (CDS). The representation of the formal model to characterize coherent sessions is also described in this section. Section 5 reports design details such as architecture decision and implementation choices. Section 6 concludes our work and proposes some directions for future enhancements of CDS.

2   Collaborative Sessions

2.1   Description

Collaborative activities are characterized by group of users physically (or virtually) distributed working jointly on common tasks. These users are involved in a collaborative session and use several collaborative tools for processing, exchanging and sharing different data types. Collaborative tools provide the basic communication services to the users registered in the session. Synchronous sessions guarantee virtual copresence of a group of users. They have more constraints in term of interactivity and are more difficult to manage than pure asynchronous sessions. Work presented in the sequel focuses on synchronous sessions.

Dynamic changes in time can appear inside collaborative sessions. Especially, at the user level, two orthogonal changes are possible [3]: (i) **User entries/exits.** Users can join and leave online sessions whenever they want. (ii) **User role changes**. An operational role is associated with a user during the lifetime of a session. A person logged with a particular role can play another role later depending on the context of the collaboration. These two changes describe the session evolution and have impact on collaborative tool space and data space.

2.2 Deployment Needs

User and role change induce modifications on the collaboration structure. Particularly, we pass from a coherent configuration with a coherent distribution of components to another new configuration where the necessary components are not present or are not available for some users. This stresses the importance of a particular coordination function that manages collaborative components distribution between involved participants when the session evolves.

An automatic deployment service appears important and necessary to ensure that all participants in the session have the appropriate set of components compulsory to perform the collaborative activity. This approach avoids a manual online session management from the connected users and so improves the quality of the collaboration process. Users concentrate on their common work.

Collaborative deployment is the main topic of our work. Requirements, solutions proposed and partially developed are presented in the sequel.

3 Deployment Analysis

Deployment of component-based distributed applications is an active research topic, close to the collaborative deployment field. A significant number of researches address deployment issues and try to solve this problem in different forms. On the basis of these researches, we propose a deployment framework that unifies different variants of this problem and serves as starting point for our collaborative deployment proposition.

3.1 Related Work

Two main directions are distinguished: deployment of monolithic software and deployment of component-based distributed applications.

In the first direction we identify two approaches depending on the target environment whether it consists on a unique host or several hosts. Java Web Start [4] provides a deployment solution of java software applications. Using JNLP (Java Network Launching Protocol), the tool automatically downloads all java archive files necessary for the execution of an application specified by a user. The Software Dock research project [5] provides a general solution for the deployment life cycle. It also deploys applications from a producer site (the release dock) to a consumer site (the field dock) using a pull-based approach. Other deployment tools are designed to support large-scale deployment such as ORYA [6] (Open enviRonment to deploY Applications).

In the second direction, the most relevant work related to the component deployment is the OMG's Deployment and Configuration (D&C) Specification [7], adopted recently. This specification describes the mechanisms by which distributed component-based applications are configured and deployed. Although it is complex, the OMG model reflects most of the deployment requirements. Other works dealing with the most known component models include: M-OSGI [8] has tried to address deployment issues of the OSGi component model. The EURESCOM P924 project [9], [10] comes with DCL (Deployment and Configuration Language), which describes configuration and distribution information for distributed applications supporting the initial and runtime deployment of CCM (CORBA Component Model).

3.2 Framework Proposition

By examining existing work, we conclude that the deployment of component-based distributed applications concerns all activities that make components available on the target environment according to the architecture of the application while satisfying various constraints resulting from application semantic requirements, network resource limitations, and resource availability of the target environment [11].

The deployment framework that we propose is shown in figure 1. High-level constraints define the architecture of an application by using ADLs (Architecture Description Language) or by using formalisms based on functional languages or graph grammars. The deployment service uses this structure and makes decisions on component choice and location to deploy them, in order to satisfy at best the application requirement imposed by the structure. The deployment process ends when a real distribution of instances of components is available onto target environment, so the global application can start running.

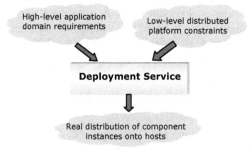

Fig. 1. Deployment framework

We aim to make the high-level requirements related to the collaborative domain. A collaborative session is thus described with a formal model that characterizes the session coherence and constitutes the input of our deployment service.

4   Collaborative Deployment Service

This section presents our model-driven approach to enable a coherent distribution of components within collaborative sessions.

4.1   Session Model

To represent the way participants of the synchronous collaborative session are exchanging information between them, a formal model, based on graphs, has been introduced [3] and is used for the control of a collaborative deployment service.

The structure of a collaboration scheme is defined by a directed graph, called the collaboration graph which describes all the active users, the components they use, the data type that they exchange, and their relationships. In this model, the nodes of a graph represent the users. The diagram relationships, represented by the edges, express the data exchanges between users. The labels used with each arrow are composed of two fields: *<Component-type>.<data-type>*. The first field gives the type of a component used in the session. The second attribute specifies the type of data produced by this component. The model in figure 2 describes an example of a coherent session state.

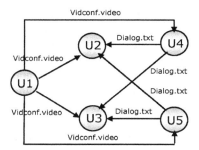

Fig. 2. Session instance

4.2 Framework Instantiation

The purpose of the deployment of component-based distributed application is to find the best configuration (in terms of distribution of components on hosts) in order to ensure optimal execution of an application. Thus for a particular component, the service decides on the most suitable component implementation and target site to instantiate it.

Deployment schema for collaborative domain follows a different goal. The hosts correspond to user's sites connected to a collaborative session. Thus hosts are well defined and the main purpose of collaborative deployment is to find components according to the needs of the group of users while satisfying several constraints. The collaborative constraints deal with (i) the site configuration (hardware and software); (ii) compatibility between components in different locations that handle the same data type and (iii) the session structure (producer/consumer).

Collaborative deployment enables initial deployment and also subsequent dynamic deployment. The initial deployment consists of distributing the components onto participant's computers before the starting of the session. The dynamic deployment must take into account the session evolution to ensure a coherent distribution of components with respect to the new session state.

According to the events that occur within the session, some changes can appear in the global state and they can influence the graph structure. From the new incoherent state where each member of the collaborative session has none or only some components, we want to reach a new coherent final state. The current session model gives the coherent state of the session where each member has the required components. If the real distribution of the components is in conformance with the graph structure then the coherence is satisfied. Otherwise, a coordinated deployment service is needed to ensure this coherence. This is the role of our deployment service detailed in this paper

4.3 Collaborative Deployment Steps

Two fundamental operations are distinguished: addition and removal of components. Addition deals with a user entry or with a user role change that adds new links between users. Removal of components corresponds to a user exit or to a user role change that remove existent links between users. In order to achieve these operations, we identify a set of distinct key steps:

The first step consists of the extraction of the deployment configuration from the session model and the comparison with component instances already deployed. This activity should determine the set of component types required on each user's site.

In case of a component removal operation, the deployment service deletes the useless component. In case of a component addition operation, the deployment service tries to discover the available components matching with the desired type. The next step consists of the context-aware selection. This activity usually is the most complex one because it deals with component decision choice. Among the returned responses, one component that satisfies the constraints must be selected for download. Then the component installation and instantiation step takes place. It covers all operations that are necessary to make a selected component ready for use, e.g., downloading the component package to its execution site and launching it.

In the following characteristics are presented for each of the aforementioned steps of the collaborative deployment process.

Extraction of the Deployment Configuration
A deployment configuration describes a particular mapping of component types to sites and interconnections topology. The deployment service entity associated to each user receives a graph describing the desired session state as input. By parsing him, it determines the set of component types required for this user.

Table 1. Deployment configuration deduced from the session instance

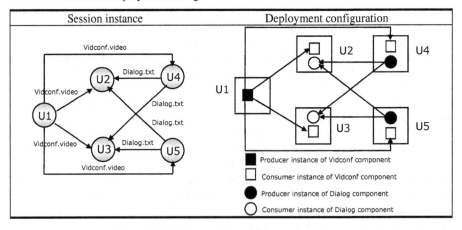

The deployment configuration implies that user U1 needs a producer instance of a videoconferencing component. U2 and U3 need a consumer instance of a videoconferencing component and both producer and consumer instances of a dialog component. U4 needs only a consumer instance of a videoconferencing component and a consumer instance of a dialog component.

By comparing with available instances already deployed on each participant site, the deployment service determines what instances must be deployed.

Once user needs are identified, the next step in the deployment process consists in removing undesired components and/or discovering components that match the components types required by a user. Component removal activity is self-explanatory. Component discovery activity, much more complex, is detailed hereafter.

Component Discovery Service
Component discovery is an important and necessary part of the deployment process. This issue has been studied in several areas especially in peer-to-peer file sharing systems like Napster, Gnutella and also in Web Services systems. Given a required component type, it returns the matching components. The discovery is done dynamically during the deployment phase. The main functionalities in a component discovery service are component provider, component requester and component broker (or matchmaker). These functionalities supply operations including: publish, discover, and retrieve. Operation links are shown in figure 3:

Fig. 3. Component discovery interaction pattern [12]

A component provider stores the components. It makes them known and available for potential users. The broker stores the component descriptors that contain their location. A requester discovers the required components by using the broker and access to components. Component broker matches existing component descriptors with requester's needs and sends responses to the requester.

The deployment service we propose is based on a peer-to-peer architecture where the discovery is decentralized. It supports both push-based and pull-based component discovery. More details are provided in the next section.

Context-Aware Selection
From the list returned by the component discovery service, the deployment service has to choose the more relevant component while satisfying constraints to deploy it onto a user's site. User's sites are heterogeneous, not only in software and hardware configurations but also in the nature of the connection to the network infrastructure. The deployment service may offer mechanisms to support different execution contexts and therefore allows taking choice at deployment time. We are still investigating this issue. A promising track comes from researchers on Semantic Web.

Besides satisfying local constraints, the deployment service has to satisfy the compatibility between components located on different remote systems. Let us consider the situation where user U1 collaborates with user U2 and sends to him a video dataflow. The producer component instance and the consumer component instance used by U1 and U2 have to be compatible to perform the communication.

We can envisage three solutions to resolve this problem. The first one relies on user decision. The participants take the choice manually. The second solution considers the choice as a collaborative decision. The set of the interested participants deduced from relationships in the session model vote to select an appropriate component. At the end, according to the vote result, the deployment service performs transfer the components to the concerned devices. The third solution takes into account the already deployed components. When a new user joins the session, the deployment service favors the selection of components currently used by other active users. This third solution seems to be the best one because it few disrupt the environment of the users already connected. Context awareness and compatibility are the main important criteria to decide if a component can be deployed or not.

Component Installation and Instantiation
This activity deals with the transfer of the component implementation to the user's site. The required archive file is moved to the new location. The deployment service launches the component instance by configuring it and starting its execution.

5 Collaborative Deployment System (CDS) Architecture

CDS is a fully distributed collaborative application that enables the dynamic deployment of components onto computers connected to a collaborative session. Our approach follows a pure peer-to-peer model. Figure 4 presents our Collaborative Deployment System architecture that implements the previous listed functionalities.

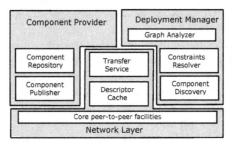

Fig. 4. Collaborative Deployment System Architecture

In the following, we detail the roles of the CDS modules.

5.1 Component Provider

Users with the Component Provider module, store locally the component packages they want to store on their hard disks and make them available to everyone for downloading. The Component Provider module implements the Provider functionality of figure 3.

Component Publisher
This module allows peers to advertise components they make available by disseminating the component descriptors. The announcement is performed in a push-based fashion using publishing mechanisms offered by the P2P Network Layer.

Within CDS, components are represented by descriptors, which are XML (eXtensible Markup Language) documents of a well-defined format. The Component descriptor contains a set of attributes that are divided into three categories: (1) Information about the component itself (unique component ID, name, description, license, version) (2) Deployment constraints. Two types of constraints can be distinguished: host and network constraints. A host constraint implies a particular configuration (memory, space, disk, operating system) needed by the component. A component which requires a considerable bandwidth cannot be deployed on a computer connected by a low bandwidth is an example of a network constraint. (3) A communication access point to the site that owns the component. The access point is used to establish a point-to-point connection in order to transfer the component package.

Component Repository
The Component Repository module stores the component packages in '.jar' files. Components must be packed up to ensure that all their elements are present. This implies that any component package contains a description of its contents: classes, images, etc. Java archive fulfils this requirement.

5.2 Deployment Manager

The Deployment Manager module associated to each user parses the current session graph and starts the discovery process. A set of the available components that match with his query are returned. After choosing one of the available components, transfer occurs between the host site and the requester's site. Nowadays, the members do this selection manually. But we aim to make this selection automatic. The Deployment Manager module implements the Requester functionality of figure 3.

Graph Analyzer
The current session instance is specified with XML and notified to each participant. By parsing this document, the graph analysis module determines the deployment configuration and identifies the component types required for each participant. The Deployment Manager uses this information and gives the order to perform the distributed search.

Component Discovery
The search capability is the central functionality of the deployment infrastructure. It involves the discovery of descriptors published among peers and includes locating components on any site. At the opposite of the push-based approach used for the announcement of descriptors, a pull-based approach is adopted. A peer may initiate the discovery by searching in its local cache for descriptors or by sending query messages to the network and waiting for response.
When a peer receives a discovery query, it checks if descriptors kept locally correspond to the search criteria specified in the query attributes and it replies directly to the requester if they match.

Constraint Resolver
Once the discovery operation is done, this module selects some of the components found and download them through the transfer service. Currently, the user does this

selection manually: from the returned results, it chooses the best components satisfying deployment constraints.

5.3 Network Layer

Core Peer-to-Peer Facilities
This module encapsulates all the connection/communication facilities needed by a peer such as retrieving and disseminating information in a peer-to-peer network.

Transfer Service
This module provides facilities to realize the download operation. It is in charge of packaging any data to be sent into an appropriate format (i.e. using XML) and using core peer-to-peer facilities for sending.

Descriptor Cache
This module contains the component descriptors. Descriptors stored come from three sources: 1) Own descriptors published. Local publishing keeps the descriptors in the local cache. 2) Other descriptors from the announcement operation achieved by other peers. 3) After a discovery operation. Discovered descriptors are stored in the local cache to speed up another discovery. The descriptor Cache module is part of the Broker functionality (figure 3) implementation.

5.4 Implementation

We have developed a first prototype that supports some functionalities for dynamic deployment of components within collaborative sessions. This implementation is written in Java and is based on the JXTA project [13]. JXTA is an open-source project promoted by Sun Microsystems, whose aim is to establish a network programming platform for P2P systems by identifying a small set of basic facilities necessary to support P2P applications. We use JXTA for our P2P Network Layer. A peergroup in the terminology of JXTA implements the current collaborative session. Participants are supported by JXTA peers and components descriptors extend the advertisement concept of the JXTA platform.

6 Conclusion

This paper has presented the approach followed for supporting dynamic deployment within collaborative sessions. By examining different deployment approaches related to the deployment issue especially in the context of deployment of component-based distributed applications, we have proposed a general framework we used for the architecture design of new collaborative deployment system (CDS).

CDS supports the following characteristics:

- From the design viewpoint, it follows a model-driven approach: the deployment is done according to a predefined coherent session model.
- From the architectural viewpoint, it is based on peer-to-peer paradigm more suitable to the deployment requirements.

Several works need to be pursued. We plan to improve CDS by introducing generic interaction patterns from the session module in order to ease the component deployment configuration extraction. We are working on providing the constraint resolver with automatic context-aware selection for components. Implementation of the prototype will be pursued in accordance with the proposed layered architecture.

References

1. Guerrero, L.A., Fuller, D.: A Pattern System for the Development of Collaborative Applications. Information and Software Technology, Vol.43, No.7, May, 2001, pp. 457-467.
2. Rodriguez Peralta, L.M., Villemur, T., Drira, K., Molina Espinosa, J.M.: Managing dependencies in dynamic collaborations using coordination diagrams. 6th International Conference on Principles of DIstributed Systems (OPODIS'02), Reims, France, December 2002, pp.29-42.
3. Rodriguez Peralta, L.M., Villemur, T., Drira, K.: An XML on-line session model based on graphs for synchronous cooperative groups. International Conference on Parallel and Distributed Processing Techniques and Applications (PDPTA'2001). Las Vegas (USA), June 2001. pp 1257-1263.
4. Java Web Start, http://java.sun.com/products/javawebstart/
5. Hall, R.S., Heimbigner, D., Wolf, A.L.: A Cooperative to Support Software Deployment Using the Software Dock. Proc. of ICSE'99: The 1999 International Conference on Software Engineering, Los Angeles, CA, May 1999, pp. 174-183.
6. Lestideau, V. and Belkhatir, N.: Providing Highly automated and generic means for software deployment Process. In the proceedings of 9th European Workshop on Software Process Technology (EWSPT 2003) held in Helsinki, Finland, September 2003.
7. OMG: Deployment and Configuration of Component-based Distributed Applications Specification. http://www.omg.org/docs/ptc/03-07-02.pdf
8. Frénot, S., Stefan, D.: M-OSGi: Une plate-forme répartie de services. Les NOuvelles TEchnologies de la Répartition (NOTERE'2004), Saida, Maroc, June 2004.
9. EURESCOM P924. http://www.eurescom.de
10. Tonghong Li Hoffmann, A. Born, M. Schieferdecker, I.: A platform architecture to support the deployment of distributed applications. IEEE International Conference on Communications, 2002 (ICC 2002), pp. 2592-2596 vol.4.
11. Kichkaylo, T., Ivan, A., Karamcheti, V.: Constrained Component Deployment in Wide-Area Networks using AI Planning Techniques. In the Proceedings of the International Parallel and Distributed Processing Symposium (IPDPS), April 2003.
12. Web Services architecture overview: The next stage of evolution for e-business. http://www-106.ibm.com/developerworks/library/w-ovr/?dwzone=ws
13. JXTA, http://www.jxta.org/

Complexity in Collaborative Online Socio-Interationist Environments: A Good Reason for Distributed Systems

Hilton José Silva de Azevedo[1] and Edson Emílio Scalabrin[2]

[1] Federal Center for Technological Education of Paraná, Av. Sete de Setembro, 3165,
80230-901, Curitiba (PR) Brazil
`hilton@ppgte.cefetpr.br`
[2] Pontifical Catholic University of Paraná, R. Imaculada Conceição, 1155,
80215-901, Curitiba (PR) Brazil
`edson.scalabrin@pucpr.br`

Abstract. Despite the technological enhancement IT has had, some main points still have no satisfactory solutions and constitute a research subject for those interested in knowledge management. It does not seem evident that the adoption of either groupware technologies or collaborative environments induces effective collaborative/cooperative behavior in team workers. If some collaborative environment projects are strongly planned they have difficulty to be integrated in the workers' daily habits. We assume that the problem may have two dimensions that shall be considered: a) the commonly accepted cycle of knowledge management is unable to cover the rich and complex cycle of social creation and validation of knowledge; b) a distributed environment architecture seems to be the best candidate to implement a system where the number, the complexity and the evolving characteristics of services that would take into account socio-interactionist dimensions of individuals and groups are necessary to reinforce collaborative behaviors. A Collaborative Online Learning Environment is discussed.

1 Introduction

In the last years the shift from the industrial based model to the information model has been pushing research in order to model and implement technologies for collaborative environments to afford concepts such as: GROUPWARE, Computer Supported Collaborative Work (CSCW), Virtual Teams or nomad workers. In most cases, it seems to be tacitly assumed that the problem of keeping or improving productivity is based on the availability of good tools to let people find the information they look for and interact with the persons they need to accomplish their tasks.

This technical approach was firstly well received inside organizations that want to find ways to differentiate themselves in a competitive global market. Despite the technological enhancement IT has had, some main points still have no satisfactory solutions and constitute a workplace for those interested in knowledge management: i) if there is a consensus about the necessity and utility of IT technologies, there is no assessment reports about the real contribution of them for workers' productivity; ii) it does not seem evident that the adoption of groupware technologies or collaborative environments induce effective collaborative/cooperative behavior in team workers; iii) if some

F.F. Ramos et al. (Eds.): ISSADS 2005, LNCS 3563, pp. 226–234, 2005.

collaborative environment projects are strongly planned (diversity of services for people interaction, knowledge base search capabilities, well planned userinterfaces) they have difficulty to be integrated in the workers' daily habits.

We assume in our research work that the problem may have two dimensions that shall be considered: a) the commonly accepted cycle of knowledge management (identifying, preserving, disseminating and updating knowledge) is unable to cover the rich and complex cycle of social creation and validation of knowledge; b) a distributed environment architecture seems to be the best candidate to implement a system where the number, the complexity and the evolving characteristics of services that would take into account socio-interactionist dimensions of individuals and group are necessary to reinforce collaborative behaviors.

This kind of approach is represented in the educational field by the Theory of Activity [Engström 99], a social theory for learning and, in the knowledge management field by the model of the Communities of Practice [Wenger 98, 01].

Section 2 presents an overview of technologies for collaborative environments. Section 3 presents the main concepts of Activity Theory and Cops. Section 4 presents some elements from the theoretical framework that is guiding the design process of a Collaborative Online Learning Environment, based in autonomous agents ([Beer 92], [Cockburn & Jennings 95], [Demazeau & Muller 90], [Scalabrin 96], [Wooldridge & Jennings 95]), whose aim is not only the development of professional competencies but also social ones. Section 5 discusses the technological and conceptual points that ask for solutions.

2 Technologies for Collaborative Environments

2.1 Technologies for Dissemination

Technologies for dissemination help information and knowledge to be distributed to users that work in computer based environments. Without such technologies workers should constantly stop their activities in order to search for the information/knowledge they need out of their working places. In this case, they would reduce the possibilities of knowledge socialization with colleagues. Technologies for dissemination can bring knowledge in both passive and active ways. In the passive mode, the user shall externalize what he/she needs by doing requesting services that will be processed and sent to the user that asked for it. In the active mode the system will try to reduce the effort the user would make to retrieve information by anticipating the users' probable requests. Depending on the way they are used, most of such technologies can be considered as either passive or active. Examples of technologies for dissemination are:

– e-mail – is the first used technology for knowledge dissemination inside most organizations. One can spontaneously send a message informing a colleague about a procedure to be done or, clarifying a discussion point he/she observed in the group (active dissemination). The same person may answer a message sent by another colleague (passive dissemination).

- data warehouse e data marts – They represent the key for active dissemination. The knowledge stored in a data warehouse is organized and characterized in order to make its retrieval easier. Anyway, the search engine shall use the warehouse to retrieve information/knowledge.
- publish-and-subscribe technology – It sends only the information/knowledge that has formerly been declared of his/her interest.
- push technology – Represents a passive form of dissemination. It uses information about the user in order to prepare or automatically send information/knowledge that is relevant for him/her. A worker can receive news as early as it is formatted and made available.
- groupware – It can be used to help people work together even if they are dispersed geographically. Groupware services can share schedules, collective writing, e-mail sending, shared database access, electronic meetings that allow its participants to see and hear each other, as well as visualize the computer screens of his/her colleagues.
- computer-based training – It allows the use of the computer as a knowledge disseminator. CBT can be seen as an instructive interactive experience between a given content and its learner. The computer offers the majority of stimuli to which the learner responds as he/she progresses, acquiring or consolidating abilities or knowledge. A CBT has a more complex ramified program for mediating and conducting than a Computer Assisted Instruction. Nowadays, the term describes all processes of computer-delivered training including CD-ROM and World Wide Web.
- Computer-Supported Cooperative Work – CSCW – is a generic term which combines the understanding of the way people work in groups with the enabling technologies of computer networking, and associated hardware, software, services and techniques. While groupware is often used as referring to real computer-based systems, CSCW means the study of tools and techniques of groupware as well as their psychological, social and organizational effects. Key issues of CSCW are group awareness, multi-user interfaces, concurrency control, communication and coordination within the group, shared information space and the support of a heterogeneous, open environment which integrates existing single-user applications. CSCW systems are often categorized according to the time/location matrix by using the distinction between same time (synchronous) and different times (asynchronous), and between same place (face-to-face) and different places (distributed).

2.2 Access Technologies

The technical infrastructure for collaborative online learning environments has to provide facilities to make people capable of searching for knowledge. These technologies take two basic shapes:

- ad hoc querying tools – they allow people to request information/knowledge by performing queries that are sent to a knowledge database.
- search-and-retrieval tools – they allow people to retrieve vast collections of information/knowledge that are frequently distributed in multiple internal and/or external servers. They use algorithms and techniques to identify and classify appropriate knowledge by using its preferences.

2.3   Sharing Technologies

Many dissemination tools may also be considered sharing technologies, because dissemination is a form of sharing. Moreover, classes of tools have evolved and are able not only to share knowledge but also promote the interaction with a look toward this knowledge.

Collaboration tools, such as groupware or brainstorming systems, allow users that may be geographically scattered to share knowledge and work with knowledge in a collaborative way. These tools, which frequently present versions with management capabilities, allow users to edit, add or even make notes on somebody else's work.

Conference tools, such as the videoconference, allow users geographically scattered to collaborate in real time while sharing data and information. Two users can compare experiences by solving a problem or sharing an optimal solution, for instance.

3   The Design of a Collaborative On-Line Learning Environment: The COLE Project

The COLE[1] (Collaborative Online Learning Environment) Project is an example of the expanded vision of how the collaboration Technologies can be used in a way to consider the social question inherent to learning. It seeks to widen the process of learning construction to beyond the traditional contents (Professional competencies), and to leverage social competencies (e.g. adaptability, negotiation of ideas, critical sense and group belonging) also important for the profile of Professional integrated to the Information Society. Different from CSCW and groupware tools that, when used without the concept of social roles, can only optimize activities of a classic productive cycle. In the COLE one uses a development and research context (Project based learning – PBL) to enrich the process of learning construction of a group of students. The theoretical ground stems from a Social Learning Theory, more precisely the Activity Theory [Engström 99], and the model of Communities of Practice [Wenger 99].

From the technological point of view, COLE may be seen as a set of services that embed dissemination, access and sharing technologies (CSCW, groupware, searchand-retrieval tools, publish-and-subscribe technology, push technology) with the intention to create social learning situations where the acting of pre-determined roles makes part of the student's continuous assessment and is seen by this as a modeling element of his identity in the group.

The reference adopted provides a set of elements that make it possible to reorganize the tools and Technologies cited in terms of the roles they represent in the individuals' activities during the learning process.

For Azevedo and Scalabrin "human collaboration in a group" means a set of intentional actions that one makes in order to help another member of a group accomplish a task or an activity that is relevant to the group. For them, the existence of interactive

---

[1] Proposto e conduzido pelo Prof. Hilton de Azevedo, no Programa de Pós-Graduação em Tecnologia – PPGTE – do CEFET-PR, com a colaboração do Prof. Edson Emilio Scalabrin, do Programa de Pós-Graduação em Informática Aplicada – PPGIA – da PUCPR

tools such as e-mail, discussion lists, forums or chat sites is not enough to configure co-operative environments, even for working or learning. This assumption is based on the present approaches of Learning Social Theory ([Engeström, 99]; [Wenger 98]). Such a theoretical model is based on the assumption that human beings continuously need to construct their identities to motivate them to participate in social activities. In such a context, every action is meaningful in terms of how people recognize themselves and are recognized by others [de Azevedo & Scalabrin 04].

According to this approach, human activities in which cooperation can be identified are those that have something more than a common objective, a shared vocabulary, and the possibility of interaction. Wenger (1998) points to engagement as one significant element. For us, it is still a fuzzy concept, in the sense that "engagement" is a broad concept that can include many others. For our purpose, we consider "engagement" as the result of social relations, in the specific activities of a given community, where people assume that specific roles and values exist, and these role and values are recognized and adhered to by everyone in the community. Roles and values help people project and reflect images of identity. If cooperation is part of such roles, then it can become a value and, through its practice, can help develop cooperative attitudes among the members of a community. Thus, cooperative-learning environments need something more than technological frameworks to allow for interaction among people. We believe that technological, economic1, and social2 models can best allow for cooperation. Through these models, people can construct their identities by assuming roles that are recognized and prized by the others who are participating in the same effective, cooperative-learning environments [de Azevedo & Scalabrin 04].

The COLE project proposes an ensemble of services allowing students to work in small groups (a maximum of 10 students per group) in order to propose solutions to a problem presented by an instructor. Learning is assumed as a discovering process and a student evaluation must consider such points as the quality of the solution proposed by the student's group, how the student uses and connects concepts belonging to the subjects under evaluation, how the student collaborates with the other group members, and whether the student acts for the benefit of the group.

The main characteristics of COLE are [de Azevedo & Scalabrin 04]:

– A pedagogical approach encouraging the student to be creative in the knowledgediscovering processes
– An assessment process that considers content-related capabilities and social capabilities, individual learning processes and their results, and collective learning processes and their results
– Students working in small groups so that they can easily learn about each other
– A PBL approach
– The use of portfolios to visualize learning processes and authorship – The use of ideas to evaluate students – One idea is made of a hypothesis (proposed by one student), some arguments (documents that the student chose in a digital library), and at least one intellectual product (a document produced by the student after reasoning about his or her hypothesis and the arguments he or she found). Arguments are related to the hypothesis by semantic links.
– The use of portfolios to organize ideas in semantic nets

- Assessments done not by evaluating students according to a final work, but by considering its quality and the contributions of every group member
- The use of document annotation – Students can make semantic marks on the documents they choose. These marks explain how the documents can contribute to an idea. Annotations are important, because they make explicit to students what they know about something and can also be used by teachers to monitor and intervene in the students' learning processes.
- An assessment method that considers both individual and group portfolios – The assessment criteria adopted may consider dimensions like richness of ideas (originality of hypotheses, robustness of argumentation, and quality of intellectual products) and collaboration (suggesting arguments or intellectual products in response to others' ideas, negotiation ability, responsibility, and responsiveness).
- A learning process composed of cycles of individual and group phases – a limited number of interactions is necessary for the students to negotiate the construction of the group portfolio, and also for teachers needing time when analyzing the data present in the learning environment and deciding how to intervene in the learning process.
- An individual phase in which every student creates and organizes his or her ideas inside his or her portfolio, studies the assessment criteria that the teachers will use, and prepares his or her arguments to convince the other group members that these arguments will benefit the group's project.
- A group phase in which students submit their ideas to their peers, who vote on the best ones to keep in the group's portfolio – before voting, students defend the quality of their ideas against the criticisms of the other group members.

In order to implement the above characteristics, many specialized and transparent services are necessary. Identifying such services is a difficult task because there were no records of cases where these kind of scenario was experienced before, neither have users been interviewed about their experience on the matter. So, we adopted two approaches: the first was to identify main concepts from the social theory of learning ([Engeström 99]; [Wenger 98]) and the second was to use the people enrolled within the project as potential future users and apply a participatory design approach with them ([de Azevedo 97]; [Barthés & de Azevedo 98]). The objective was to produce a primer that shall be object of further criticism.

Theoretical concept	Agent description	Technologies
Division of labor, Participation, Identity	Portfolio Agent is a semantic Net editor that allows students to represent their ideas and envision how they are constituted and interrelated. It shows images of a group portfolio for the agent's owner and teachers.	edition and management of semantic graphic elements, classification rules
Division of labor	Library Agent returns documents from the digital library, based on keywords selected by students. It introduces new documents in the library.	full-text searchretrieval, multi-index indexation

Division of labor	Web Search Agent helps students search sites in the Web based on the keywords related to their portfolios.	search engines over semistructured database
Shared vocabulary	Dictionary Agent helps students discover the relations among keywords in the taxonomic trees.	ontology server search-retrieval over structured database
Negotiation of meaning, assessment	Ballot Agent monitors submissions of ideas, copies agreed-upon ideas in the group portfolio and can transfer ideas from the group portfolio to an individual portfolio.	workflow manager, text-mining for communication style pattern recognition
Brokering	Broker Agent tries to identify other students who have worked on similar subjects in order to put its owner in contact with them (by pattern matching of portfolios pieces).	pattern recognition
Assessment	Diary Agent is used by teachers to store profiles of students' performances and the planning undertaken to motivate students' work.	project management tool
Reification	Living Memory agent stores all portfolios built in the online collaborative environment and returns data related to them or even pieces of data.	storage and retrieving of data

4   Discussion

In the search for flexibility of conception, construction e evolution of the COLE en-vironment, the agent model was adopted. Such model allows the definition of multi-user interfaces, the simultaneity control, the communication and coordination within the group, the information sharing space and the support for open heterogeneous en-vironments that embed the existing mono-user applications. In fact, the great contri-bution of the agent model in this scenario is a good support to heterogeneity and the necessary openness to the resulting environment. The agents can operate in both ways synchronous and asynchronous as well as face-to-face or distributes. The interest in the agent model is also the possibility of instantiating agents with high level capabilities, essential, for example, to aid in the assessment process of learners' activities, either on the individual or each group.

The COLE environment convenes a set of open agents that implement competencies with several levels of complexity. We present some elements we consider important in each agent of the COLE.

Library Agent. The assembling ontology that describes the stores objects/documents in the digital library is and important point. The exactitude and the completeness of the ontology will define the accuracy of consultations. The flexibility of consultations is also linked to the quality of the indexes associated to each concept of the ontology. The use of indexes allows the utilization of parser based in cases to implement the search mechanisms.

Dictionary Agent. The principal activity of the agent is the management of flow and roles the make part of the submission, approval/rejection of new concept. This flow may happen in a synchronous or asynchronous way, Here, an important requisite is to endow the communication interface agent with the other software agents, as well as the students and teachers.

Ballot Agent. The principal element managed by the agent is the flow involved in the submission, approval/rejection of ideas. This flow may happen in a synchronous or asynchronous way. Another important task is to provide the student with help in the elaboration of his arguments to approve or reject totally or partially an idea. This help may be achieved in the form of alerts on possible positive or negative impacts an expression may cause in an interlocutor.

Portfolio Agent. The presentation of an easy-to-handle interface is essential to motivate the student. The contribution management is the principal task of the portfolio agent, besides providing information on the impact a contribution had in the group. The information will be obtained through the identification of the ideas that are constantly enriched versus the ideas that are discontinued. Each student must receive is his computer a module for portfolio edition. The edition tools were written in Java and the net distribution will be made through the instancing of specialized mobile agents.

Web Search Agent. The principal virtue of this agent is to work in an integrated way with the ontology/dictionary agent, particularly to refine the terms of the user's solicitation in a pro-active way to reach a better result.

Broker Agent. The ideas, the arguments and the artifacts are textual. The identification of students that are working on similar themes requires the understanding of texts through the processing of natural language to decide to get them in contact. The natural language processing will be made by a parser based in cases [Schank & Riesbech 81]. This one has shown great efficiency in the comparison of texts.

Diary Agent. The assembling of profiles is a complex task because it implies the Discovery and the validation of behavior patterns. Definition, implementation and execution, in a pro-active way, of mechanisms that aid the teacher to motivate/provoke the students keep the flow of activities.

Living Memory. The difficulty concerns the structure and the indexation of portfolio content in way useful information may be extracted. The implementation of textmining techniques seems to be an alternative in the lack of elements that structure and index the contents. The necessity for text-mining also comes due to the great volume of texts generated or transferred to the environment of a portfolio.

References

de Azevedo, H. (1997). Contribution à la modélisation des connaissances à l'aide des systèmes multi-agents. Ph.D. Thesis, University of Technology of Compiègne, France, 169 (in French).

de Azevedo, H., & Scalabrin E., (2004), A Human Collaborative Online Learning Environment Using Intelligent Agents. In: Designing Distributed Learning Environments with Intelligent Software Agents. Edited Fuhua Oscar Lin. Athabasca University, Canadá. Publishing: Idea Group. ISBN: 1-59140-501-7.

Barthès, J. -P. A., & de Azevedo, H. J. S. (1998). Identifying autonomous agents for capitalizing knowledge in R&D environments. Electronic Edition (CEUR Workshop Proceedings).

Beer, R. D. (1992). A dynamical systems perspective on autonomous agents. Special Issue of the AI Journal on Computational Theories of Interac-tion and Agency.

Cockburn, D., & Jennings, N. R. (1995). ARCHON: A distributed artificial intelligence system for industrial applications. In G. M. P. O'Hara, & N. R. Jennings (Eds.), Foundations of DAI. New York: Wiley.

Demazeau, Y., & Müller, J. -P. (1990). Decentralized artificial intelligence. In Y. Demazeau, & J. -P. Müller (Eds.), Decentralized AI. Amsterdam; New York: Elsevier Science Publishers.

Engström, Y. (1999). Activity theory and individual and social transformation. In Engström et al. (Eds.), Perspectives on activity theory. London; New York: Cambridge University Press.

Fox, M. S. (1988). An organizational view of distributed systems. In Bond and Gasser (Eds.), Readings in artificial intelligence (pp. 140–150). New York: Morgan & Kaufman.

Hewitt, C. (1988). Offices are open systems. In A. Bond, & L. Gasser (Eds.), Readings in distributed artificial intelligence. New York: Morgan Kaufman.

Scalabrin, E. E. (1996). Conception et réalisation d'environnement de développement de systèmes d'agents cognitifs (Realization of an environment for developing cognitive agents systems). Ph.D. thesis, University of Technology of Compiègne, France, 169 (in French).

Schank, R. C., Riesbech, C. K. (1981). Inside Computer Understanding. Lawrence Erlbaum Associates Publishers, Hillsdale, New Jersey.

Wenger, E. (1998). *Communities of practice: Learning, meaning and identity.* London; New York: Cambridge University Press.

Wooldridge, M. J., & Jennings, N. R. (1995). Intelligent agents: Theory and practice. *The Knowledge Engineering Review*, 10(2).

Injecting Communication Faults to Experimentally Validate Java Distributed Applications*

Gabriela Jacques-Silva[1,**], Roberto Jung Drebes[1],
Taisy Silva Weber[1], and Eliane Martins[2]

[1] Instituto de Informática, Universidade Federal do Rio Grande do Sul
Caixa Postal 15064 , 90501-970 Porto Alegre, RS, Brazil
{gjsilva,drebes,taisy}@inf.ufrgs.br
[2] Instituto de Computação, Universidade Estadual de Campinas
Caixa Postal 6176, 13083-870 Campinas, SP, Brazil
eliane@ic.unicamp.br

Abstract. The use of Java to develop highly available network services and the inherent unreliability of communication systems require the validation of its fault tolerance mechanisms to avoid unexpected behavior during execution. Tools for testing distributed programs that must remain operational in a faulty environment are not common and are generally difficult to operate. One possible solution is applying a fault injector to emulate communication faults and test the behavior of the distributed application under these faults. We developed Jaca.net, an extension of the fault injector based on computational reflection Jaca, to include UDP communication faults to its fault model. Potential target applications of Jaca and Jaca.net are the ones developed in Java. Using Jaca.net, software developers can complete the test cycle validating the high level fault detection and recovery mechanisms built on their applications.

1 Introduction

By allowing computing systems to support mission critical services in our daily routines, fault tolerance is required so that these services can correspond to the reliance put upon them. An essential step in the development of reliable systems is the experimental validation phase. Delegating evaluation of the fault tolerance effectiveness to a real use scenario of the system, observing the behavior of a service under a real fault, can lead to disastrous consequences.

Many network applications need to reach a high degree of availability. Some examples are distributed programs that manage database replicas or hold a distributed consistent state, group communication and multicast applications that support cooperative work and middleware for grid computing. Another example are control systems where no single message can be lost or delayed.

---

* Project developed in collaboration with HP Brazil R&D and CNPq/Brazil Project ACERTE (#472084/2003-8)
** Sponsored by CNPq/Brazil

F.F. Ramos et al. (Eds.): ISSADS 2005, LNCS 3563, pp. 235–245, 2005.

One of the techniques used for experimental system validation is fault injection. Using this technique, we introduce faults in a target system in a controlled way, and its response is monitored under this condition. The aim is to test the efficiency of the implemented fault tolerance mechanisms and to evaluate system safety operation, providing the necessary feedback in the development cycle [1].

Networks are used as supporting infrastructure to distributed applications that must provide the high availability needed in mission critical services. This makes dependability evaluation of network applications essential. One possibility to deal with evaluation is to inject faults on the message exchange system, forcing activation of the fault detection and error recovery mechanisms. If other fault models are used for testing, in an indirect approach like injecting memory or CPU faults in the nodes running the target application, the latency until faults are manifested can be too high. To speed up their manifestation, faults can be injected directly on the message exchange system.

Java is a commonly used language to develop dependable distributed applications, making a tool for testing these applications in network faulty conditions not only useful, but required. Many communication fault injectors have been described in the literature, but none of them are appropriate to test Java-based distributed applications. They are either locked to a specific application or work at too low abstraction levels, restricted to a specific operating system kernel, which inhibits portability and platform independence. The most important advantage of injecting faults in a layer on top of the operating system communication protocol stack is the low spatial intrusion on the target system. To fill this gap, we developed Jaca.net, an extension to the Jaca fault injector [2] for dealing with communication faults. Using this tool, dependability can be more easily tested on Java-based network applications. The next section shows basic concepts of software fault injection and some tools for conducting this task. Sections 3 and 4 describe Jaca and its extension to communication faults, presenting the fault model that was added and implemented. In section 5 we demonstrate the feasibility of Jaca.net to conduct communication fault tolerance validation. We finish by presenting some concluding remarks and proposing future works.

2   Fault Injection Tools

A software fault injection tool is usually a code segment that uses whatever hooks are available in the processor or system to create an incorrect behavior in a controlled way [3]. This technique can simulate both hardware and software faults. Dealing with distributed Java applications, we are mainly interested in hardware faults emulated and injected through software. We inject the manifestations of the hardware faults as errors affecting the communication system of the application under test, not the real faults that disturb the network.

To conduct a fault injection experiment we run the test system and generate faults, monitoring and verifying how the target system behaves. The target system, in our case, is the network application under test.

One problem in using fault injection is the lack of available tools. Appropriate tools are difficult to find and use, resulting in most developers building their own injectors when needed, which increases the systems development cycle, a task that consumes both time and man power.

Some examples of communication fault injection tools are CSFI, ORCHES-TRA and ComFIRM. CSFI (Communication Software Fault Injection) [4] was one of the first tools developed exclusively to inject communication faults, and its main purpose was to evaluate the impact of faults in parallel systems. The existing version of CSFI was developed for a transputer T805 system, and thus is not applicable to general Java-based applications. Other popular environment is ORCHESTRA [5], developed specifically to test dependability of distributed protocols. It injects faults through the inclusion of an extra layer, called PFI (Protocol Fault Injection), to the protocol stack. Next, ComFIRM (Communication Fault Injection through OS Resources Modification) [6] focuses only on communication faults. It is located inside the kernel, at the lower layer of the network message handling subsystem. This reduces intrusion on the target system considerably, but the kernel after instrumentation is no longer the original kernel and the tool must be adapted to each new kernel release.

Finally, INFIMO (INtrusiveless Fault Injection MOdule) [9] is a Linux based toolkit for fault injection experimentation, which can use different fault injection techniques in a modular approach, allowing these techniques to be compared. The toolkit, however, is based on a specific operating system and library for real-time communication, which makes it difficult to extend and apply the injector to a broader class of network applications.

There are also some others tools, including GOOFI and NFTAPE, that allow their fault models to be extended. GOOFI (Generic Object-Oriented Fault Injection) [7] does not depend on any specific fault injection technique. Presumably, it could be extended to handle communication faults. NFTAPE's [8] highlights are being able to work with multiple fault models, having diverse triggering modes and accepting many target systems. To allow this multiplicity, NFTAPE introduces the concept of a LightWeight Fault Injector, LWFI. If a new fault injector needs to be built, it is only necessary to implement a new LWFI. Jaca is also an extensible tool aimed at validating Java-based object-oriented applications. It is based in computational reflection and its architecture follows a software pattern system for fault injectors [10].

Most tools presented above have strong portability impairments, that range from the development for a specific architecture (like CSFI, only applicable to transputers) to the development for a specific version of an operating system's kernel (like ComFIRM, which is only available to a specific version of Linux). Jaca does not have such limitations.

Jaca, ComFIRM and INFIMO were all in-house developed tools we could extend. Jaca, using computational reflection and being platform independent, was the most appropriate one to extend considering the goal to test Java-based network applications. The advantage to extend Jaca is having a single tool that can test all fault tolerance aspects of a network application, not only the communication subsystem and the related fault detection and recovery mechanisms.

3   Jaca Tool

Jaca offers mechanisms for high-level fault injection in Java-based object-oriented systems. Instead of acting over memory data or register contents, Jaca acts upon the object's public interface: its attributes, method parameters and return values.

Jaca uses computational reflection to inject high level faults, allowing an easy adaptation and following the specifications of any Java system. It uses a supporting platform called Javassist [11], which allows bytecodes to be transformed during load time. Thus, the needed instrumentation for injection is introduced in the bytecode, which can be applied even in cases where the source code is unavailable. This feature gives the tool independence and portability, since it can run on any platform where a Java Virtual Machine is available.

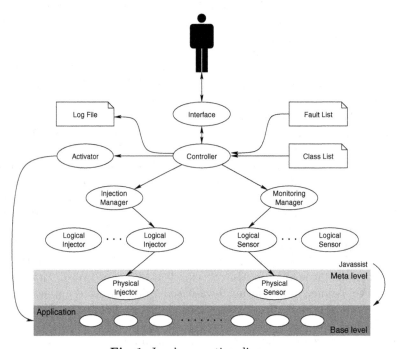

Fig. 1. Jaca's operation diagram

Jaca's operation diagram can be seen on Figure 1. Computational reflection is used in three main packages: `Injector`, `Monitor` and `Activator`. `Injector` uses the `PhysicalInjector` class for fault injection, which is implemented as a meta-object and is a subclass of the `javassist.reflect.Metaobject` Javassist class. A `PhysicalInjector` is associated to each object in the class list, as described by a configuration file used to identify which classes should be monitored. In this way, the specified objects are intercepted whenever there is a read or write into a class attribute or when a method call is issued. The injection process takes place during this interception. The kind of fault is sought in a file which contains the list of faults that should be injected during runtime. This file is interpreted by the fault manager, which passes to the injection manager, by the controller, the needed information to instantiate the logic injectors.

A similar use of the Javassist toolkit is done with the `Monitor` package. The object associated to the objects base level objects is the `PhysicalSensor` meta-object, whose only goal is to monitor the fault injection experiment. The acquired data is passed to the controller and stored in a log file. The `Activator` package uses the Javassist classes to reflect the configured classes and also to activate the target system.

4   Jaca.net: A Jaca Extension to Communication Faults

Jaca's original version can corrupt class attributes as well as method parameters and return values. Using this prior version to test network applications is not a direct procedure. The latency could be too high to have one of these possible faults manifested as an error in the message exchange system. Setting up a test scenario from the available fault model to validate the mechanisms which handle network faults is complicated and hardens the analysis of the test results. To ease testing of network applications, we developed Jaca.net extending Jaca to handle a fault model more closely associated to communication.

Had we chosen a fault injector working at lower abstraction levels, we could, for example, intercept message send and receive kernel system calls, but the tests would be specific for just one of the platforms from all of which the target can run. Dealing with Java-based distributed applications, we offer a communication fault injector where faults are inserted on a higher abstraction level. This brings operating system and node architecture independence. Most of the other existing communication fault injection tools face dependency problems, since they are usually locked to a specific operating system or a specific target application. Another advantage of having the fault injector in the same level as the application is that it only acts when the application is running, which can decrease temporal intrusion on the system as a whole. Fault injectors located inside the kernel work independently of the target application, having an overhead which is not related to the target application.

Extending Jaca's fault model was possible because the tool is based on a pattern system for fault injection tools, structured to fault model expansion. The tool extension had three phases: establishment of the fault model, decision of the moment the faults should be injected and implementation of each fault of the model. These phases are described in the following sections.

4.1   Fault Model

Faults are random and unpredictable phenomena, which can lead a system to an erroneous state. If errors are not corrected, the system may fail. A failure occurs when a service is not offered according to its specification. A fault is classified by its type. In a distributed context, we can consider the occurrence of faults based on a fault model for distributed systems, suggested by Cristian [12].

This model describes omission, timing, response and crash faults. An omission fault occurs when a node does not reply one or more requests. Timing faults occurs when a node's response occurs outside the specified time interval. A response fault occurs when the node replies incorrectly either by an incorrect request return value or an incorrect state transition. A crash fault occurs when a node completely stops responding. The specific cause of each fault does not matter to the model, since a distributed application reacts to faults that affect the message exchange system as well as a node's crash to maintain the distributed system failure-free.

Cristian's fault model can be considered protocol independent and must be mapped to the specific network protocol which the application intends to use. For Jaca.net, we consider the User Datagram Protocol, UDP, due to its popularity, and so the adopted UDP fault model is mapped from Cristian's. It considers omission, timing and crash faults, as well as ordering faults, a subtype of timing faults. Spurious message insertion and duplication are also considered: both are subtypes of response faults. Such model was chosen because it includes types of faults that are very common in distributed environments. Also, none of these faults are handled by UDP and so are directly perceived by the application, which must support detecting and correcting them.

4.2   Fault Triggering

A commonly used approach to activate communication faults is to trigger the fault during message sending. Considering that we are injecting communication faults in Java, the interception should take place on the network programming interface, like UDP sockets.

With UDP sockets, message sending is done by the send() method of the java.net.DatagramSocket class. Therefore, interception must occur when this method executes. To intercept method execution, the class must be reflectible, i.e., all the class objects must have a meta-object associated to them. Thus, every method execution of this object is intercepted and a fault can be injected. The decision of which type of fault depends on a fault configuration file. Unfortunately, the Javassist's class loader does not allow the reflection of system classes. This is due to the Java class loading algorithm, in which a user class loader cannot load such classes.

To overcome this problem we created a wrapper to the java.net. Datagram Socket class which is a subclass of it and overloads its send() method. Since the wrapper subclass is not a system class, it can be reflected by the Javassist's class loader. A simple example of a wrapper class can be seen on Figure 2. If there is a valid reference to a datagram, the packet should be sent, otherwise it should not. The method must be invoked even with a null reference because when intercepted it has to run to completion, otherwise the stack trace is not correctly cleared and execution flow is lost.

The use of wrappers could limit Jaca, since the source code of the target application would be needed to replace references from the system classes to the wrappers. If the source code is available, a simple script may be used to replace

```
─────────────── DatagramSocket_.java ───────────
import java.net.*;

public class DatagramSocket_ extends DatagramSocket
{

   public void send(DatagramPacket packet) throws java.io.IOException
   {
      if (packet)
         super.send(packet);
      else
         return;
   }
}
```

Fig. 2. Example of a system class wrapper

references from java.net.DatagramSocket to the wrapper DatagramSocket_ (notice the ending underscore). A more general approach, which does not rely on the availability of the source code, is to directly alter Java bytecodes. This is accomplished by modifying the constant_pool table in Java's .class files [13]. Such structure is analog to the symbol table of conventional object files. For this approach, we have developed a patching filter that substitutes class references, which is run before class loading.

As a future plan Jaca.net should be enhanced to support faults dealing with the Transmission Control Protocol, TCP, and Java's RMI (Remote Method Invocation) protocol. The use of TCP sockets presents problems related to fault triggering. For UDP sockets, a message can only be sent by the send() method of the java.net.DatagramSocket class. With TCP, there is a multitude of ways to write data to a socket, including input/output related operations. So, there are two challenges: implementing wrappers for each of the possible classes, and differentiating between local (file) and remote (socket) writes. Solutions to such problems are still under investigation. Intercepting remote invocations (RMI) should not present any new difficulties, since this can be done while executing the methods from the stub classes. These classes are created by the RMI compiler (rmic) and so are not considered system classes, thus Javassist's class loader is able to reflect them.

4.3   Implementation of the UDP Fault Model

UDP packet delivery is unreliable, but it is commonly used as a base for the development of fault tolerance mechanisms, where the required reliability is implemented on upper layers. One such example is the JGroups [14] group communication system used as a building block for the development of many high availability applications. It uses UDP by default as the foundation of its protocol stack, and the protocols running on top of it are responsible for safe operation.

In this case, a UDP based fault injection tool is extremely valuable to experimentally validate such layers.

Adding a new fault type to Jaca requires changes in two packages: Fault_Manager and Injector. In the first, the manager has to be changed to parse the fault list file for this new fault type. This is accomplished adding an entry in a case statement. In the Injector, the extension process begins by adapting the InjectionManager class, which is responsible for the instantiation of each logic injector required during the experiment. The PhysicalInjector class should also be altered to inject the new fault type. It is necessary to create two new classes as well: the specialized injector to the new fault and the class describing and storing fault related data. By modifying and creating these classes, Jaca is ready to inject the new fault type in future experiments. Currently, Jaca.net supports the injection of omission, crash, duplication and timing faults.

To illustrate the extension process we show how we add omission faults to Jaca's fault model. For UDP omission faults two classes were created: UdpOmissionFault and UdpOmissionFaultInjector. The first stores fault related data, while the second is the logic injector. UdpOmissionFault attributes include source and destination IP addresses, UDP ports and the fault rate, if faults are set to intermittent. Setting this type of fault requires specifying the following 8-tuple:

< 'UdpOmissionFault', duration, start, fault rate, src host, src port, dst host, dst port>

The *duration* of a fault can be transient, permanent or intermittent. The *start* of the fault injection process is also configurable, determining which is the first message where faults begin to occur (e.g. after the nth message). The socket is identified by the source and destination IP addresses (*src host, dst host*) and UDP ports (*src port, dst port*). Configuring the source is optional and is useful for multihomed hosts. Since UDP is connectionless, destination address is verified directly in each sent datagram.

Implementing a new fault model proves that the use of a tool with an extensible architecture is not only viable but also desirable. Extending a pre-existent tool has a much lower cost of development than designing and implementing a new one from scratch. In Jaca, the use of a well documented and extensible software pattern eased this extension. At a minimum, it is necessary to create only two classes for each new type of fault. The modification of other classes is straightforward. The fault management class, for instance, only requires alteration of the fault file parser.

5   Applying Jaca.net to Inject Faults in a Real Network Application

In this section we show how Jaca.net can be used with its new fault model to conduct an experiment. This gives us a qualitative view of the tool's feasibility

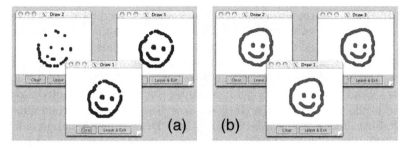

Fig. 3. Fault injection experiment without (a) and with (b) retransmission

to conduct experimental validation using fault injection: we apply Jaca.net and observe how a communication system deals with faults. This experiment mirrors the process a designer faces when trying to test fault tolerant mechanisms in network applications.

For our experiments, the chosen target was a shared whiteboard application. Every node has a local canvas in which the user can make simple drawings. These drawings are then propagated, in real time, to the other users' canvases. Since drawing events are sent as datagrams (UDP packets) to the other nodes, a lost message results in an incomplete drawing. The application must implement, if the drawings are to be consistent, detection and retransmission of faulty packets. Our target was based on a sample application for the JGroups middleware.

In the first test, we considered exclusively the UDP protocol, without any application based fault tolerance mechanism. Jaca.net was applied to a process to inject omission faults in one communication link, with a fault rate of 80%. Figure 3 (a) reflects that the injector is working as expected. The window "Draw 1" corresponds to the process where the drawing is made and faults are injected. Omission faults are injected when messages are sent, so the result of these faults should be observed in the corresponding window of the receiving end of the faulty communication link. In this case, Jaca.net injected faults in the link between processes 1 and 2. The window "Draw 2" has an incomplete drawing, since messages were not received as expected and retransmission was not made. The communication link with the process associated to window "Draw 3" was fault-free, and so the drawing on that window is a copy of the original.

The next test uses a similar shared whiteboard application, but now a transmission error detection and recovery mechanism was implemented. The chosen fault model for the application was recovery of packet loss. Whenever a UDP packet is lost the implemented timeout based detector signals the error and the packet is retransmitted. To implement the timeout we used the `setSoTimeout()` method of the `java.net.DatagramSocket` class, which enables socket timeout to expire after a specified interval, in this case, 100 milliseconds. Hence, an invocation of the `receive()` method blocks for the time passed to the `setSoTimeout()` method. If this timeout expires, an exception indicating this situation is raised. Since Jaca.net stands under the application, it is Jaca.net that catches this exception, but it raises it back to the application. When it reaches the application, the exception starts the error recovery functions and the message is retransmitted. The retransmitted message is also acknowledged, so that we can detect if it gets lost as well. While the `DatagramSocket_` wrapper class does not implement `setSoTimeout()` and other methods of the original system class, inheritance provides the needed transparency to the system.

The second test was conducted in a similar way to the first, faults also being injected in the process represented by window "Draw 1". Faulty communication was established with the process with window "Draw 2", with an omission fault rate of 10%. The difference between the first and the second experiment is that in the second, even with faults being injected, the drawing in the "Draw 2" window is identical to both other windows. Figure 3 (b) shows the expected behavior, faults being masked.

Observing this behavior the developer can conclude that the implemented error detection and recovery mechanism covers 100% of the injected faults. More complex scenarios can also be created to refine the test.

One could argue that the fault model and application chosen for testing Jaca.net is too simple, but it should be noticed that our main goal is to show how to use Jaca.net, not really the fault tolerance mechanisms of the protocol itself. Choosing a simple testing target we can reasonably expect how it behaves under the presence of faults. It is a matter of choosing a testing vector with known results, and being able to directly observe if the results under Jaca.net are consistent with real faults.

6   Concluding Remarks

This paper shows Jaca.net, an extension of the Jaca fault injector to a communication fault model. Jaca is based on a fault injection pattern system that facilitates fault model's extension through the addition of new types of faults. Jaca can corrupt attributes, parameters and return values. Jaca.net can also be used to conduct validation experiments on distributed applications developed over UDP, since it can act directly in the Java UDP sockets programming interface.

Jaca's implementation uses computational reflection, which presents several advantages for the development of software fault injectors. The selection of the Javassist reflection toolkit also maintains Jaca's portability, since it does not require modifications to the Java Virtual Machine. The impossibility of reflecting system classes, imposed by the class loading algorithm of Java, has been overcome with direct bytecode manipulation, that is, substitution of references from the system classes to our own wrappers of these classes.

The experiments presented in section 5 demonstrate how Jaca.net can be used to conduct validation experiments on network applications. Since our example application has a protocol that deals with packet loss, omission faults were chosen for validation. Other kinds of faults that could be injected using Jaca.net can be applied to test fault tolerant mechanisms in applications that tolerate a more complex fault model.

Future works include the implementation of the TCP fault model and addition of a RMI fault model to Jaca.net. Even so, Jaca.net is ready to experimentally validate fault tolerant mechanisms of UDP based distributed applications such as group communication and multicast systems and grid middleware, as well as any generic middleware developed in Java that must follows high availability specifications.

References

1. M.-C. Hsueh, T. Tsai, R. Iyer, *Fault Injection Techniques and Tools*. IEEE Computer, Volume 30, Number 4, pp. 75-82. April 1997.
2. E. Martins, C. M. F. Rubira, N. G. M. Leme, *Jaca: A Reflective Fault Injection Tool Based on Patterns*. In Proceedings of DSN 2002. Washington, USA. 2002.
3. J. Carreira, J. G. Silva, *Why do Some (weird) People Inject Faults?* ACM SIG-SOFT, Software Engineering Notes, Volume 23, Number 1, pp. 42-43. January 1998.
4. J. Carreira, H. Madeira, J. G. Silva, *Assessing the Effects of Communication Faults on Parallel Applications*. In Proceedings of IPDS'95. Erlangen, Germany. 1995.
5. S. Dawson, F. Jahanian, T. Mitton, *ORCHESTRA: A Probing and Fault Injection Environment for Testing Protocol Implementations*. In Proceedings of IPDS'96. Urbana-Champaign, USA. 1996.
6. P. P. A. Barcelos, F. O. Leite, T. S. Weber, *Building a Fault Injector to Validate Fault Tolerant Communication Protocols*. In Proceedings of PCS'99. Ensenada, Mexico. 1999.
7. J. Aidemark, J. Vinter, P. Folkesson, J. Karlsson, *GOOFI: Generic Object-Oriented Fault Injection Tool*. In Proceedings of DSN 2001. Göteborg, Sweden. 2001.
8. D. T. Stott, B. Floering, D. Burke, Z. Kalbarczyk, R. K. Iyer, *NFTAPE: A Framework for Assessing Dependability in Distributed Systems with Lightweight Fault Injectors*. In Proceedings of IPDS'2000. Chicago, USA. 2000.
9. P. P. A. Barcelos, R. J. Drebes, G. Jacques-Silva, T. S. Weber, *A Toolkit to Test the Intrusion of Fault Injection Methods*. In Proceedings of the 5th IEEE Latin-American Test Workshop. Cartagena, Colombia. 2004.
10. N. G. M. Leme, E. Martins, C. M. F. Rubira, *A Software Fault Injection Pattern System*. In Proceedings of PLoP 2001. Monticello, USA. 2001.
11. S. Chiba, *Load-time Structural Reflection in Java*. In Proceedings of ECOOP 2000. Cannes, France. 2000.
12. F. Cristian, *Understanding Fault-Tolerant Distributed Systems*. Communications of the ACM, v. 34, n. 2, pp. 56-78. February 1991.
13. T. Lindholm, F. Yellin, *The Java Virtual Machine Specification*. 2nd Edition. Addison-Wesley. 1999.
14. B. Ban, *JavaGroups - Group Communication Patterns in Java*. Department of Computer Science, Cornell University. July 1998.

Implementing Rollback-Recovery
Coordinated Checkpoints

Clairton Buligon, Sérgio Cechin, and Ingrid Jansch-Pôrto*

Graduate Program in Computer Science
Federal University of Rio Grande do Sul (UFRGS)
P.O.Box 15064, Porto Alegre, RS, Brazil
{clairton,cechin,ingrid}@inf.ufrgs.br

Abstract. Recovering from processor failures in distributed systems is
an important problem in the design of reliable systems. The processes
should coordinate their operation to guarantee that the set of *local checkpoints* taken by the individual processes form a *consistent global checkpoint* (recovery line). This allows the system to resume operation from a
consistent global state, when recovering from failure. This paper shows
the results of the implementation of a transparent (no special needs
for applications) and coordinated (non blocking) rollback-recovery distributed algorithm. As it does not block applications, the overhead is
reduced during failure-free operation. Furthermore, the rollback procedure can be executed fast as a recovery line is always available and well
identified. Our preliminary experimental results show that the algorithm
causes very low overhead on the performance (less than 2%), and high
dependency on the checkpoint size. Now we study optimizations on the
implementation to reduce checkpoint latency.

1   Introduction

Rollback-recovery treats a distributed system as a collection of application processes that communicate through a network. Processes achieve fault tolerance
by saving recovery information in a *stable storage* (which survives all tolerated
failures) periodically during failure-free execution. Upon a failure, a failed process uses the saved information to restart the computation from an intermediate
state, thereby reducing the amount of lost computation. The recovery information includes, at a minimum, the states of the participating processes, called
checkpoints. Other recovery protocols may require additional information, such
as logs of the interactions with input and output devices, events that occur to
each process, and messages exchanged among the processes [1].

Transparent rollback-recovery, which does not require any intervention on the
part of the application or the programmer, is an effective way for implementing
this approach. Some key performance considerations are related to: failure-free

---
* This research is partially supported by HP Brazil R&D and CNPq/Brazil Project
  ACERTE

F.F. Ramos et al. (Eds.): ISSADS 2005, LNCS 3563, pp. 246–257, 2005.
© Springer-Verlag Berlin Heidelberg 2005

overhead, extent of rollback, and output commit latency [2]. During failure-free operation, a rollback-recovery protocol records information about the computation's execution on stable storage. This information is used by the system to roll the computation back to a consistent state [3]. In general, the systems also send messages to the "outside word", which consists of entities that cannot recover their states (a printer, for instance). Thus, the systems must ensure that the state from which these messages are sent will never be rolled back [4], which introduces latency in sending messages to the outside world.

The overhead of checkpointing during failure-free operation includes (1) the cost of saving the checkpoints on stable storage, (2) the cost of interference between the checkpointing and the execution of processes, and (3) the cost of the communication among processes required to ensure a consistent system state checkpoints.

The cost of saving the checkpoints on stable storage depends on the checkpoint data to be saved. Thus, this overhead depends only on the amount of data handled by the fault-tolerant application; there is no straight relation to the checkpointing algorithm, and we can use a copy-on-write [2] implementation, for instance, to lower this cost. Second, checkpointing should be nonintrusive [5], that is, it should not force the processes to freeze their normal activity during checkpointing of other processes, which results in a small interference in the system execution. The third factor to be considered is the cost of communication: it is decreasing with the evolution of network technology, pushing the speed to higher levels.

There are three basic approaches to implement application–transparent rollback–recovery in distributed systems: message logging, communication-induced checkpointing (CIC) and coordinated checkpointing [1]. Message logging relies on a piecewise deterministic system model (PWD) in which nondeterministic events determine intervals of deterministic execution.

CIC protocols do not block the application during checkpointing. However, Alvisi [6] showed that some communication patterns can present a bad performance, mainly due to the number of forced checkpoints; CIC mechanisms do not scale well with the increase on the quantity of processes. Some particular communication patterns also present problems related to the prediction of the required amount of stable storage and on the placement policy for local checkpoints. That study shows that the benefit of autonomy in allowing processes to take local checkpoints at their convenience does not seem to hold.

In coordinate checkpointing algorithms, processes use additional control messages to synchronize their checkpointing activities [7],such that the collection of local checkpoints represents a *consistent state* of the whole system. This consistent global state includes the individual states of all participating processes and the states of the communication channels. And more precisely, if the state of a process reflects a message receipt, then the state of the corresponding sender reflects sending that message [1]. After a failure, failed processes can be restarted on any available machine and their address space will be recovered from their last checkpoint on stable storage [8]. Coordinated checkpointing requires processes to integrate their checkpoints in order to form a consistent global state (*recovery line*). Either blocking or unblocking approaches may be used for this. Blocking approach means that the processes stop their execution and flush all the communication channels before taking their checkpoints. This imposes high run-time overhead on the system, which makes non-blocking approach a preferable scheme [9].

Many checkpointing/recovery algorithms were proposed in the literature, but the emphasis of most of them is in the theoretical aspects. Differently, our goal is the implementation of a transparent and coordinated checkpointing/recovery algorithm and the evaluation of its performance. The checkpointing mechanisms are transparent from the application programmer point-of-view this means that no additional code is necessary in the applications and no reliable communication is needed (as usual, for many protocols). As the performance was an important concern during algorithm design, we focus our attention in this domain.

The algorithm we implemented is coordinated and nonblocking [1]. According to Prakash [5], it may be characterized as a nonintrusive algorithm. As we are interested on the performance of the distributed algorithm, we block each process just while the checkpoint is being written on stable storage. Mechanisms as copy-on-write or incremental checkpointing [2] have not been used to improve the performance.

Our paper is composed of six sections: following this introduction, we define the system model is used here, and then we briefly describe the checkpointing algorithm, which is followed by the discussion of its implementation. Next, we report and analyze the performance measurements taken from this implementation, finishing with Section 6 where our conclusions are presented.

2   System and Communication Model

A distributed computation consists of a finite set P of n processes $\{P_1, P_2, \ldots, P_n\}$ that communicate only by exchanging messages. The messages generated by the underlying distributed application will be referred to as *computation messages*. Messages generated by the processes to advance checkpoints, handle failure, and for recovery will be referred to as *system messages*. We assume that each process is executed on a processor of its own, processors do not have a shared memory, and there is no bound on their relative speeds.

In case of a temporary crash [10], a process loses its *volatile state* and stops execution according to the fail-stop model [11]. As soon as failure effect disappears, processes can resume the operation by accessing a *stable storage* to obtain the last stored state, which was saved before the failure was detected.

We do not assume reliable communication channels. This assumption simplifies the design of rollback-recovery protocols but introduces implementation complexities [1] that can reduce the system performance.

Every process P_i has an initial local state denoted $Si,0$. The subsequent local states Si,k *(k>0)* result from the execution of a sequence of events applied to the initial state. A *local checkpoint* C is a recorded state of a process. Only part of the local states is saved, so the set of local checkpoints is only a subset of those ones. Thus, Ci,x represents the x -th local checkpoint of process P_i. A *global checkpoint* is a set of local checkpoints, one for each process. A global checkpoint is consistent (forms a *recovery line*) if there are neither *orphan* nor *lost* messages [12].

3 Algorithm Description

The algorithm which we have implemented [13] does not require any process to suspend its underlying computation, does not require FIFO channels, avoids both lost and orphan messages, needs stable storage only to store two checkpoints per process, does not need an underlying reliable communication protocol and does not waste time with tentative checkpoint. The messages generated by the application (in the sender) go through the checkpoint/recovery layer before reaching the communication layer, whereas the messages which arrive (in the receiver) from the communication layer also go through the checkpoint/recovery layer before reaching the application.

Our checkpointing algorithm has been specified using Lamports' TLA+ [14], and its correction (safety properties) was proved [15]. The description shown in this paper (Figure 1) is an extract of the original specification [13].

4 Implementation

The algorithm was developed to support fault-tolerance in distributed applications by means of distributed checkpointing implementation. The library Crak [16], which originally was developed for Linux, as a kernel module through a device driver [17] for process migration, saves the state of the application process into the stable storage implemented in disk. Consequently, it is partially responsible by checkpointing and process recovery activities.

The rollback algorithm should run between the application layer and the operational system layer. We considered two alternatives: (a) to integrate the application and the rollback algorithm or (b) to construct a module for checkpointing and rollback to be inserted between the application and the operational system using **interception**. The latter was chosen due to its flexibility and transparency, as we do not need the source code of the application to insert modifications.

We implemented interception as explained by Fontoura [18], in a previous research in our Group. The implementation was divided in two parts: interception and the library Crak were implemented in the kernel space while general control, application messages control, failure detector, and checkpointing and rollback-recovery control were implemented in the user space.

The library Crak aims at a single process checkpoint and it was not developed to save network connections. Thus, our implementation can only deal with non-connection-oriented distributed applications (UDP). Figure 2 shows these modules and their interactions.

```
Interface
    SendCom(Message m);
    Deliver(Message m);
    WriteSM(int n, Checkpoint c);

Process' data structure:
    int N;    // Number of processes
    int cpid; // current process
    int mid;  // current message
    Checkpoint cur;
    Checkpoint prev;
    boolean oncp;
    boolean g[N];

Checkpoint's control structure:
    int index;
    set of Message msgSet;
    boolean bStable;

Message's data structure:
    int sender, receiver;
    int type, mid, index;

procedure takeCheckpoint(int n):
    cur.index = n;
    if (cur.bStable)
        WriteSM(1,cur);
        cur.bStable = false;
    else
        WriteSM(0,cur);
        cur.bStable = true;

procedure verify(Message m):
    if (m.index > cur.index)
        takeCheckpoint ( m.index );

procedure init():
    mid = 0;
    oncp = true;
    cur.index = 0;
    cur.msgSet = {};
    cur.bStable = false;
    WriteSM(0,cur);
    prev.index = 0;
    prev.msgSet = {};
    prev.bStable = false;
    WriteSM(1,cur);

procedure startNewCp():
    if (!oncp)
        oncp = true;
        takeCheckpoint(cur.index + 1);
        for (i=0; i<N; ++i)
            if (i==cpid) g[i] = true;
            else
                g[i] = false;
        m = new Message;
        m.sender = cpid;
        m.receiver = i;
        m.type = TREQ;
        m.index = cur.index;
        SendCom(m);
```

```
procedure sendMessage(Message m):
    m.sender = cpid;
    m.type = TAPP;
    m.mid = mid; mid = mid+1;
    m.index = cur.index;
    cur.msgSet = cur.msgSet Union m
    SendCom(m);

procedure receiveMessage(Message m):
    if(m.type == TAPP)
        verify(m);
        m2 = new Message;
        m2.sender = cpid;
        m2.receiver = m.sender;
        m2.type = TACK;
        m2.mid = m.mid;
        m2.index = cur.index;
        SendCom(m2);
        Deliver(m);

    else if (m.type == TACK)
        verify(m);
        if (Exists m2 In cur.smsg: m.mid==m2.mid)
            cur.msgSet = cur.msgSet - {m2};

    else if (m.type == TREQ)
        verify(m);
        m2 = new Message;
        m2.sender = cpid;
        m2.receiver = m.sender;
        m2.type = TAREQ;
        m2.index = cur.index;
        SendCom(m2);

    else if (m.type == TAREQ)
        g[m.sender] = true;
        if (Forall i In [0;N): g[i]==true)
            prev = cur;
            for (j=0; j<N; ++j)
                if (j!=cpid)
                    g[j] = false;
                    m2 = new Message;
                    m2.sender = cpid;
                    m2.receiver = j;
                    m2.type = TCMT;
                    m2.index = cur.index;
                    SendCom(m2);

    else if (m.type == TCMT)
        prev = cur;
        m2 = new Message;
        m2.sender = cpid;
        m2.receiver = m.sender;
        m2.type = TACMT;
        m2.index = cur.index;
        SendCom(m2);

    else if (m.type == TACMT)
        g[m.sender] = true;
        if (Forall i In [0;N): g[i]==true)
            oncp = false;
```

Fig. 1. Algorithm specification

As Figure 2 shows, the application messages are intercepted and put into Queue I. Output messages are copied to that queue and sent through the communication layer, as specified by the procedure *sendMessage* (Figure 1). Input messages carry on the checkpoint index of the sender process for comparison when are received. If the sender index is greater than the checkpoint index of the receiver, a new local checkpoint has to be taken. Thus, interception module freezes the execution of the local application module, foreseeing a writing procedure into stable memory. In addition, a control message is put into the Queue

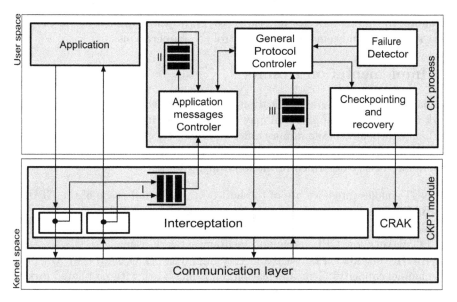

Fig. 2. Process implementation

I. The interception module sends these control messages; they are internal and do not use the network. When the control module of the application messages receives a control message, it takes a new local checkpoint, releases the application module and then the message is delivered. Concurrently, an acknowledge message is sent back to the originator of the application message. If a new checkpoint is not necessary, the application message is immediately delivered to the application and an acknowledge message is also sent back.

Finally, when an acknowledge message is received, depending on its sender index, a new local checkpoint may occur. The arrival of these messages is to release the memory previously allocated by the procedure *sendMessage* used to store the application messages. Acknowledgements are system messages and the application is unaware of them.

Checkpointing and recovery were implemented into the kernel space. The checkpoint of a single process includes the checkpoint index, the list of application messages sent but not yet acknowledged and the local state of the process, which includes the application address space, CPU registers, file descriptors, current working directory, terminal state, signal handlers, and UDP connections. Library Crak is called to save checkpoints.

Three threads are implemented in the user space module. The first thread takes the message (either sent or received) from the queue, verifies the sender index and stores it into a temporary buffer (output messages) or sends the acknowledge message (received messages). The second thread exchanges system messages: checkpointing messages and application acknowledge messages. Some of the checkpointing messages are directed to specific procedures. Finally, the third thread implements the rotation of the coordinator, avoiding a single point of failure, the failure detector and the recovery. All those threads access the same data structures and semaphores to control these operations.

5   Implementation Results

We have built a synthetic application for capturing the usage of CPU and network resources. This application may be configured: its parameters can be used to change its behavior and mimics different kinds of applications. We have chosen five sets of parameters, which resulted in five application profiles. The application profiles are briefly described in the following:

- NET: makes intensive use of the network, with small usage of the CPU;
- BAL: there is a good balance between network and CPU usage;
- CPU: high CPU usage and low network usage.
- LOW: very low CPU usage and medium network usage;
- HIGH: very low CPU usage and very high network usage (up to 10% of the channel capacity). This application sends messages, with no related processing activity. It does not wait for answers.

The three former applications are similar to typical applications, whose time is shared among processing, sending messages and waiting for answers. Notice that CPU utilization is modeled by the processing time whereas the network utilization is modeled by message-related tasks. The latter two application profiles aim at identifying the performance impact of the information attached to the messages by the checkpointing algorithm.

These five applications have run in six computers that communicate through a 100Mbps Ethernet. All these computers are Pentium IV, 2.4 GHz and 512 Mbytes of memory. One of these computers works as a server while the others are clients. Finally, we have chosen 30 seconds for the periodicity checkpoints. This rate is high for most of the real applications, thus our measurements overestimate the interference of the checkpointing algorithm.

5.1   Checkpointing Size Factor

We have designed three scenarios that differ on the checkpoint size: 0.1 Mbytes, 5 Mbytes, and 15 Mbytes. The applications were run with each of these scenarios applied. Figure 3 shows the mean time of one checkpoint. We can see that the

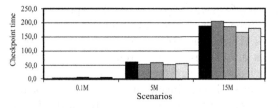

Apps	0.1 Mbytes	5 Mbytes	15 Mbytes
NET	0.4 ms	60.7 ms	182.1 ms
BAL	0.7 ms	57.2 ms	202.5 ms
CPU	1.5 ms	59.3 ms	182.8 ms
LOW	0.6 ms	50.8 ms	168.2 ms
HIGH	0.8 ms	55.8 ms	181.0 ms

Fig. 3. Checkpoint size comparison

mean time spent for checkpointing is dominated by the checkpoint size, which has a more important influence than the application profile.

The mean and standard deviation calculated from all measurements are shown in Figure 4. According to the relative standard deviation (Rsdev), the set of measured values is clustered around the average.

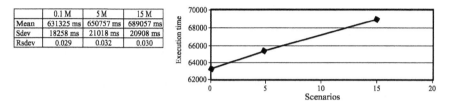

	0.1 M	5 M	15 M
Mean	631325 ms	650757 ms	689057 ms
Sdev	18258 ms	21018 ms	20908 ms
Rsdev	0.029	0.032	0.030

Fig. 4. Application execution time scenarios

Figure 4 shows a straight line connecting the three points. The correlation coefficient for these points is 0.999963. That line can be modeled by the next formula, where Cps represents the checkpoint size:

$$Time = 3868.0527 \times Cps + 631130.3802 \tag{1}$$

The line inclination (3868.0527) indicates the effect of the checkpoint size and the axis interception (631130.3802) indicates the CPU load caused by the checkpointing algorithm, interception and network usage.

5.2   Interception Factor

We have designed a scenario to investigate the effect of message interception. The mean values of the application execution time and the corresponding overhead are shown in Table 1.

Table 1. Execution time overhead caused by interception

Application	Execution time (ms)	Overhead (%)
NET	621747	0.033
BAL	654555	0.104
CPU	615087	0.090
LOW	614298	0.081
HIGH	614943	0.270
		Mean 0.115

As expected, application HIGH has the highest overhead (0.270%). In spite of this, the mean overhead is 0.115%, which represents a very low interference in the application execution time. Thus, we can use interception to augment applications with fault-tolerance and to obtain low execution time overhead.

5.3   Composition of Checkpoint and Interception Overheads

We have identified that the execution time of the application has a linear relationship with the size of the checkpoints. Thus, if we choose very small checkpoints, we may observe other factors (besides checkpoint size) that affect the execution time, causing overhead.

Table 2 shows the execution time of two scenarios: the original application augmented with the interception mechanism (WINT); and full operational with a small checkpoint size (FOPE), which adds the checkpointing to WINT scenario. In addition, OFOPE shows the overhead of full operation and OALGO shows only the overhead of the checkpointing algorithm (without interception). Finally, values in the RATIO column are the contribution of the checkpointing algorithm to the execution time overhead.

Table 2. Comparision of checkpointing and interception overhead

Application	WINT(ms)	FOPE(ms)	OFOPE	OALGO	RATIO(%)
NET	621747	627087	0.892	0.859	96.3
BAL	654555	663012	1.398	1.292	92.4
CPU	615087	625162	1.729	1.638	94.7
LOW	614298	619852	0.985	0.904	91.8
HIGH	614943	617249	0.646	0.375	58.1

As shown in column RATIO (Table 2) the interference of the checkpointing algorithm is greater than that of interception for the applications NET, BAL, CPU and LOW. Application HIGH offers a comparatively higher interception overhead due to the high message ratio it generates, which is not usual in real applications.

5.4   Messages Attached to Messages

In our checkpointing algorithm, messages sent but not yet acknowledged must be written to the stable memory with the process local state. Hence, the amount of data to be written to stable memory increases as the number of messages increases. Table 3 shows the message ratio generated by the applications (row *msg rate*), the mean number of messages saved with each checkpoint, and the overhead of stable memory to save them.

A quick inspection of Table 3 shows that each process saves a small number of messages in each checkpoint. Scenarios 5M and 15M presented overhead figures smaller than 0.1%. Scenario 0.1M had a more significant overhead (up to 12%), because of the small size of the checkpoint. Measurements show that the number of messages saved is not related to the checkpoint size. We believe that their variability is related to the number of messages but more experiments are necessary to observe the function tendency.

Table 3. Message rate and overhead

	NET	BAL	CPU	LOW	HIGH
msg rate	957 msg/s	603 msg/s	160 msg/s	483 msg/s	9725 msg/s
0.1M	6.9 msg	12.8 msg	2.1 msg	2.3 msg	4.1 msg
	6.8%	11.9%	2.1%	2.4%	4.1%
5M	10.4 msg	12.8 msg	2.9 msg	2.9 msg	2.3 msg
	0.2%	0.3%	0.06%	0.06%	0.05%
15M	11.4 msg	13.6 msg	14.2 msg	2.1 msg	3.1 msg
	0.08%	0.1%	0.1%	0.02%	0.02%

5.5 Checkpointing Overhead

Table 4 shows a comparison between the execution times of the original application and the application augmented with checkpointing. We have calculated the execution time overhead and discovered a low interference of the checkpointing algorithm in the execution time.

Table 4. Checkpointing overhead

Apps	Original apps	With Ckpts	Overhead
NET	621543 ms	627087 ms	0.892%
BAL	653874 ms	663012 ms	1.398%
CPU	614535 ms	625162 ms	1.729%

We have plotted the execution time overhead as a function of the CPU utilization, which was obtained through TOP monitor. Figure 5 shows that the execution time increases with the increase on the utilization of the CPU by the applications (as expected). Additionally, when the CPU usage is higher the execution time overhead is relatively smaller.

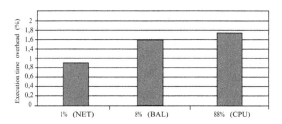

Apps	CPU Util.	Overhead
NET	1 %	0.892 %
BAL	8 %	1.398 %
CPU	88 %	1.729 %

Fig. 5. Overhead and CPU utilization

The impact of the network usage in the execution time overhead is shown in Figure 6. We have used the mean rate of the application messages as a metric for the network utilization and the results were ordered to show the influence of this metric. In this case, there is an inverse report between the number of sent application messages and the execution time overhead.

Apps	Msg rate	Overhead
NET	957 msg/s	0.892 %
BAL	603 msg/s	1.398 %
CPU	160 msg/s	1.729 %

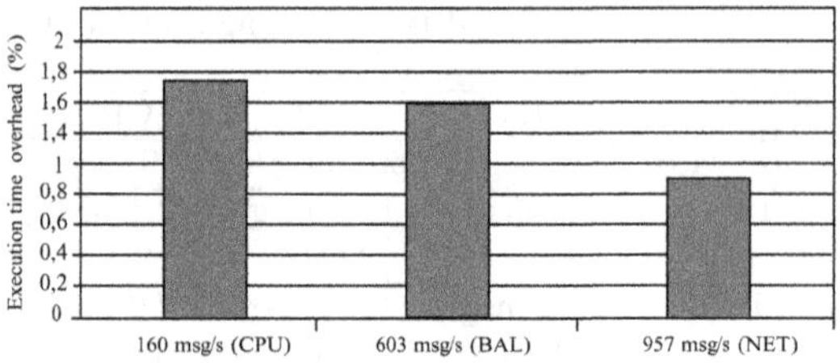

Fig. 6. Overhead and network utilization

6   Conclusions

In this paper, we described the implementation of a transparent and coordinated checkpointing/recovery algorithm and evaluated its performance. The main mechanisms used to achieve transparency (from the application programmer point-of-view) and to obtain consistent recovery lines were presented. The performance was an important concern during algorithm design: this paper proposed to show the results in this domain.

Our measurements show that the main factor in the execution time overhead is due to the checkpoint size. Comparatively, other factors produced just slight differences on the overhead values. Therefore, the execution time overhead of the coordination among processes to obtain a recovery line is small. The size of the checkpoints depends only on the application, but optimization techniques as incremental checkpointing, for instance, may be investigated aiming at still better performance results.

We have identified a small interference on the interception of the application messages. We observed an overhead of 0.27% in the worst case that was the application HIGH, which generates a message rate of 9725 msg/s. For providing fault-tolerance to our synthetic applications (NET, BAL and CPU), the implementation of the checkpointing algorithm shows a small overhead over the execution time (less than 2%).

The interference on the execution time due to CPU usage and network usage were shown. The measurements show that the algorithm is sensitive to CPU usage but this influence is less significant when the message rate increases. Even so, the overhead on the execution time in all these cases has never exceeded 2%, which is small.

All the experiments were conducted with applications running during 600s and with 20s of checkpoint interval, which is a conservative configuration. In practice, most usual applications set up longer checkpointing intervals. In that sense, our measurements overestimate the failure-free cost, since longer checkpointing intervals reduce the overhead on the execution time.

References

1. Elnozahy, E.N.; Johnson, D.B.; Wang, Y.M. *A Survey of Rollback-Recovery Protocols in Message-Passing Systems.* ACM Computing Surveys **34(3)** (2002) 375-408.

2. Elnozahy, E.N.; Johnson, D.B.; Zwaenepoel, W. *The performance of consistent checkpointing.* In Proc. 11th Symposium on Reliable Systems (1992) 39-47.
3. Chandy, K.M.; Lamport L. *Distributed snapshots: Determining global states of distributed systems.* ACM Transactions on Computer Systems **3(1)** (1985) 63-75.
4. Strom, R.E.; Yemini, S.A. *Optimistic recovery in distributed systems.* ACM Transactions on Computer Systems, **3(3)** (1985) 204-226.
5. Prakash, R.; Singhal, M. *Low-cost checkpointing and failure recovery in mobile computing systems.* IEEE Transactions on Parallel and Distributed Systems **7(10)** (1996) 1035-1048.
6. Alvisi, L. et al. *An Analysis of communication-induced checkpointing.* Technical Report, TR-99-01. Department of Computer Science. Univ. of Texas, Austin (1999).
7. Hélary, J.-M.; Mostefaoui, A.; Raynal, M. *Communication-based prevention of useless checkpoints in distributed computations.* Distributed Computing **13** (2000) 29–43.
8. Koo, R.; Toueg, S. *Checkpointing and rollback-recovery for distributed systems.* IEEE Transactions on software engineering, **SE-13(1)** (1987) 23-31.
9. Elnozahy, E.N.; Zwaenepoel, W. *Manetho: transparent rollback-recovery with low overhead, limited rollback and fast output commit.* IEEE Transactions on Computers, Special Issue on Fault-Tolerant Computing **41(5)** 526-531.
10. Cristian, F.; Aguili, H.; Strong, R. *Atomic broadcast: from simple message diffusion to Byzantine agreement.* In Proc. 15th IEEE Fault Tolerant Computer Systems (1995) 200-206.
11. Schlichting, R.D.; Schneider, F.B. *Fail-Stop processors: An approach to designing fault-tolerant computing systems.* ACM Transactions on Computer Systems **1(3)** (1983) 222-238.
12. Jalote, P. *Fault tolerance in distributed systems.* Prentice Hall (1994).
13. Cechin, S.L.; Jansch-Pôrto, I. *A New Efficient Coordinated Checkpointing.* In Proc. 2nd IEEE Latin American Test Workshop. Cancun, Mexico (2001) 56-61.
14. Lamport, L. *The temporal logic of actions.* ACM Transactions on Programming Languages and Systems **16(3)** (1994) 872-923.
15. Cechin, S.L. *TLA formal proof of rollback recovery protocol.* Technical Report (RP-319). Institute of Informatics, Federal University of Rio Grande do Sul, Porto Alegre, Brazil (2002).
16. Zhong, H.; Nieh, J. *Crak: Linux checkpointing/restart as a kernel module.* Technical Report CUCS-014-01, Department of Computer Science, Columbia University, Columbia, USA (2001).
17. Rubini, A. *Linux device drivers.* Market Books (1999).
18. Fontoura, A. B. *Evaluation of approaches for capturing the application data.* MSc. Dissertation. Instituto de Informática, Universidade Federal do Rio Grande do Sul, Porto Alegre, Brazil (2002) (in portuguese).

An Identity-Based Model
for Grid Security Infrastructure*

Xiaoqin Huang, Lin Chen, Linpeng Huang, and Minglu Li

Department of Computer Science and Engineering,
Shanghai Jiao Tong University, 200030 Shanghai, China
{huangxq,chenlin}@sjtu.edu.cn

Abstract. In this paper, we propose a grid security infrastructure based on identity cryptography. We mainly discuss the grid security authentication and authorization architecture by using Tate Pairing. We propose a private key generator security infrastructure and secure group communication scheme by using non-interaction secret sharing protocol and one round tripartite Diffie-Hellman protocol. Finally, we present the advantages and disadvantages of our ID-based security infrastructure comparing with the public key infrastructure in grid circumstance.

Keywords: Identity Cryptography, Grid Security Infrastructure, Secure Group Communication.

1 Introduction

The grid is a distributed computing system comprising a large number of computational resources. Grid security infrastructure can assure the legal users to access the resource securely. The current grid security infrastructure, Grid Security Infrastructure (GSI), consists of: User, Proxy, Mutual Authentication Process, Service, Access Control List, Backup Logs [1, 3, 4, 5, 11]. The authentication and authorization process is the core of the security model. The authentication is composed of X.509 certificates and digital signature schemes [13]. The certificate consists of user name, issuer, a public key, validity. But in recent years, cryptography based on identity is developing very quickly. Many important results have been achieved. In 1984, Shamir presented the identity-based cryptography concept [6]. In 2001, Boneh and Franklin presented an identity-based encryption scheme based on properties of the Weil and Tate pairings [7]. The properties of identity-based cryptography (IBC) may well match the qualities of grid computing. In the traditional public key cryptography, we must get users' public keys from Certificate Authority (CA). When there are thousands of users in grid circumstance, the CA will become the bottleneck. The management of the users' certificates will become difficult. But in the IBC system, the public key may be

---

* This paper is supported by SEC E-Institute: Shanghai High Institutions Grid project, the 863 High Technology Program of China (No. 2004AA104340 and No. 2004AA104280), Natural Science Foundation of China (No. 60433040 and No. 60473092) and ChinaGrid Program of MOE of China.

F.F. Ramos et al. (Eds.): ISSADS 2005, LNCS 3563, pp. 258–266, 2005.

the user's identity, for example, e-mail address. We don't need to get the user's public key from CA. We just use the user's e-mail address as the public key. It is very convenient. The advantages of ID-based system are obvious. In this paper, we propose a grid security infrastructure based on identity cryptography and mainly discuss the grid security authentication and authorization architecture by using Tate Pairing. We also propose a private key generator security infrastructure and secure group communication scheme. Finally we present the advantages and disadvantages of our ID-based security infrastructure comparing with the public key infrastructure in grid circumstance.

2   Related Work

2.1   ID-Based Encryption Scheme with Chosen Ciphertext Security

Dan Boneh and Matt Franklin presented ID-based encryption scheme in paper [7]. The bilinear maps and bilinear map groups satisfies the following properties:

1. Let $\mathbb{G}_1$ and $\mathbb{G}_2$ be two cyclic groups of prime order q for some large prime q;
2. $\mathbb{G}_1$ is the group of points of an elliptic curve over $\mathbb{F}_p$ and $\mathbb{G}_2$ is a subgroup of $\mathbb{F}_{p^2}^*$;
3. A map $\hat{e} : \mathbb{G}_1 \times \mathbb{G}_1 \rightarrow \mathbb{G}_2$ is said to be bilinear, if $\hat{e}(aP, bQ) = \hat{e}(P, Q)^{ab}$ for all $P, Q \in \mathbb{G}_1$ and all $a, b \in \mathbb{Z}$.

Setup: Suppose PKG setup the system parameters as follows:
Params=$< p, n, P, P_{pub}, G, H >$. Where p a large k-bit prime p such that $p = 2 \bmod 3$ and $p = 6q - 1$ for some prime $q > 3$. P an arbitrary parameter, $P \in E/\mathbb{F}_p$ of order q. $P_{pub} = sP$, n the message space size, a cryptographic hash function $H : \mathbb{F}_{p^2} \rightarrow \{0, 1\}^n$ for some n, a cryptographic hash function $G : \{0, 1\}^* \rightarrow \mathbb{F}_p$. The master-key is $s \in \mathbb{Z}_q$. In addition, we pick a hash function $H_1 : \{0, 1\}^n \times \{0, 1\}^n \rightarrow \mathbb{F}_q$, and a hash function $G_1 : \{0, 1\}^n \rightarrow \{0, 1\}^n$.
Encrypt: If a user has a public ID, use algorithm $MapToPoint_G$ to convert ID into a point $Q_{ID} \in E/\mathbb{F}_p$ of order q. To encrypt $M \in \{0, 1\}^n$, a user can choose a random $\sigma \in \{0, 1\}^n$, set $r = H_1(\sigma, M)$, and set the ciphertext to be:

$$C =< rP, \sigma \oplus H(g_{ID}^r), M \oplus G_1(\sigma) > \quad where \ g_{ID} = \hat{e}(Q_{ID}, P_{pub}) \in \mathbb{F}_{p^2} \quad (1)$$

Decrypt: Let $C =< U, V, W >$ be a ciphertext encrypted using the public key ID. If $U \in E/\mathbb{F}_p$ is not a point of order q reject the ciphertext. To decrypt C using the private key d_{ID} do:

1. Compute $V \oplus H(\hat{e}(d_{ID}, U)) = \sigma$.
2. Compute $W \oplus G_1(\sigma) = M$.
3. Set $r = H_1(\sigma, M)$. Test that $U = rP$. If not, reject the ciphertext.
4. Output M as the decryption of C.

2.2   Short Signatures from the Tate Pairing

As in papers [16, 8], let G_1 and G_2 denote two groups of prime order q in which the discrete logarithm is hard. There exists a computable bilinear map: $t : G_1 \times G_1 \to G_2$. If $a, b, c \in \mathbb{F}_q$ and $P, Q \in G_1$, the Tate pairing has the following properties:

$$t(aP, bQ)^c = t(aP, cQ)^b = t(bP, cQ)^a = ... = t(P, Q)^{abc} \tag{2}$$

Setup: Suppose PKG has a standard public/private key pair (R_{TA}, s). If the user's public key is Q_{ID}, then the user's private key $S_{ID} = sQ_{ID}$. The user also publishes the public parameter $R = S_{ID}P$. $P \in G_1$, $H_1 : \{0, 1\}^* \to G_1$.
Sign: If a user want to sign a message m, he computes the $V = S_{ID}H_1(m)$.
Verify: Check whether the following equation holds:

$$t(P, V) = t(R, H_1(m)) \tag{3}$$

2.3   One Round Tripartite Diffie-Hellman Protocol

Antoine Joux [9, 10] presented a new efficient one-round tripartite key agreement protocols. The definition of $\mathbb{G}_1$, $\mathbb{G}_1$ is as above. If Alice, Bob and Charlie want to get a secret share key, the protocol requires each party to transmit only a single broadcast message to establish an agreed session key among three parties.

$$\begin{aligned} A &\to B, C : aP \\ B &\to A, C : bP \\ C &\to A, B : cP \end{aligned} \tag{4}$$

After the session, A computes $K_A = (bP, cP)^a$. B computes $K_B = (aP, cP)^b$ and C computes $K_C = (aP, bP)^c$. The established session key is $K = K_A = K_B = K_C = (P, P)^{abc}$.

2.4   ID-Based Non-interaction Secret Sharing Protocol

Ryuichi Sakai [12] proposed non-interaction secret sharing protocol. ID_A and ID_B are respectively the identity information of Alice and Bob. $S_{ID_A} = sH(ID_A)$ and $S_{ID_B} = sH(ID_B)$ is respectively their secret key. s is the system secret key. The protocol is as follows:

1. Alice computes the K_{AB}, $K_{AB} = \hat{e}(S_{ID_A}, P_{ID_B})$.
2. Bob computes the K_{BA}, $K_{BA} = \hat{e}(S_{ID_B}, P_{ID_A})$.
3. Using map $\hat{e}$ properties, we can verify $K_{AB} = K_{BA}$.

Alice and Bob can get the sharing secret key $K_{AB} = K_{BA}$. The protocol doesn't need interaction.

3   Our Identity-Based Grid Authentication and Authorization Schemes

Before we discuss the grid secure authentication and authorization schemes, some important concepts should be introduced. As in paper [1, 2, 15], we define the following concepts from the security literature:

Authentication: Authentication is the process by which a user proves his identity to a requester, typically by the use of a certificate.

Authorization: Authorization is the process by which we determine whether a user is allowed to access or use a resource.

A trust domain: A trust domain is a logical, administrative structure within which a single local security policy hold.

Virtual organization: A dynamic collection of users and resources that may span multiple administrative domains and governed by the same managing rules.

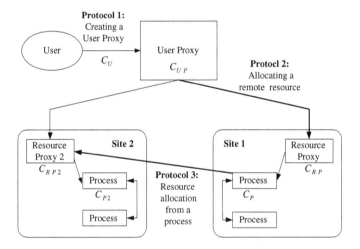

Fig. 1. Grid security infrastructure

As in paper [1], Fig.1 depicts the security architecture of Grid Security Infrastructure (GSI). It includes User, User Proxy, Resource Proxy, Process, Protocol 1, Protocol 2, Protocol 3 and Certificates et al. In the GSI, the execution of authentication of the user U is actually performed by the user proxy UP. Entities U and RP have their long-term identity certificates, denoted by C_U and C_{RP}, respectively. The user U issues the identity certificate C_{UP} to the user proxy UP. The UP requires access to a resource by authenticating with the RP. If the authentication is passed, the RP allocates the processes to the UP. If the computation resource is inefficient, the process P requests access to the resource proxy in the site 2. Then the P authenticates with the $RP2$. If the authentication is passed, the $RP2$ allocates the processes in the site 2 to the process P in site 1.

3.1 Identity-Based Grid Authentication Schemes

In the public key cryptography, there are two kinds of certificates: Identity Certificate and Authorization Certificate. The Identity Certificate is used to indicate the identity information. Usually we use the X.509 certificate form. This include: (Subject, Issuer, Public Key, Validity, Signature) [13]. Issuer is the Certificate Authority and Subject is the certificate's owner. Public Key is the owner's public key. Validity is the validity period of the certificate. Signature is the CA's signature. Authorization Certificate is the access rights to access some resources. When we use the identity-based cryptography, we neither need user's public key certificate nor verify his identity as the authentication task has been indirectly transferred to the PKG. The user needs to authenticate himself to the PKG before he receives the appropriate corresponding private key [15]. The authentication process is as follows:

1. The user sends his identity to the PKG. The PKG authenticates the identity and generates the private key for the user. For example, the identity is ID=$M_{User}\|Date$, the public key is $P_{User} = H_1(ID)$, $H_1 : \{0,1\}^* \to G_1$. If the PKG has the public/private key pair (R_{PKG}, s), where $R_{PKG} = sP$, $P \in G_1$, it generates the user's secret key $S_{User} = sP_{User}$.
2. The user also generates a key pair (R_{User}, s_1), where $R_{User} \in G_1$, $s_1 \in \mathbb{F}_q$, $(R_{User} = s_1P)$, $P \in G_1$. So the user now has two key pairs: (P_{User}, S_{User}) and (R_{User}, s_1). The before is used for signing a signature and the latter is used for generating a private key for the user proxy UP.
3. The user generates the private key and the certificate for the user proxy UP. Suppose we select $ID_1 = M_{User}\|1\|Date$ as the user proxy's identity, the UP's public key is $P_{UP} = H_1(ID_1)$ and the secret key $S_{UP} = s_1P_{UP}$. So the UP has the public/private key pair (P_{UP}, S_{UP}). The user signs the certificate for RP. The certificate may include (Issuer, Subject, Public Key, Delegate, Validity, Signature). Here the Issuer is the user, the Subject is the user proxy (i.e. ID_1), the Public Key is P_{UP}, the Delegate is a Yes flag, the Validity is the efficient period specified by the user and the Signature is signed by the user using the private key S_{User}. The signature algorithm is the short signatures from the Tate Pairing in section 2.2. The UP's certificate is short-timed.
4. The UP then use the certificate signed by the user to authenticate with RP. The RP can select a random parameter and send to the UP, the UP signs the random parameter with S_{UP}. The RP verifies the signature with P_{UP}. If it is valid and the user proxy's identity is $ID_1 = M_{User}\|1\|Date$, then the authentication is passed.
5. The process is repeated between P and $RP2$ as before. Then the user can use the resource in site 1, site 2, ..., site n. The scalability is enhanced.

3.2 Identity-Based Grid Authorization Schemes

In this section, we describe a authorization scheme for a user to access a grid resource. The steps are as follows:

1. The authorization certificate is represented by the 5-tuple: Issuer, Subject, Delegate, Authorization, Validation. Delegate is a Yes/No flag, Authorization is the description of what is being authorized and Validity is the validity period [16]. PKG forms the expression given by

$$\sigma = P_{User}\|Delegate\|Authorization\|Validity \tag{5}$$

and then forms the public/private key pair given by $S_\sigma = sQ_\sigma$ where $Q_\sigma = H_1(\sigma)$. PKG then gives the private key S_σ to the user. The authorization public key Q_{User} for the user ($Q_{User} = Q_\sigma$) is also public known. Now the user has a public/private key pair (Q_σ, S_σ) for the authorization.

2. The user generates an authorization certificate for the user proxy UP. The authorization certificate may include (Issuer, Subject, Public Key, Delegate, Authorization, Validity, Signature). In this situation, Issuer is the user, Subject is the UP, Public Key is the UP's public key, Delegate is Yes, Validity is the effective period and Signature is signed by the user using S_σ. The public key $P_{UP} = H_1(ID_{UP})$, where $ID_{UP} = M_{User}\|A\|Date$. The UP's private key can be generated by the user as before.

3. The UP sends the authorization certificate to the RP. The RP selects a random parameter to UP, the UP signs the parameter and sends back to the RP. If the verification is passed, the RP also compares the $ID_{UP} = M_{User}\|A\|Date$ and the $ID = M_{User}\|Date$. If they have the same M_{User}, the authorization is passed. The RP permits the UP to use the local resource.

4 Public Key Infrastructure Based on Identity Cryptography

As in paper [15, 16], there is a lot of virtual organizations. In each virtual organization, if there is only one PKG, this is a risky situation as the PKG is the single point of failure and becomes the workload bottleneck of the system. In a VO, there are several Trusted Communities (TCs), a TC has one PKG who is trusted by all entities (users and resources). If users are in the same TC, they can use IBC approach to communicate securely. For example, they can use the ID-Based encryption scheme in section 2.1 or short signature scheme in section 2.2. If users belong to different PKGs, for example, Alice in a PKG1 want to communicate with Bob in another PKG2, Alice needs to authenticate with PKG2 through PKG1. The architecture is in the Fig.2.

In the Fig.2, each VO has a corresponding intermediate grid PKG. When there are a lot of VOs, there are a lot of intermediate grid PKGs. At the top, there are several peer grid PKGs. When users in the different peer grid PKGs want to communicate securely, they need the peer grid PKGs to establish a cross-certificate. The X.509 specification [14] defines a cross-certification in this way: "Two CAs exchange information used in establishing a cross-certificate. A cross-certificate is a certificate issued by one CA to another CA which contains a CA signature key used for issuing certificates." According to the definition, we extend the content to the peer grid PKGs's cross-certification. Suppose a

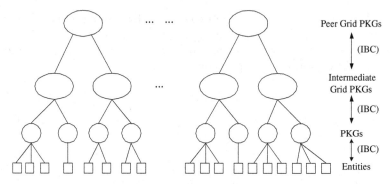

Fig. 2. A trust model for grid environment

peer grid PKG1 has a key pair (R_1, s_1), another peer grid PKG2 has a key pair (R_2, s_2), PKG1 signs a certificate (PKG1, Subject1, R_1, Validity) using the secret key s_1, PKG2 verifies the certificate using the public key R_1. If the verification is passed, then PKG2 trusts the PKG1. In the same way, PKG2 signs a certificate (PKG2, Subject2, R_2, Validity) using the secret key s_2, PKG1 verifies the certificate. If the verification is passed, the PKG1 trusts PKG2. The cross-certification between PKG1 and PKG2 is completed. The users in PKG1 can communicate securely with users in PKG2.

5   Secure Group Communication Scheme in Grid Computing

Grid systems may require any standard security functions, including authentication, access control, integrity, privacy, and nonrepudiation [1]. A computation can comprise a number of processes that will need to coordinate their activities as a group. The composition of a process group can and will change during the lifetime of a computation. Therefore, secure communication for dynamic groups is needed. So far, no current security solution supports this feature; even GSS-API has no provisions for group security contexts [1]. In our grid security architecture, there are a lot of processes. These processes need to communicate securely. They have to share a common secret key. If two processes need to get a share secret key, they can use the ID-Based non-interaction secret sharing protocol in section 2.4. If three processes need to get a share secret key, they can use the one round tripartite Diffie-Hellman protocol in section 2.3. The scheme is very simple and practical.

6   Security Analysis and Comparisons

IBC is a relatively new technology in comparison with PKI. In this field, a lot of new results have been achieved in recent years. We consider its applications in a grid system. So the grid security is based on the Identity-Based cryptography.

When the grid system is developed to a large scale, the excellence is obvious. We just use other people's e-mail address || date as the public key, rather than get other people's public key certificate from CA each time. When there are tens of thousands people using the CA, the CA will become the bottleneck. We use the short signature scheme from the Tate pairing, it is more efficient than the short signature scheme based on the Weil pairing. So our grid security authentication and authorization architecture is more practical than the traditional grid architecture based on the PKI.

In the process of grid authentication and authorization, we use the X.509 certificate form. But there is no certificate form between a user and a PKG. It is very easy for the PKG to manage the users. In the traditional PKI, the management of the certificates becomes the burden. In the ID-Based grid security architecture, the certificates among $UP\ RP\ P$ are short-timed. We also discuss the secure group communication scheme in the ID-Based grid circumstance. We use the one round tripartite Diffie-Hellman and ID-Based non-interaction secret sharing protocol, it is more efficient than the traditional authenticated group Diffie-Hellman key-exchange protocol.

However, there are two drawbacks with identity-based cryptosystems [15]. The first drawback is the need for a user to maintain an independent secure channel for the distribution of the private key. This need not be such a problem within a grid infrastructure and within a controlled and closed VO, though it does remain an important area for future research. The second drawback is that the PKG knows the private keys of all its users. This can be solved by distributed PKGs and threshold cryptography. Also members of a given VO are expected to trust the PKG anyway.

7   Conclusions

Grid computing is one of today's most important technologies. The security problem is a complicated and important problem in grid computing. Current implementations rely on a traditional PKI technology. In this paper, we introduce a new cryptography technology (Identity-based Cryptography) into the grid security. We design the grid secure authentication and authorization architecture based on ID-based cryptography. We have explored an IBC security architecture. We adopt the short signature algorithm based on the Tate pairing, it is more efficient in the implementation. Because secure group communication is seldom considered before, we propose an secret key exchange protocol based on Joux's One Round Tripartite Diffie-Hellman Protocol. The scheme is very simple and practical. The inherent qualities of IBC appear to closely match the demands of a dynamic environment in the grid circumstance where the availability of resources can change over the time frequently.

References

1. Foster, I., Kesselman, C., Tsudik., G.: A Security Architecture for Computational Grids. ACM Conference on Computers and Security, 83-9, 1998.

2. Mao, W., B.: An Identity-based Non-interactive Authentication Framework for Computational Grids. May 29, 2004.
   http://www.hpl.hp.com/techreports/2004/HPL-2004-96.pdf
3. Welch, V., Siebenlist, F. and Foster, I.: Security for grid services. Proceedings of the 12th IEEE International Symposium on High Performance Distributed Computing (HPDC'03), 2003.
4. Butler, R., Foster, D., Kesselman, I.: A National-Scale Authentication Infrastructure. IEEE Computer, 33(12). 60-66. 2000.
5. Gasser, M. and McDermott, E.: An Architecture for Practical Delegation in a Distributed System. Proc. 1990 IEEE Symposium on Research in Security and Privacy, 1990, IEEE Press, 20-30.
6. Shamir, A.: Identity-based cryptosystems and signature schemes in Proc. Crypto'84, LNCS Vol.196, Springer, pp.47-53, 1985.
7. Boneh, D. and Franklin, M.: Identity-Based Encryption from the Weil pairing," in Proc. Crypto 2001, LNCS Vol.2193, Springer, pp. 213-229, 2001.
8. Boneh, D., Lynn, B. and Shacham H.: Short Signatures from the Weil pairing. ASIACRYPT 2001, LNCS 2248, Springer-Verlag (2001), pp.514-532.
9. Joux, A.: A one-round protocol for tripartite Diffie-Hellman. Algorithm Number Theory Symposium -ANTS-IV, Lecture Notes in Computer Science 1838, Springer-Verlag (2000), pp. 385-394.
10. Joux, A.: A One Round Protocol for Tripartite Diffie-Hellman. Journal of Cryptology. Vol17, pp.263-276, 2004.
11. Introduction to grid computing with globus. http://www.ibm.com/redbooks.
12. Sakai, R., Ohgishi, K. and Kasahara, M.: Cryptosystems based on pairing. In SCIS, Okinawa, Japan, 2000.
13. Lock, R. and Sommerville, I.: Grid Security and its use of X.509 Certificates. http://www.comp.lancs.ac.uk/computing/.
14. Internet X.509 Public Key Infrastructure Certificate and CRL profile, RFC3280, 2002.
15. Lim, H.W. and Robshaw, M.J.B.: On Identity-Based Cryptography and Grid Computing. ICCS 2004, LNCS 3036, pp. 474-477, 2004.
16. Chen, L., Harrison, K., Moss, A., Soldera, D. and Smart N.P.: Certification of Public Keys Within an Identity Based System. ICS 2002, LNCS 2433, pp. 322-333, 2002.

Lineage Tracing in Mediator-Based Information Integration Systems*

Nematollaah Shiri and Ali Taghizadeh-Azari

Dept. of Computer Science & Software Engineering
Concordia University, Montreal, Quebec, Canada
{shiri,a_taghiz}@cse.concordia.ca

Abstract. The problem of identifying the data contributed to a query answer is referred to as lineage tracing. While this has been studied extensively in data warehouse systems, it is identified as a research topic in the mediator-based approach to information integration [10]. A main problem in this context is that a mediator does not store data, and hence for query processing and tracing, it has to communicate with the data sources. While this communication could be expensive, the real issue is that in some situations, after a query is being processed, lineage tracing may be more difficult, e.g., when the schema of a source has changed, or may even be impossible, e.g., when a source becomes unavailable. In this paper, we study the lineage tracing problem in mediator-based systems and propose a solution by collecting "enough" data and metadata during query processing so that tracing is possible in such situations.. We have developed a system prototype, called ELIT (for *Exploration and LIneage Tracing*). To allow more flexibility, ELIT supports lineage tracing in two modes: batch and interactive. Due to the distributed nature of the context, efficiency is of primary concern for practical reasons. We therefore investigate ways to reduce the overhead of lineage tracing in the proposed framework while processing queries. Using some basic query optimization techniques in ELIT, our preliminary experimental results show considerable increase in efficiency. This indicates the proposed ideas in the framework of ELIT could lend themselves to powerful lineage tracing and data analysis tools, by incorporating more sophisticated query optimization techniques.

1 Introduction

Information integration systems provide users a uniform interface to a multitude (possibly) heterogeneous data sources [9]. As in database systems, a user in an information integration system formulates a query, based on the actual schema or view. The underlying run-time system validates the user query for its syntax and semantics. If all is in order, the system then generates sub-queries and dispatches them to the appropriate data sources for evaluation. The results of the sub-queries are collected from the sources, combined, and sent back to the user. In many applications, it is desired to find out which atomic data contributed to a query answer, for instance for data analysis. This is known as *the lineage tracing problem* and has been studied extensively in the data warehouse approach to information integration.. For the mediator-based approach, however, this is a research problem [10]. The question is: "what is needed to

---

* This work was supported in part by grants from Natural Sciences and Engineering Research Council (NSERC) of Canada, and by Concordia University, ENCS.

F.F. Ramos et al. (Eds.): ISSADS 2005, LNCS 3563, pp. 267–282, 2005.

support lineage tracing in mediator-based systems?" For this, we need the following capabilities, in general.

- To have the schema of the data sources involved and their locations.
- To have the query itself in order to define the transformation functions. These functions should be introduced to run-time system according to the specifications of queries.
- To deal with multiple data sources, due to the distributed nature of mediator-based systems.

Let us elaborate on the issues. A data warehouse is a centralized database system defined from data sources through the operations of extraction, transformation, load, and refresh. In a mediator-based information integration system, on the other hand, there is no data stored at the mediator, and hence the actual data sources will be involved in query processing. Compared to regular query processing in mediator-based systems, accessing atomic data contributed to the query answer is more time consuming and sometimes even impossible. If it takes T_1 to retrieve the data from data sources and combine them, and takes T_2 to apply the linage tracing functions, then T $= T_1 + T_2$ is the total time that must be considered as a gap between the first attempt to access the data and the second one to provide linage tracing. Considering this gap, an inconsistency problem may arise in case some contributing atomic data are updated after time T_1 and before T_2. In this case, lineage tracing will return the new atomic data, which are different than those contributed to the query result in the first place. Another complication, which is also due to dynamic nature of mediator-based systems, is that some contributing data sources may not be available for tracing after query processing is completed. Data cashing is a possible solution to this problem, which in general seems to go against the philosophy that mediators do not store data. As this data could be large, the problem is how to manage this large cash? What data structures and algorithms are suitable and efficient in this context?

In this paper, we study lineage tracing in mediator-based information integration systems, and propose a framework to investigate possible solution techniques. We adopt a *fine-grain* approach, which amounts to having lineage tracing at the instance level. An alternative would be a *coarse-grain* approach, which provides lineage tracing at the schema level [8]. Having instance level requires having the schema level as well. This is why in mediator-based system, some operations on schemas of the original data sources are required to obtain the required schema information.

1.1 Motivating Example

We use an example of a sales application to introduce some concepts and notations, as well as an illustration of the lineage tracing problem and the issues involved in our context. In this example, we have a mediator-based information integration system that includes two different types of data sources, a conventional relational database and an XML data source. As shown in Figure 1.1, the database includes a relation schema SALES (StoreID, ItemID, NumSold, Price), with the usual meaning. The XML data file ITEM, shown in Figure 1.2, records ItemID, ItemName, and ItemCategory.

The XML file we consider in this work does not have deep nesting structure. This is just to make the parser easier to develop. Arbitrary XML and XSD files could be supposed at the cost of a more complex parser, which was not our focus in this study.

TableName	RecordNum	ColumnName	Value
...			
SALES	1	StoreID	2
SALES	1	ItemID	1
SALES	1	NumSold	800
SALES	1	Price	5
SALES	2	StoreID	2
SALES	2	ItemID	21
SALES	2	NumSold	2000
SALES	2	Price	2
...	...	...	...
ITEM	1	ItemID	1
ITEM	1	ItemName	Binder
ITEM	1	Category	Stationary
ITEM	2	ItemID	21
ITEM	2	ItemName	Pencil
ITEM	2	Category	Stationary
...	...	...	...

StoreID	ItemID	NumSold	Price
2	1	800	5
2	2	2000	2
2	4	800	35
3	3	1500	45
3	4	600	60
4	3	2100	50
4	4	1200	70
4	5	200	30
1	1	1000	4
1	2	3000	1

Fig. 1.1. SALES table (left) and Data Reference table (right)

```
...
<xs:complexType name="ITEM">
<xs:attribute name="ItemID" type="ID" use="required"/>
<xs:attribute name="ItemName" type="string" use="required"/>
<xs:attribute name="Category" type="string" use="required"/>
</xs:complexType>
...
...
<ITEM ItemID="1" ItemName="binder" Category="stationary"></Item>
<ITEM ItemID ="2" ItemName="pencil" Category="stationary"></Item>
<ITEM ItemID="3" ItemName="shirt" Category="clothing"></Item>
<ITEM ItemID="4" ItemName="pants" Category="clothing"></Item>
<ITEM ItemID="5" ItemName="pot" Category="kitchenware"></Item>
...
```

Fig. 1.2. Fragments of the XML schema XSD and XML data files for *ITEM*

We store all the data and metadata used in processing a query in a large table, called *Data Reference Table* (*DRT*), which is essentially a data pool. Figure 1.1 (right) exhibits an instance of *DRT*, built for a query on *SALES* and *ITEMS*. There is a tuple in *DRT* for each component of a data from the sources used in processing the query. For example, consider tuple 1 from *SALES* table in Figure 1.1. For each value in row 1, there is a unique tuple in *DRT*. Here we have *StoreID* as a column name having value 2 at row 1. To support lineage tracing, we apply the transformation functions to *DRT* to identify the data components, which contributed to the answer.

1.2 Our Contributions

There are many works on lineage tracing in the context of data warehouse systems [4]. The point here is that all the schema information and the data itself is available to the query processor of the database management system. In a mediator-based system, on the other hand, data has to be retrieved from the sources query processing. This makes query processing more complicated in mediator-based systems than data warehouse systems. In addition, data contributed to a query answer must be identical to the data used for lineage tracing. This latter requirement is more challenging since the data might not even be available when a user requests the system for an explanation. Moreover, in case of an update of data and/or schema in the sources, lineage tracing may not be possible unless the data and/or schema involved in answering the query is somehow captured in the first place. This should be done with care; otherwise lineage tracing may not be infeasible. For instance, a solution might require storing atomic data with the mediator, which is against the philosophy of the mediator approach. Query processing in a mediator-based approach in general requires dealing with several (possibly heterogeneous) data sources. These are all challenging issues for query processing in general and lineage tracing, in particular. Our goal has been to study different influential parameters, which resulted in the development of the current framework for lineage tracing in mediator-based data integration systems. Our focus in this work is not on data and schema integration problems, but rather assumed they are resolved and have been dealt.

The rest of this paper is organized as follows. Section 2 provides a review of related work. In section 3, we study ways to collect and store schema information from the integrated system – an essential step for lineage tracing. We use relation as the uniform model to store the collected structured and semi-structured schema information. Constraints on this modeling are discussed in [15]. In section 4, we investigate query processing and lineage tracing in the context of our proposed framework. Section 5 introduces a prototype system and reports its design features and performance evaluations. Concluding remarks and future directions are provided in section 6.

2   Related Work

In a mediator-based system, data can be analyzed for decision support systems. For business data, it is useful to provide explanation for a query result, by identifying the data in the sources contributed to the result. This process, tracing data from query answer back to the data sources and finding contributing atomic data is known as lineage tracing [4]. It is useful in many areas including: On-line data analysis processing and mining (OLAP/OLAM), scientific databases, data cleaning, authorization management, and view update problem.

In general to do the lineage tracing, we need to have the metadata, original data, and query information itself. Lineage tracing is a combination of information about atomic data structure, data transformation and a number of functions. Consider the motivating example for the sales application. We assumes that the unified repository for the system has already been created, so we can submit a query using a SQL like language and make a join between two data sources. Consider the following query:

```
Select SUM (NumSold) From SALES, ITEM
Where  SALES.ItemID = ITEM.ItemID and ItemName = 'pencil';
```

The query result is 5000 and the lineage tracing answer is shown in Figure 2.1.

StoreID	ItemID	NumSold	Price
2	2	2000	2
1	2	3000	1

ItemID	ItemName	Category
2	Pencil	stationary

Fig. 2.1. Tuples traced in *SALES* (left) and *ITEM* data sources (right)

2.1 Lineage Tracing for General Data Warehouse Transformations

This paper proposes a complete set of techniques and algorithms to retrieve original data contributed to a query answer in data warehouse systems using *fine-grained* approach, prepared by Cui and Widom [4]. Their solution focus on transformation functions, which transforms a set of input data to the output set. These functions satisfy some properties, listed below together with their applications.

1) Dispatcher: Each input data item to *dispatcher* produces zero or more output data item.
2) Filter: Each input data item to *filter* produces itself or nothing.
3) Aggregator: Each input data item is a part of the input partition including zero or more other input data items. This partition of input data items to *aggregator* produces one output data item.
4) Context-free aggregator: Any two input data items are always in a same input partition or always not.
5) Key-preserving aggregator: This property is like the aggregator, which exist a unique key for each input data item and in an input partition every subset of that partition generates the same output key for the output item.
6) Black-Box: This is neither an aggregator nor a dispatcher.
7) Inverse: A transformation T is *invertible* if there exists a transformation T^{-1} such that for each input set I, we have $T^{-1}(T(I)) = I$, and for every output set O, $T(T^{-1}(O)) = O$.

There are also some techniques such as schema mapping to transfer an input set to an output set. The result might be an intermediate set which is supposed to be used by the upcoming transformations. They present indexing as an improvement technique. There are two levels of indexing:

1) Conventional: locate data items matching a given value.
2) Functional: they are constructed for a given function F and allow us to quickly locate data items i such that $F(i) = V$ for a value V. This type of indexing is used by schema mapping functions.

Based on the input query, transformations can be combined or decomposed. There is a transformation sequence consideration to combine or decompose them. Having a sequence or order for transformation depends on each transformation itself. They proposed a set of algorithms to classify and combine transformations in an efficient way. Transformations can be done in multiple-input multiple-output way. They are all *stable* and *deterministic*. A transformation T is stable if it never produces spurious output items, i.e., $T(null) = null$. A transformation is deterministic if it always produces the same output set given the same input set. They also proposed a prototype in order to prove their solution. There are some works in the prototype to improve the efficiency. Those works show that there is a big improvement in case of indexing and combining transformations.

2.2 Tracing Data Lineage Using Schema Transformation Pathways

In this work, we define lineage tracing based on the notions *why-provenance* and *where-provenance* proposed by H. Fan and A. Poulovassilis [8]. The former refers to the source data used in processing the query without actually appearing in the query result. On the other hand, *where-provenance* refers to the actual source data that appears in the query result. Corresponding to these two types of data, they introduce two internal data structures, called *affect-pool* and *origin-pool*. They work on high-level data models, e.g., ER, OO, and relational model, as well as physical data structures. They developed a prototype, called AutoMed, which is based on a lower level data model, HDM, and define high level data models and schema transformation in HDM. They used this common data model to prevent semantic mismatch between models and metadata from different sources. This data model is similar to the internal representation in our work for creating and updating metadata information in ELIT. The authors also describe how transformation functions affect their two different data pools, called data pool and origin pool. Our *IMDS* and *DRT* tables in ELIT used are similar in sprit to their pools. The difference is in the organization. In our work, *IMDS* stores only metadata and *DRT* stores data, while this distinction is not there in [8]. In AutoMed, there are some sort of automatically reversible transformation functions to keep track of each change, which might happen to the input data set. AutoMed provides an Intermediate Query Language (IQL) to issue queries over the data sources and models.

2.3 Mapping XML and Relational Schemas Using CLIO

In this work, we use the ideas proposed in CLIO engine by Popa et. al [15] in order to map XML data sources to relational schemas. This engine has interesting features such as supporting mappings in any direction and for any combination of relational and XML schemas. It also considers constraints on source and target data. They have also proposed mapping algorithms for CLIO and established their correctness. CLIO also provides a GUI for users to browse and select appropriate interpretation. Our system prototype includes a similar GUI to browse the metadata in order to facilitate formulation of queries over the integrated schema.

3 Collecting Schema Information

Having access to metadata is essential for lineage tracing. In this phase we collect information about the schemas of the sources in the system. This information is independent of any particular user query. The assumption, however, is that the user may require an explanation, for which we have this phase to prepare. As there is no global repository maintained by the mediator, we create such a data pool during the set up of the system. Collecting schema information requires schema-mapping functions. The mapping could be complex especially when the existing data sources are of different data models. This mapping is different from schema mapping for the intermediate sets discussed in the context of data warehouse systems [4]. In *ELIT*, we support two different types of schemas: structured (relations) and semi-structured (XML). Schema mapping in this level contains information about the data sources and their individual data items used by the system. Intermediate data sets or results are those created by the transformation functions. It is required to have intermediate data sets in order to be able to retrieve the next data in a sequence of application of transformation functions. For this to be correct, intermediate results should be collected as *bags,* since lineage tracing has to identify all the data contributing to a query result. For example, consider the following user query:

```
Select   STORE.StoreName, SUM(SALES.NumSold * SALES.Price)
From     STORES, SALES, ITEMS
Where    ITEM.Category  = 'sanitary' And
         ITEM.ItemID    = SALES.ItemID And
         STORES.StoreID = SALES.StoreID
Group By STORE.StoreName;
```

Suppose the user is interested to know the contributing data in relation STORES. The first step is to produce the ItemID's used which are in "sanitary" category. This data may include duplicates since there could be several stores having the same product. At this point, the bag semantic should be used in order to avoid missing data. We then retrieve the data from Store and return the result to the user.

Intermediate results are useful for being consistent in producing the original data in case there is an update. They would be also helpful to provide a feature to the user to perform selective lineage tracing so that the user can specify which intermediate data set is of interested.

A mediator-based system may consist of several heterogeneous data sources [11]. In order to have the metadata of various data models and to be able to process queries using them, we need to have an *Integrated Metadata Schema* (*IMDS*) [12,6]. To create *IMDS,* some schema mapping is required [4]. This integrated schema allows us to (1) formulate a query referring to both structured and semi-structured data in such environment, and (2) to support lineage tracing as discussed earlier. The *IMDS* supports the former by providing some query components. It also supports the latter by providing specifications of the transformation functions required. The first application of *IMDS* is discussed in sections 4.1 to 4.5, and the second is explained in section 4.6. In addition to these applications, *IMDS* also reduces the processing overhead. This is because *IMDS* contains the necessary metadata information, used by existing user queries. This results in significant saving on references to metadata by the lineage tracing process. Since *IMDS* is created for lineage tracing, it is not a large repository with all the metadata in the network. Query evaluation is done based on the integrated schema model. At this point, schema update is a potential problem. Also, we assume the schema of data does not change while query processing. This is a reasonable assumption upon noting that such changes are not frequent. Updating metadata information is a responsibility of the system administrator usually done based on some predetermined schedule.

In order to support these functionalities, we naturally assume that information sources are cooperative in the sense that the mediator has access to the actual information sources. There are different approaches to define sources in information integration systems, including *GAV, LAV,* and *GLAV* [7]. While these approaches support query processing and extracting data, they are not sufficient for lineage tracing, as we need to have access to atomic data items. In what follows, we introduce a set of functions to extract metadata of the data sources, including table names, column names, types of data sources, and to store and manage this information as part of the *IMDS*. Note that there will be at most one tuple in this data pool of the form $(\mathcal{R}, \mathcal{T}, \mathcal{S})$ even if there is more than one user query that uses the data source $\mathcal{R}$ (a table or a XML data source) from source $\mathcal{S}$.

1. **add_Relation**($\mathcal{R}, \mathcal{T}, \mathcal{S}$): adds to the *IMDS* a new relation $\mathcal{R}$ with type $\mathcal{T}$.
2. **delete_Relation**($\mathcal{R}, \mathcal{T}, \mathcal{S}$): deletes from *IMDS* the definition of $\mathcal{R}$ which is of type $\mathcal{T}$.

3. **add_Column**($\mathcal{R}$, $\mathcal{COL}$): adds to the *IMDS* a new column definition $\mathcal{COL}$ in relation $\mathcal{R}$.

4. **delete_Column**($\mathcal{R}$, $\mathcal{COL}$): deletes from the *IMDS* the definition of $\mathcal{COL}$ in relation $\mathcal{R}$.

We next introduce an algorithm to collect the schema information. Assume there are k nodes in the system, called N = (N_1, ..., N_k), where node N_i includes m data sources D_1, ..., D_m such that each D_j is a data source which may be used in a user query. We assume that data sources at each node are unique, which the same data source D_j (with the same schema) may be used in different nodes. So in order to have all the metadata information of all data sources, the input set D has to be changed into D^k, (i.e.) having all data sources from *k* nodes in the system. The output T = (T_1,..., T_n) is a list of tables stored in the internal data structure, *IMDS*, where n = k × m. XML metadata collection algorithm, retrieves the information from an XSD file. Let X = (X_1,..., X_n) be the input XSD files and W = (W_1,..., W_m) be all the individual words in an XSD files. To collect all the words in all XSD files we use W^k.

Input: D^k, N   /* The set of data sources involved */
 Output: T   /* The IMDS – the metadata of D*/
 Algorithm: *Collecting Schema Info. Relational*
 For each N_i in N where i in [1..k]
  For each D_j in D^i where j in [1..m].
  Get the metadata information accessible by mediator
  Create T_i if there is no such information in *IMDS*.
 Return.
	Input: X, W^k /* The set of XML sources*/
	 Output: T = (T_1,..., T_n) /* The *IMDS* */
	 Algorithm: *Collecting Schema Info. XML*
	 For each X_i in X where i in [1..n]
	  For each W_j in W^i where j in [1..m].
	  Based on each identified word property
	  create T_i if there is no such information in *IMDS*.
	 Return.

4 Query Formulations and Processing

This includes query formulation, processing, and lineage tracing functions. In other words, it requires building the query, parsing, running, and then tracing its execution. As mentioned earlier, this process requires that the information about the actual sources be available to the mediator. In case a local source is a view over the actual data, lineage tracing may be incomplete. Having metadata information allows users to formulate desired queries, and to support lineage tracing. Having an integrated data model, *IMDS*, helps user use a unified query language to retrieve data from different types of data sources. This query can be mapped to the query language used by the data source involved, through the wrapper level and be evaluated over that source.

4.1 Query Building-Visual Frame Based

In this section, a query building interface will be introduced to simplify data access to heterogeneous data sources [13]. Query execution over a mediator-based system may require retrieving data from different data sources with different schema types and structures [3]. This query might involve structured and semi-structured schemas. In the previous section, we introduced *IMDS* and four mapping functions from one schema to another. We propose a frame-based query interface, using which a user can formulate the queries in a visual environment. Because of the unified schema mapping accessible to the mediator, user can execute a query having structured format but using both structured and semi structured schemas to retrieve the actual data and to produce the answer to support the lineage tracing. This query tool generates a "SQL like" statement, which can then be executed over the mediator-based system. It also facilitates formulation of queries by non-expert users. Also such an interface is useful to get query components, which are essential in our context for tracing. Details are discussed in section 4.4.

4.2 Query Type

Different query types can be executed in a mediator-based system. So for lineage tracing, a system should be able to provide query explanation with different query types. There are different query types, which can be run by the user. These types transfer an input data set to the same or different output data set. There would be some different tracing procedures based on the query types [4]. We proposed a general lineage tracing function to support different query types. *Query components* are that kind of information which is required to implement lineage tracing process. We assumed that a query having a sub query can be rewritten as a simple query without any sub queries producing the same output. Sub queries can be considered as a new data set, which can be joined to the parent query. Following examples illustrated our assumption and solution for that:

Original query:
`Select SUM(NumSold) From SALES`
`Where ItemID in( select ItemID`
`    From ITEM Where ItemName='pencil');`
	Rewritten query:
	`Select SUM(NumSold) From SALES, ITEM`
	`Where SALES.ItemID = ITEM.ItemID And`
	`    ItemName = 'pencil';`

Original query:
`Select  SUM(NumSold)  From  SALES,  ITEM`
`Where SALES.ItemID = TEM.ItemID And`
`    ItemID in (1, 2);`
	Rewritten query:
	`Select SUM(NumSold) From SALES, ITEM`
	`Where SALES.ItemID = TEM.ItemID And`
	`    (ItemID = 1 Or ItemID = 2);`

In this paper, we consider SQL queries of SELECT-PROJECT-JOIN (SPJ), possibly with aggregation, but without recursion. The current version of our system prototype supports query conditions for 'And' and 'Or' operators, using which we can simulate set operations and sub-queries.

4.3 Query Parsing

Mediator-based systems are responsible to process the queries. This includes retrieve, combine, and enrich the data using a query language. There are several types of data sources in a network and a query can request data from all of them. Therefore, efficient query processing is one of the important mediator functionalities. The first step of query processing is query parsing. The second one is query evaluation. We will discuss the query evaluation in section 4.6. Query parsing checks the input query if it is syntactically correct. To do that, it uses a parser tree. At this point we need to have the metadata information, which is physically defined in the system. For this implementation it can be done by *IMDS* as described before. Query parsing and analysis is needed before dispatching sub queries over the network. In case of an invalid query, failing to recognize this would result in waste of resources in the system. For query evaluation, we would perhaps need to apply query rewriting and query optimization before dispatching the query, in order to reduce network utilization and increase the efficiency of lineage tracing processes [16,5].

4.4 Query Components

To support lineage tracing, we need some transformation functions [4,14,1]. The role of these functions is to help users identify the data contributed to the query result. Let T be a transformation function with a set S of input data values. The output of T would be a "subset" R of S. Note that R could be S, a modified subset of S, or empty. Intuitively, this is used when applying the various conditions in the Where clause, each of which may result in filtering out tuples which do not contribute to the result. To support lineage tracing, we can view T in the reverse direction as explained before. Having such functions helps providing query explanation. To see how, let us consider the functions in Figure 4.1. Transformation function T_1 has the input set S and the output S_1, T_2 has the input set S_1 and the output set S_2, and finally T_3 has S_2 as the input and R as its output. To determine the atomic data, it suffices to apply each condition to *DRT* and find the result. To have the result of each step, however, the transformation functions must be applied in the *reverses* direction and we need the intermediate results. For example, to determine the atomic data contributed to R after applying T_3, we can obtain S_2 by applying T_3^{-1} to R.

Fig. 4.1. Sequence of applying the transformation functions

Transformation functions for a query are created whenever a valid query is dispatched over the network. Each clause in the query transfers the collection of input data from one stage to another. Each clause e.g., Where, Group BY, HAVING, etc. may transfer an input set to another. To do linage tracing in an efficient way, transformation functions must be applied in some particular order. Some of these functions reduce the output size and hence it would be better to apply such functions first. The following functions are introduced to extract and store data components:

1. **add_query** (Q, P): adds to the *IDMS* the query Q with a unique ID P.
2. **delete_query** (Q, P): deletes from the *IMDS* query Q with a unique ID P.
3. **add_tables**(Q, TL): adds the list of contributed tables TL to the *IMDS* used in query Q.
4. **delete_table**(Q, TL): deletes the list of contributed tables TL from the *IMDS* used in query Q.
5. **add_column**(Q, COL): adds the list of contributed columns COL to the *IMDS* used in query Q.
6. **delete_column**(Q,COL): deletes list of contributed columns COL from *IMDS* used in query Q.
7. **add_condition**(Q, CND, $CNDT$, CT): adds to *IMDS*, the list of conditions CND (in the Where, Group By, or Having) with type $CNDT$ in Q using connectives of type CT(i.e., And, Or, Not).
8. **delete_condition**(Q, CND): deletes from the *IMDS*, the list of conditions CND used in query Q.

The following example illustrates how these functions maybe used when processing a user query. Suppose Q1 below is a query submitted to the system from node P1:

```
Select SALES.Price, SALES.NumSold
From ITEM, SALES
Where SALES.ItemID = ITEM.ItemID And ITEM.Category = 'stationary';
```

Lineage tracing functions below are then applied to *IMDS*, in the order shown by the first column followed by the second.

add_query (Q1, P1),
add_table (Q1, ''ITEM', 'SALES''),
add_column (Q1, 'SALES.Price'),
add_column (Q1, 'SALES.NumSold'),
add_condition (Q1, 'SALES.ItemID=ITEM.ItemID', 'Where', 'And'),
add_condition (Q1, 'SALES.Category='stationary''', 'Where', 'And'),

To free the resources after lineage tracing terminates, we apply the following functions:

delete_query (Q1, P1).
delete_table(Q1, ''ITEM', 'SALES'').
delete_column (Q1, 'SALES.Price').
delete_column(Q1, 'SALES.NumSold').
delete_condition (Q1, 'SALES.ItemID=ITEM.ItemID').
delete_condition(Q1, 'SALES.Category = 'Stationary'').

Input: Q (COL, T, CON)
Output: COMP   /* Query Component */
Algorithm: Collecting Query Component
1. Find all tales T_j, where j is in [1..n]
2. Find all pair of (COL_i, F_i), where i is in [1..m]
3. Match columns and tables using the information in *IMDS*.
4. Find all conditions CON_p, where p is in [1..k]
5. Store the information in the internal data structure.
Return.

Let Q be a query with COL = $((COL_1, F_1),....,(COL_m, F_m))$ as selected columns used in Q, and F be the formula applied to these columns. T is a list of data sources referenced by Q, where T = $(T_1, ...,T_n)$. The query may have some other components, to which we refer as CON, such as WHERE, GROUP BY, and HAVING. These components may change an input set to another set while processing Q. The format of CON would be $((CON_1, CONT_1),...,(CON_k, CONT_k))$, where $CONT_i$ is the type of condition CON_i. The output is a set of query components, called COMP, stored in the internal data structure of the system.

4.5 Query Evaluation

The SQL-like user query must be mapped to the real data retrieving each schema structure in the mediator-based system. There are several algorithms for implementing each query operator. Also there is no specific algorithm for a selected operator, it depends on the efficiency plan which we expect to have while running the query. Some data factors like relation size; design specifications like existing indexes and even hardware specifications such as memory size have to be considered to implement the operations. In a mediator-based system query evaluation has to be done for several heterogeneous databases. It can be done by the mediator or by the wrapper. Again, in this case, we need to know the physical data schema of the sources and the schema types. It can be done by *IMDS*, however to do it in a more efficient way, information about physical storage, indexes, partitions and more is needed. The mediator can have this information in the integrated schema, and hence it can execute the query and retrieve the result, which are then sent back to the requester.

4.6 Lineage Tracing

We defined *Data Reference Table (DRT)*, which is a physical storage to store all data values obtained from data sources while processing a query. Because at the processing time, it is not clear which particular data items will contribute to the answer, we need to collect from data sources, all the data involved in processing the query. This strategy reduces the risk of reading invalid data contributed to the query answer if the data is updated soon after query execution. The *DRT* structure was introduced in section 1.1. Having data and metadata stored in *DRT* enables the system to provide intermediate results and also an additional option for the user to perform (or not to perform) lineage tracing. This is similar to the "Explain" feature of *Coral*, by which a user instructs the system to provide explanation [2]. Wishing to do so requires user to switch on the tracing feature at run time before submitting a query. For lineage tracing, we collect "enough" data and metadata information to which we only need to apply the transformation functions, defined earlier. For lineage tracing, we have the following functions:

1. **add_data**(Q, T, C, V): adds data to *DRT* for query Q, table T, column C, and value V.
2. **delete_data**(Q, T, C, V): deletes data from *DRT* for Q, table T, column C, and value V.
3. **apply_condition** (T, C, CND): applies condition CND to table T for column C based on the condition CND, and deletes each tuple that is not satisfied.
4. **explain_query** (Q, TL, CL, V): generates the query explanation for query Q based on its table list TL and column list CL having value V.

Input: = {T_1,…, T_n} Output: DRT Algorithm: AddData 1.Find T_i from *IMDS* for i in [1..n] 2.Get data from D_i={A1,…,Am} in T_i 3.For each COL_i^j in D_i, create a tuple with appropriate tuple id for D_i where j in [1..m]. Return.	Input: DRT, COMP Output: O (D, COL,V) Algorithm: applyCondition 1.Find all one side conditions in COMP, called OS_i, i in [1..h] 2. Apply OS_i to the *DRT* and delete those tuples in *DRT* that do not satisfy the condition OS_i. 3. Find all two side conditions in COMP called TS_i, i in [1..h] 4. Apply TS_j to the *DRT* and delete those tuples in *DRT* that do not satisfy the condition TS_i. 5. Repeat step 2 until no more tuple is deleted from *DRT*. 6. Create the output from the remaining tuples in *DRT*. Return.

The first step in lineage tracing is building the *DRT*. For this purpose, we need the information on the set of data source called T = (T_1,…, T_n) used by the query. T includes data source D_i, and data item COL_j^i, i.e., all necessary columns in each D_i. We also need the information on node N_i. All these information are stores in *IMDS*. *DRT* can be populated, while query is executing.

The inputs to the lineage tracing algorithm are *DRT*, COMP, and the query components. As mentioned above, COMP is of the form $((C_1,T_1), ..., (C_h,T_h))$. The output of lineage tracing is a set of tables together with the tuples contributed to the query answer. The output is of the form O (D, COL, V) where D is the data source, COL is the data item in D, V is its value, and, OS and TS denote one or two side conditions.

5 ELIT: A System Prototype

We have designed and implemented a prototype for lineage tracing in a mediator-based information integration system. We refer to this system prototype as *Explanation and LIneage Tracing* (**ELIT**). We require that the schema of each data source in the system be introduced to ELIT, being structured or semi-structured. This information is stored in the internal data structures of ELIT to support lineage tracing.

5.1 System Design

ELIT supports both structured and semi structured schema to do the lineage tracing. To allow semi-structured data, ELIT includes an XML parser [7]. Information in the XML file is stored in the internal data structures (*IMDS*) and it is going to be mapped as a relational table. In this case, all the information sources in the system would be treated as relational sources. ELIT has an interface for formulating and submitting queries. Once the input is prepared and submitted, ELIT generates a "SQL-like" query and this SQL like statement is then parsed for validity check. ELIT accepts query conditions with "And" and "Or." Any other types of conditions such as "In" and "Not In" for a predefined set or nested SQL statement is not currently supported in this simple prototype. They can be rewritten as a set of "And" and "Or" conditions. In the next step, after a query is parsed, a *DRT* is created (Figure 1.1 right). Regarding our example of SALES and ITEM, *DRT* would have *all* the SALES and ITEM information. It is required to get the *SALES* data from the original relational table and *ITEM* data from XML file, accessible for mediator, and store them in the *DRT*. This gives a table as shown in Figure 5.1 (left). The user can view the result of the query while data is being inserted into *DRT*.

All conditions in user query must be applied to the *DRT* and all the tuples, which do not satisfy the conditions, must be removed from *DRT*. This process can be done in two modes, *batch* and *interactive*. In the batch mode, the system does all the necessary steps for lineage tracing, in a pre-determined sequence of applications of lineage tracing functions. In the latter mode, the user may interact with the system to provide a step-by-step explanation, as desired, through the display interface. To do this, query conditions should be applied in some order as follows. First, it applies conditions of the form "A θ v", if present, where A is an attribute, v is a value, and θ is a comparison operator. We call this as "one-side-condition." Next, it considers applying conditions of the form "A θ B", which we call as "two-side-condition." Intuitively, this order results in increased efficiency by reducing the number of tuples involved in the join conditions (basically, two-side-condition). In our example, *ELIT* looks for a one-side-condition, which is ITEM.Category = 'stationary'. It then applies this condition to the *DRT* and finds 2 records with record number 1 and 2 from table *ITEM*, as

TableName	RecordNum	ColumnName	Value
SALES	1	StoreID	2
SALES	1	ItemID	1
SALES	1	NumSold	800
SALES	1	Price	5
....	...	...	...
SALES	10	StoreID	1
SALES	10	ItemID	2
SALES	10	NumSold	3000
SALES	10	Price	1
....	...	...	...
ITEM	1	ItemID	1
ITEM	1	ItemID	binder
ITEM	1	Category	Stationary
...	...	...	...
ITEM	5	ItemID	5
ITEM	5	ItemName	Pot
ITEM	5	Category	Kitchenware

Price	NumSold
5	800
2	2000
4	1000
1	3000

Fig. 5.1. *DRT* after inserting metadata and atomic data values (left) and Query result (right)

indicated under the column TableName in Figure 5.1 (left). All the tuples in *DRT* with tuple ID other than 1 or 2, and TableName = 'ITEM' are marked as deleted.

We next apply all the two-side-conditions to the remaining tuples in *DRT*. For instance, here we SALES.ItemID = ITEM.ItemID. Because of the effect of the one-side-condition, we only have values 1 and 2 in *DRT* for ItemID. Therefore, ELIT looks for tuples with TableName = 'SALES' and ItemID being 1 or 2. This identifies tuples 1, 2, 9, and 10, so tuples with numbers other than these with TableNaame = 'SALES' are marked as deleted. Figure 5.2 shows *DRT* after this step. As it can be seen, this has identified the atomic data for the query as well as details of the query answer.

Table Name	Record Num	ColumnName	Value
SALES	1	StoreID	2
SALES	1	ItemID	1
SALES	1	NumSold	800
SALES	1	Price	5
....	...	...	...
SALES	10	StoreID	1
SALES	10	ItemID	2
SALES	10	NumSold	3000
SALES	10	Price	1
....	...	...	...
ITEM	1	ItemID	1
ITEM	1	ItemName	Binder
ITEM	1	Category	Stationary
ITEM	2	ItemID	2
ITEM	2	ItemName	Pencil
ITEM	2	Category	Stationary

Table Name	Record Num	ColumnName	Value
SALES	1	StoreID	2
SALES	1	ItemID	1
SALES	1	NumSold	800
SALES	1	Price	5
....	...	...	...
SALES	10	STORE_ID	1
SALES	10	ItemID	2
SALES	10	NumSold	3000
SALES	10	Price	1
....	...	...	...
ITEM	1	ItemID	1
ITEM	1	ItemName	Binder
ITEM	1	Category	Stationary
ITEM	2	ItemID	2
ITEM	2	ItemName	Pencil
ITEM	2	Category	Stationary

Fig. 5.2. *DRT* after applying one-side-condition (left) and after applying two-side-condition (right)

This method can be applied to queries with aggregations as well. For this, we first need to find all the information from the table(s) to which we want apply the aggregations functions. We can then apply the processes of one-side and two-side conditions to identify all the atomic data relevant to the query.

5.2 Performance Evaluation

To assess our lineage tracing model, and evaluate the performance of the system prototype ELIT, we generated a range of data sets. Selecting specific columns and values makes the creation of *DRT* and lineage tracing more efficient.

	Tuples in SALES	Executing User Query	Creating DRT	Linage Tracing	Number of Records in *DRT*
FULL DRT – Non Optimized	1,000,000	2"	14 h	-	(3*5) +(4* 1000000) = 4000015
Partial DRT – Non Optimized	1,000,000	2"	10 ' 47"	11' 47"	(3*2) +(4* 100305) = 401226
Partial DRT –Optimized	1,000,000	2"	2'43"	40"	(3*2) +(4* 100305) = 401226
Partial DRT –Optimized(Using Rename)	100,000	1"	19"	5"	(3*2) +(4* 10019) = 40082
Partial DRT –Optimized(Using Rename)	1,000,000	2"	2' 43"	19"	(3*2) +(4* 100305) = 401226
Partial DRT –Optimized(Using Rename)	5,000,000	9"	22' 26"	2' 28"	(3*2) +(4* 1003050) = 4012206
Partial DRT –Optimized	10,000,000	20"	46' 15"	3'11"	(3*2) +(4* 501525) = 2006118

Fig. 5.3. Lineage tracing result

For example, in table SALES with 10^6 tuples, there are approximately 10^5 tuples with ItemID = 6. In this case, tuples related to other items are not of interest and hence ignored during this "preparation" for lineage tracing. These results in creation and management of what we call as *partial DRT*, as opposed to the complete one required in the batch mode of tracing. Figure 5.3 above, illustrates preliminary result of our performance evaluation of ELIT in supporting batch and interactive modes of lineage tracing. We have used four data sets of sizes 10^5 to 10^7 tuples, as shown in the figure. The size of the partial *DRT* for condition IetmID = 6 in the query, the complete *DRT*, as well as the corresponding query processing and lineage tracing times are provided in the table. The information in this figure indicates 14 hours to create *DRT* in a non-optimized processing for 1 million records can reduce to 46 minutes for 10^7 tuples, using the above basic "optimized" processing. For lineage tracing, the processing time ranges from 2.5 minutes to 5 seconds.

6 Concluding Remarks and Future Work

Lineage tracing is the problem of recording the history of query processing to provide users with explanation. In this work, we study this problem in a mediator-based information integration system. We illustrate the difficulties in this context and make a first attempt to address some of them. The basic idea in our proposed solution is to extract and store a pool of atomic data and metadata of information sources contributed to the query answer. We have defined and employed a number of functions together with the required algorithms to manage and manipulate the aforementioned pool to support lineage tracing. We have developed a system prototype, ELIT, which includes a number of user interfaces for "building" queries and "displaying" traces. In particular, users can formulate SQL-like queries over structured as well as semi-structured data sources through an "input query" interface. ELIT can trace summarized and aggregated data and find atomic data step-by-step as the query processing is in progress.

We are currently working on improving the efficiency of the ELIT. *DRT* is a large table, so more efficient storage management with suitable indexes is required to improve the efficiency. Another direction is to improve query rewriting technique in

ELIT to convert set definition in sub-queries into 'And' and 'Or' conditions. In the current version of ELIT, the input query interface does not need this option, however, to support lineage tracing in real application, we should allow any type of input queries. Another future direction for this work is to incorporate lineage tracing in distributed database systems. In our preliminary study of this issue, it seems to be more challenging as it requires changes in the internal structures and algorithms, most notably in the query processing and optimization components of distributed database systems. Some more details of this study can be found in [17].

References

1. Y. Arens, C. A. Knoblock, and W. Shen. *Query reformulation for dynamic information integration.* Journal of Intelligent Information Systems, 1996.
2. T. Arora, R. Ramakrishnan, W. G. Roth, P. Seshadri and D. Srivastava. *The CORAL deductive database system.* In Proc. 3rd Int'l Conference on Deductive and Object-Oriented Databases, 1993.
3. P. Buneman, S. Davidson, G. Hillebrand, and D. Suciu. *A query language and optimization techniques for unstructured data.* In Proc. of ACM SIGMOD, Pages 505–516, Montreal, Canada, June 1996.
4. Y. Cui and J. Widom. *Lineage tracing for general data warehouse transformations.* In Proc. of VLDB, 2001.
5. O. M. Duschka. *Query planning and optimization in information iIntegration.* December 1997.
6. A. Doan, P. Domings, and A. Y. Levy. *Learning source descriptions for data integration.* In Proc. Int'l Workshop on The Web and Databases (WebDB), 2000.
7. D. Draper, A. Y. Halevy, and D.S. Weld. *The Nimble XML data integration system.* In Proc. Int'l Conference on Data Engineering (ICDE), pages 155-160, 2001.
8. H. Fan and A. Poulovassilis. *Tracing data lineage using schema transformation pathways.* In Proc. Of Workshop on Knowledge Transformation for the Semantic Web, 2002.
9. H. Garcia-Molina, J. D. Ullman, and J. Widom. *Database systems: The complete book.* Prentice Hall,2001.
10. A. Halevy and C. Li. *Information integration research: Summary of NSF IDM workshop breakout session.* December 2003.
11. L. M. Haas, R. J. Miller, B. Niswonger, M. T. Roth, P. M. Schwarz, E. L. Wimmers. *Transforming heterogeneous data with database middleware: Beyond integration.* IEEE Data Eng. Bulletin, 1999.
12. A. Kementsietsidis M. A. Ren´ee J. Miller. *Mapping data in peer-to-peer systems: Semantics and Algorithmic Issues.* SIGMOD Conference, 325-336, 2003.
13. Katchaounov and T. Risch. *Interface capabilities for query processing in peer mediator system.* Uppsala university September 2003.
14. J. Widom and D. Quass. *On-line warehouse view maintenance.* In Proc. Int'l Conference on Management of Data, ACM SIGMOD, 1997.
15. L.Popa, M.A.Hernandez, Y. Velegrakis, R. J. Miller, F. Naumann, and H. Ho. *Mapping XML and relational schemas with CLIO.* Demo. ICDE, 2002.
16. Y. Papakonstantinou and V. Vassalos. *Query rewriting for semi-structured data.* In Proc. Int'l. Conf. on Management of Data, ACM SIGMOD, pages 455-466, 1999.
17. Ali Taghizadeh-Azari. *Supporting Lineage Tracing in Mediator-based Information Integration Systems.* Master thesis, Computer Science & Software Engineering, Concordia University, Montreal, Canada, February 2005.

Combining Sources of Evidence for Recognition of Relevant Passages in Texts*

Alexander Gelbukh[1,2], NamO Kang[1], and SangYong Han[1,**]

[1] Chung-Ang University, Korea
kang@archi.cse.cau.ac.kr, hansy@cau.ac.kr
[2] National Polytechnic Institute, Mexico
www.Gelbukh.com

Abstract. Automatically recognizing in large electronic texts short selfcontained passages relevant for a user query is necessary for fast and accurate information access to large text archives. Surprisingly, most search engines practically do not provide any help to the user in this tedious task, just presenting a list of whole documents supposedly containing the requested information. We show how different sources of evidence can be combined in order to assess the quality of different passages in a document and present the highest ranked ones to the user. Specifically, we take into account the relevance of a passage to the user query, structural integrity of the passage with respect to paragraphs and sections of the document, and topic integrity with respect to topic changes and topic threads in the text. Our experiments show that the results are promising.

1 Introduction

The huge amount of textual information available nowadays makes it impossible for a person to read all documents in order to find the information of intrest. Hence the necessity of development of automatic means for recognition of spots in the text carrying information corresponding to a given criterion.

Currently the most frequent approach to finding relevant information in large text collections is *document retrieval* [1, 17]. In response to a user query, a document retrieval system returns a list of documents (ranked by relevance) supposedly containing relevant information – somewhere in the text. This approach works perfectly when the documents are relatively small. However, when the documents contain more than several paragraphs, the user usually has to perform a second task: to search for the relevant information inside the text of the document. Surprisingly, current systems offer very little help in this task, which is in fact the bottleneck of the whole process.

Alternatives to document retrieval have been suggested for certain types of queries. One of such approaches is question answering [4, 6]. When the user is interested in a simple factoid question, e.g., *Who won the Nobel Peace Prize in 1992?*, returning a bunch of long documents is particularly inappropriate, being a much more meaningful reaction of the system just one phrase: *Rigoberta Menchú Tum* [6].

---

* Work done under partial support of the ITRI of Chung-Ang University, Korea, and for the first author, Korean Government (KIPA) and Mexican Government (SNI, CONACyT, The first author is currently on Sabbatical leave at Chung-Ang University.
** Corresponding author

F.F. Ramos et al. (Eds.): ISSADS 2005, LNCS 3563, pp. 283–290, 2005.
© Springer-Verlag Berlin Heidelberg 2005

However, for more complicated types of queries such an approach is not possible. For example, when the user needs to know the development of some sequence of events, e.g., *What was the history of the wars between England and France?*, or a detailed explanation on some topic, e.g., *What is the structure of an information retrieval system?*. Such information is often contained in very long documents: one can imagine, for example, a tractate on British history or a textbook on natural language processing. In this case the user would expect some help from the system to find the relevant piece of information in the long text.

An intermediate approach between full document retrieval and question answering is *passage retrieval* known also as *passage extraction*. Given a user query, a passage retrieval system returns a (ranked) list of text segments extracted from a long document (or a document collection) that contain the requested information.

In this paper we present a general architecture of a passage retrieval system and discuss the factors that contribute to assessment of passage quality and thus the ranking of retrieved passages.

The paper is organized as follows. In Section 2 we discuss our motivation and related work. In Section 3 we outline our approach and present the details on each of the sources of evidence for ranking the retrieved passages: scoring by relevance to the user query (Section 3.1) and by alignment of their boundaries to structural units of the text and to topic change points (Section 3.2). In Section 4 we present our experimental results, and in Section 5 draw conclusions and discuss possible future work.

2   Motivation and Related Work

Applications of Passage Retrieval

Most literature on passage extraction is devoted to three main applications: text comparison, summarization, and question answering.

A number of authors have noted that similarity in passages better reflects document similarity than traditional bag-of-word comparison methods. Indeed, if the same number of the same keywords is scattered across the whole text of one of the documents (and thus these keywords are unrelated to each other) but concentrated in specific places of the second one (and thus these words describe a common idea), the two documents are scarcely similar. Passage-level comparison has been suggested to solve this problem [5, 9]. The key idea is that short passages are extracted from each of the two documents, and the sets of these excerpts are compared. With this, only similar groupings of the words lead to high document similarity. Document similarity measure improved with passage extraction has been applied to document retrieval [5, 11], as well as to document clustering and classification tasks [10].

Other applications of passage extraction are related to spotting specific, or removing irrelevant, information in long texts. In text summarization, the passages extracted from the document can be combined in a kind of summary [13]. A problem in such task is that the passages must not overlap and in particular a passage cannot be a part of a longer passage. Other applications do not impose such constraints [6].

A task similar to passage extraction but with smaller pieces of text to be found is information extraction. In this task, simple patterns carrying specific information are to be detected in a large document collection or flow, usually to fill in a relational database. Full passage extraction techniques have been applied to detect the passages likely to contain the desired information, for their further processing [3].

A task where even smaller piece of information is to be found for a specific request is question answering, as discussed in Section 1. Similarly to information extraction, full passage extraction was applied to spot the relevant information in large texts [4, 6, 8].

However, as discussed in Section 1, our motivation is a direct application of passage extraction to the interactive information retrieval – a kind of question answering with questions implying some narrative (and not just a name or a number) as answer. Thus the extracted passages are to be directly presented to the user. This requires special attention to the quality of the passages, leading to the desiderata from Section 3.

Previous Work

Early passage extraction techniques concentrated on finding whole paragraphs or sections of a document most relevant to the user query [11]. They do not adapt themselves to the situation when the section or paragraph is too short or too long for a good passage.

Later, sliding windows of fixed length were used as candidates for passages [3, 8]. The research was concentrated on the selection of an optimal window size. Variable-size windows have been applied, too. However, no specific attention has been paid to check self-containedness of the passages, as described in Section 3.

The main issue in selecting the candidate windows is assessment of their quality (weighting). Traditionally, vector space model [1] is used to detect the passages relevant to a given query. Salton *et al.* [12] introduced the balance between global and local term weighting: the terms of the query that are used in many other documents (or passages) are less important, while the terms used many times in the current document (passage) are more important. We develop on this idea in Section 3.1.

Other cues on the importance of a text unit have been exploited. For example, a passage that is similar (in some measure of similarity, such as cosine measure of the vector space model) to many other paragraphs in the document, is more important [13]. This idea is quite similar to Google's PageRank algorithm [14]. Comparison using semantic units has been employed to improve the selection of important passages [9, 10]. While determining important paragraphs in a text is necessary for text summarization without customizing the summary for the given user query, it does not help much in finding passages relevant to the specific query, which might not coincide with the main topic of the document intended by its author – which is our goal in this paper.

3 The Algorithm

We consider the task of selecting passages that are likely answers to a user query, for subsequent presenting them to the user. For a piece of text to be a passage answering the question, it should:

- be relevant: contains relevant information, and
- be "a good passage" rather than a detached extract out of context.

To be as self-contained as possible, the passage should not imply information communicated in the previous part of the document; in particular, it should not refer to entities or develop on the ideas just introduces. We suggest that the passages more likely to be self-contained are those that correspond to

- structural units of the text, especially the beginning of structural units, and/or
- thematic threads in the text.

The general architecture of our approach is presented in Fig. 1. After some pre-processing of the text of the document, currently consisting mainly of stemming [16], candidate windows are generated. For our experiments we used all possible windows in a range of sizes (from 5 to 1000 words) as candidates; stricter criteria for candidate generation can be applied for sake of performance.

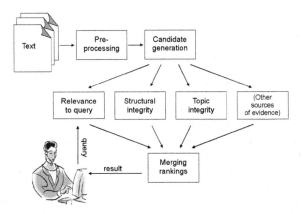

Fig. 1. The general architecture of the system.

Then each candidate window is assessed independently by its relevance to the query as well as by the criteria of self-containdess: structural and topic integrity; more assessment criteria might be added in the future. The scores assigned to a candidate window by each module are combined, and the highest scored passages are presented to the user, with the proper ranking. To combine the rankings we use multiplication; with this, the passages scored as irrelevant receive zero total score even if they are otherwise good (self-contained) passages.

Thus, we can prefer a good self-contained passage even over a more relevant but less understandable one. This does not mean that we hide relevant information from the user. Since our variable-size windows are overlapping, for a relevant but too short to be self-contained passage there usually exists a longer one containing it but properly aligned to the formal and thematic structure of the document. Its relevance score will be lower since the share of the relevant keywords in it is lower (among a greater amount of other words). However, it still presents to the user the same information, but with the necessary context added. Thus the main goal of our combined scoring is not to reject relevant passages but to extend them to be self-contained, i.e., to prefer whenever possible a slightly larger but self-contained passage.

In the following subsections we discuss each of the scoring blocks individually.

3.1 Assessing Relevance

To assess relevance, we use the classical techniques known in information retrieval. However, we take advantage of the general context of the document to performs certain disambiguation that helps matching the passage with the query.

Boolean and Vector Space Estimation

For the passages to more likely contain the full requested information, and also for sake of efficiency, we first apply Boolean selection of candidates: we only consider the windows that contain all the query terms except stopwords. This can be turned off if the returned set is too small. Then we order the retrieved set by the similarity with the query.

To compare a candidate window with a query, we use the traditional vector space similarity measure [1]. We represent both the passage and the query as vectors, being coordinates the frequencies of individual words. Then the similarity between the query q and a passage p is expressed as an angle between the two vectors in the Euclidean affine space:

$$sim(p,q) = \frac{\sum_i F_{p,i} F_{q,i}}{\sqrt{\sum_i F_{p,i}^2} \sqrt{\sum_i F_{q,i}^2}},$$

where $F_{p,i}$ and $F_{q,i}$ are the weighted frequencies of the term i in the passage and query, respectively: $F_{.,i} = w_i f_{.,i}$; the summation is by all terms occurring in the document. Here $f_{.,i}$ is the frequency of the term in the passage or query, and the meaning of the coefficients w_i is described in the following subsection.

Term Weighting in Context

We determine the importance weights w_i of individual terms combining the global context of the document collection (or language in general) with the local context of the given document. In document retrieval, the wellknown IDF weighting is used [1]: $w_i = \log (N/n_i)$, where N is the total number of documents in the collection and n_i is the number of documents containing the term i; when the large document is not a part of a collection, the figures from a general language corpus are used.

However, unlike in full document retrieval, a passage is in the linearly ordered immediate context of surrounding paragraphs. Firstly, they provide additional information on the passage that is not contained in it directly. This information is useful, for example, for word sense disambiguation and anaphora resolution. Secondly, some of the surrounding paragraphs are more closely related with the passage in question (being located nearer in the text) than others. Thus, we construct an IDF-like expression using the surrounding paragraphs. What is more, to reflect the closeness of the paragraph to the given passage, we scale the expression by a smooth function decreasing with the linear distance. Thus, we use the following expression:

$$w_i = \log\left(\frac{N}{n_i} + \sum_k e^{-a\left(\frac{d_i}{D}\right)^2} \frac{1}{n_{k,i}}\right),$$

where d_k is the distance in paragraphs from the given paragraph k to the passage in question, D is the maximal such distance in the document, $n_{k,i}$ is the number of occurrences of the term i in the paragraph k, and a is a coefficient which we determine empirically; we experimented with $a = 1$. The idea underlining decreasing of the weight of the words frequent in the document is that they are likely to express the general topic of the document already known to the user.

Additionally, we can modulate the weight of the query terms, thus controlling the desired size of the passages: the higher the weight of the query terms the longer the passages retrieved, since the noise words contribute less in the length of the vectors.

3.2 Assessing Structural and Topic Integrity

Structural Integrity
As we have discussed, "good" passages selected for presentation to the user, to be understandable should be, desirably, self-contained. We suggest that at the boundaries of the structural units of the document, such as paragraphs, sections, and chapters, the passages are less likely to develop on the ideas introduced previously or to require further explanations in the following text. Thus, we boost (score higher) those passages that begin at the structural boundaries of the document, and (in a smaller degree) those that end at such boundaries. In our experiments, the structural integrity module in Fig. 1 assigns the score 1.0 to every candidate window, and then increments it by the following values found empirically (further research is necessary to tune these values):

Boundary	Beginning of passage	End of passage
Paragraph	0.2	0.1
Section	1.0	0.3
Chapter	2.0	0.5

Topic Integrity
Structural boundaries do not always correspond to the topic changes in the text: for example, a group of paragraphs can comprise a topic thread, while some long paragraphs contain more than one topic thread [2]. For each candidate window, we estimate the strength of the topic change at its boundaries in the way much like area boundaries are detected in images: by the degree of difference between the points (in our case, words) to the left and to the right of the boundary and the degree of similarity of the points at the same side of the suspected boundary. We rely on the notion of *word relatedness* (similar to color similarity in image processing): some words are known to be related more than others, e.g., *galaxy* and *astronomer* are more related than *galaxy* and *baker*. Several word relatedness measures have been suggested [7, 15]. We use the following formula:

$$S = S(b) + 0.3 S(e), \quad S(x) = \frac{\displaystyle\sum_{i<j<x \,\vee\, x<i<j} e^{-a(x-i)^2} e^{-a(x-j)^2} R(i,j)}{1 + \displaystyle\sum_{i<x<j} e^{-a(x-i)^2} e^{-a(x-j)^2} R(i,j)},$$

where S is the topical integrity score of the window, b is the position of the beginning of the window, e of the end, $R(i,j)$ is the relatedness of the words i and j, and a is a coefficient; we experimented with $a = 0.05$. Note that proper alignment of the beginning of the passage is more important than that of the end.

4 Experimental Results

We have implemented our method in a system that given a long text and a user query, presents a list of passages that are likely to contain the requested information. For preprocessing, we only applied Porter stemmer [16]. We used low weight for the query terms to get short passages, to be able to present them in the paper. Only passages consisting of complete sentences were considered. The top three passages returned by the system for the query "wars between England and France" on the text of *A Child's History of England* by Charles Dickens, 164,772 words, are as follows:

Rank	Score	Passage
1	0.49	*The Queen's husband who was now mostly abroad in his own dominions and generally made a coarse jest of her to his more familiar courtiers was at war with France and came over to seek the assistance of England. England was very unwilling to engage in a French war for his sake but it happened that the King of France at this very time aided a descent upon the English coast.*
2	0.48	*As his one merry head might have been far from safe if these things had been known they were kept very quiet and war was declared by France and England against the Dutch.*
3	0.46	Same as 1 plus the continuation: *Hence war was declared greatly to Philip's satisfaction and the Queen raised a sum of money with which to carry it on by every unjustifiable means in her power.*

As one can see, the lack of semantic processing (ignoring the word *between* in the query) results in some passages in fact unrelated to the query, like the second passage in the table. Elements of meaning understanding can be a topic of future work.

5 Conclusions and Future Work

We have presented a method of retrieving passages suitable for presenting them to a human user. We were mostly interested in self-contaidness of the extracted passages, which should improve their understandability. This aspect is specific for passage retrieval intended for human users, as compared with full document retrieval or passage extraction for automatic use, as described in Section 2. Our first results are promising.

In the future we plan to investigate the possibility of combining the retrieved passages in a summary of the document customized for the given query. One of the additional scoring sources in Fig. 1 will penalize the candidates with pronouns in the initial part of the window, since such windows are likely not self-contained. We also plan to further exploit the context of the passage within the document for word sense disambiguation and anaphora resolution, which is not very important – and not easy – in full document retrieval but is necessary in passage retrieval. Finally, we will consider merging the passages extracted from different documents; here the term weights (1) should be adjusted to be comparable between documents.

References

1. R. Baeza-Yates, B. Ribeiro-Neto. *Modern Information Retrieval*. Addison Wesley, 1999.
2. I. A. Bolshakov, A. Gelbukh. Text segmentation into paragraphs based on local text cohesion. *Text, Speech and Dialogue* (TSD-2001), Lecture Notes in Artificial Intelligence N 2166, Springer, 2001, pp. 158–166.
3. C. Cardie. Empirical Methods in Information Extraction. *AI Magazine*, 18:4, 65_79 1997.
4. C. L. A. Clarke, G. V. Cormack, T. R. Lynam, E. L. Terra. Question Answering by Passage Selection. In *Advances in Open Domain Question Answering*, Kluwer, 2004.
5. G. V. Cormack, C. L. A. Clarke, C. R. Palmer, S. S. L. To. Passage-Based Query Refinement. *Information Processing and Management*, 36(1):133-153, 2000.
6. A. Del-Castillo-Escobedo, M. Montes-y-Gómez, L. Villaseñor-Pineda. QA on the Web: A Preliminary Study for Spanish Language. *Proc. of ENC-2004*, IEEE, 2004.
7. G. Hirst, D. St-Onge. Lexical chains as representations of context for the detection and correction of malapropisms. In: C. Fellbaum (Ed.), *WordNet: An electronic lexical database*, Cambridge, MA: The MIT Press, 1998.
8. F. LLopis, J. L. Vicedo, A. Ferrández. Passage Selection to Improve Question Answering. In: *Multilingual Summarization and Question Answering* (COLING-2002), 2002.
9. H. Mochizuki, M. Iwayama, M. Okumura, Passage-Level Document Retrieval Using Lexical Chains, RIAO 2000, pp. 491-506.
10. Y. Nakao. A Method for Related-passage Extraction based on Thematic Hierarchy. *IPSJ Transactions on Databases* 42 (SIG 10 (TOD 11)), 2001, pp. 39–53.
11. G. Salton, J. Allan, C. Buckley. Approaches to passage retrieval in full text information systems. In: 16th annual international ACM SIGIR conf. on Research and development in information retrieval, US, 1993, 49–58.
12. G. Salton, and C. Buckley. Term weighting approaches in automatic text retrieval. *Information Processing and Management*, 24(5):513–523, 1988.
13. G. Salton, A. Singhal, M. Mitra, C. Buckley. Automatic text structuring and summarization. Mani, I., Maybury, M. (Eds), Advances in automatic text summarization. MIT, 1999.
14. L. Page and S. Brin. The anatomy of a large-scale hypertextual web search engine. Proc. 7th Intl. WWW Conf., 107-117, 1998.
15. S. Patwardhan, S. Banerjee, T. Pedersen. Using Measures of Semantic Relatedness for Word Sense Disambiguation. A. Gelbukh (Ed.), Computational Linguistics and Intelligent Text Processing (CICLing-2003), Lecture Notes in Computer Science N 2588, Springer, 2003, p. 241–257.
16. M.F.Porter. An algorithm for suffix stripping. *Program*, **14** no. 3, pp 130-137, July 1980.
17. T. Strzalkowski (Ed.). Natural Language Information Retrieval. Kluwer, 1999.

A Hierarchical and by Role Multi-agent Organization: Application to the Information Retrieval

Emmanuel Adam and René Mandiau

LAMIH UMR CNRS 8530, University of Valenciennes
Le Mont Houy, 59313 Valenciennes Cedex 9, France
{emmanuel.adam,rene.mandiau}@univ-valenciennes.fr

Abstract. Web retrieval becomes more and more important for the knowledge management area, and we think that multi-agent systems are a good answer to this problem. We propose, in this paper, a centralized Information multi-agent system to help actors of technological watch cells (called CIMASTEWA). This system is an evolution of a previous project and is set-up within a n-tiers architecture, which follows the STRUTS framework. This information multiagent system that has been developed to answer to demands from technological watch cells (for example, to securitize the search, notably concerning the survey by spies, we have proposed particular search strategies).

1 Introduction

In a context of globalisation of the economy and of serious modifications in socioeconomic structures, the technical and administrative processes, which underlie the activities of a Company, are, in particular, subjects of considerable revision. Documents on paper, exchanged from hand to hand have progressively been replaced by electronic documents transmitted automatically by machines without taking the human factors, such as the notion of the group (the individuals are isolated at their work post), the levels of responsibility or even man-machine co-operation into account. Admittedly, tools for aid in co-operative work have already been suggested, some with success, but they do not tackle the overall organisation.

This fact is the base of our works. Indeed, our researches aim at set up an information management assistance system in watch cells or in laboratories. In order to take into account the human factors, such as the human cooperation or even the human-machine co-operation, we have previously developed a method (AMOMCASYS, meaning the Adaptable Modelling Method for Complex Administrative Systems) that has helped us to design and to set-up an information multi-agent systems accessible by each actor of a technological watch team [1]. We call this system a CIMASTEWA (for Centralized IMAS for TEchnological WAtch).

This paper describes firstly the underlying concept of our works, which is the holonic concept. Then, the design of the centralised IMAS, which is an extension of a previous project [2], is shown in our classical two steps: a step for the individual characterization of the agents; and a step for the design of the agents' cooperative working. Finally, this article presents some details about the build of the CIMASTEWA.

F.F. Ramos et al. (Eds.): ISSADS 2005, LNCS 3563, pp. 291–300, 2005.

2 Human Organisation Modelling

2.1 Holonic Principles

In our works, we use holonic principles (defined by Koestler [3]) in order to understand the working mechanisms of the human organisations, in which we plan to set up information multi-agent systems, and to design the multi-agents organisations.

Agents of holonic system are organized following levels of responsibility. So, a holonic multi-agent system has a hierarchical structure where each agent is responsible of a sub-holonic multi-agent system.

We have used the social rules defined in the holonic concept in order to simplify and to accelerate the design of a multi-agent society (in the [4] sense) because they provide a framework to build a fixed multi-agent society (which does not imply rigidity).

Indeed, the hierarchical structure is not sufficient to model modern organisations and bureaucracies: "the degradation of hierarchy is a necessity for organisation to prosper" [5]; the organisations are, or have to be, flexible, more decentralised, based on roles.

We find these requirements in the area of the intelligent manufacturing system, where new concepts have been proposed such as:

- the bionic manufacturing systems [6], where the organisation is seen as an organ composed of cells (called modelon), which can be merged or divided into units,
- the holonic manufacturing systems [7], based on the holonic concept,
- and more recently the fractal manufacturing systems [8], which give a hierarchical view of the organisation where each basic part (named basic fractal unit) owns an individual goals and offers services. The global coherence of the system comes from inheritance mechanisms, particularly for the goal formation process.

All of these concepts allow us to decompose recursively an organisation into entities which can be themselves decomposed into other entities. Each of these entities is autonomous, flexible and cooperates with other ones to maintain the organisation's stability. The main differences between these approaches concern [9]: the definition of entities groups, which are predefined in holonic concept and in fractal concept (with dynamic redefinition) and dynamic in the bionic concept; the dynamic reconfiguration of the system that could imply the change of data flow in the bionic and fractal concept, and that consists in evolutions of predefined strategies (canons variations) in the holonic concept.

We think that the fractal and bionic approaches are too permissive, regarding the reconfiguration capacities, for the stability whose we need for the software presented here. Moreover, holonic concepts are closer of the human organisations in which we want to integrate software agent systems.

2.2 A Holonic Multi-agent Platform

The particularity of our approach is that it uses both the notion of role and notion of hierarchy in a same multi-agent system.

We propose the use of a roles' manager: it owns the roles' list, the tasks' list linked to the roles, and the names of the agents (and theirs roles) that compose the multi-agent organisation. In our architecture, we give this role to the agent at the top of the system. Regarding to the FIPA multiagent platform architecture this agent can be considered as an extended Directory Facilitator agent.

Generally, like in the propositions of [9][10], the roles define links between agents; the interactions between agents depend of the roles. In our case, the messages are sent following the hierarchy links or between agents of a same layer (having the same supervisor).

In our proposition, a holonic agent communicate with its supervisor, its neighbours, its assistants, according to theirs roles, or not. So, we propose that each holonic agent plays also the "holonic role" that describe the tasks relative to these communication.

We define a multi-agent system as following: a multi-agent system is composed of roles and agents. Each role is composed of a name, some knowledge (resources), that are necessary to play the role, and of some skills that are composed of set of processes interacting with the knowledge and with the agents (in fact, each skill is defined by a class with classically a name, attributes and operations). An agent owns one or more roles, has a supervisor and can have some assistants and neighbours (they are the only acquaintances with which it can interact). We have built an application that allows us to deploy into a network a holonic multi-agent system from its description (by a XML file).

3   Design of a MAS into Technological Watch Departments

The case study that is presented in this article started in a technological watch department of a large company. The IMAS that we propose is composed of request agents that are eachresponsible of informations' search about a request[1], and launches search engine agents which are responsible of informations' search on a search engine. Information retrieve by the request agents are filtered by the information Responsible Agent. All this system is controlled by the Coordinator Agent that initialize the system (to establish the link to the database, to manage the roles). This information multiagent system at the end of a third-party application (cf. Figure 1) and is called CIMASTEWA (for Centralized IMAS for TEchnological Watch).

The users have access to this IMAS through their browsers by calling dynamic web pages (JSP or ASP pages for example) and dynamic web components (like java bean for instance). They record their queries in the centralized database that the coordinator agent checks periodically to detect if a request has to be done. In this case, the request is sent to the information responsible agent, which distributes it to the information agents according to a search strategy. The information agents send back their results to the information responsible agent, which filters and merges them to record them into the database.

---

[1] A request is defined by a name, a list of words that have to appear in the results (necessary words), a list of words that can appear in the results (possible words), a list of words that do not have to appear in the results (forbidden words), a list of search engines to interrogate and a date of launch

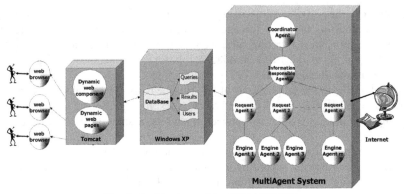

Fig. 1. Architecture of the CIMASTEWA

Our MAS is not centralized on a single computer; it runs on a computers network. So it is possible of having search principles that are sophisticated. For example, information search, in technological watch domain, entails defining securitized search strategies, such as adding 'noise' around the requests. So, in the CIMASTEWA, if a user wishes to scramble one of its requests, this one is then decomposed into elementary requests, which are launched with false keywords. Then, the Information Responsible Agent recomposes the actual results with a particular process.

Regarding the notion of cooperation, we propose to the user to share some of their requests by defining them as public, so other users have access to the public requests and to their results.

In order to design the CIMASTEWA, we have reused the methodology that we have built to analyze and model complex administrative system (AMOMCASYS) which has been applied in previous projects: firstly, the individual roles are described; secondly, the cooperative activities of the agents are defined.

3.1 Individual Design of the CIMASTEWA Agents

Four roles have to be defined in a CIMASTEWA: the coordinator agent role (CA), the information responsible agent role (IA), the request agent role (RA), and the search engine agent role (SA).

The table 1 presents the behaviour of the coordinator agent (this table is inspired from [11]). The knowledge used by the role, the function corresponding to the management of the organisation and of the interactions are defined relatively to the role itself, to the organisation and to the environment. The main activity of the role (its 'production') and the preservation functionality are also defined relatively to these three dimensions.

The roles of the other types of agents are described by the same way

3.2 Cooperative Functioning of a CIMASTEWA

After having described the individual roles of agents that compose a CIMASTEWA, we have to define the cooperative interactions between them. An extract of the processing model representing a cooperative activity within a CIMASTEWA is shown in figure 3 (annex 2).

Table 1. Definition of a coordinator agent

Dimensions/ Function	Social	Environmental	Personal
Representational	Knows the IA and RA	Knows the requests and results of the users.	Knows its name, its IP address.
Organizational	Control the coordination of actions of CIMASTEWA agents Manage the roles	Manages the database.	Checks that a request does not exist
Interactive	Is the responsible of IA.	Interacts with the database and the jsp pages	Ø
Productive	Send requests to the appropriated IA	Fills the database with results and requests provided by the IA	Modifications of knowledge, of its role.
Preservation	Checks if its contacts IA are active...	Check the database.	Deferred to its contacts.

This figure presents the recording of a new request in a CIMASTEWA. The user adds a request in the system through the JSP pages and decides to launch the request immediately. A message is sent to the coordinator agent, which informs the user if the request exists in the group database, if it is a subset of another one or if it includes requests of other actors. The request is then recorded in the user database and a message is sent to the information responsible agent. This message asks it to execute the requests not yet carry out. For this, the agent creates a request agent for each request. Each request agent creates a search engine agent for each search engine specified in the request. Each of these request agents connects to Internet in order to find results and send them to its responsible. When the request agent has received the results of each of its subordinated, it filters them (it deletes the doubles) and sends the results to its responsible. When the information responsible agent has received response from each of the request agents, it records them to the database.

Thanks to the AMOMCASYS method, we have defined other interactions between users and agents of the CIMASTEWA such as the annotation, the deletion of a result, the modifying and the deletion of a request.

4   Setting-up of the Centralised CIMASTEWA

The CIMASTEWA has been developed, mainly in java, in a small data-processing company to answer to the demand of technological watch cells and is currently used in our laboratory. The coordinator agent, the information responsible agent and the information agents have been developed in java, using the holonic multi-agent platform based on the MAGIQUE [12] multi-agent platform. Currently, the search strategy used by our information agent is a broadcast strategy: the information responsible agent sends the request that has to be launched to information agents, which are each dedicated to a search engine. So our system is able to search information on 5 classical search engines and two search engines that are specialized in magazines and documents.

We use the MAGIQUE [12] platform (for multi-agent hierarchic platform), which allows us to easily create hierarchical multi-agent systems:

- A MAGIQUE agent is an empty shell having only communication capacities (with its supervisor and its team (agents under it)).
- It is possible to give skills to an agent by associating it with Java classes, composed of functions or sub-processes.
- Messages exchanged between agents, which are called requests, consist in calls to functions or to sub-processes that are located in the skills[2].

In order to generate holonic multi-agent systems, we have defined two skills:

- HolonicOrganisationSkill, Java class that represents a holonic organisation management skill, associated to the highest multi-agent organisation supervisor. It owns the roles' list, the skills' list linked to the roles, and the names and the roles of the agents that compose the multi-agent organisation.
- HolonSkill, Java class that represent a holonic communication skill, linked to each agent. It defines the attribution of the neighbours and assistants, and the role oriented communication processes. A holonic agent is able to send a message to its neighbours or assistants having a particular role.

We have built an application that allows us to deploy into a network a holonic multiagent system from an XML file that describes it. This XML file describes the roles, the agents, theirs hierarchic relations and the methods of the skills, associated to the roles linked to the agents, that are to be launched at the start of the multi-agent organisation.

Although MAGIQUE platform is not yet FIPA compliant, we have used it to build the first version of our holonic multi-agent platform because it allows us to easily create hierarchical multi-agent systems, and because we have a long term relationship with the SMAC team who has created this platform.

However, we envisage to build a version of the holonic multi-agent platform on a FIPA compliant one, like JADE, for instance.

An extract of the code that allow us to create agents is presented in annex 1.

The main advantage of using agents, rather than an application based only on threads, is based on the flexibility offered by this technology. Indeed, for example, each agent can be situated on a remote machine, or can move on a new computer (only if it is not acting) in order to beneficiate of more resources. Likewise, an agent can dynamically learn new skills or change its skills to adapt and increase its capacity of search (for example, it is possible to add a new skill dedicated to the information pertinence evaluation, that is not taken into account currently).

The application server that we use is Tomcat, three databases have been developed (in Progress®, in Ms Access® and in MySQL, which is the version used at present). The MAS has not particular location, it only needs to have access to the database and to the Internet, in order to execute the searches.

The human computer interfaces have been developed in web pages (using jsp, javascript and css processing language) and used the STRUTS[3] framework of the Jakarta Project. Through these pages, the users can: add, modify, remove requests;

---

[2] If a request cannot be satisfied, because the agent does not know how to answer (the function asked is not present in its skills), it is stored by the platform until the agent learns to answer to it

[3] http://jakarta.apache.org/struts/

consult previous results; choose to share or not theirs requests or results; separate a request in two parts; merge results of two requests (in fact, this duplication is the first strategy of scrambling).

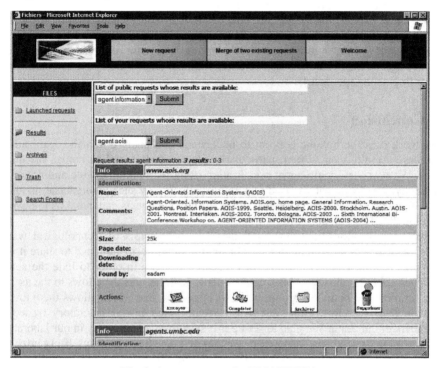

Fig. 2. A screen copy of a CIMASTEWA

The figure 2 presents a screen copy of the web page allowing to the user the consulting of personal or public results: to send them to another actor (through the user mail service), to add some information, to archive them and/or to delete them. The results proposed by the CIMASTEWA of the figure 2 come from a request on 'agent information'.

The functionality concerning the identification of interest communities of the users has not been yet added to this new IMAS. Currently, we are developing the functionality that should allow the CIMASTEWA to self-organize, according to the problem encountered during the search (no response from search engine for example).

As for perspectives, according to the user's needs, it could be interesting to have different search strategies for the Search Engine Agents. For example: if the user wants to have results rapidly, an CFP (Call For Proposition) protocol can be used with these agents; if the user wants to have all the possible results, then the requests are sent to all of them by a broadcast technique. On the other hand, according to the queries, different search strategies can be also chosen. For example: if the words used in the request correspond to specialities of information agents, then the search is organized by speciality; if some requests are subsets of other requests, then information agents are structured hierarchically.

We are currently work on the "regeneration" of some parts of the CIMASTEWA that could be break down by a technical problem such as the crash of a computer or a search engine malfunctioning. This will make our MAS more flexible and so it will more justify the use of this kind of technology.

We think that the main interest of our system is the personalisation of the search strategies that it proposes. Indeed, it is relatively easy to add skills to the agents or new kinds of agents, in response to particular needs (in case of the addition of a new kind of agents, their roles and their relations with the other agents have to be designed according to our approach).

5 Conclusion

Our work uses the holonic concept to understand and analyse human organizations and design multi-agent system particularly adapted to the studied human organizations. We propose a multi-agent organisation using both notion of role and notion of hierarchy. The tools that we used to automatically deploy such an organisation allow us to focus and develop only on the role played by the agents and avoid us to have to develop the global organisation.

We have developed a Centralized IMAS to help actors of technological watch cells, or searchers in a laboratory, that have to search information, and to share it in a cooperative aim. Our system proposes a search strategy in order to hide the actual searches asked by the users. Sharing the queries and their results allows to the user to keep in mind the notion of group, which is important, and which allows them to win time in their searches. This system is currently used in our laboratory by a few searchers of our team. We plan to set-up this system in a larger way in our laboratory in short term. Indeed, we carry out researches and developments: to self-organize the information agents in order to have the more relevant results; and to identify automatically communities of users. So, we could measure impact of our MAS on the behaviour of the searchers.

Acknowledgements

We would like to thank the team SMAC of the LIFL (University of Lille 1, France) for its cooperation during the project NIPO , which allows us to build the Holonic platform.

References

1. Adam, E., Kolski, C., Mandiau, R., Vergison, E. A software engineering workbench for modeling groupware activities. In C. Stephanidis (Ed.), Universal Access in HCI: inclusive design in the information society. Mahwah, New Jersey: Lawrence Erlbaum Associates, (2003) 1499-1503.
2. Adam, E., Mandiau, R. Bringing multi-agent systems into human organizations: application to a multi-agent information system. In M.A. Jeusfeld, O. Pastor (Ed.), Conceptual modeling for novel application domains, ER 2003 Worshops ECOMO, IWCMQ, AOIS, and XSDM, Chicago,IL, USA, October 2003 Proceedings, LNCS 2814. Berlin: Springer (2003) 168-179
3. Koestler, A. The Ghost in the Machine. Arkana Books, London, (1969).

4. Mandiau, R., Le Strugeon E. & Agimont G. Study of the influence of organizational structure on the efficiency of a multi-agent system. Networking and Information Systems Journal, 2(2) (1999) 153-179.
5. Schwarz, G.M., Organizational hierarchy adaptation and information technology, Information and Organization 12 (2002) 153–182
6. Okino, N., Bionic Manufacturing System, in J. Peklenik (Ed.) CIRP, Flexible Manufacturing Systems: Past-Present-Future (1993) 73-95.
7. Van Brussel, H., Bongaerts, L., Wyns, J., Valckenaers, P., Van Ginderachter, T., A Conceptual Framework for Holonic Manufacturing Systems: Identification of Manufacturing Holons. Journal of Manufacturing Systems, 18, 1 (1999) 35-52.
8. Kwangyeol, R. and Mooyoung, J., Agent-based fractal architecture and modelling for developing distributed manufacturing systems, Int'l J. of Production Research, Vol. 41, No. 17 (2003) 4233-4255.
9. Kendall, E. A. Role modeling for agent system analysis, design, and implementation. In First International Symposium on Agent Systems and Applications (ASA'99), Third International Symposium on Mobile Agents (MA'99), (1999).
10. Wooldridge, M., Jennings, NR., Kinny D. The GAIA methodology for agent oriented analysis and design. Journal of Autonomous Agents and Multi-Agent Systems, (2000).
11. Ferber, J. Les systèmes multi-agents, Vers une intelligence collective. InterEditions, Paris, (1995).
12. Mathieu, P., Routier, J-C., Secq, Y. RIO: Roles, Interactions and Organizations. CEEMAS 2003: Multi-Agent Systems and Applications III, Lecture Notes in Artificial Intelligence 2691. (2003)

Annex 1. Java Code for Agents' Creations and Communication

The following code is an example of agents' creations and communication. Extract of the 'go()' method of the InformationResponsibleSkill class, which is associated to the Information Responsible agent (IR agent). This code creates a Request Agent for each search asked by the users.

```
for (int i=0; i<reqToLaunch.size(); i++)
{
   Search req = (Search) reqToLaunch.elementAt(i);
   /* creation of an empty agent whose the name is the
   name of the request */
   Agent a = platform.createAgent(req.getName());
   // addition of the Holon skill
   a.addSkill(new holon.skill.HolonSkill(a));
   // connection to the boss (the current IR agent)
   a.connectToBoss(getName()); // magique method
   // holonic add -> automatically update the neighbourgs and the
supervisor assistants
   perform(a.getName() ,"setMySupervisor", new Object [] {getName()});
   // IR agent asks the request agent to request its role
   a.askNow("requestRole", new Object [] {a.getName(),
                                    "RequestResponsible"});
   // IR agent asks the request agent to initialise itself
   a.askNow("initRequestResponsible", new Object[]{req});
   // IR agent asks the request agent to perform its search
   perform(req.getNom(), "searchRequest");
   nbRequestLaunched ++;
}
```

In this code example, agents are created in local, but their creations on remote machines are similar.

Annex 2. Cooperative Working of the CIMASTEWA Agents

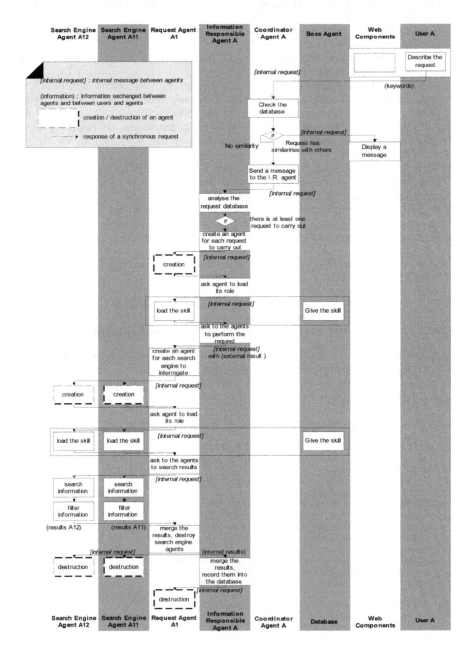

Fig. 3. Processing model of the request recording process in a CIMASTEWA

Evaluating a Scientific SPMD Application on a Computational Grid with Different Load Balancing Techniques

André Oliveira*, Gabriel Argolo*, Pablo Iglesias,
Simone Martins**, and Alexandre Plastino***

Department of Computer Science, Universidade Federal Fluminense,
Rua Passo da Pátria, 156 - Bloco E - 3º andar - Boa Viagem,
24210-240, Niterói, RJ, Brazil
{aoliveira,grocha,piglesias,simone,plastino}@ic.uff.br
http://www.ic.uff.br

Abstract. The performance of SPMD programs is strongly affected by dynamic load imbalancing factors. The use of a suitable load balancing algorithm is essential for overcoming the effects of these imbalancing factors. In this work, we evaluate the performance of a scientific SPMD parallel application when executed on a computational grid, with different kinds of load balancing strategies. The developed SPMD application computes the macroscopic thermal dispersion in porous media. A set of experiments was conducted on a computational grid composed by two geographically separated clusters. The main contribution of this work is the performance evaluation and comparison of a large variety of load balancing techniques under dynamic environment conditions. The experimental results showed the importance of choosing appropriate load balancing strategies when developing SPMD applications on a grid environment.

1 Introduction

The design of parallel applications is classically based on either *functional* or *data* parallelism. Associated with MIMD (Multiple Instruction, Multiple Data) architectures, data parallelism originated the SPMD (Single Program, Multiple Data) programming model [20]: the same program is executed on different processors, over distinct data sets. Under this model, each *task* is characterized by the data over which the common code is executed. The SPMD programming model has been widely used in parallel programming. Coding and debugging is usually simpler under this model than in arbitrary MIMD programs. Moreover, data decomposition is a natural approach for the design of parallel algorithms for many problems [12].

The performance of SPMD programs is strongly affected by dynamic load imbalancing factors, which may include: the lack of information about the processing load of each task before its execution, the dynamic creation of new tasks,

---

* Work sponsored by FAPERJ scholarship
** Work sponsored by CNPq research grant 475124/03-0
*** Work sponsored by CNPq research grant 300879/00-8 and 475124/03-0

or the variation of processor load external to the application. The use of suitable load balancing strategies is essential for overcoming these imbalancing factors. Despite the simplicity of the SPMD model, it is often hard to determine the most appropriate load balancing technique for each application, partly because of the large variety of load balancing algorithms that may be adopted [6, 7, 11, 25, 26].

Grid environments [5] emerge as powerful computing platforms where SPMD programs can be executed. They may present higher load imbalancing levels for running applications than other parallel systems like clusters or parallel machines. There are two main reasons for that: first, the machines have heterogeneous computational power and their load and availability vary dynamically, then they do not perform similarly for the same application, and second, the network links present diverse speeds, some communications are rather fast while others are quite slow. Due to these characteristics, load balancing techniques are of considerable interest in order to improve the efficiency of parallel application executions on this platform.

In this work, we evaluate and compare the behavior of nine versions of a scientific SPMD application on a computational grid, each one adopting a different load balancing algorithm. The scientific application computes the macroscopic thermal dispersion in porous media – the *thermions* application [23].

The development of the *thermions* parallel application was supported by SAMBA-Grid, a recently developed version for grids of SAMBA (Single Application, Multiple Load Balancing) [14–16] – a parallel programming tool. SAMBA-Grid is a framework which captures the structure and the characteristics common to different SPMD applications and supports their development on computational grids.

The conducted performance comparison aims to identify appropriate load balancing strategies for the characteristics of this scientific parallel application when running on a grid environment.

This paper is organized as follows. Related work is presented in the next section. The thermal dispersion computation is described in Section 3. The SAMBA-Grid framework is briefly presented in Section 4. Adopted load balancing algorithms are presented in Section 5. The computational experiments and the evaluation of the load balancing strategies are reported in Section 6. Concluding remarks are made in the last section.

2   Related Work

Similar work, in which different load balancing strategies are compared when used with SPMD applications, has been described in [6, 11, 14–16, 25, 26]. Different SPMD applications were considered in order to compute: matrix multiplication [14–16, 26], numerical integration [14–16], genetic algorithm [15, 16], recursive database queries [11], N-body simulation [6], and branch-and-bound job scheduling [25].

From the results presented in the above works, we observe that the most suitable load balancing strategy may vary with the type of the application, more precisely, with the type of load imbalancing factor considered and with the number of tasks of the application. A local-partitioned load balancing strategy, for example, obtained good results for the parallel matrix multiplication and for the parallel genetic algorithm, but had a poor performance for the parallel numerical integration.

In these works, typically, the used computational environments were networks of workstations or clusters of PCs. In [24], different load balancing algorithms were evaluated for the *thermions* application in a cluster of 32 machines. The emergent grid technology motivated us to investigate the behavior of different load balancing algorithms when associated with the *thermions* application in this new kind of computational environment.

There are some approaches for scheduling and providing load balancing for parallel applications on grids. Systems like Pace [2] and AppLeS [3] combine performance prediction techniques and resource monitoring functions to place the tasks of an application on the available machines, aiming load balancing either statically or dynamically. They need estimates of computation times for the tasks that compose the application, which are usually hard to be precise.

Other works [9, 10, 22] use the master-worker paradigm, where a single master process dispatches tasks to multiple worker processes and gathers results from them. They exploit strategies to locate processes in the available machines, intending to avoid load imbalancing and reduce execution time. Aida et al. [1] propose a hierarchical master-worker strategy that achieves much better performance than a conventional master-worker paradigm.

3   The Scientific SPMD Application

In this section, we briefly present the method used to evaluate the macroscopic thermal dispersion in porous media. More details can be found in [23]. This method is applied in an one-equation model (Equation 1) [13], which describes the thermal dispersion on a periodic porous media composed of a union of several fundamental cells. Each fundamental cell is composed of solid elements and by fluid.

$$\frac{\partial \mathcal{H}}{\partial t^*} + \vec{\mathcal{V}}^* \cdot \nabla^* \mathcal{H} = \nabla^* \cdot \left(\overline{\overline{\mathcal{K}}}^* \nabla^* \mathcal{H} \right) + \phi \tau (\vec{r}^{\,*}) \delta(t^*) \qquad (1)$$

In the previous equation, $\mathcal{H}$ is the enthalpy (energy related to the medium temperature), $\vec{\mathcal{V}}^*$ is the velocity vector field of the fluid flux in the porous media, $\overline{\overline{\mathcal{K}}}^*$ is the dispersion tensor, ϕ is the energy injected in the medium, $\tau(\vec{r}^{\,*})$ its initial normalized distribution and $\delta(t^*)$ is the Dirac distribution. ∇^* and t^* are the dimensionless nabla operator and the dimensionless time, respectively.

The thermal dispersion will be evaluated by the movement of hypothetical particles, called *thermions*, which have a fixed quantity of energy. Each *thermion* is represented by its position (x, y) in the space. This position indicates in which kind of medium the particle is. The movement of a particle is determined by a random component and, when the particle is in the fluid part, also by the flux velocity.

Initially, a large number of *thermions* is released. At each iteration, the position of all *thermions* is updated according to their step length and direction.

The direction of a particle movement to the left, right, up or down is chosen randomly. The length of each step depends on the thermal properties of the medium in which the particle is and on the velocity of the fluid flux (if the particle is in the fluid part).

After a number of steps, the particles reach their final position. From this distribution, we obtain the thermal dispersion.

Each *thermion* will go through a random way. The evaluation of the total path of each *thermion* may require different computational load if distinct solid parts have different thermal properties. In the experiments conducted in this work, the media have homogeneous thermal properties and, consequently, the computational work required for evaluating each thermion is approximately the same. This choice allowed us to evaluate more precisely the load imbalancing factor produced by the heterogeneity of the grid environment.

4   Framework SAMBA-Grid

An SPMD application can typically be structured into three major components: (a) the single code which is replicated for the execution of a task; (b) the load balancing strategy; and (c) a skeleton (which initializes and terminates the application, manages the tasks, and controls the execution of the other parts). The first component is specific to each application, but the other two usually are not. SPMD applications can thus be modeled by a *framework* [8, 18, 19, 21].

Frameworks capture design decisions common to all applications of a given domain. They act both as a specification that models applications with common structure and characteristics, and as a partial implementation that can be used as a basis for the development of these applications. Frameworks allow the programmer to focus on the specific problem at hand, reducing the programming effort. They promote reusability to a higher degree: not only parts of the code are reused, but also, and more important, the application architecture itself.

Some parts of a framework are purposely incomplete. These parts, called *hot spots*, represent the difference among distinct applications of the same domain. The developer must fill in these hot spots to obtain a complete program. This process is known as *framework instantiation*. The typical user of a framework is an application developer.

The SAMBA-Grid is a new version of the framework SAMBA [14–16], developed for grid environments. SAMBA models the class of SPMD parallel applications. Its three main hot spots are responsible for: generating the tasks, executing a single task, and dealing with the results. SAMBA allows the SPMD application designer to "plug-and-play" with different load balancing algorithms. Consequently, SAMBA simplifies the generation of distinct versions of the application for different load balancing strategies.

In order to instantiate the framework to generate the *thermions* parallel application, we implemented SAMBA's main hot spots. In this application, a task is represented by its position (x, y) in the space - a pair of reals. So, the first hot spot must generate all tasks by setting their initial position and deliver them to the task manager of the framework. Each task corresponds to the calculation of the path through which a *thermion* will go. Then, the second hot spot is the single code that will be evaluated over all *thermions*. To process the results, the third hot spot must gather the final position of the set of particles in order to obtain the thermal dispersion.

5   Load Balancing Algorithms

The design of the adopted load balancing algorithms was guided by the classification criteria described in [16, 17]. The nine currently implemented algorithms cover a broad range of classes, with a wide variety of characteristics. In this section, we briefly describe these algorithms.

1. STATIC: A central processor distributes the set of tasks among all processors, including itself. The same number of tasks is assigned to every processor. Each processor executes the tasks it received, without any dynamic load balancing.

2. MASTER-WORKER: A master processor allocates a block of tasks to each other worker processor. Each time a worker finishes the execution of its current block of tasks, it requests and receives a new one.

3. HIERARCHICAL MASTER-WORKER: This algorithm is basically the same as algorithm 2, except that the processors are hierarchically organized. The root of the hierarchy has a master role. The leaves are workers and the internal processors have both master and worker roles.

4. DISTRIBUTED, GLOBAL, COLLECTIVE: A central processor distributes the set of tasks in equal parts to all processors, including itself. Whenever a processor finishes the execution of all tasks it received, it sends a message to all others, asking them to perform a load balancing step. At this point, each processor sends to all others its internal load index (the number of tasks still remaining to be executed). Next, a collective load balancing takes place: each processor defines the necessary task exchanges to achieve exact redistribution and performs the exchanges in which it is involved.

5. CENTRALIZED, GLOBAL, COLLECTIVE: This algorithm is similar to the previous one, except that decisions are taken by a central processor. Whenever a processor finishes the execution of all tasks it received, it sends a message to all others, asking them to send their internal load indexes to a central processor. After receiving this information from all processors, this central processor defines necessary exchanges and informs each processor of the task transfers in which it is involved. Finally, each processor executes the indicated transfers.

6. DISTRIBUTED, GLOBAL, INDIVIDUAL: Once again, load balancing is triggered when a processor finishes the execution of all tasks it has received. However, in this case the goal consists in correcting an underload condition at this single (individual) processor. Whenever a processor finishes the execution of its tasks, it sends a message to all others and they send back their internal load indexes. After receiving load information from all processors, the underloaded processor sends a request for load transfer to the most loaded processor, which then sends back half of its load.

7. DISTRIBUTED, LOCAL, PARTITIONED, COLLECTIVE: This algorithm is basically the same as algorithm 4, except that the processors are partitioned into disjoint groups. All load balancing activity takes place exclusively inside each group.

8. DISTRIBUTED, LOCAL, NEIGHBORHOOD-BASED, INDIVIDUAL: This strategy is similar to algorithm 6, except that load information and load exchanges occur only between processors in the same ring-based neighborhood (which may reflect physical connections). Each processor interacts with only two neighbors. The neighborhood-based characteristic requires the use of a termination detection strategy. We use Dijkstra's algorithm [4] in our implementation.

9. HYBRID DISTRIBUTED, PARTITIONED AND MASTER-WORKER: In this algorithm, processors are partitioned into disjoint groups. Inside each group, a master-worker strategy takes place. Initially, a central processor distributes the set of tasks to all master processors. This distribution is proportional to the number of workers in each group. Whenever a master finishes the execution of its tasks, it sends a message to all others and they send back their internal load indexes. After receiving load information from all masters, the underloaded one sends a request for load transfer to the most loaded master, which then sends back half of its load, similarly to that described in algorithm 6.

6   Performance Evaluation

The computational experiments reported in this section have been carried out on the grid GridRio[1] composed by two clusters, physically located in separate cities in Brazil: Rio de Janeiro and Niterói. The first one, cluster-RJ, has 32 hosts (Pentium IV 1.7GHz) and the second one, cluster-NT, has 8 hosts (AMD Athlon 1.3GHz). The machines of each cluster are connected by Fast Ethernet and the two clusters are connected by a 34 Mbits/s link. The conducted experiments were executed on 15 hosts of cluster-RJ and 5 hosts of cluster-NT.

The middleware used is The Globus Toolkit 2.4 and the message passing library is MPICH-G2 v1.2.5.

Nine load balancing strategies have been tested and compared. They are numbered according to their description in Section 5: static (S1), master-worker (S2), hierarchical master-worker (S3), distributed (S4), centralized (S5), individual (S6), local-partitioned (S7), ring-neighborhood-based (S8), and the hybrid one (S9). In the master-worker strategy (S2) each block corresponds to one task (the evaluation of one *thermion*). The hierarchical strategy (S3) was executed with the root located in cluster-RJ. Each other node of this cluster was connected to the root. In cluster-NT, a local master was connected to the root and each other node was connected to this local master. The local-partitioned (S7) strategy was executed with two groups, corresponding to the two clusters. The main goal of the evaluation of this set of load balancing algorithms is to

---

[1] http://easygrid.ic.uff.br

identify appropriate strategies for the *thermions* application running on a grid environment.

The relative behavior of the different load balancing algorithms is assessed in terms of their elapsed times. The most suitable load balancing algorithm for a given application is considered as that leading to smallest elapsed times. We performed three groups of experiments. In the first, the total number of *thermions* (SPMD tasks) was 500; in the second it was 1 000; and 2 000 in the third.

To measure the load imbalance of an execution of a parallel application (E), we consider a *load imbalancing index* (LII) [17, 24]. The LII of E, on p processors, is defined by $LII = PIT/t_f$, as the ratio between the average of the processors idle times (PIT) and the elapsed time of the processor which was the last one to finish its tasks (t_f).

The PIT (average of the processors idle times) is defined by.

$$PIT = \frac{\sum_{i=1}^{p}(t_f - t_i)}{(p-1)}, \tag{2}$$

where t_i is the elapsed time of the ith processor $(1 \leq i \leq p)$. Note that at most $p-1$ processors become idle and contribute to PIT calculation. We can consider p subtractions (and not $p-1$) in the total sum since one of them is necessarily equal to zero.

To show the effects of the dynamic imbalancing factor produced by the grid heterogeneity, in Table 1 we present the load imbalance indexes for the static load balancing algorithm (S1) executed on the grid, on three different days, with 500, 1 000, and 2 000 *thermions* (tasks). Each value in the table represents the average of the load imbalance index obtained from five executions.

Table 1. Load imbalance for static strategy executions

	Load Imbalance Indexes		
Thermions	1st day	2nd day	3rd day
500	34%	44%	40%
1000	26%	34%	30%
2000	28%	37%	30%

For instance, in the execution with 1 000 tasks on the second day, 19 $(p-1)$ processors became idle, on average, 34% of the elapsed time of the slowest processor. In these experiments, the imbalance index ranged from 26% to 44%, illustrating the need for dynamic load balancing strategies.

Table 2 presents the behavior of all strategies for five executions with 500 *thermions*. To allow a fair comparison among all strategies, each one was executed along with the static strategy (S1), and each value in this table represents the relative time of the strategy when compared to the static one. The last row contains the average values.

Table 2. All strategies with 500 *thermions*

S2	S3	S4	S5	S6	S7	S8	S9
0.76	0.75	0.95	1.33	1.00	0.96	0.90	0.76
0.79	0.80	0.94	1.34	1.01	0.97	0.90	0.77
0.85	0.85	1.13	1.24	1.02	0.92	0.89	0.75
0.69	0.73	1.09	0.91	0.98	0.94	0.90	0.77
0.76	0.75	1.11	0.94	0.97	0.93	0.90	0.75
0.77	0.78	1.04	1.15	1.00	0.94	0.90	0.76

A straightforward comparison between the times observed for the different strategies illustrates the effectiveness of some dynamic load balancing algorithms and the importance of selecting an appropriate one. The master-worker strategies (S2, S3, and S9) were the best ones for 500 *thermions*. Their behaviors were very similar. Although we have designed the hierarchical and the hybrid strategies (S3 and S9) to avoid using excessively the communication channel between cluster-RJ and cluster-NT, the cost of this communication was not relevant when compared to the cost of each application task.

We observe that, with 500 *thermions*, the overhead imposed by the load balancing activities in strategies S4, S5, S6, and S7 presented a high computational cost and made the performance of these strategies similar or even worse than the static one.

The good behavior of the ring-neighborhood-based strategy (S8) indicates that a locally load balancing activity can take advantage of making less communication among processors.

Tables 3 and 4 present the behavior of all strategies for five executions with 1 000 and 2 000 *thermions*, respectively. Again, each strategy was executed along with the static one (S1), and each value represents the relative time of the strategy when compared to the static one. The last row contains the average values.

Table 3. All strategies with 1 000 *thermions*

S2	S3	S4	S5	S6	S7	S8	S9
0.70	0.70	0.83	0.92	0.95	0.85	0.75	0.73
0.84	0.85	0.85	0.80	1.01	1.02	0.96	0.81
0.85	0.85	0.95	1.04	0.99	1.01	0.90	0.86
0.88	0.87	0.94	1.14	0.99	0.95	0.91	0.87
0.90	0.91	1.08	1.15	1.01	0.96	0.93	0.90
0.83	0.84	0.93	1.01	0.99	0.96	0.89	0.83

Table 4. All strategies with 2 000 *thermions*

S2	S3	S4	S5	S6	S7	S8	S9
0.83	0.84	0.83	0.95	0.85	0.87	0.85	0.81
0.82	0.82	0.80	0.86	0.83	0.84	0.83	0.83
0.81	0.81	0.77	0.82	0.84	0.86	0.84	0.82
0.84	0.84	0.73	0.88	0.93	0.84	0.82	0.81
0.83	0.83	0.78	0.94	0.90	0.85	0.81	0.82
0.83	0.83	0.78	0.89	0.87	0.85	0.83	0.82

We observe that, as the number of tasks (*thermions*) increased from 500 to 2 000, the performance of the master-worker strategies (S2, S3, and S9) ranged from approximately 77% to 83%. All other strategies had the opposite behavior. For example, the performance of the distributed strategy (S4) ranged from 106%

to 78%. S4 was worse than the static strategy with 500 (*thermions*) and it was the best one with 2 000 tasks. With a larger number of tasks, not necessarily the load balancing activity of S4 (and also of S5, S6, S7, and S8) increases. The overhead of the load balancing activity in these strategies is attenuated when the number of tasks increases. The effects of task transfers performed to balance the load may last longer and may be more effective with a larger number of tasks.

Since the communication cost between the clusters is significantly higher than the communication cost in each cluster, a last experiment was performed to evaluate the effectiveness of using the grid, instead of using just only one cluster. Table 5 presents elapsed times in seconds for five executions of the master-worker strategy (S2) with 2 000 *thermions*, conducted on distinct days, in different environments: in the grid (20 procs.), in the cluster-RJ (15 procs.), and in the cluster-NT (5 procs). The last row contains the average of the elapsed times. We observe that in spite of the communication overhead imposed by the grid utilization, this environment obtained the best execution times in all runnings. We also notice that the cluster-RJ has three times more processors than the cluster-NT. However the real reduction factor is smaller than the expected one. This is due to the higher capacity of executing floating point operations of the cluster-NT, and to the intense use of this kind of operation in the *thermions* application.

Table 5. Master-worker strategy in distinct environments

1st Day			2nd Day		
Grid	Cluster-RJ	Cluster-NT	Grid	Cluster-RJ	Cluster-NT
28.20	42.00	50.84	25.79	40.59	52.78
28.49	41.96	50.39	26.04	40.52	54.30
27.57	41.74	49.53	25.25	40.34	52.08
24.23	35.31	40.05	25.16	40.18	52.06
24.66	35.46	42.60	25.34	40.21	52.08
26.63	39.29	46.68	25.52	40.37	52.66

7   Conclusions

The main contribution of this work is the performance evaluation and comparison of nine different load balancing algorithms for a scientific parallel application on a grid environment.

In the conducted experiment, load imbalance was due to the heterogeneity and dynamical behavior of the grid computational environment.

The reductions in elapsed times clearly illustrate the need for efficient dynamic load balancing algorithms for this type of time-consuming application running on a computational grid. The master-worker strategies (S2, S3, and S9) led to the best results. However we observed a tendency for the other strategies (S4, S5, S6, S7, and S8) to become more competitive with a larger number of tasks.

The study of distinct load balancing algorithms for the *thermions* application clearly illustrated the need for tuning and choosing the best strategy for a given SPMD application executing on a grid environment.

SAMBA-Grid has also proved itself to be an effective tool for the development and tuning of SPMD applications on grids, helping the task of identifying appropriate load balancing strategies.

Many questions have arisen and will lead us to future work. To answer them we intend to evaluate distinct parameters in some load balancing strategies, such as: the number of tasks per block in the master-worker strategy, the location of the root in the hierarchical master-worker strategy, or even the topology of the neighborhood can also be an important parameter to be evaluated in the neighborhood-based strategy.

We think the next important step in this work is to propose a cost model for each relevant load balancing strategy in order to help predicting the most suitable strategy for a specific SPMD application running on a grid environment.

References

1. K. Aida, Y. Futakata, and S. Hara, "High-Performance Parallel and Distributed Computing for the BMI Eigenvalue Problem", *Proceedings of the 16th International Parallel and Distributed Processing Symposium*, 2002, CD-ROM/Abstracts.
2. J. Cao, D.P. Spooner, S.A. Jarvis, S. Saini, and G.R. Nudd, "Agent-based Grid Load Balancing using Performance-driven Task Scheduling", *Proceedings of 17th International Parallel and Distributed Processing Symposium*, 2003, CD-ROM/Abstracts.
3. F. Berman, R. Wolski, S. Figueira, J. Schopf, and G. Shao, "Application Level Scheduling on Distributed Heterogeneous Networks", *Proceedings of Supercomputing*, 1996.
4. E. Dijkstra, W. Seijen, and A. Gasteren, "Derivation of a Termination Detection Algorithm for a Distributed Computation", *Information Processing Letters* 16, 1983, pp. 217–219.
5. I. Foster, *The Grid: Blueprint for a New Computing Infrastructure*, Morgan Kaufmann Publishers, 1998.
6. M.A. Franklin and V. Govindan, "A General Matrix Iterative Model for Dynamic Load Balancing", *Parallel Computing* 22, 1996, pp. 969–989.
7. M. Furuichi, K. Taki, and N. Ichiyoshi, "A Multi-Level Load Balancing Scheme for Or-Parallel Exhaustive Search Programs on the Multi-Psi", *Proceedings of the II ACM SIGPLAN Symposium on Principles and Practice of Parallel Programming*, 1990, pp. 50–59.
8. E. Gamma, R. Helm, R. Johnson, and J. Vlissides, *Design Pattern - Elements of Reusable Object Oriented Software*, Addison-Wesley, 1994.
9. J-P. Goux, S. Kulkarni, M. Yoder, and J. Linderoth, "An Enabling Framework for Master-Worker Applications on the Computational Grid", *Proceedings of the Ninth IEEE International Symposium on High Performance Distributed Computing*, 2000.
10. E. Heymann, M.A. Senar, E. Luque, and M. Livny, "Adaptive Scheduling for Master-Worker Applications on the Computational Grid", *Proceedings of the First IEEE/ACM International Workshop on Grid Computing*, 2000, pp. 214-227.

11. S. Lifschitz, A. Plastino, and C.C. Ribeiro, "Exploring Load Balancing in Parallel Processing of Recursive Queries", *Proceedings of the III Euro-Par Conference, Lecture Notes in Computer Science* 1300, 1997, pp. 1125–1129.
12. T.G. Mattson, "Scientific Computation", in *Parallel and Distributed Computing Handbook* (A.Y. Zomaya, editor), McGraw-Hill, 1996, pp. 981–1002.
13. C. Moyne, S. Didierjean, H.P.A. Souto, and O.T. da Silveira Filho, "Thermal Dispersion in Porous Media: One-Equation Model", *International Journal of Heat and Mass Transfer* 43, 2000, pp. 3853–3867.
14. A. Plastino, C.C. Ribeiro, and N. Rodriguez, "A Tool for SPMD Application Development with Support for Load Balancing", *Proceedings of the International Conference ParCo'99*, Imperial College Press, 2000, pp. 639–646.
15. A. Plastino, C.C. Ribeiro, and N. Rodriguez, "A Framework for SPMD Applications with Load Balancing", *Proceedings of the XII Brazilian Symposium on Computer Architecture and High Performance Computing*, 2000, pp. 245–252.
16. A. Plastino, C.C. Ribeiro, and N. Rodriguez, "Developing SPMD Applications with Load Balancing", *Parallel Computing* 29, 2003, pp. 743–766.
17. A. Plastino, V. Thomé, D. Vianna, R. Costa, and O.T. da Silveira Filho, "Load Balancing in SPMD Applications: Concepts and Experiments", in *High Performance Scientific and Engineering Computing: Hardware/Software Support* (L.T. Yang and Y. Pan, editors), Kluwer Academic Publishers, 2004, pp. 95–107.
18. W. Pree, *Design Patterns for Object-Oriented Software Development*, Addison-Wesley, 1995.
19. W. Pree, *Framework Patterns*, SIG Books & Multimedia, 1996.
20. M.J. Quinn, *Parallel Computing: Theory and Practice*, McGraw-Hill, 1994.
21. J. Rumbaugh, M. Blaha, W. Premerlani, F. Eddy, and W. Lorensen, *Object Oriented Modeling and Design*, Prentice-Hall, 1991.
22. G. Shao, F. Berman, and R. Wolski, "Master/Slave Computing on Grid", *Proceedings of the 9th Heterogeneous Computing Workshop*, 2001, pp. 3–16.
23. H.P.A. Souto, O.T. da Silveira Filho, C. Moyne, and S. Didierjean, "Thermal Dispersion in Porous Media: Computations by the Random Walk Method", *Computational and Applied Mathematics* 21, 2002, pp. 513–543.
24. V. Thomé, D. Vianna, R. Costa, A. Plastino, and O.T. da Silveira Filho, "Exploring Load Balancing in a Scientific SPMD Parallel Application", *Proceedings of the IV International Workshop on High Performance Scientific and Engineering Computing with Applications in conjunction with the XXXI International Conference on Parallel Processing*, 2002, pp. 419–426.
25. M.A. Willebeek-LeMair and A.P. Reeves, "Strategies for Dynamic Load Balancing on Highly Parallel Computers", *IEEE Transactions on Parallel and Distributed Systems* 4, 1993, pp. 979–993.
26. M.J. Zaki, W. Li, and S. Parthasarathy, "Customized Dynamic Load Balancing for a Network of Workstations", *Journal of Parallel and Distributed Computing* 43, 1997, pp. 156–162.

Increasing the Training Speed of SVM, the Zoutendijk Algorithm Case

Rodolfo E. Ibarra Orozco[1], Neil Hernández-Gress[1],
Juan Frausto-Solís[2], and Jaime Mora Vargas[1]

[1] Department of Computer Science
ITESM, Campus Estado de México
Carretera Lago de Guadalupe Km. 3.5, Atizapán de Zaragoza,
52926 Estado de México
Tel: 5864-5555 Ext. 5690
{rodolfo.ibarra,ngress,jmora}@itesm.mx
http://www.laas.fr/~hdez/
[2] Department of Computer Science
ITESM, Campus Cuernavaca
Reforma 182-A, Colonia Lomas de Cuernavaca, Temixco, 62589 Morelos, México
juan.frausto@itesm.mx

Abstract. The Support Vector Machine (SVM) is a well known method used for classification, regression and density estimation. Training a SVM consists in solving a Quadratic Programming (QP) problem. The QP problem is very resource consuming (computational time and computational memory), because the quadratic form is dense and the memory requirements grow square the number of data points. The support vectors found in the training of SVM's represent a small subgroup of the training patterns. If an algorithm could make an approximation beforehand of the points standing for support vectors, we could train the SVM only with those data and the same results could be obtained as trained using the entire data base.

This paper introduces an original initialization by the Zoutendijk method, called ZQP, to train SVM's faster than classical ones. The ZQP method first makes a fast approximation to the solution using the Zoutendijk algorithm. As result of this approximation, a reduced number of training patterns is obtained. Finally, a QP algorithm makes the training with this subset of data. Results show the improvement of the methodology in comparison to QP algorithm and chunking with QP algorithm.

The ideas presented here can be extended to another problems such as resource allocation, considering that allocation as a combinatorial problem, that could be solved using some artificial intelligent technique such as Genetic algorithms or simulated annealing. In such approach ZQP would be used as a measure for effective fitness.

1   Introduction

A Support Vector Machine (SVM) is an algorithm for classification, regression, and density estimation. It was developed by Vladimir Vapnik [1]. Training a

F.F. Ramos et al. (Eds.): ISSADS 2005, LNCS 3563, pp. 312–320, 2005.

Support Vector Machine (SVM) consists in solving a Quadratic Programming (QP) problem. While solving this QP problem, SVM's solves two problems that classical Neural Networks have: 1) choose an optimal topology and 2) adjust the parameters of the network. Since the number of variables in the QP problem is equal to the number of training patterns, the optimization problem becomes challenging, because the quadratic form is dense and the memory requirements grow square the number of data points. The support vectors represents a small subgroup of the training patterns. If an algorithm could detect beforehand what points will be the support vectors, the SVM could be trained only with those data and the same results could be obtained as trained using the entire data base. In this paper we propose an original methodology that first reduces the number of training patterns and then the QP algorithm makes the training with this subset of the data.Some examples of methods based on this idea can be found in [16], [17], [18] and [19].

The ideas presented here can be extended to another problems such as resource allocation, considering that allocation as a combinatorial problem, that could be solved using some artificial intelligent technique such as Genetic algorithms or simulated annealing. In such approach ZQP would be used as a measure for effective fitness [20].

This paper is organized as follows: The second section describes the optimization problem generated by s SVM and the Chunking method that is used to deal with a large number of vectors. In section three we describe how selecting remarkable vectors for an initial working set can reduce the training time. The section three describes the Zoutendijk algorithm. In section five, experimental results while training well-known benchmarks are discussed to show the capability of the ZQP method. Finally, we finish giving some conclusions.

2   Support Vector Machines

Support Vector Machines is a well-known technique for training separating functions in pattern recognition tasks and for function estimation in regression problems [8]. In several problems has shown its generalization capabilities. In classification tasks, the main idea can be stated as follows: given a training data set characterized by patterns $x_i \in \Re^n$, $i = 1, \ldots, n$ belonging to two possible classes $y_i \in \{1, -1\}$ there exists a solution represented by the following optimization problem.

$$Maximize \quad F(\boldsymbol{\Lambda}) = \boldsymbol{\Lambda} \cdot \mathbf{1} - \frac{1}{2}\boldsymbol{\Lambda} \cdot H\boldsymbol{\Lambda} \tag{1}$$

$$subject \ to:$$

$$\boldsymbol{\Lambda} \cdot \boldsymbol{y} = 0 \tag{2}$$

$$0 \leq \boldsymbol{\Lambda} \leq C\mathbf{1} \tag{3}$$

where $\boldsymbol{\Lambda}$ is a vector containing the Lagrange multipliers (λ_i), C is a penalization constant defined by the user, and H is a symmetric, semi-positive definite, quadratic nxn matrix with elements $H_{ij} = y_iy_jk(x_i, x_j)$.

$k(x_i, x_j)$ represents the so-called kernel trick and is used to project the data into a Hilbert space F of highest dimension using simple functions for the computation of the dot products of the input patterns.

$$k(x_i, x_j) = \phi(x_i)^T \phi(x_j), \quad i, j = 1, \ldots, n \tag{4}$$

And the decision function is defined as:

$$f(x) = sgn\left(\sum_{i=1}^{n} y_i \lambda_i \cdot k(x_i \cdot x_j) + b\right) \tag{5}$$

The solution to the problem formulated in eq. (1) is a vector $\lambda_i \geq 0$ for which the λ_i^* strictly greater than zero are the so called support vectors (SV's). Geometrically, these vectors are on the border of the decision funtion. While solving the optimization problem, constraints (2) y (3) are satisfied and thus (1) is maximized.

2.1   Chunking Algorithm

Chunking algorithm brakes down the problem into smaller QP sub problems (or chunks) that are optimized iteratively. This algorithm is based on the idea that the solution of the QP problem is the same as if we remove vectors with $\lambda = 0$. The idea is to structure the sub problems with non-zero vectors values as well as the M worst examples that violate KKT conditions and then solves the sub problem. The QP sub problem is initialized with the results of the previous one. The general chunking procedure is described as:

1. Decompose the original training data base randomly in:
   a) Training data set (TRN).
   b) Testing data set (TST).
2. Optimize the reduced TRN by classical QP optimization.
3. Obtain the Support Vectors by the previous optimization.
4. Test the Support Vectors in TST by the generalization function (see eq. 5).
5. Recombine Support Vectors and testing errors on a new training Set (TRN-new).
6. Repeat from step 2 until no errors are found by 4.

Algorithm 1. Chunking Algorithm

The first chunk (TRN) is composed using q training patterns randomly selected $(q \ll n)$ from the original data set. Even when the starting point of the algorithm is blind (the solution can be near or far from the real one) by using the chunking procedure, training time for SVM is reduced as revealed in [1] and [4].

3   The Zoutendijk Algorithm

[11] [12] This algorithm belongs to the methods of feasible directions [13]. This class of methods solves a nonlinear programming problem by moving from a feasible point to an improved feasible point. The following strategy is typical of feasible directions algorithms: Given a feasible point $\boldsymbol{x}_k$, a direction $\boldsymbol{d}_k$ is determined such that for $h > 0$ and sufficiently small, the following two properties are true: (1) $\boldsymbol{x}_k + h\boldsymbol{d}_k$ is feasible, and (2) the objective value at $\boldsymbol{x}_k + h\boldsymbol{d}_k$ is better than the objective value at $\boldsymbol{x}_k$. After such a direction is determined, a one- dimensional optimization problem is solved in order to calculate h_k. This leads to a new point $\boldsymbol{x}_{k+1}$ and the process is repeated. Since primal feasibility is maintained during this optimization process, these procedures are often refered to as primal methods.

For the special case of optimizing a SVM, the Zoutendijk algorithm consists in solving the next four steps:

---

1. Find $\boldsymbol{d}_k$, which is the optimal solution of:

$$Maximize \quad f(\boldsymbol{d}) = 1 - (\boldsymbol{H}\boldsymbol{\Lambda}) \cdot d \qquad (6)$$

$$subjet \ to \qquad (7)$$

$$\boldsymbol{Y} \cdot \qquad \boldsymbol{d} = 0 \qquad (8)$$

$$1 \leq \boldsymbol{d} \leq 0 \quad for \ \lambda_i = C \qquad (9)$$

$$0 \leq \boldsymbol{d} \leq 1 \quad for \ \lambda_i = 0 \qquad (10)$$

$$-1 \leq \boldsymbol{d} \leq 1 \quad otherwise \qquad (11)$$

2. If $\nabla f(\lambda_k) \cdot \boldsymbol{d}_k = 0$, stop.
3. Calculate h_k

$$h_k = \frac{d \cdot 1 - dH\Lambda}{2dHd} \qquad (12)$$

4. Let $\boldsymbol{x}_{k+1} = \boldsymbol{x}_k + h_k\boldsymbol{d}_k$. Let k=k+1. Go to step 1.

Algorithm 2. Zoutendijk algorithm

4   The ZQP Method

The ZQP method works as follows:

1. Train the SVM using the Zoutendijk algorithm with a very low penalization constant C.
2. Reconstruct a reduced Hessian matrix with the data set that reach the value of C (H_{new} is smaller than H_{old}).
3. Solve the new problem with a QP solver using a normal C.

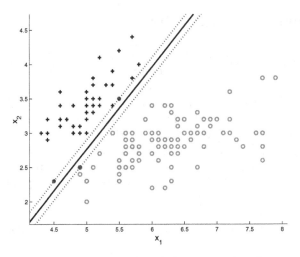

Fig. 1. Training with the whole training data base

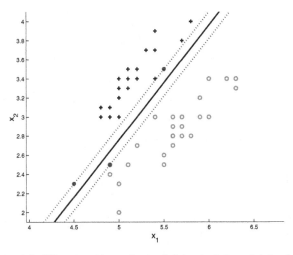

Fig. 2. Training with QP using the subset of data training obtained by Zoutendijk algorithm

For the Iris database, figures (1) and (2) show that if a SVM is trained with all the training data base (figure 1) or with a subset where the SV's are contained (figure 2), the same decision function is obtained. We use this fact to implement a fast method initializing a subset containing the Support Vectors. Finally, with this reduced subset, a QP is performed.

In order to reduce the training time of the Zoutendijk algorithm, the penalization constant C is set to a low value. Having a small C penalization constant, the algorithm is very fast in training an approximated solution.

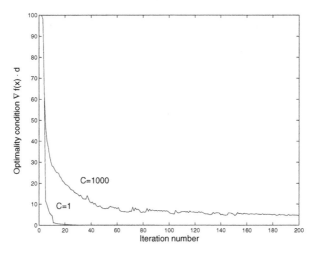

Fig. 3. Convergence of the Zoutendijk algorithm with two different C

Figure 3 shows that the algorithm's convergence is faster having a small C penalization than a bigger one. When this kind of training is performed the result is a vector Λ having two types of values:

1) $\lambda_i = 0$ and
2) $\lambda_i > 0$.

It's important to note that the support vectors are a subset contained in the $\lambda_i > 0$.

This is very useful because, as we have already discussed, a small set including the support vectors is trained using a small number of resources.

One drawback on the Zoutendijk algorithm is related to the construction of the Hessian matrix within the global data set. As we have mention this is very time and memory consuming. To deal with this problem decomposition algorithms, like Chunking [1], Osuna [2] or SMO [3], are used.

We use the ZQP method to solve the generated subproblem in each iteration of the Chunking algorithm, instead of using the traditional QP algorithm.

5 Results

In this section, the results of the ZPQ method are compared to the original QP algorithm available in Matlab. Some benchmarks are used as database: Pima Indians diabetes [21], Iris [21]

5.1 Iris Benchmark

This benchmark is maybe the most known database in different pattern recognition researches. It contains 4 attributes and 2 classes where each class refers to a type of iris plant. Total instances are 150 where 50 belong to a class and the rest to other. Results are presented in Table 1.

Table 1. Comparison of the SVM training of the Iris database with traditional Chunking with QP versus the training with Chunking and the ZQP algorithm

	Trainnig with QP	Trainning with the ZQP algorithm
Examples	150	150
kernel	polynomial	polynomial
Degree	2	2
Chunk size	30%	30%
C	1000	0.001
SV	11	11
Total training time	0.6176	0.5547
Std. Dv.	0.1077	0.1108
Error	0 %	0 %

Table 1 shows that the Chunking with ZQP algorithm is a little faster than the traditional training with QP. In this case the training time is very similar because the data base is very small.

5.2 Pima Indians Diabetes Benchmark

Pima Indians diabetes benchmark is used to observe if a patient shows signs of diabetes according to World Health Organization criteria. The number of instances is 768 having 8 attributes.

Table 2 shows that the training time of the Chunking with QP algorithm is each the same that the chunking with the ZQP method. This is because the number of support vectors is similar to the number of examples and this provokes that the number of examples that can be eliminated with Zoutendijk is very small.

Table 2. Comparison of the SVM training of the Pima Indians Diabetes database with traditional Chunking with QP versus the training with Chunking and the ZQP algorithm

	Trainnig with QP	Trainning with the ZQP algorithm
Examples	768	768
kernel	polynomial	polynomial
Degree	2	2
Chunk size	10%	10%
C	1000	0.001
SV	608	608
Total training time	195.8	195.1466
Std. Dv.	18.12	19.11
Error	0 %	0 %

Table 3. Comparison of the SVM training of the Phonemes database with traditional Chunking with QP versus the training with Chunking with the ZQP algorithm

	Trainnig with QP	Trainning with the ZQP algorithm
Examples	1027	1027
kernel	RBF	RBF
Gamma	2	2
Chunk size	10%	10%
C	1000	0.001
SV	329	329
Total training time	271.35	235.5911
Std. Dv.	41.8011	12.6499
Error	0 %	0 %

5.3 Phonemes

Table 3 shows that the training time of the Chunking with QP algorithm is faster than the Chunking with the ZQP method. This is because the number of support vectors is considerably smaller than the number of examples.

6 Summary and Conclusions

SMV presents good classification, regression and density estimation results, but his principal problem lies on the prohibitive training time. This paper presents a hybrid approach for the solution of the QP problem generated by a SVM. In this work we compared the hybrid method, Zoutendijk with Quadprog (ZQP), against the normal approach that is using the only the QP algorithm and the results show that the hybrid approach has a better behavior that the Quadprog optimizer.

References

1. VAPNIK, V. Statistical Learning Theory. *Journal of the Association for Computing Machinery*, 40:741–764, 1993.
2. OSUNA E. et al. "Suppot Vector Machines: Training and applications". In *Massachusetts Institute of Technology*, Marzo de 1997.
3. PLATT, JOHN. Fast Training of Support Vector Machines using Sequential Minimal Optimization. Microsoft Research. MIT Press, 1998.
4. BOSER, B.E., GUYON I., VAPNIK,V. A training algorithm for optimal margin classifiers *Proceedings of the 5th Annual ACM Workshop on Computational learning Theory*, 1992, pp. 144-152.
5. VECKMAN, VOJISLAV. Learning and Soft Computing. In *MIT Press, Cambidge Massachusetts*, 2001.
6. CRISTIANINI, N., SHAWE, J. An Introduction to Support Vector Machines and other kernel-based learning methods. Cambridge University Press, 2002.

7. VAPNIK, V. An Overview of Statistical Learning Theory. *IRRR Transactions on Neural Networks, Vol. 10, no.5, september 1999.*

8. VAPNIK, V. and CHERVONENKIS, A. J. One the uniform convergence of relative frequencies of events to their probabilities. Theory of probabilities and its applications, vol. 16, pp. 264-280, 1971.

9. VAPNIK, V., Minimization of expected risk based on empirical data. Proc. of the 1st World Congress of the Bernoulli Society VNUSCIENCEPRESS, vol. 2, Utrecht, the Netherlands, pp. 821-832, 1987.

10. VAPNIK, V. and CHERVONENKIS, A. J. The necessary and sufficient conditions for consistency in the empirical risk minimization method Pattern Recognition and Image Analysis, vol. 1, no. 3, pp. 283-305, 1991.

11. FRAUSTO, JUAN, RIVERA, RAFAEL et al. Fast hard Linear Problem resolution using Simulatead Annealing and Datzing's Rule. *Proc. of IASTED Int. Conf. in Artificial Intelligence and Soft Computing (ASC 2001),* May 2001.

12. FRAUSTO, JUAN, RIVERA, RAFAEL. A simplex Genetic Method for Solving the Klee Minty Cube. *Transactions on Systems, WSEAS, 2(1) pp 232-237.ISSN 1109-2777,* April 2002.

13. BAZARAA, M., SHETTY, C.M. Nonlinear Programing, Theory and Algorithms. *School of Industrial and Systems Enginnering, Georgia Institute of Technology, Atlanta, Georgia. Jhon Wiley & Sons,* 1979.

14. VAŠEK CHVÁTAL. Linear programming. *W.H. freeman and Company, New York,* 2000.

15. FLORES R, HERNÁNDEZ A. Uso de algoritmos genéticos para detección de vectores de soporte en el entrenamiento de Máquinas de Soporte Vectorial. Memorias del Primer Congreso Mexicano de Computación Evolutiva, México 2003.

16. VAŽIANGRONG, ZHANG, FANG, LIU. A Pattern Classification Method Based on GA and SVM. *Signal Processing, 2002 6th International Conference on, Volume: 1, 26-30 Pages: 110-113 vol.1,* Aug. 2002.

17. RYCHETSKY, M., ORTMANN, S., ULLMANN, M. AND GLESNER, M. "Accelerated training of Support Vector Machines." *IJCNN '99. International Joint Conference on Neural Networks,* July 1999.

18. MING-HSUAN YANG, AHUJA, N.A. *A Geometric Approach to Train Support Vector Machines. Computer Vision and Pattern Recognition, 2000.* Proceedings. IEEE Conference on, June 2000.

19. GARCÍA, A. HERNÁNDEZ, N. Reducing the training speed of Support Vector Machines By Barycentric Correction Procedure. WSEAS TRANSACTIONS. on SYSTEMS. Issue 3, Volume 3, May 2004. ISSN 1109-2777.

20. STEPHENS, C. MORA, J. Effective fitness as an alternative paradigm for evolutionary computation I: General Formalism GENETIC PROGRAMMING AND EVOLVABLE MACHINES Issue 4, Volume 1, October 2000. ISSN 1389-2576.

21. BLAKE, C.L. and MERS. UCI Repository of machine learning databases. http://www.ics.uci.edu/ mlearn/MLRepository.html, Department of Information and Computer Science, 1998.

Video Motion Detection Using the Algorithm of Discrimination and the Hamming Distance

Josué A. Hernández-García, Héctor Pérez-Meana, and Mariko Nakano-Miyatake

SEPI ESIME Culhuacan, National Polytechnic Institute, Av. Santa Ana #1000,
San Francisco Culhuacan, C.P. 04430 Edificio 2, 3er Piso México D.F, Mexico
josue_a_hdez@hotmail.com
hmpm@calmecac.esimecu.ipn.mx

Abstract. Several video detection systems that use a simple system of motion detection (if something moves, is generated an alarm) have been proposed, for this reason we trust part of the process to the human interpretation. Recent studies have demonstrated that a person is almost impossible to kindly watch a static scene in a monitor more than 20 minutes, doing that traditional systems of video monitoring as CCTV systems are little reliable, also, it is necessary to add numerous and annoying the false alarms generated by the few elimination of irrelevant information (color, light, shade, etc.) within the scene. The artificial vision nowadays allows having an automatic system of monitoring with the capacities to identify real threats and alert of security at the same time that they are happening. This paper presents a method of video motion detection that bases its use on an algorithm of discrimination able to eliminate the irrelevant information caused by natural effects (sun, moon, wind, etc.) or animals, maintaining the maximum of details on the image, allowing a better detection of motion through the distance of Hamming doubly justified, reducing in this way rate of false alarms, obtaining a method of motion detection automatic and reliable. In this paper is mentioned the comparison with other techniques, demonstrating itself that the proposed method gives better results. The obtained results show the basic characteristics of this method of detection.

1 Introduction

An accurate video monitoring system must cover necessarily certain requirements (trustworthiness, quality of image, low number of false alarms, interoperability with other systems etc.) if we want that it can get to be really usable and with the possibility to improve through future investigations with no need to modify all its stages [2]. The video monitoring is nowadays the used system more for the monitoring of places like buildings, banks, governmental offices, malls, prisons, airports etc. [1]. At present great part of these systems gets to have a high cost of maintenance, requires great capacity of storage when being recording the 24 hours of the day with necessity of human intervention the 24 hours to be able to determine if it is a real alert or no, because these systems are not able to detect the difference between no significant motions, like leaves moving by the wind and the significant motions as a person jumping a fence [3]. Making this class of systems is time ineffective. On the other hand these monitoring systems do not guarantee that all the irregular events are detected because at any moment the security guards can have some kind of distraction causing that they turn their attention another object, it give as result, a momentary abandonment of the monitored which could be important [2].

F.F. Ramos et al. (Eds.): ISSADS 2005, LNCS 3563, pp. 321–330, 2005.
© Springer-Verlag Berlin Heidelberg 2005

An ideal system of video monitoring would be able to imitate, totality, the sense of the human vision, without tired or distraction problems, considering that through the eyes we received information of the objects position of the surroundings, determined the free way of obstacles, distinguished what it moves of the static thing, we calculated trajectories, we distinguished between people, objects and animals, we detected the presence of possible dangers, etc. [4], nevertheless it until the moment is practically impossible. But, taken in consideration the powerful systems of computation present, we can establish several analogies between the human and artificial vision, since both have a sensorial element (the eye and the camera) and a processor of the information (the brain and the computer) [4] allowing create video monitoring systems able to distinguish the different elements within a scene with no need to be analyze by human during the 24 hours of day, affirming that it is not to replicate the sense of Human Vision.

The artificial vision consists of teaching to the computers " to see ", allowing that certain processes interpret what " they see " and thus to be able to make decisions in order to give resolution to the problems [3]. The figure 1 showed the form in which a computer interprets an analogical image in a digital image.

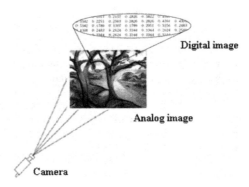

Fig. 1. Representation of computational vision

With the computation systems present not only is possible to obtain and analyze the patterns of a scene through the artificial vision, also it allows to store the information that we wish at the moment that is necessary and combining it with the communication technology is possible controlled the monitoring systems centrally in safe way using cryptographic methods to protect data that are transmitted and received by the network. In this way we only store and forward the important information, taking advantage of the resources to the maximum, obtaining in this way a reliable, automatic and versatile system. So that a video monitoring system present, covers the future necessities about security, is necessary that it bases its system on this technology, if we do not taken in consideration these points, these systems in a moment got to be obsolete.

2   Motion Detection

The basic idea is simple: the motion detection within a scene where normally is without motion [1]. The different types of motion that exist are:

- Object Motion.
- Changes in illumination.
- Changes in structure, forms or size of the object.

The simplest method for video motion detection is that is based on the difference of images, being less precise if it is applied directly on an image that has not been processed previously. Other systems are based on the graphic differentiation of the images to make the motion detection (figure 2), these systems transform the image matrix to vector, later each vector is compared with the vector bases and if the new vector exceeds certain scale in respect to the vector bases goes on an alarm indicating the movement presence, the problem that presents this method, is that, does not consider the changes in the scene caused by natural effects as well as the distinction between animals, objects and people because the image is not analyzed before comparing it graphically.

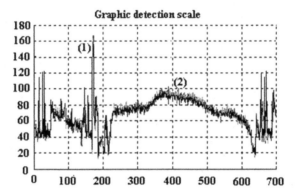

Fig. 2. Detection method based on an image graphic scale. Image with movement (1), and image without movement (2)

Taken in consideration the importance of eliminate the irrelevant information in the scene, in order to obtain a precise detection with the used method of detection, different methods were created trying to discriminate the irrelevant information by techniques of edge detection using mask of Sobel and the motion detection by the difference of brightness between 4 images taken different pixels by image and base their final result in the use of hierarchic rules. Problem that presents this method of discrimination is loss of details that edge detector presents over the image when is using on this (details which they can be important for the motion detection), diminishing in this way the effectiveness of the brightness differentiation.

Analyzing the previous we could observe the importance that has the elimination of irrelevant information, but, conserving the maximum of details on the scene to increase the effectiveness of the used method of detection. The method proposed in this paper (figure 3) is able to eliminate and to diminish the irrelevant information in the scene by an algorithm of discrimination and a motion detection based on the distance of Hamming doubly justified.

In the figure 3 is possible to be observed a blue box that the discrimination algorithm includes and a red box that the stage of motion detection contains on the processed image.

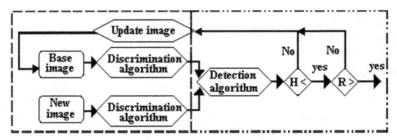

Fig. 3. Block diagram of the proposed detection system

3   Discrimination Algorithm

The elimination of irrelevant information and the details preservation within a scene, are the first stage that must have a system of motion detection, which is very important, for the efficiency and precision of the system, to greater number of details greater precision [2].

Systems of motion detection that fulfill some of these two points, using, graphics scales for the discrimination of irrelevant information or edge detectors like Sobel, Prewitt, Canny, etc. obtaining efficient but little precise systems or vice versa [2].

Through this algorithm is obtained considerably increases the level of motion detection, diminishing the common errors of detection; the principal function of this algorithm is discrimination or elimination of irrelevant information, conserving the maximum of details in the image, allowing a better motion detection, the algorithm is formed by 4 stages as it showed in the figure 4.

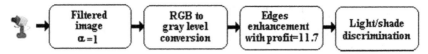

Fig. 4. Block diagram of the algorithm to discrimination

3.1   Image Filtering

The filtering is a technique to modify or to improve an image, a filter can emphasize or attenuate some characteristics and is an operation of neighborhood, where the value of pixel given in the processed image calculates by some algorithm that taken in consideration the values from pixels from the vicinity from the original image [5].

In this stage a Unsharp filter is used with a value of $\propto$ determined, this type of filtrate helps to eliminate or to diminish the noise and at the same time emphasizes the characteristics of the image, this stage is very important, if we do not considering it we could have variations in our reading from the beginning which could cause an incorrect detection of movement, diminishing the reliability of the system [2].

In the equation (1) showed the equation that is used to create the Unsharp filter the value of alpha can vary from 0,1 to 1.

$$\frac{1}{(\alpha+1)}\begin{bmatrix} -\alpha & \alpha-1 & -\alpha \\ \alpha-1 & \alpha+5 & \alpha-1 \\ -\alpha & \alpha-1 & -\alpha \end{bmatrix} \qquad (1)$$

3.2 Convertion from a RGB Image to Gray Level Image

In motion detection system colors within an image are irrelevant, since it is not of interest to know how it is color of the elements of the zone, that we know, is watching or the color of clothes of the person who access a prohibited place, things for our interests, is to detect the moment when that person is invading a prohibited zone or to detect when the object that must not have movement has it, by this, in the second stage becomes an image RGB to an image gray scale. This type of change not only helps to eliminate the irrelevant part of the color also is an important factor for discrimination of irrelevant information caused by natural elements (sun, moon, etc.), which can cause to changes in the values of pixels of the image matrix, causing differences in respect to the original image, and, if the discrimination of these elements is not taken into account will have false alarms [2].

3.3 Edges Enhance

Edges enhances in an image has the opposed effect to the elimination of noise; it consists on to emphasize or to stand out those pixels that has a value of gray different to that of their neighbors [5].

To be able to have it enhances of acceptable edges it is necessary to eliminate the noise that can have the image by filter, previously since of not making it the effect of noise is multiplied [2]. Edge enhances consists on increasing the gain of the high frequencies, according to the equation (2).

$$\text{Resulting image} = [(\text{Original Profit}) \times (\text{Image}) - \text{Low frequencies}] \times \frac{1}{9} \qquad (2)$$

The importance of applying an edges enhances and not an edges detector is that edges enhances eliminates a percentage greater of light and shade, maintains the maximum of details on the image and it allows to make a second elimination of light and shade in the image even conserving, the maximum of details in the image, which can not be done applying to a edges detector [2].

3.4 Final Discrimination

In the last stage of discrimination, the second elimination of irrelevant information in the image is made eliminated pixels which value greater 20, for this is used the equation (3), which makes a multiplication between pixels of matrix with the same matrix, obtaining a maximum of elimination of light and shade.

$$C(x, y) = A(x, y) \bullet B(x, y) \qquad (3)$$

The results obtained when applying the algorithm of discrimination to a scene, are observed in the figure 6, in his figure we can observe the conservation of detail in the scene and the discrimination of irrelevant information like light variations or the movements of leaves in trees caused by natural effects. The results application of this algorithm offers give the possibility of make a better detection within the scene.

Fig. 5. Original Image

Fig. 6. Processed image

4 Detection Algorithm

Different algorithms exist that can be used for motion detection, as the discreet Fourier transformed, parallel approach, tracking contours, space differentiation etc. The suitable selection of this algorithm will depend, to a large extent, of application system and the compatibility with the seen algorithm of discrimination previously, in other way, the algorithms combination that offers better results.

The distance of Hamming is a method that allows to compare 2 images, pixel by pixel giving like result of that single comparison 2 values [1 0] that is similar to say [equal different], allowing a better analysis of scene, allowing a better detection [6]. Like the differentiation, the distance of Hamming offers good results when the scene to compare has been processed previously.

The temporary differentiation between images is a method that offers good results if it is applied of suitable way, its means that the image has been processed previously (elimination of irrelevant information) before being applied [7]. The temporary differentiation consists of reducing the existing difference between two possibly different patterns, taking on memory that it is necessary to standardize the obtained values to avoid possible errors in the result.

Combining both methods we managed to obtain an algorithm able to detect significant movements, with great exactitude, the algorithm this formed by two stages as showed in figure 7.

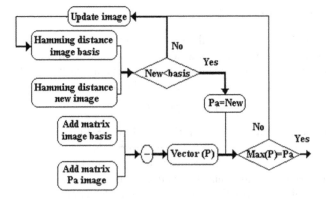

Fig. 7. Block diagram of detection algorithm

The operation of this algorithm is based on two stages, in the first stage compute the range of Hamming of the second scene with the scene bases, if the result exceeds a determined scale, is indicated to the system that can be a possible significant movement and a pointer is created indicating in that scene was detected the movement, calling to the second stage of the algorithm, if the result does not exceed the determined scale, the image bases is updated and the following scene is compared now with the new image bases. The fact to change the image constantly bases, serves the system to be able to adapt to the natural changes that surround the scene.

In the second stage 4 scenes are taken counting from the scene where registry possible motion and one or two scenes later, depending on number of previous scenes available. We calculated the temporary difference of these scenes with respect to the scene bases, and if the maximum value of this differentiation agrees with the position of the scene calculated in the distance of Hamming registered in the pointer, the result will be the detection of a significant motion.

5   Experimental Results

The tests were made in MATLAB, using 2 different sequences of image where the variations by irrelevant information are well-known, something that is very important to note is the run time system, because the intention of these systems is not to make videos with quality of films. The rates of recording with low rates as 1 or 2 frames per second will be able to capture any criminal act virtually. The run time of this algorithm is enough short comparing it with other systems (0,5 to 0,8 sec.) and covering the rate with recording required in these systems.

The first test that we made was with a short sequence of 4 different scenes (figure 8) in each scene are different variations from no significant motions like the motions from leaves, the position of some objects among others to the detection of an intruder in the monitoring place. Frame 4 where the significant motion is, and which must being detected by our system.

Fig. 8. Sequence of 4 frames taken by the movement detection system

The first results are obtained when applying the algorithm of discrimination in 4 scenes obtaining to conserve details in the image and eliminating unnecessary information of the scene. The sequence of images processed by the discrimination algorithm is observed in (figure 9).

Fig. 9. Sequence of 4 processed frames

The algorithm of detection is applied from the second scene, the distance of Hamming is calculated in the second image taking in consideration that the result does not have to exceed the scale indicated in case of doing it take 3 sequences more and the second stage of the algorithm is applied. In this test it observed that significant motion is in the last frame where the first trigger of the system goes on. In the figure 10 is possible to observed results in graphic form of the distance of Hamming.

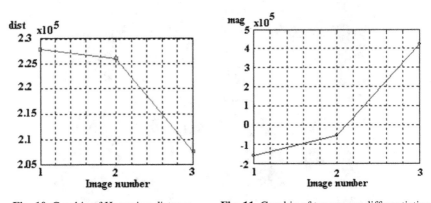

Fig. 10. Graphic of Hamming distance   **Fig. 11.** Graphic of temporary differentiation

Fig. 12. Sequence of 6 frames taken by the system

Fig. 13. Sequences of 6 processed frames

Now taking the first trigger generated by the distance from Hamming the second stage of this algorithm is applied, where temporary differentiation of the 4 scenes is compute, and the position of the maximum with the first trigger is compared if both agree the system shoots to the second trigger generating an alarm. In the figure 11 the graphic representation of the result of this is observed second stage. Observing both graphics we can note that the last points that represent the 4 frame are connected, reason why the system interprets this result like detection of a significant motion and that is correct. The second test where made taking 6 different sequences now (figure (12)), in different scene, making the same procedure that in previous test. The obtained results are the following ones.

In this last sequence could observed that significant movement appears in scene 4 and 5, being more well-known in scene five. The results in application of the algorithm of detection are observed in the figure 14. It is possible to observe that the distance that exceeds the scale is the pertaining to scene 5, goes on the first trigger and it is verified with the second stage shown in the figure (15).

It is possible to be observed in both graphics that the detection point is connected in the scene 5 which is where the significant motion appears, having then like result of both tests, a reliable motion detection.

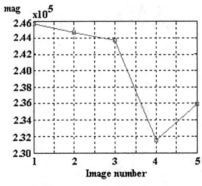

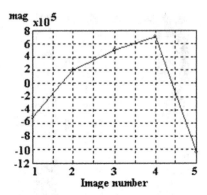

Fig. 14. Graphic of Hamming distance   **Fig. 15.** Graphic of temporary differentiation

6 Conclusions

The detection system proposed, has demonstrated contain better efficiency and exactitude in the different made tests that some used systems at the moment. Giving to beginning to application of better video monitoring systems, considering that even is possible to improve this method having like objective getting to develop to a video system monitoring able to make tasks similar to human vision. Since the great importance and application that the artificial vision has generated in the present time, force to look for better detection systems to us but that simultaneously they are able to save space in storage with possibility of remote control with no need of human intervention.

Acknowledgments

The authors specially thank to the National Science and Technology Council (CONACYT) and National Polytechnic Institute for the support during the realization of this research.

References

1. Bernard J. T. Jones, Low Cost Outdoor Video Motion And Non-Motion Detection; ASTRA Developments Ltd; Lundegaardsvej, 23 Hellerup, DK 2900, Denmark.
2. Josue A. Hernandez, Hector P. Meana, Algorithm of Discrimination for Motion Detection, SEPI Culhuacan IPN, CICINDI-2004, pp. 1-9
3. IT-Deusto company, Object Video System Proyect. España-2004, pp. 1-3.
4. Arturo De La Escalera Hueso, Computation Vision; Pearson Education S.A., Madrid, 2001, pp. 5-23
5. M. C. José Jaime Esqueda Elizondo, Image Processing Tools; Instituto Tecnologico De Ciudad Madero, 2002, pp. 7-21
6. Mathwork Co. Manual Engineering of image processing, pp. 155-202
7. Ling Guan, Sun-Yuan Kung, Multimedia Image And Video Processing; CRC Press; Boca Raton London, 2002, pp. 100-134.

An Efficient and Grain Preservation Mapping Algorithm: From ER Diagram to Multidimensional Model

Yen-Ting Chen[1,2] and Ping-Yu Hsu[3]

[1] Department of Business Administration, National Central University,
Jhongli City, Taoyuan 320, Taiwan, R.O.C.
[2] Department of Information Management, Lunghwa University of Science
and Technology, Taoyuan 333, Taiwan, R.O.C.
s1441001@cc.ncu.edu.tw
[3] Department of Business Administration, National Central University,
Jhongli City, Taoyuan 320, Taiwan, R.O.C.
pyhsu@mgt.ncu.edu.tw

Abstract. Many practitioners and researchers advocate that the designs of the data models of the data warehouses should incorporate the source data as much as possible to answer the finest levels of queries. On the other hand, the source data are very likely to come from systems designed with ER Diagrams. Therefore, many researches have been devoted to design methodologies to build multidimensional model based on corresponding source ER diagrams. However, to the best of our knowledge, no algorithm has been proposed to systematically translates an entire ER Diagram into a multidimensional model with hierarchical snowflake structures. The algorithm proposed in the paper promised to do so with two characteristics, namely, grain preservation and minimal distance from each table to the fact table. Grain preservation characteristic guarantees that translated multidimensional model has cohesive granularity among entities. The minimal distance characteristics guarantees that if an entity can be connected to the fact table in the derived model with more than one paths, the one with the shortest hops will always be chosen. The first characteristic is achieved by translating problematic relationships between entities with weight_factor attributes in bridging tables and enhancing fact tables with unique primary keys. The second characteristic is achieved by including a revised shortest path algorithm in the translating algorithm with the distance being calculated as the number of relationships required between entities.

1 Introduction

As enterprizes worldwide strive to compete on real time management, providing valuable information in time to managers to help them perform timely decisions has become a critical mission for MIS departments in organizations worldwide. Among the related applications installed, data warehouses play a vital role for integrating, storing, and querying data. The data collected in data warehouses come from various transactional processing systems, such as, ERP, POS, etc. The

F.F. Ramos et al. (Eds.): ISSADS 2005, LNCS 3563, pp. 331–346, 2005.

collected data are cleaned, integrated and organized into structures designed for easy access and quick comprehension, for the purpose of decision making [11, 12]. With its wide applications, many researches have been devoted to the study of proper models of data presentation [1–5, 7–10, 12, 13, 15–21]. The dominant data model for representing a data warehouse is multidimensional modelling[1], also known as a *malposition* model, which is composed of a fact table in the center and a set of dimensional tables in the peripheral. The fact table stores measures of performance indicators which managers are interested to know and dimensional tables provide the viewpoints or entry points to view the data. A fact table and corresponding dimensional tables are linked by storing the primary keys of dimensional tables in the fact table. Figure 1 is excerpted from [13] and shows a sample multidimensional model with a fact table and three-dimensional tables. The grain is the level of detail at which measurements or events are stored [13, 20]. To have cohesive querying results, the multidimensional models designed must have consistent grains, as pointed out by Inmon & Kimball [11, 13]. After the grain is declared, all measures in the fact table and all dimension tables must adhere to the grain. Otherwise, unexpected query result may be returned. Following is an example of the grain mismatch. In a typical supermarket visit, customers may buy several products in one transaction and the dollar amount of each product is aggregated into a total. Given a multidimensional model recording the total dollar amount of each transaction, the grain is in the level of transaction. (shown in Figure 2). If products are also stored as a dimension in the model, then querying the transaction amounts from product dimension will return figures that not only include amount of the product but also the amounts of other products purchased in the same transaction. The difference is due to the grain mismatch in the fact and the dimension table. The grain of the fact table is in transaction level, which may contains more than one products. Therefore, designing a model with coherent facts and dimensions is vital in designing multidimensional models.

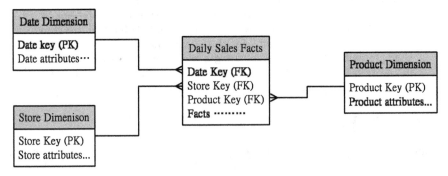

Fig. 1. A Sample Multidimensional Model; source [13]

---

[1] Multidimensional model is also referred as dimensional model in some studies

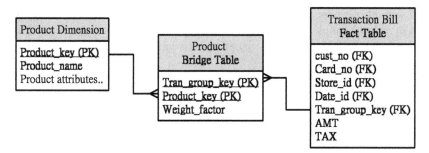

Fig. 2. The many-to-many relationship between the fact and dimension tables

On the other hand, data in a data warehouse are populated from source systems whose data probably are modeled by ER diagrams [6]. Therefore, the source ER diagrams show the most finest granular data that can be stored in a corresponding multidimensional model. If a systematic approach can be found to build multidimensional models to store data retrieved from the source systems modeled by ER diagrams, the work of model designers can be greatly reduced and more importantly, the errors committed can also be dramatically reduced.

Therefore, practitioners and researches have strived to propose methodologies to design multidimensional models from existing ER diagrams [3, 5, 8, 9, 14–16, 19–21]. Even though [12, 16, 20] acknowledged the importance of grain consistence, they provide only vague guidelines for the mapping and do not specify any concrete algorithms to perform task. Moody and Kortink [16] proposed a three-step method,including classifying entities, identifying hierarchies and producing dimensional models, for developing a dimension model from entity relational models. They also presented five optional schemas in the paper, from simple flat schema to complex snowflake schema. Song et al.[20] presented five methods to handle many-to-many relationships from an ERD to a dimension model. The possible solutions can be either adding a bridge table, denormalizing the dimensional table by positional-flag attributes or non-positional attribute, lowering the grain of the fact table to the dimension grain level, or lowering the grain of the fact table by separating data from the fact table.Bonifati et al. [4] presented a method to design a data mart. The method consists of three steps: top-down requirement analysis to elicit and consolidate user-requirements, bottom-up data model extract to form candidate data mart, and consolidation to derive the ideal data marts. Similarly, Cabibbo and Torlone [5] proposed method to obtain a Multidimensional schema from an underlying operational databases. The schema consists of a finite set of dimensions, a finite set of F-tables, and a finite set of level descriptions of the dimensions. Golfarelli et al. [8] presented a graphical conceptual model (Dimensional Fact model) for data warehouses and a semi-automated methodology to construct a tree-structured fact schema from an Entity-Relation schema. Marotta et al. [15] provided a set of transformation rules to trace the mapping between source logical schema and data warehouse logical schema. Tryfona et al., [21] presented a new model, the starER model, to make semantics richer than traditional multidimensional model to record many-to-many relationships between fact and dimensional tables.Boehnlein et al. [3] proposed the SERM model to visualize existence dependencies between data object types.

The approach proposed in the paper differs from the other approaches in following ways:

(a) the algorithm systematically performs ER Diagrams to multidimensional model translation, given the fact table identified,
(b) the algorithm guarantees that adding a new entity to the structure does not change the grain of existing entities,
(c) the snowflake structure proposed by the algorithm takes the fewest relationship to connect dimensions and the given fact table.

The remainder of this paper is organized as follows: Section 2 formally defines grain preservations. Section 3 presents the ER to multidimensional translation algorithm. Section 4 explains how the two characteristics are achieved by the algorithm.

Section 5 uses a case to demonstrate the algorithm. Finally, the summary and future work is presented in Section 6.

2   Grain Preservation

As Kimball pointed out [13], a multidimensional model in general contains a fact table and a set of dimension tables. Each dimension table has a primary key which is also a foreign key of the fact table. The primary key of the fact table is the composition of all the foreign keys stored in the dimension tables.

If grain mismatch happens between the fact table and any of the dimension tables then the query result may be wrong [13, 20]. The erroneous queries return values that aggregate individual measures more than one time. Hence, a multidimensional model with the consistent grain should aggregate at most one copy of individual measure, regardless of the dimensions users querying along. Before formally defining grain preservation, we need to define two operators, namely, $\sum$ and $\star$.

Definition 1 *Given a table, T, with m of its attributes are measures,namely, $a_{i1}, \ldots, a_{im}$, and n of its attributes are weight factors, namely, $a_{j_1}, \ldots, a_{j_n}$.*

- $\sum a_{ik} = \sum_{t \in T} t.a_{ik}$, for $1 \le k \le m$
- $\sum(T) = \langle \sum a_{i1}, \ldots, \sum a_{im} \rangle$.
- $\star(T) = \{t' | \forall a \in \text{attriubtes of } T, t \in T, (a \notin \{a_{i1}, \ldots, a_{im}\} \to t'.a = t.a) \wedge (a \in \{a_{i1}, \ldots, a_{im}\} \to t'.a = t.a * t.a_{j_1} * \ldots * t.a_{j_n})\}$

With the $\star$ operator, a measure can be refined to finer grain. Table 1 shows a sample table with customer# as a non measure attribute, amount and cost as measures and weight_factor$_1$, weight_factor$_2$ as weight factor attributes.

Table 2 shows the result of applying $\star$ operator on Table 1.

Table 1. A sample Table

customer#	amount	cost	weight_factor$_1$	weight_factor$_2$
c125	50	30	0.4	0.2
c125	50	30	0.6	0.8
c125	50	30	0.4	0.8
c125	50	30	0.6	0.2
c127	40	30	1.0	1.0

Table 2. Applying $\star$ to Table 1

customer#	amount	cost	weight_factor$_1$	weight_factor$_2$
c125	4	2.4	0.4	0.2
c125	24	14.4	0.6	0.8
c125	16	9.6	0.4	0.8
c125	6	3.6	0.6	0.2
c127	40	30	1.0	1.0

In a multidimensional model with snowflakes, a table can be added as a dimension table, which connects to the fact table directly, or as a table in the snowflake hierarchy, which is composed by a set of tables connected as a tree with the fact table as the root. A table added to a multidimensional model without breaking the existing grain provides an entry point to correctly summary measures.

Definition 2 *Given a multidimensional model with a fact table, F, and a table T, if adding T to the multidimensional model results in a path of $F, D_1, \ldots, D_k, T$ connecting T to F, and $\sum(\star(F \bowtie D_1 \ldots \bowtie D_k \bowtie T)) = \sum(F)$, where $\bowtie$ is a natural join operator then the addition is called* Grain Preservation.

3   The Mapping Algorithm

The section shows a relationship translation algorithm, which translates entities and relationships in an ER diagram to dimension tables in a multidimensional model while keeping grain preservations and taking the least join operators.

Given the ER diagram of a source system, the entities connecting to others with some many-to-many relationships and including additive numeric attributes are candidates for being the fact tables [12]. The paper assumes that a table in the source ER diagram is identified as the fact table which contains several fact attributes, also known as measures.

Given a source ER diagram with $\langle E, R \rangle$, where E is the set of entities and R is the partial functions of relationships in the ER Diagram. $R : E \times E \to \{$'1-1','1-M','M-1','M-N'$\}$, where '1-1','1-M', 'M-1' and 'M-N' denote the cardinality of the relationships.

A multidimensional model is a $\langle DE, DR \rangle$, where DE is the set of tables in the model, and DR is the partial function of relationships between the tables. Every entity in E, and DE is assumed to have a primary key.

3.1   Naive Mapping Rules

The naive mapping rules analyze the R between entities in the source ER diagram and translate corresponding entities and relationships into multidimensional model. Translation of '1-M' and 'M-to-N' relationships may produce grain mismatch if they are not handled carefully. As pointed out in [12, 13, 20],the mismatch can be corrected by lowering the grain in the fact tables or the grain in the dimension tables. In the case of snowflaked multidimensional model, we argue that lowering the grain of dimension tables should be more preferable since the same methodology can be applied to lower the grains of tables down in the snowflake hierarchy.

If $R(E_i, E_j)$ exists and $E_i \in DE$ then E_j is added to the DE in following ways:

– Rule#1: $R(E_i, E_j) =$ 'M-to-1'
  In this case, the translation is straightforward.

$$DE = DE \bigcup \{E_j\}$$
$$DR = DR \bigcup \{DR(E_i, E_j) = R(E_i, E_j)\}$$

Figure 3 shows an example of such cases.

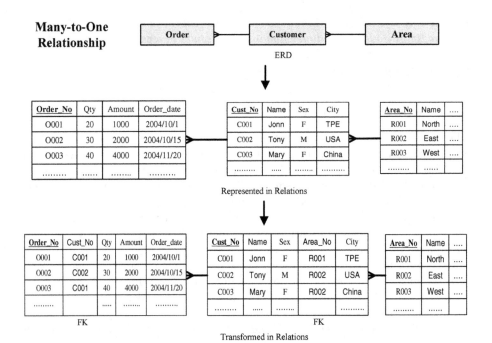

Fig. 3. Transformation in a 'many-to-one' relationship

- Rule#2: $\boldsymbol{R}(E_i, E_j) =$ '1-to-M'
  Since the grain of E_j is finer than the grain of E_i, an attribute of weight factor is added to E_j to tune the grain of E_j.

$$\boldsymbol{E}'_j = \boldsymbol{E}_j + \text{weight\_factor}$$
$$\boldsymbol{DE} = \boldsymbol{DE} \bigcup \{E'_j\}$$
$$\boldsymbol{DR} = \boldsymbol{DR} \bigcup \{\boldsymbol{DR}(E_i, E'_j) = \boldsymbol{R}(E_i, E_j)\}$$

Figure 4 shows an example of '1-M' relationship translation.

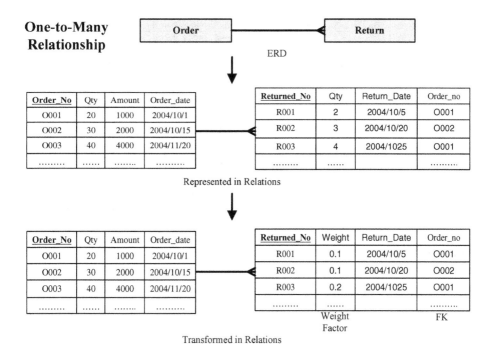

Fig. 4. Translation of a 'one-to-many' relationship

- Rule#3: $\boldsymbol{R}(E_i, E_j) =$ 'M-to-N'
  Since The grains in the two tables are incompatible, a bridging table $\boldsymbol{B}$ is added to tune the grain. The table has two foreign keys coming from E_j, and E_i, respectively, and an attribute of weight_factor[12, 20]. The foreign key from E_i groups entries in E_j so that the combinations of the entries have the same grains as the corresponding entries in the E_i. The attribute of weight_factor records the contribution of the entries in the group. The summation of weight_factor in each group should be equal to one.

$$\boldsymbol{B} = \langle weight\_factor \rangle$$
$$\boldsymbol{DE} = \boldsymbol{DE} \bigcup \{E_j, \boldsymbol{B}\}$$

$$DR = DR \bigcup \{DR(E_i, B) = \text{`1} - to - M\text{'}\}$$

$$DR = DR \bigcup \{DR(B, E_j) = \text{`}M - to - 1\text{'}\}$$

Figure 5 shows such an example. The algorithm of transformation rules is shown in Figure 6.

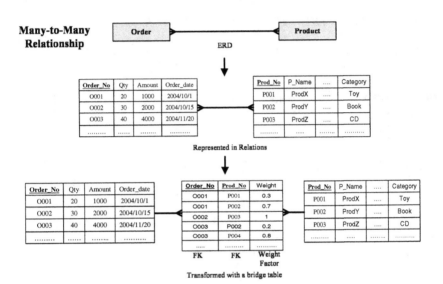

Fig. 5. Translation of a 'many-to-many' relationship

Algorithm: MR
Input: E_0 //the fact table
          $\langle E, R \rangle$ //the original ERD
Output: $\langle DE, DR \rangle$ //the desired multidimensional model

    Begin
        $\langle L_0, L \rangle = \text{Shortest\_distance}(E_0, \langle E, R \rangle)$
        $DE = \{E_0\}$
        While $\exists E_i, E_j \in E$
            and $E_i \in DE \wedge E_j \notin DE$
            and $L(E_0, E_j) = L(E_0, E_i) + min(L_0(E_i, E_j), L_0(E_j, E_i))$ do {
            case $R(E_i, E_j)$ {
                when (1,1) then apply rule#1
                when (M,1) then apply rule#1
                when (1,M) then apply rule#2
                when (M,N) then apply rule#3
            }
        }
        Return $\langle DE, DR \rangle$
        End;

Fig. 6. Relationship Translation Rules

3.2   Applying the Mapping Rules to an ER Diagram

This section further explains the process of building an entire multidimensional model from a given source ER diagram. The algorithm proposed assume that a fact table in the source ER diagram has been identified and strives to find a multidimensional model with the least number of number of relationships.

Since an ER Diagram can be translated to more than one multidimensional model, the major decisions lie on the selection of relationships to form the translated multidimensional model. The point is illustrated by following example.

Example 1 *An original ERD as shown in Figure 7(A) that includes several loop relationships. A loop among the snowflake tables causes problems in aggregating measures when querying data. A loop means there are more than one path to join a given table in the loop to the fact table. The different path may aggregate measures differently and cause confusion. Therefore, loop in the given ER diagram has to be broken when translating the ER diagram into a multidimensional model.*

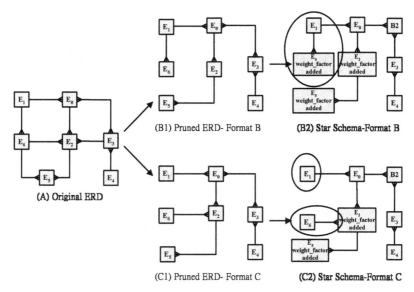

Fig. 7. An example of the same ERD being transformed into different multidimensional models

A loop can be broken in several ways. For example, the original ER diagram shown in 7(A) can be translated to two different ERDs (in Figure 7(B1)(C1)). Next, different multidimensional models (see Figure 7(B2)(C2)) are generated by applying the naive mapping rules shown in section 3.1. The differences between the two figures are highlighted in circles.

Hence, given an ER diagram, there are more than one way to build a corresponding multidimensional model. The paper proposes to use a shortest path algorithm to derive the multidimensional model where each entity has the shortest path to the fact table. The distances between entities and the fact table are counted by the number of relationships between them, since the more the relationships, the more join operators are needed to perform queries. Readers will find that the calculation of distances can be changed to many other formula, such as the estimated numbers of tuples participated in each join, without jeopardizing the integrity of the algorithm.

To compute the shortest distance between the fact table and all other tables, an initial distance matrix has to be built. The initial matrix is formed by scanning the entire ER diagram and for each entity pair that are connected by relationships other than 'M-to-N', the initial value of 'one' is assigned. For relationships that are 'M-to-N', an initial values of 'two' are assigned to the corresponding entries since a bridging table will be needed in the translation. After deriving the initial matrix, the algorithm then calculates the shortest path matrix, which is asymmetric. The diagonal elements are filled with zeros.

Zeros in diagonal entries of the distance matrix represent that the distance between an entity and itself is zero. Such an assumption may in contradiction to entities with self reference relationship in ER Diagrams. However, in the paper, the translated multidimensional model is assumed to be free of self reference relationships. The assumption is based on the widely adopted practice that most self reference relationships are flatten into corresponding entities to save query processing time. The algorithm of the Shortest Distance Computing is shown in Figure 8.

4   Correctness Proof

The section proves that given an ER diagram of $\langle E, R \rangle$ with a fact table identified, the algorithm of MR returns a $\langle DE, DR \rangle$, which satisfies *Grain Preservation* in the process and all tables are connected to fact tables with the least relationships.

Theorem 1 *Given an ER diagram and a fact table, the process of adding entities to $\langle DE, DR \rangle$ by algorithm MR is* Grain Preservation.

Rationale
Only the addition of entities with relationships of '1-to-M' and 'M-to-N' may challenge grains of a multidimensional model. However, since the summary of weight_factors in each group in the two cases have to equal to one, the grain is still be kept according to Definition 2.

The fewer the relationships between entities and the fact table in a multidimensional model, the more efficient the queries issued from the entity can be processed.

Theorem 2 *Given an ER diagram and a fact table, the multidimensional model discovered by algorithm MR connecting each entity to the fact table with the least number of relationships.*

Algorithm: Shortest_Distance
Input: E_0 //the fact table
           $\langle E, R \rangle$ //the original ERD
Output L_0: Initial Distance Matrix
        L : Shortest Distance Matrix
        Begin
            Fill L_0 with ∞
            // scan the original ERD and assign initial value to each relationship
            for i=0 to $| E |$ do {
                for j=1 to $| E |$ do {
                    for each $R(E_i, E_j)$ do {
                        if $R(E_i, E_j)$ = 'M-to-1' then $L_0(E_i, E_j) = 1$
                        elseif $E(E_i, E_j)$ = '1-to-1' then $L_0(E_i, E_j) = 1$
                        elseif $R(E_i, E_j)$ = '1-to-M' then $L_0(E_i, E_j) = 1$
                        elseif $R(E_i, E_j)$ = 'M-to-N' then $L_0(E, E_j) = 2$
                    }
                }
            }

            //Computing shortest path matrix
            for i = 0 to $|E|$ {
                for j = 0 to $|E|$ {
                    for k = 0 to $|E|$ {
                        $L(E_j, E_k) = \min(L(E_j, E_k),\ L(E_j, E_i) + L(E_i, E_k))$
                    }
                }
            }
            return L_0, L
        End;

Fig. 8. Computing the Shortest Distance Between Entities and the Fact Table

Rationale
The distances between entities to the fact table are computed by the relationships needed to connect the two tables. MR adds only one relationship to the multidimensional model when needed, which is the most efficient way found up to date [20] when keeping the grains of fact tables are mandatory. Besides, the MR algorithm uses the shortest path algorithm to find the paths with the least relationships to connect entities with the designated fact table.

5   A Sample Case

In order to show the translation process, a sample is demonstrated in the section. Figure 9(a) shows a sample ER Diagram derived from a commercial sales order tracking system. The designated fact table is the order table. With several loops in the ER diagrams, the diagram can be translated into more than one multidimensional model. The initial distance between connected entities are marked in

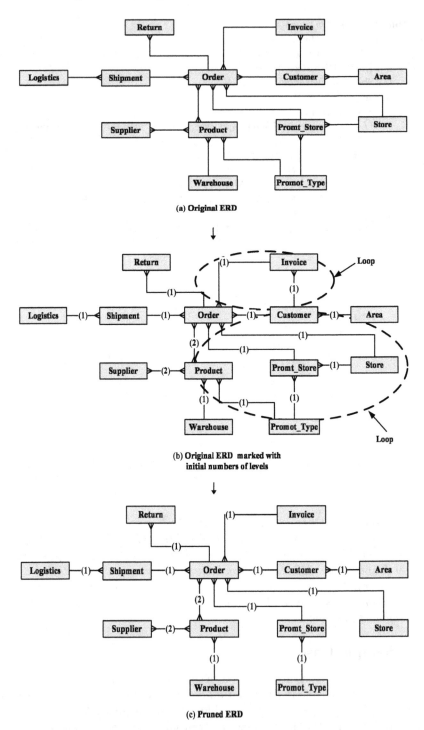

Fig. 9. Computing Distances between Dimensions and the Fact table

Figure 9(b). The calculated shortest distances between each entity and the fact table is shown in Figure 9(c).

The corresponding shortest distance matrix is shown in Table 3.

Table 3. the shortest distance matrix from entity Order to other entities

	Ordr	Rtrn	Inv	Logs	Shp	Cust	Area	Sup	Prdt	PmtS	Str	WH	PmtT
order	0	1	1	2	1	1	2	4	2	1	1	3	2
Return	∞	0	2	3	2	2	3	5	3	2	2	4	3
Invoice	∞	∞	0	3	2	1	2	6	4	3	3	5	4
Logisitcs	∞	∞	∞	0	1	3	4	6	4	3	3	5	4
Shipments	∞	∞	∞	∞	0	2	3	5	3	2	2	4	3
Customer	∞	∞	∞	∞	∞	0	1	5	3	2	2	4	3
Area	∞	∞	∞	∞	∞	∞	0	6	4	3	3	5	4
Supplier	∞	∞	∞	∞	∞	∞	∞	0	2	4	5	3	3
Product	∞	∞	∞	∞	∞	∞	∞	∞	0	3	3	1	1
Promt_Store	∞	∞	∞	∞	∞	∞	∞	∞	∞	0	1	3	1
Store	∞	∞	∞	∞	∞	∞	∞	∞	∞	∞	0	4	2
Warehouse	∞	∞	∞	∞	∞	∞	∞	∞	∞	∞	∞	0	2
Promot_type	∞	∞	∞	∞	∞	∞	∞	∞	∞	∞	∞	∞	0

The algorithm MR is then applied to translate selected relationships and corresponding entities into a multidimensional model. The transformation process is illustrated in the following steps and also shown in Figure 10:

(a) The designated fact entities *Order* is added into **DE** (identified as Step 1 in Figure 10).
(b) Based on the elements in the first row in the shortest distance matrix to transform relationships. Entity *Return, Invoice, Shipment, Customer, Promot_Store, Store,* and *Data warehouse* are candidates since their distances to Entity *Order* are the shortest. Assuming Entity *Return* is processed first. Since the relationship between *Return* and *Order* is one-to-many; a weight_factor attribute is added into *Return*. *Return* is added into **DE** and the **R**(*Order, Return*) is added to **DR** (identified as Step 2 in Figure 10).
(c) With the addition of Entity *Return* to **DE**, the eligible entities becomes Entity *Invoice, Shipment, Customer, Prmot_Store, Store*. Assuming *Invoice* is processed next. Since the relationship between *Invoice* and *Order* is many-to-one, the *Invoice* dimension in added into **DE** and the relationship of **R**(*Order, Invoice*) is added to **DR** (identified as Step 3 in Figure 10).
(d) Entities *Shipment, Promot_Store, Customer* and *Store* are added to the model as in previous steps (identified as Step 4 through Step 7 in Figure 10).
(e) Entity *Product* is processed then, the relationship between *Product* and *Order* is many-to-many; a bridge table *Prod_B* with a weight_factor attribute will be added in between to tune the grain, the relationships of **R**(*Order, Prod_B*) and **R**(*Prod_B, Product*) are added to **DR** (identified as Step 8 in Figure 10).

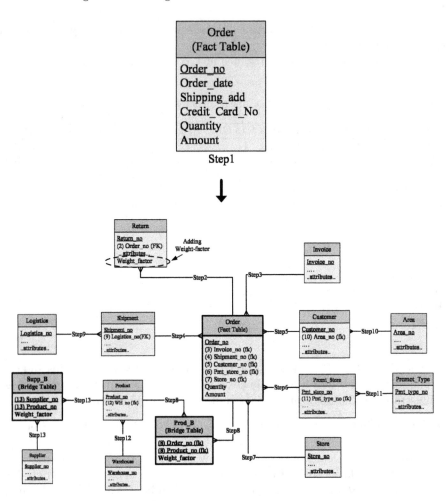

Fig. 10. The Translated multidimensional model $\langle DE, DR \rangle$

(f) With addition of all entities in level one, Entity *Logistics*, *Promot_type*, *Area*, *Warehouse* and *Supplier* are becoming eligible to be processed next. Entity *Logistics*, *Promot_type*, *Area*, *Warehouse* are process as entity *Invoice* done in Step 5 (identified as Step 9 through Step 12 in Figure 10).

(g) Finally, Entity *Supplier* is processed, the transformation process is same as Entity *Product*; thus, a bridge table *Supp_B* is added into **DE** and two relationships **R**(*Product*, *Supp_B*) and **R**(*Supp_B*, *Supplier*) are added to **DR** (identified as Step 13 in Figure 10).

6   Summary and Conclusions

As enterprizes place top priority on real time management, Data Warehouse systems have become critical information analytical tools. However, most companies suffer from the lack of experienced Data Warehouse design professionals to effectively design multidimensional models. On the contrary, people with ERD concepts and experiences are far more widely available. Hence, deriving data warehouse schema from ER diagram may be one of the best way to create multidimensional models. However, a corporate Data Warehouse is not easy to be built by inexperienced Data Warehouse team in a short time. The techniques and mapping rules presented here will be valuable for them to have a quick and correct start. This paper presents a tool to derive data warehouse schema from ER diagrams. The transformation rules presented in this paper give Data Warehouse team a great tool to start with.

The main contribution of this paper providing an efficient and correct algorithm to translate ER diagrams into multidimensional model. The algorithm is efficient because every dimension table in the formed proposed hierarchy is connected to the fact table through the least expensive path. The algorithm is correct in that while adding new entities to existing multidimensional models, it still preserves the grain of the original dimensional model.

The issue of data warehouse model design should also include user requirement taking, verification and integration of the requirement with atomic grain data. Therefore, the work presented in this paper is just a foundation for further research of systematic data warehouse schema design.

Acknowledgement

The authors would like to acknowledge the financial support by the National Science Council, Taiwan, through the project no. NSC93-2416-H-008-010.

References

1. L. Baekgaard and F. Alle. Event-entity-relationship modelling in data warehouse environment. In *ACM Second International Workshop on Data Warehousing and OLAP (DOLAP)*, pages 9–14, Kansas City, Missouri, USA, November 6 1999. ACM.
2. P.A. Bernstein and E. Rahm. Data warehouse scenarios for model management. In *ER (2000) Conference Proceedings*, pages 1–15, Salt Lake City, Utah, USA, October 2000. Springer.
3. M. Boehnlein and A. Lbrich. Deriving initial data warehouse structures from the conceptual data models of the underlying operational information systems. In *ACM Second international Workshop on Data Warehousing and OLAP (DOLAP)*, pages 15–21, Kansas City, Missouri, USA, November 1999.
4. A. Bonifati, F. Cattaneo, S. Ceri, A. Fuggetta, and S. Paraboschi. Designing data marts for data warehouse. In *ACM Transactions on Software Engineering and Methodology*, volume 10 of *4*, pages 452–483, October 2001.
5. L. Cabibbo and R. Torlone. A logical approach to multidimensional databases. In *In Proceedings of the International Conference on Extending Data Base Technology*, pages 183–197, Balencia, Spain, March 1998.
6. P. P.S. Chen. The entity-relationship model -toward a unified view of data. *ACM Transactions on Database Systems*, 1(1):9–36, March 1976.

7. E. Franconi and U. Sattler. A data warehouse conceptual data model for multi-dimensional aggregation. In *Proceedings of the International Workshop on Design and Management of Data Warehouses (DMDW'99)*, pages 13–1 13–10, Heideliberg, Germany, 1999.

8. M. Golfarelli, D. Maio, and S. Rizzi. Conceptual design of data warehouses from er schemes. In *Proceedings of the Hawaii International Conference On system Sciences*, Kona, Hawaii, January 1998.

9. M. Golfarelli and S. Rizzi. A methodological framework for data warehouse design. In *ACM First International Workshop on Data Warehousing and OLAP*, pages 3–9, Washington D.C., United States, November 1998.

10. B. Husemann, J. Lechtenborger, and G. Vossen. Conceptual data warehouse design. In *Proceedings of the International Workshop on Design and Management of Data Warehouse(DMDW2000)*, page 6, Stockholm, Sweden, 2000.

11. W.H. Inmon. *Building the Data Warehouse*. New York: John Wiley & Sons, Inc., third edition, April 2002.

12. R. Kimball, L. Reeves, M. Ross, and W. Thornthwaite. *The Data Warehouse Life cycle Toolkit*. New York: John Wiley & Sons, Inc., 1998.

13. R. Kimball and M. Ross. *The Data Warehouse Toolkit*. New York: John Wiley & Sons, Inc., second edition, 2002.

14. T.M. Krippendorf and I.Y. Song. The translation of star schema into entity-relationship diagrams. In *Eighth International Conference and Workshop on Database and Expert-systems Applications (DEXA'97)*, pages 390–395, Toulouse, France, September 1997.

15. A. Marotta and R. Ruggia. Data warehouse design: A schema-transformation approach. In *Proceedings of the XXII International Conference of the Chilean Computer Science Society (SCCC 2002)*, pages 153–162. IEEE-CS, November 2002.

16. D. L. Moody and M. A.R. Kortink. From enterprise models to dimensional models: A methodology for data warehouse and data mart design. In *Proceedings of the International Workshop on Design and Management of Data Warehouse(DMDW2000)*, page 5, Stockholm, Sweden, 2000.

17. B. Pedersen and C.S. Jensen. Multidimensional data modeling for complex data. In *Proc. of 15th ICDE*, pages 336–345, Sydney, Austrialia, March 1999.

18. F. Ravat, O. Teste, and G. Zurfluh. Towards data warehouse design. In *Proceedings of the 1999 ACM CIKM International Conference on Information and Knowledge Management*, pages 359–366, Kansas City, Missouri, USA, November 1999.

19. C. Sapia, M. Blaschka, G. Hofling, and B. Dinter. Extending the e/r model for the multidimensional paradigm. In *Proceedings of the Workshops on Data Warehousing and Data Mining: Advances in Database Technologies, LNCS Vol. 1552*, pages 105–116. Springer-Verlag, 1998.

20. I.Y. Song, C. Medsker, W. Rowen, and E. Ewen. An analysis of many-to-many relationships between fact and dimension tables in dimensional modeling. In *Proceedings of the International Workshop on Design and Management of Data Warehouses (DMDW'2001)*, pages 13–1 13–10, Interlaken, Switzerland, June,4 2001.

21. N. Tryfona, F. Busborg, and J.G.B. Christiansen. starer: A conceptual model for data warehouse design. In *ACM Second International Workshop on DataWarehousing and OLAP (DOLAP)*, pages 3–8, Kansas City, Missouri, USA, November 1999.

Quadratic Optimization Fine Tuning for the Learning Phase of SVM

Miguel González-Mendoza[1,2], Neil Hernández-Gress[2], and André Titli[3]

[1] LAAS-CNRS. 7, avenue du Colonel Roche, 31077 Toulouse Cedex 4, France
mgonza@laas.fr
[2] ITESM-CEM. Carretera Lago de Guadalupe Km. 3.5, Atizapán de Zaragoza,
Estado de México, C.P. 52926, México
{mgonza,ngress}@itesm.mx
[3] INSA Toulouse. 135 avenue de Rangueil, 31077 Toulouse Cedex 4, France
Andre.Titli@insa-tlse.fr

Abstract. This paper presents a study of the Quadratic optimization Problem (QP) lying on the learning process of Support Vector Machines (SVM). Taking the Karush-Kuhn-Tucker (KKT) optimality conditions, we present the strategy of implementation of the SVM-QP following two classical approaches: i) active set, also divided in primal and dual spaces, methods and ii) interior point methods. We also present the general extension to treat large scale applications consisting in a general decomposition of the QP problem into smaller ones. In the same manner, we discuss some considerations to take into account to start the general learning process. We compare the performances of the optimization strategies using some well-known benchmark databases.

1 Introduction

Support Vector Machines (SVM), are a learning technique derived from the statistical learning theory and can be applied in pattern recognition, regression and density estimation problems. Among its basic characteristics, they provide a convergence to a globally optimal solution including a complexity system control capacity.

The construction of SVM involves the solution of a quadratic optimization problem in which special training patterns are identified: the support vectors to construct the optimal hyperplane. Implementing a solver for this type of optimization problems is not a trivial dilemma due to memory and computation requirements particularly for large training sets. Several researches as [13], [14], [18], use the fact that the value of the quadratic form is the same if the rows and the columns corresponding to zero are removed from the Karush-Kuhn-Tucker (KKT) multipliers matrix. By iterative optimization of simple problems, one obtains the problem solution.

This paper is organized as follows: Section two describes the optimization problem which arises when one tries to construct a SVM. Section three explains how it can be solved using well-adapted optimization methods. Then we describe in which way optimization methods can manage a large number of learning vectors using a decomposition strategy in section four. Section five compares the performance, in terms of time, of the two proposed QP strategies versus a well known QP pr-loqo by means of some benchmarks. We conclude, in section six, with comments on current and future work.

F.F. Ramos et al. (Eds.): ISSADS 2005, LNCS 3563, pp. 347–357, 2005.

2 Support Vector Machines

The learning process in SVM involves a quadratic optimization problem that offers the architecture and the parameters of a decision function representing the largest possible margin [18]. These parameters are represented by the vectors in the class boundary and their associated Lagrange multipliers.

With the aim of taking into account nonlinearities, the SVM can built the optimal hyperplane in a Hilbert space of higher dimension than the input space. This space is the result of the transformation of data $\mathbf{x}_i$ through a function $\phi(\mathbf{x})$. Fortunately, we only need the internal product between the vectors mapped. So, we can use the kernel functions:

$$k(\mathbf{x}_i, \mathbf{x}_j) = \phi(\mathbf{x}_i)^{\mathrm{T}} \phi(\mathbf{x}_j) \tag{1}$$

satisfying the Mercer conditions (Gaussian, polynomial, single layer perceptron, ...) [14] to avoid the explicit calculation of $\phi(\mathbf{x})$.

For simplicity reasons, we only consider the pattern recognition case, while noticing that the development is similar for the three paradigms. So, to build a SVM for two non–linearly separable learning sets, even in a high dimension space, with a non–linear decision function, one has to optimize the following quadratic optimization problem (QP):

Maximize
$\boldsymbol{\alpha}$

$$L_D(\boldsymbol{\alpha}) = \sum_{i=1}^{\ell} \alpha_i - \frac{1}{2} \sum_{i,j=1}^{\ell} \alpha_i \alpha_j y_i y_j k(\mathbf{x}_i, \mathbf{x}_j) \tag{2}$$

Under the constraints
$$\sum_{i=1}^{\ell} y_i \alpha_i = 0, \tag{3}$$

$$0 \leq \alpha_i \leq C \qquad i = 1, \dots, \ell \tag{4}$$

where α_i are the Lagrange multipliers introduced to transform the original formulation of the problem with linear inequality constraints into the above representation. The parameter C controls the misclassification level on the training data and therefore the margin. A large C corresponds to assign a higher penalty to the errors, decreasing the margin, while a small C tolerate more errors, growing the margin.

Once one has the solution, the decision rule is defined like:

$$f(\mathbf{x}) = \mathrm{sign}\left(\sum_{i=1}^{\ell} \alpha_i y_i k(\mathbf{x}_i, \mathbf{x}) + b\right) \tag{5}$$

Evidently, only the non-zero Lagrange multipliers will affect the decision rule. Due to this, the vectors associated to such multipliers are called *support vectors*. Geometrically, these vectors are at the margin defined by the separator hyperplane.

3 Optimization Strategies to Solve SVM-QP

Let us define the matrix $\mathbf{Q}$ as $(\mathbf{Q})_{ij}=y_i y_j k(x_i,x_j)$, $i,j=1, \dots, \ell$, and the vectors $\boldsymbol{\alpha}=[\alpha^1,\dots, \alpha^\ell]^{\mathrm{T}}$, $\mathbf{1}=[1^1,\dots, 1^\ell]^{\mathrm{T}}$, $\mathbf{y}=[y^1,\dots, y^\ell]^{\mathrm{T}}$ and $\mathbf{C}=[C^1,\dots, C^\ell]^{\mathrm{T}}$, the SVM-QP (2)-(4) written in matrix form is:

Minimize

$$q(\alpha) = \frac{1}{2}\alpha^T Q\alpha - 1^T \alpha \qquad (6)$$

α

Under the constraints

$$y^T\alpha = 0, \qquad (7)$$

$$0 \le \alpha \le C \qquad (8)$$

The symmetric semi-definite positive, SSDP, matrix Q guarantees a global minimum α^* thanks to its (strict) convexity making problem (6)-(8) a problem of convex programming, [1].

3.1 Optimality Conditions

Optimality conditions are crucial, because they allow to recognize the solution and to establish the strategy of implementation for algorithms. In general, QPs must satisfy first and second order conditions, but the convexity of the problem (6)-(8) makes any first order critical point a global solution, [3].

Using the classical Lagrange duality theory and associating Lagrange multipliers $\gamma \in \Re$ to (7), $\beta=[\beta^1, ..., \beta^l]^T$ and $\chi=[\chi^1, ..., \chi^l]^T$ to (8), primal Lagrangian is:

$$L_P(\alpha, \beta, \chi, \gamma) = \frac{1}{2}\alpha^T Q\alpha - 1^T \alpha + \gamma y^T \alpha - \beta^T \alpha + \chi^T (\alpha - C) \qquad (9)$$

which is necessary to minimize respect to α and to maximize compared to γ, β and χ. Thus the set of stationary conditions is:

$$y^T\alpha = 0, \alpha \ge 0 \text{ and } C - \alpha \ge 0 \qquad \text{(primal feasibility)} \qquad (10)$$

$$Q\alpha - 1 + \gamma y - \beta + \chi = 0, \ \beta \ge 0 \text{ and } \chi \ge 0 \qquad \text{(dual feasibility)} \qquad (11)$$

$$\beta^T\alpha = 0 \text{ and } \chi^T(\alpha - C) = 0 \qquad \text{(complementary conditions)} \qquad (12)$$

which are, with exception of the KKT conditions (12), linear functions of α, γ, β and χ. Consequently, one can obtain the solution of the SVM-QP (6)-(8) by finding a nonnegative solution for the ℓ equations (10) which also satisfies the ℓ equations (10)-(12). We can also find the dual problem of the SVM-QP (6)-(8):

Minimize

$$L_D(\beta, \chi, \gamma) = \frac{1}{2}(1 - \gamma y + \beta - \chi)^T Q^{-1}(1 - \gamma y + \beta - \chi) - \chi^T C \qquad (13)$$

α

Under the constraints

$$\beta \ge 0, \qquad (14)$$

$$\chi \ge 0, \qquad (15)$$

which has the same KKT conditions and, therefore, the same solution (saddle point).

3.2 Algorithms for Quadratic Optimization Problems

Essentially, there are two types of algorithms for the resolution of QPs:

- *Active set methods* are also divided in *primal* methods, which aim for dual feasibility by keeping primal feasibility and the complementary conditions, and *dual* methods, which point for primal feasibility by keeping dual feasibility and the complementary conditions. These last, are only applicable when $\mathbf{Q}$ is a positive definite matrix. They gather simplex linear programming methods in the case of QP, [1].

- **Interior point methods**, which aim for the complementary conditions by keeping primal and dual feasibility at the same time.

For each method, we propose a specific implementation to solve the specific SVM QP (6)-(8).

3.3   Active Set Methods

Active set methods seek, after having found a feasible point during an initial phase, a solution around the edges and the faces of the feasible set by solving a sequence of equally constrained quadratic problems, EQP. Three basic approaches can be used to solve EQP: 1) full-space approach, 2) range-space approach and 3) null-space approach. For each one of these three approaches, one can use direct methods (Cholesky factorization) or iterative (combined gradient). For more details, see [3].

Primal Active Set Methods

In primal active set methods, certain inequality constraints are indexed by an active set A, and they are also seen as equality constraints while the remainder is isolated as a whole inactive set N (complement of A). The method adjusts active set A in order to identify correct active constraints in the solution of (6)-(8). Each iteration k tries to find the solution of an EQP. For that, the origin changes to $\boldsymbol{\alpha}^{(k)}$ and searches a correction $\boldsymbol{\delta}^{(k)}$ which solves:

$$\text{Minimize} \quad \frac{1}{2}\boldsymbol{\delta}^\mathrm{T}\mathbf{Q}\boldsymbol{\delta} - \boldsymbol{\delta}^\mathrm{T}\mathbf{g}^{(k)} \quad \text{with } i \in A, \qquad (16)$$

$$\text{Under the constraints} \quad \mathbf{a}_i^\mathrm{T}\boldsymbol{\delta} = 0,$$

with $\mathbf{g}^{(k)} = \mathbf{1} + \mathbf{Q}\boldsymbol{\alpha}^{(k)}$, defined as $\nabla q(\boldsymbol{\alpha}^{(k)})$ of function (6). If $\boldsymbol{\delta}^{(k)}$ satisfies inactive constraints, the following iteration is $\boldsymbol{\alpha}^{(k+1)} = \boldsymbol{\alpha}^{(k)} + \boldsymbol{\delta}^{(k)}$. Otherwise, to find the best feasible point, the solution of (16) is found by searching in direction of $\boldsymbol{\delta}^{(k)}$, $\mathbf{s}^{(k)}$, with a step $\eta^{(k)}$, obtaining:

$$\eta^{(k)} = \min\left(1, \min_{\substack{i:i \notin A \\ \mathbf{a}_i^\mathrm{T}\mathbf{s}^{(k)} < 0}} \frac{b_i - \mathbf{a}_i^\mathrm{T}\boldsymbol{\alpha}^{(k)}}{\mathbf{a}_i^\mathrm{T}\mathbf{s}^{(k)}} \right) \qquad (17)$$

to find $\boldsymbol{\alpha}^{(k+1)} = \boldsymbol{\alpha}^{(k)} + \eta^{(k)}\mathbf{s}^{(k)}$. If $\eta^{(k)} < 1$, the new constraint becomes active, defined by the set of indices p, minimizing (17), by adding it to the active set $A^{(k)}$.

If $\boldsymbol{\alpha}^{(k)}$ (i.e. $\boldsymbol{\delta}^{(k)} = 0$) solves current EQP, it is possible to calculate Lagrange multipliers $\boldsymbol{\beta}$ for the active inequality constraints by using any method to solve EQP. Vector $\boldsymbol{\beta}^{(k)}$ must satisfy the set of stationary conditions (10)-(12). If dual stationary conditions, $\boldsymbol{\beta} \geq \mathbf{0}$, are not satisfied, it is necessary to find the set q of indices for which $\beta_q^{(k)} < 0$ solving:

$$\min_{i \in A} \beta_i^{(k)}. \qquad (18)$$

Algorithm 1 synthesizes the primal active set method:

Algorithm 1. Primal active set method

---

1. Let's the initial point $\mathbf{x}^{(1)}$, active set A and $k=1$.
2. If $\delta^{(k)}=0$ does not solve (16), then to go to step 4.
3. Calculation of Lagrange multipliers $\beta^{(k)}$ and solve (18) ; if $\beta\geq0$ then finish with $\alpha^*=\alpha^{(k)}$, otherwise remove q of active set A.
4. Solve (16) for $\mathbf{s}^{(k)}$.
5. Find $\eta^{(k)}<1$ to solve (17) and compute $\alpha^{(k+1)}=\alpha^{(k)}+\eta^{(k)}\mathbf{s}^{(k)}$.
6. If $\eta^{(k)}<1$, add p to active set A.
7. $k=k+1$ and to go to step 2.

Dual Active Set Methods

For our research, we propose a SVM QP (6)-(8) fine tuning of the dual active overall algorithm, proposed by Goldfarb and Idnani, [8], with modifications of Powell, [15]. This method calculates a solution without taking into account the constraints through a Cholesky factorization, obtaining a triangular system. Sequence $\alpha^{(k)}$, $\beta^{(k)}$, satisfy KKT conditions (12) excepting primal feasibility (10). Initially, $\alpha=-\mathbf{Q}^{-1}\mathbf{1}$ is the minimization of the dual QP without constraints (13), $A=\varnothing$, and $\beta=0$ are the vertex in the dual space. Iteration k consists on the following steps:

Algorithm 2. Dual active set method

---

1. Take some q such as constraint q is not accomplished for (6) and add it to A.
2. If $\mathbf{a}_q^{(k)}\in\text{span}\{\mathbf{a}_i,\ i\in A\}$ then decrease the index in one equality constraint which will become positive in step 3.
3. Move through the solution of the EQP.
4. If $\beta_i\downarrow0$, $i\in A$, remove i from A and go to step 3.

The iteration is completed when the EQP solution is found in step 3. More significant iterations continue until having a primal feasibility in step 1 (α is an optimal solution) or until the inexistence of indices in A to be decreased in step 2. Because QP (13)-(15) is the dual of SVM QP (6)-(8), Goldfarb and Idnani's method is equivalent to primal active set method, applied to the this dual QP, [8].

3.4 Interior Point Methods

Primal-dual methods, usually known as interior point methods, solve the problem in primal space (space of α variables) at the same time as in dual space (space of the Lagrange multipliers γ, β and χ). In general, interior point algorithms introduce relaxation variables $\mu\in\mathfrak{R}^+$ in the stationary conditions. For the SVM QP (6)-(8), the stationary conditions (10)-(12) and the relaxation variables μ_1, $\mu_2\in\mathfrak{R}^+$ form the set of perturbed conditions:

$$\mathbf{y}^T\alpha=0,\ \alpha+\mathbf{t}=\mathbf{C},\ \alpha\geq0\text{ and }\mathbf{t}\geq0 \qquad \text{(primal feasibility)} \qquad (19)$$
$$\mathbf{Q}\alpha-\mathbf{1}+\gamma\mathbf{y}-\beta+\chi=0,\ \beta\geq0\text{ and }\chi\geq0 \qquad \text{(dual feasibility)} \qquad (20)$$
$$\mathbf{BA}=\mu_1\mathbf{I}\text{ and }\mathbf{XT}=\mu_2\mathbf{I} \qquad \text{(complementary conditions)} \qquad (21)$$

where $\mathbf{A}=\text{diag}(\alpha)$, $\mathbf{B}=\text{diag}(\beta)$, $\mathbf{X}=\text{diag}(\chi)$ et $\mathbf{T}=\text{diag}(\mathbf{t})$. These algorithms handle perturbations μ_1 and μ_2, in such a way they tend towards zero and give place to an approximated solution to the stationary conditions (10)-(12) with the desired precision. The solution is unique and resides inside the primal–dual space:

$$\alpha \geq 0,\ t \geq 0,\ \chi,\ \beta \geq 0,\ \chi \geq 0. \tag{22}$$

There are several types of interior point algorithms, all having a common mathematical base with the logarithmic barrier function, [4], but they can be summarized in three principal ones: affine scaling methods, potential reduction methods and central trajectory methods. Last ones are the most used in practice and the only type of interior point algorithm considered in this paper.

A primal dual central trajectory algorithm is composed of an iterative process which starts with a point strictly inside of (22). At each iteration, it estimates a value of perturbations μ_1 and μ_2, representing a point of the central trajectory, nearer of the optimal solution than the current point. Then, it tries to take a step towards this point of the central trajectory, [16].

Let $(\alpha,\ t,\ \chi,\ \beta,\ \chi)$ the current point and $(\alpha+\Delta\alpha,\ t+\Delta t,\ \gamma+\Delta\gamma,\ \beta+\Delta\beta,\ \chi+\Delta\chi)$ the point of the central trajectory corresponding to the target values μ_1 and μ_2. Equations defined for the point of the central trajectory are:

$$\mathbf{y}^T\Delta\alpha = -\mathbf{y}^T\alpha \tag{23}$$

$$\Delta\alpha + \Delta t = C - \alpha - t \tag{24}$$

$$Q\Delta\alpha + \gamma\Delta y - \Delta\beta + \Delta\chi = 1 - Q\alpha + \gamma y + \beta - \chi \tag{25}$$

$$\mathbf{B}^{-1}\Delta\mathbf{B} + \Delta\mathbf{A} = \mu_1\mathbf{B}^{-1} - \mathbf{A} - \mathbf{B}^{-1}\Delta\mathbf{B}\,\Delta\mathbf{A} \tag{26}$$

$$\mathbf{X}^{-1}\Delta\mathbf{X} + \Delta\mathbf{T} = \mu_2\mathbf{X}^{-1} - \mathbf{T} - \mathbf{X}^{-1}\Delta\mathbf{X}\Delta\mathbf{T} \tag{27}$$

This set of equations is almost a linear system for the direction vectors ($\Delta\alpha,\ \Delta t,\ \Delta\gamma,\ \Delta\beta,\ \Delta\chi$). Nonlinearities appear in conditions (26)-(27).

Predictor-Corrector Method

Predictor-corrector methods are the most effective methods of linear programming, [5], [16], [17] to find a solution of equations (23)-(27). The *predictor* step decrease the μ and "delta" terms, appearing on the right side, for solving the resulting linear system for "delta" variables. The *corrector* step estimate an adapted target value of μ and restores "delta" and μ terms of the right side by using the current estimates and the resulting system is again solved according to "delta" variables. Resulting directions are used to go at the new point in the primal–dual space.

The basic step in iteration k calculates the Newton's direction, associated to conditions (23)-(27):

$$\begin{pmatrix} Q & 0 & y & -1 & 1 \\ y^T & 0 & 0 & 0 & 0 \\ 1 & 1 & 0 & 0 & 0 \\ 1. & 0 & 0 & B^{-1(k)}. & 0 \\ 0 & 1. & 0 & 0 & X^{-1(k)}. \end{pmatrix} \begin{pmatrix} \Delta\alpha^{(k)} \\ \Delta t^{(k)} \\ \Delta\gamma^{(k)} \\ \Delta\beta^{(k)} \\ \Delta\chi^{(k)} \end{pmatrix} = \begin{pmatrix} 1 - Q\alpha^{(k)} + \beta^{(k)} - \chi^{(k)} \\ -y^T\alpha^{(k)} \\ C - \alpha^{(k)} - t^{(k)} \\ \mu_1 B^{-1(k)} - A^{(k)} - B^{-1(k)}\Delta B^{(k)}\Delta A^{(k)} \\ \mu_2 T^{-1(k)} - T^{(k)} - X^{-1(k)}\Delta X^{(k)}\Delta T^{(k)} \end{pmatrix} \tag{28}$$

where $\alpha^{(k)}$. and $t^{(k)}$. indicate the scalar product between two vectors (element by element). This system is reduced to a quasi-definite system and it is solved by using Cholesky factorizations. It is not guaranteed that $(\alpha^{(k)}+\Delta\alpha^{(k+1)}, t^{(k)}+\Delta t^{(k+1)}, \gamma^{(k)}+\Delta\gamma^{(k+1)}, \beta^{(k)}+\Delta\beta^{(k+1)}, \chi^{(k)}+\Delta\chi^{(k+1)}) > 0$. Instead, one establishes:

$$(\alpha,t,\gamma,\beta,\chi)^{(k+1)} = (\alpha,t,\gamma,\beta,\chi)^{(k)} + v((\Delta\alpha,\Delta t,\Delta\gamma,\Delta\beta,\Delta\chi)^{(k+1)}) \tag{29}$$

where $v \leq 1$ ensures $(\alpha,t,\gamma,\beta,\chi)^{(k)} + v(\Delta\alpha,\Delta t,\Delta\gamma,\Delta\beta,\Delta\chi)^{(k+1)} > 0$. The algorithm can be paraphrased as follows:

Algorithm 3. Predictor-corrector interior point method

---
1. Check optimality with the specified tolerances.
2. Establish the new target values μ.
3. Solve the Newton's system of (28) with these targets.
4. Carry out a Newton's step (29) towards Newton's direction of with, possibly, steps of different width in the primal and dual spaces.

For more information on interior point methods, see [1], [2], [16] and [17].

4   Large Scale SVM-QP Implementation

Optimization algorithms to solve the SVM-QP (6)-(8), described in the preceding section, are operational to solve problems of less than 2000 examples. Beyond this limit, depending on memory and processing capacities, we cannot use any QP technique without some modifications. For large-scale databases, it is difficult to calculate and store the matrix $\mathbf{Q}$ of the vector products $k(\mathbf{x}_i,\mathbf{x}_j)$, because of data-processing limitations. Consequently, one must find more effective methods for this kind of problems and be able to find the optimal solution in a minimal time, with a moderate request of data-processing resources.

4.1   General Decomposition Technique

Several authors, [9], [13], [14], [18], introduced the idea to break up the SVM-QP (6)-(8) into smaller sub-problems, easier to treat. All strategies consider two key points:

- *optimality conditions*, which make possible to check if the algorithm has optimally solved the problem, for the SVM QP (6)-(8) optimality conditions (10)-(12), and
- *strategy of implementation*, which defines the implementation of the objective function, associated with variables violating optimality conditions, if a particular solution is not the global solution.

The solution of the SVM-QP (6)-(8) is optimal if and only if KKT conditions (12) are satisfied, knowing that matrix $\mathbf{Q}$ is semi-definite positive. KKT conditions have a simple form to check them; the SVM-QP can be solved when, for any i, $i = 1, \ldots, \ell$:

$$\alpha_i = 0 \quad \rightarrow \quad y_i g(\mathbf{x}_i) > 1 \tag{30}$$
$$0 < \alpha_i < C \quad \rightarrow \quad y_i g(\mathbf{x}_i) = 1 \tag{31}$$
$$\alpha_i = C \quad \rightarrow \quad y_i g(\mathbf{x}_i) < 1 \tag{32}$$

with $g(\mathbf{x}_i)$, the argument of the sign decision function (5):

$$g(\mathbf{x}_i) = \sum_{j=1}^{\ell} \alpha_j y_j k(\mathbf{x}_j,\mathbf{x}_i) + b \tag{33}$$

In order to incorporate optimality conditions, implementation strategy must take into account the fact that a significant part of Lagrange multipliers of α_i are equal to zero in the solution. In a similar way to primal active set methods, a solution is to divide the training set in an active set A, also known as working set, and its complement N. Then one can rewrite the SVM-QP (6)-(8) as follows:

$$\text{Minimize} \atop \alpha_A, \alpha_N \quad q(\alpha_A, \alpha_N) = \frac{1}{2} \begin{bmatrix} \alpha_A \\ \alpha_N \end{bmatrix}^T \begin{bmatrix} Q_{AA} & Q_{AN} \\ Q_{NA} & Q_{NN} \end{bmatrix} \begin{bmatrix} \alpha_A \\ \alpha_N \end{bmatrix} - \begin{bmatrix} 1_A \\ 1_N \end{bmatrix}^T \begin{bmatrix} \alpha_A \\ \alpha_N \end{bmatrix} \qquad (34)$$

$$\text{Under the constraints} \quad \begin{bmatrix} y_A \\ y_N \end{bmatrix}^T \begin{bmatrix} \alpha_A \\ \alpha_N \end{bmatrix} = 0, \qquad (35)$$

$$\begin{bmatrix} 0_A \\ 0_N \end{bmatrix} \leq \begin{bmatrix} \alpha_A \\ \alpha_N \end{bmatrix} \leq \begin{bmatrix} C_A \\ C_N \end{bmatrix}, \qquad (36)$$

in which we can replace any $i \in A$, by any $j \in N$, without modifying the cost function. The idea is to only have the support vectors in the active set A. In this manner, the inactive set N is formed by zero-multipliers α_N.

Algorithm 4. Decomposition algorithm of the SVM-QP

---
1. Election of an active unit initial A of size n_A.
2. Solve the QP (6)-(8), defined by active set A.
3. While there is any $j \in N$ violating $y_j g(x_j) > 1$.
   a) shift the n_A most erroneous vectors x_j to active set A,
   b) shift all vectors x_i with $\alpha_i = 0$, $i \in A$, to inactive set N, and return to step 2

The solution of this problem will be the solution of the SVM-QP (6)-(8), if it verifies the optimality conditions (30)-(32), in particular $y_j g(x_j) > 1$, $j \in N$ ($\alpha_j = 0$). If it is not the case, then α_j, corresponding to x_j, must be different to zero and, consequently, it is necessary to shift it to active set A. Certainly, we can make the same for vectors x_i, associated $\alpha_i = 0$, to N. Algorithm 4 summarizes the decomposition algorithm of the SVM-QP. To introduce better than a random initial working set, we ca use a gaussian search and accelerate the learning process, [7].

An extreme form of decomposition is the sequential minimal optimization, SMO, suggested by Platt, [14], but we did not use it because it finds a sub-optimal solution.

5   Experiments and Results

In this section, we present the application of our two adapted QP-SVM implementations: a dual active set algorithm (QP_1) and an interior point algorithm (QP_2). We compare these methods with a second interior point method called pr-loqo (QP_3), [16]. For every strategy, we coupled a decomposition algorithm (QP_i+Dec). All implementations are in C language and have also a complete toolbox link in matlab for data manipulation and visualization.

Table 1. Characteristics of the UCI data sets: N_{Ler} is the number of elements used in the learning set, N_{test} for the number of observations in the test set and N the total database size. n_{num} and n_{cat} denote respectively the number of numerical and categorical attributes, n is the total number of attributes

	N_{ler}	N_{test}	N	n_{num}	n_{cat}	n
wbc	455	228	683	9	0	9
bld	230	115	345	6	0	5
iri	100	50	150	4	0	4
hea	1000	541	1541	7	6	13
adu	5000	40222	45222	6	8	14
wine	125	53	178	13	0	13
glass	150	64	214	10	0	10
sonar	140	68	208	60	0	60

Table 2. Optimized hyperparameter values of the SVM for the UCI data sets: *kernel* is the type of the kernel, σ its corresponding parameter, C the regularization parameter, to the corresponding learning and test performance P_L and P_{test}, respectively. n_{sv} (%) represents the number of support vectors found and its percentage according the leaning set

	kernel	σ	C	P_L	P_{Test}	n_{sv} (%)
wbc	Gaussian	1.4	100	1.0	0.9780	64 (14.065 %)
bld	Gaussian	0.22	840	0.9085	-	192 (55.65%)
iri	Polynomial	2	1120	0.9876	-	9 (6%)
hea	Gaussian	0.34	150	0.9086	-	660 (42.83%)
adu	Polynomial	3	70	0.9632	0.9213	936 (23.4%)
wine	linear	-	100	1.0	0.9732	11 (8.8%)
glass	Polynomial	5	100	1.0	0.9532	23 (15.33%)
sonar	Polynomial	2	0.01	0.9863	0.8592	84 (57.53%)

We used eigth benchmark problems commonly referred in the literature. This fact makes them very suitable for benchmarking purposes. We restrict the study to binary datasets: the Wisconsin breast cancer database (wbc), the heart disease diagnosis test (hea), the sonar test (son), the adult dataset (adu), the BUPA liver disorders dataset (bld), the Iris data set (iri), and a wine recognition dataset (win). Table 1 summarizes the principal characteristics of these databases. Data and their description are available in [11].

5.1 Learning Rate of SVM Implementations

Algorithms' performance in terms of separation accuracy and optimal solution is almost the same for the three implementations, showing a difference no greater than 1×10^{-5}. All experiments were carried out on sun SunBlade$_{100}$ Workstations. For the kernel types, we employed gaussian and polynomial kernels and all give inputs were normalized to [-1,1]. The regularization parameter C and kernel parameter σ were chosen using a cross-validation procedure. Table 2 reports the optimal hyper parameters.

5.2   Time Performance of SVM Implementations

Table 3 shows the result of the three SVM-QP implementations. On one hand, dual active set method, QP_1, show, in general, a little better performance than QP_2 and QP_3. Both QP_1 and QP_2 have superior results than QP_3, even using the decomposition algorithm. On the other hand, the decomposition algorithm diminishes, substantially, the learning time for all three implementations.

Table 3. Time performance of SVM implementations using the UCI data sets: QP_i are the SVM-QP implementations and QP_i+Dec add the decomposition algorithm. n_{sv} (%) indicates the number of support vectors and its percentage on the learning set

	QP_1	QP_2	QP_3	QP_1+Dec	QP_2+Dec	QP_3+Dec
wbc	**16.656 sec**	71.747 sec	184.816 sec	**1.02 sec**	1.102 sec	2.625 sec
bld	**3.097 sec**	5.657 sec	49.095 sec	**1.558 sec**	9.183 sec	38.843 sec
iri	**1.065 sec**	19.649 sec	4.259 sec	**0.018 sec**	0.038 sec	0.082 sec
hea	-	-	-	**495.95 sec**	1284.21 sec	4646.65 sec
adu	-	-	-	**1960.59 sec**	5830.2 sec	24951.9 sec
wine	**0.077 sec**	0.482 sec	3.987 sec	**0.024 sec**	0.027 sec	0.196 sec
glass	**0.421 sec**	3.887 sec	8.349 sec	**0.038 sec**	0.114 sec	0.528 sec
sonar	**0.375 sec**	1.701 sec	5.717 sec	**0.379 sec**	1.95 sec	3.237 sec

6   Conclusions

Support Vector Machines are an important methodology in Machine Learning. The kernel based representation allows representing the learning problem as a QP. Moreover, the optimization of the SVM QP is a delicate problem due to processing, memory and time constraints.

In this paper we presented a study of classical optimization techniques in order to implement this particular QP problem, following an adapted strategy implementation for each technique, instead of a general one. In one hand, active set methods show their performance in terms of time face to interior-point methods (Accuracy was not evaluated because all strategies find the same solution). On the other hand, utilization of a good basis of optimality conditions in both methodologies shows better results in terms of time.

References

1. Altman, A. and Gondzio, J.: Regularized Symmetric Indefinite Systems in Interior Point Methods for Linear and Quadratic Optimization. Optimization Methods and Software 11-12, pp. 275-302. (1998).
2. Andersen, E. D., et al.: Implementation of interior-point methods for large-scale linear programming. Technical Report 1996.3, Logilab, HEC Geneva, Section of Management Studies, University of Geneva, Switzerland, (1996).
3. Fletcher, R.: Practical Methods of Optimization. John Wiley & Sons; 2nd edition, May (2000).
4. Freund, R. M. and Mizuno, S.: Interior Point Methods: Current Status and Future Directions. Optima, Vol. 51, pp. 1-9, (1996).

5. Gertz, M. and Wright, S. J.: Object-Oriented Software for Quadratic Programming. Report ANL/MCS-P891-1000, Argonne National Laboratory, Mathematics and Computer Science Division, (2001).
6. González-Mendoza, M.: Etude du problème d'optimisation dans les Machines à Vecteurs de Support. Mémoire de DEA INSAT, LAAS-CNRS, Toulouse, France. (2000).
7. González-Mendoza, M, Titli, A., Hernández-Gress, N.: Boosting Support Vector Machines in Density Estimation Problems. IEEE Information Processing and Management of Uncertainty, IPMU 2002 Symposium, July 1-5. Annecy, France, (2002).
8. Goldfarb, D. and Idnani, A.: A numerically stable dual method for solving strictly convex quadratic programs. Mathematical Programming, 27, pp. 1-33 (1983).
9. Joachims, T.: Making large-scale support vector machine training practical. In Advances in Kernel Methods: Support Vector Machines. B. Schölkopf, C. Burges, A. Smola editors, MIT press, Cambridge, MA, pp. 169-184. (1998).
10. Kaufman, L.: Solving the quadratic programming problem arising in support vector classification. In B. Schölkopf, C. J. C. Burges and A. J. Smola, editors, Advances in Kernel Methods, chapter 10, pages 147-167. MIT press (1998).
11. Keogh, E., Blake, C. and Merz, C.J.: UCI repository of machine learning databases, http://kdd.ics.uci.edu (1998).
12. Moré, Jorge J. and Wright, S. J.: Optimization Software Guide. SIAM Publications, (1993).
13. Osuna, E. et al: Support Vector Machines: Training and Applications. Report of the Center of Biological and Computational Learning MIT. Paper No. 144 (1997).
14. Platt, J. C: Fast Training of support vector machines using sequential minimal optimization. In B. Schölkopf, C. J. C. Burges and A. J. Smola, editors, Advances in Kernel Methods, chapter 12, pages 185-208. MIT press (1998).
15. Powell, M. J. D.: ZQPCVX A fortran subroutine for convex quadratic programming. Technical Report DAMTP/83/NA17, University of Cambridge, UK, (1985).
16. Smola, A. J.: Learning with Kernels. PhD thesis, Technische Universität Berlin. (1998).
17. Vanderbei, R. J.: Linear programming: Foundations and Extensions. Kluwer academic Publishers, Hingham, MA. (1997).
18. Vapnik, Vladimir N.: Computational Learning Theory. John Wiley & Sons (1998).

WFCTA (Weighted Fair Channel Time Allocation) and Its Analysis for HR-WPAN*

WoongChul Choi[1], KwangSue Chung[2], Seung Hyong Rhee[2], and Jin-Woong Cho[3]

[1] Department of Computer Science
wchoi@daisy.kw.ac.kr
[2] Department of Electronics Engineering
KwangWoon University, Seoul, Korea 139-701
[3] Korea Electronics Technology Institute

Abstract. The IEEE 802.15.3 standard does not specify how to schedule CTA (Channel Time Allocation)s in CTAP (Channel Time Allocation Period) of a superframe. In this paper, we propose a novel scheduling algorithm for channel time allocation of 802.15.3-based HR-WPAN (High Rate Wireless Personal Area Networks), named *WFCTA* (Weighted Fair Channel Time Allocation). The proposed *WFCTA* inherently has properties which are necessary for various QoS provisioning, because it is based on TDMA, applied by WFQ algorithm. We explain and compare four implementation cases of *WFCTA*. We also analyze its worst-case performance in terms of both link utilization and fairness and verify it by simulation.

Keywords: IEEE 802.15.3, HR-PAN, WFQ (Weighted Fair Queueing), superframe, beacon, CTAP (Channel Time Allocation Period), CTA (Channel Time Allocation)

1 Introduction

A piconet is a wireless ad hoc data communications system which allows a number of independent data devices (DEVs) to communicate with each other. It is distinguished from other types of data networks in that communications are normally confined to a small area around a person or an object that typically covers at least 10 m in all directions and envelopes the person or the object whether stationary or in motion. A piconet is a building block of 802.15.3-based WPANs, and is a wireless ad hoc data communications system which allows a number of independent data devices (DEVs) to communicate with each other[1][2].

In a piconet, time is divided into superframe (Fig. 1). A typical superframe is composed of three parts – a beacon, a CAP (Contention Access Period) and a CTAP (Channel Time Allocation Period). The beacon is used for synchronization and contains information on the piconet. The CAP is used for signaling and sending data. QoS sensitive data in a piconet is transmitted in CTAP, which is TDMA-like medium access period. CTAP is basically contention-free period. Once a DEV is allocated CTA (Channel Time Allocation)s, it can use those channel allocations exclusively.

---

* This research has been conducted by the Research Grant of KwangWoon University in 2004 and by CUCN (Center of Excellence in Ubiquitous Computing and Networking).

F.F. Ramos et al. (Eds.): ISSADS 2005, LNCS 3563, pp. 358–367, 2005.

While the IEEE 802.15.3 standard document mentions the structure of a super-frame and the purposes and usage of each part of a superframe, it does not specify how to allocate CTAs in CTAP. Since CTAs are important, especially to QoS sensitive communication, we apply WFQ (Weighted Fair Queueing) algorithm to channel time allocation, because WFQ and its variations have been widely researched and proven to be very effective to traffics with QoS requirements. In this paper, we propose a scheduling algorithm for channel time allocation, named *WFCTA* (Weighted Fair Channel Time Allocation), and analyze its performance. The proposed *WFCTA* inherently has properties which are suitable for various QoS requirements [3][4][5][6].

The rest of this paper is organized as follows. In Section 2, we review the specification of the IEEE 802.15.3 standard. We provide the problem statements in Section 3 and detailed description of *WFCTA* and its performance analysis in Section 4. We conclude the paper in Section 5.

2   IEEE 802.15.3 MAC Protocol

An 802.15.3 piconet consists of several components. The basic component is a DEV. One DEV is required to assume the role of the piconet coordinator (PNC) of the pi-conet. The PNC provides the basic timing for the piconet with the beacon. Addition-ally, the PNC manages the quality of serice (QoS) requirements, power save modes and access control to the piconet.

Timing in the 802.15.3 piconet is based on the superframe, which is illustrated in Fig. 1. The superframe consists of three parts – beacon, contention access period (CAP) and channel time allocation period (CTAP). The boundary between the CAP and CTAP periods is dynamically adjustable. The beacon is used to set the timing allocation and to communicate management information for the piconet. It consists of the beacon frame as well as any announcement commands sent by a PNC as a beacon extension. A beacon is transmitted at the beginning of each superframe carrying WPAN-specific parameters, including power management, and information for new devices to join the ad hoc network. The CAP is used to communicate commands or asynchoronous data if it is present in the superframe. Its period is reserved for trans-mitting non-QoS data frames such as short bursty data or channel access requests made by the devices in the network. The medium access mechanism during the CAP period is carrier sense multiple access/collision avoidance (CSMA/CA). The remain-ing duration of the superframe is reserved for CTAP to carry data frames with spe-cific QoS provisions. The CTAP is composed of channel time allocations (CTAs), including management CTAs (MCTAs). CTAs are used for commands, isochronous (real-time) streams and asynchronous (non real-time) data connections. MCTAs are a type of CTA that is used for communications between the DEVs and the PNC[1][2].

The type of data transmitted in the CTAP can range from bulky image or music files to high-quality audio or high-definition video streams. CTAs are allocated for isochrnous and asynchronous streams. If a DEV needs channel time on a regular basis, it makes a request to the PNC for isochronous channel time. If resources are available, the PNC allocates time in a CTA for the DEV. If the requirements for the data change, then the DEV is able to request a change to the allocation. For asynchro-nous allocation, a channel time request is a request for a total amount of time to be used to transfer its data, rather than requesting recurring channel time. The PNC is then able to schedule time for this request when available based on the channel time requirement. Finally, power management is one of the key features of the 802.15.3 MAC protocol, which is designed to significantly lower the current drain while being connected to a WPAN. In the power save mode, the QoS provisions are also maintained.

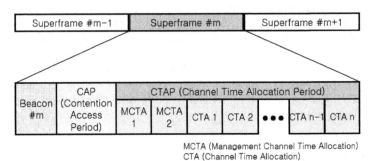

Fig. 1. 802.15.3 piconet superframe structure

3 Problem Statement

Channel access in the CTAP is based on a TDMA method in which all CTAs have the guaranteed start times and durations. The guaranteed start times enable both power saving and good QoS characteristics. All the CTAs for the current superframe are broadcast in the beacon.

The PNC divides the CTAP into channel time allocations (CTAs). A DEV that is given a CTA is guaranteed that no other DEVs will compete for the channel during the indicated time duration of the CTA. A DEV with a CTA may or may not make use of all the allocated time duration within the CTA. The selection of a stream, command or asynchronous data for transmission during a CTA is determined locally by the DEV depending on the number of pending frames and their priorities.

While a TDMA is specified for the channel access method, there is no specification about the channel allocation method in 802.15.3 specification[1]. Even though a simple channel allocation method could achieve a basic QoS (Quality of Service), a better method is required to meet various QoS requirements for various types of data transmitted in 802.15.3-based networks. Fundamentally, the goal of QoS is to provide better and more predicable network service by providing dedicated resource such as channel time allocation. By doing this, QoS enables a certain connection to be provided with such service. Many mechanisms have been proposed for QoS provisioning and among them, WFQ (Weighted Fair Queueing) has been the most widely researched topic for such purpose[3][4][5][6]. In WFQ and its variations, the key parameter is weight, which represents the fair amount or portion of service that a certain connection is expected to receive by a scheduling system. The characteristics of WFQ are that both throughput and service delay are guaranteed to be bounded even in the worst case. By such characteristics, WFQ and its variations have been proved to be very effective in QoS provisioning for various types of traffics. Therefore, we apply WFQ method to channel allocation for CTAP.

4 *WFCTA* (Weighted Fair Channel Time Allocation)

WFCTA is a channel time access method which uses WFQ (Weighted Fair Queueing) algorithm for providing QoS. It uses a TMDA-based channel access method and the concept of weight in WFQ algorithm for service fairness.

WFCTA works as follows. Each DEV sends a request of a certain weight to its PNC based on service requirement and then the channel time allocations are computed in terms of virtual clock based on the requested weights. The computed channel time allocations are then used by the corresponding DEVs, similar to WFQ algorithm (Fig. 1) where the virtual start and finish times are stamped for every backlogged packets and used for scheduling.

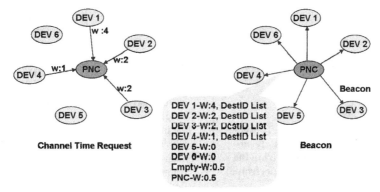

Fig. 2. Example of Case DI and DII in Table 1

The computation and scheduling of CTAs is done in one of two ways – in a central way or in a distributed way. In a central way (Case CI and CII in Table 1), the PNC computes all the CTAs and then sends such information at every superframe interval in a beacon. In a distributed way (Case DI and DII in Table 1), the PNC sends all of the received information of weight to DEVs in a beacon, and the DEVs in a piconet computes all of the CTAs based on the received information. Therefore, the difference is what kind of information is sent to DEVs by the PNC and where the computation for scheduling CTAs is executed. The choice between the two depends on the computation complexity and the power consumption of the PNC for the computation.

Another decision that has to be made is the time when an update of weight occurs. When a DEV wants to change its weight so that it can receive an increased or decreased service, it will notify the PNC it belongs to about the change. Then the CTA needs to be computed again. There are also two ways to do that. One way (Case CI and DI) is that the updated CTA is known to DEVs only using a beacon, which means that the update will be known only at each superframe. The other way (Case CII and DII) is that, whenever an update occurs, the update is immediately notified to DEVs during the current superframe. So the difference is whether the updated CTA is notified during a current superframe or at each beacon of a superframe by the PNC. The choice depends on how long a superframe is and how often weight updates occur. If updates are frequent and a superframe interval is short, then the updated CTA will be sent in a beacon of each superframe. Otherwise, the other way will be more efficient. Table 1 summarizes four cases.

Table 1. Four cases of implementation of *WFCTA*

		Which computes virtual time for CTAs?	
		PNC does	**each DEV does**
When to process weight update?	**Inter-CTA (= weight is adjustable only at each superframe)**	**CASE CI** – PNC computes all of the relative weights and sends the information to DEVs – changes of weight will be effective at the beacon of the next superframe	**CASE DI** – PNC sends all the information of weight requests to DEVs and each DEV computes the relative weights locally – changes of weight will be effective at the beacon of the next super-frame
	Intra-CTA (= weight is immediately adjustable during the current superframe)	**CASE CII** – PNC computes all of the relative weights and sends the information to DEVs – changes of weight is immediately notified during the current CTA	**CASE DII** – PNC sends all the information on weight requests to DEVs and each DEV computes the relative weights locally – changes of weight is immediately notified during the current CTA

4.1 Performance Analysis: Link Utilization and Fairness

For performance analysis, consider WFQ in wired networks and wireless networks. The difference of applying WFQ to such networks lies in how to share available link capacity when the state of a flow changes to OFF state. Specifically, in wired networks, flows that share link capacity immediately share the available bandwidth when a flow changes to OFF state without any further management, i.e. such a state change does not require any state notification to other sharing flows in wired networks. So the WFQ scheduler only keeps on scheduling backlogged packets based on the virtual clocks of backlogged packets.

On the contrary in wireless networks, there is no central place for packets or for channel time in 802.15.3 networks to be queued, therefore, a DEV can not know whether other DEVs will send a packet or not during its allocated channel time. For that reason, information on when a DEV will not use the allocated CTAs should be exchanged among the DEVs in a piconet. Specifically, suppose that a DEV has been allocated a set of CTAs but it changes to OFF state so that it does not need to use its allocated CTAs. Then it should let others know the fact so that its allocated CTAs should be shared among other active DEVs, which is similar to what happens in wired WFQ. Otherwise, underutilization of link bandwidth will occur.

Similar procedure is required for a DEV whose state changes to ON state. When a DEV changes to ON after OFF, it needs to claim its CTAs again. In order to do that, it has to send a request for its CTAs, but has to wait for the request to be processed for the DEV. While any newly backlogged packet in wired networks immediately receives its fair amount of service for the weight, the DEV in wireless networks has to wait even when its weight is reserved. As a result, the amount of service during that time interval is unfairly used by other DEVs. From this observation, performance analysis of *WFCTA* is done in terms of two key performance parameters of link utilization and fairness.

Since the CTAs of a DEV that changes to its state OFF should be shared as soon as possible, and that changes to its state ON should be immediately notified, Case CI is the slowest or worst of the four cases in Table 1. in terms of the reaction to such an event. Therefore, the performance of Case CI is the worst in terms of those two performance parameters. Based on that observation, we can induce the worst-case performance for those parameters of *WFCTA* by analyzing the performance of Case CI.

To analyze the performance of Case CI, assume that a DEV changes its state to OFF state with rate λ and it changes to its state to ON state with rate β, where $\lambda, \beta > 0$. Assume also that the moment of state change is based on a CTA slot to make the analysis tractable. The length of a superframe is assumed to be fixed with T where T > 0. Then when the DEV changes its state to OFF during the first superframe interval T, it will wait for the next superframe start time of 2T to let others share its CTAs. If the DEV changes its state to OFF not during the first superframe interval T, but during the second superframe interval 2T, then it will wait for the next superframe start time of 3T and so on. Therefore, the expected value of the time when the DEV is discovered to go to its state OFF is

$$\{\sum_{i=0}^{\infty} \int_{iT}^{(i+1)T} \lambda e^{-\lambda x} dx\} * (i+1)T = \frac{T}{1-e^{-\lambda T}} \tag{1}$$

Then the expected duration of the time that the DEV has to wait for until the next superframe is

$$\sum_{i=0}^{\infty} \int_{iT}^{(i+1)T} \lambda e^{-\lambda x} \{(i+1)T - x\} dx = \frac{T}{1-e^{-\lambda T}} - \frac{1}{\lambda} \tag{2}$$

For fairness, similar derivation can be made to the above. When a DEV changes its state to ON during the first superframe interval T, it will wait for the next superframe start time of 2T to receive CTAs. If the DEV changes to its state ON not during the first superframe interval T, but during the second superframe interval 2T, then it will wait for the next superframe start time of 3T and so on. Then by applying the procedures of (1) and (2), the same results with the replacement of a parameter λ to β can be drawn.

Fairness, a key metric of WFQ, is defined as

$$\left| \frac{W_i(t_1, t_2)}{w_i} - \frac{W_j(t_1, t_2)}{w_j} \right| < \Delta \tag{3}$$

where w_i, w_j are the weights of DEV i, j and $W_i(t_1,t_2)$, $W_j(t_1,t_2)$ are the amount of service that DEV i, j have received during the time interval t_1 and t_2 (t_1, t_2 are in CTAP). Therefore, substituting the values to (3) shows the fairness of *WFCTA*. Since this is for Case CI, which is the worst, for other cases, especially for Case DII, it is obvious that both link utilization and fairness is better than those of Case CI from the observation which was made in the previous section. Therefore, the following proposition holds.

Proposition 1. Bounded Link Underutilization of *WFCTA* by a DEV
Assume that the rate of state change to OFF state of a DEV is an exponential random variable with parameter λ and that the length of a superframe is fixed with T where T > 0. Then the link underutilization of *WFCTA* by a DEV is bounded by

$$C - \text{CTA\_during\_}(\frac{T}{1-e^{-\lambda T}} - \frac{1}{\lambda})\text{\_interval} \approx C - \frac{w_i(\frac{T}{1-e^{-\lambda T}} - \frac{1}{\lambda})}{C} \quad (4)$$

where C is the wireless link capacity of CTAP of a superframe, w_i is the weight of DEV i, and $w_i(\tau)$ is the amount of service that DEV i has received during the time interval τ (τ is in CTAP).

Proof. The proof is based on mathematical analysis in (1).   □

Proposition 2. Bounded Fairness of *WFCTA*
Assume that the rate of state change to ON state of a DEV is an exponential random variable with parameter β and that the length of a superframe is fixed with T where T > 0. Then the fairness of *WFCTA* is bounded by

$$\left| \frac{W_i(t_1,t_2) - w_i(\frac{T}{1-e^{-\beta T}} - \frac{1}{\beta})}{w_i} - \frac{W_j(t_1,t_2)}{w_j} \right| \quad (5)$$

where w_i, w_j are the weights of DEV i, j and $W_i(t_1,t_2)$, $W_j(t_1,t_2)$ are the amount of service that DEV i, j have received during the time interval t_1 and t_2 (t_1 and t_2 are in CTAP). $w_i(\tau)$ is the amount of service that DEV i has received during the time interval τ (τ is in CTAP).

Proof. The proof is based on mathematical analysis in (2).   □

4.2 Simulation

We have implemented *WFCTA* method in *ns-2*[7] with the CMU wireless exten-sions[8] and 802.15.3 modules developed by Intel[9]. The piconet configured for this experiment has 10 DEVs and 1 PNC. We assume that there is no CAP in the super-frame, and only CTAP is in the superframe. The link capacity is 50Mbps and the frame length is 10Kbyte. The simulations are excuted on Linux 2.4.20 on a Pentium 3.0 Ghz PC with 516Mbytes main memory.

The result of Fig 3 and 4 are obtained by applying (4). As the result shows, the link utilization is worse for Case CI and DI than for Case CII and DI. And also link utilization becomes worse as the value T grows larger. The result of Fig 5 and 6 are obtained by applying (5). The result shows that fairness for Case CII and DII is better than that of Case CI and DI, which conforms to the observations in the previous section. Notice that, for both link utilization and fairness, the results from analysis and the simulation results of Case CI and DI are almost identical.

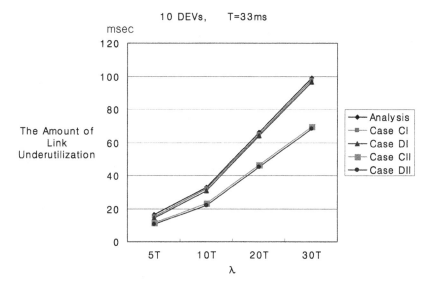

Fig. 3. Link underutilization of *WFCTA* by (4). C = 50Mbits/sec, $w_i = 0.1$

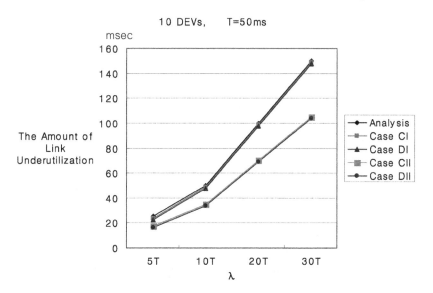

Fig. 4. Link underutilization of *WFCTA* by (4). C = 50Mbits/sec, $w_i = 0.1$

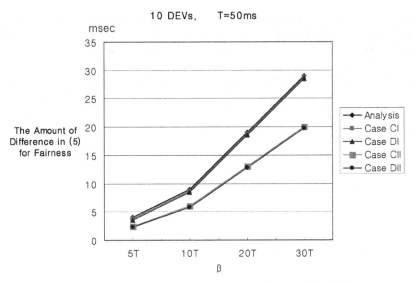

Fig. 5. The amount of difference in (5) for fairness of *WFCTA*

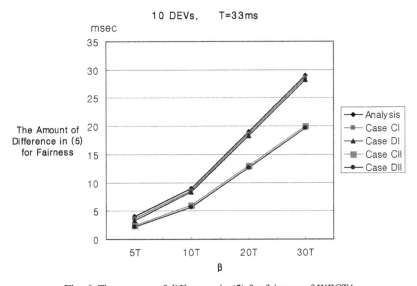

Fig. 6. The amount of difference in (5) for fairness of *WFCTA*

5 Conclusion

In this paper, we proposed a novel scheduling algorithm for channel time allocation for 802.15.3 HR WPAN, named *WFCTA* (Weighted Fair Channel Time Allocation). *WFCTA* is based on TDMA, applied by WFQ algorithm, because WFQ algorithm has many outstanding features for various QoS provisioning such as fairness and bounded service delay. Therefore, the proposed *WFCTA* inherently has such properties. There are four cases of its implementation, and their comparisons are summarized in Table 1. We analyze its performance in terms of link utilization and fairness, and show the worst case performance. We also conducted a simulation, and verified that the performance of Case CII and DII are better than that of CI and DI, which conforms to the intuition that weight update requests should be handled as soon as possible for better performance.

References

1. "Draft Standard for Part 15.3: Wireless medium Access Control and Physical Layer Specifications for High rate Wireless Personal Area Networks (WPAN), " Draft P802.15.3, Nov. 2001
2. Karaoguz, J.,"High-rate wireless personal area networks", Communications Magazine, IEEE, Dec. 2001 pp. 96-102
3. Zhang L., "Virtual Clock: a new traffic control algorithm for packet switching networks." ACM SIGCOMM, Sep. 1991 pp. 19-29
4. T. Nandagopal, S. Lu, and V. Bharghavan, "A Unified Architecture for the Design and Evaluation of Wireless Fair Queueing Algorithms, " ACM MOBICOM, Aug. 1999 pp132-142
5. T. S. Ng, I. Stoica, and H. Zhang, "Packet Fair Queuing Algorithms for Wireless Networks with Location-dependent Errors," IEEE INFOCOM, Mar. 1998 pp. 1103-1111
6. S. Lu, V. Bharghavan, and R. Sirkant, "Fair Scheduling in Wireless Packet Networks," IEEE/ACM Trans. Net. vol. 7, no. 4, Aug. 1999 pp. 473-489
7. http://www.isi.edu/nsnam/ns
8. The CMU Monarch Project, *Wireless and mobile extensions to ns*
9. R. Mangharam and M. Demirhan, "Performance and simulation analysis of 802.15.3 QoS", IEEE 802.15-02/297r1, Jul. 2002

Performance Analysis of Two Approaches to Service Discovery in Mobile Ad Hoc Networks

Dante Arias-Torres[1] and J. Antonio García-Macías[2]

[1] Universidad Autónoma Benito Juárez de Oaxaca, Faculty of Sciences,
5 de Mayo 111, Oaxaca de Juárez, Oaxaca, México
[2] CICESE Research Center, Computer Science Department,
Km. 107 Carretera Tijuana-Ensenada, Ensenada, México

Abstract. In recent years, diverse solutions for service discovery in mobile ad hoc networks have been proposed. These solutions basically follow two approaches: the first one considers routing and service discovery as separate activities (i.e. implementing independent protocols for each activity); the second one integrates routing and service discovery into a single protocol. Based on this second approach we extend the AODV routing protocol to also perform service discovery. We analyze and compare the performance of both approaches. The results show that the integration of routing and service discovery reduces the amount of traffic generated and the time necessary to find a service.

1 Introduction

The technological revolution of recent years encompasses radical changes; we are in the transition from the personal computer era (one device per person) to the era of ubiquitous computing where people will use, at the same time and sometimes without knowing it, many digital platforms, anywhere, anytime [1]. In such an environment, interactions between devices will be carried out spontaneously and transparently, being very common the formation of mobile ad-hoc networks (MANETs) [2] with these devices.

In these scenarios, the resources can be represented as services, which can be offered by devices (such as printers, sensors, personal computers, etc.) or by specialized software [3]. The presence of ad-hoc networks between devices and the representation of resources as services does not suffice to have an ubiquitous computing environment; it is also necessary to have a mechanism that allows discovering available resources.

The problem of service discovery has been studied extensively, and solutions such as Jini [4], SLP [5], UPnP [6], etc., have been proposed. These mechanisms have been developed for fixed networks with pre-established infrastructure, thus, they can not be applied to networks with limited resources, where nodes move frequently and where there is not a fixed computing infrastructure available (e.g., mobile ad-hoc networks) [7]. Therefore, there is a real need for developing service discovery solutions that address the specific requirements of ad-hoc networks.

F.F. Ramos et al. (Eds.): ISSADS 2005, LNCS 3563, pp. 368–376, 2005.

Traditionally, service discovery has been considered as an application layer function. In this approach, a service discovery protocol is in charge of finding the address of the service-providing node and sometimes of providing additional information, like attributes and access mechanisms; whereas a routing protocol finds the route between clients and the service provider. This approach has been adopted by service discovery protocols like NOM [8], JESA [9], and Allia [10].

It is important to emphasize that routing and service discovery are not independent activities, since once a service request is received by a provider, it is necessary to establish a route to the client so it can notify its presence, for the case of active service discovery; also, a client needs a route to the service provider announced in a passive service discovery [9]. Moreover, there are several intrinsic characteristics of ad hoc networks that motivate a new approach combining routing and service discovery [11, 12].

In fixed networks (or even in mobile networks with very limited mobility), once a service provider is located, the same route will be used during the whole service provisioning process, as the provider will remain in the same place. Thus, in this type of networks, service discovery can be completely detached from routing and other lower layer activities. Also, in order to provide scalability for service discovery, fixed networks usually rely on registry servers that maintain service information.

All these assumptions do not hold for ad hoc networks: First, as nodes move frequently, it is not possible to guarantee that the route to a service provider will remain the same along the service lifetime. The unpredictable nature of ad hoc networks imply varying conditions in nodes density, link status, available bandwidth, available services, etc. Frequent mobility in ad hoc networks, along with the fact that nodes may leave the network (e.g., when a user suddenly turns off its device) imply that the network topology may vary, that routes in the network can change, that network partitioning can occur, and that previously available services may become unavailable. Thus, given all these conditions we can say that a) ad hoc networks can not rely on registry servers, and b) service discovery and routing are more tightly coupled that in fixed networks.

As new proposals emerge for both approaches (combining and separating routing and service discovery), it is only natural to compare them both and evaluate their benefits and shortcomings. Reid et al. [11] have compared SLP and DSR with extensions for service discovery. Nevertheless, SLP is not a protocol designed for mobile ad hoc networks; thus, we consider that it would be more useful to evaluate the two approaches for service discovery comparing only protocols specifically designed for mobile ad hoc networks.

In this paper we analyze and compare two approaches for service discovery in MANETs. The first approach combines routing and service discovery into a single protocol; we follow this approach and propose extending the AODV [13] routing protocol to perform service discovery as it discovers routes. The second approach separates routing from service discovery, clearly preserving the separation of functions recommended by the OSI model; we take the NOM protocol [8] as an example of this approach.

This document is organized as follows: section 2 describes the two protocols under analysis, section 3 describes the experimental setup for such analysis, section 4 compares the results of the simulations, and section 5 presents some conclusions.

2   Overview of AODV-SD and NOM

In this section we will give an overview of how two protocols for service discovery work. These protocols represent two different approaches: AODV-SD is our proposed extension to the AODV routing protocol to manage service discovery; on the other hand, NOM is a protocol that represents the approach of managing service discovery at the application layer.

2.1   Service Discovery with AODV

Koodli and Perkins have outlined some ideas regarding extensions to ad hoc on-demand routing protocols to support service discovery [12]. Noting that these ideas can be applied to the AODV protocol [13], we have designed and implemented a solution, which we called AODV-SD, as described next.

In order to perform service discovery with AODV, it is necessary to extend the formats of the RREQ and RREP messages [13]; new fields are defined, but also actions that nodes along the network perform when receiving these extended messages.

Whenever a node requires a service, it performs a lookup in its services table, which contains information about services it provides as well as those provided by other nodes. The information about others services is acquired when the node participates in a service discovery process, while the information about the services it offers is set when the node is initialized (or when a new service is initialized within the node). Each row in this table contains the service identifier (a string that uniquely identifies the service), the service port, the protocol used, its IP address, a lifetime, a list of attributes that varies with the type of service, and a URL path. A lifetime is used to keep information up to date, which is mandatory in ad-hoc networks where there are frequent changes in topology. Figure 1 shows the structure of the services table.

Service ID	Port	Protocol	IP Address	Lifetime	Attributes List	URL Path

Fig. 1. Services Table

If a node meets the following conditions: its services table contains the required information about the service, it has a valid route to the service provider, and the service lifetime is still valid, then it can contact the service provider to use the service; otherwise, the node initiates a service discovery process, sending an RREQ message with extensions, known as SREQ. Recall that these extensions are fields added to a regular RREQ, so it is possible to locate the service (IP address of the service provider), as well as a route to it, simultaneously.

An extension to the RREQ message includes a Type field to identify a SREQ message, the length of the extension, the length of Service ID field, length of the Attributes List field, a Service Identifier, and lastly an Attributes List with an optional value, used to include restrictions in the required service. Figure 2 shows the format of SREQ messages.

1 byte	1 byte	1 byte	1 byte
Type	Length	Length Service ID	Length Atributes List
Service ID			
Atributes List			

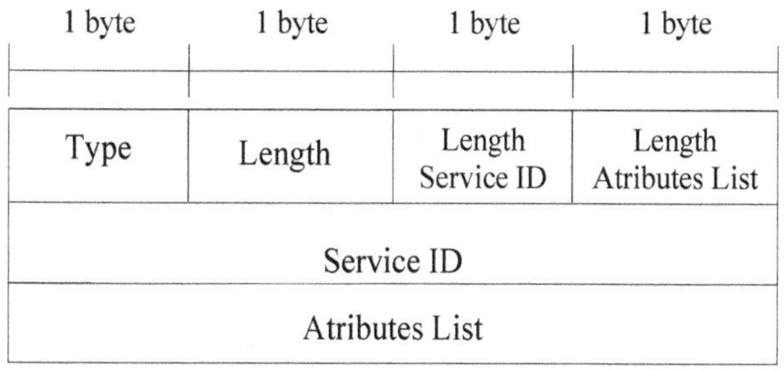

Fig. 2. Format of SREQ messages

When a node receives an SREQ it executes the following actions. First, it determines if there is valid association (service name, IP address) for the required service in its services table; that is, if it provides the service or if it knows a valid route to a node that can provide it. If any of these criteria are met, the node issues an RREP message with extensions for service discovery, also known as SREP, and sends it to the requesting node. Of course, both SREQ and SREQ messages are transmitted through the network according to the rules of the AODV protocol, so the route to the service provider will be found, as well as the reverse route. An extension to the RREP message includes the following fields: a Type to identify SREP messages, the Length of the extensions, a service Lifetime, the Length of the service URL, and finally the URL itself. Figure 3 shows the format of SREP messages.

1 byte	1 byte	1 byte	1 byte
Type	Length	LifeTime	
URL Length	URL		

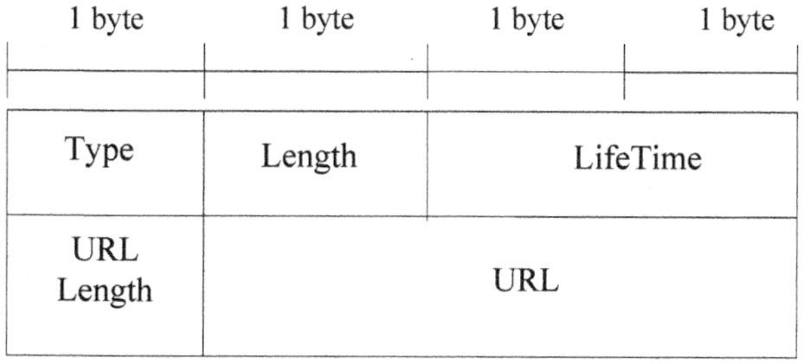

Fig. 3. Format of SREP messages

If a node contains an association (service name, IP address) to a service, but does not have a valid route to it, then it assigns this IP address as the address to resolve issuing an SREQ. Any node receiving an SREQ with a valid destination address send an SREP if it has a route to the destination node or if it knows an equivalent route to the service required. Otherwise, if it does not have information about the service required, or a route to the destination node, it will only forward the SREQ message.

If a node receives an SREP and has information about the service required, it compares its lifetime with the one contained in its services table; if the information in the table is more recent, then it discards the message received and issues an SREP with that information. Otherwise, it will simply send the message to its destination.

Although we have developed an implementation for our proposed mechanism (AODV-SD), such implementation will not be presented in this paper; this is due to the fact that, for the performance comparison, an implementation for NOM was not available. So, we have used a simulation tool to analyze the behavior of both AODV-SD and NOM.

2.2   NOM Service Discovery Protocol

NOM is a service discovery protocol for mobile ad hoc networks, proposed by Doval and O'Mahony [8] that operates above the network layer. NOM operates in a completely distributed fashion, each node monitoring the messages of the applications and the network and reacting according to the message type received: either forwarding the message received if it doesn't apply to the current node, creating and forwarding an appropriate query-reply message if the node should respond to the query, or creating a query message and inserting it into the network. The basic algorithm follows these steps:

1. Receive a NOM message. If the message has already been processed, ignore it.
2. If the message is a query-initiate message, build the query message and send it to the neighbors.
3. If the message is a query message, check whether this node contains the information requested on the query. If so, create a query-reply message and send it to the neighbors so it can go back to its destination. If the message's number of hops is past the TTL limit, ignore it. If the information requested is not in the current node, increment the number of hops in the message and re-send the query message to the node's neighbors.
4. If the message is a query-reply message, check whether the request was sent by this node. If the query was sent by this node, return the result to the application layer that made the request. If the query was not sent by this node, increment the number of hops in the query-reply message and resend it to the node's neighbors.

3   Simulation Model

We used the NS-2 network simulator, with CMU's wireless extensions, to evaluate both approaches to service discovery, represented by NOM and AODV-SD. All experiments use AODV as the routing protocol and the distributed coordination function (DCF) of IEEE 802.11b as the MAC protocol. The nominal transmission range is 100 meters and a raw capacity of 11Mbits/sec was assumed. Two configurations of nodes were chosen, one with 50 nodes randomly placed on a square 1000m x 1000m flat space and another with 100 nodes randomly placed on a square 1500m x 1500m flat space. Nodes move following the random waypoint model with pause time constant at 30 seconds and maximum speed of 2 m/s. To simulate a realistic network, 5 UDP connections between pairs of nodes are set up with CBR traffic between them. The CBR packet size is 512 bytes and each packet is sent every 0.25 seconds. Simulations are run for 600 simulated seconds. Each data point represents an average of five runs with identical traffic models, but different randomly generated mobility scenarios. For fairness, identical mobility and traffic scenarios are used across protocols. Without loss of generality, five services are offered in the network. In order to simulate a realistic behavior, service requests are randomly generated, i.e., the ID of the node requesting the service is uniformly distributed over the whole set of node IDs, as well as the time of the request and the type of service required. We consider two performance metrics to evaluate both protocols:

1. Control message overhead. The amount of messages generated by the service discovery protocol and by the routing protocol. This metric allows us to observe the efficiency of a service discovery protocol regarding the use of the available bandwidth.
2. Service acquisition time. The time that elapses between the sending of the first request for a service and the reception of the first valid reply. This metric allows us to observe how fast a service discovery protocol performs its functions.

4   Results

Using the simulation model explained in the previous section, two experiments were made. In the first one (Fig. 4 and 5), we measured the amount of control messages generated by both service discovery protocols when service requests are made. The numbers of service requests considered are 50, 100, 150 and 200; these numbers are chosen so that we have sufficient number of request to calculate the performance, but at the same time we do not overload the network.

Figures 4 and 5 show the results for both protocols with 50 and 100 nodes. These include AODV packets and service discovery packets (no MAC packets are included). It can be seen from both diagrams that AODV-SD generates a smaller amount of control messages than the NOM protocol, independently of the amount of requests made. So, AODV-SD makes a better use of the bandwidth.

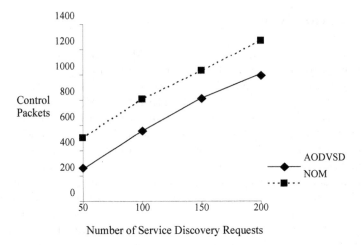

Fig. 4. Control Packets vs. Service Requests (50 nodes)

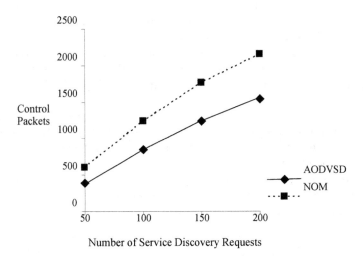

Fig. 5. Control Packets vs. Service Requests (100 nodes)

This is the outcome of making a route between the client and service provider during the service discovery process. This avoids that the service provider initiates a route discovery for the client. Whereas in the case of protocols like NOM, it is necessary to initiate a route discovery if the service provider does not have a route to the client.

In the second experiment we measured the acquisition time for a service. In this experiment, we keep the number of service requests at 50 while we increase the service redundancy. The number of replicated services for each service type is considered to be the service redundancy. For example, if a network has only a web service and a mail service and the service redundancy is three, then there are three web services and three mail services. We decided to analyze service redundancy for both protocols, as this shows what happens in a realistic scenario where there is more than one provider for a service. Figure 6 shows the results for both protocols, with 50 nodes and values of service redundancy of 1, 2, 3 and 4.

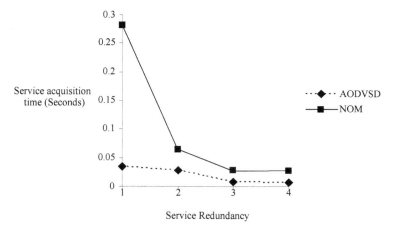

Fig. 6. Service Acquisition Time vs. Service Redundancy

It can be seen from the diagram that the approach taken by AODV-SD allows finding a service faster than the approach used by a protocol like NOM, independently of the number of providers for a service. The reason for this is that in AODV-SD a service provider does not need to consume additional time in the discovery of a route to a client. Moreover, it can be observed that route acquisition latency decreases as the service redundancy increases. This can be explained as follows: when there are more nodes in the network which provide a service, it is likely that a node will take less time to find a service closer to the node on average. Although, as the Figure 6 shows, AODV-SD finds a provider for a service faster than NOM.

5   Conclusions

In this paper two service discovery approaches are compared, one that separates routing and service discovery (NOM) and another that combines these two activities (AODV-SD). We show that the approach followed by AODV-SD finds a service faster and with a smaller amount of messages than the approach followed by the NOM protocol. Experimental results suggest that these benefits are independent of the quantity of nodes, the services, and the service requests made. The decrease in the number of messages generated has a positive impact on energy conservation, which is an important factor in ad hoc networks. Given these facts, we conclude that an approach to service discovery in mobile ad hoc networks based on integration of routing and services discovery surpasses the performance of an approach based on the separation of these activities. Thus, we suggest that a cross-layer approach in ad hoc networks brings benefits that justify violating the principles of strict layering found in traditional networks.

Acknowledgment

We wish to acknowledge the financial support provided by the Mexican Science and Technology council (CONACYT), for the development of the work presented in this paper.

References

1. Weiser, M.: The computer for the twenty-first century. Scientific American (1991)
2. Corson, S., Macker, J.: Mobile Ad Hoc Networking (MANET): Routing protocol performance issues and evaluation considerations. RFC 2501 IETF (1999)
3. Helal, S., Desai, N., Verma, V., Lee, C.: Konark. a service discovery and delivery protocol for ad hoc networks In: Proceedings of the Third IEEE Conference on Wireless Communication Networks (WCNC) New Orleans, Lousiana, USA (2003)
4. Sun Microsystems.: Jini Specifications v2.0 (2004)
5. Guttman, E., Perkins, C.: Service Location Protocol, version 2. RFC 2608 IETF (1999)
6. UPnP Forum.: UPnP Device Architecture v1.0.1 (2004)
7. Cheng, L.: Service advertisement and discovery in mobile ad hoc networks In: Proceedings of the Workshop on Ad Hoc Communications and Collaboration in Ubiquitous Computing Environments New Orleans Louisiana USA (2002)
8. Doval, D., O'Mahony, D.: Nom: Resource location and discovery for ad hoc mobile net-works In: Proceedings of the First Annual Mediterranean Ad Hoc Networking Workshop, Med-hoc-Net Italy (2002)
9. Preub, S.: JESA service discovery protocol In Proceedings of Networking 2002. Lectures Notes in Computer Science, Vol. 2345. Springer-Verlag, Berlin Heidelberg New York (2002) 1196-1201
10. Ratsimor, O., Chakraborty, D., Tolia, S., Kushraj, D., Kunjithapatham, A., Gupta, G., Joshi, A., Finin, T.: Allia: Alliance-based Service Discovery of Ad-Hoc Environments In ACM Mobile Commerce Workshop (2002)
11. Reid, B., Varshavsky, A., de Lara, E.: Cross-Layer Service Discovery, Selection and Re-discovery in Multihop Mobile Ad Hop Networks. submitted for publication
12. Koodli, R., Perkins, C.: Service Discovery in On-demand Ad Hoc Networks. IETF draft (2002)
13. Perkins, C., Belding-Royer, E., Das, S.: Ad Hoc On-Demand Distance Vector (AODV) Routing. RFC 3561 IETF (2003)

BCTMA (Bi-directional Cut-Through Medium Access) Protocol for 802.11-Based Multi-hop Wireless Networks*

WoongChul Choi[1], JinWoo Han[1], Byung Joon Park[1], and JiMan Hong[2]

[1] Department of Computer Science
wchoi@daisy.kw.ac.kr
[2] Department of Computer Engineering,
KwangWoon University, Seoul, Korea 139-701

Abstract. In DCF of 802.11-based multi-hop wireless networks, a channel access sequence of 4-way handshake with RTS-CTS-DATA-ACK is used to forward a single packet. For multi-hop packet forwarding, multiple channel accesses with this 4-way handshake are required, and this might entail multiple collisions, which, in turn, results in poor end-to-end performance. To eliminate the overhead of these multiple channel accesses and, as a result, to reduce the possible number of collisions, the DCMA (Data-driven Cut-through Medium Access) protocol has been proposed[5]. We name the scheme used in the DCMA protocol the *forward cut-through scheme*. In this paper, we propose *BCTMA (Bi-directional Cut-Through Medium Access)* protocol for high performance 802.11-based multi-hop wireless networks by combining both *forward and backward cut-through schemes*. We have implemented *BCTMA* protocol in *ns-2*[9]. We conducted a comprehensive simulation to study the performance improvements. The simulation results indicate that the performance is significantly improved and the number of dropped packets due to collisions can be significantly reduced as much as a half.

Keywords: Forward cut-through scheme, Backward cut-through scheme, BCTMA (Bi-directional Cut-Through Medium Access) protocol, DCF (Distributed Coordination Function), Wireless multi-hop networks, IEEE 802.11

1 Introduction

End-to-end performance improvement has been an important issue not only in wired networks, but in multi-hop ad-hoc wireless networks as well. Unlike in wired networks where packets are transmitted in a full duplex mode, packets can be transmitted only in a half-duplex mode in ad-hoc wireless networks. As the transmission medium is shared by nodes in a transmission zone, the medium access control protocol is also important. In IEEE 802.11-based MAC protocol[1], two medium access control protocols are specified - PCF (Point Coordination Function) and DCF (Distributed Coordination Protocol) which is often used as a referred scheme for multi-hop ad-hoc wireless networks. Since DCF is based on CSMA/CA (Carrier Sense Multiple Access with Collision Avoidance), a host that has packets to send can send only when the medium becomes available. Because of these reasons, the end-to-end performance of ad-hoc wireless networks is inherently poor.

---

* This work was supported by grant No. R01-2002-000-10934-0 (2005) from the Basic Research Program of the Korea Science & Engineering Foundation and by the Research Grant of KwangWoon University in 2003.

F.F. Ramos et al. (Eds.): ISSADS 2005, LNCS 3563, pp. 377–387, 2005.

DCF is a contention-based medium access protocol, so collision can occur. To avoid collision, collision avoidance protocols such as RTS-CTS-DATA-ACK handshake are used in DCF of 802.11-based networks. But even with that mechanism, collisions can occur due to several reasons, so the problem of collision in wireless networks needs to be investigated from different views – one for the cause of the collisions and the other for its aftermath. For the cause of a collision, the hidden/exposed terminal problem is one main reason[6]. The research efforts on the procedure after a collision are about fine tuning the parameters such as back-off interval for retransmission[3].

In order to forward a single packet in DCF, a channel access sequence of 4-way handshake with RTS-CTS-DATA-ACK is used. For multi-hop packet forwarding, multiple channel accesses with this 4-way handshake are required, and this might entail multiple collisions, which, in turn, results in poor end-to-end performance. To eliminate the overhead of these multiple channel accesses, the DCMA (Data-driven Cut-through Medium Access) protocol has been proposed[5]. We name the scheme used in DCMA protocol the *forward cut-through scheme*. In this paper, we develop a *backward cut-through scheme* and propose *BCTMA* (Bi-directional Cut-Through Medium Access) protocol by combining both schemes. We make an extension for 802.11-based MAC protocol in DCF mode to implement the BCTMA protocol. With the *BCTMA* protocol, we show by simulation how significantly the performance improves.

The rest of this paper is organized as follows. In Section 2, we review the related work and briefly describe the specification of the IEEE 802.11 background in Section 3. We provide the problem statements and detailed description of the *BCTMA* protocol in Section 4. Section 5 and 6 discusses simulation and the results. We conclude the paper in Section 7. In this paper, the terms of packet and frame are used interchangeably.

2 Related Works

There have been many research efforts to improve the performance of 802.11-based wireless networks. The efforts can be categorized into two - one for the collision avoidance in terms of the hidden/exposed terminal problem and the other for how to handle a collision. Fujii *et al.* [7] propose a MAC protocol where a high-power node forwards the RTS and CTS packets from a low-power node to improve success rate performance of a data, by reducing collisions that occur after connection establishments, regardless of the size of the transmission range. Dutkiewicz [8] tries to find out the optimum transmit range to maximize data throughput in ad-hoc wireless networks. The author presents a simulation study stating that under a wide set of network and load conditions multi-hop networks have lower performance than single-hop networks, data throughput is maximized when all nodes are in range of each other and also shows that the addition of relay-only nodes does not significantly improve throughput performance of multi-hop networks. In [6], Bharghavan proposes Dual Channel Collision Avoidance (DCCA), which employs two channels for signaling and data in order to avoid collisions efficiently in all cases of hidden/exposed receivers and senders, and Fair Collision Resolution Algorithm (FRCA), which seeks to fairly resolve collisions with both consideration for spatial locality of stations and back-off advertisement, in order to provide better channel utilization and delay properties compared to IEEE 802.11 standard. Cali *et al.* [3] propose a method that estimates the number of active stations via the number of empty slots, and exploit the estimated value to tune the contention window value based on their analytic model.

3 IEEE 802.11 MAC Protocol

IEEE 802.11 provides two medium access control protocols, PCF (Point Coordination Function) which is a centralized scheme and DCF (Distributed Coordination Function) which is a fully distributed scheme. DCF is also known as the basic access method, and is a CSMA/CA (Carrier Sense Multiple Access with Collision Avoidance) protocol. A node that has a packet to send changes its state to the contention state, which means that it needs to perform carrier-sensing first. If it finds the medium idle, then it can transmit the packet. Otherwise the node is waiting for the on-going transmission to terminate. To avoid any collision with other nodes when the medium is available, a slotted binary exponential backoff mechanism is used.

In DCF protocol (Fig. 1), the frame exchange sequence between a source and a destination node is RTS (Request to Send)-CTS (Clear to Send)-DATA-ACK (Acknowledgement). There is a time interval between frames and there are four IFSs defined in IEEE 802.11 – SIFS (shortest interframe space), PIFS (PCF interframe space), DIFS (DCF interframe space) and EIFS (extended interframe space). The IFSs provide priority levels for accessing the medium. The SIFS is the shortest of the interframe spaces and is used after RTS, CTS and DATA frames to give the highest priority to CTS, DATA and ACK, respectively. In DCF, when the medium is idle, a node waits for the DIFS time interval before initiating a transmission.

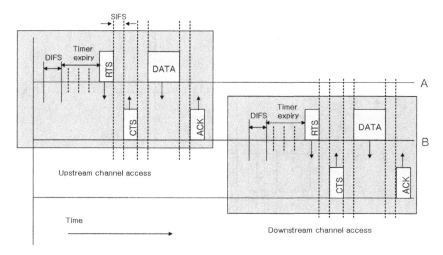

Fig. 1. Packet forwarding operation of DCF of 802.11 MAC protocol

Each node in IEEE 802.11 maintains a NAV (Network Allocation Vector) which indicates the remaining time of the on-going transmission sessions. NAV is called virtual carrier sensing, corresponding to physical carrier sensing. This information is contained in the RTS, CTS and DATA packets, so whenever nodes receive those packets, they extract the information and update their NAVs. Therefore, the medium is considered to be busy if a node senses a signal either physically or virtually, i.e. is in duration of its NAV.

4 BCTMA (Bi-directional Cut-Through Medium Access) Protocol

4.1 Forward Cut-Through Scheme in 802.11 DCF Protocol

To eliminate the overheads of multiple channel accesses, the Data-Driven Cut-Through Medium Access (DCMA) scheme has been defined as a simple extension of the 802.11 DCF[5]. DCMA combines the ACK (to the upstream node) with the RTS (to the downstream node) in a single ACK/RTS packet that is sent to the MAC broadcast address. The payload of the ACK/RTS packet contains the MAC address of the upstream node and the downstream node. The reservation for the downstream hop is attempted only after successfully receiving the DATA packet from the upstream node. Since the downstream node (and all other neighboring nodes of the forwarding node) is assured to be silent till the completion of the ACK from the forwarding node, this forwarding cut-through scheme gives a preferential and contention-free channel access to the downstream transmission. Cut-through in DCMA fails when the downstream node fails to respond to the ACK/RTS with a positive CTS. The forwarding node then simply queues the packet in the NIC queue and resumes the normal 802.11 channel access.

The timing diagram in Fig. 2 explains the operation of DCMA. Assume that node A has a frame to send to node B. Node A sends an RTS to node B. Assuming that its

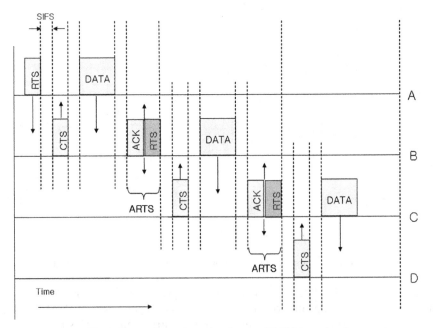

Fig. 2. Forward cut-through scheme of DCMA protocol

NAV is not busy for the proposed transmission duration, B replies with a CTS. B receives the DATA packet, and then sends an RTS/ACK control packet with the ACK part addressed to A and the RTS part addressed to C.

Since the DATA packet is transmitted to the downstream node and so is the combined control packets of ACK/RTS, we name this *Forward Cut-Through Scheme*. *Forward Cut-Through Scheme* can be aliased as *Downstream Cut-Through Scheme*.

4.2 Backward Cut-Through Scheme in 802.11 DCF Protocol

In *Backward Cut-Through Scheme*, a CTS is combined with the DATA from a downstream node, if any, and the DATA from the upstream node is combined with the ACK for the previous DATA transmission. The timing diagram in Fig. 3 explains this *backward cut-through scheme*. The payload of the CTS/DATA packet contains both the MAC addresses of the upstream node and the downstream node. So does the payload of DATA/ACK.

The reasoning for this scheme is that both nodes in the downstream and the upstream are in the listening mode while they are in any state of the 4-way handshake. By taking advantage of this silence and the listening state they are in, up to two access sequences of 4 way handshakes are processed only in one access. As a result, the possible number of collisions can be reduced, while the end-to-end throughput can be increased.

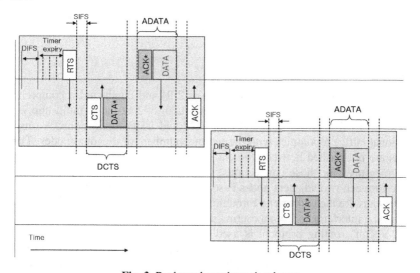

Fig. 3. Backward cut-through scheme

If the transmission of the DATA in a CTS/DATA packet (DCTS) is not answered by the ACK in the DATA/ACK (ADATA), the scheme simply queues the DATA and will resume the normal 802.11 access or another *backward cut-through scheme* in the next channel access time. This same rule applies to the case where the ACK in the DATA/ACK (ADATA) packet is not successfully transmitted to the node in the upstream. *Backward Cut-Through Scheme* can be aliased as *Upstream Cut-Through Scheme*.

By combining both schemes into one, we develop a new efficient protocol called *BCTMA* (Bi-directional Cut-Through Medium Access) protocol in the following Fig. 4.

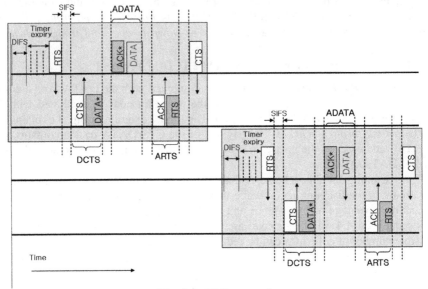

Fig. 4. *BCTMA* protocol

5   Simulation

We have implemented *BCTMA* scheme in *ns-2*[9] and conducted a comprehensive study to evaluate the performance enhancements of 802.11-based multi-hop wireless networks. We perform the simulation for TCP and UDP connections. We use two-dimensional lattice topologies with the various numbers of diagonal nodes. The connections are established between the end nodes of both diagonals, and the performance is measured for those connections. Link capacity is assumed 2Mbits/s and the distance between two adjacent nodes is set to 250m. The metrics for the performance improvements are the end-to-end throughput and the number of collisions. In order to minimize the interference from a routing protocol, the DSDV (Destination Sequenced Distant Vector) routing protocol is used. DSDV[2] is one of the proactive routing protocols where the route update packets are sent periodically and incrementally as the topology changes. Since the topology used in the simulation is fixed, the route updates are sent periodically only, and that fact is taken into account to calculate the performance metrics. The performance values are evaluated after running simulations for 300 *ns-2* simulation seconds. The simulations are conducted on Linux 2.4.20 on a Pentium 3.0 Ghz PC with 516Mbytes main memory. The version of *ns-2* is *ns-2.27*.

6   Results

Fig. 5, 6 and Fig. 7, 8 show the simulation results of end-to-end throughput and throughput improvements for 4 bidirectional TCP and UDP connections. Fig. 5 and 6 show that throughputs by the *BCTMA* protocol are always better and Fig. 7 and 8 examine the specific value of difference between two protocols. While the difference in throughput is approximately 1.5Mbytes/300secs for TCP and 0.5Mbytes/300s for UDP, it can be said from Fig. 5, 6 and 7, 8 that wireless networks with more hops have a better ratio of throughput improvement comparing to the amount of the end-to-end throughput itself. In addition, throughput improvement for TCP connections is greater than that for UDP connections. The reason for this is that TCP has an end-to-end rate adaptation mechanism, while UDP does not. Therefore, the transmission rate at a sender node is constant for UDP, so the throughput improvement is not much.

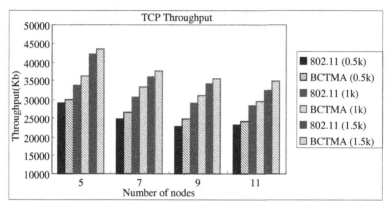

Fig. 5. End-to-end throughput for 4 bidirectional TCP connections with frame size of 0.5Kbytes, 1Kbytes, and 1.5Kbytes

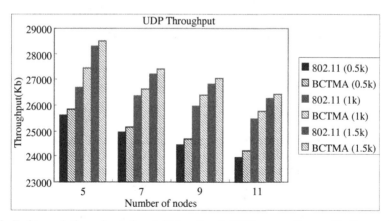

Fig. 6. End-to-end throughput for 4 bidirectional UDP connections with frame size of 0.5Kbytes, 1Kbytes, and 1.5Kbytes

Fig. 9 and 10 show the number of collisions for TCP and UDP connections. In Fig. 9, the number of collisions represents the aggregated number of frame losses and drops at every hop and is significantly reduced as much as 30%. Similar thing can be said for UDP connections in Fig. 10. In fact, this reduction in the number of collisions is the most outstanding feature of our protocol.

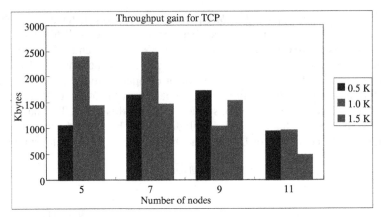

Fig. 7. End-to-end throughput gain for 4 bidirectional TCP connections for frame size of 0.5, 1.0, 1.5Kbytes

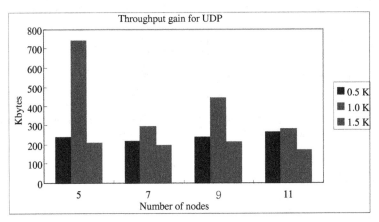

Fig. 8. End-to-end throughput gain for 4 bidirectional UDP connections for frame size of 0.5, 1.0, 1.5Kbytes

Finally, we examine the value of throughput cost defined as (frame_loss_and_drop_in_bytes / end-to-end_throughput_in_bytes), which means how much it costs in order to transmit a packet successfully from one end to another end. This value is especially important because it is related to the power consumption. Fig. 11 and 12 show the result and tell that the *BCTMA* protocol works more efficiently than 802.11 protocol. Considering our simulation runs for 300 simulation seconds, which are approximately 5 simulation minutes, the longer the running time is, the greater the difference will be.

7 Conclusion

In this paper, we proposed and implemented *BCTMA (Bi-directional Cut-Through Medium Access)* protocol for high performance 802.11-based multi-hop wireless

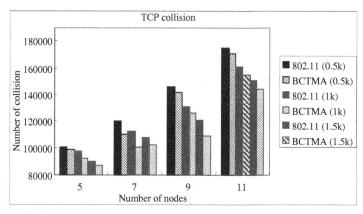

Fig. 9. The number of collisions for 6 bidirectional TCP connections

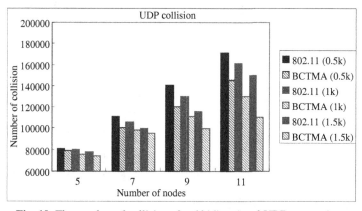

Fig. 10. The number of collisions for 6 bidirectional UDP connections

networks by combining *forward cut-through scheme* with *backward cut-through scheme*. Forwarding a single packet to one hop in DCF of 802.11-based wireless networks costs a 4-way handshake of RTS-CTS-DARA-ACK. Forwarding a single packet to multi-hop requires multiple sequences of 4-way handshake, which is likely to entail multiple numbers of collision, especially in the network with many active connections. Collisions negatively affect the end-to-end performance of connection-oriented protocols such as TCP, because the binary back-off scheme is triggered at the MAC layer of the node when a collision occurs. Due to this back-off scheme, the packet transmission rate between the nodes becomes slow, which, in turn, curbs the transmitting rate at the transport layer of a sender. There has been much research to prevent a collision, and the approach in this paper is using cut-through scheme in the transmission of a DATA packet, i.e., 4-way handshake is used to assure that the communicating nodes are in ready state in terms of listening or forwarding a packet, and our approach is to take advantage of it to reduce the number of these 4-way sequences.

Using the *BCTMA* protocol, the end-to-end performance of wireless multi-hop networks significantly improves in terms of throughput and the number of collisions.

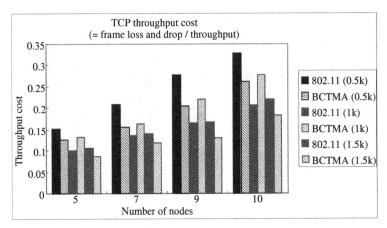

Fig. 11. Throughput cost of 6 bidirectional TCP connections. Throughput cost is defined as how much frame is lost or dropped for a successful packet transmission

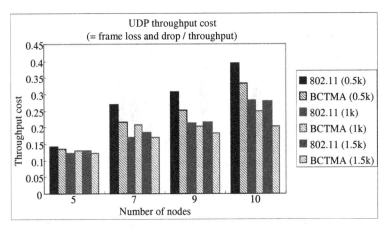

Fig. 12. Throughput cost of 6 bidirectional UDP connections. Throughput cost is defined as how much frame is lost or dropped for a successful packet transmission

The simulation results show that the throughput is increased as much as about 20% and the number of collisions is decreased as much as a half, comparing to those performance parameters with the legendary 802.11 wireless MAC protocol.

For future work, we aim to put the modified code in the MAC device drive in our testbed, and collect the data on the actual end-to-end performance. We believe that the actual performance parameters conform to the simulation results presented in this paper.

References

1. IEEE: IEEE Standard for Wireless LAN-Medium Access Control and Physical Layer Specification, IEEE 1997
2. Perkins, C., Bhagwatt, P.:Highly Dynamic Destination-Sequenced Distance-Vector Routing for Mobile Computers. Computer Communications Review, Oct. 1994, pp. 234-244

3. F.Cali, M.Conti, E.Gregori: IEEE 802.11 protocol: design and performance evaluation of an adaptive backoff mechanism, IEEE Journal of Selected Areas in Communications, vol. 18, no. 9, 2000, pp. 1774-1786
4. J.P. Monks, V.Bharghavan, W.-M.W.Hwu,: A Power Controlled Multiple Access Protocol for Wireless Packet Networks, IEEE INFOCOM 2001, pp. 219-228
5. A.Archaya, A.Misra, S.Bansal : A Label-Switching Packet Forwarding Architecture for Multi-hop Wireless LANs, ACM WoWMoM 2002, pp. 33-40
6. V.Bharghavan: Performance Evaluation of Algorithms for Wireless Medium Access, Proceedings of IEEE International Computer Performance and Dependability Symposium, 1998
7. Fujii, T., Takahashi, T., Bandai, T., Udagawa, T., Sasase, T.: An efficient MAC protocol in wireless ad-hoc networks with heterogeneous power nodes, Wireless Personal Multimedia Communications, 2002 pp. 776-780
8. Dutkiewicz, E.: Impact of transmit range on throughput performance in mobile ad hoc networks, IEEE ICC 2001 pp.2933-2937
9. http://www.isi.edu/nsnam/ns/

Some Security Issues of Wireless Systems

Eduardo B. Fernández, Saeed Rajput,
Michael VanHilst, and María M. Larrondo-Petrie

Dept. of Computer Science & Engineering, Florida Atlantic University,
777 Glades Road, Boca Raton, FL 33431-0991
{ed,saeed,mike,maria}@cse.fau.edu

Abstract. Wireless systems have found wide acceptance in many industries such as military and healthcare. These systems appear under a variety of architectures including fixed networks, cellular networks, and ad hoc networks. We survey some security problems, of interest to researchers, in wireless systems when used in these environments. Most studies of the security of these systems emphasize cryptographic aspects, we concentrate on other security aspects, such as operating systems, access control, web services, and location awareness.

1 Introduction

Wireless systems have found wide acceptance in many industries such as military, healthcare, business, manufacturing, retail, and transportation. These systems appear under a variety of architectures including fixed networks, cellular networks, and ad hoc networks. The challenges posed by the industries to each of these technologies are unique, especially for healthcare and military applications.

We survey some security problems in wireless systems. We do not attempt to be comprehensive but to give a general overview of some problems of interest to researchers. Most studies of the security of these systems emphasize cryptographic aspects. While important, they are not the only issues and we concentrate on other aspects. Background information about security aspects of wireless systems can be found in [1], [2] ,and [3], and about the structure of the networks and protocols in [4].

We start by discussing some general issues that define the context for our discussion. Then we consider the effects of the type of industry on application security. Next we talk about access control aspects and the effect of the operating system on security. We look then at web services and end with the effect of location awareness on security.

2 General Issues

When compared to wired networks, there are four generic limitations of all wireless devices: 1) limited power, 2) limited communications bandwidth, 3) limited processing power, and 4) relatively unreliable network connection. The bandwidth available to wireless systems is usually at least an order of magnitude less than that available to a wired device. The processing power is limited due to the limited space/cost of fixed wireless devices typically used for Wi-Fi networks, and is further limited due to power constraints in other wireless devices. The unreliability of the network connection is universal in all wireless networks. Protocols have been designed to take this

F.F. Ramos et al. (Eds.): ISSADS 2005, LNCS 3563, pp. 388–396, 2005.

lack of reliability into account and to try to improve it. However, in designing these protocols, choices have to be made about the size of the packets and frames to be used. Such decisions can have a profound impact on the effectiveness and efficiency of cryptographic protocols and other security measures. To this we add the fact that there is a large variety of devices using different architectures, several operating systems, and diverse functionality. On top of everything, security needs for wireless devices are greater than those of regular wired-network devices. This is due to the very nature of their use; they are mobile, they are on the edge of the network, their connections are unreliable, and they tend to get destroyed accidentally or maliciously. These devices can also be stolen, lost, or forgotten. Thus, we need more security processing. Security processing can easily overwhelm the processors in wireless devices. This challenge, which is unique to wireless devices, is sometimes referred to as the *security-processing gap*. Non-fixed wireless devices such as cellular handsets and ad hoc network devices such as sensors are severely handicapped due to their very low battery power. Even though significant advances are expected in computation and communication speed over the next decade, it is still expected that they will lag behind the power available to fixed computers due to the need for miniaturization. To make things worse, only modest improvements to battery power are expected. The battery limitation in mobile wireless devices is sometimes called *battery gap* and refers to the growing disparity between increasing energy requirements for high-end operations needed on such devices and slow improvements in battery technology.

Finally, ad hoc wireless networks have their own security challenges. Due to their extremely small device size (*smart dust* [5]), their battery life and processing power are further limited. However, security needs are even greater, since some security processing is needed just for the device to be able to function properly and be able to communicate in their routing protocols.

When it comes to the general service provider industry (internet and cell phone companies), they are mostly interested in providing cellular service and hotspot services. While the security issues of cellular networks are relatively well understood, those of Wi-Fi networks are not. Important issues are authentication of users on hotspots, wireless-hop security (the part of the ISP network that is wireless), and seamless security association transfer from one domain (e.g. the cellular network) to the other (e.g. the Wi-Fi network). An interesting direction here is authorization of devices once authenticated. This has to come from application semantics as we discuss below.

With the increase in functions, the typical problems found in larger systems are also appearing in portable devices. One of these problems is viruses [6]. The first portable virus to appear was Liberty, followed shortly by Phage. The WML (Wireless Markup Language), a script language used by WAP can also be a source of possible attacks [7] [8]. The devices do not distinguish between script code resident in the phone from the one downloaded from potentially insecure sites, all of them execute with the same rights. An infected device can be used to launch denial of service attacks on other devices or the network. Similarly to wired systems, wireless systems need up-to-date antivirus programs. Companies such as Symantec, McAfee, and Trend Micro have specialized products for handheld devices. A problem here is that in some devices because of space and processing limitations, antivirus programs and other protection devices, such as firewalls and IDS, may not be feasible.

3 Applications and Security

For the healthcare industry both Wi-Fi and sensor networks are important. Issues in these networks are similar to the ones we discussed in the previous section in the context of service providers. The difference in this case is that the consequences of an error are severe, especially when it involves wireless bedside monitoring or a dispensing device communicating with the server. The area of sensor networks (biometric sensors) is still a research area. When we consider the collection of data from sensors, the issues of confidentiality, integrity, and non-interference also arise. HIPAA regulations have brought renewed concern about patient privacy and new models are being proposed [9]. A model defined at the application level, say using UML (Unified Modeling Language), must be mapped to the lower levels of the wireless networks; it is an open problem how to do this in a systematic way. The use of patterns, discussed in the last section, could provide a handle for this mapping.

The military has applications for all types of wireless devices. Their need for security in all areas is more rigorous. However, in their case, survivability of the network is very important, i.e. it is vital that theft or destruction of one device does not compromise the information stored on that device, or worse, the security of the entire system. In case of ad hoc networks, it is vital that removal of a few nodes does not affect the communication capabilities of the devices, which opens interesting research areas to develop authentication and security protocols that are friendly to such changes. The US Department of Defense recently issued Directive 8100.2 that requires encrypting all information sent in their networks according to the rules of the Federal Information Processing (FIP) standard [10]. The provision also calls for anti-virus software. It is interesting to observe that their concern is mostly about message transmission and they don't seem to be worried about the other aspects of security, such as the ones discussed in this paper. This is also true for the NIST recommendations for wireless security in federal agencies. Apparently they were considering only simple applications; however, the increasing use of web services opens up many new possibilities for military uses, including battlefield communications, sensor networks, and soldier location and identification.

Another important application is mobile e-commerce. This includes mobile banking, wireless payment services, shopping, reservations, and many others. Many of the required functions can be secured using cryptography (see [11] for a survey), but access to specific services requires at least some type of Role-Based Access Control (RBAC), as discussed below.

4 Access Control to Sensitive Information
in or Through the Device

We should consider access control to:

- *Resources in the device.* The portable device may contain files that need to be restricted in access and it is the function of its operating system to perform this control. Control of types of access is important; for example, a user may play a song, but she should not copy it. This type of control can complement other types of digital rights management. The device may contain passwords to access networks, encryption keys, lists of people, etc.; all this data needs protection.

- *Resources provided by other mobile network devices.* This is the most interesting case for research. Because of the variety and unpredictability of potential users, access decisions must be based on attributes (roles, groups, qualifiers) and trust [12, 13]. For the same reasons and because of the variety of resources, rights must be created dynamically [14, 12]. In addition, it is not clear where the access rights should be kept because of the lack of a centralized repository for authorization rules (no device can hold large tables) [14].
- *Resources in wired networks.* When portable devices need to access applicationrelated data from corporate databases some type of Role-Based Access Control (RBAC) may be necessary. Management and enforcement of application and institution constraints can be performed following PMI (Privilege Management Infrastructure) [15]. PMI is a standard of ITU X.509. There is some work on RBAC models that integrate the wireless access with access from the wired network users. One of these papers [16] uses a hierarchic role structure, which doesn't appear as very useful for practical situations because it is not easy to build meaningful hierarchies for complex applications. More flexible models are needed.

5 Operating Systems

Portable devices have evolved from having ad hoc supervisors to standard operating systems. Some systems use the Java run-time system as supervisor. High-end cell phones run complete operating systems such as Palm OS (now being replaced by Cobalt), Microsoft Windows CE (renamed PocketPC), Symbian, or Linux; and provide IP networking capabilities for web browsing, email and instant messaging. Some typical security features include:

- *A unique device identifier* – this can be accessed by applications.
- *A kernel configuration with enhanced protection* – this allows the use of the protected kernel mode, instead of the full-kernel model.
- *Digital authentication in the dial-up boot loader* – the dial-up boot loader is a program in ROM used to upgrade the OS image file (NK.bin) using flash memory or a remote server. The OS image file should be signed using digital encryption to verify its integrity before it is downloaded.

In addition, these operating systems include support for the standard cryptographic protocols.

The security of the operating system is fundamental for any system because it controls all the resources and provides support for the execution of applications. There is an overemphasis on cryptography, while aspects such as memory protection and file authorization have been neglected in most products, although this is changing (Cobalt includes memory protection). Memory protection is important in the creation of compartments to stop the propagation of viruses, while as mentioned above, file authorization is necessary to protect cryptographic keys and to enforce digital rights management. Downloaded contents, such as music, wallpaper, and games need to be protected. Current devices have no protection or protection based on cryptographic means. The study of these aspects provides a potentially fruitful research direction, in particular protection of digital rights without resorting solely to cryptography.

6 Web Services

A web service is a component or set of functions accessible through the web that can be incorporated into an application. Web services expose an XML interface, can be registered and located through a registry, communicate using XML messages, and support loosely-coupled connections between systems. Web services represent the latest approach to distribution and are considered an important technology for business integration and collaboration. Figure 1 shows the architectural layers of web services architectures. Each layer is regulated by a variety of security standards [17].

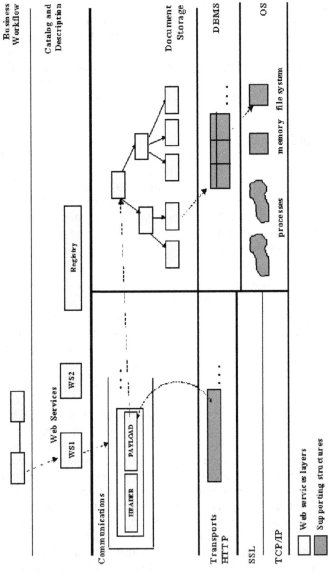

Fig. 1. Web services architectural layers

Wireless devices can access web services using SOAP (Simple Object Access Protocol) but web services still are not widely used in portable devices. The limited processing power of portable devices and the lack of network reliability are a serious obstacle for a full implementation. However, using appropriate gateway middleware, it is possible for portable devices to access web services. Most access to web services from mobile devices now goes through a WAP gateway and most of the use of web services for mobile systems is now between servers [18]. However, this situation is changing and predictions indicate that web services in cell phones will be arriving soon [19] [20] [21]. In fact, Nokia just announced a Service-Oriented Architecture for smart mobile phones [22]. Security will be an important issue for this generation of smart and complex devices.

The richness of web services brings along a new set of security problems [17]. All the attacks that are possible in wired systems are also possible in wireless systems using web services, e.g., viruses, buffer overflow attacks, message interception, denial of service, etc. Web services introduce several extra layers in the system architecture and we have to consider the unique security problems of these layers. Since these are layers that run on top of the platform layers, the security of the platforms is still fundamental for the security of the complete system. Wireless systems using web services have to face, in addition, the general vulnerabilities of wireless networks and may also add new security problems to these networks, although this aspect has not been explored in detail. There is also a variety of standards for web services security and a designer of wireless devices should follow at least the most important ones to be able to have a credibly secure system. On the other hand, the extra layers bring more flexibility and precision for security; for example, encryption can be applied at the XML element level, authorization can be applied to specific operations in a web service interface. This greater security precision allows applying policies in a finer and more flexible way.

Web services make possible convenient implementations of location-based services, where information is pushed to the device depending on its location. We discuss below additional problems that may occur in that case.

7 Location Awareness

Because mobile devices are usually connected to networks, it is possible to track their position. For example, the US Federal Communications Commission mandates that cell phones must be able to be located within 300 meters of their actual location. In some cases the user of the device may want others to know her whereabouts but in other cases she might not [23]. Even in the first case, only authorized persons should have access to location information. That means that we need to control access to location information. This is another aspect of access control, related to the discussion in Section 4. Ease of determining location also raises privacy concerns [24] [25].

Location can also be used to get access to physical resources; for example, doors in a building could be controlled depending on the location of an authorized user. In some cases nomadic users may want to access the resources provided by some physical devices, e.g., printers or storage devices. A device may establish its web presence through physical registration [26]. The position of the user is important to decide which resources would be more convenient for him to access.

Location can be absolute or relative. Examples of absolute location are geospatial representation (typically longitude and latitude) or civic (address, city, region, country). The position of the mobile entity with respect to other known locations is an example of a relative location.

Work on this area requires finding new models of access control based on location information, as well as standard characteristics such as roles, certificates, and identity. For example, access control to location information may need to be performed in a distributed way [27] [14]. An overview of access control situations is given in [28]. Another direction is finding ways to preserve privacy; for example, [14] proposes the use of logical borders and anonymous IDs, based on the concept of personal profiles and context-aware agents, and [29] considers preventing unnecessary information to be disclosed to third parties. Contexts are important for privacy and access control. A context is an evolving, structured, and shared information space [30].

8 Conclusions

There is serious concern about the vulnerabilities of wireless systems. The easy access to the medium by attackers is a negative aspect, compounded by the design errors in the early protocols [31] [32] [33]. It is true that Wi-Fi is becoming more secure and Bluetooth appears reasonably secure but they (and WAP) cover only some of the security layers. A basic security principle indicates that security is an all-layer problem, securing one or more layers is not enough [34]. With some of the layers still insecure, it is not possible to have true security.

Third generation systems will have voice quality that is comparable to public switched telephone networks. Voice over IP over WiFi will bring its own set of security problems. In addition, the new systems will have higher data rates, symmetrical and asymmetrical data transmission rates, support for both packet and circuit switched data services, adaptive interface to the Internet to reflect common asymmetry between inbound and outbound traffic, more efficient use of available spectrum, support for wide variety of mobile equipment, and more flexibility. All of these are the potential sources of new security problems. The pervasiveness of mobile devices makes their users want them to work together. For example, a cellular phone extracting phone numbers from a PDA or a digital camera storing its pictures in a laptop. This will lead to new interoperable architectures [35], which in turn, will bring new security problems. The proliferation of small devices in all places leads to *ubiquitous computing*, security issues for that environment are discussed in [36]. Anonimity, traceability, and traffic analysis are aspects that will become more important in that environment and they are all related to the protection of the metadata of the wireless structure. Usability of the security interfaces is another possible problem due to the limited sizes of these interfaces [8].

We have indicated some aspects that offer promising avenues for future work. We are working on some of these issues but there are several areas that appear neglected and could be a good source of ideas for future research. A general approach that appears promising is the use of security patterns, which can help designers build secure systems [34]. Several patterns have been found in the Bluetooth architecture, including versions of the Broker, Layers, Lookup, and Bridge patterns [37]. Some patterns for ubiquitous computing have appeared [38]. However, no specific security patterns for wireless systems have been described. Patterns are part of the more general area of software architecture and the methods and approaches of that area should be more explored for possible use in security [39].

Acknowledgements

This work was supported by a grant from the Defense Information Systems Agency (DISA), administered by Pragmatics, Inc. Tami Sorgente, Alvaro Escobar, and Andrei Bretan provided valuable comments that helped improve this paper.

References

1. Fernandez, E. B., Jawhar, I., Larrondo-Petrie, M. M., and Van Hilst, M.: An overview of the security of wireless networks. In: Ilyas, M. (ed.): Handbook of Wireless LANs, CRC Press (2004)
2. Rajput, S.: Wireless security protocols. In: Ilyas, M. (ed.): Handbook of Wireless LANs, CRC Press (2004)
3. Elliot, G. and Phillips, N.: Mobile commerce and wireless computing systems, Addison-Wesley, 2004.
4. Stallings, W: Wireless Communications and Networks, Prentice-Hall (2002)
5. Warneke, B., Last, M. Liebowitz, B. and Pister, K.S.J.: Smart dust: communicating with a cubic- millimeter computer. In: Computer, IEEE, January (2001)
6. Foley, S. and Dumigan, R.: Are handheld viruses a significant threat? In: Communications of the ACM, Vol. 44, No 1 (2000) 105-107
7. Ghosh, A.K. and Swaminatha, T.M.: Software security and privacy risks in mobile ecommerce. In: Communications of the ACM, Vol. 44, No. 2 (2001) 51-57
8. Josang, A., and Sanderud, G.: Security in mobile communications: Challenges and opportunities. In: Proceedings of the Australasian Information Security Workshop (2003)
9. Fernandez, E. B., Larrondo-Petrie, M. M., and Sorgente, T.: Security Models for Medical and Genetic Information. In: Proceedings of the IADIS International Conference (e- Society 2004), Avila, Spain, July 2004, (2004) 509-516
10. http://www.dtic.mil/whs/directives/corres/html/81002.htm
11. Thanh, D.V.: Security issues in mobile eCommerce. In: Proceedings of the 1st International Conference on Electronic Commerce and Web Technologies (EC-Web 2000), Vol. 1875, Springer Verlag (2000) 467-476.
12. Kagal, L., Finin, T., and Joshi, A.: Trust-based security in pervasive computing environments. In: IEEE Computer, December 2001, (2001) 154-157.
13. Zhang, K., and Kindberg, T.: An authorization structure for nomadic computing. In: Proceedings of SACMAT'02, ACM (2002) 107-113.
14. Di Pietro, R. and Mancini, L.V.: Security and privacy issues of handheld and wearable wireless devices. In: Communications of the ACM, Vol. 46, No. 9 (2003) 75-79
15. Chadwick, D.W.: An X509 role-based PMI, (2001)
   http://www.permis.org/files/article1_chadwick.pdf
16. Lee, Y.R. and Park, D.G.: The ET-RBAC-based privilege management infrastructure for wireless networks. In: Proceedings of EC-Web (2003) 84-93
17. Fernandez, E.B., Sorgente, T. and Larrondo-Petrie, M.M.: Web services security: Standards and research issues, in preparation.
18. Gralla, P.: Mobile web services: Theory vs. reality.
   http://SearchWebServices.com, 10 February 2004.
19. Pilioura, T., Tsalgatidou, A. and Hadjiefthymiades, S.: Scenarios of using web services in M-commerce. In: ACM SIGecomm Exchanges, Vol. 4, No 4, January 2003, 28-36

20. Yuan, M.J.: Access web services from wireless devices. In: Java World, August 2002, http://www.javaworld.com/javaworld/jw-08-2002/jw-0823-wireless.html

21. Yuan, M. J.: Securing wireless J2ME: Security challenges and solutions for mobile commerce applications. In: IBM DeveloperWorks, IBM, 1 June 2002 http://www-106.ibm.com/developerworks/wireless/library/wi-secj2me.html

22. Yuan, M.J. SOA and web services go mobile, Nokia-style, 6 July 2004, http://www.sys-con.com/story/?storyid=45531&DE=1

23. Dogac, A. and Tumer, A.: Issues in mobile electronic commerce. In: Journal of Database Management, Jan.-March (2002) 36-42

24. Hong, J.I., and Landay, J.A.: An Architecture for privacy-sensitive ubiquitous computing. In: Berkeley EECS Annual Research Symposium, Berkeley, California, 2004; http://www.eecs.berkeley.edu/BEARS/STARS.html

25. Schilit, B. Hong, J. Gruteser, B. M.: Wireless Location Privacy Protection. In: IEEE Computer, December 2003

26. Barton, J., Kindberg, T., and Sadalgi, S.: Physical registration: Configuring electronic directories using handheld devices. In HPL-2001-119, Hewlett-Packard Co. (2001) http://www.hpl.hp.com/techreports/2001/HPL-2001-119.pdf

27. Hengartner, U. and Steenkiste, P.: Implementing access control to people location information. In Proceedings of SACMAT'04 (2004) 11-20

28. Larrondo-Petrie, M. M., VanHilst, M., Ferrnandez, E.B., Escobar, A., and Bretan, A.: Location-based access control, submitted for publication.

29. Gorlach A., Heinemann, A., and Terpstra, W.W.: Survey on location privacy in pervasive computing. In: Proceedings of 1st Workshop on Security and Privacy at the Conference on Pervasive Computing (SPPC), Vienna, April 2004.

30. Coutaz, J., Crowley, J.L., Dobson, S., and Garlan, D.: Context is key. In: Communications of the ACM, Vol. 48, No. 3, March 2005, (2005) 49-53.

31. Arbaugh, W.: Wireless security is different. In: Computer, IEEE, August 2003, 99-102.

32. Juul, N.C., and Jorgensen, N.: WAP may stumble over the gateway (security in WAP-based mobile commerce). http://www.dat.ruc.dk/~nielsj/research/papers/wap-ssgrr.pdf

33. Saarinen, M.-J.: Attacks against the WAP WTLS protocol. In: Proceedings of Communications and Multimedia Security (1999) http://www.jyu.fi/~mjos/wtls.pdf

34. Fernandez, E.B.: A methodology for secure software design. In: Proceedings of the 2004 International Conference on Software Engineering Research and Practice (SERP'04), Las Vegas, NV, 21-24 June 2004

35. Schilit, B.N., and Sengupta, U.: Device ensembles. In: IEEE Computer, December 2004, 56-64.

36. Stajano, F.and Anderson, R.: The resurrecting duckling: Security issues for ubiquitous computing. In: Security & Privacy 2002, Supplement to IEEE Computer, Vol. 35, No. 4, April 2002, (2002) 22-26. http://www.computer.org/security/supplement1/sta/

37. Gamma, E., Helm, R., Johnson, R., Vlissides,J.: Design Patterns: Elements of Reusable Object-Oriented Software, Addison-Wesley, Boston, MA (1995).

38. Landay, J.A., and Borriello, G.: Design patterns for ubiquitous computing, In: Computer, IEEE, Vol. 36, No. 8, August 2003 (2003) 93-95.

39. Medvidovic, N., Mikic-Rakic, M., Mehta, N.R., and Malek, S.: Software architectural support for handheld computing. In: IEEE Computer, Vol. 36, No. 9, September 2003, (2003) 66-73.

Overview the Key Management in Ad Hoc Networks*

Gerardo del Valle and Roberto Gómez Cárdenas

ITESM-CEM, Depto. Ciencias Computacionales, Km 3.5 Lago Guadalupe,
51296, Atizapan Zaragoza, Edo México, Mexico
{A00472042,rogomez}@itesm.mx

Abstract. The aim of this paper is to show some solutions for key management in ad hoc networks. The major problem in providing security services in such infrastructure less networks is how to manage the cryptographic keys that are needed. In order to design practical and sufficient key management systems it is necessary to understand the characteristics of ad hoc networks and why traditional key management systems cannot be used.

1 Introduction

Ad hoc networking is a networking paradigm for mobile, self-organizing networks. Typically the network nodes are interconnected through wireless interfaces and unlike traditional networks lack specialized nodes, i.e. routers, that handle packet forwarding. Instead every node in the network functions as a router as well as an application node and forwards packets on behalf of other nodes. Ad hoc networks have the ability to form "on the fly" and dynamically handle the joining or leaving of nodes in the network. An example is when three people with ad hoc networking enabled PDAs come within communication range of each other. The three PDAs could then automatically create an ad hoc network used to exchange data.

The ad hoc networks generally have the following characteristics [2]:

Dynamic network topology: The network nodes are mobile and the topology of the network may change frequently. Nodes may move around within the network but the network can also be partitioned into multiple smaller networks or be merged with other networks.

Limited bandwidth: The use of wireless communication typically implies a lower bandwidth than that of traditional networks. This may limit the number and size of the messages sent during protocol execution.

Energy constrained nodes: Nodes in ad hoc networks will most often rely on batteries as their power source. The use of complex algorithms there may not be possible.

Limited physical security: The use of wireless communication and the exposure of the network nodes increase the possibility of attacks against the network. Due to the mobility of the nodes the risk of them being physically compromised by theft, loss or other means will probably be bigger than for traditional network nodes.

By definition a mobile ad hoc network does not rely on any fixed infrastructure; instead, all networking functions (e.g., routing, mobility management, etc.) are per-

---

* The work described here was supported by the Computer Security Research Group at ITESM-CEM

F.F. Ramos et al. (Eds.): ISSADS 2005, LNCS 3563, pp. 397–406, 2005.

formed by the nodes themselves in a self organizing manner [1]. For this reason, securing ad hoc networks is challenging and in some applications requires a shift in paradigms with respect to the traditional security solutions. The security is an important issue for ad hoc networks; one of the major problems in providing security services in ad hoc networks is how to manage the cryptographic keys that are needed. In order to design practical and efficient key management systems it is necessary to understand the characteristics of ad hoc networks and why traditional key management systems cannot be used.

In the rest of this paper the main key management protocols for ad hoc networks are presented. At the end we explain our conclusions and propose several solutions.

2   Key Management

As in any distributed system, in ad hoc networks the security is based on the use of a proper key management system. As ad hoc networks significantly vary from each other in many aspects, an environment-specific and efficient key management system is needed.

The security in networking is in many cases dependent on proper key management. Key management consists of various services, of which each is vital for the security of the networking systems. The services must provide solutions to be able to answer the following questions: Trust model, Cryptosystems, Key creation, Key storage and Key distribution [9].

The key management service must ensure that the generated keys are securely distributed to their owners. Any key that must be kept secret has to be distributed so that confidentiality, authenticity and integrity are not violated. For instance whenever symmetric keys are applied, both or all of the parties involved must receive the key securely. In public-key cryptography the key distribution mechanism must guarantee that private keys are delivered only to authorized parties. The distribution of public keys need not preserve confidentiality, but the integrity and authenticity of the keys must still be ensured. We showed several solutions for key management in ad hoc networks.

3   Partially Distributed Certificate Authority

This solution proposed by Zhou and Hass [3] uses a (k, n) threshold scheme to distribute the services of the certificate authority to a set of specialized server nodes. Each of these nodes is capable of generating a partial certificate using their share of the certificate signing key skCA, but only by combining k such partial certificates can a valid certificate be obtained

The solution is suitable for planned, long-term ad hoc networks. Since it is based on public key encryption it requires that the all the nodes are capable of performing the necessary computations. Finally it assumes that subsets of the nodes are willing or able to take on the specialized server role.

3.1   System Overview

The system contains three types of nodes; client, server and combiner nodes. The client nodes are the normal users of the network while the server and combiner nodes are part of the certificate authority. The server nodes are responsible for generating partial certificates and storing certificates in a directory structure allowing client nodes to request for the certificates of other nodes. The combiner nodes which are also server nodes are responsible for combining the partial certificates into a valid certificate. The system also has an administrative authority which will be termed the dealer. The dealer is the only entity in the system that has knowledge of the complete certificate signing key skCA.

Every node in the network has a public/private key pair and it is the responsibility of the dealer to issue the initial certificate for the nodes public key as well as distributing the public key pkCA of the certificate authority which is needed to verify the certificates. [3]

The certificate authority as a whole has a public/private key pair, pkCA/skCA of which the public key is known to all network nodes. The private skCA, is shared among the server nodes according to Shamir's secret sharing scheme. [3]

3.2 Certificate Renewal

The certificates are only valid for a certain amount of time and therefore need to be renewed before they expire. When a node wishes to renew its certificate, it must request a certificate renewal from a minimum of k server nodes. If the request is granted, each of these k server nodes generates a partial certificate with a new expiration date. These partial certificates are then sent to a combiner, which could be one of the k servers, which then combines the partial certificates.

If any of the servers are compromised they may generate an invalid partial certificate which they then send to the combiner. The certificate produced by the combiner will then also be invalid. If a node changes its private/public key pair it will need to update its certificate with the new public key, this is accomplished in a similar way as the renewal.

3.3 Certificate Retrieval

The server nodes are responsible for storing the certificates of all nodes in the network. This allows any nodes requiring the public key of any other nodes to simply request the corresponding certificate from any of the server nodes.

This service requires that all nodes must register their certificate with the servers when they initially join the network. The servers must also have a mechanism of synchronizing their certificate directories in the case of updates and renewal. [3].

3.4 Analysis

This solution requires that a server- and organizational/administrative infrastructure is available and therefore is only applicable to a subset of ad hoc network applications. Viewed from a functional standpoint the solution has a number of faults or weaknesses of which the lack of a certificate revocation mechanism is the most critical. Any solution based on certificates should, considering the risk of compromise in ad hoc networks, provide such a mechanism.

Also the solution requires that the server nodes store all of the certificates issued. This requires a synchronization mechanism that propagates any new certificates to all the servers. It also must handle the case when the network has been segmented and later re-joined.

4 Fully Distributed Certificate Authority

This solution is first described by Luo and Lu in [4]. Its uses a(k, n) threshold scheme, to distribute a RSA certificate signing key to all nodes in the network. It also uses verifiable and proactive secret sharing mechanisms to protect against denial of service attacks and compromise of the certificate signing key.

This solution is aimed towards planned, long-term ad hoc networks with nodes capable of public key encryption. However, since the service is distributed among all the nodes when they join the network, there is no need to elect or choose any specialized server nodes.

4.1 System Overview

In this solution, the capabilities of the CA (Certificate Authority) are distributed to all nodes in the ad hoc network. Any operations requiring the CA's private key skCA can only be performed by a coalition of k or more nodes. The services provided by the CA can be grouped as certificate related services and system maintenance services. The certificate related services include certificate renewal and revocation. The system maintenance services include incorporating joining nodes into the CA. This service is called share initialization.

The system maintenance also includes proactively updating the shares of the CA's private key to protect it from being compromised. This service is termed share update. [4]

The availability of the service is based on the assumption that every node will have a minimum of k one-hop neighbors and that the nodes are provided with a valid certificate prior to their joining the network. The system then provides services to maintain and update these initial certificates. [4]

4.2 Certificate Renewal

Since certificates are only valid for a limited time period they must be renewed before they expire. When a node p wishes to renew its certificate cert it requests a certificate renewal from a coalition of k of its one-hop neighbors. Each node i in the coalition then first checks that the old certificate has not already expired and that it has not been revoked. If they agree to serve the request they each generate a new partial certificate certi and return it to node p. Node p then combines the k partial certificates to obtain its updated certificate certupdated. [4]

4.3 Certificate Revocation

The certificate revocation mechanism is based on the assumption that all nodes monitor the behavior of their one-hop neighbors and maintain their own certificate revocation lists. If a node discovers that one of its neighbors is incorrect it adds its certificate to the CRL (certificate revocation list) and floods an accusation against the node [4]. Any node receiving such an accusation first checks its CRL to verify that the accusation did not originate from a node whose certificate has been revoked. If the accuser certificate has been revoked the accusation is ignored. However, if the accusation originated from a valid node, the accused node is marked as suspect.

4.4 Analysis

Similar to the partially distributed CA this solution requires an organizational/administrative infrastructure to provide the registration and initialization services. The main benefit of this solution is its availability and that it, unlike the other certificate based solution proposed, provides a certificate revocation mechanism.

Since all nodes are part of the CA service, it is sufficient that a requesting node has k one-hop neighbors for the CA service to be available. The amount of network wide traffic is also limited.

The cost of achieving this high availability is a set of rather complex maintenance protocols, e.g. the share initialization and the share update protocols. A larger number of shares are also exposed to compromise since each node has its own share as compared to only the specialized server nodes in the partially distributed solution. The parameter k therefore may need to be chosen larger since an attacker may be able to compromise a larger number of shares between each share update. This in turn affects the availability of the service. The solution must also provide for a synchronization mechanism in the case of network segmentations.

The certificate revocation method proposed assumes that each node is capable of monitoring the behavior of all its one-hop neighbors. This assumption however may be too strong in certain ad hoc networks.

5 Self-issued Certificates

This solution is proposed by Hubaux [5] and provides a public key management solution similar to PGP in the sense that certificates are issued by the users themselves without the involvement of any certification authority. Unlike the public key based solutions, this one is intended to function in spontaneous ad hoc networks where the nodes do not have any prior relationship. However, due to this it requires an initial phase during which its effectiveness is limited and therefore it is unsuitable for short-term networks. Since it is based on public key encryption it requires that the nodes have sufficient computational capacity.

5.1 System Overview

Like PGP, deals with the problem of distributing public keys in an authenticated manner. Unlike traditional PKI solutions, in PGP the public keys are not certified by some trusted third party[6]. Instead each user has the capability of certifying the public keys of other users. It is then up to each user to determine how much trust to place in a specific certificate.

In PGP, public key servers, i.e. certificate directories are used to distribute certificates; however in ad hoc networks no such servers are available and therefore the solution proposed by Hubaux relies on the users to distribute and store the certificates themselves. Each user stores a small number of certificates that have been issued. When two users wish to authenticate each others public keys, they tried to find a certificate chain using only the certificates stored in their combined local certificate repositories.

5.2 Analysis

The main benefit of this solution is that it does not require any form of infrastructure neither routing, server or organizational/administrative. However it lacks a certificate revocation mechanism. Also like PGP it has problems during its initial stages before the number of certificates issued reaches a critical amount.

This solution also assumes the PGP terminology is called trusted introducers or even meta-introducers. A trusted introducer is a user that is trusted to introduce other users, i.e. issue certificates to other users. A meta-introducer is a trusted introducer that is trusted to introduce other trusted introducers. [6]

6 Secure Pebblenets

This solution proposed by Basagni [7] provides a distributed key management system based on symmetric encryption. The solution provides group authentication, message integrity and confidentiality.

This solution is suitable for planned and distributed, long-term ad hoc networks consisting of low performance nodes that are unable to perform public key encryption

6.1 System Overview

All network nodes share a secret group identity key kGI which is used to provide authentication and to derive additional keys used to provide confidentiality. The group identity key's crypto-period lasts for the whole duration of the network while the keys used to provide confidentiality are updated on regular intervals.

The network's lifetime is divided up in time periods, each consisting of three phases. During the operational phase the nodes use the group identity key kGI to provide authentication and message integrity, and a traffic encryption key kTEK to provide confidentiality.

To enable the distributed update of the traffic encryption key, the network is segmented into clusters during the cluster generation phase. Each cluster has a node designated as the cluster head. During the key update phase one of the cluster heads is elected key manager and is responsible for generating a new traffic encryption key and distributing it to the other cluster heads. Each of the cluster heads then distributes the new traffic encryption key to its cluster members.

The solution is intended to be used in large ad hoc networks consisting of nodes with limited processing, storage and power resources. Therefore public key cryptography is not feasible.

Due to the complexity involved in key distribution, authentication is limited to group membership since this only requires that all nodes in the network share one cryptographic key. If authentication of individual nodes is required, $n*(n-1)/2$ symmetric keys need to be managed. [7]

Since the network lifetime consists of a number of time periods during which the nodes update the encryption key, the nodes must maintain a loosely synchronized clock.

6.2 Non-cryptographic Parameters

Prior to joining the network all nodes must be equipped with the following parameters:

- The key update period, update.
- A unique node id, idi.
- A statistical average delay Δ.

The key update period specifies the time between key updates. The shorter update period used the higher security is obtained, however the shorter the update period is, the more resources are used.

Each node must have a unique id, which is used during the cluster generation phase and to elect the key manager.

The statistical average delay, Δ, is used to minimize the risk of multiple nodes becoming key managers. [7]

6.3 Cryptographic Parameters

The following cryptographic parameters are used by the network nodes.

- Group identity key kGI: used as seed for other keys and for authentication.
- Traffic encryption key kTEK: used for encryption of application data.
- Cluster key kC: used to encrypt intra cluster communication.
- Backbone key kB: used for encryption of cluster head communication.
- Hello key kH: used during cluster head selection.

The group identity key kGI and the traffic encryption key kTEK are used during the operational phase while the other keys are only used during the cluster generation and the key update phase. The backbone and the hello keys are derived from the group identity key kGI.

The traffic encryption key is randomly generated by the key manager during each key update phase and the cluster key kC is generated by each cluster head and used for intra cluster communication.

6.4 Non-cryptographic Functions

During the cluster generation and the key update phase all nodes need to be able to calculate a weight that represents their current status with regard to remaining battery power, distance to other nodes etc. This weight is then used to determine which nodes that become cluster heads and finally which node that becomes the key manager.

6.5 Cryptographic Functions

The following cryptographic functions are required by all nodes in the network:

- One-way hash function.
- Symmetric encryption algorithm.
- Secure key generation algorithm.

The hash function and the symmetric encryption algorithm are used to provide authentication and confidentiality while the secure key generation algorithm is needed to generate a new traffic encryption key kTEK, during the key update phase. [7]

6.6 Key Update Phase

During the key update phase one of the cluster heads become the key manager and generate a new traffic encryption key that will be distributed among the other cluster heads.

To select a key manager all cluster heads first decide whether they are a potential key manager. This is done by checking whether any of its neighboring cluster heads has a higher weight. If not, the node decides it is a potential key manager.

After an exponential delay with the average Δ the potential key manager then generates a new traffic encryption key TEK ki tek which is subsequently distributed to all other cluster heads over the cluster backbone. [7]

6.7 Analysis

This solution based on symmetric cryptography requires an organizational/administrative infrastructure that initializes the network nodes with the shared group identity key kGI and additional parameters such as tupdate.

The main weakness of this solution is that it requires that the nodes maintain a tamper-resistant storage. Such a requirement excludes the use of standard networking devices since these typically don't include any tamper-resistant memory. If the group identity key is compromised then all the network nodes need to be re-initialized with a new group identity key.

Finally since only group authentication is supported this solution is not applicable in applications where the communication is peer-to-peer.

7 Demonstrative Identification

This solution proposed by Balfanz [8] presents a mechanism for trust relationships in local ad hoc networks where the network nodes have no prior relationship with each other. Examples of such local ad hoc networks could be a group of people at a meeting wishing to setup a temporary network or a PDA wishing to temporarily connect to a printer.

Since the solution does not require that the nodes have any prior relationship, it is suitable for spontaneous, localized ad hoc networks. It is unsuitable for distributed ad hoc networks since it requires that the nodes be in a close proximity of each other during the initial bootstrapping. It allows the participating nodes to have diverse capabilities, i.e. some limited to symmetric encryption while others are capable of public key encryption.

7.1 System Overview

To establish initial trust, two nodes first exchange authentication data, termed pre-authentication data over a location-limited channel, which is separate from the main wireless links. Examples of such channels are infrared, physical contact, audio etc.

This solution requires that all network nodes be equipped with the same location-limited communication device, e.g. infrared or audio and it only permits the key-exchange in local ad hoc network, i.e. ad hoc networks where the nodes are in close proximity to each other.

Two different two-party key-exchange protocols are presented. The basic protocol requires that both parties are capable of performing public key cryptography, the single public key protocol only requires that one party has this capability. [8]

7.2 The Basic Protocol

For two nodes A and B capable of public key cryptography to exchange a secret encryption key the following steps are performed [8]:
1. Using the location-limited channel node A sends Hash(pkA) to node B and node sends Hash(pkB) to node A.
2. Switching over to the main wireless channel the nodes now exchange their public keys.
3. If the verification was successful any public key based key-exchange protocols, e.g. Diffie-Hellman can now be used to exchange a shared secret.

7.3 Single Public Key Protocol

In the case that one of the nodes is not capable of public key cryptography the following protocol can be used [8]:
1. Using the location-limited channel, node A (capable of public key cryptogra phy) sends node B, Hash(pkA), and node B sends node A, Hash(sB), where sB is a secret generated by B.
2. Switching over to the main wireless channel node A sends node B, pkA.
3. Node B authenticates the received key pkA* by verifying that Hash(pkA*)= Hash(pkA)
4. If the verification was successful, node B sends EpkA(SB*) to node A.
5. Node A decrypts the received message EpkA(sB*) and verifies that Hash(sB*) =Hash(sB). If the verification is successfully both nodes have successfully authenticated themselves and share a secret sB which can be used to generate a shared encryption key.

This protocol assumes that the public key algorithm used has a computationally cheap encryption function. RSA is an example of such an algorithm.

7.4 Analysis

All previous solutions have required either a organizational/administrative infrastructure or some sort of social interaction as in the solution based on self issued certificates. The use of demonstrative identification however allows the formation of a secure ad hoc network in a purely self-configured way. As an example two users need only to point their PDAs towards each other. The PDAs then automatically exchange the authentication information required to secure the following communications.

A possible down-side is that the networking devices must be equipped with some sort of location-limited channel. However since the majority of portable devices, e.g. PDAs and laptops are equipped with an infrared interface this should not be a problem. Also this solution is only applicable for localized ad hoc networks. An advantage of this solution is that it is applicable even for devices that do not have a user friendly interface, e.g. printers, projectors etc.

8 Conclusions

The solutions presented in this paper differ significantly in their requirements, functionality and complexity. However, they can be grouped into different categories depending on different criteria.

The partially and fully distributed CA solutions are similar and are appropriate for large distributed ad hoc networks such as military battlefield networks or disaster area networks. The solutions based on self issued certificates have a number of issues that make it questionable if it is appropriate for an ad hoc networking environment. Even if these issues are resolved the question is if the PGP approach is realistic in such a dynamic networking environment as ad hoc networks.

The Secure Pebblenets solution is appropriate for group-oriented ad hoc networks where the network nodes are distributed and do not have the resources or the need for public key based solutions. For highly spontaneous ad hoc network applications, such as collaborative networking or personal area networking, the solutions based on demonstrative identification is preferable.

While we can never expect to provide 100 percent security for ad hoc networks, we can prevent from several attacks taking precautions to protect potential vulnerabilities. The protection is our best defense against most of the attacks and we can utilize some solutions presented in this paper to guarantee authentication, confidentiality and integrity.

References

1. C.E. Perkins, Ad Hoc Networking. Addison Wesley Professional,Dec. 2000.
2. J. Mackar and S. Corson, RFC 2501, "Mobile Ad hoc Networking (MANET): RoutingProtocol Performance Issues and Evaluation Considerations", IETF 1999
3. L. Zhou and Z. J. Haas, "Securing Ad Hoc Networks", IEEE Networks, Volume 13, Issue 6 1999
4. H. Luo and S. Lu, "Ubiquitous and Robust Authentication Services for Ad Hoc Wireless Networks", Technical Report 200030, UCLA Computer Science Department 2000
5. J-P. Hubaux, L. Buttyán and S. Capkun, "The Quest for Security in Mobile Ad Hoc Networks",ACM 2001
6. S. Garfinkel, PGP: Pretty Good Privacy, O'Reilly & Associates 1995,ISBN 1-56592-098-8
7. S. Basagni, K. Herrin, E. Rosti and Danilo Bruschi, "Secure Pebblenets", ACM 2001
8. D. Balfanz, D. K. Smetters, P. Stewart and H. Chi Wong, "Talking To Strangers: Authentication in Ad-Hoc Wireless Networks", Internet Society, Conference Proceeding of NDSS Conference 2002
9. Kärpijoki Vesa, "Security in Ad Hoc Networks", Telecommunications Software and Multimedia Laboratory 2002D Kanh, The History of Steganography, Proceedings: Information Hiding. First International Workshop, Cambridge UK pp1-5 1996

On Performance Improvement
for 802.11-based Multi-hop Ad Hoc Wireless Networks*

WoongChul Choi, YongSuk Lee, Byung Joon Park, and Kuk-Hyun Cho

Department of Computer Science, KwangWoon University, Seoul, Korea 139-701
wchoi@daisy.kw.ac.kr

Abstract. Collision due to the hidden terminals in contention-based medium access control protocols is one of the main reasons of the poor end-to-end performance of wireless networks. In this paper, we present a novel approach for MAC protocol improvements for 802.11-based multi-hop ad-hoc wireless networks to reduce unnecessary collisions, resulting in performance enhancement. Our main idea is to reduce unnecessary collisions by introducing a new time interval, named *CAI* (Collision Avoidance Interval) for the node in the carrier sensing zone[6]. Specifically, in the context of 802.11, the four-way handshake is specified as a collision avoidance medium access protocol and the protocol behavior for the node in the carrier sensing zone is required to be modified when it senses a signal for CTS, such that the node defers transmitting a frame during *CAI*, unlike during EIFS in the 802.11 specification. We carry in-depth analysis of the protocol behavior and have conducted a comprehensive simulation to study the performance improvements. The simulation results show that the end-to-end performance is greatly increased and the number of dropped frames due to collision is significantly reduced as much as one half, and so is the throughput cost.

Keywords: Ad-hoc wireless networks, IEEE 802.11, MAC, Collision, CAI (Collision Avoidance Interval)

1 Introduction

End-to-end performance improvement has been an important issue not only for wired networks, but for ad-hoc wireless networks as well. Compared to wired networks, there are several differences that affect performance, and the two main differences are communicating in half-duplex mode in a single channel and possible collisions. Because of these reasons, the end-to-end performance of ad-hoc wireless networks is inherently poor[3].

In the IEEE 802.11-based MAC protocol[1], two medium access control protocols are specified – PCF (Point Coordination Function) and DCF (Distributed Coordination Protocol). DCF is often used as a referred scheme for multi-hop ad-hoc wireless networks, and is a contention-based medium access protocol – a host that has frames to send can send them only when the medium is available, which means it works in a simplex mode. There has been some research work to overcome this limitation.

---

* This work was supported by grant No. R01-2002-000-10934-0 (2005) from the Basic Research Program of the Korea Science & Engineering Foundation and by the Research Grant of KwangWoon University in 2003

F.F. Ramos et al. (Eds.): ISSADS 2005, LNCS 3563, pp. 407–416, 2005.

To avoid collisions, collision avoidance protocols such as RTS-CTS-DATA-ACK handshake are used in 802.11-based networks, but even with that mechanism, collisions can occur due to several reasons, so the problem of collisions in wireless networks needs to be investigated from different views – one for the cause of the collision and the other for its aftermath.

For the cause of a collision, there are two categories in the research. One is about the power control of transmitting a packet in an area where multiple nodes are coexistent, trying to send packets. In such an environment, the number of collisions would be large without a power control mechanism[6]. The other is about the hidden/exposed terminal problem[5]. Since packets in wireless networks can be transmitted by transmit energy, only one node can send a packet at one moment in a range covered by the power. Because of that, the hidden/exposed terminal problem can occur[5], and it necessarily entails the problem of collision as well. The research efforts on the procedure after a collision are about fine tuning the parameters such as back-off interval for retransmission[3][4][6].

The range covered by the power necessary for transmitting a frame has two disjoint areas, called the transmission range and the carrier sensing zone (Fig. 1)[6]. In the transmission range, a node can sense and decode a signal correctly, whereas a node can sense but can not decode it correctly in the carrier sensing zone. To avoid a collision, a node is required to sense the medium first before transmitting a frame. If it finds the medium busy, the behavior of the node in IEEE 802.11 specification is as follows. If the node is in the transmission range, it can decode the signal correctly, so it can also recognize NAV (Network Allocation Vector) which indicates the remaining time of on-going transmission sessions, therefore, it defers transmitting a frame during that NAV interval. But if it is in the carrier sensing zone, the node can not decode the signal, so it can not recognize NAV.

In this paper, we address the importance of the protocol behavior in the carrier sensing zone and show that the behavior is required to be modified to avoid unnecessary collisions to improve performance. With these modifications on the MAC protocol, we show how significantly the performance improves by both in-depth analysis of the protocol behavior and by simulation. We use the terms of packet and frame interchangeably in this paper, although the former is usually used for layer 3 terminology, and the latter for layer 2[7], and if the distinction is required, it will be clarified in the context.

The rest of this paper is organized as follows. In Section 2, we review the related work. We provide the problem statements in Section 3 and detailed description of our solution in Section 4. Section 5 and 6 discuss simulation and the results. We conclude the paper in Section 7.

2   Related Work

There have been many research efforts to improve performance of 802.11-based wireless networks. The efforts can be categorized into the collision avoidance in terms of power control for transmitting a packet, the hidden/exposed terminal problem and how to handle a collision. Jung et al. [6] propose a power control protocol where MAC protocol uses a maximum power level for RTS-CTS and a minimum power level for DATA-ACK, combined with using a maximum power level for

DATA periodically to avoid any potential collision and show the throughput and power saving improvement. Bharghavan *et al.* [5] investigate a hidden/exposed terminal problem in a single channel wireless LAN. They modify the basic binary exponential backoff algorithm for fair use of bandwidth. They examine the basic RTS-CTS-DATA message exchange, classify the hidden/exposed terminal problem in four cases and propose solutions for each case. Kanth *et al.* [3] perform a simulation for performance of TCP controlled file transfers over multiple wireless networks and discuss the reasons for the poor performance. They suggest a simple modification of the 802.11backoff algorithm, such that they use only two back-off windows of size 128 and 256. Lin *et al.* [4] propose a mechanism called distributed cycle stealing for improving the performance of DCF protocol of 802.11. They investigate the issue of efficient channel utilization, where all the communications should obey power-distance constraints, which guarantee that all transmissions would not disturb each other during all communication periods.

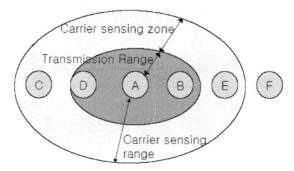

Fig. 1. Two disjoint areas of carrier sensing zone and transmission range, both of which constitute the carrier sensing range for node A. We assume that node A is the sender and node B is the receiver and transmission range from a frame transmitting source is one hop and carrier sensing rage is two hops. Then node C and E is said to be in the carrier sensing zone of the sender side

3   Problem Statement

Consider a simple fixed chain topology like Fig. 1. Assume that node A is a sender, node B is a receiver and all the nodes have data frames to send. Suppose that node A initiates a frame transmission to node B with RTS-CTS-DATA-ACK mechanism. Fig. 2 shows how the 802.11 protocol proceeds for each node.

In this situation, node D is in the transmission range when node A sends an RTS to node B. Likewise, node E is in the transmission range when node B answers with a CTS to node A. Therefore, both nodes D and E can decode the NAV specified in RTS and CTS correctly, so they defer transmitting their frames during the NAV interval. However, since node C and node F are in the sensing zone, they can not decode the NAV field in RTS and CTS frame. In case when a node senses a signal but can not decode it, IEEE 802.11 specifies that the node set NAV for EIFS (Extended Inter-Frame Space). So node C and node F set NAV after sensing respective signals. After that, their behavior and the aftermath differ. Now node A starts transmitting a DATA frame, which can be sensed by node C, but not by node F. For node C, this sensing happens before NAV expires, so it defers its frame transmission again. As a result, node C waits until a frame transmission from A to B ends. However, for node F, after NAV expires, it can not sense any signal at all, so it thinks the medium is idle and proceeds to the operation to send a DATA frame, i.e. switches to its state to the contention mode. If it tries to transmit a frame, then a collision will occur.

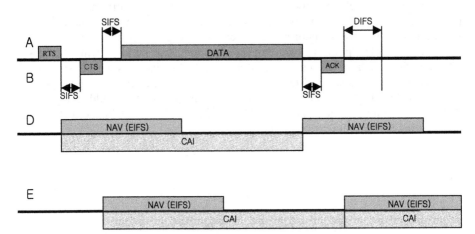

Fig. 2. Comparison of the packet exchange sequences and the state changes of 802.11 specification and the modified protocol for the topology in Fig. 1. For nodes D and E, the control packets above the line show how 802.11 proceeds, while the CAIs below the line show how the modified protocol proceeds

In Table 1, various parameter values are shown for each control frame and IFSs with the data link capacity of 2 Mbit/s. As shown in Table 1, the transmission time is 4383④s for a DATA frame length of 1Kbytes while the duration time of EIFS is only 349④s, therefore, the duration time of EIFS is too short to prevent a collision. As shown in Phase III (Fig. 2), when node F tries to transmit a frame after EIFS, then a collision with node B always occurs, which results in discarding the DATA frame that node B is receiving. Once a collision occurs for a DATA frame, the sender (node A) will increase the contention window and execute the binary backoff process of data link layer and then tries to transmit that frame again. Contention window starts from 32-aSlotTime[1], and the next contention window size is 64-aSlotTime, and so on, therefore, the next retransmission will happen during the interval of [0, 1280s], which is still too short for a successful frame transmission. Considering wireless networks where the end-to-end performance is inherently poor and where transmitting in the half-duplex mode is one of generic properties, a frame loss due to collision greatly affects not only performance but also energy efficiency in negative way. In addition, if the lost frame is for a TCP connection, it results in packet loss. This, in turn, will increase the size of the contention window of TCP layer and the binary backoff mechanism of TCP layer will be executed at the source node. These sequences of TCP will negatively affect the end-to-end performance as well, and it is obvious that the consequence will become worse as the number of connections and the capacity of the transmission increases.

Table 1. Parameter values for various frame type and space for 802.11 networks. Transmission time and IFSes (Inter-Frame Spaces) are for the data link capacity of 2 Mbits/s in *ns-2*[8]. The length of RTS, CTS and ACK are 20, 14, 14 bytes, respectively by [1]

Frame Type and Space	Time (Value)
RTS (Request To Send)	352s
CTS (Clear To Send)	304s
DATA (1Kbytes)	4383s
ACK (Acknowledgement)	304s
SIFS (Short Inter-Frame Space)	10s
DIFS (Distributed Inter-Frame Space)	50s
EIFS (Extended Inter-Frame Space)	349s
aSlotTime[1] (for Contention Window)	20s

One possible solution is to increase the value of aSlotTime such that the contention window is set to a larger value than the transmission time between the two nodes[3]. However, considering the property of ad-hoc networks where nodes can move any time so the topology always changes, it is not a n ultimate solution. And also, even in fixed ad-hoc wireless networks, the relative role of the nodes continuously changes. For example, in Fig. 1, the role of the sender and the receiver changes if the direction of a flow of a connection changes, for example, in bi-directional connections.

For these reasons, protocol behaviors should be different for a node in the transmission range and in the carrier sensing zone.

4 Protocol Improvements

We first make one assumption for protocol improvements that nodes in the carrier sensing zone can tell the types of a frame. Even though this assumption might be arguable because nodes in the sensing zone can not decode signal correctly from the definition (Fig. 1), there are three good and practical reasons for the assumption. First, this assumption is not impractical at all. Although nodes in the carrier sensing zone often fail to decode signal correctly, there might be a good possibility that it can tell the type of the frame it receives, considering that decoding a signal is related to the strength of power the signal carries. Second, our protocol is completely compatible with the legendary 802.11 MAC protocol, so it does not give any negative effect at all on 802.11 MAC protocol even when all the nodes in the carrier sensing zone can not decode signals correctly. Third, there can be several feasible ways to improve the capability of the nodes in the carrier sensing zone to distinguish the type of frames. For example, if the length of a frame can be helpful to do that, the length of frames can be adjusted. In fact, as shown in Table 1, the length of RTS, CTS and ACK are 20, 14, 14 bytes, respectively[1]. Our simulation results show that this capability of frame distinction is very helpful for collision avoidance at any cost.

Now we describe our MAC protocol improvements in detail. We first define a term *CAI* (Collision Avoidance Interval). *CAI* is defined for a node in the carrier sensing zone and is defined as a time interval from the moment when the node in the carrier sensing zone senses a CTS signal until the virtual length of a DATA frame is transmitted. Therefore, it is a time interval necessary for transmitting a frame by a transmitting node. From the motivation in the previous section, NAV, which is set to

EIFS in IEEE 802.11, is too short for a collision to be prevented, so we use *CAI* instead of NAV. While in *CAI*, the node defers transmitting a frame, like in NAV, even when the node has a frame to send. But there are two important differences in the protocol behavior. The first difference is that the node resets to *CAI* whenever it senses another CTS signal while in the carrier sensing zone, so it can be repeatedly set to *CAI*. The reason for this is because of ad-hoc networking property – nodes can move anytime, so the relative location and the role of a node continuously changes. Even in fixed ad-hoc wireless networks, signals can be received from any directions. The second difference is that the node in *CAI* will answer to a control frame from other nodes, especially to ACK, which means that the node now exits from *CAI* interval. This situation, that a node receives an ACK while in *CAI*, tells the possibility that the location or the topology of the networks has been changed, so *CAI* for the node has become invalid.

```
Recv() { /* When a frame is received */

    …. /* original operation */
    /* new protocol behavior starts when sensing CTS or ACK*/

    set Min_CAI_Value;
    /* User defines Min_CAI_Value.
    For example, Min_CAI_Value = tx_value(1KByte) */
    if (CTS or ACK sensing) {
    /* Min_CAI_Value <= CAI
                    <= Last_Forward_Frame_Size */
    if (Minimum_CAI_Value
            > Last_Forward_Frame_Size)
            start CAI <- Min_CAI_Value;
        else   start CAI <- Last_Forward_Frame_Size;
        /* CAI replaces backoff timer */
        /* the value of CAI is chosen between
            Min_CAI_Value and the frame sent just before (
            Last_Forward_Frame).
            The reason for Last_Forward_Frame is that it is likely that the
        frame that the node senses is for
            Last_Forward_Frame. The reason for defining
            Min_CAI_Value is because of performance – if not, the frame
        length could be short for control frames such as RTS, CTS or ACK,
        which are short frames in Table 1, and therefore, will cause  per-
        formance degradation. */
    }
}
/* back to the original operation of 802.11 MAC protocol */
```

Fig. 3. *CAI* and the procedure for MAC protocol improvements

From the above description on the modification, the cost for the misinterpretation of frame type is a waste of *CAI* only. In Fig. 3, the procedure for MAC protocol improvements is presented and commented. Notice that the value of *CAI* is automatically tuned to the length of current data frame. Fig. 2 shows how collision can be avoided using *CAI*.

5 Simulation

We have implemented the proposed protocol improvements in *ns-2*[8] and conducted a comprehensive study to evaluate the performance enhancements of 802.11-based multi-hop ad-hoc wireless networks. The main metrics for performance evaluation are the end-to-end throughput, the number of collisions and throughput cost. We perform simulations for TCP and UDP bidirectional connections for various numbers of connections of 4, 6, 8. The simulations are executed for the chain topologies like Fig. 1. Transmission range and carrier sensing range are assumed 1 hop and 2 hops, respectively, and link capacity is assumed 2Mbits/s[1]. The distance between two adjacent nodes is set to 250m. *CAI* is set to the length of (2*SIFS + 1*ACK + 1 * DATA frame) to allow one virtual DATA frame transmission. The length of a DATA frame is assumed to be 0.5, 1, 1.5 Kbytes. In order to minimize the interference from a routing protocol, DSDV (Destination Sequenced Distant Vector) routing protocol is used. DSDV[2] is one of the proactive routing protocols and the route update packets are sent periodically and incrementally as the topology changes. Since the topology used in the simulation is fixed, the route updates are sent periodically only, and that fact is taken into account to compute the performance metrics. The performance values are evaluated after running simulations for 400 *ns-2* simulation seconds. The simulations are conducted on Linux 2.4.20 on a Pentium 3.0 Ghz PC with 516Mbytes main memory. The version of *ns-2* is *ns-2.27*.

6 Results

Fig. 4 and 5 show the simulation results of end-to-end throughput and throughput gains for 4 bidirectional TCP and UDP connections. Fig. 4 and 5 show that throughputs by our modified protocol are always better. The difference in throughput is ap-

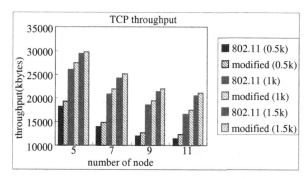

Fig. 4. End-to-end throughput for 4 bidirectional tcp connections with frame length of 0.5, 1.0, and 1.5Kbytes

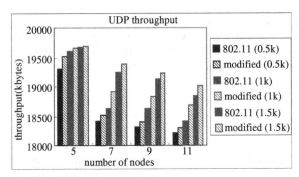

Fig. 5. End-to-end throughput for 4 bidirectional ucp connections for frame length of 0.5, 1.0, and 1.5Kbytes

proximately 1Mbits/400secs for most cases, but it can be said from Fig. 4 and 5 that wireless networks with more hops have better ratio of throughput gain, comparing to the amount of the end-to-end throughput itself. For example, consider the case for 11 nodes. The end-to-end throughputs for TCP connections are approximately 21Mbits/400sec for 1.5K frame length, but the throughput gain for that case is almost 1Mbits/400sec, so it is about 8% gain.

Fig. 6 and 7 show the comparisons of the number of collisions for TCP and UDP connections. In Fig. 6, the number of collisions represents the aggregated number of frame losses and drops at every hop and is significantly reduced as much as 30%. Similar claim can be made for UDP connections in Fig. 7. In fact, this reduction in the number of collisions is the most outstanding feature of our modified protocol.

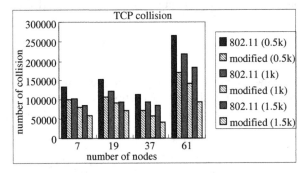

Fig. 6. The number of collisions for 6 bidirectional tcp connections for frame length of 0.5, 1.0, and 1.5Kbytes

So far, the performance of the modified protocol was verified in Fig. 4,5 and Fig. 6,7. Finally, we examine the value of throughput cost defined as

$$Throughput\ cost = (frame\_loss\_and\_drop\_in\_bytes\ /\ end\text{-}to\text{-}end\_throughput\_in\_bytes) \tag{1}$$

which means how much it costs to transmit a packet successfully from one end to another end. This value is especially important because it is related to the power consumption. Fig. 8 and 9 show the result and tell that the modified protocol works more

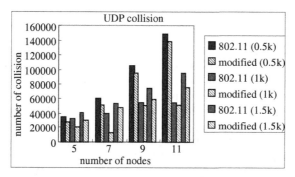

Fig. 7. The number of collisions for 6 bidirectional udp connections for frame length of 0.5, 1.0, and 1.5Kbytes

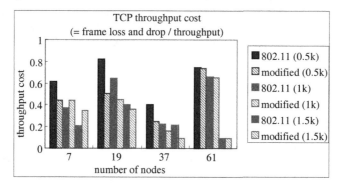

Fig. 8. Throughput cost of 8 bidirectional tcp connections for frame length of 0.5, 1.0, 1.5Kbytes. Throughput cost is defined as how much frame is lost or dropped for a successful packet transmission (1)

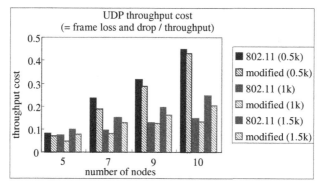

Fig. 9. Throughput cost of 8 bidirectional udp connections for frame length of 0.5, 1.0, 1.5Kbytes

efficiently than the conventional 802.11 protocol. Considering our simulation runs for 400 simulation seconds, which is approximately 7 simulation minutes, the longer the running time is, the greater the difference will be. One comment is that the results are consistent for traffic mix with TCP and UDP with various lengths of frames.

7 Conclusions

In this paper, we addressed the importance of the protocol behavior in the carrier sensing zone to prevent unnecessary collisions, and showed that the protocol behavior is required to be modified by in-depth analysis of the protocol behavior. We defined a term *CAI* to avoid unnecessary collision and this interval is used for a node in the carrier sensing zone instead of NAV when the node senses CTS signal. We conducted a comprehensive simulation study to examine how the performance of the modified protocol in multi-hop wireless ad-hoc networks improves. Our improved MAC protocol is completely compatible with the IEEE 802.11 specification, so it can be coexistent with the legendary 802.11-based wireless MAC protocol. With the improvements in the MAC protocol, the number of collisions is decreased as much as 30% and the throughput gain is as much as 8% for 400 simulation seconds. In addition, throughput cost, which is defined to measure how much it costs to transmit a packet successfully from one end to another, can be saved as much as 30%. As a result, we can verify that the end-to-end performance is significantly improved by our MAC protocol enhancements.

References

1. IEEE: IEEE Standard for Wireless LAN-Medium Access Control and Physical Layer Specification, IEEE 1997
2. Perkins, C., Bhagwatt, P.:Highly Dynamic Destination-Sequenced Distance-Vector Routing for Mobile Computers Computer Communications Review, Oct. 1994, pp. 234-244
3. Kanth, K., Ansari, S., Melikri, M.H.: Performance enhancement of TCP on multihop ad hoc wireless networks, IEEE International Conference on Personal Wireless Communications 2002, pp. 90 –94
4. Lin, C.R., Chien-Yuan Liu: Enhancing the performance of IEEE 802.11 wireless LAN by using a distributed cycle stealing mechanism, IEEE International Workshop on Mobile and Wireless Communications Network 2002, pp. 564 –568
5. V.Bharghavan, A.Demers,S.Shenker,L.Zhang: MACAW:A Media Access Protocol for Wireless LAN's, Proceedings of SIGCOMM 1994, pp. 212-225
6. Eun-Sun Jung, Vaidya, N.H.: An energy efficient MAC protocol for wireless LANs, , IEEE INFOCOM 2002, pp. 837-845
7. http://www.cisco.com
8. http://www.isi.edu/nsnam/ns/

Analysis of Context Transfer in Seamless IP Mobility

Christian P. García-Martinez and J. Antonio García-Macías

Computer Science Department, CICESE Research Center
Ensenada, Baja California, México
{cpgarcia,jagm}@cicese.mx

Abstract. As mobile devices roam between wireless cells, performing handovers, mobility is managed by protocols like Mobile IP and micro-mobility protocols. However, these protocols do not manage how to transfer context from cell to cell as the devices move. Context transfer mechanisms aim for performance improvements in the process of handover, so that the applications running on mobile nodes can operate with minimal disruption, thus allowing seamless mobility. In this paper we propose mechanisms that enable context transfer between access routers offering internet connectivity for mobile nodes; we use an actual implementation to test the performance of context transfer for different services and analyze the benefits that can be obtained using these mechanisms.

1 Introduction

Cellular communication networks, such as current 3G (and emerging 4G) networks are rapidly converging with more traditional, wired and wireless, data networks. In this convergence, the Internet Protocol (IP) is clearly the de facto standard as the network layer bearer. However, as IP and its related protocols were not originally designed with mobility of nodes as a requirement, new challenges had to be solved, such as the problem of how to route the packets to Mobile Nodes (MNs) when these change their point of attachment to the network. Among many proposals, Mobile IP [3] has emerged as the standard that solves this problem; however, it does not provide seamless mobility due to the high cost of signaling and registration procedures incurred. That is why, many proposals have been made overcome the limitations of mobile IP. It has been observed that intra-domain mobility is highly dynamic and can not be properly handled with Mobile IP; this has led the research toward the study of micro-mobility approaches [1].

Context transfer has emerged as one of the problems that must be solved to achieve seamless mobility in IP networks. In general, context is the information on the current state of a service, required to re-establish the service on a new subnet without having to perform the entire protocol exchange between the MN and the Access Router (AR) from scratch. In this paper we propose mechanisms that enable context transfer between access routers offering Internet connectivity for mobile nodes; our proposal includes means for representation of contexts for services. RFC 3374 [8] describes the main reasons why Context Transfer procedures may be useful in IP networks.

The remainder of the paper is organized as follows: Section 2 overviews related work. Section 3 describes potential customers for Context Transfer Protocol (CTP). Section 4 describes the CTP; there, we also propose a format to represent the context of two candidate services (MLD and HC). Section 5 discusses our experience with its implementation; we provide conclusions and mention some future work.

F.F. Ramos et al. (Eds.): ISSADS 2005, LNCS 3563, pp. 417–424, 2005.
© Springer-Verlag Berlin Heidelberg 2005

2 Related Work

The work of Koodli and Perkins [12] was one of the first that mentioned context transfer in mobile networks. There are a couple of Internet drafts on generic context transfer protocols [9, 11] proposed by the IETF Seamless Mobility (Seamoby) working group [5]. These proposals have not been evaluated through analytical, simulation or test bed means; the exact deployment scenarios are not clear yet. It is also unclear how these protocols represent the different types of context meant to be transferred. The IRTF Micro-mobility research group was working on these topics, but they have been dormant for about a year. There is a new IRTF Mobility Optimizations (MOBOPTS) [6] research group that is working on this but to date, they haven't presented any related proposal.

3 Why Context Transfer?

Mobile nodes improve the performance of their connections across wireless media by establishing various kinds of state (context), in order to use the available bandwidth securely and economically [8]. For example, a particular node establishes the Header Compression (HC) service by collecting enough information about its data streams to get synchronized with its AR and then be able to send and receive compressed packets. This state information is needed to keep the service available. Once the mobile move to another subnet, it is required to re-establish the service by the same process it used to initially establish it, and delay-sensitive traffic may be seriously impacted. An alternative is to transfer the context of the service to the new subnet so that the service can be re-established quickly, rather than establish it from scratch. The context transfer may be advantageous in minimizing the impact of host mobility on certain cases. In the following paragraphs we describe two of the candidate services we consider good examples to evidence the benefits of context transfers.

Multicast Listener Discovery (MLD). We consider the transfer of context of MLD [13] as an example of how context transfer can improve the performance of an IP layer handover. The purpose of MLD is to enable each IPv6 router to discover the presence of multicast listeners on its directly attached links, and to discover specifically which multicast addresses are of interest to those neighboring nodes. This information is then provided to whichever multicast routing protocol is being used by the router, in order to ensure that multicast packets are delivered to all links where there are interested receivers. MLD is a good example to show the benefits of context transfer because every node must perform two MLD messaging sequences per subscription on the wireless link to establish itself as an MLD listener. If this state information is transferred to the new router it is possible to avoid these messaging sequences.

Header Compression (HC). The use of bandwidth constrained links in wireless networks suggests the use of bandwidth saving HC schemes. A number of HC schemes have been proposed for existing Internet protocols, one of them is Robust Header Compression (RoHC) [2]. In some cases, for example using IPv6/UDP/RTP, the headers can be reduced from 84 bytes to 1 byte, and therefore, can reduce the load on the wireless link by 50-70% [4]. The HC process is stateful; the compressor and the decompressor, both maintain records to represent the expected content of protocol headers, so that headers fields that have the expected values do not need to be retransmitted, since they can be inferred. Establishing HC generally requires from 1 to 5 packets exchanges between the last hop router and the mobile node with full or partially compressed headers before full compression is available [2]. During this period, the MN will experience an effective reduction in the available bandwidth equivalent to the uncompressed header information sent over the air. An approximate quantitative estimate for the amount of savings in handover time can be obtained as follows. A RTP/UDP/IPv6 message contains 84 bytes only in their headers; as we said before, from 1 to 5 messages with full headers are required. Let's say 3 messages are sent before the MN and the AR are synchronized, that means about 252 bytes in headers. Some representative numbers can be obtained by assuming bandwidths of 20 kbps or 100 kbps. With these two bit rates, the savings from not having to send these messages with full headers are 110 and 20 ms. If there are more data streams being compressed, the amount of time saved could be significantly more.

4   Context Transfer Protocol Proposal

We believe that it may be advantageous to bundle the context transfer signaling between the MN and network, or between access routers, together with other handover signaling. We use a micro-mobility protocol that had simplicity as one of its main design requirements [7]. When a handoff request is sent, specific information is piggybacked to the new access router indicating that context transfer will take place (if any). Previous work has explored the issue of finding out if it is possible to perform context transfer [10]; it also describes mechanisms for Candidate Access Router Discovery (CARD), which allows knowing the characteristics of the new access router before the handover.

4.1   CTP Overview

Context transfer takes place in response to a context transfer trigger; which could be a handoff request or an explicit context transfer request sent to the previous AR (pAR). The MN initiates the process by sending a Context Transfer Request (CTR) message to the pAR. Once the pAR has received the message, it generates a Context Transfer (CT) message, which contains all the state information associated to the mobile node and capable of being interpreted by the nAR. The nAR receives the context and relocates the state information in order to offer the same treatment to the data flows as the pAR did. Performing context transfer in advance of the MN attaching to the new AR (nAR) can increase handover performance. In order to make this happen, certain conditions must be met. For example, pAR must have sufficient time and knowledge about the impending handover. This has proven to be feasible [10].

Every messsage has the format illustrated in figure 1, the header is the same for all messages and is comprised by a Type field, which indicates the type of the message (e. g. CTR); a Length field that contains the size of the complete message; a Flags field that contains indicators as Version, need for Acknowledgement, sequence number; and an authorization token required to ensure that the MN has the rights to exchange messages within the domain. The Data Block varies depending on the type of message.

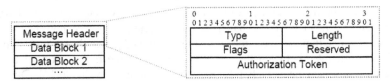

Fig. 1. Generic message format

The context data structure needs appropriate encapsulation for communication and processing, figure 2 shows the format of a data block for a CT message. The field Context Type indicates the interpretation of the next context blocks. The context type defines how the state information is organized. In section 4.2 we present a specific representation for the state information of MLD and Robust Header Compression. The amount of information in a Context Data Block is not fixed, due to the fact that a node could have any number of data streams being treated by the same service. For instance: multiples audio/video sessions using RoHC.

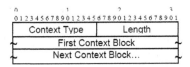

Fig. 2. Context Data Block format

The messages will use UDP as the transport protocol for the Context Transfer Request and Context Transfer Data messages. Signaling messages will use ICMP.

4.2   Feature Context Representation

Every context type requires a different way of representation due to the differences between the state information of the services. Despite these differences, we can organize the context in a generic way as follows: a MN has associated data streams, data streams could have associated different services, and each service has associated state information which is called service context. We have identified and represented the context of two candidate services (MLD and RoHC). Figure 3a shows the specific data that need to be transferred to enable the MLD service in a nAR; this is what is carried on the Context Block field showed in figure 2. The Subnet Prefix on the nAR Wireless Interface field contains a subnet prefix that identifies the interface on which multicast routing should be established, as sometimes a router has more than one interface to the same link and it is necessary to perform the router part of MLD only over one of those interfaces. The Subscribed IPv6 Multicast Address field contains the multicast address for which multicast routing should be established.

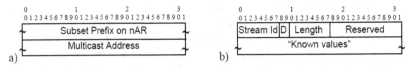

Fig. 3. a) Representation of MLD context. b) Representation of RoHC context

In order to determine the information that needs to be transferred to enable the RoHC service in the nAR, it is necessary to know how the header fields can be classified based on their behavior during the session lifetime. RFC 3095 [2] allow us to distinguish those fields that can be inferred and those that are known. Once they are identified it is necessary to get the values for each instance of the fields, and then associate each instance with a data stream ID. This is how the context feature data for this service is built. This information is sent to the nAR so it can reconstruct the headers, gathering the data received in the context transfer, the data inferred by the service and the data contained in the compressed headers.

5 Experimental Analysis

As we have previously stated, much of the research activity regarding seamless IP mobility found in the literature has produced mainly design requirements, architectural proposals, functional specifications, and simulations results. We feel that in order to advance the understanding on the requirements, reach, and limitations of seamless mobility, it is necessary to start devising actual implementations of the proposals and test them in experimental setups.

In order to better understand the (hopefully positive) impact of context transfer on the process of handover, we implemented our proposal for a context transfer protocol and conducted experimental tests. The testbed platform included standard desktop computers acting as access routers (pAR, nAR, gateway AR); these were running Mandrake Linux 9.2, and were connected to the local network through 10 Mbps hubs, while the backbone had transfer rates of up to 100 Mbps. Mobile nodes (laptops) were also running Mandrake Linux 9.2 and were connected to the local network through IEEE 802.11b access points, with a nominal rate of 11 Mbps. The repository containing the capabilities for nodes in the network was placed at the same level as the gateway AR, and used an OpenLDAP v2.1.25 server. Mobile nodes, as well as ARs, were loaded with daemons to perform different functions such as triggering a handover, handling context transfer, managing micro-mobility, etc. We conducted a series of experiments to determine the performance of our proposed solutions (see Figure 4). The first set of experiments was conducted to test the performance of the candidate access router discovery (CARD) process, as follows:

1. The mobile node receives level 2 beacons from the access points it can listen to.
2. A module that triggers seamless mobility gathers a list with the MAC addresses of these access points; this list is sent to the pAR along with the mobile node identifier.
3. The pAR consults the capabilities repository to query for the capabilities and IP addresses corresponding to the nodes in the list of MAC addresses. We tested a worst-case scenario where the cache in the AR does not contain any of the required information, so it has to query the repository located at the gateway AR (the root of the domain); this query was forced by asigning a time-to-live of zero to any cached information. Based on the information retrieved, the target access router (TAR) selection is made (the nAR is determined).
4. Once the nAR is determined, it is necessary to identify the services it can handle, in order to encapsulate the context information that should be transferred.

5. The pAR then triggers a handover to the nAR by indicating the micro-mobility module that it should do so.
6. Immediately after, the encapsulated context is transferred.

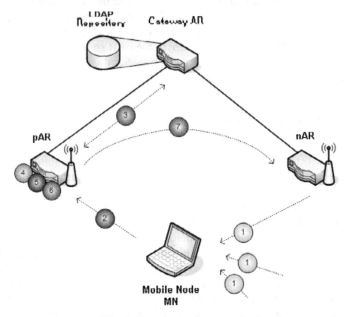

Fig. 4. Experimental tests setup

The LDAP repository had information about several network elements in the administrative domain, such as: the capabilities of 10 different routers, and the capabilities of 10 access points (each one associated to a different AR). Using the scenario described above, experiments were repeated over a dozen times and execution times were recorded. The average time it took for the CARD process, nAR selection and context encapsulation was observed to be around 51 milliseconds, with an standard deviaton of 1.5 milliseconds.

A second set of experiments was conducted in order to determine the latency of the context transfer process (step 7 in Figure 4). We used the following typical scenario as the basis for these experiments:

"A user with a WiFi-equipped laptop participates in a videoconference session (where UDP is the transport protocol); this videoconference involves 10 other participants. In order to save bandwith in the wireless connection, the mobile is using header compression, as specified in RFC 3095 (RoHC). This means that at least 10 UDP/IP microflows are being serviced by RoHC; the approximate size of these microflows is 300 bytes".

The context transfer is carried out by our proposed CTP, from the pAR to the nAR. We repeated the test over a dozen times with varying context sizes (ranging from 300 to 3000 bytes, incrementing by 300), recording the time it took for the context to be transferred, and obtained the average time, as well as the standard deviation and variance. The micro-mobility protocol implemented in our test platform was developed at

INPG [7]. Figure 5 graphs the context transfer latency, where each point represents a time average from the repeated tests. The handover latency, which is practically a constant, is superposed as a reference. The graph shows that transferring contexts with a size less than 2000 bytes is done before a handover concludes. This means that when the MN starts communicating via the nAR, all the services it had at the pAR will already be available at the nAR. So, the question is: how convenient it is to perform context transfer when it exceeds the handover latency?

Assuming that only 2 messages are sent per subscription, the mobile node should sent 144 bytes for each subscribed address. Now, considering that the report message for the two modalities allowed by the protocol should be sent, then the mobile node should send 288 bytes for each subscription. Considering bit rates of 20 Kbps and 100 Kbps, then the time for sending the 288 bytes would be of 115 and 23 milliseconds, respectively. Obviously, as the number of subscribed multicast addresses grows, so does the number of messages that the mobile node should send and the benefits of transferring the context, instead of reinitializing the service, become more evident.

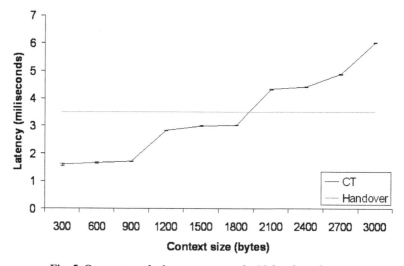

Fig. 5. Context transfer latency compared with handover latency

The case of the header compression service can be analyzed similarly. Let us suppose that this service is compliant with RFC 3095 [2], which specifies Robust Header Compression (RoHC). Let us also assume a microflow using IPv6 as its network protocol and RTP/UDP at the transport layer. Then, each packet has a RTP/UDP/IPv6 header that is 84 bytes long. RFC 3095 recommends receiving at least 3 to 5 consecutive messages in a microflow to properly synchronize the compressor and decompressor, and thus be able to provide the header compression service. Supposing that only 3 packets are needed, then 252 bytes in complete headers have to be sent before achieving the required synchronization. Again, considering bit rates of 20 Kbps and 100 Kbps, then the time it would take to send the headers (252 bytes) would be 100 and 20 milliseconds, respectively. Analogously, when the number of microflows using the header compression service is increased, the benefits of performing context transfer becomes more evident.

6 Conclusions

To date, many interesting proposals have been made for using context transfer to speed up handovers. Some of them are sophisticated and complex, so short-time applicability would be difficult; in fact, many of these proposals have not been implemented and only specifications and simulation results have been offered. That is why our proposal is meant to be simple but functional for a controlled environment, enabling the identification of requirements that only experimental tests can provide. We consider this to be an step through an evolutive process that will add more features that will bring us closer to a more comprehensive mobile environment. The results of our experimental analysis indicate that context transfer can be achieved before completing a handover in most typical situations, according to the context size of different services. Thus, in these situations context transfer can be considered instead of reinitializing services after a handover. A current problem for developing more a more comprehensive experimental platform is that several of the service candidates for context transfer are either not implemented or their implementation is not freely available (e.g., the RoHC service). Also, interoperability among different wireless technologies (WLAN, cellular, WPAN, etc.) is still a great challenge.

Acknowledgements

Financial support for this project was provided by the Mexican Council for Science and Technology (CONACyT).

References

1. A.T. Campbell, J. Gomez, S. Kim, C.Y. Wan, Z.R. Turanyi, and A.G. Valko, "Comparison of IP micromobility Protocols", IEEE Wireless Communications, 9(1):72–82, 2002.
2. C. Bormann, "Robust Header Compression (ROHC)", RFC 3095, IETF, July 2001.
3. C.E. Perkins, "Mobile IP Support", RFC 2002, IETF, October 1996.
4. C. Westphal and R. Koodli, "IP Header Compression: A Study of Context Establishment", IEEE Wireless Communications and Networking Conference, New Orleans, USA, 2003.
5. IETF. Seamless Mobility (SeaMoby) Working Group. Homepage: http://www.ietf.org/html.charters/seamobycharter.html.
6. IETF. IP Mobility Optimizations (Mobopts) Research Group. Homepage: http://www.irtf.org/charters/mobopts.html
7. J. Antonio García Macias, "Mobile Communication Architecture with Quality of Service", Ph. D. Thesis, Institute National Polytechnique de Grenoble, January 2002.
8. J. Kempf, "Problem Description: Reasons for Performing Context Transfers between Nodes in an IP Access Network", RFC 3374, IETF, September 2002.
9. J. Loughney, "Context Transfer Protocol", Internet Draft, IETF, January 2004. (Work in progress)
10. Juan M. Oyoqui and J. Antonio Garcia Macias, "Context Transfer for Seamless Mobility", 4th Mexican International Conference on Computer Science, (ENC) Tlaxcala, Mexico, Sept. 2003.
11. R. Koodli R. and C. E. Perkins, "A Context Transfer Protocol for Seamless Mobility", Internet Draft, IETF, August 2002.
12. R. Koodli R. and C. E. Perkins, "Fast Handovers and Context Transfers in Mobile Networks", ACM Computer Communication Review, vol. 31, number 5, 2001.
13. S. Deering, "Multicast Listener Discovery for IPv6", RFC 2710, IETF, October 1999.

An Introduction to Evolutionary Algorithms and Their Applications

Carlos A. Coello Coello

CINVESTAV-IPN, Evolutionary Computation Group, Dpto. de Ing. Elect./Secc. Computación
Av. IPN No. 2508, Col. San Pedro Zacatenco, México, D.F. 07300, Mexico
ccoello@cs.cinvestav.mx

Abstract. This paper provides a brief introduction to evolutionary algorithms including some of their applications. Our discussion includes short descriptions of genetic algorithms, evolution strategies, evolutionary programming and genetic programming. Then, a few case studies involving applications of evolutionary algorithms in real-world problems are analyzed. In the final part of the paper, some of the current research directions in this area are provided.

1 Introduction

The idea of developing search and optimization techniques based on the mechanism of natural selection is not new (see for example [1]). However, it was until the 1960s when the three main techniques based on this notion were developed. These approaches, which are now collectively denominated "evolutionary algorithms", have been very effective for single-objective optimization [2–4, 1].

This paper provides a brief introduction to evolutionary algorithms through the description of each of their main paradigms. Besides describing each basic algorithm and associated operators, we will also provide a list of some of their representative applications. In the last part of the paper, we will describe some of the emerging biologicallyinspired paradigms that may become the dominant heuristics of the XXI century.

The remainder of this paper is organized as follows. Section 2 provides some basic concepts related to evolutionary algorithms. Section 3 discusses a few representative case studies of applications of evolutionary algorithms in real-world problems. After that, we provide some of the current research trends in the area in Section 4 and our conclusions in Section 5.

2 Basic Notions of Evolutionary Algorithms

The famous naturalist Charles Darwin defined *Natural Selection* or *Survival of the Fittest* as the *preservation of favorable individual differences and variations, and the destruction of those that are injurious* [5]. In nature, individuals have to adapt to their environment in order to survive in a process called *evolution*, in which those features that make an individual more suited to compete are preserved when it reproduces, and those features that make it weaker are eliminated. Such features are controlled by units called *genes* which form sets called *chromosomes*. Over subsequent generations not only the fittest individuals survive, but also their fittest genes which are transmitted to their descendants during the sexual recombination process which is called *crossover*.

F.F. Ramos et al. (Eds.): ISSADS 2005, LNCS 3563, pp. 425–442, 2005.
© Springer-Verlag Berlin Heidelberg 2005

Early analogies between the mechanism of natural selection and a learning (or optimization) process led to the development of the so-called "evolutionary algorithms" (EAs) [6], in which the main goal is to simulate the evolutionary process in a computer. There are three main paradigms within evolutionary algorithms, whose motivations and origins were independent from each other: evolution strategies [3], evolutionary programming [7], and genetic algorithms [8]. Additionally, some authors consider genetic programming [9] as another paradigm, although this approach can also be seen as a special type of genetic algorithm. Each of these four types of evolutionary algorithm will be discussed next in more detail.

2.1 Evolution Strategies

When working towards his PhD degree in engineering at the Technical University of Berlin, Ingo Rechenberg came across some optimization problems in hydrodynamics that could not be solved using traditional mathematical programming techniques [10]. This led him to the development of a very simple optimization algorithm which consisted of applying a set of random changes to a reference solution. The approach was later called "evolution strategy" and it was formally introduced in 1964 [11]. The original evolution strategy was called (1+1)-ES, because it consisted of a single parent that was mutated (i.e., subject to a random change) to produce an offspring. Then, the parent was compared to its offspring and the best from them was selected to become parent for the following iteration (or generation).

In the original (1+1)-EE, a new individual was produced using:

$$\overline{x}^{t+1} = \overline{x}^t + N(0,\overline{\sigma})$$

where t refers to the current *generation* (or iteration) and $N(0,\overline{\sigma})$ is a vector of independent Gaussian numbers with median zero and standard deviation $\overline{\sigma}$. It is important to emphasize that an "individual" in an evolution strategy contains the set of decision variables of the problem. No encoding is used in this case. So, if the decision variables are real numbers, then such real numbers are directly put together as a single vector for each individual.

Let's consider the following example of a (1+1)-ES:
Let us assume that we want to **maximize**:

$$f(x_1, x_2) = 100(x_1^2 - x_2)^2 + (1 - x_1)^2$$

where: $-2.048 \leq x_1, x_2 \leq 2.048$

Now, let us suppose that our population consists of the following (randomly generated) individual:

$$\overline{x}^t, \overline{\sigma} = (-1.0, 1.0), (1.0, 1.0)$$

Let us now suppose that the mutations generated are the following:

$$x_1^{t+1} = x_1^t + N(0, 1.0) = -1.0 + 0.61 = -0.39$$
$$x_2^{t+1} = x_2^t + N(0, 1.0) = 1.0 + 0.57 = 1.57$$

Now, we compare the parent with its offspring:

Parent: $f(x_t) = f(-1.0, 1.0) = 4.0$

Child: $f(x_{t+1}) = f(-0.39, 1.57) = 201.416$

Since: $201.416 > 4.0$ the offspring will replace its parent in the following generation.

Rechenberg [12] stated a rule for adjusting the standard deviation in a deterministic way such that the evolution strategy could converge to the global optimum. This is now known as the "1/5 success rule", and it consists of the following:

$$\sigma(t) = \begin{cases} \sigma(t-n)/c & \text{if } p_s > 1/5 \\ \sigma(t-n)*c & \text{if } p_s < 1/5 \\ \sigma(t-n) & \text{if } p_s = 1/5 \end{cases}$$

where n is the number of decision variables, t is the current generation, p_s is the relative frequency of successful mutations (i.e., those mutations in which the offspring replaced its parent) measured over a certain period of time (e.g., $10n$ individuals) and $c = 0.817$ (this value was theoretically derived by Schwefel [3]). $\sigma(t)$ is adjusted at every n mutations.

Over the years, several other variations of the original evolution strategy were proposed, after the concept of population (i.e., a set of solutions) was introduced. The most recent versions of the evolution strategy are the $(\mu + \lambda)$-ES and the (μ, λ)-ES. In both cases, μ parents are mutated to produce λ offspring. However, in the first case (+selection), the μ best individuals are selected from the union of parents and offspring. In the second case (i.e., ,selection), the best individuals are selected only from the offspring produced.

In modern evolution strategies, not only the decision variables of the problem are evolved, but also the parameters of the algorithm itself (i.e., the standard deviations). This is called "self-adaptation". Parents are mutated using:

$$\sigma'(i) = \sigma(i) \times \exp(\tau' N(0,1) + \tau N_i(0,1))$$
$$x'(i) = x(i) + N(0, \sigma'(i))$$

where τ and τ' are proportionality constants that are defined in terms of n.

Also, modern evolution strategies allow the use of recombination (either sexual, when only 2 parents are involved, or panmictic, when more than 2 parents are involved in the generation of the offspring).

Some representative applications of evolution strategies are the following [3]:

- Routing and networking.
- Biochemistry.
- Optics.
- Engineering design.
- Magnetism.

2.2 Evolutionary Programming

Lawrence J. Fogel introduced in the 1960s an approach called "evolutionary programming", in which intelligence is seen as an adaptive behavior [13, 7].

Evolutionary programming emphasizes the behavioral links between parents and offspring, instead of trying to emulate some specific genetic operators (as in the case of the genetic algorithm [2]).

The basic algorithm of evolutionary programming is very similar to that of the evolution strategy. A population of individuals is mutated to generate a set of offspring. However, in this case, there are normally several types of mutation operators and no recombination (of any type), since evolution is modelled at the species level in this case and different species do not interbreed. Another difference with respect to evolution strategies is that in this case, each parent produces exactly one offspring. Also, the decision of whether or not a parent will participate in the selection process is now determined in a probabilistic way, whereas in the evolution strategy this is a deterministic process. Finally, no encoding is used in this case (similarly to the evolution strategy) and emphasis is placed on the selection of the most appropriate representation of the decision variables.

We will now show an example of the way in which evolutionary programming works. Let us consider the finite automaton from Figure 1. The transition table corresponding to this automaton is the following:

Current State	**A**	**A**	**B**	**B**	**C**	**C**
Input Symbol	0	1	1	0	0	1
Next State	B	c	B	C	C	A
Output Symbol	a	b	c	b	a	b

Considering the type of problem at hand, several mutation operators are possible. For example: change an output symbol, change a transition, add a state, delete a state and change the initial state. The goal is to make this automaton able to recognize a certain set of inputs (i.e., a certain regular expression) without making a single mistake.

Some representative applications of evolutionary programming are the following [1]:

- Forecasting.
- Generalization.
- Games.
- Automatic control.
- Traveling salesperson problem.
- Route planning.
- Pattern recognition.
- Neural networks training.

2.3 Genetic Algorithms

Genetic algorithms (originally denominated "genetic reproductive plans") were introduced by John H. Holland in the early 1960s [14, 15]. The main motivation for creating the genetic algorithm was the solution of machine learning problems.

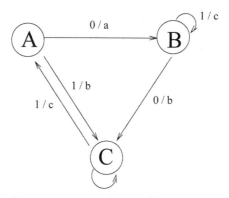

Fig. 1. Finite automaton with 3 states. Symbols to the left of "/" are input symbols. Symbols to the right of "/" are output symbols. The initial state is A

Genetic algorithms emphasize the importance of sexual recombination (which is the main operator) over the mutation operator (which is used as a secondary operator). They also use probabilistic selection (like evolutionary programming and unlike evolution strategies).

The basic operation of a Genetic Algorithm is illustrated in the following segment of pseudo-code [16]:

```
generate initial population, G(0);
evaluate G(0);
t:=0;
repeat
    t:=t+1;
    generate G(t) using G(t-1);
    evaluate G(t);
until a solution is found
```

First, an initial population is randomly generated. The individuals of this population will be a set of chromosomes or strings of characters (letters and/or numbers) that represent all the possible solutions to the problem.

1	0	0	1	1	0	1

Fig. 2. Example of the binary encoding traditionally adopted with the genetic algorithm

One aspect that has great importance in the case of the genetic algorithm is the encoding of solutions. Traditionally, a binary encoding has been adopted, regardless of the type of decision variables of the problem to be solved [2]. Holland [8] provides some theoretical and biological arguments for using a binary encoding. However, over the years, other types of encodings have been proposed, including the use of vectors of real numbers and permutations, which lend themselves as more "natural" encodings for certain types of optimization problems [17, 18].

Once an appropriate encoding has been chosen, we apply a fitness function to each one of these chromosomes in order to measure the quality of the solution encoded by the chromosome. Knowing each chromosome's fitness, a selection process takes place to choose the individuals (presumably, the fittest) that will be the parents of the following generation. The most commonly used selection schemes are the following [19]:

- *Proportionate Reproduction:* This term is used generically to describe several selection schemes that choose individuals for birth according to their objective function values f. In these schemes, the probability of selection of an individual from the th class in the th generation is calculated as

$$p_{i,t} = \frac{f_i}{\sum_{j=1}^{k} m_{j,t} f_j} \qquad (1)$$

where k classes exist and the total number of individuals sums to n Several methods have been suggested for sampling this probability distribution, including Monte Carlo or *roulette wheel* selection [20], *stochastic remainder* selection [21, 22], and *stochastic universal* selection [23, 24].

- *Ranking Selection:* In this scheme, proposed by Baker [25] the population is sorted from best to worst, and each individual is copied as many times as it can, according to a non-increasing assignment function, and then proportionate selection is performed according to that assignment.

- *Tournament Selection:* The population is shuffled and then is divided into groups of elements from which the best individual (i.e., the fittest) will be chosen. This process has to be repeated k times because on each iteration only m parents are selected, where

$$m = \frac{population\ size}{k}$$

For example, if we use binary tournament selection ($k = 2$), then we have to shuffle the population twice, since in each stage half of the parents required will be selected. The interesting property of this selection scheme is that we can guarantee multiple copies of the fittest individual among the parents of the next generation.

- *Steady State Selection:* This is the technique used in Genitor [26], which works individual by individual, choosing an offspring for birth according to linear ranking, and choosing the currently worst individual for replacement. In steady-state selection only a few individuals are replaced in each generation: usually a small number of the least fit individuals are replaced by offspring resulting from crossover and mutation of the fittest individuals. This selection scheme is normally used in evolving rule-based systems in which incremental learning (and remembering what has already been learned) is important and in which members of the population collectively (rather than individually) solve the problem at hand [27].

After being selected, *crossover* takes place. During this stage, the genetic material of a pair of individuals is exchanged in order to create the population of the next generation. There are three main ways of performing crossover:

1. *Single-point crossover:* A position of the chromosome is randomly selected as the crossover point as indicated in Figure 3.
2. *Two-point crossover:* Two positions of the chromosome are randomly selected as to exchange chromosomic material, as indicated in Figure 4.

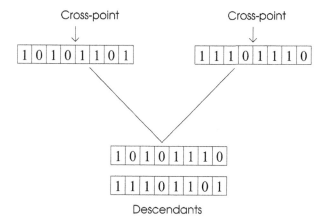

Fig. 3. Use of a single-point crossover between two chromosomes. Notice that each pair of chromosomes produces two descendants for the next generation. The cross-point may be located at the string boundaries, in which case the crossover has no effect and the parents remain intact for the next generation

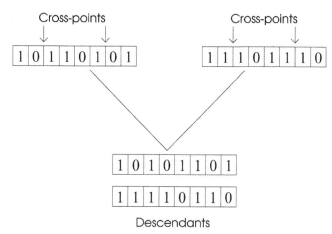

Fig. 4. Use of a two-point crossover between two chromosomes. In this case the genes at the extremes are kept, and those in the middle part are exchanged. If one of the two cross-points happens to be at the string boundaries, a single-point crossover will be performed, and if both are at the string boundaries, the parents remain intact for the next generation

3. *Uniform crossover:* This is a relatively recent crossover operator proposed by Syswerda [28] which can be seen as a generalization of the two previous crossover techniques explained in this paper. In this case, for each bit in the first offspring it decides (with some probability p) which parent will contribute its value in that position. The second offspring would receive the bit from the other parent. See an example of 0.5-uniform crossover in Figure 5. Although for some problems uniform crossover presents several advantages over other crossover techniques [28], in general, one-point crossover seems to be a bad choice, but there is no clear winner between two-point and uniform crossover [29].

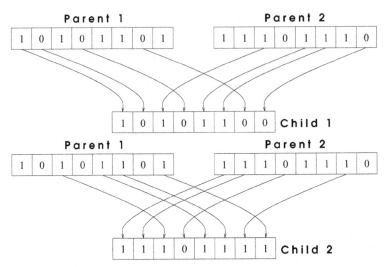

Fig. 5. Example of uniform crossover (using 50% probability) between two chromosomes. Notice how half of the genes of each parent goes to each of the two children. First, the bits to be copied from each parent are selected randomly using the probability desired, and after the first child is generated, the same values are used to generate the second child, but inverting the source of procedence of the genes

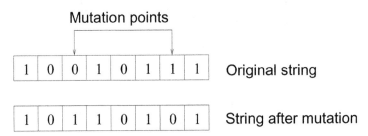

Fig. 6. An example of mutation using binary representation

Mutation is another important genetic operator that randomly changes a gene of a chromosome. If we use a binary representation, a mutation changes a 0 to 1 and vice-versa. An example of how mutation works is displayed in Figure 6. This operator allows the introduction of new chromosomic material to the population and, from the theoretical perspective, it assures that – given any population – the entire search space is connected [16].

If we knew in advance the final solution, it would be trivial to determine how to stop a genetic algorithm. However, as this is not normally the case, we have to use one of the two following criteria to stop the GA: either give a fixed number of generations in advance, or verify when the population has become homogeneous (i.e., all or most of the individuals have the same fitness).

Traditionally, genetic algorithms do not have a self-adaptation mechanism. Therefore, one of their main drawbacks is that their parameters tend to be fine-tuned in an empirical manner.

Some representative applications of genetic algorithms are the following [2]:

- Optimization (numerical, combinatorial, etc.).
- Machine learning.
- Databases (optimization of queries, etc.).
- Pattern recognition.
- Grammar generation.
- Robot motion planning.
- Forecasting.

2.4 Genetic Programming

One of the original goals of artificial intelligence (AI) was the automatic generation of computer programs that could produce a desired task given a certain input. During several years, such a goal seemed too ambitious since the size of the search space increases exponentially as we extend the domain of a certain program and, consequently, any technique will tend to produce programs that are either invalid or highly inefficient.

Some early evolutionary algorithms were attempted in automatic programming tasks, but they were unsuccessful and were severely criticized by some AI researchers [1]. Over the years, researchers realized that the key issue for using evolutionary algorithms in automatic programming tasks was the encoding adopted. In this regard, Koza [9] suggested the use of a genetic algorithm with a tree-based encoding. In order to simplify the implementation of such an approach, the original implementation of this sort of approach (which was called "genetic programming") was done under LISP, taking advantage of the fact that such programming language has a built-in parser.

The tree-encoding adopted by Koza obviously requires of different alphabets and specialized operators for evolving randomly generated programs until they become 100% valid. Note however, that the basic principles of this technique may be generalized to any other domain and, in fact, genetic programming has been used in a variety of applications [9].

The trees used in genetic programming consist of both functions and terminals. The functions normally adopted are the following [9]:

1. Arithmetic operations (e.g., +, -, $\times$, $\div$)
2. Mathematical functions (e.g., sine, cosine, logarithms, etc.)
3. Boolean Operations (e.g., AND, OR, NOT)
4. Conditionals (IF-THEN-ELSE)
5. Loops (DO-UNTIL)
6. Recursive Functions.
7. Any other domain-specific function.

Terminals are typically variables or constants, and can be seen as functions that take no arguments. An example of a chromosome that uses the functions F={AND, OR, NOT} and the terminals T={A0, A1} is shown in Figure 7.

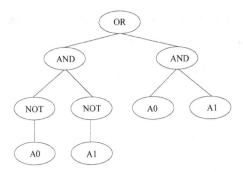

Fig. 7. An example of a chromosome used in genetic programming

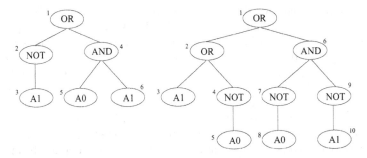

Fig. 8. The tree nodes are numbered before applying the crossover operator

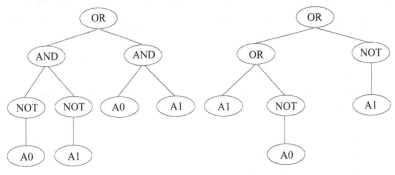

Fig. 9. The two offspring generated after applying the crossover operator

Crossover can be applied by numbering the tree nodes corresponding to the two parents chosen (see Figure 8) and (randomly) selecting a point in each of them such that the subtrees below such point are exchanged (see Figure 9, where we assume that the crossover point for the first parent is 2 and for the second is 6). Typically, the sizes of the two parent trees will be different as in the example previously shown. It is also worth noticing that if the crossover point is the root of one of the parent trees, then the whole chromosome will become a subtree of the other parent. This allows the incorporation of subroutines in a program. It is also possible that the roots of both parents are selected as crossover points. Should that be the case, the crossover operator will have no effect and the offspring will be identical to their parents.

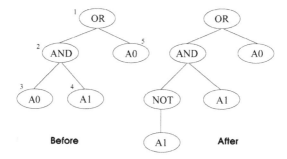

Fig. 10. An example of mutation in genetic programming

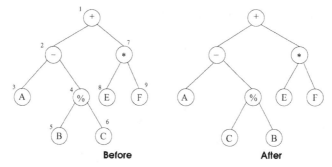

Fig. 11. An example of permutation in genetic programming

Normally, genetic programming implementations impose a limit on the maximum depth that a tree can reach, as to avoid the generation (as a byproduct of crossover and mutation) of trees of very large size that could produce a memory overflow [30].

Mutation in genetic programming takes place through a (random) selection of a certain node tree. The subtree below the chosen node is replaced by another tree which is randomly generated. Figure 10 shows an example of the use of this operator (the mutation point in this example is node 3).

Permutation is an asexual operator used in genetic programming to emulate the effect of the inversion operator adopted with genetic algorithms [2]. This operator reorders the leaves of a subtree placed below a (randomly chosen) node. Its goal is to strengthen the union of allelic combinations with good performance within a chromosome [8].

Figure 11 shows an example of the use of the permutation operator (node 4 was selected in this example). In Figure 11, the symbol '*' indicates multiplication and '%' indicates "protected division", referring to a division operator that keeps our program from generating a system error when the divisor is zero.

In genetic programming is also possible to protect or "encapsulate" a certain subtree which we know to contain a good building block, as to avoid that it is destroyed by the genetic operators. The selected subtree is replaced by a symbolic name that points to the real location of the subtree. Such subtree is separately compiled and linked to the rest of the tree in an analogous way to the external classes of object oriented languages. Figure 12 shows an example of encapsulation in which the right subtree is replaced by the name (**E0**).

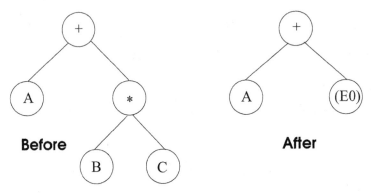

Fig. 12. An example of encapsulation in genetic programming

Normally, it is also necessary to edit the expressions generated during the evolutionary process as to simplify them. However, the simplication rules to be adopted normally depend on the problem at hand. For example, if the output of our program are Boolean expressions, we could apply rules such as the following:

(AND X X) X
(OR X X) X
(NOT (NOT X)) X

Finally, genetic programming also provides mechanisms to destroy a certain percentage of the population such that we can renovate the chromosomic material after a certain number of generations. This mechanism, called **execution**, is very useful in highly complex domains in which our population may not contain a single feasible individual even after a considerably large number of generations.

Despite the obvious differences and motivations of each of the aforementioned paradigms, the trend in the last few years has been to decrease the differences among the paradigms and refer (in generic terms) simply to evolutionary algorithms when talking about any of them.

It is worth indicating that the ever-growing popularity of evolutionary algorithms in a variety of application domains tends to be related to their good reputation as "optimizers" (either for single-objective or for multi-objective problems [31, 32]). This is remarkable if we consider that some of them (namely, genetic algorithms) were not originally proposed for that type of application and that their use in optimization tasks has been questioned by some well-established researchers in the evolutionary computation community [33]. Apparently, the reported success of evolutionary algorithms has resulted sufficiently convincing for practitioners and therefore their popularity [4].

3 A Few Real-World Applications

Next, we will briefly review a few interesting real-world applications of evolutionary algorithms that have been reported in the specialized literature. Note that our coverage of such applications will be shallow (for the sake of saving space), but the interested reader is referred to further references in case of having interest in any of them.

3.1 Improved Satellite Constellation Design and Optimization

Improving satellite constellation design is of great interest to any users of satellite communications (e.g. cell phones, television), location (e.g. global positioning system) and/or observation (e.g. weather). Many of today's satellite constellation designs rely on the "Walker Constellations," a series of designs developed in 1970, which have rarely been improved upon. These constellations make use of symmetric constellations with circular orbits. Dr. William Crossley (from Purdue University) has used genetic algorithms to search the constellation design space, producing constellation designs not previously envisioned but with performance equal to or greater than comparableWalker or "streets of coverage" constellations. The designs produced by the genetic algorithm took some seasoned satellite engineers by surprise. Dr. Crossley is now experimenting with multiobjective genetic algorithms and has been able to generate constellation designs that outperform constellations that have been under development for several months. The genetic algorithm used in this case, required just a few days to produce such designs. For more details, see [34].

3.2 Telecommunication Network Design

Prof. Benjamín Barán and his research group in Paraguay used parallel multiobjective evolutionary algorithms [32] to design an optimal telecommunication network in which the objectives were to minimize cost and maximize performance. The network was modelled using graphs and encoded adopting integers. Reliability was estimated using Monte Carlo simulations, and the cost of each configuration produced was computed by adding up the costs of every link added to the topology. The authors also considered a minimum acceptable reliability. In their study, the authors used a well-established problem in the area to validate their approach. The results produced by the evolutionary algorithms adopted outperformed the best solution previously reported for the problem used as a reference. For more information, see [35].

3.3 Design of Mobile Telecommunication Networks

Meunier and his colleagues used a multi-objective evolutionary algorithm to design a mobile telecommunication network that consists of positioning base stations in potential sites such that 3 objectives are fulfilled: minimize the number of sites used, maximize the amount of traffic held by the network and minimize the interferences. The authors also considered two constraints: (1) all the service test points must me covered with a minimum radio field value that must be greater than the receiver sensitivity threshold of the mobile and (2) the cellular network must be able to ensure the communication continuity from the starting cell to the target cell, when a mobile is moving toward a new cell. This is a combinatorial optimization problem with a high computational cost associated with the evaluation of each potential solution. The authors used parallelism and tested their genetic algorithm on a large and realistic highway area generated by the France Telecom's research laboratory (CNET). Results indicated that the use of evolutionary algorithms is a very promising alternative in this type of problem. For further details, see [36].

4 Some Current Research Trends

In recent years, other biologically-inspired metaheuristics have become increasingly popular in a wide variety of applications [37]. It is expected that several of these approaches are eventually adopted in biometric applications. Representative examples of these new metaheuristics are the following:

- **Particle Swarm Optimization:** Proposed by Kennedy and Eberhart [38, 39], this metaheuristic simulates the movements of a group (or population) of birds which aim to find food. The approach can be seen as a distributed behavioral algorithm that performs (in its more general version) multidimensional search. In the simulation, the behavior of each individual is affected by either the best local (i.e., within a certain neighborhood) or the best global individual. The approach uses then the concept of population and a measure of performance similar to the fitness value used with evolutionary algorithms. The approach introduces the use of flying potential solutions through hyperspace (used to accelerate convergence) and allows individuals to benefit from their past experiences. This technique has been successfully used for both continuous nonlinear and discrete binary optimization [40, 41, 39].
- **Artificial Immune Systems:** Computationally speaking, our immune system can be seen as a highly parallel intelligent system that is able to learn and retrieve previous knowledge (i.e., it has "memory") to solve recognition and classification tasks. Due to these interesting features, several researchers have developed computational models of the immune system and have used it for a variety of tasks, including classification and pattern recognition [42–44].
- **The Ant System:** This is a metaheuristic inspired by colonies of real ants, which deposit a chemical substance on the ground called pheromone [45–47]. This substance influences the behavior of the ants: they tend to take those paths where there is a larger amount of pheromone. Pheromone trails can thus be seen as an indirect communication mechanism among ants. From a computer science perspective, the ant system is a multi-agent system where low level interactions between single agents (i.e., artificial ants) result in a complex behavior of the entire ant colony. The ant system was originally proposed for the traveling salesman problem (TSP), and most of the current applications of the algorithm require the problem to be reformulated as one in which the goal is to find the optimal path of a graph. A way to measure the distances between nodes is also required in order to apply the algorithm [48]. Despite this limitation, this approach has been found to be very successful in a variety of combinatorial optimization problems [45, 49].
- **Cultural Algorithms:** Cultural algorithms were developed by Robert G. Reynolds as a complement to the metaphor used by evolutionary algorithms, which had focused mainly on genetic and natural selection concepts [50]. Cultural algorithms are based on some theories originated in sociology and archaeology which try to model cultural evolution. Such theories indicate that cultural evolution can be seen as an inheritance process operating at two levels: (1) a micro-evolutionary level, which consists of the genetic material that an offspring inherits from its parents, and (2) a macro-evolutionary level, which consists of the knowledge acquired by individuals through generations. This knowledge, once encoded and stored, is used to guide the behavior of the individuals that belong to a certain population

[51, 52]. The main goal of cultural algorithms is to increase the learning or convergence rates of an evolutionary algorithm such that the system can respond better to a wide variety of problems. Cultural algorithms have been successfully applied to different optimization tasks [53–55].

5   Conclusions

In this paper, we have tried to provide a brief, but general overview of evolutionary algorithms and some of their applications. The main emphasis has been to illustrate the fact that evolutionary algorithms are a viable alternative to solve complex, real-world problems for which no other approach provides acceptable results in a reasonably short time.

It is noted, however, that due to their heuristic nature, evolutionary algorithms cannot guarantee that the solution that they find is the global optimum (in fact, the result obtained may vary from run to run, due to their stochastic nature). That is the reason why evolutionary algorithms must be consider as an alternative only after unsuccessfully trying deterministic (e.g., mathematical programming) techniques.

Despite their limitations, there is overwhelming evidence regarding the effectiveness of evolutionary algorithms to solve real-world problems when compared with other (either deterministic or heuristic) approaches.

Acknowledgments

The author acknowledges support from CONACyT through project No. 42435-Y.

References

1. Fogel, D.B.: Evolutionary Computation. Toward a New Philosophy of Machine Intelligence. The Institute of Electrical and Electronic Engineers, New York (1995)
2. Goldberg, D.E.: Genetic Algorithms in Search, Optimization and Machine Learning. Addison-Wesley Publishing Co., Reading, Massachusetts (1989)
3. Schwefel, H.P.: Numerical Optimization of Computer Models. Wiley, Chichester, UK (1981)
4. Bäck, T., Fogel, D.B., Michalewicz, Z., eds.: Handbook of Evolutionary Computation. Institute of Physics Publishing and Oxford University Press, New York (1997)
5. Darwin, C.R.: The Variation of Animals and Plants under Domestication. Second edn. Murray, London (1882)
6. Bäck, T.: Evolutionary Algorithms in Theory and Practice. Oxford University Press, New York (1996)
7. Fogel, L.J.: Artificial Intelligence through Simulated Evolution. Forty Years of Evolutionary Programming. John Wiley & Sons, Inc., New York (1999)
8. Holland, J.H.: Adaptation in Natural and Artificial Systems. University of Michigan Press, Ann Arbor, Michigan (1975)
9. Koza, J.R.: Genetic Programming. On the Programming of Computers by Means of Natural Selection. The MIT Press, Cambridge, Massachusetts (1992)
10. Rao, S.S.: Engineering Optimization. Theory and Practice. Third edn. John Wiley & Sons, Inc. (1996)

11. Fogel, D.B., ed.: Evolutionary Computation. The Fossil Record. Selected Readings on the History of Evolutionary Algorithms. The Institute of Electrical and Electronic Engineers, New York (1998)
12. Rechenberg, I.: Evolutionsstrategie: Optimierung technischer Systeme nach Prinzipien der biologischen Evolution. Frommann–Holzboog, Stuttgart, Germany (1973)
13. Fogel, L.J.: Artificial Intelligence through Simulated Evolution. John Wiley, New York (1966)
14. Holland, J.H.: Concerning efficient adaptive systems. In Yovits, M.C., Jacobi, G.T., Goldstein, G.D., eds.: Self-Organizing Systems – 1962. Spartan Books,Washington, D.C. (1962) 215–230
15. Holland, J.H.: Outline for a logical theory of adaptive systems. Journal of the Association for Computing Machinery **9** (1962) 297–314
16. Buckles, B.P., Petry, F.E., eds.: Genetic Algorithms. Technology Series. IEEE Computer Society Press (1992)
17. Michalewicz, Z.: Genetic Algorithms + Data Structures = Evolution Programs. Third edn. Springer-Verlag, New York (1996)
18. Rothlauf, F.: Representations for Genetic and Evolutionary Algorithms. Physica-Verlag, New York (2002)
19. Goldberg, D.E., Deb, K.: A comparison of selection schemes used in genetic algorithms. In Rawlins, G.J.E., ed.: Foundations of Genetic Algorithms. Morgan Kaufmann, San Mateo, California (1991) 69–93
20. Jong, A.K.D.: An Analysis of the Behavior of a Class of Genetic Adaptive Systems. PhD thesis, University of Michigan (1975)
21. Booker, L.B.: Intelligent Behavior as an Adaptation to the Task Environment. PhD thesis, Logic of Computers Group, University of Michigan, Ann Arbor, Michigan (1982)
22. Brindle, A.: Genetic Algorithms for Function Optimization. PhD thesis, Department of Computer Science, University of Alberta, Edmonton, Alberta (1981)
23. Baker, J.E.: Reducing Bias and Inefficiency in the Selection Algorithm. In Grefenstette, J.J., ed.: Genetic Algorithms and Their Applications: Proceedings of the Second International Conference on Genetic Algorithms. Lawrence Erlbaum Associates, Hillsdale, New Jersey (1987) 14–22
24. Grefenstette, J.J., Baker, J.E.: How Genetic Algorithms work: A critical look at implicit parallelism. In Schaffer, J.D., ed.: Proceedings of the Third International Conference on Genetic Algorithms, San Mateo, California, Morgan Kaufmann Publishers (1989) 20–27
25. Baker, J.E.: Adaptive Selection Methods for Genetic Algorithms. In Grefenstette, J.J., ed.: Proceedings of the First International Conference on Genetic Algorithms. Lawrence Erlbaum Associates, Hillsdale, New Jersey (1985) 101–111
26. Whitley, D.: The GENITOR Algorithm and Selection Pressure: Why Rank-Based Allocation of Reproductive Trials is Best. In Schaffer, J.D., ed.: Proceedings of the Third International Conference on Genetic Algorithms. Morgan Kaufmann Publishers, San Mateo, California (1989) 116–121
27. Mitchell, M.: An Introduction to Genetic Algorithms. The MIT Press, Cambridge, Massachusetts (1996)
28. Syswerda, G.: Uniform Crossover in Genetic Algorithms. In Schaffer, J.D., ed.: Proceedings of the Third International Conference on Genetic Algorithms, San Mateo, California, Morgan Kaufmann Publishers (1989) 2–9
29. Michalewicz, Z.: Genetic Algorithms + Data Structures = Evolution Programs. Second edn. Springer-Verlag (1992)
30. Banzhaf,W., Nordin, P., Keller, R.E., Fancone, F.D.: Genetic Programming. An Introduction. Morgan Kaufmann Publishers, San Francisco, California (1998)
31. Osyczka, A.: Evolutionary Algorithms for Single and Multicriteria Design Optimization. Physica Verlag, Germany (2002) ISBN 3-7908-1418-0.

32. Coello Coello, C.A., Van Veldhuizen, D.A., Lamont, G.B.: Evolutionary Algorithms for Solving Multi-Objective Problems. Kluwer Academic Publishers, New York (2002) ISBN 0-3064-6762-3.
33. Jong, K.A.D.: Genetic Algorithms are NOT Function Optimizers. In Whitley, L.D., ed.: Foundations of Genetic Algorithms 2. Morgan Kaufmann Publishers, San Mateo, California (1993) 5–17
34. Ely, T., Crossley, W., Williams, E.: Satellite Constellation Design for Zonal Coverage Using Genetic Algorithms. Journal of the Astronautical Sciences **47** (1999) 207–228
35. Duarte Flores, S., Barán Cegla, B., Benítez Cáceres, D.: Telecommunication network design with parallel multi-objective evolutionary algorithms. In: Applications, Technologies, Architectures, and Protocols for Computer Communication. Proceedings of the 2003 IFIP/ACM Latin America conference on Towards a Latin American agenda for network research, La Paz, Bolivia, ACM Press (2003) 1–11
36. Meunier, H., Talbi, E.G., Reininger, P.: A Multiobjective Genetic Algorithm for Radio Network Optimization. In: 2000 Congress on Evolutionary Computation. Volume 1., Piscataway, New Jersey, IEEE Service Center (2000) 317–324
37. Corne, D., Dorigo, M., Glover, F., eds.: New Ideas in Optimization. McGraw-Hill, London (1999)
38. Kennedy, J., Eberhart, R.C.: Particle Swarm Optimization. In: Proceedings of the 1995 IEEE International Conference on Neural Networks, Piscataway, New Jersey, IEEE Service Center (1995) 1942–1948
39. Kennedy, J., Eberhart, R.C.: Swarm Intelligence. Morgan Kaufmann Publishers, San Francisco, California (2001)
40. Eberhart, R., Shi, Y.: Comparison between Genetic Algorithms and Particle Swarm Optimization. In Porto, V.W., Saravanan, N., Waagen, D., Eibe, A., eds.: Proceedings of the Seventh Annual Conference on Evolutionary Programming, Springer-Verlag (1998) 611–619
41. Kennedy, J., Eberhart, R.C.: A Discrete Binary Version of the Particle Swarm Algorithm. In: Proceedings of the 1997 IEEE Conference on Systems, Man, and Cybernetics, Piscataway, New Jersey, IEEE Service Center (1997) 4104–4109
42. Dasgupta, D., ed.: Artificial Immune Systems and Their Applications. Springer-Verlag, Berlin (1999)
43. Nunes de Castro, L., Timmis, J.: Artificial Immnue System: A New Computational Intelligence Approach. Springer Verlang, Great Britain (2002) ISBN 1-8523-594-7.
44. Nunes de Castro, L., Von Zuben, F.J.: Learning and Optimization Using the Clonal Selection Principle. IEEE Transactions on Evolutionary Computation **6** (2002) 239–251
45. Dorigo, M., Caro, G.D.: The Ant Colony Optimization Meta-Heuristic. In Corne, D., Dorigo, M., Glover, F., eds.: New Ideas in Optimization, London, McGraw-Hill (1999) 11–32
46. Colorni, A., Dorigo, M., Maniezzo, V.: Distributed Optimization by Ant Colonies. In Varela, F.J., Bourgine, P., eds.: Proceedings of the First European Conference on Artificial Life, MIT Press, Cambridge, MA (1992) 134–142
47. Dorigo, M., Maniezzo, V., Colorni, A.: The Ant System: Optimization by a colony of cooperating agents. IEEE Transactions on Systems, Man, and Cybernetics – Part B **26** (1996) 29–41
48. Dorigo, M., Maniezzo, V., Colorni, A.: Positive Feedback as a Search Strategy. Technical Report 91-016, Dipartimento di Elettronica, Politecnico di Milano, Italy (1991)
49. Bonabeau, E., Dorigo, M., Theraulaz, G.: Swarm Intelligence. From Natural to Artificial Systems. Oxford University Press, New York (1999)
50. Reynolds, R.G.: An Introduction to Cultural Algorithms. In Sebald, A.V., Fogel, L.J., eds.: Proceedings of the Third Annual Conference on Evolutionary Programming. World Scientific, River Edge, New Jersey (1994) 131–139

51. Renfrew, A.C.: Dynamic Modeling in Archaeology: What, When, and Where? In van der Leeuw, S.E., ed.: Dynamical Modeling and the Study of Change in Archaelogy. Edinburgh University Press, Edinburgh, Scotland (1994)
52. Durham, W.H.: Co-evolution: Genes, Culture, and Human Diversity. Stanford University Press, Stanford, California (1994)
53. Chung, C.J., Reynolds, R.G.: CAEP: An Evolution-based Tool for Real-Valued Function Optimization using Cultural Algorithms. Journal on Artificial Intelligence Tools **7** (1998) 239–292
54. Jin, X., Reynolds, R.G.: Using Knowledge-Based Evolutionary Computation to Solve Nonlinear Constraint Optimization Problems: a Cultural Algorithm Approach. In: 1999 Congress on Evolutionary Computation, Washington, D.C., IEEE Service Center (1999) 1672–1678
55. Saleem, S.M.: Knowledge-Based Solution to Dynamic Optimization Problems using Cultural Algorithms. PhD thesis, Wayne State University, Detroit, Michigan (2001)

Distributed Anticipatory System

Marco A. Ramos, Alain Berro, and Yves Duthen

Institut d Reccherche en Informatique de Toulouse, (IRIT)
IRIT-UPS, route de Narbonne-31062
{maramos,alain.berro,yves.duthen}@univ-tlse1.fr
http://www.irit.fr

Abstract. In this paper we present an introduction to computing anticipatory systems. The internals aspects of anticipation will be explained. The concepts of incursion are proposed to model anticipatory systems. A simple example of computing anticipatory systems will be simulated on computer that includes an anticipatory model.

Keywords: anticipatory system, anticipation, agents.

1 Introduction

Anticipatory systems (AS) are systems where change of state is based on information pertaining to present as well as future states [13]. Cellular automata can be used for the visualization of the observations by different observers. The exchange of observations among observers can be shown to generate (a) uncertainty about the delineations in the observed system at each moment in time and (b) uncertainty about the dynamics of the interaction over time. The conditions for meta-stabilization or globalization by synchronization of the anticipation at a next-order level are specified. Cellular organisms, industrial processes, global markets, certainly the central nervous systems provide many examples behavior where output is the result of future not only present state.

Simulation studies of social systems have used evolutionary models from biology for heuristic reasons, but often without sufficient reflection of the metaphors on which these models are based. For example, in their foundational study of the simulation of social systems, [7] used the metaphor of "growing artificial societies". Human beings are then considered in terms of their behavior. In general, multi-agent models begin with the specification of the activity at the nodes. The relations among the agents are modeled using a (more or less complex) function. The results of these simulations can be appreciated in terms of the quality of modeling the observable phenomena. The epistemological assumptions of this approach, however, have remained biological: even if reflexivity is declared in the model, the exchange of meaning among agents is considered as a means to the ends of improving performance of agents [1], [3].

Using the biological model of anticipatory systems [13], the simulation studies will enable me, among other things, to distinguish the dynamics of the interactions from those of the aggregates of actions [17]. First, I will abstract the anticipatory model from its biological basis using [4] formalization. Second, the concept of anticipation is elaborated for a multi-agent system. In a third step, a system which is both socially distributed and anticipatory will be decomposed into an observing system and a system under observation. In a next section, the quality of the observation is varied. The

F.F. Ramos et al. (Eds.): ISSADS 2005, LNCS 3563, pp. 443–451, 2005.

interaction among observers can then be distinguished from the interaction among observations.

Anticipatory systems were defined as systems that contain a representation of the system itself [13], [5]. The internal representations can be used by the system for the anticipation because the system's parameters can be varied and recombined internally. A biological system can use this degree of freedom for anticipatory adaptation, that is, by making a selection in the present among its possible representations in a next exhibition.

In electrical engineering, this model has been used to simulate the future behavior of systems that contain delays in their operation [6]. In order to make these models relevant for social systems theory, however, we have to specify additionally how the exchange of meaning among anticipatory agents may result in an anticipatory feed back on the information and meaning processing among them. Let us perform this analysis step by step. I shall first specify the anticipatory model and then combine this mechanism with multi-agent modeling in a next step. Using a cellular automaton the generation of an observer will be made visible as a possible result of the interaction between these two mechanisms (anticipation and environment). After the specification of possible differences among observers in terms of their perspectives, I turn in the final parts of this study to the exchange of observations as a next-order level of the communication.

The study of anticipatory systems requires a model of the system that is sufficiently complex to accommodate representations of the system within the model. These systems do no longer model an external world, but they entertain internal representations of their relevant environments in terms of the ranges of possible further developments. The possibility of anticipation in systems can thus be considered as an analytical consequence of the complexity of the model. This additional complexity is found by using the time dimension not as a given, but as another degree of freedom available to the system. This degree of freedom allows for active adaptation to changes in the environment through anticipation by inverting the arrow of time.

Research on anticipatory systems draw heavily upon advancement in intelligent artificial as well biological artificial life and learning theory [2], and there is growing interest in anticipatory systems, ranging from plant and traffic control to intelligent agents in the internet. Although anticipatory systems have been studied by a number of researches in the context of mathematical biology [13], [8], automata theory, and as Rosen points out, their epistemological roots may be trace back to Aristotle's view on causality, it only recently that the advent of modern computing technologies makes it possible to employ them for complex systems regulation and management [14].

2 Cognition

The study of cognition is posing a fascinating a fascinating and challenging question to systems theorists: *How does the anticipation of future events in the brain takes place (through seemingly timeless memory) and what are the implications of such a process to the development of anticipatory control systems capable of learning?*. In brain research, a number of theoretical and clinical studies have emerged in recent years pointing to the importance of anticipation in various control functions involving the central nervous system. In kinesiology, the question of how the process of movements specification proceeds whit reference to brain structures has occupied a central importance and has been addressed by Goldberg through the dual promoter systems hypothesis which identifies two major sources of informational constraints that are used to control motor functions: an intrinsic source related to intentionality and an extrinsic source related to external conditions [15]. The first source enables a human to function in an anticipatory adaptive mode using information that is derived from intrinsic models structured from past experience, while the second source enables motor responses that are reactive to environmental conditions.

3 Prediction

The simple method of predicting the future is based on the assumption that the future will be like the recent past and present; the common example is the statement "tomorrow will be about the same weather as today" is of this type. This primitive method of forecasting the weather is correct about 70% of the time, but nonetheless, the likelihood of correct weather forecasting using such a no change heuristic decreases exceedingly rapidly as the anticipation time increases.

Prediction over a longer period of time requires consideration of not only the present state of a system, but also its rate of change. A somewhat better method of forecasting is based on the assumption that the "rate of increase or decrease is about constant." Such forecasting heuristics are often used, for example in demography. Generally, forecasting over a long period calls for increasing the complexity of the model by which future values are predicted. In a number of cases such an increase of complexity gives good results, since in increases the probability of accurate forecasting aver longer periods. Nevertheless in such cases as well, the period of accurate forecasting is determined by the properties of the process, as reflected in the constancy of the coefficients in the prediction formula (state, rate of change acceleration, etc.).

Predictions about the future of a system have been taken into account in preview control, an approach that was developed by Tomizuka. In preview control future information is considered as probabilistic in kind and the control problem seen as a problem of time-delay [16]. The situation is illustrated en Fig. 1 where a discrete control problem that lasts n time steps is considered. The system's present is denoted as $t = i$. Tomizuka postulated that up to certain time n_{la} past i, reliable predictions about the future can be made and utilized by the controller at i. This part of the future is considered "deterministic". Further away into the more distant future we have a time zone, called "probabilistic", where prediction are generally not reliable enough to be successfully used by a controller.

Thus, the future is divided into deterministic and probabilistic parts as seen in the Fig. 1. The controller is assumed to make use of preview information whit respect to a command signal (desired trajectory) from the present time i up n_{la} time units into deterministic future. The quantity, n_{la} is the preview time (or length of anticipation) and is usually shorter than n, the problem duration, and often one or two time steps. To make the solution applicable to a broader class of problems, measurement time delay, observation noise and driven noise were included in formulating the problem. The solution shows how to utilize the local future information obtained by finite preview (n_{la}) in order to minimize an optimally criterion evaluated over the problem duration n. It was found that preview dramatically improved the performance of a system relative to no preview optimal performance, and heuristic criterion about the preview time, n_{la} was suggested, by example.

$$n_{la} \approx 3 \text{ x (longest closed loop plant time constant).}$$

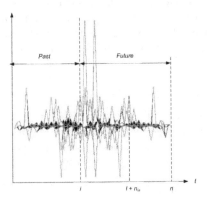

Fig. 1. Prediction in finite control

4 Derivation of the Anticipatory Model

When one simulates a process in discrete time steps, it becomes possible to evaluate the behaviour of a system over time using a forward or a backward appreciation of the differential equation. When these different formulations can be provided with other appreciations, an anticipatory model is analytically generated. In general, the differential equation $dx/dt = f(x(t))$ can be written as a difference equation (in discrete time) either as follows:

$$x(t + \Delta t) = x(t) + \Delta t f(x(t)) \tag{1a}$$

or equivalently backward as:

$$x(t - \Delta t) = x(t) - \Delta t f(x(t)) \tag{1b}$$

It follows that:

$$x(t) = x(t - \Delta t) + \Delta t f(x(t)) \tag{1c}$$

The latter function allows for the following rewrite after one time-step Δt:

$$x(t + \Delta t) = x(t) + \Delta t f(x(t + \Delta t)) \tag{1d}$$

In this formulation the state of a system at time $(t + \Delta t)$ depends on the state at the present time t, but also at the next moment in time $(t + \Delta t)$. The prediction 'includes' (or 'implies') its own next state. [3] Proposed that this evaluation be labelled *incursion*. The behaviour of incursive models can be very different from recursive ones, even when the two models are based on the same equations. As will be demonstrated below, the incursive subroutine may balance the recursive one and thus counteract on instabilities (e.g., emerging bifurcations) in an evolving system. These effects of anticipations are highly relevant for understanding social systems because as noted social systems are driven both historically and by the expectations available and exchanged within them.

For example, the price of a commodity can be considered as its expected value on the market. The price is based both on an intrinsic value and on the feedback from the market system. The intrinsic factor stems from the historical production given factor prices, while the feedback of the market originates in the present on the basis of the dynamics of current supply and demand. This economic system can be modelled using the anticipatory version of the well known logistic or Pearl-Verhulst equation for the growth of biological systems. The use of the traditional that is, only forward format of this model is ill advised, since the two sub dynamics of production and diffusion are then not sufficiently distinguished in terms of the dynamics over time. Production proceeds historically along the time axis, while diffusion takes place under competitive conditions in the present. The selection mechanism in this case, the market can be considered as an evolutionary feedback term on the historical development [5].

The following model is known as the logistic map:

$$x(t) = ax(t-1)\{1 - x(t-1)\} \tag{2}$$

This equation models, for example, the growth of a population. The feedback term $\{1 - x(t)\}$ inhibits further growth of the system represented by $x(t)$ as the value of $x(t)$ increases over time. The 'saturation factor' generates the bending of the well-known sigmoid growth curves of systems for relatively small values of the parameter $(1 < a < 3)$. For larger values of a, the model bifurcates $ata \geq 3.0$ or increasingly generates chaos $(3.57 < a < 4)$.

An anticipatory equivalent of the logistic equation can be formulated as follows [3]:

$$x(t) = ax(t-1)\{1 - x(t)\} \tag{3}$$

In this model the selection pressure prevailing in the present is analytically independent of the previous state of the system that produced the variation. The recursion on $x(t-1)$ can be considered as the historical representation. Note that one needs theoretical reasons for the assumption that the feedback of saturation is experienced by the system in its present state. For example, technological systems, which develop within an economy, experience interaction with the market at each moment in time. In other words, the horizontal diffusion in the market stands in orthogonal relation to the historical development of the technology over time. However, the results of the interactions are continuously input to a next cycle that builds both recursively on the previous state and in cursively experiences another feedback of the market at a next moment in time [4].

As noted, an incursive model can be expected to have properties different from those of the recursive one from which it is derived. For example, this model does not exhibit bifurcation or chaos for larger values of the parameter a. Let us first fully specify the model analytically and then in a next section demonstrate and discuss the behavioural differences by using cellular automata for the visualization of the effects in a social system of exchange relations.

The analytical reformulation of the Equation 3 proceeds as follows:

$$x(t) = ax(t-1)\{1 - x(t)\} \tag{4}$$
$$x(t) = ax(t-1) - ax(t-1)x(t)$$
$$x(t) + ax(t-1)x(t) = ax(t-1)$$
$$x(t)\{1 + ax(t-1)\} = ax(t-1)$$
$$x(t) = \frac{ax(t-1)}{\{1 + ax(t-1)\}} \tag{5}$$

Equation 4 specifies $x(t)$ as a function of $x(t-1)$, but it is analytically equivalent to a model for incursion embedded in historical recursions as specified in Equation 3. In the case of pure incursion (that is, only environmental determination in the present as represented by the second term of Equation 3, one would no longer be able to produce a simulation because one would loose the historical development of the system in the model. In other words, the anticipatory model containing both recursive and incursive factors imports the global or system's perspective into systems, which are developing historically. The incursive term enriches the historically developing system with an orientation towards the future.

5 General Approach

A system that make decisions in the present on the basis of what may be happening in the future is based in two important aspect, firstly the language that is utilize for formulate the behavior anticipative and the method of prediction for access to future states.

A system is described by a set of differential equation of the form

$$x(t+1) = Ax(t) + Bu(t) + w(t);$$
$$x(t_0) = x_0$$
$$y(t) = Cx(t) + v(t) \tag{6}$$

Where

$\quad \{u(t)\}$ $r \times 1$ input sequence;
$\quad \{y(t)\}$ $m \times 1$ output sequence;
$\quad \{x(t)\}$ $n \times 1$ state sequence;
$\quad$ **A, B, C** $\quad$ appropriate transition matrices;
$\quad x_0 \quad$ some initial state;
$\quad w(t), v(t) \quad$ noise terms.

A system is called anticipatory if $x(t+1)$ and $y(t)$ in equation (6) are not uniquely determined by $x(t)$ and $u(t)$ alone use information pertaining to some future state $x(t + \Delta t)$ and input $u(t + \Delta t)$. In the equation (6) we observe that it is rather difficult to in clued future information in this formulation, except by containing it whiting the noise terms as in the case of nondeterministic systems. Another point of view, however, is to look at the equation sing "=" as assign operators ":=" for example;

$$x(t+1) := Ax(t) + Bu(t) + w(t)$$

$$y(t) := Cx(t) + u(t) \qquad (7)$$

Where, the assignment operator, ":=" is an *if/then* rule, which assigns the right hand side (RHS) of equation (7) to the left hand side (LHS) upon update. Now we are in the realm of logical implication where we can easily include terms such as $x(t + \Delta t)$, and $u(t + \Delta t)$ in *if / then* rules is well known an provides an interesting alternative and enhancement of formulations such as equation (6) particularly for the purpose of qualitative and complex systems modelling. Thus, an anticipatory system can be described by a finite collection of fuzzy *if / then* rules

$$R^N = \{R^1, R^2, L, R^n\} \qquad (8)$$

Each rule is a situation / action pair, denotes as $x \rightarrow u$, where both present and anticipated situations are considered in the LHS and current action in the RHS. The rules of equation (8) may be rewritten as

$$R^N = \{x^1 \rightarrow u^1, x^2 \rightarrow u^2, L, x^n \rightarrow u^n\}$$
$$= \phi_{j=1}^n (x^j \rightarrow u^j) \qquad (9)$$

Where ϕ is an appropriate implication operator [18]. In many cases we can further partition the set of rules in equation (9) into rule-base (RB) with each rule-base being responsible for one action, for example,

$$R^n = \bigcup_{p=1}^r [RB^p] \qquad (10)$$

Rule base in equation (10) can be to reflect temporal partitions, that is we can have rules that describe the state of the system at t, for example of the form

$$x(t) \rightarrow u(t) \qquad (11)$$

As well as rules that describe the possible state of the system some time latter,

$$x(t + \Delta t) \rightarrow u(t) \qquad (12)$$

Thus an anticipatory fuzzy algorithm can infer the current action $u(t)$ on the basis of the present state $x(t)$ as well as anticipated ones $x(t + \Delta t), x(t + 2\Delta t), L, x(t + n\Delta t)$. Generally, the rules of equation (10) describe relations of a more general type than that of function. Such mappings have the linguistic form of fuzzy *if / then* rules for example,

$$\text{if } x \text{ is } A(t) \text{ then } y \text{ is } B(t) \qquad (13)$$

Where x is a fuzzy variable whose arguments are fuzzy sets denoted as A, and y is a fuzzy variable whose arguments are the fuzzy sets B. similar rules pertaining to future states are of the form,

$$\text{if } x \text{ will be } A(t + \Delta t) \text{ then } y \text{ is } B(t). \qquad (14)$$

Anticipatory control strategies may be based on global fuzzy variables such as performance where a decision at each time t is taken in order to maximize current as well as anticipated performance pertaining to $(t + \Delta t)$. Performance in this case is a fuzzy variable with an appropriate set fuzzy value that summarizes information about its change of state.

6 Simulation

In a dynamic multi-agent, the anticipation of actions may be is crucial to survive. We focus on the anticipation of the motion of agent who follows a well-defined periodic path. An anticipatory mechanism is proposed in [19]. To anticipate the movement of a patrolling agent, we build a model of the movement. This model allows the explicit simulation of the future motion of the agent. These predictions are directly used to improve escape or pursuit abilities and to obtain infiltration and ambush behaviors.

7 Resulted

We have tested our algorithm on periodic movement. The motion is evaluated according to criteria linked whit predictions: the track reliability is the right prediction rate, during one period. The first test is learning and knows the environment; we define critical points, that the agent has visit, figure 2. The problem is that the environment exist the elements that the agent have avoid for example the rock or the wall.

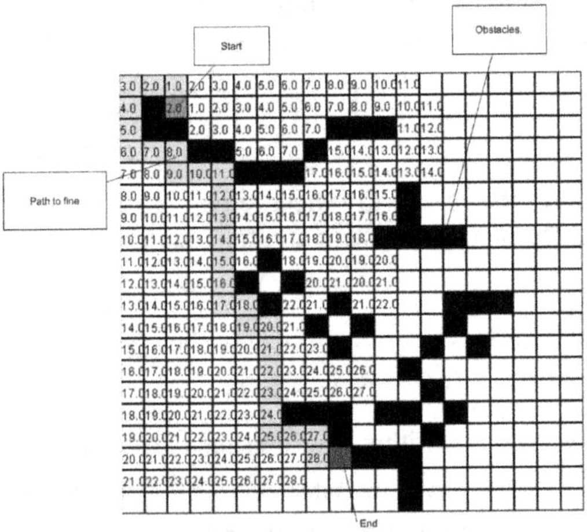

Fig. 2. Playoff model of movement

The model performs a linear approximation of motion so as to anticipate the next position. When the agent accelerates, the anticipation happens to be wrong and the model is updated. In order to do so, edges are adapted permanently to fit to the motion. This dynamical adaptation is made through experience, justifying the notion of learning.

8 Conclusion

The system anticipatory presented in this paper endows an agent capabilities in front of a patrolling guard without equivalent in the video game research literature [20]. We have mathematically demonstrated how this system could be used. The systems anticipative to give a new way for to solve problems with the solution are based in any event of the past.

References

1. Axelrod, R. (1997). The Complexity of Cooperation: agent-based models of competition and collaboration. Princeton: Princeton University Press.
2. D. C. Dennet, Consciousness Explained. Boston, MA: Little Brown, 1991.
3. Dittrich, P., T. Kron, & W. Banzhaf, On the Formation of Social Order: Modeling Luhmann's Double Contingency Problem. Paper presented at Simulating Society V, Kazimierz Dolny, 21-24 September 2001
4. Dubois, D. M. (1998). Computing Anticipatory Systems with Incursion and Hyperincursion. In D. M. Dubois (Ed.), Computing Anticipatory Systems: CASYS'97, AIP Proceedings Volume 437, pp. 3-29. American Institute of Physics, New York: Woodbury.
5. Dubois, D. M. (2000). Review of Incursive, Hyperincursive and Anticipatory Systems Foundation of Anticipation in Electromagnetism. In D. M. Dubois (Ed.), Computing Anticipatory Systems CASYS'99. AIP Proceedings Vol. 517, pp. 3-30. Melville, NY: American Institute of Physics.
6. Dubois, D. M. (2002). Theory of Incursive Synchronization of Delayed Systems and Anticipatory Computing of Chaos. In R. Trappl (Ed.), Cybernetics and Systems (Vol. 1, pp. 17-22). Vienna: Austrian Society for Cybernetic Studies.
7. Epstein, J. M., & R. Axtell. (1996). Growing Artificial Societies: Social Science from the Bottom Up. Cambridge, MA: MIT Press.
8. Leftery H. Tsoukalas (1998). NeuroFuzzy Approches to Anticipation. IEEE Transactions on systems, man and cybernetics, vol. 28, No. 4.
9. Leydesdorff, L. (2001). Technology and Culture: The Dissemination and the Potential 'Lock-in' of New Technologies. Journal of Artificial Societies and Social Simulation, 4(3), Paper 5, at <http://jasss.soc.surrey.ac.uk/4/3/5.html>.
10. Luhmann, N. (1984). Soziale Systeme. Grundriß einer allgemeinen Theorie. Frankfurt a. M.: Suhrkamp.
11. Luhmann, N. (2002). The Modern Sciences and Phenomenology. In W. Rasch (Ed.), Theories of Distinction: Redescribing the descriptions of modernity (pp. 33-60). Stanford, CA: Stanford University Press.
12. Nelson, R. R. & S. G. Winter (1982). An Evolutionary Theory of Economic Change. Cambridge, MA: Belknap Press of Harvard University
13. R. Rosen, Anticipatory Systems. New York: Pergamon, 1985.
14. L. H. Tsoukalas and Ikonomopoulos, (1992). "Uncertainty modeling in anticipatory systems," in Analysis and Management of Uncertainty. Amsterdam, The Netherlands. pp. 79-91.
15. G. Goldberg, (1991). "Microgenetic theory and dual premotor systems hypotesis," in Cognitive Microgenesis, R. E. Hanlon, Ed. New York: Spring-Verlag, pp. 35-52.
16. M. Tomizuka and D. E. Whitney, (1975) "Optimal finite preview problems (why and how is future information important),
17. Giddens, A. (1979). Central Problems in Social Theory. London, etc.: Macmillan.
18. T. Terano, K. Asai, and M. Sugeno, (1992). Fuzzy Systems Theory and Applications. Boston, MA: Academic.
19. Butz, M. V., Sigaud, O. and Gérard, P. (2003) Internal Models and Anticipation in Adaptive Learning Systems. LNCS 2684: pp 87-110, Spring Verlag.
20. Steve Rabin. (2002) AI Game Programming Wisdom. Charles River Media, INC.

Memory as an Active Component of a Behavioral Animation System

David Panzoli, Hervé Luga, and Yves Duthen

Research Institute on Informatics of Toulouse (IRIT)
Université Toulouse 1, 31042 Toulouse Cedex
{panzoli,luga,duthen}@irit.fr

Abstract. Our research is interested in behavioral animation among virtual reality applications. A major concern in this field is animating background actors and modeling their interactions. The aim is to provide virtual agents behaviors enabling them to evolve an autonomous and coordinated way in dynamic environments.

The behavior is modeled through the standard perception/decision/action loop where the characteristics of the decision module determine the agent abilities. The artificial intelligence "cognitive" agents have reasoning capabilities upon symbolic representations of the objects surrounding them, the way humans do. The artificial life agents possess the reactive and adaptive features from life imitation techniques.

The canvas of behavioral animation combine both approaches in order to obtain autonomous, coherent, reactive and adaptive agents. The so-called "hybrid" agents are for the most cognitive agents including reactive features. Two properties follow: they handle symbolic information and they store it in a memory regarded as a passive module.

We propose a different approach, focused on memory. We consider memory as an active component of cognition and reasoning or intelligence as the emergent expression of its operating. While keeping an "artificial life" view, we propose an original hybrid architecture which avoids the traditional reactiveness/cognition dichotomy and relies on distributed implicit mental representations.

Our model is a neural networks based architecture where two dimensions are considered: Whereas a vertical dimension models the procedural perception/action associations which form the reactiveness of a behavior, a horizontal dimension introduces the semantic concept association.

1 Background

Behavioral animation researchers aim at making virtual entities able to evolve in virtual worlds in a realistic way. To that end, they attempt to provide autonomous, reactive, coherent and adaptive features to the agent's behaviors. From the realism of these behaviors depend the quality of the animation in artistic productions and particularly the user's immersion in virtual communities, industry training simulations but also video games.

F.F. Ramos et al. (Eds.): ISSADS 2005, LNCS 3563, pp. 452–464, 2005.

Building one entity's behavior is to model its interactions with the environment on the one hand and with the other entities or users on the other. Modeling involves either manual rule writing by human experts or automatic learning procedures. The interaction can be summarized as the selection, for every perception, of an appropriate action with the aim of reaching a goal or fulfilling number of conditions. We often speak about *decision* or "action selection". Depending on the field of research, this fundamental question can be tackled in different ways.

Conditioning, where the decision is a simple association between perception and action, is a first illustration: someone who gets an electric shock after touching some electrical equipment is likely to build a cause and effect association in his/her brain in order to prevent a further accident. This kind of *reactive* behavior is often favored by artificial life approaches.

However, conditioning cannot stand for all the properties of human intelligence. For example, if I tell you not to make contact with a certain electric equipment because you could be electrocuted, you probably won't experience it to consider it as highly dangerous. From the artificial intelligence point of view, concepts exist somewhere in the brain that represent 'danger' and 'electric equipment' and which will be associated. From this new approach, we can derive two capital points: The appearance of *mental representation* on which the decision will rest. The distinction between experience-based and reasoning-based knowledge. In contrast with AL reactiveness, the notion of *cognition* arises.

1.1   Different Approaches

As underlined by Joanna Bryson in [3], the general problem of cognitive modeling can be addressed as shown in the equation 1:

$$P \xmapsto{f} R \xmapsto{g} R' \xmapsto{h} A \qquad (1)$$

f transforms a perception P into a useful mental representation R. The fundamental process of intelligence, also called *action selection*, is addressed through g which applies on R to create R', a mental representation of the desired action. Finally, R' is transformed into a motor or neural action A by the function h. The interesting points of this formalization are the very nature of mental representations R and R' and the processing behind g.

The AI approach is purely cognitive. It aims at endowing agents reasoning abilities on symbolic environment representations such as long term action planning, communication, etc. f and h are hence really complex since they support transformation from a perception to a symbolic representation and eventually to a motor action. g can often be brought back to a logic rule.

The artificial life approach considers symbolic representations are not mandatory to obtain intelligent behaviors. On the contrary, it can possibly turn disabling when a decision must be taken quickly. Indeed, a lot of studies in biology and ethology shows insects merely link their sensors to their effectors. Although they are deprived of all symbolic access they behave brilliantly.

In this approach, mental representations of an object or an action are really close to the stimuli itself. To recapture our general model in equation 1, f and h only ought to fit stimuli to the structure employed for implementation (neural networks, classifier systems, etc.). g still means associate perception and action but no longer with logical rules, but in a rather more reactive way, inherent to the structures introduced previously. As a result, actions from environment perceptions are instantaneous, which termed *reactive approach*, in contrast with the processing time cognitive models traditionally require.

Following the example of artificial life, the behavioral animation approach also criticizes the lack of reactivity of cognitive models. Meanwhile, they also reproach reactive agents the limited set of their abilities and their incapacity to plan mid-term or long-term actions.

To fill the gaps of the previous two approaches, they propose a new approach where reactive and cognitive features are blended. *Hybrid agents* are thus allowed to fire quick reaction when survival is at stake (running away from a predator) but also to plan purpose-driven behaviors when no threat is in sight.

1.2   Hybrid Models of the Behavioral Animation

For the qualities mentioned in section 1.1, hybrid models are nowadays widely used in behavioral animation. Among the most famous, one may quote Rodney Brooks' *Subsumption Architecture*, the *HPTS* model from Stéphane Donikian and Innes Ferguson's *TouringMachine*.

Brook's "subsumption architecture" [2] is historically the first to consider the lack of traditional cognitive approaches. Working in robotics, he deems essential the reactivity of behaviors. This is the reason why he defines an architecture where every behavior is modeled as a predefined automate and competes for the control of the agent. His architecture is *layered* and *hierarchical*. So, lower layers' reactive behaviors serving the agent's survival have precedence over more advanced layers' cognitive behaviors used for long term goal fulfillment. Hence, an agent can be assigned objectives which don't prevent it from reacting instinctively to dangers, threats or opportunities to fulfill another mid-term goal. Finally, the agent's world knowledge is modeled through global variables at the disposal of every automate.

The HPTS *(Hierarchical Parallel Transition System)* model of Donikian [10] and its improvement HPTS++ [9] take back Brook's architecture principles, with the intent to generalize them. In particular, Donikian is interested in virtual humans. In HPTS++ the world representation is managed by a specific module, *BCOOL* by Fabrice Lamarche [16], which deals with a database of every known objects of the simulation.

Ferguson's TouringMachine [12] is a genuine hybrid agent in that the reactive and cognitive features are present as functionally and structurally separate modules. Indeed, the decision stage is addressed within three communicating layers, as represented in figure 1:

A reactive layer holds the entire set of the agent's basic behaviors and enables it to react without complex reasoning.

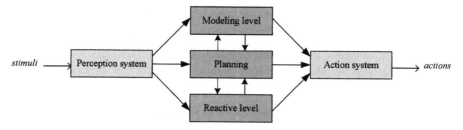

Fig. 1. Architecture of Ferguson's agent

A modeling layer stores symbolic information about the world. Provided the use of AI inference operators, this module can access cognition.

A planning layer, also known as behavior layer, acts as a medium between reactivity and cognition so that we usually employ the term of *arbitration*. It makes plans from reactive layer behaviors in order to fulfill modeling layer goals.

We can make a note of this architecture which establishes the general organization of a hybrid agent.

1.3   Restrictions and Drawbacks

Although these *behavior oriented* architectures are above all reactive, we can say that in a general way, hybrid agents are cognitive agents integrating reactive features, which means they entail AI programming.

Despite their indisputable strength, we assert these models suffer from several drawbacks:

The basic behaviors are automates and need manual expert programming. Hence, programming a virtual human requires to discriminate every one of its behaviors and to know how to reproduce it as an automate or in a logic rules shape. Besides, the chaining of these distinct behaviors raise the question of continuity.

The world's symbolic representation also requires the user to define every object in the simulation and every interaction possibilities it offers. Furthermore, and here is the most problematic point as far as we are concerned, memory is regarded as a passive module, working in parallel with cognitive processes.

As a consequence of all these restrictions, every model produced is non-adaptive, since it can't maintain its own consistency when the environment changes and non-evolutionary since improving it boils down to rewriting the whole system.

2   Goals

For the purpose of animating autonomous entities, from the *animat*[1] to the virtual human, our goal is to achieve a reactive and cognitive behavioral module.

---

[1] An animat is an agent whose behavior is inspired from an animal which has to survive in a hostile environment

In order to get rid of the limitations mentioned above, we intend to keep an artificial life perspective, which basically means:

- The module should not be split into structural components.
- The behaviors should not be user defined rules, but rather emerge from a learning procedure.

For these reasons, we have intentionally chosen the cognitive sciences approach to the detriment of artificial intelligence techniques.

3   Human Memory

Cognitive psychology is a variation of experimental psychology. Classic or experimental psychology is based on *behaviorism*, which studies the way the brain operates through a single stimulus/response cycle. Conversely, *cognitivism* advocates inner representations in the brain and rather considers a more realistic stimulus/organism/response cycle. The above-mentioned organism which is basically the memory, is the center of interest of cognitive psychology. As the single tangible organ forming the brain, memory not only plays a significant part in cognition but is the very location of cognition.

Ralph W. Gerdard considers memory can be summarized as the modification of behavior by experience. According to him, memory operating involves several stages:

1. The making of an impression by an experience.
2. The retention of some record of this impression.
3. The re-entry of this record into consciousness as recall or recognition.

Alan Baddeley thinks this approach is simplistic because remembering someone's name does not necessarily modify the behaviour. Nevertheless, this definition points out some outstanding ideas. First, a memory record is closely associated to the impression of an experience, which means the trace of a collection of *stimuli*. Then, the recall or recollection is not the issue of some computation but the reactivation of the impression.

In less than a century, human memory has been formalized by several cognitive psychology theories, all of them coming from experiments centered on particular brain operating properties.

Historically, the first theory supposed to model the human brain is Richard Atkinson and Richard Shiffrin's modal model also called "stage theory" [1]. This model focuses on brain structures pointed out by experimental issues on memory size and duration. Figure 2 shows the classic partition between sensory store, short term store and long term store memory.

Little time elapsed before this theory was challenged. The fact some memory items disappear after about twenty seconds when others can last for ages is not contested. Yet, the existence of separate units inside the brain is disputed. Therefore, instead of being concerned with so-called physiological partitions in the brain, the mind research community started studying memory processes.

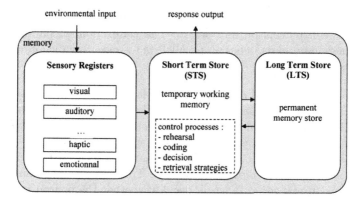

Fig. 2. Atkinson-Shiffrin model for memory

3.1 Knowledge and Skills

Among all the ways human memory can be addressed, mental or inner representations constitute a good starting point. Neal Cohen and Larry Squire distinguish two types, procedural memory and declarative or semantic memory which work different by ways [5].

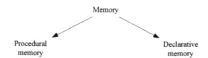

Fig. 3. Squire and Cohen types of memory

Declarative and procedural memory. Procedural memory is the *"know-how"*. It deals with actions, skills and conditioning. It expresses everything one can do but can not talk about. For instance, it would not be easy for a tennis player to describe the way he hits the ball though he can precisely handle it.

Declarative memory, similarly called *"know-what"*, embeds every knowledge that can be verbally expressed. This knowledge goes from autobiographic and contextualized knowledge such as the menu of our last dinner to conceptual knowledge as the year World War II ended.

3.2 Parallel Distributed Processing

The *Parallel Distributed Processing* theory (a.k.a. PdP) by Rumelhart and Mc-Clelland [23] relies on two previous experimental issues: Karl Lashley's showed knowledge in the brain is distributed [17]. Warren McCulloch and Walter Pitts formalized the neuron [18].

The PdP binds mental representations to neurons, and cognition to their activity. More simply, knowledge is regarded as a set of distributed neuronal configurations and the propagation of the signal through the neurons stands for the link between perception and action. The *connectionism* paradigm, which regroups these hypothesis, relies on parallelism to reject any dichotomy between reactivity and cognition.

Neural nets. An artificial neural network is formed and powered by the interconnection of simple and elementary information processing units called formal neurons. The McCulloch and Pitt artificial neuron works the same way its biologically model does: Its task is to spread a signal from its inputs *(dendrites)* to its output *(axone)* under certain conditions. In order to achieve it, the sum of the potentials at every input is computed. This value is then compared to a threshold and an activation function decides whether the neuron is to produce an output signal or not.

The organization of the cells, herein called layout, is the key of the power of the network. Following the tasks neural nets can carry out, there are many kinds of layouts. Two of them are presented below:

The simple "perceptron" of Frank Rosenblatt [21] is among the most famous. It is composed of an input layer connected to an output layer. The multi-layered perceptron of Marvin Minsky and Seymour Papert [19] includes n hidden layers between the input and the output layers, allowing it to deal with non linearly separable problems such as the XOR logic door. Learning the network relies on error-correction mechanisms introduced in section 3.5.

Kohonen networks of Teuvo Kohonen [15] propose a matrix layout and a self-organization rule based learning. They are mainly used for classification problem solving.

Wether it is a perceptron or a Kohonen, a network is not built from user defined rules but trained to fit what the user expects it to do. This point is further addressed in section 3.5.

How can the memory and the brain be modeled better than with life imitation based structures ? Indeed, some mental abilities turn out to be explained by neural network properties. Generalization process, which is defined as "the degree to which learning about one stimulus transfers to another" can be fully described through an attractive neural networks property: the *signal completion*. Conversely, another feature called *negative patterning* can explain how two very close stimuli can be discriminated by memory. *(see [13], chapter 4)*.

3.3   Semantic Association

Situated at a higher abstraction level, semantic networks [6, 11, 24] consider human memory as an associative memory to account for information spreading among brain structures. All of these networks are based on the *"spreading activation theory"* by Alan Collins and Ross Quillian [7]. According to them, semantic memory is a network of concepts linked to each other through experience. Propagation rules allow activated concepts to activate in turn concepts in their neighborhood.

Experimental tests about familiarity, typicality and the *priming effect*[2] account for such an organization.

3.4 Memory Abstraction

Beyond neural networks, the memory's abstraction faculty is studied by the *"Levels of Processing"* from Fergus Craik and Robert Lockhart [8]. Through experimentations, they find out that a collection of random letters is quickly forgotten whereas it can last a whole week if they form a word. Thus, they express the following theory:

The more processing a memory *item* involves, the longer it is likely to be held in memory. Furthermore, the stimulus seems to acquire more semantic meaning according to the time granted to this processing. These results led Craik and Lockhart to represent human memory as a multilayered structure, where the deepest[3] layers might present the greatest complexity or abstraction and the best durability.

3.5 Memory and Learning

In section 3.1, two types of memory were dissociated due to the nature of knowledge they were storing. Experimentations led in relation to learning reveal these types of memory were involving different learning procedures.

Skill practicing. Procedural memory learning is conscious and often intentional. As human skills heavily rely on training and practicing, we usually use the term of "skill strengthening".

In a neural networks framework, proceedings have been designed to make a network able to resolve given problems. They consist of decreasing a deviation value computed between the current and the ideal solutions, in an iterative error/correction cycle. The most famous is the "backpropagation theory" by David Rumelhart [22], initiated by the Widrow-Hoff learning rule [25] and the Rescola-Wagner model [20].

Such methods can be compared to human practice. Indeed, according to Mark Gluck and Catherine Myers *([13], chapter 3)*, similar mechanisms occur during human learning. So the brain is able to appreciate an action consequence and compute inner structural changes to tend to a minimal deviation.

Mere exposure learning. According to Donald Hebb [14], declarative memory only relies on associative laws. Learning someone's name cannot be regarded as learning to play football. At first, learning new semantic knowledge is an unconscious process. Then, hearing one person's name is usually sufficient to hold it in memory for long, without involving any practice.

---

[2] The priming effect explains why a souvenir is more often retrieved if one have been given a semantically close cue

[3] The "Levels of Processing" theory can also be found as "Depth of Processing" in the literature

Perceptual learning, or "mere exposure learning" to employ Donald Hebb's terminology, tries to explain how knowledge can be held in memory whereas it has not undergone any conscious practice. Hebb's *long term potentiation* [14], or "synaptic plasticity" law, states that co-activated neurons tend to strengthen their connexions. In other words, a multimodal stimulus entering the brain through every sensor is known to activate several neurons inside the brain. When reinforcing their connexions, these neurons build a distributed structure which can be viewed as the mental representation of the original stimulus. The latter can be compared to a *pattern* which has a symbolic meaning, even if it cannot be explicitly expressed.

In this section, we have introduced several cognitive psychology theories and statements which have led us to distinguish two types of memory of different natures and operating modes. To make an analogy with behavioral animation, we could connect procedural memory to the reactive feature and semantic memory to the cognitive feature.

4   Proposed Model

We propose a behavioral hybrid architecture in which memory is not regarded as a passive module but on the contrary plays the leading part. As a matter of fact, we intend to reproduce the functional structures and features of memory exhibited by cognitive psychology theories.

4.1   General Architecture

The general architecture is supported by two theories introduced in section 3. An overview is presented as figure 4.

From a conceptual point of view, we will split the architecture into two separate but overlapping dimensions to fit Squire and Cohen theory. The vertical dimension stands for procedural memory and the horizontal dimension is at the root of semantic memory.

For a number of reasons, the implementation will call for connectionism. For instance, neural networks have the particularity to provide continuous outputs, which is helpful to avoid behavior colliding or rough transitions. Moreover, as seen in subsection 3.2, generalization and specificity, which are two inherent features of human memory, go along with neural networks.

Thus, we will combine a multilayer perceptron and a Kohonen network in order to obtain a bi-dimensional network, in which will be hosted two different kinds of representation and learning.

The vertical dimension is the place for procedural memory and therefore the model reactivity. It is made up of a perceptron, similar to those employed in artificial life solving methods. On the one hand, the input layer gathers every agent's perception *(see 4.2)*. On the other, the output layer regroups every action the agent is able to. Both of them are connected through a hidden layer forming the horizontal dimension. Supervised learning techniques as backpropagation shall be used to train the agent's skills.

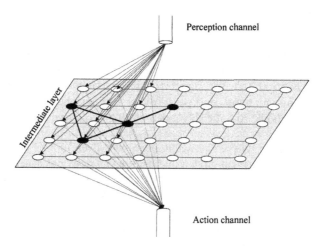

Fig. 4. Proposed architecture for a behavioral controller

The horizontal dimension is a re-representation of the previously cited hidden layer, as a Kohonen network. In this way, all the neurons of the layer are connected to each other, likely to reinforce or weaken the links between them thanks to Hebb's unsupervised learning rules. We aim at building an associative memory where neurons or groups of neurons would be associated to form complex patterns to eventually get non symbolic environment representations.

4.2 Perception and Action

In artificial life, learning and evolving mechanisms produce *situated agents*. The "situated cognition theory" [4] maintains that every human thought or action is adapted to its environment. Behavioral animation speaking, the abilities of the agent emerge from its interactions with the environment. Consequently, perception and action are a crucial point in the conception of the agent's architecture.

An agent's perception channel as shown in figure 4 is a vector conveying the usual external informations as sight (as a vision matrix) and touch (collision), but also inner or "visceral" states (fear, hunger, mood, etc.). In the same manner, communication is seen as a sense (audition), and messages from an agent to the other as environmental stimuli.

These prior choices are accounted by the fact that an "our-way built" agent cannot attain symbolic level reasoning. The differentiation between an obstacle and another virtual world's agent shall emerge during the semantic representation construction inside its memory.

The entity's action channel is subjected to the same constraints: its physical actions and its communication are represented in the same way and use the same circuits. For instance, speaking is nothing but an action in the environment.

4.3 Learning

After having specified it's sensors and effectors, there remains to define learning methods in order to allow the agent to behave in a realistic way. The goal of such methods is to enable the agent to create relevant associations between perceptions on the one hand, and perceptions and actions on the other.

We made the choice to split the learning into two successive stages:

1. An *exposure* stage where the agent perceives a number of stimuli from the environment. During this first stage, the agent does not learn how to react but builds mental representations with storing patterns, associating them to create abstraction classes or links between co-occurring events. This "perceptual learning" applies Hebb's learning rules to the horizontal matrix.
2. After the mental representation of the agent's world is complete, the *training* stage takes place. This stage, we term "vertical conditioning", uses Rumelhart error/correction mechanisms to refine action selection.

Across the first stage, we expect the agent to create representations and associations which shall enable it, during the second stage, to fire actions from the basis of perceptions which are not explicitly linked. We intend to reveal behaviors situated above the simple reactivity, that would be qualified of intelligent.

5   Conclusions and Perspectives

This model of human memory, presenting its main properties and its activity, must be able, as a behavioral module, to help virtual agents going above simple conditioning. By enabling them to build complex representations from stimuli associations, we expect them to behave in the same way a traditional AI hybrid agent would.

However, the model as it is presented is not scalable. It does not allow us to build a virtual human scale behavioral module. Yet, in order to obtain more complex behaviors, we must access high abstraction level knowledge representations. To do so, we raise the need to introduce a notion of modularity in order to build and train larger modules.

By analogy with Craik and Lockhart layers, supported by the depth of processing theory, we could view a complex system as an association in cascade of the simple described above modules. The perception channel data could then acquire more semantic sense while they would go down through the multiple layers. The levels of competence of an agent would then be defined by the architecture layers and its intelligence by their number.

To conclude, we do not expect our model to show more complex behaviors than AI based models, given AI techniques permit to produce virtually every kind of behavior. With the use of artificial life techniques such as interaction-guided learning, we just think we can free the animation designer from all the expertise required to build complex systems.

References

1. Richard C. Atkinson and Richard M. Shiffrin. Human memory: A proposed system and its control processes. In *The Psychology of Learning and Motivation: advances in research and theory, Vol. 2*, New-York: Academic Press, 1968. K.W. Spence.
2. Rodney A. Brooks. A robust layered control system for a mobile robot. *IEEE Journal of Robotics and Automation*, pages 14–23, 1986.
3. Joanna Bryson. Cross-paradigm analysis of autonomous agent architecture. *Journal of Experimental and Theoretical Artificial Intelligence (JETAI)*, 12(2):165–189, 2000.
4. William J. Clancey. *Situated Cognition: On human knowledge and Computer Representations*. Cambridge University Press, 1997.
5. Neal J. Cohen and Larry R. Squire. Preserved learning and retention of pattern analyzing skill in amnesia: Dissociation of knowing how and knowing that. *Science*, 210:207:209, 1980.
6. Alan M. Collins and M. Ross Quillian. Retrieval time from semantic memory. *Journal of Verbal Learning and Verbal Behavior*, 8:240–248, 1969.
7. Allan M. Collins and Elizabeth Loftus. A spreading activation theory of semantic memory. *Psychological Review*, 82:407–428, 1975.
8. Fergus I. M. Craik and Robert S. Lockhart. Levels of processing: A framework for memory research. *Journal of Verbal Learning and Verbal Behavior*, 11:671–684, 1972.
9. Stéphane Donikian. Modélisation, contrôle et animation d'agents virtuels autonomes évoluant dans des environnements informés et structurés. Habilitation à diriger les recherches, août 2004.
10. Stéphane Donikian and Eric. Rutten. Reactivity, concurrency, data-flow and hierarchical preemption for behavioral animation. In *Fifth Eurographics Workshop on Programming Paradigms in Graphics*, volume 1995, Maastricht (Nederlands), 1995. springer-verlag.
11. Scott E. Fahlman. *NETL: a system for representing and using real world knowledge*. MIT Press, Cambridge, MA, 1979.
12. Innes A. Ferguson. Touringmachines: Autonomous agents with attitudes. *IEEE Computer*, 25(5):51–55, 1992.
13. Mark A. Gluck and Catherine E. Myers. *Gateway To Memory*. MIT Press, nov. 2000.
14. Donald Hebb. *The Organisation Of Behavior*. Wiley, 1949.
15. Teuvo Kohonen. Self-organized formation of topologically correct feature maps. *Biological Cybernetics*, 43:59–69, 1982.
16. Fabrice Lamarche. *Humanoïdes virtuels, réaction et cognition: une architecture pour leur autonomie*. PhD thesis, Université de Rennes I, décembre 2003.
17. Karl S. Lashley. *Brain mechanism and intelligence: A quantitative study of injuries to the brain*. Chicago University Press, Chicago, 1929.
18. Warren S. McCulloch and Walter Pitts. A logical calculus of the ideas immanent in nervous activity. *Bulletin of mathematical biophysics*, 5:115–133, 1943.
19. Marvin Minsky and Seymour Papert. *Perceptrons: an Introduction to Computational Geometry*. MIT Press, 1968.
20. Robert Rescorla and Allan R. Wagner. A theory of pavlovian conditionning: Variations in the effectiveness of reinforcement and non-reinforcement. In A. Black and W. Prokasy, editors, *Classical Conditionning II: Current Research and Theory*, pages 64–99, New-York, 1972. Appleton-Century-Crofts.

21. Frank Rosenblatt. The perceptron: probabilistic model for information storage and organisation in the brain. *Psychological Review*, 65:386–408, 1958.
22. David E. Rumelhart, Geoffrey E. Hinton, and Ronald J. Williams. Learning internal representations by error propagation. In D. Rumelhart and J. McClelland, editors, *Parallel Distributed Processing: Exploration in the microstructure of cognition*, pages 318–362, Cambrigde, MA, 1986. MIT Press.
23. David E. Rumelhart and James L. McClelland. *Parallel Distributed Processing: Explorations in the Microstructure of Cognition*, volume 1 and 2. MIT Press, MA, 1986.
24. John F. Sowa. *Conceptual structures. Information Processing in Mind and Machine.* Addison Wesley, Reading. MA. USA, 1984.
25. Bernard Widrow and Marcian E. Hoff. Adaptative switching circuits. *Institute of Radio Engineers, Western Electronic Show and Convention Record*, 4:96–104, 1960.

Growing Functional Modules, a Prospective Paradigm for Epigenetic Artificial Intelligence

Jérôme Leboeuf Pasquier

Departamento de Ingeniería de Proyectos,
Centro Universitario de Ciencias Exactas e Ingeniería, Universidad de Guadalajara
J. Guadalupe Zuno 48, Los Belenes, Zapopan, Jalisco, México
jleboeuf@dip.cucei.udg.mx

Abstract. Epigenesis postulates that intelligence may arise in a system thanks to an adequate developmental process interacting with its environment. Robotics constitutes the most suitable field to implement this approach. This paper presents the underlying concept, an earlier proposal and a potential implementation of a prospective paradigm named Growing Functional Modules. This paradigm has been conceived to allow the design and the automatic development of a distributed and dynamic architecture able to gradually control an epigenetic robot. An illustration is given applying the paradigm to create a simple artificial brain for a mushroom shaped robot.

1 Introduction

Epigenesis, introduced by Jean Piaget, states that to gain true intelligence, a system must satisfy three fundamental characteristics: its embodiment, its situatedness in an environment and its involvement in an epigenetic developmental process [1]. Considering computer science, the most natural field satisfying the first two characteristics is robotics; nonetheless, artificial systems that could fit the third criterion are often based on rigid models, rarely focused on learning and quite always disconnected from perception. In spite of this fundamental limitation, epigenetic robotics attracted many researchers during the last few years [2,3,4,5] due to its invaluable reward: building intelligent machines by means of a developmental process, which means freeing their realization from a huge programming task.

To evaluate the potential of an earliest model of artificial brain, we designed a mushroom shaped robot, called hOnGo [7]. The acting and sensing systems of hOnGo were minimal: three actuators and a dozen of sensors. Neither task nor functionalities were programmed; but an artificial brain was provided and a prior and global goal was integrated: phototaxis[1]. Both, the method of implementation and the representation of the developmental process seem to be sufficiently robust and versatile to be applied for the design of other epigenetic robots and, moreover, to establish the fundamentals of a new paradigm, named "Growing Functional Modules". This paper presents the underlying concept, an earlier proposal and a potential implementation of this prospective paradigm.

---

[1] Light seeking

F.F. Ramos et al. (Eds.): ISSADS 2005, LNCS 3563, pp. 465–471, 2005.
© Springer-Verlag Berlin Heidelberg 2005

2 Two Prior Postulates

The two postulates described at continuation have a fundamental impact on the conception of the upcoming paradigm.

Our first postulate concerns learning, and states that the emergence of a coherent behavior, intelligent or not, on an epigenetic robot presupposed an expending hierarchical learning. Such learning begins with the lowest level (handling of joints, involvement[2] of basic sensing), i.e. it concerns mainly modules directly coupled to actuators and sensors; during this phase the brain discovers its rudimentary abilities. Then slowly, learning spreads to control basic motion like coordination of actuators and primitive sensing where simple patterns emerge as the result of the association of input stimuli. Finally, learning should produce behavior focused at satisfying the global goals, and this, leaning on its sensing area whose patterns have evolved to conform proper concepts. Acquisition of basic skills is stimulated when trying to satisfy global goals like positive phototaxis in our example. This postulate concerning learning directly shapes the growth of the architecture components: low level modules (mainly those coupled with actuators) are required and consequently developed to satisfy basic skills, meanwhile gradually but slowly, growing affects higher modules structures; learning then slows down as success rate in satisfying goals increases. Nevertheless, contrary to the learning process mentioned above, interconnection of modules is not strictly hierarchic; for example, two modules occupying different positions in the hierarchy may both request goals to a third one.

Our second postulate, concerning design, states that distribution and interconnection of the modules conforming the brain should result from the robot's design. This previous assertion may be inferred as follow: as a principle in our architecture, to allow its enhancement, each module needs some feedback in order to evaluate the effects produced when triggering specific actions. Nevertheless, potential data conforming this feedback is not exhaustive, for example, while designing a robotic leg, sensing may take into account joints angles, high and size of steps, pressure on the foot, strength required, etc. For practical reasons, the corresponding set of sensors must be minimized. Therefore, a relevant and sufficient response must be defined during the designing phase to provide an adequate and sufficient feedback to each module of the brain. In particular, the corresponding task must consider the finality of the application which presupposes from the designer, a precise forecast of the kind of data each module requires to process and has to produce, and this considering the global interconnection of these modules. For example, efficiency in motion constitutes a universal criteria, consequently the input of a module in charge of "finding out" optimum trajectories should include energy cost and distance covered; in turn, such data may result from lower modules. Therefore, this specific designing phase, part of the proposed epigenetic approach, substitutes programming and conforms the upcoming paradigm. Thus growing functional modules, together with actuators and sensors conform the basic components involved in this design. The resulting architecture is encoded and initially provided to the system in charge of controlling the associated robot. Additionally, the designing phase also establishes the communication protocol between the robot and its controller.

---

[2] Initially, values transmitted by sensors have no meaning at all. Gradually, these values are associated with static or dynamic states inside the brain

Introducing a designing phase comports obviously a frustrating aspect. Nevertheless such task is required not only for pragmatic reasons: deciding which actuators and sensors to integrate on the robot responds to an intrinsic logic on how to combine potential sensing and acting to pursue some finality; but also for efficiency motive. A simulation of an early version of the architecture [8] corroborates that last fact: the brain was supposed to evolve by its own, selecting the pertinent information to treat and finding the way to organize the modules. To accomplish this operation, a few rules were implemented: for example, one rule states that "lowest modules always assume that all sensors values altered shortly after triggering one of their assigned actions, were under their control". Then, according to such rule, when two modules claim the same sensor, a higher module was created and given the control over this sensor and both lower modules. Though our preliminary results were successful, the convergence of this architecture shows to be extremely slow, its structures redundant and excessively large.

Hence, the modules constituting the brain grow slowly beginning with the lowest levels controlling their respective actuators and extending gradually to higher levels in charge of global behavior. On a similar manner, the Sensing Area should construct its knowledge combining elemental recognition abilities to facilitate the emergence of significant patterns and concepts, guided by processes similar to those of the Acting Area. As no experiment strengthens it, this ultimate statement is still hypothetic though integrated in the proposed paradigm.

3 Growing Functional Modules

3.1 Sharing Common Characteristics

As mentioned previously, the basic design units are conformed by modules. In particular, those belonging to the Acting Area must share some common characteristics to, among others, allow their interconnection:

- Initially they have no internal structure, but a set of internal "mechanisms" in charge of building some accurate structures, an associated set of "actions" and a sensing feedback.
- They try to satisfy some input goals, triggering a selective sequence of actions. In the case of lower modules, these actions correspond to specific commands to actuators; otherwise, they are constituted by goals aimed at other modules.
- In order to evaluate the accomplishment of a goal, a feedback should be provided by the Sensing Area. In case of a simple application, the Sensing Area may be omitted and the feedback provided directly by sensors. This feedback leads the growing and adaptation of internal structures.
- When immersed in a stable context, the internal structure converges to produce effective sequences of actions satisfying each achievable goal; if not, the internal structures grow and adapt in an intent to satisfy input goals; eventually they fail in this attempt.

Concerning the denomination "Growing Functional Modules": the word "Growing" characterizes the dynamic internal structure of these modules while the word "Functional" refers to the property of these modules to combine lower abilities to engender higher ones. For example, a specified height of a leg may be obtained when reaching certain angles on its joints (which does not conform a unique solution). In fact, after a while, the graphic representation of this module will mimic the mathematical function representing the relation between the height of a leg and the angles of its joints [6]. The key factor of the architecture is given by the dynamic internal structure of each module which allows local adaptative abilities, and additionally generates a gradual bottom-up integration of skills according to the intrinsic mechanical capabilities of the robot.

3.2 Communication Between Modules

Two kinds of messages are transmitted between Acting modules:

- Activation messages which occurs when a module solicits a lower one to reach a specific goal. Modules did not return any answer to these solicitudes, they just produce a sequence of actions focused on reaching the goal and eventually fail. Some of the highest modules do not receive any solicitude as they are in charge of satisfying the initial purposes like, according to our previous example, maximizing positive phototaxis.
- External inhibition is a less common kind of message which emerges under atypical conditions and characterizes the incompatibility of some modules while propagating simultaneously. An illustration of this phenomenon is given in [7] when the hOnGo robot assimilates a physical property expressing that standing on its foot constitutes a prior condition to orienting its hat.

In practice, communications between modules represent a minor fraction of the total processing time, especially if compared with the time dedicated to process each autonomous structure. This distributed nature of the architecture provides the system an additional advantage since the control may be spread out on processors in charge of controlling distinct parts of a robot.

3.3 Towards a Library of Modules

According with the object oriented representation, each module composing the architecture is considered as an instance of its corresponding class. Furthermore, all these classes are derived from an upper one whose standard interface ensures the interconnectivity of all these modules. So, the designer would dispose of a library containing several classes of modules to elaborate a desired architecture. The main difficulty appears when trying to define a suitable content for the library: the potential and limitations of this representation are under studies meanwhile the requirements of complex applications are unknown. In consequence, such lack of information leads to a pragmatic approach consisting in programming and adding specific modules whenever required. The programming task may result complex and laborious as some modules required over five thousands lines of source code to implement the whole set of mechanisms involved in its dynamic structure; even so they are reusable for other applications if matching the standard interface allowing their incorporation to the GFM library.

Such added modules may contain a made to measure architecture defined to match a peculiar task or implement existing ones, like those based on Competitive Learning whose characteristics may be adapted to fit those mentioned in paragraph 3.1 and 3.3:

for example, it may consist in associating a specific action or "meaning" (if implemented in the Sensing Area) to each Voronoi Set. The module in charge of "probing
trajectory" constitutes an example of a made-to-measure structure, different from
those mentioned earlier and described in [6]. Its function consists in generating sequences alternating the height and length of each step to bring up suitable motion.

4 Designing hOnGo

The entire design process of hOnGo and its major achievements constitute the object
of a forthcoming paper. Meanwhile, a graphic representation of the virtual version of
hOnGo is presented figure 1 and a brief description of its design using Growing Functional Modules with its corresponding graphic representation (figure 2) illustrate the
current thesis.

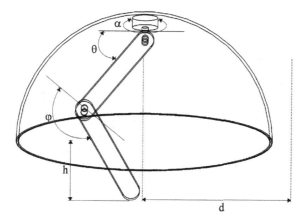

Fig. 1. hOnGo's graphic representation

   The architecture is in fact composed by seven modules, but two of them are integrated as second levels:

- Module A: in charge of controlling joints angles, is assigned the associated ele-
  mentary actions $\{-\delta\theta, \delta\theta, -\delta\varphi, \delta\varphi\}$. A first level A1 learns correlations between
  the real position of both articulations (θ, φ) and the height h of the body while the
  second level A2 learns the correlation with the distance l from the foot to its
  "zero" position. Values of pressures p_1 and p_2 on the front and back part of the foot
  are also processed by this module to generate internal inhibition.
- Module B: controls hat rotation triggering the elementary actions $\{-\delta\alpha, \delta\alpha\}$; level
  B1 learns correlation with direction of motion d while level B2 learns correlation
  with orientation of the hat o.
- Module C: in charge of coordinating the trajectory of one steps s, controls its
  height and length, taking into account efficiency. Efficiency e is obtained "computing" the length of a step and the energy spent to produce it.
- Module D: focused in maximizing the incoming light energy v whilst moving the
  robot closer and orienting correctly its solar panel. Moreover, this module tries to
  find a correlation within its input values, finding thus the most effective way to
  reach its goal.

– Module E plays an inhibitory role over "orienting the hat" and "changing direction", traducing thus that, depending on the contact the foot applies to the ground, the rotation of the hat affects only one of these controls at a time.

Each of these modules, in charge of a specific task, builds its own cellular network according to its particular set of mechanisms. At last, the resulting architecture issued of the designing phase, should produce a coherent behavior thanks to the developmental skills integrated into such representation.

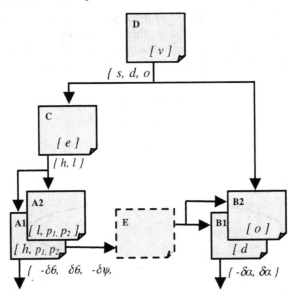

Fig. 2. Growing functional modules conforming the architecture of hOnGo's Acting Area

5 Conclusion

Though in its primary phase of conception, the Growing Functional Modules paradigm offers a strong potential for epigenetic artificial intelligence and, in particular, its most suitable field of application: robotics. From a preliminary experience gained during the implementation of hOnGo, a few classes of modules have been defined and developed, taking into account both their functionality and universality. Under the described principle, the architecture of the brain, generated during a previous designing phase, comes out from the robot's physical characteristics, in particular the selection and distribution of its sensors and actuators defined to fulfill some global goals.

After having elaborated a consistent library of modules, the promising benefit of this methodology, should consist in freeing the implementation of its programming task. The dynamic structure inside each module evolves through time to fulfill its specialized function, contributing to a global behavior focused on satisfying global goals. Besides, the distributed character of this architecture allows to spread control over the system, a significant advantage in robotics.

The actual challenge resides in defining a suitable content for such a library and in programming its components. Besides, more complex applications are required to evaluate the capacity and limitations derived from this prospective paradigm.

References

1. Ziemke, T., Situated and Embodied Cognition, Introduction to the Special Issue of the Cognitive Systems Research Journal 3, Elsevier (2002) 271-274
2. Lungarella, Max and Metta, Giogio, Beyond Gazing, Pointing and Reaching. A Survey of Developmental Robotics. In Prince, Berthouze, Kozima, Bullock, Stojanov and Balkenius (Eds.). Proceedings of the Third International Workshop on Epigenetic Robotics: Modeling Cognitive Development in Robotic Systems 101. Boston MA USA (2003) 81-89
3. Prince, Christopher G., Introduction: the Second International Workshop on Epigenetic Robotics. In Prince, Demiris, Marom, Kozima, Bullock and Balkenius (Eds.). Proceedings of the Second International Workshop on Epigenetic Robotics: Modeling Cognitive Development in Robotic Systems. Lund University Cognitive Studies Vol. 94. Lund Sweden (2002)
4. Berthouze, Luc and Prince Christopher G., Introduction: the Third International Workshop on Epigenetic Robotics. In Prince, Berthouze, Kozima, Bullock, Stojanov and Balkenius (Eds.). Proceedings of the Third International Workshop on Epigenetic Robotics: Modeling Cognitive Development in Robotic Systems. Lund University Cognitive Studies Vol. 101. Lund Sweden (2003)
5. Prince, Christopher G., Demiris Y., Introduction to the Special Issue on Epigenetic Robotics, International Society for Adaptive Behavior (2003) Vol. 11(2) 75-77
6. Leboeuf, Jérôme: Facing Combinatory Explosion in NAC Networks. Advanced Distributed Systems, Lecture Notes in Computer Science, Third International School and Symposium ISSADS 2004 Guadalajara Mexico. Larios, Ramos and Unger (eds.). Springer (2004) 252-260
7. Leboeuf, Jérôme: Nac, an Artificial Brain for Epigenetic Robotics, Proceedings of the World Automation Congress 2004, 10th International Symposium on Robotics and Applications, Seville Spain. Robotics: trends, principles and applications Vol. 15. Jamshidi, Ollero, Martinez de Dios (eds.) TSI Press Series (2004) 535-540
8. Leboeuf, Jérôme: A Self-Developing Neural Network Designed for Discrete Event System Autonomous Control in Mastorakis, N. (eds.): Advances in Systems Engineering, Signal Processing and Communications, Wseas Press (2002) 30-34

Specifying Agent's Goals in 3D Scenarios Using Process Algebras

Fabiel Zúñiga, Félix Ramos, and H. Ivan Piza

Research and Advanced Studies Center (CINVESTAV)
Prolongación López Mateos Sur No. 590, Guadalajara, Jalisco, México
{fzuniga,framos,hpiza}@gdl.cinvestav.mx
http://www.gdl.cinvestav.mx

Abstract. This paper presents a method to specify agent's goals using process algebras. Formal specification of agent's goal is important in goal oriented works because it allows more detailed description about what we want an agent to do and also is possible to detect possible problems. In this paper we present the method we use to specify formally agent's goals in GeDA-3D a platform useful to implement distributed applications where a 3D interface is useful.

1 Introduction

This paper describes how we can use process algebras [3, 4] like LOTOS [5, 6] to specify the way in which we want an agent (or a set of agents) to accomplish its (theirs) goals. This work focuses in agents which have to accomplish a set of goals, and particularly, this method is used in GeDA-3D a platform to design and run dynamic virtual environments described in [1, 2]. The work presented in [2] shows a platform that allows users to generate virtual scenes. Such generation involves two phases: 1) description of the attributes, arrangement and intentions of the virtual characters participants throughout a natural language, and 2) graphical simulation of a dynamic scene during which the characters interact with each other in order to achieve individual and/or collective goals. Every agent controls the behavior of an intelligent virtual object and enforces it to accomplish a goals-specification defined in a declarative description; an agent receives the goals specification and it resolves and sends back to the environment a set of primitive actions for the object to perform.

We give a goals-specification to an agent in order to give a more detailed definition about the way these goals must be reached. The global behavior of the agent will not only try to reach the defined goals, it will try to accomplish the whole specification. For example, suppose there exist the following goals an agent is able to reach: g1, g2 and g3, then we can construct expressions like the following ones:

- $g_1; g_2; g_3$. Prefix operator: The agent will have to reach the goal g_1, later the goal g_2 and finally the goal g_3.
- $g_1 [] g_2$. Choice operator: The agent can reach the goal g_1 or g_2.
- $g_1 ||| g_2$. Parallel composition operator: The agent must reach the goals g_1 and g_2 without concerning the order in which they are reached.

The article is organized as follows. Section 2 describes the syntax and semantics used to construct goals- specifications. Section 3 describes how an agent can handle the specification, and how it determines if it has reached such specification. Section 4 generalizes a single agent's goals-specification to collective agents' goals-specification and finally, section 5 summarizes the conclusions.

F.F. Ramos et al. (Eds.): ISSADS 2005, LNCS 3563, pp. 472–482, 2005.

2   Goals Specification

This section describes the syntax and semantic of the specification language. We have based the syntax in LOTOS language [5] because it is a specification language having the following principles we are interesting on: Formal definition, Process algebra, Interleaving concurrence and executability. LOTOS has a defined syntax and semantic, and because LOTOS semantic is defined operationally, it is possible to implement this semantic in an interpreter, which for a behavior expression can enumerate the set of possible next actions. This property allows us to implement a function that gives the next goal to try to reach in a specific time in order to accomplish the whole specification. In this context we use goals instead of actions.

The Action Prefix Operator. The action prefix operator, written as a semicolon ;, expresses sequential composition of goals. This operator is used to sequentially order goals. For example, g1; g2 denotes a behavior where goal g1 must be executed before goal g2. If g1 can not be reached, g2 is offered.

Choice Operator. The choice operator [] denotes the choice between two or more alternative behaviors. The choice operator is commutative and associative. So, $g_1 \,[]\, g_2$ is equivalent to $g_2 \,[]\, g_1$ and $g_1 \,[]\, g_2 \,[]\, g_3$ is equivalent to both $(g_1 \,[]\, g_2) \,[]\, g_3$ and $g_1 \,[]\, (g_2 \,[]\, g_3)$.

Interleaving Operator. The interleaving operator ||| is used to express the concept of parallelism between behaviors when no synchronization is required.

$$((g_1; g_2) \,|||\, (g_3; g_4)) \equiv (g_1; (g_2; g_3; g_4 \,[]\, g_3; (g_2; g_4 \,[]\, g_4; g_2)) \,[]\, g_3; (g_4; g_1; g_2 \,[]\, g_1; (g_4; g_2 \,[]\, g_2; g_4))).$$

Enable Operator. The enable operator >> has a similar function as the action prefix operator, which expresses the sequential composition of a goal with a behavior expression. The >> is used to express the sequential composition of two behavior expressions. For example, if A and B are two behavior expressions, A >> B is read, A enables B. A must be reached successfully in order for B to be enabled. This is the only condition under which B is enabled.

Disable Operator. The disable operator [> models an interruption of a behavior expression by another behavior expression. So, A [> B means that, at any point during which the agent is trying to reach A, there is a choice between starting to reach one of the next goals from A or one of the first goals from B. Once a goal from B is chosen, B continues being reached, and the remaining goals of A are no longer possible. If A can not be reached, the first goal from B is offered, while if A is reached, B is not tried to be reached.

Guarded Behavior. A behavior expression can be preceded by a logical expression, called a guard ([exp]→), which enables a behavior expression if its logical value is true. A guard has the following form:

$$[exp] \rightarrow A$$

where *exp* is a logical expression and A is a behavior expression.

Definition 1 Goals-Specifications Set. Let G and E be non-empty sets of goals and logical expressions respectively. Then, the set GS of goals-specification expressions based on G and E is the smallest set of expressions satisfying the following:

- If $g \in G$ then $g \in GS$.
- If $\varphi, \psi \in GS$ then $\varphi \Theta \psi \in GS$, where $\Theta \in \{;, [], \|, >>, [>\}$
- If $\varphi \in GS$ then $[\lambda] \to \varphi \in GS$, where $\lambda \in E$.

If γ is a goals-specification based on G and E, then $\gamma \in GS$.

3 Specification Fulfillment

This section presents how an agent can handle the specification, and how it determines if it has accomplished the specification

Definition 2 Parallel Composition. Let G_A and G_B be rooted trees as they are defined in Graph theory [7, 8]. We define a parallel composition G_{AB} over these trees as a tree which satisfies the following property:

- $\alpha = \alpha_1, \alpha_2, ..., \alpha_n$ and $\beta = \beta_1, \beta_2, ..., \beta_m$ are paths in G_A and G_B respectively from the root to a leaf, if and only if, the set of paths $\Psi_{\alpha\beta}$ belongs to G_{AB}, where $\Psi_{\alpha\beta} = \{\psi \mid \psi = \psi_1, \psi_2, ..., \psi_w, w = n + m, \psi_i \in \alpha \cup \beta$, if $\psi_i = \alpha_j$ then $\neg\exists \psi_k = \alpha_r$ where $i>k$ and $j<r$, or $j=r$ and if $\psi_i = \beta_j$ then $\neg\exists \psi_k = \beta_r$, where $i>k$ and $j<r$, or $j=r \}$

Intuitively, G_{AB} is a tree that contains all the possible paths representing routes in G_A and G_B without concerning the order in which the nodes among G_A and G_B are reached. Figure 1 and 2 show an example. The algorithm shown in figure 3 generates G_{AB}.

Proposition 1. The Parallel Composition Algorithm generates a tree representing the parallel composition over two trees.

Proof. Let $\alpha = \alpha_1, ..., \alpha_n$ and $\beta = \beta_1, ..., \beta_m$ be paths in G_A and G_B respectively from the root to a leaf. Let $\psi = \psi_1, ..., \psi_w$, be a path in $\Psi_{\alpha\beta}$. $\alpha_1 =$ root in G_A and $\beta_1 =$ root in G_B. By lines 1 to 7 in *PCA* (Parallel Composition Algorithm) $\psi_1 = \alpha_1$ or $\psi_1 = \beta_1$. Therefore, path ψ_1 exists in G_{AB}.

Let suppose that $\psi_1, ..., \psi_i$ is a path in G_{AB} ($i \leq w$). In some point in the recursion of *PCA* $G_{AB} = \psi_i$ (current node, lines 40 to 42 in *PCA*).

If $i = w$, as $\psi \in \Psi_{\alpha\beta}$, then $\psi_i = \psi_w$, $\psi_i \in \{\alpha_n, \beta_m\}$ and there exists a ψ_k where $k < i$ and $\psi_k \in \{\alpha_n, \beta_m\} - \{\psi_i\}$, thus, *PCA* ends to such path (lines 8 to 13) and $\psi \in G_{AB}$.

If $i < w$, each element $\omega \in \Omega = \{\omega \mid \omega$ is a ψ_i's child$\} \cup \{\omega \mid \omega$ is a ψ_k's child, where k is the greatest integer which satisfies that ψ_k belongs to the path which ψ_i does not, and $k < i\}$ is added as child to ψ_i (lines 11 to 39). $\psi_1, ..., \psi_i, \omega$ satisfies the parallel composition property for every $\omega \in \Omega$, so, there exists a $\omega' = \psi_{i+1}$. Consequently, $\psi_1, ..., \psi_i, \psi_{i+1} \in G_{AB}$. And $\psi \in G_{AB}$.

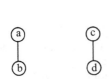

Fig. 1. G_A and G_B trees

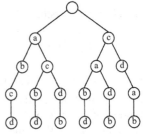

Fig. 2. G_{AB} tree resulting

Parallel_Composition(G_A, G_B, G_{AB})

1   If G_{AB} = empty then
2        $G_{AB} \leftarrow$ new node with empty value; // root
3   add G_A root as child in G_{AB};
4   add G_B root as child in G_{AB};
5   Parallel_Composition (G_A, G_B, first child in G_{AB});
6   Parallel_Composition (G_A, G_B, second child in G_{AB});
7   end if

8   if G_{AB} = leaf node in G_A and first ancestor in G_{AB} belonging to G_B = leaf then
9   return;
10   end if

11   if G_{AB} = leaf node in G_B and first ancestor in G_{AB} belonging to G_A = leaf then
12   return;
13   end if

14   if $G_{AB} = \alpha_i$ where $\alpha_i \in G_A$ then
15   for each child ω of α_i do
16   add ω as child in G_{AB};
17   end for
18       $\theta \leftarrow$ first ancestor in G_{AB} belonging to G_B
19   if $\theta \neq$ leaf then
20   for each child ω of θ do
21   add ω as child in G_{AB};
22   end for
23   else if θ = empty then
24   add G_B root as child in G_{AB};
25   end if
26   end if

27   if $G_{AB} = \beta_i$ where $\beta_i \in G_B$ then
28   for each child ω of β_i do
29   add ω as child in G_{AB};
30   end for
31       $\theta \leftarrow$ first ancestor in G_{AB} belonging to G_A
32   if $\theta \neq$ leaf then
33   for each child ω of θ do
34   add ω as child in G_{AB};
35   end for
36   else if θ = empty then
37   add G_A root as child in G_{AB};
38   end if
39   end if

40   for each child ω of G_{AB} do
41   Parallel_Composition (G_A, G_B, ω);
42   end for
end Parallel_Composition

Fig. 3. Parallel Composition Algorithm

Therefore, if $\alpha = \alpha_1, ..., \alpha_n$ and $\beta = \beta_1, ...,\beta_m$ be paths in G_A and G_B respectively from the root to a leaf, then the set of paths $\Psi_{\alpha\beta}$ belongs to G_{AB}.

Let $\psi_1, ..., \psi_w$, be a path in G_{AB} from the root to a leaf. By lines 1 to 7 in *PCA* we can see that ψ_1 is the root node from G_A or G_B. By lines 11 to 39 in *PCA*, $\psi_i \in \Omega =$ $\{\omega \mid \omega$ is a ψ_{i-1}'s child$\} \cup \{\omega \mid \omega$ is a ψ_k's child, where k is the greatest integer which satisfies that ψ_k belongs to the path which ψ_{i-1} does not, and $k < i\}$ ($1 < i \leq w$). But ψ_i does not break the parallel composition property. *PCA* ended the path in ψ_w, therefore, ψ_w is a leaf. Thus, $\psi_w \in \{\alpha_n, \beta_m\}$ for some leaf α_n and β_m (where n and m are the depth plus one of α_n and β_m respectively) and there exists a ψ_k where $k < w$ and ψ_k $\in \{\alpha_n, \beta_m\} - \{\psi_w\}$, therefore $w = n + m$.

Thus, $\psi_1, ..., \psi_w$ satisfies the parallel composition property. And consequently $\psi_1, ..., \psi_w \in \Psi_{\alpha\beta}$ for some path $\alpha \in G_A$ and for some path $\beta \in G_B$.

Therefore, the Parallel Composition Algorithm generates a tree representing the parallel composition over two trees.

3.1 Goals-Specification Graph

The algorithm shown in figure 4 generates a graph describing the behavior of a goal's specification. Such algorithm generates a rooted tree containing all the possible paths which satisfy the specification. Any path from the root to a leaf satisfies the specification.

A path from the root to a leaf shows an order in which the goals can be reached, so the arc (v_i, v_{i+1}) means that v_i is reached before v_{i+1}. As we defined above, in some expressions the next goal is offered only if the previous one is reached, and in some cases if the previous one can not be reached, the next goal is offered. Therefore, the algorithm labels the arcs with >> symbol where it is necessary to reach a goal in order to some other can be offered. If the arc (v_i, v_{i+1}) is labeled with >>, it means that v_i has to be reached in order to v_{i+1} can be offered. In the same way, the algorithm also labels the arcs with [> symbol where it is present the disable operator.

The algorithm also labels the arc (v_i, v_{i+1}) with the logical expression λ if the goal v_{i+1} is preceded by a guard in the way $[\lambda] \rightarrow v_{i+1}$.

Specification_Graph (behavior_expression)
1   if behavior_expression is a goal without guard then
2   return behavior_expression;
3   end if

4   L_exp = guard in left expression in behavior_expression;
5   L_BExpr ← left expression in behavior_expression;
6   Op ← operator in behavior_expression;
7   R_ex = guard in right expression in behavior_expression;
8   R_BExpr ← right expression in behavior_expression;

9   L_B Expr_Tree ← Specification_Graph (L_BExpr);
10   If (L_exp ≠ empty)
11   r ← new node;
12   add L_BExpr_Tree tree as child in r;
13   set L_exp as label in (r, L_BExpr_Tree root) arc;

Fig. 4. Specification Graph Algorithm

```
14     L_BExpr_Tree ← r;
15   End if

16   R_BExpr_Tree ← Specification_Graph (R_BExpr);
17   If (R_exp ≠ empty)
18      r ← new node;
19      add R_BExpr_Tree tree as child in r;
20      set R_exp as label in (r, R_BExpr_Tree root) arc;
21      R_BExpr_Tree ← r;
22   End if
23   BExpr_Tree ← new node with empty value; // root

24   if Op = ; then
25      BExpr_Tree ← L_BExpr_Tree;
26      for each descendant ω of BExpr_Tree do
27         if ω = leaf then
28            add R_BExpr_Tree tree as child in ω;
29         end if
30      end for
31   else if Op = [ ] then
32      add L_BExpr_Tree tree as child in BExpr_Tree;
33      add R_BExpr_Tree tree as child in BExpr_Tree;
34   else if Op = ||| then
35      Parallel_Composition (L_BExpr_Tree, R_BExpr_Tree, BExpr_Tree);
36   else if Op = >> then
37      BExpr_Tree ← L_BExpr_Tree;
38      for each descendant ω of BExpr_Tree do
39         if ω = leaf then
40            add R_BExpr_Tree tree as child in ω;
41            set >> as label in (ω, R_BExpr_Tree root) arc;
42         end if
43      end for
44   else if Op = [> then
45      r ← new node;
46      add L_BExpr_Tree tree as child in r;
47      BExpr_Tree ← r;
48      for each descendant ω of BExpr_Tree do
49         if ω ≠ leaf then
50            add R_BExpr_Tree tree as child in ω;
51            set [> as label in (ω, R_BExpr_Tree root) arc;
52         end if
53      end for
54   end if
55   return  BExpr_Tree;
   end Specification_Graph
```

Fig. 4. (Continued)

3.2 Example

Imagine a combat game. Two empires compete each other by the land. We want to give a goals specification to a soldier belonging to one of these empires. We have three kinds of agents in these empires: the king, soldiers and miners. Each one of these agents has a set of skills. A soldier is capable to: look for the closest enemy miner agent, look for the closest enemy soldier agent, look for the enemy king, catch the agent it has found, attack an agent and defend from an agent. These skills may be developed using evolutionary algorithms or learning algorithms [9, 10, 11, 12], we do not want to give an action specification telling to the agent how we want it to perform the actions. The agents have its own behavior and we only want to give a detailed specification about what we want it to do instead of how we want it to do.

Figure 5 shows a description example about what an agent has to do; this description shows what we want an agent to do using the natural language. Figure 6 shows an equivalent description using a goals specification as we have defined in this work. Figure 7 shows the specification graph gotten by the specification graph algorithm.

Look for an enemy miner or soldier, catch it and attack it. In the same time, if the king is near, catch it and attack it.

Fig. 5. Description example to a soldier agent

g_1 = *Look for an enemy miner*
g_2 = *Look for an enemy soldier*
g_3 = *catch*
g_4 = *attack*
g_5 = *attack king*
e = *King near*

$$((g_1 \; [] \; g_2) >> g_3 >> g_4) \; ||| \; [e] \rightarrow g_5$$

Fig. 6. Goals specification of figure 5

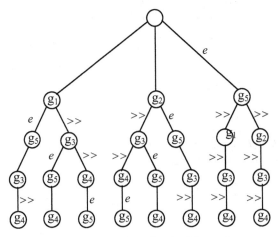

Fig. 7. Specification Graph of figure 6

4   Collective Agents' Goals-Specification

This section generalizes a single agent's goals-specification to collective agents' goals-specification.

Definition 3 Collective-Goals-Specifications Set. Let A, G and E be non-empty sets of agents, goals and logical expressions respectively. Then, the set CGS of collective goals-specification expressions based on A, G and E is the smallest set of expressions satisfying the following:

- If $g \in G$ and $a \in A$ then $(a, g) \in CGS$.
- If $\varphi, \psi \in CGS$ then $\varphi \Theta \psi \in CGS$, where $\Theta \in \{[], |||, >>\}$
- If $\varphi \in CGS$ then $[\lambda] \to \varphi \in CGS$, where $\lambda \in E$.
- If $\varphi, \psi \in CGS$ and $\forall (a_i, g_k), (a_j, g_w) \in \varphi \cup \psi \, a_i = a_j$, then $\varphi \Theta \psi \in CGS$, where $\Theta \in \{;, [>\}$

If Γ is a collective-goals-specification based on A, G and E, then $\Gamma \in CGS$.

4.1 Goals-Specifications Based on Collective-Goals-Specifications

We can specify a collective-goals-specification to give a detailed description about we want a set of agents to do. But in the practice, it is better to have the goals-specification to each agent. So, this section introduces a method to get the corresponding goals-specification to a specific agent taken from the collective-goals-specification. Let assume the goal labels belonging to a collective-goals-specification are all different, so, g_1 and g_2 could be the same goal.

Definition 4 Goals-Specifications to Collective Agents. Let A, G and E be non-empty sets of agents, goals and logical expressions respectively. And let CGS be the set of collective goals-specification expressions based on A, G and E. Let $\Gamma \in CGS$ and $\alpha \in A$. γ is a goals-specification based on Γ to α if:

- $\forall \chi \in G \, (\alpha, \chi) \in \Gamma$ if and only if $(\alpha, \chi) \in \gamma$.
- if $(\beta, \chi) \in \gamma$ then $\beta = \alpha$.
- σ is a sequence of goals reached by all $a \in A$, where α accomplished γ, if and only if σ is a path from the root to a leaf in the Goals-Specification Graph of Γ.

Definition 5 Goals-Specifications to Collective Agents. Let Γ be a collective-goals-specification, T_Γ represents the equivalent binary tree gotten recursively in the following way:

- If $\Gamma = (a, g)$ or $\Gamma = [\lambda] \to (a, g)$, $T_\Gamma = \Gamma$.
- If $\Gamma = [e] \to \varphi$,
  - $T_\Gamma \gets e$
  - add T_φ tree as child in T_Γ.
- Let $\Gamma = \varphi \Theta \psi$ where $\Theta \in \{;, [\,], |||, >>, [>\}$
  - $T_\Gamma \gets \Theta$
  - add T_φ tree as child in T_Γ.
  - add T_ψ tree as child in T_Γ.

Definition 6 $\alpha_{\chi\delta}$. Let A, G and E be non-empty sets of agents, goals and logical expressions respectively. And let CGS be the set of collective goals-specification expressions based on A, G and E. Let $\Gamma \in CGS$, $\alpha \in A$ and $\chi, \delta \in G$. $\alpha_{\chi\delta}$ is the smallest sub-tree of T_Γ satisfying the following:

- $(\alpha,\chi), (\alpha,\delta) \in \alpha_{\chi\delta}$.
- If $(\alpha,\upsilon) \in \alpha_{\chi\delta}$ then $(\alpha,\upsilon) = (\alpha,\chi)$ or $(\alpha,\upsilon) = (\alpha,\delta)$.

Definition 7 Own Specification. Let A, G and E be non-empty sets of agents, goals and logical expressions respectively. And let CGS be the set of collective goals-specification expressions based on A, G and E. Let $\Gamma \in$ CGS and $\alpha \in$ A. Γ is own of α, denoted by $\alpha{:}\Gamma$, if and only if $\forall (a, \chi) \in \Gamma$ a = α. Clearly $\alpha{:}\Gamma$ is a goals-specification to α based on G and E ($\alpha{:}\Gamma \in$ GS based on G and E, see definition 2.1).

Definition 8 Sequence Events. Let A, G and E be non-empty sets of agents, goals and logical expressions respectively. And let CGS be the set of collective goals-specification expressions based on A, G and E. Let $\Gamma \in$ CGS, $\alpha \in$ A, $\chi \in$ G and let E $= E \cup \{\alpha\chi \mid (\alpha, \chi) \in \Gamma\}$. The sequence events related to (α, χ) is the conjunction of the following conditions:

- True if $\neg\exists \; \varphi\Theta\psi \mid (\alpha, \chi) \in \psi$ and $T_{\varphi\Theta\psi}$ is a sub-tree of T_Γ. Where $\Theta \in \{;, [], \|\|, >>,$ [>\}
- $\alpha\delta$ if $(\alpha,\delta) >> (\alpha, \chi)$ is a sub-tree of T_Γ
- True if $\forall \; \varphi\Theta\psi \mid (\alpha, \chi) \in \psi$ and $T_{\varphi\Theta\psi}$ is a sub-tree of T_Γ, $\Theta = \|\|$
- $e \mid (\alpha, \chi) \in \varphi$ and $[e]{\rightarrow}\varphi \in$ is a sub-tree of T_Γ
- ω_1 or ... or ω_n if $\varphi{>>}\psi$ is a sub-tree of T_Γ and $(\alpha, \chi) \in \psi$ and $\neg\exists \; p{>>}q \mid (\alpha, \chi) \in$ q and $d(>>, (\alpha, \chi))$ in $p{>>}q < d(>>, (\alpha, \chi))$ in $\varphi{>>}\psi$, where $d(a, b)$ is the distance from a to b in T_Γ, $\omega_i = \alpha\delta_{i1} \ldots \alpha\delta_{im}$ is a path in φ specification graph, n = leaves number in φ specification graph (number of paths).

Intuitively, the sequence events related to (α, χ) specifies the events that have to hold before the agent α try to reach the goal χ.

Let A, G and E be non-empty sets of agents, goals and logical expressions respectively. And let CGS be the set of collective goals-specification expressions based on A, G and E. Let $\Gamma \in$ CGS and $\alpha \in$ A. The algorithm shown in figure 8 generates a goals-specification γ based on Γ to an agent α.

```
goals-specification( Γ )
1    substitute all μ of T_Γ by an suitable symbol (μ becomes a leaf in T_Γ), where μ is
     the largest sub-tree satisfying α:μ
2    for each φΘψ ∈ Γ where Θ = [ ] do
3        let e be a new event | e ∉ E
4        substitute φΘψ by [e]→φ Θ [¬e]→ψ in Γ
5        E←E ∪ e
6    end for
7    while there exist a α_χδ in T_Γ
8        φ ← [(α,χ) sequence event] → χ
9        ψ ← [(α,δ)sequence event] → δ
10       θ ← α_χδ root // node without children
11       add φ as child in θ
12       add ψ as child in θ
13       let τ be a suitable symbol
14       substitute α_χδ by (α,τ)
15   end while
end goals-specification
```

Fig. 8. Goals-Specification Algorithm

4.2 Example

Let $\Gamma = ((A_1, g_1) >> (A_2, g_2)) \ ||| \ (((A_3, g_3) [ ] (A_4, g_4)) >> ((A_1, g_5) \ ||| \ (A_2, g_6)))$ be a collective-goals-specification based on $A = \{A_1, A_2, A_3, A_4\}$, $G = \{g_1, g_2, g_3, g_4, g_5, g_6\}$ and $E = \varnothing$. The goals-specifications to each agent based on Γ are:

- $[True] \rightarrow (A_1, g_1) \ ||| \ [A_3g_3$ or $A_4g_4] \rightarrow (A_1, g_5)$
- $[A_1g_1] \rightarrow (A_2, g_2) \ ||| \ [A_3g_3$ or $A_4g_4] \rightarrow (A_2, g_6)$
- $[e_1] \rightarrow (A_3, g_3)$
- $[\neg e_1] \rightarrow (A_4, g_4)$

Now it is possible to remove the symbols that become unnecessary in order to make the goals-specification clearer:

- $(g_1 \ ||| \ [A_3g_3$ or $A_4g_4] \rightarrow g_5)$ to agent A_1.
- $([A_1g_1] \rightarrow g_2 \ ||| \ [A_3g_3$ or $A_4g_4] \rightarrow g_6)$ to agent A_2.
- $([e_1] \rightarrow (A_3, g_3))$ to agent A_3.
- $([\neg e_1] \rightarrow (A_4, g_4))$ to agent A_4.

5 Conclusions

We have presented a method to specify agent's goals using process algebras, particularly using LOTOS. This type of specification is used to give a more detailed description about what we want an agent to do instead of how we want it to do.

We showed the necessary algorithms to transform the specifications in a graph (rooted tree) containing all the possible ways an agent has in order to accomplish such specification, and we generalize a single agent's goals-specification to collective agents' goals-specification.

This work is used in a platform to design and run dynamic virtual environments representing virtual scenes, where the user describes attributes and intentions of the virtual characters throughout a natural language. The user (scenarist) generates a description defining the environment and the agent's intentions, and an interpreter generates a goals specification to each involved agent as we have defined above. Then the agents receive such goals specification, and they resolve and send back to the environment a set of primitive actions for the agent to perform.

References

1. Félix Ramos, Fabiel Zúñiga, Hugo I. Piza. *A 3D-Space Platform for Distributed Applications Management*. International Symposium and School on Advanced Distributed Systems 2002 (ISSADS 2002). Guadalajara, Jal., México. November 2002. ISBN 970-27-0358-1
2. H. Iván Piza, Fabiel Zuñiga, Félix R. Ramos. A Platform to Design and Run Dynamic Virtual Environments. To be published in CyberWorlds-2004. Tokyo, Japan.
3. J.F. Groote and M.A. Reniers. Algebraic process verification. In J.A. Bergstra et al., editor, Handbook of process algebra, chapter 17. Elsevier, 2001.
4. Joost-Pieter Katoen, Rom Langerak and Diego Latella. Modelling Systems by Probabilistic Process Algebra: An Event Structures Approach. Department of Computer Science, University of Twente. Proceedings of the IFIP TC6/WG6.1 Sixth International Conference on Formal Description Techniques, VI, p.253-268, October 26-29, 1993.

5. Logrippo, L. and Haj-Hussein. *An Introduction to LOTOS: Learning by Examples*. Computer Networks and ISDN Systems, 23(5) pp 325- 342, 1992.
6. L. Drayton, A. Chetwynd, G. Blair. An introduction to LOTOS through a worked example. Distributed Multimedia Research Group, School of Engineering, Computing and Mathematical Sciences, Lancaster University, Bailrigg, Lancaster LA1 4YR.
7. Diestel, Reinhard. Graph Theory. Series: Graduate Texts in Mathematics , Vol. 173. 2nd ed., 2000, XIV, 313 p. 122 illus., Softcover. ISBN: 0-387-98976-5.
8. Journal of Graph Theory. Copyright © 2004 Wiley Periodicals, Inc., A Wiley Company. Volumes 12 45-47. Online ISSN: 1097-0118. Print ISSN: 0364-9024.
9. Thomas Bäck, Frank Hoffmeister, Hans-Paul Schwefel. "A Survey of Evolution Strategies". University of Dortmund. Department of Computer Science XI. Germany.
10. T Bäck, D. Fogel and Z. Michalewicz. "Handbook of Evolutionary Computation". Oxford University Press, New York, February 1997
11. J. H. Holland. "Adaptation in Natural and Artificial Systems". University of Michigan Press, Ann Arbor, 1975.
12. Xin Yao. A review of Evolutionary Artificial. Neural Networks. Commonwealth Scientific and Industrial Research Organisation Division of Building, Construction and Engineering. Australia

A New Approach for Offer Evaluation in Multi-agent System Negotiation Based in Evidential Paraconsistent Logic

Fabiano M. Hasegawa, Bráulio C. Ávila, and Marcos A.H. Shmeil

Pontifical Catholic University of Paraná – PUCPR, Brazil
{fmitsuo,avila,shm}@ppgia.pucpr.br

Abstract. This paper presents a *Paraconsistent Approach* based on a heuristic of multi-valued decrement list followed by formalization into Evidential Paraconsistent Logic to evaluate offers in a negotiation session. The mission of an organization stands for its goals and also leads corrections likely to occur in the posture adopted by the organization before the society. In order to fulfill the goals of the organization, this one needs to interact with other components of the society. Within an organization each individual responsible for the sale and purchase of either commodities or services detains knowledge concerning possible values of the criteria used to represent a determined commodity or service which may be either offered or accepted in a negotiation. So, an offer may be seen as an inconsistency caused by the previous individual knowledge of the negotiator and the incoming offer. When compared to the *Utility Value Approach*, the Paraconsistent one converges toward the negotiation ending with fewer interactions.

Keywords: Multi-agent Systems, Negotiation, Offer Evaluation, Paraconsistent Logic.

1 Introduction

Within an organization, each individual responsible for the sale and purchase of commodities or services detains knowledge concerning possible values of the criteria used to represent a determined commodity or service which may be either offered or accepted in a negotiation. This knowledge is part of the organizational knowledge that stands for the "truth" about the world, the world from the organization's point of view. In a negotiation, an offer may cause a conflict with the previous individual knowledge of the negotiator. This conflict may be seen as an intra-case inconsistency [1]. In the intra-case inconsistency the case which is stored in a base causes contradiction with the domain previous knowledge.

This work describes a new approach for offer evaluation based on a multi-valued decrement list heuristic followed by formalization into Evidential Paraconsistent Logic (*EPL*) [2, 3] to evaluate offers in a negotiation. The *EPL* is used to represent the rules and offers that describe how consistent the offer is according to the individual knowledge of the negotiator. If the offer is consistent

F.F. Ramos et al. (Eds.): ISSADS 2005, LNCS 3563, pp. 483–494, 2005.

and is "true" for the negotiator, it is then accepted. The ARTOR – ARTificial ORganizations [4] – is a Multi-Agent System (*MAS*) which simulates a society of organizations – each organization owns agents responsible for the operations of purchasing and selling either commodities or services. Within this *MAS* a new approach is undertaken by the supply executor agent and by the selection executor agent which are, respectively, responsible for the operations of purchase and sale.

Section 2 presents how a negotiation using the *Utility Value Approach* is achieved in ARTOR. In section 3 the *Paraconsistent Approach* is detailed and explained. Section 4 presents the results of tests as well as the comparison between the *Paraconsistent Approach* and the *Utility Value Approach*. Finally, in section 5 some conclusions are inferred.

2   Negotiation in ARTOR

The mission of an organization [5] stands for its goals and also leads corrections likely to occur in the posture adopted by the organization before the society. In order to fulfill the goals of the organization and achieved the mission, this one needs to interact with other components of the society [6, 7]. The negotiation process is a decision making process, which helps the agents to satisfy their goals.

It is possible to simulate a society of artificial organizations through ARTOR, it provides means to simulate the inner and outer environment of an organization [4]. Each organization is composed of three classes of agents:

- *cover agent*: which stands for the organization;
- *administrator agent*: responsible for planning and coordination;
- *executor agent*: responsible for operational tasks.

Another important component of the society is the *News_Stand*, a public blackboard [8] known by every organization. The *News_Stand* is used for news exchanging – about business – among organizations.

In a negotiation within ARTOR a conflict occur when the distance calculated in the evaluation phase – see Subsection 2.1 – is either negative or positive, giving rise to the positive and negative conflict types [9].

2.1   Using the Utility Value Approach to Evaluate an Offer

In ARTOR, the commodity or service that an organization is willing to sell or buy is represented by a Criteria List (*CL*) [4]. The Criteria List é composed of Selection Criterion (*SC*) which determines the dimensions used to describe and assess the commodity or service. The Criteria List can be seen as a list of constraints which the supply or consumer organization must follow in order to reach an agreement. The Criteria List is defined by[1]:

$$CL_{product1}(SC_1, SC_2, ..., SC_n)$$

---

[1] This representation of the *CL* was modified to bear continuous values

each SC_i is the tuple $SC_i(Id_i, Vd_i, Tp_i, Va_i, Pr_i, Sm_i)$, where:

- Id_i: is the identification of the Selection Criterion;
- Vd_i: is the default value that satisfies the executor agent;
- Tp_i: contains information about the type of value. Represented by $(Tv_i : TUn_i : Un_i)$, where:
  - Tv_i: indicates the attribute domain which belongs to the set $\{discrete, continuous\}$;
  - TUn_i: type of value which may be $\{unit, real, date\}$;
  - Un_i: is the value of a unit. For instance, 30 for a unit of the date type.
- Va_i: is represented by the ordered pair (Vac_i, Fed_i), where:
  - Vac_i: is a list of valid values (constraints) for SC_i if $Tv_i = discrete$. If $Tv_i = continuous$ then Va_i will be the ordered pair (Min, Max), where Min is the minimum value for the SC_i and Max maximum one;
  - $Fed_i \in \{left, right, none\}$, where:
    * $left$: the values that better satisfy are on the left of Vd_i;
    * $right$: the values that better satisfy are on the right of Vd_i;
    * $none$: any value satisfy.
- Pr_i: utility of the SC_i for organization;
- Sm_i: stands for the status of the Selection Criterion according to the instantiation of the value, where:
  - grounded: the first offer using the SC_i will be made with a value;
  - free: the first bid using the SC_i will be made without a value.

The agents responsible for the negotiation uses the Possibility Space (PS) – defined from the Criteria List – which contains all the possible values for each Selection Criterion and it is used to evaluate and to create offers. Each Selection Criterion has a weight according to its utility[2] for the organization – a type of SC may be more important than other. The utility, in Economics, is an analytical concept which represents a subjective pleasure, the advantage or the satisfaction derived from the consumption of commodities, and explains how consumers divide their limited resources among the commodities consumed [10].

The offer utility value is used to assess an offer and according to the result it will be either accepted or not. The offer utility value is defined by the sum of all utility values of the dimension instances of the Criteria List.

$$offer\_utility = \sum_{i=0}^{j} instance\_utility_i.$$

The instance utility value is obtained as follows:

$$instance\_utility = (Pr_i \times relative\_instance\_value)$$

The relative instance value for a Selection Criterion is the relative position of the value in the domain of values Vac_i (Values Constraints) of the SC_i –

---

[2] In this work, the minimum utility is 1 and the maximum one is 10 for both approaches

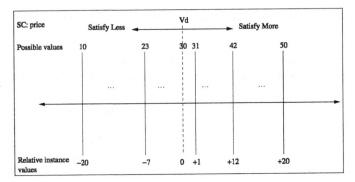

Fig. 1. Relative instance value example for *SC* price

see Figure 1. If the relative instance value is positioned on the side that better satisfies – the side indicated by Fed_i (Favorable Evolution Direction) in relation to the value that satisfies Vd_i (default value) – the relative value will be positive, otherwise it will be negative. The relative instance value of a discrete value will be 1 if it exists in the domain of the values Vac_i, otherwise the relative value will be −1. For example:

$$..., SC(price, 30, cont : real : 1, [[10, 50], right], 10, ground), ...$$

$$offer(..., [price, 42], ...)$$

$$instance\_utility = (10 \times 12) = 220$$

3   Offer Evaluation Through the Paraconsistent Approach

In a computer system, the paraconsistent reasoning and representation could be achieved using the ParaLog_e. The ParaLog_e [11, 12] is an interpreter of Evidential Paraconsistent Logic *EPL* based on *Annotated Paraconsistent Logic* [2, 3, 13]. The *EPL* is infinitely valued and its truth values belong to the lattice $\tau = \langle |\tau|, \leq \rangle$, where:

$$|\tau| = \{\mu 1 \in \Re | 0 \leq x \leq 1\} \times \{\mu 2 \in \Re | 0 \leq x \leq 1\}.$$

In the *EPL* a proposition p owns two annotated values $p : [\mu 1, \mu 2]$. The annotated value $\mu 1$ is the favorable evidence to p and the value $\mu 2$ is the contrary evidence to p.

It is possible to obtain from the $[\mu 1, \mu 2]$ the Contradiction Degree (*CtD*) and the Certainty Degree (*CD*) in which the proposition lies [2]. The *CtD* stands for the distance between the inconsistent ($\top$) and the undetermined ($\bot$) truth values. The *CD* stands for the distance between the true (v) and the false (f) truth values.

In the paraconsistent approach the Criteria List is a little different[3] from the Criteria List presented in the previous session. Now each SC_i is the tuple $SC_i(Id_i, Tp_i, Va_i, Pr_i, Sm_i)$, where:

- Id_i: is the identification of the Selection Criterion;
- Tp_i: contains information about the type of value. Represented by $(Tv_i : TUn_i : Un_i)$, where:
  - Tv_i: indicates the domain of the value that belongs to the set $\{discrete, continuos\}$;
  - TUn_i: is the type of value that may be $\{unit, real, date\}$;
  - Un_i: is the value of a unit. For instance 30 for a unit of the date type.
- Va_i: if $Tv_i = discrete$ then Va_i will contain a list of valid values for the SC_i. If $Tv_i = continuous$ then Va_i will be the ordered pair (S_less, S_more), where S_less is the value that less satisfies and S_more is the value that more satisfies;
- Pr_i: utility of the SC_i;
- Sm_i: stands for the status of the Selection Criterion according to the instance value, where:
  - *grounded*: the first bid using the SC_i will be made with a value;
  - *free*: the first bid using the SC_i will be made without a value.

3.1 Paraconsistent Approach Architecture

The offer evaluation by using the *Paraconsistent Approach* begins when an offer is received by the agent executing the selection. First the offer is translated into annotated facts and annotated evaluation rules that use the representation formalism of the *EPL* – Subsection 3.2. So it is obtained as output a text file that contains the facts that represent the offer and the rules of evaluation – Figure 2. The text file is loaded in the ParaLog_e and a query of the rules is made. The outcome of this query is the favorable evidence ($\mu 1$) and the contrary evidence ($\mu 2$) in relation to the offer. The CD and the CtD are obtained from $[\mu 1, \mu 2]$ and they are converted into discrete values by the algorithm Para-Analyzer – Subsection 3.3 – into resulting logical status. The resulting logical status is used to assess the offer. If the resulting logical status is t and the CD is equal or greater than 0.6 then the offer is accepted. Otherwise, a decrement value is chosen according to the resulting logical status and used in the creation of a counter-offer – Figure 3.

3.2 Translating Offers to the EPL Representation Formalism

In ARTOR, an offer contained in a message of negotiation is a list composed of ordered pair $(SC_I D, SC_V alue)$. For instance:

```
[[color, black], [price, 5], [payment_term, 0], [quantity, 80]]
```

---

[3] Due to the use of the *EPL* it is not necessary to use a reference value that indicates the satisfaction point to assess a Selection Criterion. The evidential values associated to the Selection Criterion indicate the negotiator's satisfaction in relation to the instance value of this Selection Criterion

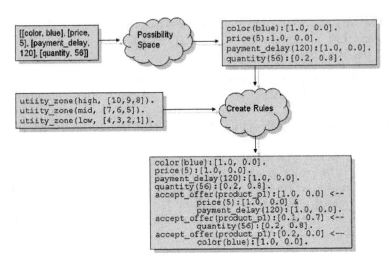

Fig. 2. Translating offers and creating evaluation rules

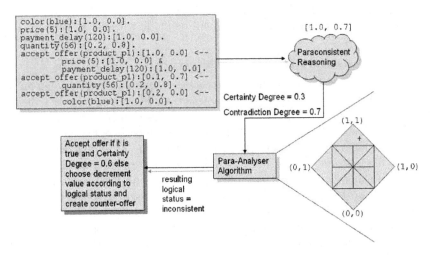

Fig. 3. Evaluating an offer

The *paraconsistent_mapping* module is responsible for translating the Selection Criteria of an offer into annotated facts. It is also responsible for creating the annotated rules that will be used to evaluate the offer. The value of a Selection Criterion is mapped into evidential values $[\mu1, \mu2]$ according to the organization's Possibility Space and the restrictions. The restrictions indicate, for a determined Selection Criterion, which values are not accepted.

If the Selection Criterion belongs to a discrete domain then the Selection Criterion instance value is mapped into evidential values as follows:

- $SC\_ID(Value) : [1,0]$ if $Value \in Va$;
- $SC\_ID(Value) : [0,0]$ if $Value \notin Va$;
- $SC\_ID(Value) : [0,1]$ if the value fits a restriction for the Selection Criterion.

If the Selection Criterion belongs to the continuous domain then the Selection Criterion instance value is mapped into evidential values as follows:

- $SC\_ID(Value) : [\mu1, \mu2]$ is equal to e, where $e \in E$ ($e = [\mu1, \mu2]$) according to the index k obtained by the function $P(x)$;
- $SC\_ID(Value) : [1,0]$ if $S\_less \leq S\_more$ and $Value > S\_less$ and $Value > S\_more$;
- $SC\_ID(Value) : [0,1]$ if $S\_less \leq S\_more$ and $Value < S\_less$ and $Value < S\_more$;
- $SC\_ID(Value) : [1,0]$ if $S\_less > S\_more$ and $Value < S\_less$ and $Value < S\_more$;
- $SC\_ID(Value) : [0,1]$ if $S\_less > S\_more$ and $Value > S\_less$ and $Value > S\_more$;
- $SC\_ID(Value) : [0,1]$ if the value fits a restriction for the Selection Criterion.

The function $P(x)$ returns the index k which is associated to the element e ($e = [\mu1, \mu2]$) – belonging to the set E – which corresponds to the evidential values, of the instance value, in relation to the contained in the individual knowledge base of the negotiator agent. The function $P(x)$ is defined by:

- $P(x) = -1$ if $x < S\_less$;
- $P(x) = 0$ if $x = S\_less$;
- $P(x) = \frac{10}{\frac{(S\_more - S\_less)}{Vd}} \times \frac{(Value\_SC - S\_less)}{Vd}$

  if:
  - $S\_less \leq x \leq S\_more$;
  - $S\_less \geq x \geq S\_more$.
- $P(x) = 10$ if $x \geq S\_more$.

The evidential values contained in the set E were created through an idiosyncratic heuristic. The set E used in this work corresponds to $E = \{-1 - 0 : 1, 0 - 0 : 0, 1 - 0.1 : 0.0, 2 - 0.2 : 0.8, 3 - 0.3 : 0.7, 4 - 0.4 : 0.6, 5 - 0.5 : 0.5, 6 - 0.6 : 0.4, 7 - 0.7 : 0.3, 8 - 0.8 : 0.2, 9 - 0.9 : 0.1, 10 - 1 : 0\}$.

The offer evaluation in the *Paraconsistent Approach* uses a set of rules which are composed of the facts that represent the Selection Criteria of an offer. These rules correspond to the beliefs of the negotiatior about how much an offer worth for the organization. A rule represented on the formalism of the *EPL* also owns associated evidential values. The facts are grouped in the rules according to their utility for the organization. Three zones of utility that group the facts were defined, and are defined by the *utility_zone/2* predicate:

```
utility_zone(high, [10, 9, 8]).
utility_zone(mid, [7, 6, 5]).
utility_zone(low, [4, 3, 2, 1]).
```

Thus, the respect for the utility of the facts is guaranteed. For instance, a fact that represents a Selection Criterion with low utility and fulfills perfectly what the organizations seeks, will not have much influence on the offer acceptance.

After grouping of the facts in the rules, the evidential values of the rules are obtained in a similar manner to the one used to find the evidential values of the facts. The *rule_evidences*/2 predicate represents all possible combinations of evidential values that may be used in the rules:

```
rule_evidences(Utl, L).
```

There are ten *rule_evidences*/2 predicates and each one corresponds to a utility (*Utl*) associated to a set L, which contains the evidential values[4] to be mapped into a rule. The set L, used for the mapping of a determined rule, will be chosen according to the Selection Criterion of bigger utility. Because, the Selection Criterion of bigger utility dominates the other Selection Criteria which compose the rule.

Once the set L – associated to a utility – was chosen, the rule will take the evidential values indicated by the element l ($l = [\rho 1, \rho 2]$) of the set L. The element l is found through the index j ($0 \leq i \leq 10$) through the function $R(x)$:

$$R(x) = \frac{10}{N} \times (\sum_{i=0}^{n} Evl_i)$$

In $R(x)$, N indicates the quantity of facts the rule owns, and Evl_i is the favorable evidence of each fact belonging to this rule.

The output of the *paraconsistent_mapping* module is a temporary text file which contains the Selection Criteria of an offer and the respective evaluation rules.

3.3   Evaluating an Offer Through the Para-analyzer Algorithm

The Para-analyzer algorithm is responsible for converting the Contradiction Degree (*Ctd*) and Certainty Degree (*CD*) gotten through the evaluation rules – see Section 3 – and the output is a logical status. This is achieved interpolating them in the lattice and the convergence point is the resulting logical status. The resulting logical status is defined in the lattice. It is possible to define a lattice with more logical statuses than the basic set – $| \tau |= \{\top, t, f, \bot\}$ – presented in Section 3. The more logical statuses the greater the precision in the analysis of the *CtD* and of the *CD*. This work uses a lattice with 12 logical statuses[5] – Figure 4.

The sensibility of extreme values may be regulated by using the control limits. There are four limit values:

---

[4] The values of the evidential values contained in the set L were also created from a idiosyncratic heuristic

[5] Where: $\top$: inconsistent; t: truth; f: false; $\bot$: indeterminate; $\top \rightarrow t$: inconsistent toward truth; $At \rightarrow \top$: almost truth toward inconsistent; and so on

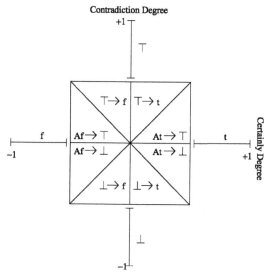

Fig. 4. Lattice with 12 logical status represented in the *CtD* and *CD* graphic

- *Sccv*: *Superior Certainly Control Value* limits the *CD* next to the truth;
- *Iccv*: *Inferior Certainly Control Value* limits the *CD* next to the false;
- *Sctcv*: *Superior Contradiction Control Value* limits the *CtD* next to the inconsistent;
- *Ictcv*: *Inferior Contradiction Control Value* limits the *CtD* next to the indeterminate;

According to tests, the increase of the *Sccv* corresponds to an increase of the minimum utility so that the organization accepts the offer. The increase of the *Iccv* corresponds to a decrement in the relaxation when the organization creates an offer or counter-offer. In this work the value used for the *Sccv* is 0.6, and for the other superior and inferior limits 0.5 and −0.5, respectively. Each resulting logical status may be used to generate either simple or complex actions in the agent. In this work the resulting logical status determines the decrement value which will be used to generate a new offer or counter-offer. The closer a resulting logical status of an offer is to the state *t* the smaller the decrement to be used in the counter-offer will be.

4   Tests and Results

In this scenario there are three organizations: one Consummer Organization (*CO*) which uses both approaches and two Supply Organization (*SO*). The Supply Organization that uses the *Utility Value Approach* is named Utility Supply Organization (*USO*) and the one that uses the *Paraconsistent Approach* is named Paraconsistent Supply Organization (*PSO*).

The Possibility Space values used in tests are the same in both approaches. The *CO* commodity specifications is:

```
[size={M, L} priority 1,
 model={sport, regular} priority 1,
 color={blue, black} priority 1,
 price={5, 30} priority 10,
 payment period={120, 0} priority 7,
 quantity={80, 50} priority 4]
```

The *SO's* commodity specification is:

```
[size={S, M} priority 4,
 model={sport, regular} priority 4,
 color={blue, black} priority 4,
 price={40, 5} priority 5,
 payment period={0, 120} priority 5,
 quantity={80, 50} priority 10]
```

In the continous Selection Criteria the first value is the maximum satisfaction value and the second value is the minimum satisfaction value. According to the strategy used, the initial offer made by the *CO* is:

```
[[size, M], [model, sport], [color, blue],
 [price, 5], [payment period, 120], [quantity, 80]]
```

The negotiation session was limited to a number of 50 interactions. If at the end of a session a *SO* does not make an offer that the *CO* accepts, then the negotiation is ended without winners. In the Tables 1, 2 and 3 the accepted offer has the following syntax: [size, model, color, price, payment period, quantity].

Table 1. Result of a negotiation between the *CO* using both approaches and the *SO* using the *Utility Value Approach*

CO DV	USO DV	Interactions	Utility/CD	Accepted Offer
15	15	28	-27	[m, sport, blue, 10, 120, 56]
4-20	15	6	0.6	[m, sport, blue, 10, 120, 56]

According to tests, where the *CO* uses both approaches, the decrement value (*DV*) that achieve less interactions for the *USO* (organization which uses the *Utility Value Approach*) is 15 – Table 1. The range of values that achieve less interactions for the *PSO* (organization which uses the *Paraconsistent Approach*) is $\{4, 8, 12, 16, 20\}$ – Table 2. These decrement values are used in the tests in order to compare the approaches.

In Table 3 we try to compare the results of a negotiation session. At the first line the *CO* uses the *Utility Value Approach* with decrement value set to 15, the

Table 2. Result of a negotiation between the *CO* using both approaches and the *SO* using the *Paraconsistent Approach*

CO DV	PSO DV	Interactions	Utility/CD	Accepted Offer
15	4-20	6	53	[m, sport, black, 5, 120, 64]
4-20	4-20	5	0.8	[m, sport, black, 8, 120, 64]

Table 3. Result of a negotiation between the *CO* using both approaches, the *PSO* and the *USO*

CO DV	PSO DV	USO	Interactions	Winner	Utility/CD	Accepted Offer
15	4-20	15	6	PSO	42	[m, regular, black, 5, 120, 64]
4-20	4-20	15	5	PSO	0.8	[m, sport, black, 8, 120, 64]

PSO uses the decrement values set to $4 - 20$ and the *USO* uses the decrement value set to 15. The *PSO* reach an agreement with the *CO* in first place with 6 interactions. In the second negotiation session the *CO* uses the *Paraconsistent Approach* and the decrement values set to $4 - 20$. The *PSO* and *USO* uses the same decrement values as the ones used in the first test. The winner of the second negotiation session was the *PSO* with 5 interactions. In the tests carried out one could observe that the *Paraconsistent Approach* obtained a good result in the accepted offer when compared along with the *PSO* and *CO PS's* – see Table 3.

5   Conclusions

The *Paraconsistent Approach* converges toward the end of a negotiation with fewer interactions when compared to the *Utility Value Approach* – see Tables 1, 2 and 3.

The gain in the approach is due to the use of a list of decrement values instead of a set one. The *EPL* allows that the list of decrements to be used in a suitable manner, according to a logical interpretation. The *EPL* provides an interpretation which is closer to the one used by the human beings when they are trying to get more confidence to their beliefs.

The results obtained in this work may be improved if different decrement values and evidential values are used. The time of an offer evaluation using the *Paraconsistent Approach* is 654 milliseconds and the average time of an offer evaluation using the *Utility Value Approach* is 2 milliseconds. The evaluation time for the *Paraconsistent Approach* could decrease if the paraconsistent reasoning was implemented on the agent instead of using an external interpreter like Para-Log_e. The computer used in tests has the following specification and softwares: CPU AMD Thunderbird 1.4 Ghz, 256Mb RAM, Video Card GeForce 2 mx440 AGP 64Mb, HDD Samsung 20Gb 5200RPM, Conectiva Linux 9, SWI-Prolog 5.2.4 and ParaLog_e.

References

1. Racine, K., Yang, Q.: On the consistency management of large case bases: the case for validation. In: Verification and Validation Workshop 1996. (1996)
2. da Costa, N.C.A., e.a.: Lógica Paraconsistente Aplicada (Applied Paraconsistent Logic). Atlas, São Paulo (1999)
3. Subrahmanian, V.S.: Towards a theory of evidential reasoning in logic programming. In: Logic Colloquium '87, Spain, The European Summer Meeting of the Association for Symbolic Logic (1987)
4. Shmeil, M.A.H.: Sistemas Multiagente na Modelação da Estrutura e Relações de Contratação de Organizações (Multi-Agent System Applied in Modelling Structures and Relations to Contract Organizations). PhD thesis, Faculdade de Engenharia da Universidade do Porto, Porto (1999)
5. Drucker, P.F.: Introdução à Administração (Introduction to Administration). Pioneira, São Paulo (1998)
6. Zlotkin, G., Rosenschein, J.S.: Negotiation and task sharing among autonomous agents in cooperative domains. In Sridharan, N.S., ed.: Proceedings of the Eleventh International Joint Conference on Artificial Intelligence, San Mateo, CA, Morgan Kaufmann (1989) 912–917
7. Rosenschein, J.S., Zlotkin, G.: Rules of Encounter: Designing Conventions for Automated Negotiation among Computers. MIT Press, Cambridge (1994)
8. Engelmore, R., Morgan, T.: Blackboard Systems. Addison - Wesley Publishing Company (1998)
9. Oliveira, e.: Negotiation and conflict resolution within a community of cooperative agents. In: Proceedings of The First International Symposium on Autonomous Decentralized Systems, Kawasaki, Japan (1993)
10. Samuelson, P.A., Nordhaus, W.D.: Economia (Economy). McGraw-Hill de Portugal Lda, Portugal (1990)
11. da Costa, N.C.A., Prado, J.P.A., Abe, J.M., Ávila, B.C., Rillo, M.: Paralog: Um prolog paraconsistente baseado em lógica anotada (paralog: A paraconsistent prolog based in annotated logic). In: Coleção Documentos. Number 18 in Série: Lógica e Teoria da Ciência. Instituto de Estudos Avançados, Universidade de São Paulo (1995)
12. Ávila, B., Abe, J., Prado, J.: Paralog_e: A paraconsistent evidential logic programming language. In: XVII International Conference of the Chilean Computer Science Society, Chile, IEEE Computer Science Society Press (1997)
13. Blair, H.A., Subrahmanian, V.S.: Paraconsistent foundations for logic programming. Journal of Non-Classical Logic 5 (1988) 45–73

A Voice-Enabled Assistant in a Multi-agent System for e-Government Services

Emerson Cabrera Paraiso[1,2] and Jean-Paul A. Barthès[1]

[1] Université de Technologie de Compiègne, Laboratoire Heudiasyc,
BP 20.529, Compiègne, France
{eparaiso,barthes}@hds.utc.fr
[2] Pontifícia Universidade Católica do Paraná, Computer Science Department,
CEP: 80.215-901, Curitiba, Paraná, Brazil

Abstract. This paper describes the design of a voice-enabled Personal Assistant to support users (civil servants) advising citizens in an e-Government multi-agent system. We present the assistant intelligent interface architecture, emphasizing the role of ontologies to knowledge handling and how the natural language dialogue is conducted. We also present a system overview, where agents are encapsulated as WEB Services. The main goal of this approach is to offer a system capable of performing tasks through an intuitive interface, allowing experienced and less experienced users to interact with it in an easy and comfortable way.

1 Introduction

In the past few years many countries have undertaken ambitious programs to introduce e-Government. Currently, public services are made available through complex workflows, which imply an interaction and collaboration among different organizations. E-Government strategies are a means to increase efficiency, effectiveness, transparency and citizen satisfaction, all essential pillars of a public administration mission. In this context, Terregov [1] is a European project focusing on the needs for flexible and interoperable tools to support e-Government services, using emerging e-Government interoperable frameworks. The project integrates the dimensions of technological R&D, involves pilot applications and socio-economic research in order to offer a European reference for the deployment of interoperable e-Government services in local governments. In this paper, we present a voice-enabled Personal Assistant that we are testing in the context of Terregov to support users (civil servants) giving information to citizens. The Personal Assistant (PA) has a speech-enabled interface allowing users to interact in English in order to control it, or to ask it to perform tasks ranging from listing conditions to receive a specific allowance to the indication of the nearest social care service. In our approach, tasks are performed by service agents that belong to a multi-agent system. The main goal of this approach is to offer a system capable of performing tasks with an intuitive interface, allowing experienced and less experienced users to interact with it in an easy and comfortable way. The agent-based approach is very appropriate for this kind of project and is also used at SOCEVO project [2]. The SOCEVO project aims at developing an agent-based service-oriented infrastructure to support construction and management of new collaborative environments for virtual organizations. However, in our system, a special attention is given to user support and interaction.

F.F. Ramos et al. (Eds.): ISSADS 2005, LNCS 3563, pp. 495–503, 2005.
© Springer-Verlag Berlin Heidelberg 2005

The rest of the paper is organized as follows. First, we describe our intelligent speech interface and how it works, highlighting the role of ontologies for handling knowledge. Then, we present how the Personal Assistant works in the context of a multi-agent system (MAS). Finally, we offer a conclusion and indicate some perspectives.

2   An Ontology-Based Speech Interface for Personal Assistants

In order to understand our approach, presented in the next section, we are going to briefly present the Personal Assistant we are working with and list some assumptions we made.

2.1   The Personal Assistant

Personal assistants are agents that help humans to do their daily work. The main goal of such an agent is to reduce the user's cognitive overload. They are used to interface a user to a multi-agent system. There are many types of agent models used in multi-agent systems. Among them, we selected cognitive agents. The main advantage of cognitive agents is the possibility of designing intelligent behaviors by specifying a set of skills. In addition, such agents run independently of any particular task to solve. Our Personal Assistant agent is built around three main blocks: the user interface, an *Assistancy* module, mainly responsible for controlling the dialogue, and a fixed body, called the Agent Kernel (further information is given in [3]). In general, the Personal Assistant belongs to a community of agents (artificial and human agents) totally independent but belonging to a cluster. Often, there are two types of artificial agents: Service Agents that provide a particular type of service corresponding to specific skills, and Personal Assistants. In that case the Personal Assistant is in charge of all exchanges of information among participants (human agents).

For the design of our speech interface we made some assumptions related to the Personal Assistant and its operation [4]:

- the Personal Assistant works concurrently with all the user's activities;
- the Personal Assistant may ask questions or start a dialogue if a previous user command cannot be executed, was misunderstood, or if the agent needs additional information to solve a problem;
- the Personal Assistant may alert the user when an event has occurred (e.g., incoming electronic message, or incoming response to a search request).
- Some assumptions concern the interaction:
- the nature of the application leads us to a master-slave relationship where the user commands his Personal Assistant;
- the user makes statements that may be questions or declarative sentences;
- the user may change the context of the conversation after a few utterances, introducing a break in the chain of discourse;
- emotion and affective states are considered less important since we are working with daily professional activities.

To increase the quality of assistance that a Personal Assistant may offer, we are developing vocal conversational interfaces. Conversational interfaces as defined by

Kölzer [5], let users state what they want in their own terms, just as they would do speaking to another person. Of course, the interaction is more complex, but the complexity is handled by the system. Although this approach does not fit all situations, the combined use of Personal Assistants and conversational interfaces is more suitable in applications where:

a) the domain is limited and well defined, as for instance, knowledge management projects or leaning environments;
b) user's actions are complex and require previous knowledge of the domain;
c) the user needs to be guided to execute a task;
d) a traditional graphical user interface may be too cumbersome, due to several menu and sub-menus options, dialogue boxes and so on;
e) the user needs to memorize past actions or navigation steps;
f) a display is not available or the user has her hands busy.

2.2 The Speech Interface Architecture

The global architecture is shown Fig. 1. It has three parts: (i) graphical and speech user interface (GSUI) modules; (ii) linguistic modules; and (iii) agency modules.

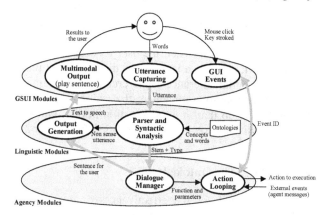

Fig. 1. Interface diagram

GSUI modules produce outputs or collect the user's inputs, like capturing voice and handling GUI events. Linguistic modules are responsible for lexical and syntactical analysis and context verification. Agency modules are directly connected to the agent kernel, which can "intelligently" manage the dialogue and the interface with the help of ontologies. The architecture is detailed in the following paragraphs.

GSUI Modules. They are modules responsible for capturing user utterances (whenever the user says something). An utterance is defined by Kemble as any stream of speech between two periods of silence [6]. It can be a single word, or contains several words (a phrase or a sentence). Utterances are captured using a commercial automatic speech recognition engine that returns the recognized result for each word. The *Utterance Capturing* module concatenates all the words forming an utterance. A process running independently analyzes each utterance.

Linguistic Modules. Like in most dialogue systems, we process each utterance sequentially. The process of interpreting an utterance is done in two steps: (i) parsing and syntactic analysis; and (ii) ontology application. The results are sent to the dialogue manager continuously, or back to the user when they do not make sense.

The parsing algorithm works bottom-up. It replaces each utterance stem with its syntactic category (verb, noun, adverb, etc.) with the help of a lexicon file and a set of grammar rules. We limited the space of dialogue utterances to Directives Speech Act classes – inform, request, or answer – since they define the type of expected utterances in a master-slave relationship (see [7] for further details). In our application, a typical utterance could be: *"I need a list of all conditions to receive an RMI[1]."* According to our taxonomy this is an order utterance and can be processed by the grammar rules. If a sentence is not well formed, according to the grammatical structure, or if it is out of the domain, then it is classified as a nonsensical utterance. In this case, the user is invited to reformulate his sentence. The occurrence of nonsensical utterances is rare, since our system tries to act with minimal information, but nevertheless may occur.

Agency Modules. Agency modules are responsible for controlling the dialogue and the assistance. The mixed-initiative and task-oriented dialogue mechanism is coordinated by *Dialogue Manager* module. It is capable of choosing an appropriate dialogue model at the beginning session. In our case, a dialogue model contains a list of possible interactions to follow to accomplish a given action. Each dialogue session is conducted as a task with sub-tasks. When the user requests an action, the *Dialogue Manager* tries to execute it, creating a task that is dispatched by the *Action Looping* module. However, if the initial utterance lacks crucial information, e.g., an action parameter, it initiates sub-tasks to complement the action list, asking additional information from the user. To do that, it uses an action library. Once the action list is complete, the Personal Assistant executes it with support from other agents.

2.3 Knowledge Handling: The Ontologies

Knowledge handling is crucial for the effectiveness of our architecture. Domain knowledge is used here to further process the user's statements and for reasoning. To do so, we use ontologies. The main purpose of an ontology is to enable knowledge sharing and reuse. The key components that make up an ontology are a vocabulary of basic terms and a precise specification of what those terms mean. In this context, ontologies have been used to help interpreting the context of messages sent by others agents, and to keep a computational representation of knowledge useful at inference time. Ontologies have been used in many projects, from Semantic WEB content [9] to representing user profiles [10].

We are using a set of task and domain ontologies, separating domain and task models for reasoning. As suggested by Allen in [11], this is interesting for domains where task reasoning is crucial. Besides, using domain knowledge separately reduces the complexity of the linguistic modules and allows a better understanding of statements. In a recent work, Milward and Beveride [12] describe how scripted dialogue

---

[1] RMI: Minimal Resource Allocation

systems are moving to a new generation of practical systems based on domain knowledge and task descriptions.

The ontologies play a key role at the semantic interpretation time since the meaning of utterances can be inferred by looking for concepts and their attributes. Precisely, the module responsible for applying the ontology to the utterance is interested in finding the list of verbs that indicate the task to be executed and the domain concepts. The corresponding keywords are concepts of the ontology directly related to a list of actions. To illustrate how this mechanism works, consider the excerpt of ontology shown Fig. 2.

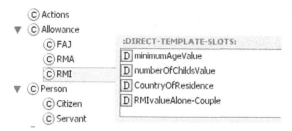

Fig. 2. Excerpt of the domain ontology: The RMI concept and its attributes

Consider the following short scenario: an unemployed person, citizen of France, may ask for an allowance (e.g. FAJ, RMA or RMI) to a social care service. To be eligible to receive the RMI allowance, four conditions must be satisfied. The candidate must:

1) live in France;
2) be older than 25;
3) have no dependent child, and;
4) have income not superior to 417,88 € per month.

In the excerpt of the ontology shown Fig. 2 (here represented using Protégé [13]), a concept called *Allowance* have 3 sub-concepts: FAJ, RMA and RMI, which means 3 types of allowances. Concepts have attributes (e.g. RMI has 4 attributes). *Person* is the general type of *Citizen* and *Servant*. Note that a set of actions (ex: list, start, shown Fig. 3) may be applied to each concept.

Given this scenario, a possible user's utterance is:

USER: *List all conditions to receive a RMI.*

To treat this utterance, the parser verifies the context of the input. It verifies that it is an order related to the domain (remember that the parser classifies all utterances as an *order* or a *question* or an *answer*). To do that, it uses the domain ontology and the lexicon. The lexicon contains thousands of words enriched with the list of all concepts and attributes of the ontology.

Since the utterance is an order and since it is related to the application domain, the parser module returns a matrix containing the list of tokens and their syntactic classification. By looking up the tokens in the ontology, it finds that the token list is an action (Fig. 3). It finds also that RMI is an object. At this point, we have a competence list with its parameters. Next, the *Dialogue Manager* module takes control of the dialogue.

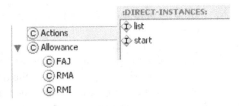

Fig. 3. The *Actions* instances

After parsing and semantic analysis, the *Dialogue Manager* is able to start a new task, since it is related to the domain (according to our first ontology presented Fig. 2). Tasks in our system are represented as shown Fig. 4, with a list of parameters (Fig. 4a shows the *Start a RMI Application* task model).

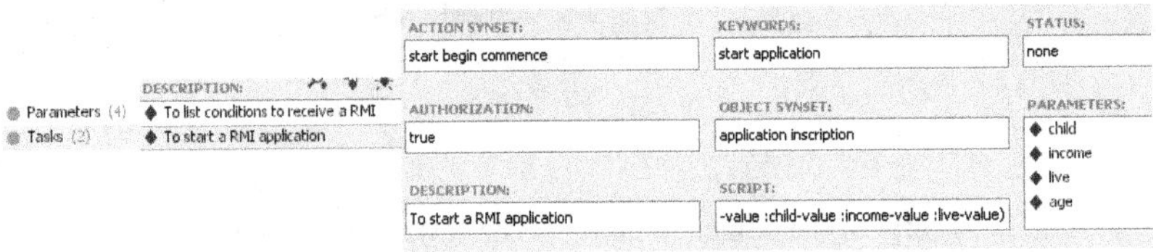

a) A task instance

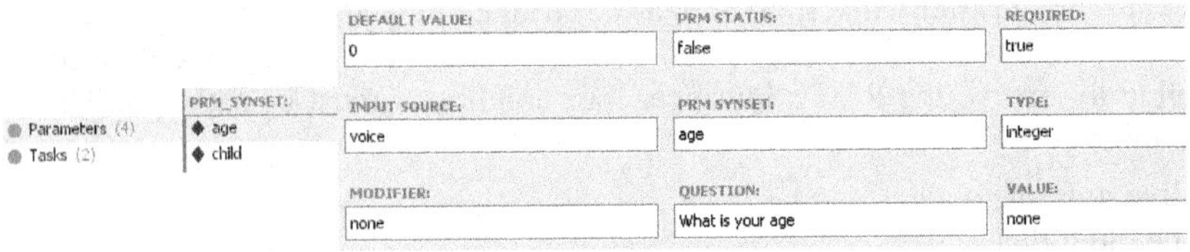

b) A parameter instance

Fig. 4. Task model example

Depending on the task, some task parameters must be filled. In general such parameters come from the user, as is the case of parameter *age* (Fig. 4b). In order to obtain this information, the *Dialogue Manager* may ask the following question "*What is your age*" stored in the appropriate parameters field.

All tasks are stored in an ontology in memory. When a dialogue session starts, the *Dialogue Manager* module pushes a task onto the stack of tasks when an utterance related to the task is given. Many tasks may be handled at simultaneously (including tasks of the same type). When all fields are filled, the *Dialogue Manager* sends the task for execution. Tasks are executed by other agents as described later.

3   A Multi-agent System for e-Government Services

Fig. 5 shows the system's architecture, where Personal Assistants are in charge of all exchanges of information among users. In this architecture, agents are totally independent and may be classified as Service Agents or Personal Assistants. Service Agents are agents that provide a particular type of service corresponding to specific skills. They are implemented and encapsulated by means of web services.

For operating the system, we give a Personal Assistant to each human participant (a civil servant). A Personal Assistant can use some service agents locally. They constitute its staff (see Fig. 5). These staff agents may also delegate sub-tasks to other agents in order to accomplish a complex task.

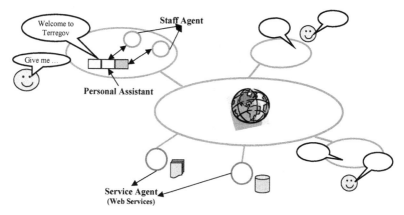

Fig. 5. The system overview

In our system all agents are cloned from a generic agent, first proposed by Ramos in [14]. The generic agent contains all the basic structure that allows an agent to exist and to communicate with other agents. Originally, agents use an ACL to communicate [15]. However, in this multi-agent system, agents are developed as WEB services (Fig. 6). In this case a gateway is needed to convert ACL messages into SOAP [16] messages and vice versa. An ACL message contains a set of one or more message parameters. Precisely which parameters are needed for effective agent communication will vary according to the situation; the only parameter that is mandatory in all ACL messages is the *performative*, although it is expected that most ACL messages will also contain *sender*, *receiver* and *content* parameters. SOAP provides a simple mechanism for exchanging structured and typed information between peers in a decentralized, distributed environment using XML. A SOAP message is an XML document information item that contains three elements: `<Envelope>`, `<Header>`, and `<Body>`.

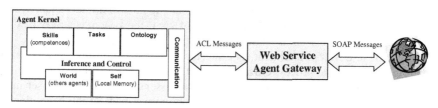

Fig. 6. Service agent structure

The gateway acts as a bridge between Web Service clients that wish to access agent services in a transparent fashion (see [8] for further information on integrating Web Services and agents).

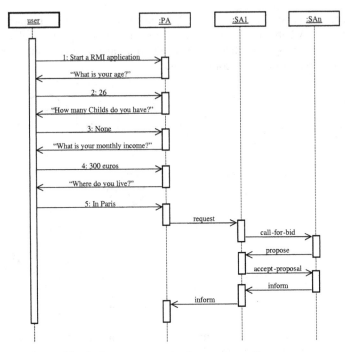

Fig. 7. Agent communication sequence diagram

Agents are completely independent and communicate when needed. As shown Fig. 7, communications may occur between human agents and their Personal Assistant, and between the Personal Assistant and service agents to accomplish a task. The later may delegate tasks to other agents. Fig. 7 shows the sequence diagram resulting from the exchange between the user and the Personal Assistant, where the Personal Assistant collects information to be able to delegate the execution of the task *Start an RMI application*, followed by the negotiation of the task execution among several service agents.

4 Conclusions and Future Work

In this paper, we presented a voice-enabled assistant applied in a multi-agent system for e-Government services. From the user point of view, the system is a Service Center and the Personal Assistant is its Service Provider.

Our goal is to develop intelligent user interfaces that enable unsophisticated users, such as civil servants, to process citizen's request readily and efficiently.

Since the application is a Personal Assistant, an essential feature of the user interface is respected: predictability. It was an assumption we made at the beginning: to provide correct responses and act according to the user request. Impossible requests, like those out of context, are easily handled since the system uses a competence list described as an ontology.

An important direction for future work is allowing users to access their assistant by different means, such as telephone or personal digital assistants (PDA). User mobility may impose interesting constraints to be tackled in the next versions of the speech interface.

Acknowledgments

Emerson Cabrera Paraiso would like to thanks CAPES – Brazil (grant 1306-02-2) and Pontifícia Universidade Católica do Paraná - Brazil that supported him in this research.

References

1. Terregov Project Web Site: http://www.terregov.eupm.net/.
2. SOCEVO: Service Oriented Collaborations Enviroment for Virtual Organisations, at http://www.it.swin.edu.au/centres/ciamas/tiki-index.php?page=SOCEVO.
3. Barthès, J.-P. A.: MASH Environments for Corporate KM. In: Proceedings of the Knowledge Management Workshop of IJCAI 2003, Acapulco, Mexico, (2003).
4. Paraiso, E. C., Barthès, J.-P. A., Tacla, C. A.: A Speech Architecture for Personal Assistants in a Knowledge Management Context. In: Proceedings of ECAI - European Conference on Artificial Intelligence, Valence, Spain, (2004).
5. Kölzer, A.: Universal dialogue specification for conversational systems. In: Proceedings of IJCAI 99 – Workshop on Knowledge and Reasoning in Practical Dialogue Systems, (1999).
6. Kemble, K.A.: An Introduction to Speech Recognition. Voice Systems Middleware Education - IBM Corporation, (2001).
7. Paraiso, E.C., Barthès, J.-P. A.: Une interface conversationnelle pour les agents assistants appliqués à des activités professionnelles. In: Proceedings of 16th Conférence Francophone sur l'Interaction Homme-Machine, Namur, Belgique, (2004), pp. 243-246.
8. Integrating Web Services into Agentcities Recommendation, at http://www.agentcities.org/rec/00006/.
9. Oberle, D., Staab, S., Studer, R., Volz, R.: Supporting application development in the semantic web, ACM Transactions on Internet Technology (TOIT), 2005, (to appear).
10. Middleton, S. E., De Roure, D. C., Shadbolt, N. R.: Capturing Knowledge of User Preferences: Ontologies in Recommender Systems. In: Proceedings of the International Conference on Knowledge Capture (KCAP'01), ACM Press, pp. 100-107, (2001).
11. Allen, J., Ferguson, G., Stent, A.: An Architecture for More Realistic Conversational Systems. In: Proceedings of Intelligent User Interfaces 2001 (IUI-01), Santa Fe, NM, (2001).
12. Milward, D., Beveride, M.: Ontology-Based Dialogue Systems. In: Proceedings of International Joint Conference on Artificial Intelligence IJCAI – 03, Acapulco, Mexico, (2003).
13. Gennari, J., Musen, M. A., Fergerson, R. W., Grosso, W. E., Crubézy, M., Eiksson, Noy, N., Tu, W.: The Evolution of Protégé: An Environment for Knowledge-Based Systems Development. 2002 – Report available at: http://smi.stanford.edu/pubs/SMI_Abstracts/SMI-2002-0943.html.
14. Ramos, M. P.: Structuration et évolution conceptuelles d'un agent assistant personnel dans les domaines techniques. PhD dissertation (in French), presented at UTC in December 2000.
15. FIPA Interaction Protocol Library Specification, http://www.fipa.org/specs/fipa00025/PC00025C.html.
16. SOAP Version 1.2 Specification Assertions and Test Collection, 2003, http://www.w3.org/TR/2003/REC-soap12-testcollection-20030624/.

CAS – An Interface Generator in Natural Language to Information System

Cezar Augusto Schipiura and Edson Emílio Scalabrin

Program of After-graduation in Technology in Health (PAGTH),
Pontifical University Catholic of the Paraná (PUCPR), Brazil
cezarschp@yahoo.com.br, edson.scalabrin@pucpr.br

Abstract. With the Web popularization, the digital inclusion comes motivating the research and development of engines of more sophisticated search each time concentrating in the concepts of the Web Semantics that incorporates semantic elements in the formatting of their concepts and propitiates a search with bigger intelligence. Such intelligence characterizes for the quality or precision of the knowledge retrieved or returned in reply to one determined request, involving a structure of how the knowledge is represented, accessed, retrieved, manipulated and enriched. The intention of this process is to enable to the executive professionals to interact naturally with computers using the natural language where the computers understand the submitted questions it and answer using the same terms of the question in understandable way, guiding them in complex decisions, allowing that they can occupy of nobler tasks, the businesses of their company.

1 Introduction

Our proposal has an ambitious conceptive that it consists of the definition of a system architecture involving software modules, that, given a ontology of domain constructed in a database, and a set of templates, automatically generates a concept memory through ontology and indexed taxonomies in way to allow to a great number of combinations between concepts representing concepts of the real world, making possible the performance of a process that understands questionings received in natural language, elaborating answers for such questions in the same terms that had been elaborated to it.

The implementation of the modules of the memory follows the principles of dynamic memory of Roger Schank [1]; the mechanism for the understanding of the phrases exchanged between the modules is based on the idea of parser established in cases of Martin [2] and Riesbeck [3] and the indexation and search considers a complementation with the implementation of the concepts of the CBR of Kolodner [4]. This mechanism will operate on a specific structure of data captured of one part of datamart constructed on a relational data base management system[5], where the concepts with their indices are represented, composing part of the memory.

1.1 Implementation Conceptive

Under this scene the CAS, considers the implementation of a system that enable to question and to get answers in natural language, where both questions and answers is received, understood and answered of automatic form for the modules system CAS it

F.F. Ramos et al. (Eds.): ISSADS 2005, LNCS 3563, pp. 504–515, 2005.

supplies a set of software layers that allow to generate and to test such memory. The test consists to stress the memory, being submitted to answer it a great set of questions in natural language. Of more pragmatic form, system CAS is structured around software modules, witch are explicated in Fig. 1 (GQR Architecture):

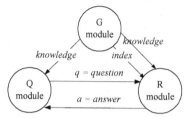

a) a module G (Generator), that from a database and of a accurate information by domain specialist, generates a memory structure constructing, in particular, an ontology of domain;
b) a module Q (Questioner), that given to an ontology of domain (in the taxonomy form) and a set of templates, automatically generates a great set of interrogative phrases in natural language;
c) a module R (Responder), that from a ontology of domain and the knowledge of domain generated by module G, is capable to understand and to answer the questions generated by module Q;

2   The Construction of Memory of Concepts

The memory created from the relational Base becomes flexible, therefore it allows reorganizations through relationships created by the engineers of the knowledge through templates. The concepts of the memory are constructed from tables of the database [5].

2.1   The Concepts Generated from the Database

The first step, executed for the CAS, is to extract of the base the names of tables and the respective relationships, executing, thus, the first phase of the construction of the structure of the memory that will take the form of graphs. Tables inside represent entities of a database and, in this way they will be placed in the memory in frames that will compose ontology. Placed independently, these frames (treated following as concept) will be related ones with the others first with the relationships defined in the database and, after with the enrichment of the knowledge of the engineer of the knowledge. These relationships will form the taxonomies that complement the direction of the ontology's in contexts, contexts these that will be used for understanding of questions and generation of answers.

2.2   The Procedures that Determine the Transformation of the Concepts

The process of transformation of the RDB in the memory of concepts follows some rules in the application of the transformation procedures as related to follow:

a) Procedure of the Increase of the Schema

With the participation of the engineer of the knowledge, the project is enriched with complements of information that are part of the domain, but is not expressed in the database.

[P01] Specification of Names of Concepts

So that it has an understanding of the CAS in the interpretation of the questionings in natural language, the names given to tables by the designers of the database, that, normally, are codes that state a summary of that the table means; it is necessary to inform to the CAS the real names of the concepts so that the phrases are elaborated and understood naturally. For this control, the CAS defines for each concept a value and a name, being that the name is internally controlled to have access the contents of the database (as a key) and the value, external expressed and used for indexation and understanding of the real concepts. In this way, for instance, one table that deals with register in cadastre of customers is codified as "DMCLI001" in the database and, such name will have to be substituted by a real representation as "Customer".

[P02] Specification of the Values That Determine the Concepts

Each concept must have a name that will have to be gotten amongst the properties of the same table, that is, of the columns of the table, which is the characteristic that corresponds to the description of the proper table. This is another information that is not explicit in the relational database. In this way, in table DMCLI001 (customer), for instance, the field is used "customerName" that it will be defined as "customer name" to contain the name of the customer; in table DMPRD005, the field "productName", as "product name" etc. With the definitions of the real names of tables and fields, module G will instance concepts of the database.

b) Explaining the Relationships Not Defined in the RDBMS

The relationships defined in the database through Primary key and Foreign Key will be transformed into taxonomies that will give context to the relationships. We know for Date (2000) that a RDBMS defines all the relationships in the terms of the: a) one for one (1:1), b) one for many (1:N), c) many for one (N:1) or d) the multi valued relationships, many for many (N:N), where the intermediate tables are created so that the RDBMS can support such representation.

[P03] Relationships of Composition

Amongst the relationships that are considered in the CAS, the representation of the composition, in the RDB, is only explained in the programming of the methods and not in the relationship of tables. This relationship defines that a concept is composed for a set of others. Following our example, we have a Product among others that he is composed for pieces (components). This style of relationships will have to be informed to the module G for increase of the base in the construction of the memory, therefore they are not discovered automatically in the base.

[P04] Elimination of Intermediate Tables

The tables of Relationships created for representation of the relations multi valued will have simply to be eliminated of the list so that the module G, when finding them in the RDB and not in the increased base of data, creates a multi valued relationship of participation or composition (see [P03]) between tables, where the concepts is completed with their characteristics.

[P05] To Discover the Characteristics Used in the Dialogues
Inside of tables is defined codes that reference the characteristics (columns) of each concept (table). This codification follow an identical standard to the definition of the table names, internationally followed, that facilitates the manipulation of data through the names of the columns. In this way, the columns are codified with codes that will have to be renamed so that the CAS interprets in correct way the concepts, for instance, 'customerName' for 'Customer Name', or 'customerState' for 'State ', or still 'customerDistrict' for 'District', etc.

c)Increased Data
The module G will have, then, in the all, database enriched with the explicit information in the RDB and the methods of the Information System. This information will be transformed into taxonomies in the structure of the memory.

2.3   Rules of Data Recovery

The Module G, in the sequence, searches the relation's among concepts in the system tables. They will be described to follow the rules and the types of relations/taxonomies that are mounted by the CAS when composing the Concept Memory in accordance with some rules, which will be presented in the follow:

[R01] Relationship "One for One" (1:1)

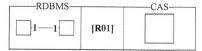

Fig. 2. – The relationship "one for one" happens in a RDB, when, in some situations, it is needed to divide a table, keeping the same primary key for the two. Amongst these situations, we can cite: i) when the fields of one table can not be filled by being optional, being able to admit null values; ii) when some data are very constantly updated ; or iii) when one or more fields are very extensive to be kept inside of the same table with other data. These tables form one meaning only and, thus, the CAS elaborates one same concept.

[R02] Relationship "One for Many" (1:N)

Fig. 3. – The Module G interprets the relation "one for many" as a relation where one meant collaborates with another one with some (or all) their characteristics. We can cite the relation between a industry and a car. The industry is not part of the car, but collaborates with its name (quality, fame) in its characteristics. In the database we say that a industry produces (or it possess) many cars and a car alone can belong to only one industry. We perceive that he is in the concept enclose where they are the foreign keys. The Module G internally keeps the information of the relation "one for many", however what it goes to characterize in the structure of the memory it is the relation enclose (grouping) with partnership (participant).

[R03] Relationship Many for Many (N:N)

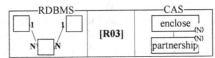

Fig. 4. – The multi valued relationship "many for many" is represented by an intermediate table, as cited in [P03]. In the edition of concepts, the user will have to eliminate such tables of the list, making possible to the module to make the interpretation through the relation that it represents: of composition or participation.

2.4   The Taxonomies and Preliminary Index of Concepts

The taxonomies, that also will generate the preliminary index, are constructed from the relationships defined in the RDB and later from the data edited for the engineer of the knowledge, that will serve to form a preliminary indexation of concepts in the memory, where each relation have multiple dimensions with particular definitions. The CAS retrieve the relations between concepts in tables of the database supplied as entered, from which, the taxonomies are mounted by a process of transformation of the classic relations of a relational model in hierarchic relations defined by a set relations with definite semantics. Such taxonomies thus are defined:

(i) *parent/son* – all the hierarchic relationship between two entities. This relation does not define sharing of characteristics;

   (i.i) *domain/instance* – the relation defines enters the entity in itself and their instances;

   (i.ii) *compound/component* – it defines the entities that are one part another one, that is, a group of entities that form one third with proper characteristics;

   (i.iii) *owner/property* – separate the entities in their properties (characteristic) or relates in an entity, diverse properties;

(ii) *enclose/partnership* – the relationship of grouping for characteristic equivalents among concepts defines. This relation defines sharing of characteristics that can be multiple.

2.5   The Templates Indexer of Answers to the Questions

The module Q possess, in their memory, templates that they are base for make generic questions that can use in any base of knowledge and has resources that they are in accordance with allow to the make templates according the definition of the logic of business domain of the base that is incorporating. Of this form, for each new domain one becomes necessary to mount templates that they represent the business logic that will complement generic templates. The concepts of the memory if do not modify with the creation of templates of domain, therefore these have as function to increase the possibilities of dialogues between the modules Q and R. In other words, these templates will supply to the module Q the parameters necessary to formulate consultations on the content of the base of knowledge of the module R. The creation of templates of domain is a task of the engineer of the knowledge.

Structure of templates

> **[object:enclose:partnership:property/partnership:instnce/property/partnership]**
> It cites me the [object] that had been [enclose] to the [partnership] of the
> [property/partnership] of the [instnce/property/partnership]
> *r:is/are: instanceobject/enclose/propertypartnership=instnce/property/partnership*

Fig. 5. – Templates are structuralized of form to combine with the indexes of relationships of this form:

1. **Structure of index** – it will be used to index templates of the group, that is, the module R, to interpreting the question and to activate the concepts through parser, will search a structure that takes care of to the recognized case.
2. **Structure of the question** – it will be used by modules Q and R, the first one the forms through will have as base to elaborate questions of all combination the concepts of the dynamic memory that take care of to the group; as to recognize the questions with the aid of the dictionary lexicon.
3. **Structure of the reply** – The module R to search the concepts in the memory will use it to elaborate the answer for the questions received.

3 Application Scenario: Data Mart of Management of Selling Strategy

3.1 The Database Origin

The module G generates the structure of the memory from a project elaborated on a RDB supplied as entered to the module. The memory created will become flexible for the successive reorganizations the measure that new concepts go being indexed. The result of this phase requires the intervention of the user for increase of that preliminarily it was extracted.

The elaboration of a memory structure consists of retrieving the concepts and relationships of the database increased with the not explicit knowledge in the relational database, executing the procedures [P01], [P02], [P03], [P04] and [P05] and applying the rules [R01], [R02] and [R03]. We go to take, as example; the project represented in Fig. 6 and to pass step by step the procedures and described rules previously.

3.2 Cases Decided for the CAS

The scene will be described in the form of a set of cases, where each in case that it involves a question and a reply. These questions are generated and answered respectively by modules Q and R.

Case 1: Question: "Tell me the products that had been sold to the customers of the state of the Paraná".

Reply: "The products that had been sold to the customers of the state of the Paraná are computer, printer and scanner".

Case 2: Question: "How many budgets generated for vendor Cezar Augusto Schipiura that had generated sale in the October month".

Reply: "The budgets generated for vendor Cezar Augusto Schipiura that had generated sale in the October month totalize 25"

3.3 The Module G, Ontology Generator and the Structure Base of the Memory of Concepts

The recognition of the database initially, through SQL commands, the module G recognizes concepts of the database, showing the concepts discovered for parameters. With each table specification the module G creates concepts that will result in a concept memory.

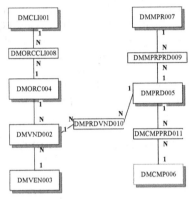

Fig. 6. -Tables are recognized in the BDR: DMCUS001, DMSAI002, DMVEN003, DMBUD004, DMPRD005, DMCMP006, DMMPR007 and the tables of relationship DMBUDCUS008, DMMPRPRD009, DMPRDSAI010, DMCMPPRD011.

1. Specification of the names of concepts[P01]
   DMCLI001 = "Customer",
   DMVND002 = "Vendor",
   DMSEI003 = "Sailing",
   DMBUD004 = "Budget",
   DMPRD005 = "Product",
   DMCMP006 = "Component",
   DMMPR007 = "Raw Material".
   The relationship tables will be treated in the process [P04].

TableName	Attribute name to CAS Understand
DMCUS001	CustomerName
DMSAL002	SaleDate
DMVEN003	VendorName
DMBUD004	BudgetDate
DMPRD005	ProductName
DMCMP006	ComponentName
DMMPR007	RawMaterial

2. Fig. 7. – Specification of the values that determine concepts [P02]

3. Relationships of composition [P03]

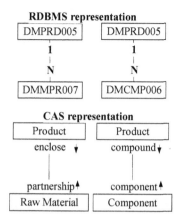

Fig. 8. – All products is prepared from the raw material and made up of components, however this representation does not differ in the diagramming of the RDB. After constructed the product, the Raw Material contributes with their characteristics, on the other hand, the component will be part of the product always that it to exist. Still a Raw Material participates of other products with the same characteristics, and components will have different functions in each type of product. Thus one understands that the Raw Material is a participant of the product and the component composes the product. The generation of this difference is described in the rules [R01], [R02], [R03].

4. Elimination of intermediate tables [P04]

As cited in the process [P01], the intermediate tables will have to be eliminated, because they are unnecessary in the form as the Module G structure the concepts. They are: DMBUDCUS008, DMMPRPRD009, DMPRDSAI010 and DMCMPPRD011.

5. To identify to the characteristics used in the dialogues [P05]

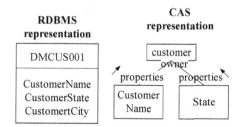

Fig. 9. – Each relevant characteristic of each concept will have to be described in the publisher of concepts, in way to explain, as each dialogue will have to be understood. These fields will be transformed into properties of their concepts (to owner).

The Memory of Concepts

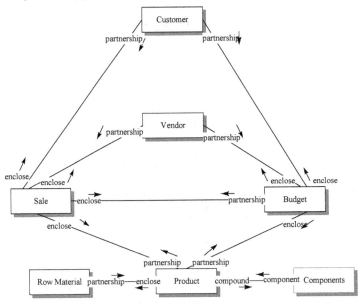

Fig. 10. – After all this process of transformation the module will have in the memory a multidimensional structure as demonstrated in parts and complemented in Fig.11.

Representation of Real Concepts
The instances then are placed in the linked ontology's and between itself as demonstrated in the fig. 10, representing in the memory, the concepts with their felt relationships and of the real world (fig. 11).

Indexation of the Memory
The first step is the generation of the tree of indices in the memory, which makes possible the search of the concepts in the memory.

[I-P01] – To Identify to the Types of Relationships
The first function executed for the module R is the creation of the types of indices leaving of the possible relationships defined by the module G: concept, compound, component, domain, instance, enclose, partnership, to owner and property.

[I-P02] – To Bind to the Concepts to the Indexes
The module R covers all the structure of the memory and binds, through one link of memory, each concept to its index, or either, for each taxonomy that possess the concept, a reference in the tree of indices is created. The concepts with more than a taxonomy will be referenced in some points of the tree, as for instance, the concept "product" have relationships, at the same time as compound, domain and enclose, being referenced for links in these three indexes.

[I-P03] – To Create an Index for the Concepts from Templates
From the relationships specified in templates the not foreseen possibilities of relationship in the database, that is, templates are created in the memory, representing the

concepts, are on to the concepts of the memory. In this task, the module R covers templates and binds each concept, by means of its name, to its respective indices of the memory.

4   Recognition of a Question

Let us retake case 1 previously cited:

"Tell me the products that had been sold to the customers of the State of the Paraná". The process of established parser in cases of Martin[2] and Riesbeck[3] recognize the concepts through the terms, activating the concepts:

Product: concept of the question [concept];

Been Sold: parser, through if the dictionary of lexicons, recognize the concept sale [enclose];

Customers: one enclose of product [partnership];

State: one property of the concept customer [property];

Paraná: one instance of one property [instance]

1. the recognized structure is reorganized in the following way:

Tell me the [concept] that had [enclose] to the [partnership] of the [property] of the [instance].

2. from this recognition, the module R searches in the structure of indices one template whose structure takes care of to the received question:

[concept:enclose:partnership:property/partnership:instnce/property/partnership]

3. finding the index, on to this index it finds template of the reply:

r:is|are: instanceconcept|enclose|propertypartnership=instnce/property/partnership

5   Elaboration of the Reply

When is encountered the structure that provides make the answer, the module R instance a generic search engine in the memory, with parameters for template of the answer and the recognized concepts with the respective meanings in the form of the index.

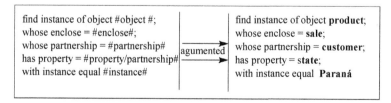

Fig. 11. – Represents of the ontology's of real concepts and to the indices represented in figure 10, we perceive as the module R finds the concepts and elaborates the answers without any difficulty:

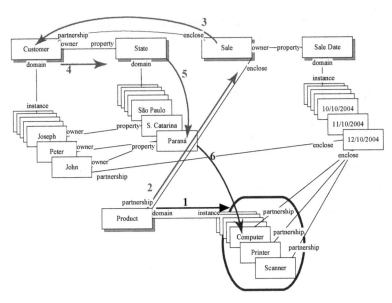

With the following conclusion:

> *The products that had been sailed to the customers of the State of the Paraná are Computer, Printer and Scanner.*

6 Conclusion

The construction of a memory is a complex process that also requires a particular modeling and sophisticated mechanism of search. System CAS contributes in the simplification of this process by means of a set of heuristic, that it allows to construct the base of the memory of modules Q and R from a database, saving considerable efforts. This study in it allowed identifying them four modules, where each one implements a particular ability. They are: (i) to generate, to leave of a prompt information and database of a domain specialist, a memory structure constructing in particular a ontology of domain; (ii) to generate, from one given to ontology of domain (in the form of a taxonomy) and a set of templates, automatically a great set of interrogative phrases in natural language; (iii) to understand and to answer, from a ontology and knowledge of domain, questions in natural language; and (iv) to analyze the quality of the questions and the generated answers. The automatic and exhausting generation of questions made for the module Q opens possibilities to test itself, for stress, domain modules.

References

1. Schank, Roger C1999: "Dynamic Memory Revisited" Cambridge University Press, Cambridge
2. Martin, Charles Eugene, (1993), "Direct Memory Access Parsing" University of Chicago, Departament of Computer Science – Technical Report CS 93-07, June 23.

3. Riesbeck, Christopher K; Schank, Roger C,(1981), "Inside Computer Understanding" Laurence Erlbaum Associates, New Jersey

4. Kolodner, Janet (1993) "Case -Based Reasoning" Morgan Kaufmann Publishers, Inc – São Mateo, Canadá .

5. Date C J. (2000). "Introdução a Sistemas de Banco de Dados". 7ªed. Rio de Janeiro: Publicare consultoria e serviços.

6. Rich, Elaine; Knight, K, (1994), "Inteligência Artificial" Makron Books do Brasil Editora Ltda. 2ª ed. São Paulo.

7. Araribóia, G.(1988), "Inteligência Artificial: Um curso prático". Livros Técnicos e Científicos, Editora Ltda – Rio de Janeiro.

A Formal Approach to Model Multiagent Interactions Using the B Formal Method

Hind Fadil and Jean-Luc Koning

INPG-CoSy, 50 rue Laffemas, BP 54, 26902 Valence cedex 9, France
{Hind.Fadil,Jean-Luc.Koning}@esisar.inpg.fr
http://www.esisar.inpg.fr/lcis/cosy

Abstract. This paper is within the scope of methodical approaches for producing flexible and reliable formal specifications of interactions protocols between agents in a multiagent system. The basic idea behind it is to define the agents as an abstract machines described by their behavior. Such machines are able to create agents, interact with other agents of a same working group via roles usin precise communication protocols. Our goal is to model the interaction between agents with a formal method that is able to check and then prove our initial UML specification. In order to obtain the final specification with this approach, we chose to use the B method and illustrated it with a case study.

Keywords: multiagent system, formal specification, B method, interaction protocols.

1 Introduction

1.1 Specification and Multiagent Systems

Specification is one of the main steps in software life-cycles. Such a step is supposed to give a non ambiguous description of the software's functionality. Besides, it is the basis for the development steps that follow like design, coding and property checking.

There are several methods and tools capable of tackling this specification process, that enable the execution of specifications, the checking of properties and compilation or generation of code.

Specifying multiagent systems must respect some fundamental characteristics. Since they heavily rely upon their interaction with the environment, it is necessary to describe the logical side effects of the system and its environment.

Any multiagent system encompasses the following elements [1]:

- the environment, that is shared by all the system agents. An agent may partially or totally have control over it.
- a set of objects located within the environment, that can be created, deleted or modified by the agents.
- a set of agents that are the active entities of the system.
- a set of links that join the objects and the agents together.
- a set of operations that enable to create, convert and manipulate agents and objects.

F.F. Ramos et al. (Eds.): ISSADS 2005, LNCS 3563, pp. 516–528, 2005.

The agents are autonomous entities able to make decisions, act at a precise moment, interact and cooperate between them via interaction protocols in order to accomplish specific tasks. Such agents can play various roles during a communication process.

Besides, they may belong to groups depending on their role [2] [3] (see Figure 1).

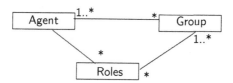

Fig. 1. Entity relationship diagram for agents, roles and groups

In this paper, we present a way to give a specification model of multiagent system using the B method [4] [5] in order to be able to derive proofs on the system's behavior. We exemplify our approach on the Contract Net Protocol [6] as it has become a *de facto* interaction protocol application in the multiagent domain.

Figure 2 depicts the *Contract Net Protocol* expressed as a UML *sequence diagram*. When invoked, an initiator agent sends a *call_for_proposal* message to another agent that responds by aggreeing (or not) with the proposal before a given deadline. This aggreement is defined by three kinds of response messages regarding the proposal: accept, refuse or not understood. The X in the diamond indicates an "*exclusive or*" decision. If a proposal is offered, the Initiator has a choice of either accepting or rejecting the proposal. When the Participant receives a proposal acceptance, it will inform the Initiator about the proposal execution.

Thus, an agent can ask for some help from the others to achieve a task. If one of the other agents considers itself capable of performing the task, it informs the initiator agent. This initiator must chose between all the alternatives. The selected agent can ask for some complementary information, and they will both communicate for the task duration.

The interest in this protocol is that it allows the agents to cooperate to solve the initial problem, divide dynamically the work and integrate their result.

1.2   The B Method

The B method [7] enables to specify, design and code software systems. It follows the entire life-cycle of a software, from specification to code. It is based on first order predicates, set theory and inference rules. A refinement process enables to derive the implementation from a B specification. It is a way to translate the information (data and operations) of an abstract machine into actual code.

With B, checking the correctness of a software system amounts to undergoing a mathematical proof. Each refinement level is checked and must be correct

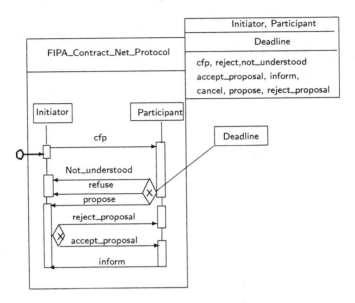

Fig. 2. Contract Net Protocol

up to the highest level of abstraction. A B specification is a set of the independent processes or machines that can be linked together using some "INCLUDES" clauses.

A B machine consists of two pieces: a static and a dynamic one. The static piece of the machine holds the *variables* definition and type, the *invariants* which are the properties the machine must satisfy, the machine dependencies that are represented by clauses such as *included*, *imported* or *sees*, and the initial state of the machine which is the clause *Initialization*.

The dynamic piece of the machine contains the operations header and body that represent the internal evolution of the machine variables.

The B method is capable of proving an actual specification via a set of proofs obligations. These proofs obligations must me valid for the operations to preserve the various *invariants*.

In the following sections, we will specify the agents as well as the Contract Net Protocol specification (section 2) using the B method and illustrate our specification by an interaction scenario (section 3).

2   Overall Specification

2.1   Agent Specification

An agent can be viewed as a set of attributes, operations, actions and interaction messages. It can be represented as an abstract machine in B. This machine consists of a heading, a set of data (static part) and a set of operations (dynamic part).

The static part (figure 3) shows the *Invariant* clause which is an important piece of the machine. This clause identifies the variable types and the constraints they should satisfy.

MACHINE
  M_AGENTS
SETS
  $AGENTS=\{agent\_voy, agent\_vol1,$
  $agent\_vol2\};$
  $GROUPES = \{groupe\_voyage\};$
  $ROLES = \{gest\_voy, gest\_vol\};$
  $PROTOCOL=\{cnet, other\}$
VARIABLES
  $agents, roles, assigned\_roles,$
  $current\_roles, groupes, part\_of, protocols, supporte$
INVARIANT
  $agents \subseteq AGENTS \land$

  $protocols \subseteq PROTOCOL \land$
  $groupes \subseteq GROUPES \land$
  $roles \subseteq ROLES \land$
  $part\_of \in agents \leftrightarrow groupes \land$
  $assigned\_roles \in agents \leftrightarrow roles \land$
  $current\_roles \in agents \nrightarrow roles \land$
  $current\_roles \subseteq assigned\_roles \land$
  $supporte \in agents \leftrightarrow protocols$
INITIALISATION
  $agents, roles, assigned\_roles, supporte,$
  $protocols, groupes := \emptyset , \emptyset , \emptyset , \emptyset ,\{cnet\}, \emptyset$
  $\| \ current\_roles, part\_of := \emptyset , \emptyset$

Fig. 3. Static part of the machine *M_Agents*

We have called this machine *M_Agents*. It makes use of four sets: AGENTS, GROUPS, ROLES and PROTOCOL. The first three have been initialized in order to use them in the remaining of the paper.

AGENTS contains all types of agents in the system and GROUPS contains all types of groups in the system. Any agent belongs to one or several groups, and a group has zero or more agents. The relationship between an agent and a group is denoted by *part_of*.

An agent can play zero or more roles. The corresponding relationship is *assigned_roles*. The *current_role* relationship indicates an agent's current role. At any given moment any agent plays its current role.

The agents support one or several protocols. The relationship is denoted *supported*. In this paper we only use one protocol, i.e. the Contract Net Protocol.

The dynamic part of the *M_Agents* machine (figure 4) contains the operations for manipulating the agents. The necessary operations are the ones for creating and deleting an agent, adding a role to an agent, changing the role of an agent, etc.

2.2   Contract Net Protocol Specification

The Contract Net Protocol is a machine that manages the contract process between two agents. The abstract machine of this protocol is called *C_Net*. It includes the *M_Agent* abstract machine to enable the use of all the variables and operations as well as verify the invariants.

The *C_Net* machine manages the set of messages exchanged between the initiator agent and the other participating agents.

The set MESSAGES contains all possible messages exchanged between two agents that use this protocol. There are eight types of messages [6]: "*cfp*", "*pro-*

OPERATIONS

create_agent(ag) = **PRE**
   $ag \in AGENTS \wedge ag \notin agents$
THEN
   $agents := agents \cup \{ag\}$
END;
create_roles(rl) = **PRE**
   $rl \in ROLES \wedge rl \notin roles$
THEN
   $roles := roles \cup \{rl\}$
END;
creat_current(rr, ag)=**PRE**
   $rr \in roles \wedge ag \in agents \wedge (ag \mapsto$
   $rr) \in$ $assigned\_roles \wedge (ag \mapsto rr) \notin$
   $current\_roles$
THEN
   $current\_roles := \{ag \mapsto rr\}$
END;
add_roles(rl, ag)= **PRE**
   $rl \in roles \wedge ag \in agents$
THEN
   $assigned\_roles := assigned\_roles \cup \{ag$
   $\mapsto rl\}$

END;
delete_roles(rl, ag)=**PRE**
   $rl \in roles \wedge ag \in agents \wedge (ag \mapsto$
   $rl) \in assigned\_roles \wedge (ag \mapsto rl) \notin$
   $current\_roles$
THEN
   $assigned\_roles := assigned\_roles - \{ag \mapsto$
   $rl\}$
END;
change_roles($r1, r2, ag$)=**PRE**
   $r1 \in roles \wedge r2 \in roles \wedge ag \in agents$
   $\wedge (ag \mapsto r1) \in current\_roles \wedge (ag \mapsto$
   $r2) \notin current\_roles \wedge$
   $(ag \mapsto r2) \in assigned\_roles$
THEN
   $current\_roles := \{ag \mapsto r2\}$
END;
add_protocol(pr, ag)= **PRE**
   $pr \in protocols \wedge ag \in agents$
THEN
   $supporte := supporte \cup \{ag \mapsto pr\}$
END

Fig. 4. Dynamic part of the machine *M_Agents*

pose", "*reject_proposal*", "*not_understood*", "*accept_proposal*", "*refuse*", "*inform*", "*cancel*".

The set STATES indicates the possible agent states of the *Initiator* or the *participants*. The set DEADLINE owns two states: *in_time* indicates that the deadline has not expired and *time_out* indicates that the deadline has expired.

The messages exchanged between the agents are stored in variable *messages_exchanged*:

$$messages\_exchanged \in \text{MESSAGES} \leftrightarrow (agent\_group \leftrightarrow agent\_group)$$

This variable contains the agents sender, the agent receiver and the message exchanged between them. In order to carry out the protocol, the machine's dynamic portion uses five operations that process the exchanged messages.

The *starting_system* operation allows the initiator agent to send a "*cfp*" message to all the other agents of the same groups. This operation will be called by the role machine of the Initiator agent. The role will be given the name of the agent thadit starts the communication. The *starting_system* operation checks the name of the agent *ag_ini*. It gives the agent the *Initiator* state and gives to the other agents in the group the *Participant* state. It initializes the deadline at *in_time* and add the **cfp** message in the set of the messages exchanged of this communication. See Figure 5.

Operation *send_response(msg, ag_ini, ag_part)* checks whether the participating agent (*ag_part*) that received a "*cfp*" message responded to the initiator agent (*ag_ini*) using a "*propose*", "*not_understood*" or "*refuse*" message:

$$msg \in \{refuse, not\_understood, propose\}$$

Operation *response(msg, ag_ini, ag_part)* checks whether the deadline has expired, and the initiator agent (*ag_ini*) that received the "*propose*" message

Starting_system(ag_ini)= PRE
 $ag\_ini \in agent\_groupe$
THEN
 $deadline:=in\_time$ ||
 $state:=((agent\_groupe\text{-}\{ag\_ini\}) \times \{Participant\}) \cup \{ag\_ini \mapsto Initiator\}$
 || $messages\_exchanged :=$
 $messages\_exchanged \cup (\{cfp\} \times \{\{ag\_ini\} \times \mathbf{dom}(state \rhd \{Participant\})\})$
END;

Fig. 5. *starting_system* operation

send_response(msg,ag_part ,ag_ini) =
    PRE
    $ag\_part \in agent\_groupe \wedge state\ (ag\_part\ )= Participant \wedge ag\_ini \in agent\_groupe \wedge$
    $state(ag\_ini\ )=Initiator \wedge$
    $messages\_exchanged^{-1}(\{ag\_ini \mapsto ag\_part\}\ ) \doteq cfp \wedge$
    $deadline=in\_time \wedge$
    $msg \in MESSAGES \wedge$
    $msg \in \{refuse ,not\_understood ,propose\}$
    THEN
    $messages\_exchanged := messages\_exchanged \cup\{msg \mapsto \{ag\_part \mapsto ag\_ini\ \}\ \}$

    END;

Fig. 6. *send_response* operation

from the participating agent (ag_part) responded using an "*accept_proposal*" or "*reject_proposal*" message.

response(msg,ag_ini ,ag_part) =
    PRE
    $ag\_part \in agent\_groupe \wedge ag\_ini \in agent\_groupe \wedge state(ag\_part\ ) = Participant \wedge$
    $state\ (ag\_ini\ ) =Initiator \wedge$
    $messages\_exchanged^{-1}(\{ag\_part \mapsto ag\_ini\ \})= propose \wedge$
    $deadline =time\_out \wedge$
    $msg \in MESSAGES \wedge$
    $msg \in \{accept\_proposal ,reject\_proposal\ \}$
    THEN
    $messages\_exchanged:= messages\_exchanged \cup \{msg \mapsto \{ag\_ini \mapsto ag\_part\ \}\}$
    END;

Fig. 7. *response* operation

Finally, the participating agent sends an "*inform*" message to initiator agent via the *inform_msg* operation.

inform_msg($msg\ ag\_part ,ag\_ini$)=
    PRE
    $ag\_part \in agent\_groupe \wedge ag\_ini \in agent\_groupe \wedge state\ (ag\_part\ ) = Participant \wedge$
    $state\ (ag\_ini\ )=Initiator \wedge$
    $messages\_exchanged^{-1}(\ \{ag\_part \mapsto ag\_ini\ \}\ )= accept\_proposal \wedge$
    $msg =inform$
    THEN
    $messages\_exchanged := messages\_exchanged \cup \{msg \mapsto \{ag\_part \mapsto ag\_ini\ \}\ \}$
    END;

Fig. 8. *Inform* operation

We have used the operational B for this protocol because the operations of the M_CNET machine are called by roles machines that communicates with a Contract Net Protocol. Therefore we do not need to use any B event [8]. The operational B is sufficient to specify a Contract Net Protocol machine . We will explained this point in the next section dedicated to the specification of the Travel System Scenario that makes use of the Contract Net Protocol.

3   Specification of the Travel System Scenario

Let us study the scenario of an electronic travel agency where the agency is an entity that has to organize some travel. It contacts flight agencies (*agent_vol1* and *agent_vol2*), a hotel agency (*agent_hotel*) and a rental car agency (*agent_cars*) [9] as shown in Figure 9.

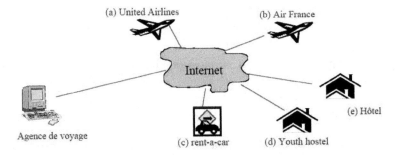

Fig. 9. Scenario of the electronic travel agency

We focus here on how the prices put forward by the flight agents (*agents_vol1* and *agents_vol2*) are chosen as described in Figure 10.

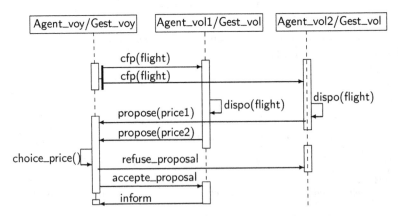

Fig. 10. Scenario of a choice between price alternatives

The agent that organizes the travel sends the call for proposal to two agents belonging to the groups *agent_vol1* and *agent_vol2*. This agent checks if a flight is available or not. In our scenario, the two agents suggest an air fare to the initiator agent (*agent_voy*). This later compares them and selects the cheapest.

In our scenario the (*agent_voy*) chose the first proposition. After that, the participant agent which was selected informs the initiator agent of its proposition.

The following sections present the specification of *agent_voy* and *agent_vol1* as well as the specification of the role played by *agent_voy* (namely *gest_voy*) and the role played by *agent_vol1* and *agent_vol2* (namely *gest_vol*).

Our specifications only relate to this scenario which makes use of the Contract Net Protocol.

3.1   Specification of the Initiator Agent

Users have asked the initiator agent to find the *agent_voy* best price of a particular flight. This agent starts the communication by sending a "*cfp*" message to all the agents that belong to the work group, i.e., the participating agents. In other words, this participating agent plays the *gest_vol* role.

An abstract machine is used for each agent and each roles. The *agent_voy* specification is given in figure 11.

```
MACHINE
    Agent_Voy
INCLUDES
    Gest_Voy
SETS
    VILLES; TASKS = {Find_fligth, Find_hotel}
VARIABLES
    ag_role, agent_name, choice_propose, task
INVARIANT
    task ∈ TASKS ∧
    ag_role ∈ ROLES ∧
    agent_name ∈ AGENTS ∧
    agent_name ∈ agent_groupe ∧
    state(agent_name) = Initiator ∧
    choice_propose ∈ agent_groupe → BOOL
INITIALISATION
    ag_role, agent_name,   task   :=   gest_voy,
    agent_voy, Find_fligth ||
    choice_propose := ∅
OPERATIONS
    cfp_agent_voy(dtdep, dtar, vdep, var) =
        PRE
```

```
    task=Find_fligth ∧
    ag_role  =  gest_voy ∧  dtdep ∈
    NAT ∧
    dtar ∈ NAT ∧ dtdep < dtar
    ∧ vdep ∈ VILLES
    ∧ var ∈ VILLES
THEN
    cfp_voy(agent_name, dtdep, dtar)
END;
resp_propose=
    ANY ag_part WHERE
    ag_part   ∈   agent_groupe   ∧
    state(ag_part)  =  Participant  ∧
    agent_name ∈ agent_groupe ∧
    messages_exchanged⁻¹ ({ag_part
    ↦ agent_name}) = propose ∧
    deadline=time_out ∧
    choice_propose(ag_part)=TRUE
THEN
    send_accept(agent_name, ag_part)

END
```

Fig. 11. The travel agent machine

The *agent_voy* agent plays the *gest_voy* role. Machine *gest_voy* is included using keyword INCLUDE thus allowing the use of the operations, variables, sets and invariants of the included machine. Machine *gest_voy* will call the *C_NET* machine that specifies the Contract Net Protocol. The *gest_voy* role specification is given in Figure 12.

MACHINE
  Gest_Voy
INCLUDES
    M_CNET
VARIABLES
    date_depart, date_arrivee,cprice
INVARIANT
    date_depart $\in$ **NAT** $\wedge$
    cprice $\in$ **NAT** $\wedge$
    date_arrivee $\in$ **NAT** $\wedge$
    date_arrivee $\geq$ *date_depart*
INITIALISATION
    date_depart, date_arrivee,cprice := 0, 0, 0
OPERATIONS
    cfp_voy(*ag_ini,dtp,dta*) =
      PRE
        ag_ini $\in$ *agent_groupe* $\wedge$
        dtp $\in$ **NAT** $\wedge$ *dta* $\in$ **NAT** $\wedge$
        dta > *dtp*
      THEN
        Starting_system(*ag_ini*) ||
        date_depart := *dtp* ||
        date_arrivee := *dta*
      END;
    compare_price(*p1,p2*)=
      PRE
        p1 $\in$ **NAT** $\wedge$ *p2* $\in$ **NAT**
      THEN
        cprice:=min({*p1,p2*})

END;
send_accept(*ag,agp*)=
  PRE
    ag $\in$ *agent_groupe* $\wedge$ *agp* $\in$
    agent_groupe $\wedge$
    state(*agp*) = *Participant* $\wedge$
    state(*ag*) = *Initiator* $\wedge$
    messages_exchanged $^{-1}$ ({*agp* $\mapsto$
    ag}) = *propose* $\wedge$
    deadline = *time_out*
  THEN
    response(*accept_proposal,ag,agp*)
  END;
send_refuse(*ag,agp*)=
  PRE
    ag $\in$ *agent_groupe* $\wedge$ *agp* $\in$
    agent_groupe $\wedge$
    state(*agp*) = *Participant* $\wedge$
    state(*ag*) = *Initiator* $\wedge$
    messages_exchanged $^{-1}$ ({*agp* $\mapsto$
    ag}) = *propose* $\wedge$
    deadline = *time_out*
  THEN
    response(*reject_proposal,ag,agp*)
  END

END

Fig. 12. The travel manager role machine

For space reasons machine *agent_voy* uses only two operations here. Operation *cfp_agent_voy(dtdep, dtar, vdep, var)* triggers the sending of message "*cfp*" where *dtdep, dtar, vdep, var* are volatile pieces of information such as dates and places of the flight. This operation calls operation *cfp_voy(ag_ini, dtp ,dta)* in the *gest_voy* role machine (figure 12) which in turn calls operation *Starting_system(ag_ini)* in the *C_Net* machine that is included in the *gest_voy* machine. Then, the *gest_voy* role follows the Contract Net Protocol procedure and respects the related invariants.

Operation *resp_propose* processes the "*propose*" messages received from the participating agents. This operation checks whether the deadline has expired and whether the "*propose*" messages have been received from the participating agents. If the initiator agent chooses one proposition, it calls operation `send_accept`(ag, agp) from the *Gest_voy* machine, where *ag* is the initiator agent that plays the *Gest_voy* role and *agp* is a participating agent. The *Gest_voy* machine also calls operation `response`(`accept_proposal`, ag, agp) from the *C_Net* machine in order to send an answer.

It is the *agent_voy* machine that starts the communication and synchronizes the call of operations.

3.2   Specification of the Participating Agent

We have studied only the specification of agent *Agent_vol1* because it plays the same role as *Agent_vol2*.

This specification is presented in the figure 13.

MACHINE
  Agent_Vol
INCLUDES
  Gest_Vol
VARIABLES
  ag_role, agent_name, available
INVARIANT
  $ag\_role \in ROLES \wedge$
  $agent\_name \in AGENTS \wedge$
  $agent\_name \in agent\_group \wedge$
  $available \in \mathbf{BOOL} \wedge$
  $state(agent\_name) = Participant$
INITIALISATION
  $ag\_role, agent\_name := gest\_vol, agent\_vol1$
  $\| \; available :\in \mathbf{BOOL}$

OPERATIONS

  verif_avail_agent$(dtdep, dtar, v1, v2)$ $=$
    PRE
      $ag\_role = gest\_vol$
        $\wedge \; dtdep \in \mathbf{NAT} \wedge dtar \in \mathbf{NAT}$
        $\wedge \; dtdep < dtar \wedge$
        $v1 \in LOCALITE \wedge$
        $v2 \in LOCALITE \wedge$
        $agent\_name \in agent\_group \wedge$

      $state(agent\_name) = Participant \wedge$
      $(v1 \mapsto v2) \in voyage \quad \wedge$
      $messages\_exchanged^{-1} (\{state^{-1}$
      $(Initiator) \mapsto agent\_name\}) = cfp$
    THEN
      $available := avail$
    END;

  propose_price$(dd, da, vd, va) =$
    PRE
      $state(agent\_name) = Participant \wedge$
      $dd \in \mathbf{NAT} \wedge da \in \mathbf{NAT} \wedge$
      $vd \in LOCALITE \wedge$
      $va \in LOCALITE \wedge$
      $available = \mathbf{TRUE} \wedge$
      $messages\_exchanged^{-1} (\{state^{-1}$
      $(Initiator) \mapsto agent\_name\}) = cfp \wedge$
      $deadline = in\_time$
    THEN
      propose_pr$(agent\_name, state^{-1}$
      $(Initiator), price((vd, va)))$
    END

END

Fig. 13. The flight agent machine

This agent plays the *gest_vol* role. Machine *Gest_vol* is given in Figure 14.

The *Agent_vol* machine uses variable *name_agent* which identifies the name of an agent. This name should belong to the set *agent_group ag_role* ∈ ROLES and uses variable *ag_role* to designate the role played by *agent_name*.

In its dynamic section, this machine contains some internal operations such as *verify_avail* and *propose_price*. The first operation checks whether agent *agent_name* has received the *"cfp"* message from the group's initiator agent. If the flight data are correct and if the flight is available. This operation returns a boolean value: *available*.

The operation *propose_price(dd, da, vd, va)* checks whether the flight is available and whether agent *Agent_name* has received a *"cfp"* message, and if the deadline has not expired. If this is true the operation *propose_pr(ag, agi, pp)* of the *Gest_vol* machine is called. Then this *Gest_vol* machine launches operation **send_response(propose, ag, agi)** from the *M_Cnet* machine. *ag* is the sender agent, *agi* is the receiver agent, and *pp* is the flight fare. This price amount is given by the *Gest_vol* machine with the help of the *price* variable: $price \in voyage \rightarrow NAT$ and $voyage \in$ PLACES $\leftrightarrow$ PLACES where PLACES is a set of cities.

In this case *agi* is the initiator agent that sends the *"cfp"* message.

MACHINE
  Gest_Vol
INCLUDES
  M_CNET
SETS
  PLACES
VARIABLES
  voyage,date_dep, date_arr, price, avail
INVARIANT
  avail ∈ **BOOL** ∧
  voyage ∈ *PLACES* ↔ *PLACES* ∧
  price ∈ *voyage* → **NAT** ∧
  date_dep ∈ *voyage* → **NAT** ∧
  date_arr ∈ *voyage* → **NAT** ∧
  dom(*date_dep*) = **dom**(*date_arr*)
INITIALISATION
  voyage,price, date_dep, date_arr := ∅ , ∅ ,
    ∅ , ∅ ||
  avail:=**FALSE**

OPERATIONS
  Verif_avail(*d1,d2,vd,va*) =
    PRE *d1* ∈ **NAT** ∧ *d2* ∈ **NAT** ∧ *vd*
    ∈ *PLACES* ∧ *va* ∈ *PLACES* ∧ (*vd* ↦
    va)∈*voyage*
    THEN
    avail :=**bool**(*date_dep* $^{-1}$ (*d1*)=(*vd* ↦
    va) ∧ *date_arr* $^{-1}$ (*d2*)=(*vd* ↦ *va*)

∧ *date_dep* $^{-1}$ (*d1*)=*date_arr* $^{-1}$
(*d2*))
END;

pr ← **prices**(*vd,va*) =
  PRE
  vd ∈ *PLACES* ∧ *va* ∈ *PLACES* ∧ (*vd*
  ↦ *va*) ∈ *voyage*
  THEN
  pr:=*price*((*vd* ↦ *va*))
  END;

propose_pr(*ag,agi,pp*) =
  PRE
  agi ∈ *agent_groupe* ∧ *ag* ∈
  agent_groupe ∧
  pp ∈ **NAT** ∧ *state*(*ag*) = *Participant* ∧
  state(*agi*) = *Initiator* ∧
  messages_exchanged $^{-1}$ ({*agi* ↦ *ag*}) =
  cfp ∧
  deadline=*in_time*
  THEN

  send_response(*propose,ag,agi*)
  END

END

Fig. 14. The flight manager role machine

The following figure shows the various calls between the machines.

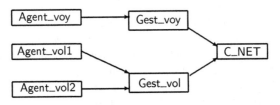

Fig. 15. The calls of the machines

4   Conclusion and Future Work

Several papers have been published on how to use B's formal specification in different systems [10] and also on the way to go from a semi-formal specification (like UML) to a formal specification with B method or the reverse [11][5]. In this article, we have shown how the B method can be used to specify the interaction aspect of a multiagent system, and how an interaction protocol can be formally specified.

In order to do so one needs to study the multiagent system and get the specification for the agents, roles and finally the Contract Net Protocol. Our specification is at an abstract level which has led us to derive abstract proofs. All our specifications have been proved.

A number of works have been published on formal specification of multiagent system using the Z method [12][13]. The present work's originality is that it gives a formal specification of the Contract Net Protocol with B, a method that is based on the sets theory. In the past, to our knowledge this interaction protocol has only been specified using ACL, Promela, etc.

We chose to use the B method because of its simplicity, ease of understanding. Besides it is a structured language that enables to proove the specification validity by a set of the obligation proofs. B also naturally leads to the refining of a specification and the generation of code (Ada, C). There are efficient industrials tools for using B such as ATELIER B [14].

In the long run, we intend on adding other properties to our multiagent system and thus refine our specification at a lower level in order to obtain a complete specification and then be able to implement our system.

Acknowledgment

The authors would like to thank Akram IDANI for his valuable comments on this paper and his help in checking the various B specifications.

References

1. Ferber, J.: Multi-Agent Systems: An Introduction to Distributed Artificial Intelligence. 1st edition edn. Addison-Wesley Pub Co (1999)
2. Odell, J., Nodine, M., Levy, R.: A metamodel for agents, roles, and groups. In Odell, J., Giorgini, P., Müller, J., eds.: gent-Oriented Software Engineering (AOSE) IV. Lecture Notes on Computer Science, Berlin, Springer (2005)
3. Bauer, B.: UML classe diagrams revisited in the context of agent-based systems. In Wooldridge, M., Ciancarini, P., Weiss, G., eds.: Agent-Oriented Software Engineering (AOSE 01), Montreal, Canada, Springer-Verlag (2001) 1–8
4. Bicarregui, J.: Formal methods into practice: case studies in the application of the B method. IEE Proceedings on Software Engineering **144** (1997) 119–133
5. Tatibouet, B., Hammad, A., Voisinet, J.: From an abstract B specification to UML class diagrams. In: 2nd IEEE International Symposium on Signal Processing and Information Technology (ISSPIT'2002), Marrakech, Morocco (2002)
6. Odell, J., Van Dyke Parunak, H., Bauer, B.: Representing agent interaction protocols in UML. In Ciancarini, P., Wooldridge, M., eds.: Proceedings of First International Workshop on Agent-Oriented Software Engineering, Limerick, Ireland, Springer-Verlag (2000) 121–140
7. Abrial, J.R.: The B-Book: Assigning Programs to Meanings. Cambridge University Press (1996)
8. Abrial, J.R., Mussat, L.: Introducing dynamic constraints in B. In: B'98: Recent Advances in the Development and Use of the B Method. Volume 1393 of LNCS., Springer-Verlag (1998) 83–128

9. Yoo, M.J., Merlat, W., Briot, J.P.: Modeling and validation of mobile agents on the Web. In Fishwick, P.A., Hill, D.R., Smith, R., eds.: 1998 International Conference on Web-based Modeling and Simulation. Volume 30 of Simulation Series., San Diego CA, USA, The Society for Computer Simulation (1998) 23–28

10. Malioukov, A.: An object-based approch to the B formal method. In Bert, D., ed.: Second International B Conference: Recent Advances in the Development and Use of the B Method (B'98). Volume 1393 of Simulation Series., Montpellier, France, Springer-Verlag, Heidelberg (1998) 162

11. Laleau, R., Mammar, A.: An overview of a method and its support tool for generating B specifications from UML notations. In: International Conference on Automated Software Engineering (ASE2000), Grenoble, France, IEEE CS Press (2000)

12. d'Inverno, M., Fisher, M., Lomuscio, A., Luck, M., de Rijke, M., Ryan, M., Wooldridge, M.: Formalisms for multi-agent systems. The Knowledge Engineering Review **12** (1997)

13. Hilaire, V., Koukam, A., Gruer, P., Muller, J.P.: Formal specification and prototyping of multi-agent systems. In: Engineering Societies in the Agents' World. Volume 1972 of Lecture Notes in Artificial Intelligence. Springer Verlag (2000)

14. Casset, L.: Development of an embedded verifier for java card byte code using formal methods. In: Formal Methods Europe (FME'02). Volume 2391 of Lecture Notes in Computer Science., Springer-Verlag (2002)

Behavioral Self-control
of Agent-Based Virtual Pedestrians

Emmanuelle Grislin-Le Strugeon, David Hanon, and René Mandiau

LAMIH-UMR 8530, Universite de Valenciennes,
59313 Valenciennes Cedex 9, France
{Emmanuelle.Grislin,David.Hanon,Rene.Mandiau}
@univ-valenciennes.fr
http://www.univ-valenciennes.fr/LAMIH

Abstract. Agents need some kind of autonomy to act in open and dynamic environments. However, the resulting behavior is not always well adapted to the situation. The use of models that combine different reasoning levels creates other difficulties. The management of the control transfer and balance between abstract time-consuming reasoning processes and reactive quick low-level behaviors are particularly complex. Our model is based on the self-observation and control of agents. The main topic is the inconsistency detection used to transfer the control between contiguous levels. This is detailed in the context of virtual pedestrians design.

1 Introduction

In open and dynamic environments, correct behaviors of autonomous entities are difficult to achieve. Indeed, the autonomy (see [4] for a recent study of this notion) given by internal drives or low-level goals, is well-adapted to enable reactivity to events, but its interaction with the environment can generate unexpected behaviors, such as blocking states. The autonomy provided by high-level goals is based on more abstract knowledge about their environment and themselves, which enables a larger view and understanding of the world. However, deeper reasoning processes are also more computationally expensive, and this creates some difficulties in several application domains. For instance, the reasoning time of autonomous virtual entities are constrained by the simulation cycle time. In such contexts, it seems interesting to reserve high level reasoning activities to solve situations in which they are really necessary.

In order to handle situations with the suited level of reasoning, the agents must be able to identify which is this level in every situation. In a more restricted approach, the model presented here is an attempt to give the agents the ability to change their reasoning level on the base of the recognition of inconsistencies in their own behavior. The first part insists on the multi-level models that are required by specific application domains, and their inherent difficulties. The second part presents the model, based on a self-observation and control. The third part gives application details in the context of the pedestrian behavior design. The last part concludes, and gives some research perspectives.

F.F. Ramos et al. (Eds.): ISSADS 2005, LNCS 3563, pp. 529–537, 2005.

2   A Multi-level Reasoning Model

Symbolic and emergent models have their own advantages and drawbacks. In some cases, it is impossible to choose one approach against another. We consider agents models that involve more than one reasoning process. Faced to opposite requirements, such models answer by the possibility to activate different levels of reasoning associated to different representations of themselves and the environment.

For example, in our application context, the problematic is to model virtual pedestrians that exhibit two opposite abilities: the ability to dynamically plan its route, taking into account some constraints about the environment and its own behavior, and the ability to quickly react to an open and dynamic world, with possible unexpected situations. The first ability is well adapted to long-term decisions, the second one runs well to activate short-term urgency behaviors. An intermediate ability has been added to control the navigation of the agents; this is quite usual in virtual pedestrian models [1] [12].

These are different levels of autonomy that require different knowledge and reasoning processes. Each of them, separately taken, possesses its specific problematic, but our interest is in the interaction between these different reasoning levels, that may produce both contradictory and complementary decisions. Planning, plan adaptation and follow-up are essential to show realist behaviors that are directed by some goals and not as erratic ones. However, low-level actions can not be totally controlled by higher levels, because there are real-time constraints. The speed of the decisions production is crucial, the reflex actions are important, especially when the software includes user's actions, like the events produced by a player. The consequence is the necessity of the integration of different levels of reasoning in the agent model.

In the Artificial Intelligence domain, hybrid systems incorporate several mechanisms or techniques that come from different approaches into one common model. Hybrid agents are usually defined as agents that include both cognitive-like and reactive-like elements. This can be generalized to models that include more than one reasoning process, situated at more than one abstraction level. A common problematic of these models is the control transfer between the layers. Horizontal layering (see for instance [6]) with a central control system can lead to bottlenecks, whereas vertical approaches (see for instance [9]) create strong dependencies between the layers.

According to the virtual reality constraints, the low level is essential to generate the system's responses within the bounded delays requested by the animation run. However, short-term knowledge and reasoning generate short-term decisions, which result in a behavior that may seem inconsistent to the observers of a longer period. Thus, it is interesting to keep a constant activity of the most reactive layer but under an observation activity of the upper layers that can intervene when the resulting behavior shows some difficulty. This approach can be classified into the vertical category but the low level is not completely and not continuously dependent of the upper ones. The interaction among the agent model levels is studied in the specific objective of the self-detection of inconsistent behaviors. An open and dynamic environment does not always enable to determine totally safe behaviors for the agents. Usual situations are obviously studied, allowing the refinement process of some simulation parameters. However, the difficulty to parameter reactive behaviors in simulation contexts is well known. Bryson [3] showed that in very dynamic situations, agents be-have better when they ignore some information. She noticed either that even learning methods are not always the appropriate solutions. We do not look for an optimal behavior, supposed to be too dependent of elements that are difficult to model, such as the behavior of a player. We would rather try to give the agent the competence to evaluate its behavior and change it when it is no more suited to the current situation.

3 Behavioral Self-control

The self-control of the agent behavior consists in placing the lower abstraction levels decisions under the control of the higher ones. Local actions of the agent acquire some significance when they are placed in a global context and according to medium or long-term goals.

3.1 General Principle

The general principle of the self-control process is based on some basic cases of con-trol flows transfer among the reasoning levels of the agent (Figure 1).

Interaction Between Contiguous Levels. The interaction occurs between contiguous levels. They operate as hierarchical ones. Two contiguous levels share some states and actions representations.

Top-Down Control. The level i has higher abstraction knowledge than the level $(i-1)$, and thus has some higher semantic understanding of the current situation, which is required and used to control it. Higher the level is, longer is the term of its goals.

Bottom-up Updates. Only the lowest level can perceive low-level states of itself and the environment. Thus, updates of the agent self-representation come from the lowest level to cause chaining modifications in the higher levels.

Compared to other multi-layered agent or character's architectures (see for exam-ple [5]), this model shares with Bryson [3] the idea that the control of the low layers by the higher ones can not occur at any time. Some constraints are only visible at low levels. That is why high level goals must be seen as global directives that are trans-lated by low levels into more concrete actions. Our model presents a new approach whose aim is to find some solutions to give the agent the ability to determine whether its own behavior is appropriate or not.

3.2 Actions and States Observation

In order to make behavior control, the agent has to observe its own actions and states. The actions are decisions products; the states are the results of the actions realization. To model these elements, we chose Petri nets, a well-known representation, that al-lows dynamic aspects modeling and provides analysis possibilities [10]. In the Petri net formalism, the observation of actions and states consist in the analysis of the tran-sitions triggering and the places marking. The evolution of the agent's state can be represented as the trace of the triggered transitions and/or marked places, and can be also seen as a word in the grammar of this representation.

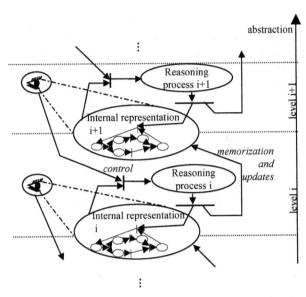

Fig. 1. Self-observation and control principles applied to a multi-level architecture

3.3 Inconsistency Detection

The inconsistency detection is based on a memory of the decisions of actions and the states of the agent. The decisions can be modeled as states of "commands", thus we will only study states modeling in the following.

The states are memorized and then forgotten in order to always keep a trace with a length that is sufficient according to the inconsistencies to be detected. For instance, if we want to detect the deficiency defined by the property p, that requires the observation of n successive states, the process will apply on sequences of n states $s = a_1$ $a_2 \dots a_n$, where a_i is the observed state at the step (or time) i. At the step t of the simulation, the self-observation applies to the $(t-1)$ to $(t-n)$ past states.

In the model, this process is realized by the memorization of the marking of the places that must be controlled. Each of them is associated with a memory place that stocks its markings, which are associated to their dates (see Figure 2a).

3.4 Self-control

When the self-observation reveals a deficiency in the agent behavior, self-control consists in introducing behavior modifications. Using the Petri net formalism, the detection of an inconsistent behavior generates the marking of the inconsistency detection place, which is used to control the transitions representing the agent's behavior. The inconsistency places are precondition places for some transitions. In this way, they can be used to select the action to make at the next step. In a first attempt, the self-control is a behavior "censor" because it can inhibit some decisions (figure 2a). In a second approach, the self-control can be used to switch the control between two levels of reasoning, and especially to transfer the control to the immediately higher level (figure 2b).

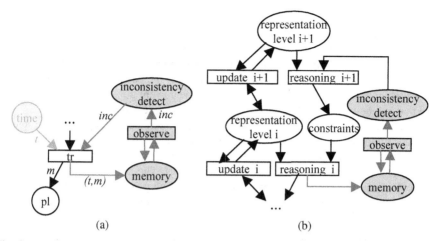

Fig. 2. (a) Model of a simple place (pl) marking memorization and observation, to control an associated transition (tr); (b) Principle of updates and controls between contiguous reasoning level

4 Application to Virtual Pedestrians

We developed a multi-level model of agent for the software called RESPECT[1], whose objective is to teach road safety to children as pedestrians in a urban environment. The child player moves its avatar in a virtual city, including vehicles and other virtual pedestrians. The other pedestrians are aimed at contributing to the realism of the environment. The pedestrians and the vehicles must react to each other's and to the player's actions; the play must be configurable in terms of road environment; some characteristics of the virtual entities are also configurable.

4.1 The Three-Levels Model

For our virtual reality application, the model of the autonomous pedestrians includes three levels. This division is usual to autonomous characters and more generally to autonomous agents (see for examples [2], [8], [9]).

Level 1. The low level is closed to the "physical" actions. It delivers commands to move the body of the characters, in a first limited way as a vector of two differential values applied to its acceleration and orientation. The underlying model is a reactive model based on an actions merging mechanism [7]. The internal representation at this level includes "raw" information coming from the agent's sensors, about the agent's physical state (position, orientation, speed...) and the set of the perceived objects. These are quickly evaluated to determine with which it is going to be in collision, and the urgency of the reaction. The selection of an action is a process, which can run independently from the other layers "reasoning products".

---

[1]   Research supported by the interdepartmental land transport research and innovation program PREDIT (France)

Level 2. The intermediate level observes the actions realized at the first level and updates some measures and states. The internal representations at this level are used to classify the current situation according to two main aspects.

One of the representations is the plan. The knowledge of the position is used to update the evolution in the plan. The achievement of the current goal, and the acquisition of the next one are managed at this level. The current goal is provided as an input data that can be taken into account in the reasoning process of the level 1.

Another part of the second level knowledge is dedicated to represent the agents' interaction situations. Given the memorized previous situation and the current one, the mutual interaction of two agents is classified into one of four categories (namely, *front crossing, side crossing, following, overtaking*). The knowledge of the situation category is provided as a mean for the level 1 decision process to select the appropriate action to do. It is another input data from level 2 to level 1, but like the previous one, it can be ignored by the first level in case of emergency.

Level 3. The highest level includes the representation of the scenario and the ability to plan the agent's route. The achievement point of the global task is known at this level. The own tasks and objectives of the agents are generated here.

4.2 Behavior Measures and Data Flows Control

The transfer of the control between the three levels is based on two main criteria that qualify the situation in terms of urgency and consistency.

The urgency of the situation is a first criterion to control the data flows among the different layers. Critical situations are mostly handled by the reactive layer, whereas anticipation can be applied when the situations match the predicted ones. In our application context and in a first approach, the urgency is measured by the time before collision. It is measured by the lowest level that can let the control to its upper level when the resulting value is low enough.

The consistency of the behavior is another criterion, which is used to select the active reasoning processes. At Level 2, the first level information and the memory of past decisions are used to update two measures (Figure 3):

- a measure of the agent's satisfaction relatively to its current goal achievement. For example, the navigation, which is the transition from a goal to another, is controlled at this level;
- a measure of the consistency relatively to its medium-term (for instance, 10 simulations steps) behavior.

Similarly to the previous one, Level 3 observes the decisions made at its underlevel (Figure 3). Two measures similar to the previous ones are made:

- the satisfaction measure represents the plan achievement,
- the consistency measure applies to the long-term (for instance, 100 simulation steps) behavior.

4.3 Examples of Inconsistency Detection and Self-control

As examples, the detection processes of two inconsistency behaviors are described.

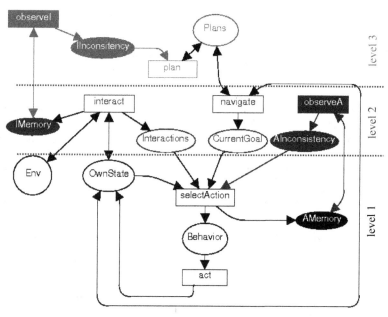

Fig. 3. The behavioral model of the pedestrian agent (observation and detection actions are color filled elements)

Dithering Detection. A dithering behavior is here defined as a sequence that includes repeated opposite actions or decisions. For example, a dithering behavior of the virtual pedestrian can be a succession of rotation decisions to the right, then to the left, then to the right, and so on. Theses actions are produced by the first reasoning level, the most reactive one. Their observation is made by the second level in order to detect the eventual oscillations.

Two actions a_i and a_j are said contradictory ones if they verify a specific condition $c(a_i, a_j)$. In our application context, the oscillation behavior is verified when there exists at least k contradictory actions in a sequence of n simulation steps, that is:

$$|C| \geq k, \text{with constant } k \text{ and } C = \{i \in [t-n, t-1], c(a_i, a_{i+1})\}$$

The detection of a dithering behavior triggers a change in the level of reasoning. More abstract knowledge is used in the decision process. For instance, the reaction to the view of an obstacle can create oscillations at a first reactive level. At the upper level, the knowledge of the interaction category is used to activate a persistent behavior. For example, an interaction situation that is recognized belonging to the following category induces a behavior of minimal distances maintaining and no more a reactive avoiding behavior.

Mutual Blocking Detection. This type of inconsistent behavior is defined by a sequence of states that shows both a lack of evolution toward the goal and a lack of change in the interaction situation with another mobile. The measure of evolution toward the goal is made on the sequence of the agent's positions relatively to the same current goal.

Having a goal g_k that is active in the time interval $[t_k,t]$, the goal achievement is measured on a period of more than n steps to give a first indication.

At time t, having a goal g_k which is active since t_k, and a goal achievement measure $a(p_t,g_k)$, if it is possible to find a state p_{t-d} at time $(t-d)$, such as $(d{\geq}n)$ and $(t-d{\geq}tk)$, the lack of evolution is detected iff $a(p_{t-d},gk){\leq}a(p_t,gk)$

The past states are evaluated in the anti-chronological order; the lack of evolution is thus the most recent one. Having a lack of evolution detected at time (t-d), there is then a search made on the interactions that could have cause the blocking situation. At time (t-d), the interacting situation s_{t-d} is described by an ordered set of couples (o_i,c_j) made of one mobile obstacle and one interaction category. The changes are observed in the time interval [t-d,t], changes in the classification of the interaction with o_i or its "disappearing" since one of the next steps, thus in one of the interacting situations s_{t-l} with l in [t-d,t].

At time t, having an interaction situation s_t, for each interacting object o_i such as $(oi,cj){\in}st$, any object o_i can be suspected to be a cause of the blocking situation iff $\forall l{\in}[0,d]\,(oi,cj){\in}st-l$

The conjunction of these two properties leads to the detection of an inconsistency. The observation actions are made by the third level on data that are accessible by the second level. In case of inconsistency detection, some regulation actions must be made. In a first attempt, only the dual interactions are considered. The classification of interacting situation is based on a model that considers the agents two by two. In this context, the action consists in a local re-planning that takes into account the first suspect obstacle.

5   Conclusion and Perspectives

The combination of different levels of abstraction in one common reasoning model requires a kind of control. Especially when different layers provide potentially opposite decisions, the problem consists in shifting the activity from one behavioral module to another. In order to handle unpredictable situations, our model is based on the control of low reactive layers by more abstract reasoning processes, in an a posteriori manner. Past activities and states are evaluated to detect eventual inconsistencies along medium and long-term periods.

In case of inconsistency detection, the agent must find the cause of such a situation. We did not treated this second phase as far as it should be. Our future work includes the study of the methods that can be used to find the reason for the inconsistent behavior from the information provided by the different levels. Another aspect consists in the representation and processing of the agents interactions. The interaction between agents should consider multiple interactions including more than two of them. For example, the blocking situation can be created by more than two agents.

The model presented here is built on the idea that the inconsistent behavior is due to a wrong model or a wrong reasoning process of the agent about its environment. But the inconsistency can come from the environment. In this case, even high abstract representation would not be of any help. Thus, when the agent does not succeed in modeling the behavior of some environmental elements, the control should be transferred to a lower level. However, it seems difficult to determine whether the inconsistency is due to the agent's own deficiency or to an environmental element's behavior.

References

1. Badler N., Bindiganavale R., Bourne J., Allbeck J., Shi J., Palmer M.: Real time virtual humans. International Conference on Digital Media Futures, Bradford, UK, April (1999)
2. Bonasso, R.P., Kortenkamp, D., Miller, D.P., Slack, M. Experiences with an architecture for intelligent, reactive agents. In Wooldridge, M., Müller, J.P., Tambe, M. (eds.): Intelligents Agents – Proceedings of the 1995 Workshop on Agent Theories, Architectures, and Languages (ATAL-95), Lecture Notes in AI, vol. 1037, Springer-Verlag (1996), 187–202
3. Bryson, J.: Cross-Paradigm Analysis of Autonomous Agent Architecture. Journal of Experimental and Theoretical Artificial Intelligence (JETAI), vol 12, n°2 (2000) 165–189
4. Carabelea, C., Boissier, O., Florea, A.: Autonomy in Multi-agent Systems: A Classification Attempt. Workshop on Autonomy in Multi-Agent Systems, Melbourne, July (2003)
5. Donikian, S.: HPTS: a Behavior Modelling Language for Autonomous Agents. In the proceedings of the Fifth International Conference on Autonomous Agents (Agents 2001), Montreal, Canada, May, ACM Press (2001) 401–408
6. Ferguson I. A.: Integrated Control and Coordinated Behavior: a Case for Agent Models. In the proceedings of ECAI- 94 Workshop on Agent Theories, Architectures and Languages (1994) 203–218
7. Hanon D., Grislin-Le Strugeon E., Mandiau R.: A behavior based architecture for the control of virtual pedestrians. In Vadakkepat, P., Wan, T.W., Chen, T.K., Poh, L.A. (eds.): Proceedings of the Second International Conference on Computational Intelligence, Robotics and Autonomous Systems CIRAS, CIC, National University of Singapore, Singapore, dec. (2003) 125–132
8. Laird, J.E., Rosenbloom, P.S.: The evolution of the Soar cognitive architecture. In Steier, D.M., Mitchell, T.M. (eds.): Mind Matters: A Tribute to Allen Newell, Lawrence Erlbaum Associates (1996) 1–50
9. Müller, J.P.: The Design of Intelligent Agents, A layered Approach. Lecture Notes in AI, vol. 1177, Springer-Verlag (1996)
10. Peterson, J.L.: Petri Net Theory and the Modelling of Systems. Prentice-Hall, New Jersey (1981)
11. Reynolds, C.W.: Steering Behaviors For Autonomous Characters. Game Developers Conference (1999)
12. Thalmann, D.: Concepts and Models for Inhabited Virtual Worlds. In proceedings of the First International Workshop on Language Understanding and Agents for Real World Interactions, Sapporo, Japan, July 13 (2003)

Security Challenges
of Distributed *e*-Learning Systems

Roberto Gómez Cárdenas[1] and Erika Mata Sánchez[2]

[1] ITESM-CEM, 52926 Edo. de México, México
`rogomez@itesm.mx`
[2] LRIA, EPHE – Université Paris 8 41, rue Gay Lussac, 75005 Paris
`emata@univ-paris8.fr`

Abstract. Security considerations play an increasingly important role for distributed computing. In today's Internet age, academia requires sharing, distributing, merging, changing information, linking applications and other resources within and among universities and other related organizations. Because *e*-learning systems are open, distributed and interconnected, then security becomes an important challenge in order to insure that interested actors only have access to the right information at the appropriate time. The purpose of this paper is to give an in-depth understanding of most important security challenges that can be relevant for distributed *e*-learning systems.

1   Introduction

The proliferation of components and open systems yields economic and interoperability benefits, but present new security challenges. In distributed systems, the potential danger is multiplied because the openness and distributed nature of these systems result in more potential access points for an attacker.

With more and more critical systems becoming open, distributed, interconnected and manufactured with component applications, the end result is that these systems are increasingly vulnerable to attacks. Accordingly, intrusion detection systems that can be detect cyber attacks, and security tools that can be used to mount a response do exist. However, an approach to integrate them in order to increase the survivability of distributed applications is needed; especially in distributed e-learning domain, where most today's proposals for architectures and systems are standards-driven but regardless of the security concerns.

E-learning systems can be characterized with large and dynamic user population and resource pool, dynamic resource acquisition and release, dynamic creation and destruction of a variety of network connections. At the same time, *e*-learning trends are demanding a greater level of interoperability for applications, learning environments and heterogenous systems. These characteristics make the security issues quite challenging.

The purpose of this paper is to give an in-depth understanding of most important security challenges that can be relevant for today's and future distributed *e*-learning systems. In order to achieve this, our paper is organized as follows:

F.F. Ramos et al. (Eds.): ISSADS 2005, LNCS 3563, pp. 538–544, 2005.

in section 2, an overview of security requirements for distributed computing with emphasis on Internet environments is given. Section 3 is devoted to the presentation of e-learning domain and its emerging trends from a technological viewpoint. Major security challenges of distributed e-learning applications are described in section 4. Finally, we present our conclusions.

2   Security for Distributed Applications

In [6], the author presents several approaches in which distributed systems can increase security of Information Systems. However, the approach of this paper is quite different. In widely distributed information systems, including the Web, it is often necessary to establish exclusive relationships of mutual trust between widely dispersed system elements, thus permitting the dynamic formation of closed domains within an otherwise open system and, in particular, to permit two-way exchanges between unambiguously and undeniably identified users. This capability lies at the heart of electronic commerce, and hence much effort has been expended on the development of appropriate sophisticated cryptographic security protocols [7].

Clearly, secure data exchange within distributed systems brings major advantages to its users. However, any data exchanges entails some risks and vulnerabilities. Cryptographic protocols must take into account attacks such as "The Man in the Middle", in which an unauthorized person can obtain access into a system by pretending to be an authorized user. Another attack example, known as replay attack [10], consists in capturing a message or a piece of a message wherewith, at any time later, an intruder gets into a system. Nevertheless, these are only two examples of possible vulnerability issues, we can mention another ones such as IP spoofing, hijacking, smurfing or DoS (Denied of Service).

Security requirements have to be focused on how an attack may manifest itself in various system layers and how to respond to them. At the application level, an attack may result in one or more requests being blocked indefinitely; one or more requests timing out or throwing exception despite multiple attempts; and/or one or more objects crashing, perhaps repeatedly on restarts. At the network level, symptoms of an attack may include abnormal traffic volume in a network segment; unexpected content and/or overload or crash of network devices. At the operating system level, attack symptoms may include unusual programs or scripts, or unusual processes and CPU load; and/or unusual pattern of network interface and system calls.

With widespread use of the internet as a core networking and cooperative computing infrastructure, concerns about security and risks have spread to stakeholders in every line of e-learning systems. Accordingly, security issues in distributed learning environments are difficult to address, given the diverseness of the clients, servers, databases, legacy and components that must be integrated. Whereas individual environments, legacy components may have their own security policies and mechanisms, in a distributed environment, security must be designed and developed across the Internet and intranets.

In a client/server environment, security policies and mechanisms must be designed to support authentication, authorization, confidentiality and accountability.

- Authentication involves validating the end users' identity prior to permit them server access.
- Authorization defines what rights and services the end user is allowed once server access is granted.
- Confidentiality keeps information from being disclosed to anyone not authorized to access it.
- Accounting provides the methodology for collecting information about the end user's resource consumption, which can then be processed for billing, auditing, and capacity-planning purposes.

The confidentiality issue is particularly important when client and servers are separated by networks.

Two key concepts for the development of secure systems are the security policy and enforcement mechanism [5]. The security policy is defined as the set of laws, rules and practices that regulate how an organization manages, protects and distributes sensitive information [1]. Once the security policy is defined, it must be captured and followed at application runtime via an enforcement mechanism which represents the set of centralized and distributed software to insure that the security policy is maintained and never violated. In general, security policies are application dependent, and consequently, data security requirements vary widely from application to application.

In order to begin to address security authorization, and authentication for distributed computing, the critical first step is to identify, delineate, and explain the key security requirements. This is accomplished by focus our attention on information access and control, security handlers and processing, and legacy of component applications.

2.1   Information Access and Control

User security privileges are a key concern when defining the security policy for distributed computing. The types of users of distributed applications, e-Learning in our particular, need different types of information at different times based on their needs potentially dynamically changing needs. Questions related to information access should be organized following security requirements that would be spelled out in the policy (which is more static); information that should be passed to users in normal operating solutions; and also, information that must be available on demand in dynamic situations.

2.2   Security Handlers/Processing

Security handler is a piece of software that is responsible for managing some portion of an application's security policy. Once the security policy have been determined, an essential requirement is to consider steps, approaches, and techniques that are necessary to maintain and enforce that policy in a dynamic, distributed and interoperative environment via security handlers that interact across it.

Historically, security has been managed at a centralized level, with a common system providing access to a shared repository of information. Nevertheless, in a client/server, distributed computing environment, such an approach will need to be expanded and evolved in order to meet more complicated and diverse requirements.

Security requirements and policy to the maintenance and enforcement at runtime, it's necessary to define and develop various security techniques to insure that the right information is getting to the right users at the right time. Accordingly, users must be sure that the information they are receiving is correct, accurate, and timely. Also, in some situations, authorized users must be able to circumvent the prescribed or default limits on information availability for requesting and receiving larger volumes of authorized information.

Security for distributed, interoperable environments, such as e-Learning environments, have only been minimally considered and must be the focus of active research and problem solving in present and coming years.

2.3 Needs of Legacy Components

An integrated, interoperative distributed application is composed of new and existing software. Custom new software, proven legacy systems, and new and future component applications must all interact in order to use information in innovative ways. Also, the level of support for security that the offer must be considered. Hence, the integration of security into distributed computing environment that allows legacy component applications to be managed and controlled is an important problem to be solved.

3 Distributed e-Learning Environments

E-learning refers the use of Internet technologies to deliver a broad array solutions that enhance knowledge and performance [9].

Despite current technological advances in e-learning, emerging trends are demanding a greater level of interoperability for components, applications, environments and systems, which are usually developed for a particular institution/organization and provide very similar functionalities. In this sense, most important outcomes in the active learning technology standardization process (LTS), could be defined in two levels. The first one deals with specifications for information models; this level is mature enough and some de-facto standards are available as LOM specification (Learning Objects Metadata) from IEEE. And the second level deals with definition of architectures and software interfaces and components which are responsible for managing information models of the first level. Despite important contributions of this level, it is still in infancy and there is a lot of work to do before to achieve suitable standards. An overview of main areas in the standardization process of learning technologies is presented in [3].

With focus on this second level of LTS process, previous work [8] presents a proposal towards an open e-learning architecture for enabling interoperability among heterogeneous systems. The main idea was to define a higher level services as part of such open reference architecture by using REBOL (Relative Expression-Based Object language) as tool for development and implementation.

3.1 A Brief Overview of REBOL

REBOL (Relative Expression-based Object Language) is a messaging language for distributed Internet applications. REBOL was designed about 1998 in order to solve one of the fundamental problems in computing: the exchange and interpretation of information between distributed computer systems. REBOL accomplishes this through the concept of relative expressions (which is how it got its name). Relative expressions, also called "dialects", are representation of code as well as data. REBOL applications are called Reblets, and both dialects and reblets are lightweight distributed applications. REBOL is a robust development language and has a consistent architecture which goes from a small size virtual machine interface called CORE, to an Internet Operating System, called IOS.

REBOL IOS is a collaborative, multimodal system for interacting with distributed applications. It adopts a client/server model based on TCP/IP internet protocols; interconnections between client/server, client/client or server/server, are made via HTTP tunnelling or via direct peer-to-peer links through a web server that is used as a gateway for connecting to IOS server. All communications from client to server and back are encrypted using session-based keys. Information about Rebol could be found in [2].

In order to enable REBOL as technological support for developing e-learning services, it could be integrated or mapped into standard recommendations or information models such as LTSA (Learning Technologies Standard Architecture), metadata, learning objects, etc. Accordingly, Rebol facilities for e-learning include:

- Metadata for building learning objects thanks to REBOL file system architecture, which consists in a collection of filesets formed with a name for identification and metadata about fileset (its properties, users, access privileges, icons, folders, etc.). Also, filesets can be public and shared by all users, or private and shared by a set of specific users or a group.
- Learning environment via distributed desktop interface, which enables access to learning resources anytime, anywhere; both over the network or locally.
- Security. IOS communications are encrypted RSA session key exchange. Messages, files, system requests, status replies and metadata are encrypted.
- Control access by user/password authentication. Passwords are encoded by server using SHA1 (Secure hash standard one) hash values with salt randomization [7].

Despite REBOL advantages for e-learning and its security considerations. Interoperability of existing components and applications with new client/server applications in the distributed computing environment is still one of the major concerns. Security must be incorporated to all levels of an e-learning system; this involves understanding the way that security can be handled by existing applications.

3.2   The Needs of e-Learning Security

While putting learning systems on the Internet offers potentially unlimited opportunities for increasing efficiency and reducing cost, it also offers potentially unlimited risk. The Internet provides much greater access to data, and to more valuable data, not only to legitimate users, but also to hackers, disgruntled employees, criminals, and corporate spies.

On the other hand, the increasing use of standard interfaces and protocols has provided major advantages for the user community; this also facilitates the initial access for an attacker.

The increasingly use of virtually standard databases, spread sheets and other generic software applications and components, and of standard hardware processors together with the continuing evolution and dissemination of hacking tools and techniques, makes the attacker's subsequent deeper intrusion into our information systems ever easier. Furthermore, such attacks are difficult to detect and harder to trace to their source, and the hacker can work from a location where s/he is essentially safe from legal retribution, thus making such attacks ever more tempting [4].

4   Summarizing Security Challenges

From previous sections, we can summarize the major security challenges of distributed e-learning environments.

1. To exploit the services of various mechanisms including replication management, access control, and packet filtering to formulate the response to such symptoms. One of the benefits of focusing on symptoms is that many kinds of attacks produce similar symptoms, so that the capacity to cope with a finite number of symptoms results in the ability to mitigate the effects of many attacks.
2. Connecting application and Infrastructure Attacks affect the availability and quality of system resources and an application needs awareness of these effects to cope with and survive them. However, the gap between application and infrastructure restricts application awareness of these changes. A middleware which bridges this gap between application and infrastructure to produce adaptive responses that are unpredictable to the attacker.
3. The ability to adapt to changing environmental and operational conditions is key to surviving the symptoms of intrusions. However sophisticated intruders predict adaptive responses and design their attacks to thwart them. Therefore, the ability to produce adaptive responses that are unpredictable to the hacker, is needed.

4. Because network attacks usually target specific applications or exploit infrastructure vulnerabilities, a requirement for security measures is to position the adaptation control and coordination among the different mechanisms whose capabilities are used in the adaptive response, in the middleware that mediates between the application and the infrastructure.

Finally, security mechanisms deployed in e-learning systems must be standard based, flexible and interoperable, to ensure that they work with others' systems. They must also work in multi-tier architectures with one or more middle tiers such as web servers and application servers.

4.1   Conclusions

Security is a growing concern as the Internet grows up from a research vehicle into a general information exchange tool. In the future, dependable distributed systems for open networks can no longer be designed without taking malicious attacks into account.

Software architects and system designers must be aware of potential solutions that are appearing on the horizon in support of security for distributed computing applications.

References

1. The orange book. Department of defense (dod) trusted computer system evaluation criteria (tcsec), DoD 5200.28-STD, 1985. GPO: 008-000-00461-7.
2. Rebol. relative expression-based object language. web site: http://www.rebol.com/, 1998.
3. L. Anido, M. Fernandez, M. Caeiro, J. Santos, J. Rodriguez, and M. Llamas. Educational metadata and brokerage. *Computers and Education*, 38(4):351–374, May 2002.
4. R. Benjamin, B. Gladman, and B. Randell. Protecting it systems from cyber crime. *The Computer Journal*, 41(7):429–443, 1998.
5. P. S. A. Demurjian. Security, authorization and authentication for entreprise computing. CSE Technical Report TR-03-99, Dept. of Computer Science and Engineering, University of Connecticut, 1999.
6. R. Gómez. Distributed systems and computer security. *Proc. of the 4th. International Conference On Principles of DIstributed Systems, OPODIS2000*, pages 20–22, December 2000.
7. V. Hassler. *Security Fundamentals for E-Commerce*. Computer Security Series. Artech House, 2001.
8. E. Mata and M. Bui. Interoperability among distributed e-learning systems. *Proc. of the 4th. International Conference on Information Technology Based Higher Education and Training, ITHET03*, pages 191–194, July 2003.
9. M. Rosenberg. e-Learning: Strategies for Delivering Knowledge in the Digital Age. Mc.Graw Hill, 2001.
10. P. Syverson. A taxonomy of reply attacks. *Proc. of the Computer Security Foundations Workshop VII*, 1994. IEEE CS Press.

A Component-Based Transactional Service, Including Advanced Transactional Models

Colombe Hérault, Sergiy Nemchenko, and Sylvain Lecomte

LAMIH / ROI / SID, UMR CNRS 8530, Université de Valenciennes,
Le Mont Houy, 59313 Valenciennes Cedex 9, France
{Colombe.Herault,Sergiy.Nemchenko,Sylvain.Lecomte}
@univ-valenciennes.fr

Abstract. The component-based model is one possible response to the increased heterogeneity of distributed systems. This model allows developers to focus on applicative logic and leaves the implementation of the technical aspects to the component platform. However, the technical services themselves do not reap the advantages provided by the components. In this paper, we propose structuring the technical services as Fractal components. We demonstrate the benefits of such a proposition through a precise decomposition of the transactional service. We also introduce an application that uses our component-based transactional service. In order to show the feasibility of our solution, we present a prototype, which is both a component-based transactional service and a solution for building such a composition. The preliminary test results for our prototype are also presented.

Keyword: transaction, technical service, component-based model, adaptability.

1 Introduction

Nowadays, computers in distributed systems are becoming more and more heterogeneous: they range from powerful, highly rated connected servers to wireless connected personal digital assistants with small batteries and little memory. The programmers of new distributed applications have to both manage this heterogeneity and deal with the portability of applications among the different devices and networks, according to the demands of the various environments. One good response to system heterogeneity is to build component-based programs. Such programs assemble software blocks that can later be interchanged if one component proves better suited to the environment than another. The component-based model marks a clear separation between functional and non-functional code. Because of this separation, the programmer can focus on the applicative logic of the application, leaving the non-functional elements, embodied by the technical (or non-functional) services, to the platform. Given the needs of the new applications, these technical services must be adapted to the specific environment.

Despite the existence of other models, platforms provide only the flat model for the transaction service, one of the principal technical services. However, other models, such as the Open Nested Transaction (ONT) or the Closed Nested Transaction (CNT), are often better suited to new applications like Business to Business E-commerce. Moreover, depending on the execution environment, one of these models may be

F.F. Ramos et al. (Eds.): ISSADS 2005, LNCS 3563, pp. 545–556, 2005.

more suitable than the other. For these reasons, we believe that technical services should be provided in the form of a composite of components, which would allow service providers to select the version the most suitable for a specific environment.

This article develops and explains our analysis. Section 2 introduces the different transactional service models. Section 3 provides further details about component-based models and their transactions. In section 4, our example of an application that can be executed using several different transaction models, depending on the environment, demonstrates that an adaptable transactional service is desirable. Section 5 describes how the component-based transactional service should be built and used. Section 6 presents our precise decomposition of the transactional service; by breaking the service down into its component parts, we make it possible for platforms to employ several transaction models instead of just one. In section 7, we propose a two-part prototype: the first part comprises a general solution for use with any component-based technical service and the second is our implementation of a component-based transactional service, including OLTP and ONT models. The preliminary results of prototype tests are also provided in this section. In section 8, we present our conclusions and discuss several possible evolutions for our research.

2 Different Transaction Models

The Transactional Service (TxS) is one of the most important technical services in distributed applications. This mechanism allows reliable applications [11] to be created. The Transaction Manager (TM) assures that transaction boundaries are maintained [6]. There are several transactional models. Flat transactions are well-suited to short applications. If a long application needs to access data at the same time as a short application, the short application is particularly penalized, especially if the applications are accessing a remote database [17, 8]. Other problems include the expensive commit protocols of many remote databases and a high probability of total aborts, resulting from the length of time that resources are locked. To resolve these difficulties, advanced transaction models have been proposed, which optimize application execution by relaxing some of the transaction properties.

In previous work [5], we have justified the advantages of the Open Nested Transaction model for distributed applications, particularly in the B2B context. The Open Nested Transaction (ONT) model was proposed by J. Gray in 1981 [12]. This model is based on relaxing the isolation constraint. So, when a sub-transaction commits, all the updates are visible to all the other transactions, without waiting for the root-transaction to be validated. In this way, the ONT model increases the parallelism between transactions. However, the relaxation of the isolation constraint also has some inconveniences, principally the need for compensation in order to preserve data coherency in certain situations, particularly when the ONT's mother-transaction aborts [19, 14, 3].

3 Transaction and Component-Based Models

In this section, we present the advantages of component-based platforms for the development of scalable distributed applications. These platforms allow the different tasks necessary to the development of an application to be better distributed. We begin with a general description of the component-based programming model, then move on to describe existing component-based platforms, and finish with a brief explanation of transaction management in these platforms.

3.1 Component-Based Models

A component is an autonomous and intelligent software module. It can be executed on different platforms, under different operational systems [22, 16]. A component has one or more interfaces, the configurable properties that allow the component to be personalized, as well as certain technical constraints, such as security or transactional needs, for example. To be used, a component must be deployed on an application server. Application servers propose technical services, including but not limited to transactional, persistency and security services, and these services may manage several components. The component code contains only the business logic. Deploying the application requires, among other things, configuring the data sources, distributing tasks on a given execution platform and determining the security policy for a given assembly of components.

There are currently four main component-based platforms: Microsoft .NET platform [23], the OMG's CORBA Component Model [7], Enterprise Java Beans [9], and frameworks for assembly components: FRACTAL [10] and AVALON [2]. There are numerous implementations of Sun's Enterprise Java Beans (EJB) specification that have been proposed, including IBM's WebSphere [24] and the ObjectWeb consortium's JONAS [18]. The EJB model essentially relies on Sun technologies such as RMI/GIIOP for the request transport. However, some of the services proposed are inspired from the CORBA world. The transactional service is one of these. Frameworks for assembly components such as FRACTAL and AVALON are both frameworks designed to build components as a composite of other components. Fractal components benefit from dynamic composability, through which the composite component is seen as a single unit. Monitoring the building and binding of composite components is possible through the different controllers, thus providing the system with a representation of itself. In addition, fractal composites allow two different component composites to share a common component. One implementation of this model, called Julia, is proposed by the Objectweb consortium.

3.2 Transactions in the Component-Based Model

Industrial component specifications support only flat transactions. These component-based models provide two transaction demarcation modes: transactions managed by the user and transactions managed by the container. In the first mode, the user calls the TM's methods, whereas in the second, it is the container (or the membrane in Fractal) that determines transaction policy using the transaction attributes.

Researchers at the University of Valenciennes have proposed extending the ONT model to include supported transactional models for use with component-based platform [5, 21]. The main issue of this model is the compensation mechanism. This mechanism is based on the use of compensator-components and Compensation Managers (CM) have been proposed by the authors of «Advanced transactional model for component-based model» [5]. They argue that each business-component that supports an ONT model must have an associated compensator. This compensator contains the methods that manage the compensation process, that actually do the compensation and that manage the component life cycle.

4   The Need for an Adaptable Transactional Service

The separation of business logic from technical services simplifies the creation of applications, as well as allowing those applications to be reused, either in their entirety or in their component parts. Often, the same business logic can be used in several different situations. As a result, the requirements for technical services can also vary. Currently, technical services do not allow their functions to be adapted to the environment. For example, as shown by in [20], the transaction management needs of a smart card are not the same as those of a powerful application server, but the service proposed for both is the same. The first way is to embed a transaction monitor light in the smart card (figure 1.a).

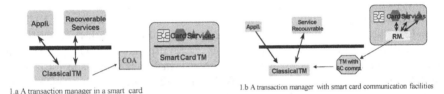

1.a A transaction manager in a smart card   1.b A transaction manager with smart card communication facilities

Fig. 1. Transaction monitors a) in a smart card, b) with smart card communication facilities

This transaction monitor has to comply with the existing transaction monitor, and must be adapted to the smart card properties. In this case, to communicate with the existing transaction monitor, the smart card uses an adaptation object (COA) [25], which translates orders from the transaction monitor in the card using a specific communication protocol. The second way, shown in figure 1.b, is to adapt an existing transaction manager to create a new interface for communication with the smart card. In this case, the transaction monitor translates the orders directly. In both cases, the transaction monitor must be modified, either to allow it to adapt to the smart card capacities, or to add an interface allowing communication with a smart card.

The fact that monitors can support different kinds of transactions (flat, CNT, ONT, etc) would seem to argue in favor of adaptable transaction monitors. For example, an application executed in a centralized computer with short transactions would not require more than a flat transaction model with a one-phase commit protocol. On the other hand, flat transactions would not be suitable for the same application executed in the distributed mode, with frequent disconnections, and a two-phase commit protocol would be needed rather than the one-phase protocol mentioned above. The second situation would require using a transactional service to provide advanced distributed transactions. Such advanced services mechanisms, of course, would be more expensive and necessitate higher capacity servers.

Using the component model to create technical services makes it possible to adapt the technical services to the environment, either statically or dynamically. If an application is to run on a computer with restricted capacities (e.g. PDA or smart card), then the technical services have to be small and compact. However, an application deployed on a powerful server can offer more choice in the services provided.

5 The Transactional Service as a Composition of Components

The previous section explained why adaptable transactional services are desirable. Other technical services, such as persistence, naming/trading and security, could also profit from increased adaptablity. This section proposes one way of making technical services adaptable, using the transactional services as an example. First, we explain the benefits of constructing technical services as composites of components, and then, we define how to create an applicative component using several technical services.

5.1 Definition of a Technical Service Using Fractal

One good way to implement an adaptable technical service is to develop it as a combination of components [15]. Using the component-based model, each subtask can be modeled as a mini-component, and the technical service itself is just the composite of those components. Each of the mini-components can easily be interchanged with any other component providing a different version of the same function. Thus, adapting the technical service to a new environment simply requires generating a different composite. The component-based technical service thus obtained has the same characteristics as a component (reusable, can separate meta-data, etc).

Still, to make it easy to use, this technical service should be a single component and not a scattered composition, which is possible if the Fractal component model is used. The Fractal model is both recursive and reflexive [4]. Its recursivity permits a composition of components to be seen both as a composite component and as a single component, and its reflexivity permits the different interceptors and controllers to be used to reveal the individual components (its content) as well as the connections between them (its bindings). Moreover, the Fractal model allows new interceptors and controllers to be incorporated, and thus new functions to be added to the components. In this way, the Fractal model permits the technical service that we have defined as a composition of components to be seen as one composite component (fig. 2), thus allowing the different models of a component-based technical service to be accessed through its different interfaces. For example, as is shown in figure 2, TS1 is accessible through two interfaces (P1 and/or P2).

Certain technical services, however, require "callback" methods, such as those defined in EJB for the *javax.ejb.SessionBean* interface or the compensation methods used in the transactional service. These methods, which are used by the technical service, require that the developer know about both the technical service and the applicative logic of the component in order to write them. In our proposition, we label these methods "*callback components*". These callback components are provided with the application, but are written separately; there is, after all, no need to add them to the composition if the technical service that is running them is not part of the composition. For example, in fig. 2, the Technical Service TS1 requires callback methods be implemented for each component: the component CB1_AC corresponds to the "Applicative Component" (AC); CB1_AC1 corresponds to AC1; and CB1_AC2 corresponds to AC2.

5.2   An Applicative Component Composition Involving Technical Services

In order to use the component-based technical services that we defined earlier, we propose certain rules for composing applicative components, call-back components and technical services. The composite obtained by following these rules allows technical services to be added to or removed from the composition. These new component-based technical services allow component-based technical services, applicative components and their respective call-back components to be gathered together in one composition (Fig. 2a). All of these components work together to allow the applicative component (AC) to benefit from the Technical Service (TS1) through its interface P2 (Fig. 2b).

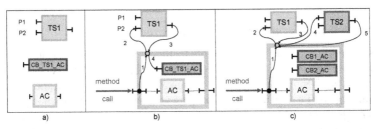

Fig. 2. a) an applicative component (AC), a call-back component (CB_TS1_AC), and a technical service (TS1), b) composition of the three components, c). Composition involving 2 technical services and an applicative component

Let's analyze the composition presented in Figure 2.b: the applicative component (AC) is combined with its call-back component to become a new composite applicative component. An interceptor (black circle) and a controller (empty circle), dedicated to technical services management, have been added to the membrane of the component; this membrane is represented in the diagram as a rectangle surrounding the component. ("Membrane" is part of the Fractal vocabulary, and its meaning approaches that of "container", as used in EJB or CCM component-based models.) The interceptor allows method calls to be reified as they take place. The interceptor delegates this treatment to the associated controller (arrow 1) before and after the execution of the method, or if an error occurs, during the execution of the method. This controller manages the use of the technical service (arrow 2). The result of the execution of the technical service is sent back to the controller (arrow 3).

Consider the example of a transactional service. A transaction is begun prior to the execution of the applicative method. After the execution, the transaction is committed. If an error occurs during the execution, the controller asks the transactional service to stop the transaction and compensate for its effects [5]. In order to do so, the transactional service uses the "call-back" component (CB_TS1_CA) (arrow 3 and 4).

The composite component described above is a good way to provide the adaptability we think is necessary. Fig. 2c) illustrates how the execution of technical service operations is managed by one controller (arrow 1), allowing the different technical services to be executed one after the other (arrows 2 & 3, and 4 & 5), thus facilitating the addition or removal of other technical services, for example, the TS2 shown in the diagram.

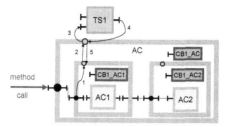

Fig. 3. Composition involving a single technical service and a composite applicative component

The composition shown in figure 3 is valid for both primitive and composite components, and it allows the recursive aspect of the Fractal component-based programming to be preserved. In a composite component, the component and each of its sub-components possess an interceptor and a controller dedicated to technical service management. The technical services are first sollicited when passing through the interceptor of the composite component (AC in figure 3), and then again when passing through each of the composition's sub-components.

This composition works well with our previous propositions. One application, including all of its subcomponents, can use one or several technical services, and they can access the most appropriate version of the technical service through one of its interfaces. In addition, the non-functional and functional codes remain separate, fulfilling one of the objectives of component-based programming. This solution is not specific to the transaction service, and can be applied to any other component-based technical service.

6   The Decomposition of the Transactional Service into Components

In the previous sections, we have shown the advantages of treating any technical service as a Fractal composite-component. In section six, we propose a decomposition of the transactional service that offers many advantages. Two TxS are presented: the first provides only flat transactions, and the second provides both ONT and flat transactions.

The first transaction service uses the functions of the Transaction Manager that supports this transactional model. All the technical services have to provide the same interface in order to be used by our controllers. Because this interface differs from the one provided by the TM, an "Interpreter" component is added at the TxS entry point (figure 4 a). This "Interpreter" component translates the commands received from the controller into commands understood by the transaction manager. As a result, the TxS contains a composite component, comprised of the TM and its Interpreter.

The second TxS supports both ONT and flat transactions. The corresponding TM has two interfaces, one for each transactional model. Interpreters are needed at each interface. However, the TM functions are not sufficient for managing ONT. The TxS assures the possible ONT compensations. This mechanism, described in section 2.2, supposes the use of a Compensation Data Object (CDO) descriptor that contains all the information necessary for locating the corresponding compensator [21]. The applicative component's controller generates the information required by the CDO and sends it to the TxS, prior to executing the applicative component (AC) method. The interpreter creates a CDO descriptor and sends it to the transaction manager at the beginning of a new ONT.

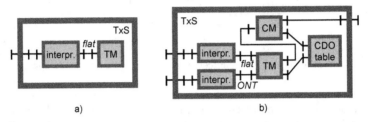

a)   b)

Fig. 4. A Transactional Service that supports a) flat transactions and b) both ONT and flat transactions

There are two ways to end a transaction. If a transaction is committed, then the TxS must save the CDO corresponding to this ONT. The TxS does so by sending the CDO to the component, "CDO_Table", once the ONT has been committed. However, if a transaction rollback is called, the TM determines whether compensation is necessary. If it is, then the TM calls the compensation process, managed by the "Compensation Manager" (CM) component. The CM locates the compensation descriptor in the "CDO_Table" and calls the compensation of the corresponding transaction, using the callback method of the component described by the CDO. The definitive schema of a TxS able to support ONT is presented in figure 4b).

7   The Prototype

Given that our proposition is based on the Fractal model, we have chose Julia, the implementation proposed by the ObjectWeb consortium, as the support for our prototype. This prototype has two parts. The first is a tool for composing component-based technical services and applicative components. It aims at building an appropriate composition to enable an applicative component to use the component-based technical services. Its technical implementation is not detailed, but it is based on theoretical principles detailed in section 5.2. The second is the component-based transaction service. Its objectives are explained in section 7.1. Then, the preliminary results of the prototype test runs are presented and analyzed in section 7.2.

7.1   The Objectives of Prototype

In this section, we present an analysis of the execution of our prototype in order to validate our stated objectives: the design of technical services that are adaptable to the variety of environments and needs. The software prototype has not been optimized for execution, but rather is open to future modifications. This software establishes a clear separation between the individual software blocks and allows each step of an execution to be verified as it is completed.

Our first objective in producing this software prototype was to prove that our proposed solution to the problem of technical service adaptability worked. We created a few applications that modify the resources of the transaction, in this case a database (DB) and ran them with using our component-based transactional service. During execution, we verified the following information: the state of the DB before and after the execution of an operation, and the demarcations of the transaction (the instants marking the beginning of a transaction and its end). The analysis of the results proves that the proposed model functions correctly. Our second objective was to detect any internal contradictions and contradictions with other products resulting from the use of our prototype. The modifications concerning the use of a universal technical service interface, with specific component specifications, have been completed.

The next step will be to test our prototype against the benchmark. For the moment, we have not attempted to execute a complete benchmark test series, like the one described by J. Gray [13]. The following section presents the preliminary speed measurement results for the different transaction management implementations.

7.2   The Measurement

We tested the simple application described in the preceding paragraphs. This application modifies certain DB fields within the scope of a transaction. Using this application allowed us to focus on transaction management. The business logic (modification of the DB) is primitive and is used only to fill the transactions. There are several ways to structure the implementation of an application and the management of its transactions (figure 5).

The simplest application is presented by figure 5a. In this case, the user program demarcates the transaction by calling the TM and interrogates the DB directly. The basic TM, which provides only flat transactions, is employed for this program. Another implementation strategy (figure 5b) allows the "cost" of adding ONT to the TM to be evaluated. In this case, a TM supports the flat transactions and the ONT. In the next implementation strategy, the business logic is extracted from the user program for use by the component accessing the DB (figure 5 c).

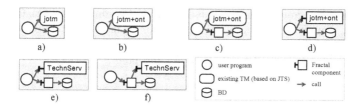

Fig. 5. The different implementation strategies

Figure 5d represents the first step towards the component-based transactional service model discussed in this paper. The TM is represented as component. Figure 5e shows the use of the interpreters described in the previous section, installed at the entry to the TM. The implementation strategy shown in figure 5f represents the goal of the research presented in this paper: a component-based application, supporting both classic and advanced transactions, with transactions managed by the business-component. The only modification needed to move from 5d to5f is to put transaction demarcation into the "hands" of the business component controller.

The follows tools were used to create the application. The components were generated using Julia1.0.6. The transaction managers included JOTM1.4.1 as well as our extension of this JOTM1.4.1 for ONT support. The database was the Mckoi SQL Database v1.00. The choice of the programming language, Java, was dictated by our chosen TM and the Julia implementation. The applications were compiled using jdk1.4.1. The tests were executed on a P3 700MHz, 384Mb operating under Windows2000. The results of our tests are presented in table 1. Execution times are expressed in milliseconds. One thousand accesses to the DB were completed for each implementation. Each query was performed in the scope of a flat transaction.

Table 1. Tests results

model	a)	b)	c)	d)	e)	f)
time (msec)	6 314	6 236	258 289	258 009	258 653	254 897

The analysis of the measurement results shows that introducing ONT support to the TM does not degrade the execution of flat transactions (models 6a and 6b). However, the use of the component model considerably reduces the speed of operations (model 6c). This reduced speed has two explanations. The first is the cost of the component model. In the component-based application, a container surrounds the program code. As a result, programs are easier to create, but running speed diminishes. The second explanation for such a significant impact on operation speed is the choice of the component model itself. In this prototype, Fractal specifications are used, which appears to slow things down. However, the Fractal specifications provide the recursiveness needed for a generous component-based model, so this problem must be worked around. There are as of yet no industrial implementations of this specification, and only one version is available for research today. Therefore, the component-based model has not yet been optimised.

The use of a component-based transaction manager and technical service (models 6c, 6d, 6e) does not visibly affect to the running speed of flat transactions. By performing transaction demarcation via the applicative component in model 6f, execution is slightly accelerated in relation to that of the user program (model 6e). One explanation may be that controllers in the applicative component are compiled with ASM (a Java bytecode manipulation framework proposed by Objecteweb [1]) and may be faster. We are currently working on clarifying this point.

8   Conclusion

In this paper, we have made two theoretical proposals based on the properties of the component-based model and the transactional services. According to basic component-based programming principle, constructing technical services as compositions of components means that the global compositions inherit all the valuable characteristics of the individual components. In addition, this component-based model allows the component platform to provide the most adapted version of a technical service to its components by offering technical services with several interfaces, each implementing a different model. To facilitate the use of our proposed component-based technical services, we have also proposed a composition that incorporates an applicative component with a variety of technical services that provide mechanisms for automating their use. We have shown the benefits of such a solution using the example of the transactional service, implementing two models (OLTP and ONT) with a Transaction Manager, a Compensation Manager and a CDO table. This composition allows each part of the service to be easily modified.

Our proposals were tested in a software prototype, which provides a tool for building composite applications using technical services and proves the feasibility of our general solution for the use of technical services as we defined them. In our future research, we plan to focus on demonstrating that the proposed solution can be applied to any technical service, and not just the transaction service. We are currently looking into the naming/trading service, which may be broken down into three main parts: one common to both the trading and the naming service, one specific to the trading service and one specific to the trading service. In addition, we would like to provide a dynamic version of our prototype. This dynamic version would allow the system to choose which technical service model to apply to a specific component, while evolving in a versatile environment, thanks indications about the bandwidth and storage capacity, for example.

The second part of the prototype is a component-based transaction service that offers two different models. This prototype of the transaction service accepts the ONT model, which has not yet been implemented in existing component platforms. It also allows a component to access the most appropriate transaction model. Moreover, the fact that the service is component-based insures an evolving solution. Still, the implemented ONT model is primitive. For example, the prototypical Transaction Service does not yet support cascading compensations, a situation that arises when one compensation provokes other compensations. The development of more complex ONT models is currently being investigated in our laboratory. Complete benchmark testing is being considered for future research.

Acknowledgement

The authors wish to thank Nadia Bennani for her helpful comments on this paper.

References

1. http://asm.objectweb.org/
2. http://avalon.apache.org/
3. G. Alonso, R. Vingralek, D. Agrawal, Y. Breitbart, A.E. Addabi, H.J. Schek, G. Weikum, "Unifying Concurrency Control and Recovery of Transactions", Proceedings of the EDBT Conference, 1994.
4. E. Bruneton, T. Coupaye, J.-B. Stefani, "Recursive and Dynamic Software Composition with Sharing", Proceedings of the 7th ECOOP International Workshop on Component-Oriented Programming (WCOP'02), Malaga, Spain, 2002.
5. N. Bennani, T. Delot, S. Lecomte, S. Nemchenko, D. Donsez, "Advanced transactional model for component-based model", IEEE International Symposium on Advanced Distributed Computing (ISADS), 2002
6. P.A. Bernstein, E. Newcomer, "Principles of Transaction Processing", Morgan Kaufman Publishers, Inc, San Francisco, California, 1997
7. Object Management Group, "CORBA Components. Specification", OMG TC Document orbos/99-02-05, 1999.

8. U. Dayl, M. Hsu, R. Ladin, "A Transactional Model for Long-Running Activities", Proceedings of the VLDB Conference, 1991.
9. Sun MicroSystems, "Enterprise JavaBeans Specification, Version 2.1", 2001.
10. http://fractal.objectweb.org/index.html.
11. T. Freund, T. Storey, "Transactions in the world of Web services", IBM, 2002
12. J. Gray, "The Transaction Concept: Virtues and Limitations", Proceedings of the VLDB Conference, 1981.
13. "The Benchmark Handbook, for database and transaction processing systems", Second edition, Edited by J.Gray, Digital Equipment Corporation, Morgan Kaufmann publishers, Inc, San Francisco, California, 1993
14. C. Hasse, G. Weikum, "A Performance Evaluation on Multi-Level Transaction Management", Proceedings of the VLDB Conference, 1991.
15. C. Hérault, N. Bennani, T. Delot, S. Lecomte, M Thilliez, "Adaptability of Non-Functional Services for Component Model, Application to the M-Commerce", IEEE International Symposium on Advanced Distributed Computing (ISADS), Guadalajara, Jalisco, Mexico, November 11-15, 2002.
16. G. T. Heineman, W. T. Council, "Component-Based Software Engineering, Putting the Pieces Together", Addison Weysley, 2001.
17. S. Jajodia, L. Kerschberg, "Advanced Transaction Models and Architecture", Kluwer Academic Publishers, 1997.
18. Java Open Application Server (JOnAS) for EJB, Objectweb, 2001.
http://www.objectweb.org.
19. H.F. Korth, E. Levy, A. Silberschatz, "A Formal Approach to Recovery by Compensating Transactions", Proceedings of the VLDB Conference, 1990.
20. S. Lecomte, "Smart card oriented transactional services and transactional system integrating smart card", PhD thesis, university of Lille, France, 1998.
21. S. Nemchenko, "Compensation management of ONT in component-based models", 7th International Forum "Radio electronics and youth in the XXI century", 2003, Ukraine.
22. R. Orfalie, D. Harkey, J. Edwards, "Client/Server Survival Guide, 3thrd edition", Vuibert, 1999.
23. T. Thai, H.Q. Lam, "NET Framework Essentials", O'Reilly & Associates, 2001.
24. O. Takagiwa, A. Spender, A. Stevens, J. Bouyssou, "Redbook: Programming J2EE APIs with WebSphere Advanced", IBM Corp., 2001.
25. J.J. Vandewalle, "OSMOSE: Modélisation et implémentation pour l'interopérabilité de services carte à microprocesseur", PhD Thesis, university of Lille, Mars 1997.

Author Index

Lecture Notes in Computer Science

For information about Vols. 1–3593

please contact your bookseller or Springer